ISBN 978-0-428-68099-2
PIBN 10201400

FB &c Ltd, Dalton House, 60 Windsor Avenue, London, SW19 2RR.
Company number 08720141. Registered in England and Wales.

CATALOGUE

OF THE

LIBRARY

OF

HARVARD UNIVERSITY

IN

CAMBRIDGE, MASSACHUSETTS.

CATALOGUE

OF THE

LIBRARY

OF

HARVARD UNIVERSITY

IN

CAMBRIDGE, MASSACHUSETTS.

Catalogorum idem plane munus est in *Republica literaria*, quod in *Romana* fuit olim *Nomenclatorum*; indicant enim *Doctrinæ Candidatis* nomina illorum, quos *prensare*, quos *colere*, quorumque *ope uti* oporteat, ut honores, quos ambiunt, consequi possint: quamque præterea jucundæ, quam doctis omnibus desideratissimæ illorum prodeant impressiones, eruditorum ubique scripta epistolæque abunde testantur.

MIDDLETON.

VOL. I.

CAMBRIDGE:
E. W. METCALF AND COMPANY,
Printers to the University.

1830.

PREFACE.

THE present Library of Harvard College dates its origin from the destruction of Harvard Hall, with its valuable contents,* by fire, in the year 1764. The General Court, which, in consequence of the prevalence of the small pox in Boston, was then sitting in Cambridge, and occupying the room appropriated to the Library, immediately voted to erect a new building; and Harvard Hall was in a short time fully replaced by the present edifice of the same name. A corresponding zeal was manifested by other friends of the institution, to furnish the new hall with a library and philosophical apparatus. The General Court of New-Hampshire, which at that time had no college of its own to provide for, granted, at the instance of Governor Wentworth, three hundred pounds sterling towards restoring the Library; "The Society for Propagating the Gospel in

* Library, Philosophical Apparatus, &c. The Library was a very valuable collection of more than 5000 volumes. Among the principal Contributors to it were the Rev. John Harvard, the founder of the University, the Hollises, and several other names of great celebrity, as Sir Kenelm Digby, Richard Baxter, Governor Winthrop, Dr. Gale, Dr. Lightfoot, Dr. Watts, Dr. Mead, Bishop Berkeley, Bishop Sherlock, Dr. Hales. A particular statement of the different benefactions is necessarily deferred for the present. What is now proposed is to give some account of the *existing* library.

New England and Parts Adjacent" gave the same sum, and "The Society for Propagating the Gospel in Foreign Parts," one hundred pounds sterling; Thomas Hollis Esq. of London redoubled his generous efforts to assist the College in its distress; other public-spirited and enlightened individuals came forward with their contributions upon the occasion; so that a very few years supplied the loss of what had been the accumulation of more than a century. The Library increased so rapidly, that, in 1790, when the last Catalogue was printed, it consisted of about twelve thousand volumes,—an amount, which, considering the situation of the country during a great part of the time it was collecting, and notwithstanding the donations from abroad, reflects no small credit on the character and spirit even of those days of patriotism and of public virtue.*

The impulse thus opportunely given, was happily continued; benefactors succeeded benefactors; and the Library now contains, besides many thousand tracts, upwards of thirty thousand bound volumes, with every prospect of increasing as fast as it has done at any former period.

Harvard College Library is almost entirely the fruit of individual munificence. Its records exhibit a long list of donors, whose names will be indissolubly associated with the establishment; but the present occasion admits of a distinct tribute to those persons only, whose contributions to the Library have been such, as to form observable stages in its growth, or to attract particular attention for their splendour and magnitude.

---

* It will be recollected that, during the same period, heavy expenses were also incurred for building the new hall, replacing the philosophical apparatus, &c.; and that the opportunities, subsequently enjoyed for acquiring wealth, had not then been afforded.

The name, which in this connexion first presents itself to the mind, is the ever-memorable one of Hollis in England. Next to that of the immortal founder of the University, it stands pre-eminent for its claims to a grateful recollection. Comprehensive benevolence seems to have been a distinguishing trait of character in the family of Hollis,—a benevolence, which was not confined within the limits of party or of country, and which was no less enlightened than it was liberal and enlarged. It was principally to supply the intellectual and moral wants of men, that this benevolence diffused itself abroad, that it crossed seas and oceans, and visited remote countries. Several individuals of that family were benefactors of Harvard College. Two of them displayed a most remarkable degree of generosity. The first was the excellent Thomas Hollis, who founded two professorships, one of Theology, and one of Mathematics and Natural Philosophy, and, besides various other benefactions, contributed largely to the library and philosophical apparatus, which were afterwards burnt. His death took place in 1731. He was great uncle to our other distinguished friend, who bore his name, and inherited his estate and his virtues.

Two large quarto volumes, compiled by Archdeacon Blackburne, are devoted to an exhibition of the latter Thomas Hollis's "deeds of peace." In one of the tributes to the memory of this extraordinary man, which appeared soon after his decease, and which are preserved in those volumes, it was justly observed, "that in his death Liberty lost her champion, Humanity her treasurer, and Charity her steward." To benefit mankind was, indeed, the great business of his life ; and, possessing a fortune which happily seconded his generous nature, he applied himself to the execution of his disinterested purposes, with all the zeal and dili-

New England and Parts Adjacent" gave the same sum, and "The Society for Propagating the Gospel in Foreign Parts," one hundred pounds sterling; Thomas Hollis Esq. of London redoubled his generous efforts to assist the College in its distress; other public-spirited and enlightened individuals came forward with their contributions upon the occasion; so that a very few years supplied the loss of what had been the accumulation of more than a century. The Library increased so rapidly, that, in 1790, when the last Catalogue was printed, it consisted of about twelve thousand volumes,—an amount, which, considering the situation of the country during a great part of the time it was collecting, and notwithstanding the donations from abroad, reflects no small credit on the character and spirit even of those days of patriotism and of public virtue.*

The impulse thus opportunely given, was happily continued; benefactors succeeded benefactors; and the Library now contains, besides many thousand tracts, upwards of thirty thousand bound volumes, with every prospect of increasing as fast as it has done at any former period.

Harvard College Library is almost entirely the fruit of individual munificence. Its records exhibit a long list of donors, whose names will be indissolubly associated with the establishment; but the present occasion admits of a distinct tribute to those persons only, whose contributions to the Library have been such, as to form observable stages in its growth, or to attract particular attention for their splendour and magnitude.

---

* It will be recollected that, during the same period, heavy expenses were also incurred for building the new hall, replacing the philosophical apparatus, &c.; and that the opportunities, subsequently enjoyed for acquiring wealth, had not then been afforded.

The name, which in this connexion first presents itself to the mind, is the ever-memorable one of Hollis in England. Next to that of the immortal founder of the University, it stands pre-eminent for its claims to a grateful recollection. Comprehensive benevolence seems to have been a distinguishing trait of character in the family of Hollis,—a benevolence, which was not confined within the limits of party or of country, and which was no less enlightened than it was liberal and enlarged. It was principally to supply the intellectual and moral wants of men, that this benevolence diffused itself abroad, that it crossed seas and oceans, and visited remote countries. Several individuals of that family were benefactors of Harvard College. Two of them displayed a most remarkable degree of generosity. The first was the excellent Thomas Hollis, who founded two professorships, one of Theology, and one of Mathematics and Natural Philosophy, and, besides various other benefactions, contributed largely to the library and philosophical apparatus, which were afterwards burnt. His death took place in 1731. He was great uncle to our other distinguished friend, who bore his name, and inherited his estate and his virtues.

Two large quarto volumes, compiled by Archdeacon Blackburne, are devoted to an exhibition of the latter Thomas Hollis's "deeds of peace." In one of the tributes to the memory of this extraordinary man, which appeared soon after his decease, and which are preserved in those volumes, it was justly observed, "that in his death Liberty lost her champion, Humanity her treasurer, and Charity her steward." To benefit mankind was, indeed, the great business of his life; and, possessing a fortune which happily seconded his generous nature, he applied himself to the execution of his disinterested purposes, with all the zeal and diligence of the most ardent votary of wealth or of power. One of his principal employments was to collect the most valuable books in the various branches of learning, especially such as were intimately connected with the highest interests of man, and to forward them, as presents, to those places where they were most wanted. This University partook largely of his bounty. It was, indeed, a favorite object of his regard. Immediately after the fire above mentioned, he subscribed two hundred pounds sterling towards replacing the philosophical apparatus; but, with a just appreciation of the importance of a good library, his chief care was to furnish books. He began to send them as early, probably, as 1758, and continued to do it till within three or four years of his death, which took place in 1774. It appears, therefore, that some of the books, presented by him, were destroyed with the old library; the greater part, however, having been transmitted subsequently to that event, still remain, and in all respects abundantly verify the accounts which have been given of his great care and judgment in selecting and procuring them.*

---

* Besides the intrinsic value of the works presented by Mr. Hollis, there is much about them, which indicates a lively interest in his benevolent occupation. The binding is always in the best style; on the covers are curious emblematical decorations; and the books often contain notes and remarks in his own hand-writing. Such expressions as "Ut Spargam!" "Felicity is Freedom," &c. frequently occur; and sometimes bibliographical and other notices of considerable extent. A few specimens of these will not, it is believed, be unacceptable to the reader.

Stephens's Thesaurus Græcæ Linguæ, for example, is accompanied with the following notice; "T. H. has been looking out, above two years, for a fine copy of Harry Stephens' Greek Thesaurus for Harvard College. At length he has purchased one out of the Library of the learned Dr. Samuel Chandler. It can hardly be

To enumerate all the works he gave would require more room than the limits of this Preface will allow. Suffice it to say, that they comprise many of the most valuable productions of human genius and industry, in various languages, ancient and modern, and in all the departments of science and literature. At his decease he left five hundred pounds sterling to be applied to the same object; and this, with the addition of some unexpended interest, now constitutes a fund of three thousand dollars, the interest of which is laid out in the purchase of books.

Mr. Hollis has been thus particularly noticed, not only on account of his general claims to respect and admiration, but because, from the amount and quality of his benefactions, and from the period at which they were received, he may justly be considered as the father of Harvard College Library.

The gentleman, to whom he bequeathed his estate,

---

imagined what difficulty there is, even where money and industry are not wanting, to procure *good* copies of the old and best editions of classical and prime authors." In the Thesaurus Linguæ Arabicæ of Giggeius, he says; "This is a fine copy of a very scarce work. T. H. has been particularly industrious in collecting Grammars and Lexicons of the oriental *Root* languages, to send to Harvard College, in hopes of forming by that means, assisted by the energy of the leaders, always beneficent, a few *prime Scholars*, honours to their country, and lights to mankind," &c.

In the splendid large-paper, *loyal* copy of Walton's Polyglott Bible (remarkable more particularly as containing a *Dedication to Charles the Second*,) he writes thus; "Thomas Hollis, an Englishman, a Lover of Liberty, civil and religious, citizen of the world, is desirous of having the honor to present this set of books, (a gift originally of the author of it to Edward Hyde, Earl of Clarendon, Chancellor of England,) to the public library of Harvard College, at Cambridge, in New England. Pall Mall, Aug. 12, 1764."

Thomas Brand-Hollis Esq., manifested a similar regard for our University. In the course of several years he presented it with many excellent books; and he gave it one hundred pounds at his decease.

It was the intention of the Hon. Thomas Hancock of Boston, the liberal founder of the Professorship of Hebrew and other Oriental Languages, to subscribe five hundred pounds sterling towards the restoration of the Library; but his death suddenly taking place before the completion of his purpose, it was voluntarily executed by his nephew and heir, the celebrated John Hancock, "who at the same time still farther enriched the Library by a large collection of chosen authors," and subsequently demonstrated his continued "affection to the College" by repeated instances of bounty.

The Antiquities of Herculaneum and Piranesi's Views of Rome, in twenty large folio volumes, were presented to the Library, in 1772, by Thomas Palmer Esq. of Boston. At the beginning of the Revolution he left this country, and resided principally in London till his decease, which took place in 1820; when, "to prove his affectionate regard to the society in which he received his education," and unmindful of past injuries and vexations, he magnanimously bequeathed to our University his excellent miscellaneous library of nearly twelve hundred choice and costly volumes.

A large collection of valuable books was presented to the Library in 1784, by Thomas Lee Esq. of Cambridge.

Mr. Samuel Shapleigh, the worthy Librarian of the University, bequeathed, in 1800, the sum of three thousand dollars, the interest of which was to be applied to the purchase of books in modern literature.

To the liberality of the Hon. Israel Thorndike of Boston the College is indebted for repeated benefactions of great value: particularly for the celebrated library of the late Professor Ebeling of Hamburgh, containing upwards of thirty-two hundred volumes, and consisting chiefly of the most important works on American History, in several languages; with a collection of ten thousand maps, charts, and views, which is probably unrivalled by any other collection of a similar kind in the world.

An important addition to the Class of "Works on America," consisting of Mr. Warden's valuable collection of nearly twelve hundred volumes, besides maps, prints, and charts, was made by Samuel A. Eliot Esq. of Boston, son of Samuel Eliot Esq., who endowed the Professorship of Greek Literature with a fund of twenty thousand dollars.

Another son of the same munificent benefactor, William H. Eliot Esq. of Boston, presented a copy of the great national French work, "Description de l'Egypte," a work, which, high as its value is at present, will no doubt be rendered more and more valuable by the inquiries now prosecuting into the wonders of Egyptian antiquity and art, of which, as well as of the natural objects and features of that interesting region, this magnificent work is an immense treasury.

The Hon. Christopher Gore, many years before his decease, gave an earnest of that munificence and regard for the interests of education, so splendidly manifested towards the University in his Will, by enriching the Law Library with a large number of rare and important works in different branches of jurisprudence.

The Boylston Medical Library, consisting of more than eleven hundred volumes, with other benefactions to the College, attest the liberality of the late Ward Nicholas Boylston Esq., nephew and heir of Nicholas Boylston Esq. of Boston, the generous founder of the Professorship of Rhetoric and Oratory.

A large number of excellent works on Natural History and a "chosen collection of the most ancient Greek poets," were presented to the Library by the late Dr. Francis Vergnies of Newburyport.

The sum of two thousand dollars, given to the University by the Hon. Peter O. Thacher, "from a fund left him in trust by the late William Breed Esq. of Boston, for objects of charity, or for the promotion of learning, piety, and religion among the rising generation," was applied by the Corporation to the purchase of books for the Library.

Among the distinguished benefactors of our library may be numbered the Hon. John Adams and the Hon. John Quincy Adams, late Presidents of the United States; and the Hon. Nathan Dane of Beverly, the liberal founder of the Dane Professorship of Law.

To names, thus endeared to the University and to literature, may be added those of Dr. Franklin, Lieut. Gov. Dummer, Thomas Wibird Esq. of New-Hampshire; Jasper Mauduit Esq., Granville Sharp Esq., and John Nichols Esq. of London; the celebrated Goethe of Germany; the Hon. Thomas Hubbard, David Sears Esq., William Hubbard Esq., and Edward Brooks Esq. of Boston; to each of whom, as well as to many others, the University is indebted for valuable donations to the Library.

Its acknowledgments are also due to many learned societies, both in this country and in Europe, for the gratuitous transmission of their important and interesting publications; to the Royal Antiquarian and Horticultural Societies of London; to the American Philosophical Society of Philadelphia; to the American Academy of Arts and Sciences; and to several Historical Societies of this and other states.

Valuable presents have also been made by several American authors and publishers, who have thus generously set the example of doing for this library voluntarily what in England is required for some of the public libraries by law.

Harvard Hall has four spacious rooms, of which, two on the ground floor are appropriated to the departments of Natural Philosophy and Mineralogy, and two on the second floor contain the principal library.* The judicious and convenient disposition of the books according to their subjects, which was introduced by that accomplished scholar, Joseph G. Cogswell Esq., has been continued with respect to those received since he had charge of the Library, so far as circumstances would permit. Many of the books, however, which have been added to the Library for several years past, have been excluded from their appropriate places by the want of room. This want is now very sensibly experienced; and in a short time another apartment will be indispensably requisite. It is most ardently hoped, that means will at no distant period be furnished by the public-spirited friends of the University and of literature, to erect a new building for the exclusive use of this department, in some respects more eligibly situated than the present, and ample enough to accommodate a library, that shall rival the great repositories of learning in Europe, and correspond more nearly to what may be reasonably expected of the first Library in our country.

---

* The Library rooms contain twenty alcoves. Over the windows of several of them are inscribed the names of *Hollis*, *Hancock*, *Lee*, *Palmer*, *Thorndike*, *Eliot*. The apartments are also decorated with pictures and busts, particularly of some of the principal benefactors of the University and great men of our country, executed by Copley, Stuart, and other distinguished artists.

It is unnecessary to offer any statement of what the Library contains in the several departments of knowledge, as that is sufficiently apparent from the Catalogue, particularly the Systematic Index. The books are principally from the first presses in Europe. A long list might be given, in which the arts of typography, of engraving, and binding have exhausted all their powers of execution and embellishment. The Library contains many rare and valuable works, which are probably to be found no where else in this country. It has some books, which were printed in the fifteenth, and many in the sixteenth century. It has also a number of curious manuscripts in the Greek, Latin, Oriental, and other languages. In those time-hallowed productions, which are an indispensable part of every great library, ours may be considered as rich. It has a solid foundation to build upon; but much remains to be done, before the superstructure will be completed.

It may be proper, however, to observe that the Corporation have recently bestowed much of their attention upon this important interest. Liberal appropriations have been already made by them, and additional ones are expected, for the increase of the Library. Orders have been sent to Europe for a large number of works, none of which came in season to be inserted in this catalogue. But, till a supplement can be given to the public, it may be of use to state generally, that in the list of the books ordered are included, such of the best dictionaries in the ancient and modern languages, as are not already in the Library; the Biographia Britannica by Kippis and others; Hansard's Parliamentary History and Debates; the great French Biographical Dictionary; many of the first Mathematical works; the most esteemed accounts of recent travels in Asia and other parts of the world; many celebrated works in the Belles-Lettres, History, Theology, and other branches of learning; the Transactions of the Royal Edinburgh and Irish Academies; the Memoirs of the Academy of Turin; the Memoirs of the Royal Academy of Berlin;—also the volumes that are wanting to complete the great collections, of which we have already a part; as the Transactions of the Royal Society of London, the Archæologia published by the London Society of Antiquaries, the Asiatic Researches, the Memoirs of the French Academies and Institute, those of the Göttingen Academy of Sciences and of the Imperial Academy of St. Petersburgh, the Acta and Nova Acta Eruditorum, and the Memoirs of the Spanish Royal Academy of History. The department of jurisprudence has also been recently enriched with large and valuable additions, and will receive all the attention necessary to render it worthy of the distinguished advantages enjoyed at the Law School of the University.

In looking over the Catalogue, authors and others will discover many deficiencies, which they may often have it in their power to supply; and by doing this they will render a service, which will be gratefully acknowledged. All publications relating to this country are naturally expected to find a place in our library. It has already a greater number of works upon America, than are to be found in any other; still the collection is far from being complete; many works are wanting, especially of a recent date, all of which it is exceedingly desirable to obtain. A public library like this, is a particularly suitable repository for state papers, political, religious, and other tracts, reports and proceedings of ecclesiastical bodies and of societies instituted for various purposes, for local publications, occasional pamphlets, and public documents of every description; it being a place, where they will not only have the best chance of being preserved, but will be accessible to all persons, who may at any time wish to consult them.

The benefits, conferred by the Library, are rendered as extensive as possible by the liberality of its regulations. A ready admittance, and the requisite information and facilities for examining and consulting the works, are afforded to all visitors. Books are loaned to all the Undergraduates, to the Members of the Theological and Law Schools, to all persons residing in Cambridge for purposes of study, to the Members of the Faculty, Corporation, and Board of Overseers, and to all regularly ordained Clergymen living within ten miles of the College; and persons, not coming within the provisions of the law, may, by application to the Corporation, obtain the use of any books, which are proper to be taken from the Library. The privileges, granted to individuals, are not exceeded by those enjoyed at any other institution of a similar kind, and are believed to be in all respects as great as a due regard to general accommodation and to the preservation of the books would permit. These facts will, of course, be all taken into consideration in estimating the importance of augmenting the Library. A fund, from which so many minds are constantly drawing their chief supplies, to pour them again, with incalculable effect, over the whole community, should be as rich, as munificence and zeal for the promotion of learning can render it.

The Catalogue of the books consists of two parts, an Alphabetical List and a Systematic Index. The general principles, adopted in preparing the Alphabetical List, have been, to describe the books in the words of their respective titles; to use the peculiar, and often uncouth, orthography found in each work, whether in the English or in any other language; and to put the works under the names of the authors or compilers, where they were known, and, where they were not known, either under some important words in the titles, or under the names of those subjects of which they respectively treat; with such references, in many cases, from one to another, as it was thought would be found useful. Some deviations, chiefly accidental, occur. In some instances anonymous works, which merely relate to particular persons or their writings, are put under the names of those persons; but an attentive reader, it is believed, will be in little danger of mistake from this circumstance.

Some observations respecting the Systematic Index will be found in the volume which contains that part of the work.

NOTE. Besides the Public Library, there are very respectable libraries belonging to some of the societies in the University; and it may also be mentioned, among the advantages enjoyed at this seat of learning, that within one hour's walk are various other repositories of learning, particularly the noble collection of the Boston Atheneum, second in extent and value to no other collection, probably, in this country, with the exception of Harvard College Library.

BENJAMIN PEIRCE, *Librarian.*

Cambridge, March, 1830.

ALPHABETICAL CATALOGUE.

CATALOGUE.

A

ABÆLARDUS, PETRUS. Abælardi et Heloisæ Opera. 4to. Paris. 1616.
———, ———. Epistolæ. 8vo. Lond. 1718.
Abarbanel, Leon. Dialogos de Amor, trad. en Leng. Castel. 4to. Venet. 1568.
Abbadie, Jacques. La Vérité de la Religion Chrétienne. 3 vols. 12mo. Rotter. 1689.
———, ———. Truth of the Christian Religion, tr. by H. Lussan. 2 vols. 8vo. Lond. 1694.
———, ———. La Divinité de Notre Seigneur Jésus Christ. 12mo. Amst. 1729.
Abbot, Abiel. Statement of Proceedings of the First Church in Coventry, with Mr. Abbot's Farewell Address. 8vo. Bost. 1811.
Abbot, Abiel. Address on Intemperance. 8vo. Camb. 1815.
———, ———. The Same. 12mo. Bost. 1815.
———, ———. Sermons to Mariners. 12mo. Bost. 1812.
———, ———. Artillery Election Sermon. 8vo. Bost. 1802.
Abbot, Charles. Law of Merchant Ships and Seamen, with Annotations by J. Story. 8vo. Newburyport. 1810.
Abbot, Hull. Artillery Election Sermon. 8vo. Bost. 1735.
———, ———. Sermon on the Rebellion in Scotland. 8vo. Bost. 1746.
———, ———. Sermon against Profane Swearing and Cursing. 16mo. Bost. 1746.
Abbot, Robert, (Bp.) De Gratia et Perseverantia Sanctorum. 12mo. Francof. 1618.
Abdollatiphi, Bagd. Vita, Auctore Ibn Abi Osaiba; e Codicibus MSS. Bodleianis descripsit, et Latine vertit, J. Mousley. 4to. Oxon. 1808.
Abeille, J. Essai sur nos Colonies et sur le Rétablissement de Saint Domingue. 8vo. Paris. 1805.
———, —. Abhandlung über der Entdeckung von America, aus dem Französischen. 12mo. Halle. 1788.
Abela, Gio. Fr. Descrittione di Malta. fol. Malta. 1647.
———, —, —. Descriptio Melitæ. (Græv. Thes. Sicil.)

Abernethy, John. Sermons on Various Subjects, with his Life. 2 vols. 8vo. Lond. 1748.

———, ——. The Same. 4 vols. 8vo. Lond. 1762.

———, ——. Tracts and Sermons, occasionally published. 8vo. 1751.

———, ——. Discourses on the Being and Perfections of God. 2 vols. 8vo. Lond. 1743.

———, ——. The Same. 2 vols. 8vo. Lond. 1757.

———, ——. The Same 2 vols. 8vo. Lond. 1767.

———, ——. Answer to Mastertown's Apology. 8vo. Belfast. 1724.

Abernethy, John. Surgical Observations. 2 vols. 8vo. Lond. 1804—6.

———, ——. Surgical Works. 3 vols. 8vo. Lond. 1817.

Abicht, J. G. De Lupsu Murorum Hierichunt. (Ugol. vol. 32.)

Abicht, J. H. System der Elementarphilosophie. 8vo. Erlangen. 1795.

———, ——. Preisschriften über Metaphysik. 8vo. Berlin. 1796.

Abingdon, Earl of. Thoughts on Burke's Letter to the Sheriffs of Bristol. 8vo. Oxford.

Abli, R. Abr. dictus Segel, Clypei Terræ Liber. fol. Amst. 1734.

Aborigines of America. See Researches. See Indians.

Abravanele, (vel Aburbanel) Isaac. De Capite Fidei. Lat. a Vorstio. 4to. Amst. 1638.

———, ——— ———. Idem. 4to. Franeq. 1684.

———, ——— ———. De Statu et Jure Regio. (Ugol. vol. 24.)

———, ——— ———. De Judicum et Regum Differentia. (Ugol. 24.)

———, ——— ———. De Pœna Excidii. (Ugol. 30.)

Abridgment of the Statutes. 9 vols. 8vo. Lond. 1725—37.

Abul-Feda, Ismael. De Vita et Rebus Gestis Mohammedis. fol. Oxon. 1723.

Abul-Pharajius, Greg. Historia Dynastiarum, Arabice et Latine, ab E. Pocockio. 2 vol. 4to. Oxon. 1663.

———, ——. Specimen Historiæ Arabum. 4to. 1650.

Abul Walidi Ibn Zeiduni. Risalet, Arabice et Latine; cum Notulis, cura J. J. Reiskii. 4to. Lips. 1755.

Academia Cæsarea. Vide Nova Acta.

Academia, Geo. Aug. Pentecostes Sacra pie Celebranda. 4to. Gottingæ.

———, —— ——. De Fundamento Theologiæ Recentioris, etc. 4to. Gottingæ. 1814.

Academia Gissena. Poetica, per nonnullos Professores. 12mo. Giessæ Hass. 1617.

Academia Lipsiensis. Pietatis Monumenta in Seculi Undevicesimi Initiis. 4to. Lips. 1801.

Academia Lugduno-Batava. Annales, 1815—1817. 4to. Lug. Bat. 1817.

Academia Scientiarum Imperialis Petropolitana. Commentarii. 1726—57. 20 vol. 4to. Petropoli. 1728—61.

Academia Witebergensis. Scripta publice proposita a Professoribus. 5 vols. 12mo. Wit. 1560—3.
Academia Real Española. Diccionario de la Lengua Castellana. 6 vol. fol. Madrid. 1726—39.
——— —— ———. Diccionario de la Lengua Castellana. Quint. ed. fol. Madrid. 1817.
——— —— ———. Ortografia de la Lengua Castellana. 12mo. Madrid. 1770.
——— —— ———. The Same. 12mo. Madrid. 1815.
——— —— ———. Gramatica de la Lengua Castellana. 12mo. Madrid. 1796.
——— —— ———. Fuero Juzgo en Lat. y Castel. fol. Madrid. 1815.
Academia Real de la Historia. Memorias. 5 vol. 4to. Madrid. 1796—1817.
Academia Real das Sciencias. Memorias para a Hist. de S. Vincente, por Gaspar da Madre de Deos. 4to. Lisboa. 1797.
Académie de Bavière. Vide Swinden.
Académie Française. Dictionnaire. 2 vol. 4to. Lyon. 1777.
——— ———. Same. 5me. ed. 2 vols. Paris. 1799.
Académie Royale des Inscriptions et Belles Lettres. Histoire et Mémoires depuis son établissement in 1663, jusques et compris l'année 1775 et une partie de 1776; avec les Tables de Matières jusques et compris le volume 32. 41 vol. 4to. Paris. 1717—80.
Académie Royale des Sciences. Histoire et Mémoires depuis son établissement en 1666 jusqu'à 1767. 82 vol. 4to. Paris. 1733—70.
——— ———. Mémoires de Mathématique et de Physique présentés à l'Académie. 4 vol. 4to. Paris. 1750—63.
——— ———. Machines et Inventions approuvées par la même. 6 vol. 4to. Paris. 1735.
——— ———. Elémens d'Astronomie et Tables Astronomiques; par Cassini. 2 vol. 4to. Paris. 1740.
——— ———. Méridienne de Paris; par Cassini. 4to. Paris. 1744.
——— ———. Géométrie de l'Infini. 4to. Paris. 1727.
——— ———. Voyage, et Mesure des Trois Degrés du Méridien; par M. de la Condamine. 2 vol. 4to. Paris. 1751.
——— ———. Mémoires; par Fontaine. 4to. Paris. 1764.
——— ———. Tables des Matières, années 1666—1740. 5 vol. 4to. Paris. 1734—47.
——— ———. Idem. 1751—60. 4to. Paris. 1758.
——— ———. Arts et Métiers. 18 vol. fol. Paris. 1761—78.
——— ———. Historia Academiæ. Vide Du Hamel.
Académies et Sociétés. Collection Académique, composée des Mémoires, Actes, ou Journaux des plus célebres Académies et

Sociétés Littéraires de l'Europe. 29 vol. 4to. Dijon, Auxerre, Paris, et Liege. 1754—87.
Academy of Natural Sciences of Philadelphia. Journal. Vol. I. and Part I. with Nos. 7, 8, 9, 10, and 11, of vol. II. 8vo. Philad. 1817—22.
Academy. See American.
Acarete, M. du Biscay. Account of a Voyage up the River de la Plata, and thence over land to Peru. 8vo. Lond. 1698.
Accademia Italiana di Scienze, Lettere, ed Arti. Atti. tomo primo. 4to. Livorno. 1810.
Accademici della Crusca. Vocabolario. 6 vol. fol. Firenze. 1729—38.
——— —— ———. Idem. 6 vol. fol. Napoli. 1746—8.
Accum, Frederick. Catalogue of the Apparatus employed in Chemistry, Mineralogy, &c. 12mo. Lond. 1812.
———, ———. Analysis of Minerals. 12mo. Lond. 1804.
———, ———. Theor. and Pract. Chemistry. 2 vols. 8vo. Lond. 1803.
———, ———. Elements of Crystallography after the Method of Haüy. 8vo. Lond. 1813.
Accursius, Bonus. Elegantiæ Latinæ. 12mo. Antv. 1535.
Achenwalls, H. H. Anmerkungen über Nordamerika. 12mo. Frank. und Leips. 1769.
Acherley, Roger. Britannic Constitution. fol. Lond. 1744.
———, ———. Free Parliaments. 8vo. Lond. 1731.
Acontius, Jac. Stratagemata Satanæ. 12mo. Oxon. 1654.
Acosta, Christoph. Aromata et Medicamenta in Orientali India nascentia. Vide Garcia.
———, ———. Idem. Vide Clusius.
———, ———. Des Drogues et Médicamens qui naissent aux Indes. Vide Colin.
Acosta, Jos. De Natura Novi Orbis. 12mo. Col. Agrip. 1596.
———, —. De Promulgatione Evang. apud Barbaros. 12mo. Col. Agrip. 1596.
———, —. Historia delle Indie, trad. in Ital. da Salodiano. 4to. Venet. 1596.
———, —. Histoire Naturelle et Morale des Indes Orient. et Occid. trad. en Français par R. R. Cauxois. 8vo. Paris. 1598.
Acrelius, I. Beskrifning om de Swenska Församlingars Forna och Närwarande Tilständ, uti Nya Swerige sedan Nya Nederland. 4to. Stockholm. 1759.
Acres, Joseph. Sermon on the True Method of Propagating Religion and Royalty. 8vo. Lond. 1714.
———, ———. Sermon from Psalm lxxviii. 4. 8vo. Lond. 1714.
Acropolita, Geo. Historia Byzant. (Script. Byz.)
Acta Apostolorum. Vide Hearne.
Acta Eruditorum. 50 vol. 4to. Lips. 1682—1731.
—— ———. Supplementa. 7 vol. 4to. Lips. 1692—1721.
—— ———. Nova. 34 vol. 4to. Lips. 1732—67.
—— ———. ———. Supplem. tom. prim. 4to. Lips. 1735.
—— ———. Indices Generales Primi Actorum Decennii, nec non Supplementorum Tomi Primi. 4to. Lips. 1693.

Acta Literaria Suecica. 1720—39. 4 vols. 4to.
—— ———— Hafniensia, An. 1778. 4to. Hafniæ.
Acta Synodi Nationalis Dordrecti habitæ, 1618—19. 4to. Dort.
——, Vide Nova Acta.
Actius, Thomas. De Ludo Scacchorum in Legali Methodo. 4to Pisauri. 1583.
Acts of Queen Anne. 4 vols. fol. Lond. 1711.
—— — ——— ——. 2 vols. fol. Lond. 1713.
—— — George II. 1732—3. fol. Lond. 1732—3.
Actuarius, Joh. De Actionibus et Affectibus Spiritus Animalis, a J. F. Fischero. 8vo. Lips. 1774.
Acugna, Christophe d'. Relation de la Rivière des Amazones, tr. par Gamberville. 12mo.
———, ————. Relation of the Great River of Amazons in S. America. 12mo. Lond. 1698.
Acusilaus. Fragmenta. (Vide Pherecydes.)
Adagia, id est, Proverbiorum, Parœmiarum, et Parabolarum Collectio. fol. Francof. 1656.
Adair, James. History of the American Indians. 4to. Lond. 1775.
Adam, Alex. Summary of Geography and History. 2 vols. 8vo. Edin. 1794.
———, ——. Roman Antiquities. 8vo. Edin. 1792.
———, ——. The Same. 8vo. Phil. 1807.
———, ——. The Same. 8vo. N. York. 1814.
———, ——. His Life and Character. 8vo. Edin. 1810.
Adam, Rob. Ruins of the Palace of Diocletian at Spalatro. fol. Lond. 1760.
Adam, Tho. Paraphrase on the Eleven First Chapters of Paul's Epistle to the Romans. 8vo. Lond. 1771.
Adams, Amos. Sermons, with a Hist. View of the Planting of N. England. 2 vols. 8vo. Bost. 1756.
———, ——. Artillery Election Sermon. 8vo. Bost. 1759.
———, ——. Sermon on the Death of Mrs. Lucy Dudley. 8vo. Bost. 1756.
———, ——. Concise History of the Planting of New England. 8vo. Lond. 1770.
Adams, Eliph. Connecticut Election Sermon. 16mo. N. Lond. 1710.
Adams, Geo. On the Microscope, &c. 4to. Lond. 1787.
———, ——. The Same. 4to. Lond. 1798.
———, ——. Lectures on Natural and Experimental Philosophy. 5 vols. 8vo. Lond. 1799.
———, ——. Astronomical and Geographical Essays. 8vo. Lond. 1789.
———, ——. Geometrical and Graphical Essays. 8vo. Lond. 1797.
Adams, Hannah. Narrative of her Controversy with Dr. Morse. 8vo. Bost. 1814.
———, ————. Summary History of New England. 8vo. Dedham. 1799.
———, ————. View of Religions. 8vo. Bost. 1801.
———, ————. The Same. 8vo. Bost. 1817.

Adams, John. Sermon on the Death of the Rev. Thomas Staynoe. 8vo. Lond. 1708.
——, ——. Ahab's Evil; a Funeral Discourse. 8vo. Lond. 1714.
——, ——. Consecration Sermon. 12mo. Lond. 1708.
——, ——. Sermon before the Queen. 8vo. Lond. 1707.
Adams, John, (Rev.) Poems. 16mo. Bost. 1745.
Adams, John, (Rev.) History of Spain to the Death of Ferdinand the Sage. 3 vols. 8vo. Lond. 1793.
Adams, John, (President) History of the Dispute with America from its Origin in 1754; written in 1774. 8vo. Lond. 1784.
——, ——, ——. Consideratien op de Memorie aan H. H. MM geadresseerd door John Adams. 8vo. Leid. 1781.
——, ——, ——. Memorial to their High Mightinesses the States General of the United Provinces of the Low Countries, with other Papers relative to the United Provinces, acknowledging the Independence of the United States. 8vo. The Hague. 1782.
——, ——, ——. Defence of the American Constitutions. 3 vols. 8vo. Lond. 1787—8.
——, ——, ——. Défense des Constitutions Américaines, avec des Notes de M. de la Croix. 2 vols. 8vo. Paris 1792.
——, ——, ——. Geschiedenis van het Geschil tusschen G. Britannie en Amerika. 8vo. Amst. 1782.
——, ——, ——. Discourses on Davila. 8vo. Bost. 1805.
——, ——, ——. Letters on Government, to Samuel Adams. 8vo. Bost. 1802.
——, ——, ——. Essay on Canon and Feudal Law. 8vo. Phil. 1783.
——, ——, ——. Correspondence originally published in the Boston Patriot 8vo. Bost. 1809.
——, ——, ——. Twenty-Six Letters on the American Revolution, written in Holland, in 1780. 12mo. N. York. 1789.
——, ——, ——. Novanglus, published in 1774—5. 8vo. Bost. 1819.
——, ——, ——. Patriotic Addresses to him, with his Answers. 12mo. Bost. 1798.
——, ——, ——. Correspondence with the late William Cunningham. 8vo. Bost. 1823.
Adams, J. Q. Answer to Paine's Rights of Man. 8vo. Lond. 1793.
——, ——. Oration, July 4th, 1793. 8vo. Bost. 1793.
——, ——. Address to the Massachusetts Charitable Fire Society. 8vo. Boston. 1802.
——, ——. Letter to the Hon. H. G. Otis, on the State of our National Affairs. 8vo. Bost. 1808.
——, ——. Remarks on the above. 8vo. Bost. 1808.
——, ——. Lectures on Rhetoric and Oratory. 2 vols. 8vo. Camb. 1810.
——, ——. Inaugural Oration at Cambridge. 8vo. Bost. 1806.
——, ——. Reports upon Weights and Measures. 8vo. Washington. 1821.
——, ——. Address, July 4th, 1821. 2d ed. 8vo. Camb. 1821.

Adams, Joseph. Observations on Morbid Poisons, Phagedæna, and Cancer. 8vo. Lond. 1795. (2 copies.)

——, ——. Observations on Morbid Poisons, Chronic and Acute. 4to. Lond. 1807.

——, ——. On Epidemics.

——, ——, Life of Hunter.

Adams, Jos. (Rev.) Sermon on the Necessity and Importance of Rulers, Civil and Ecclesiastical. 4to. Portsm. 1760.

Adams, Nathaniel. Annals of Portsmouth. 8vo. Exeter. 1825.

Adams, Robert. Narrative of his Shipwreck on the Coast of Africa and Residence in Tombuctoo. 4to. Lond. 1816.

——, ——. The Same. 8vo. Bost. 1817.

Adams, Samuel. On the Conduct of the Society for Propagating the Gospel. 8vo. Lond. 1765.

Adams, Samuel. Correspondence with John Adams on Government. 8vo. Bost. 1802.

——, ——. Rede den Aug. 1, 1776.

Adams, T. M. Cool Address to the People of England on the Slave Trade. 8vo. Lond. 1788.

Adams, Wm. Essay in answer to Hume on Miracles. 8vo. Lond. 1752.

——, ——. The Same. 8vo. Lond. 1754

——, ——. Sermon on the Nature and Obligation of Virtue. 2vo. Lond. 1754.

——, ——. ——. Thanksgiving Sermon on the Conquest of Canada. 12mo. N. Lond. 1761.

Adams, Wm. Election Sermon. 8vo. Bost. 1685.

Adams, Zabdiel. Sermon on the Nature, Pleasure, and Advantages of Church Music. 12mo. Bost. 1771.

——, ——. Sermon at the Ordination of the Rev. Charles Stearns. 8vo. Bost. 1782.

——, ——. Election Sermon. 8vo. Bost. 1782.

Adamus, Fr. De Rebus Gestis in Civitate Firmana Fragmenta. (Grævius, Thes. Sicil.)

Adamus, Melchior. Vitæ Germanorum Clarorum. 12mo. Francof. 1615.

——, ——. Idem. 12mo. Francof. 1663.

——, ——. Vitæ Germanorum Theologorum. 8vo. Haidelb. 1620, et Francof. 1618.

——, ——. Idem. 8vo. Francof. 1653.

Adamus de Domerham. De Rebus Gestis Glastoniensibus. Vide Hearne.

Adanson, Mich. Histoire Naturelle de Sénégal. 4to. Paris. 1757.

——, ——. Familles des Plantes. 2 vol. 8vo. Paris. 1763.

——, ——. Voyage to Senegal, &c. From the French. 8vo. Lond. 1759.

Addenda to the Statutes. fol. Lond. 1708.

Addington, Stephen. Christian Minister's Reasons for Baptising Infants. 12mo. Lond. 1771

Addison, Alex. Reports in Pennsylvania. 8vo. 1800.

Addison, John. Works of Anacreon and Sappho, translated into English Verse; with the original Greek. 12mo. Lond. 1735.

Addison, John. The Works of Petronius Arbiter in Prose and Verse, from the Latin, with his Life. 12mo. Lond. 1736.
Addison, Joseph. Freeholder. 8vo. Lond. 1758.
———, ———. La Religion Chrétienne, tr. de l'Anglais. 8vo. Lausanne. 1757.
———, ———. Works. (Baskerville's ed.) 4 vols. 4to. Birmingham. 1761.
———, ———. Works, excepting his Spectator, collected by Tickell. 6 vols. 12mo. N. York. 1811.
———, ———. Table of Remarks in his Travels. (Som. Tr. I.)
———, ———. Discourse on Ancient and Modern Learning. 6th. ed. 4to. Lond. 1739.
———, ———. Spectator. 8 vols. 12mo. Glasg. 1745.
———, ———. The Same. 8 vols. 8vo. Lond. 1797.
———, ———. The Same. 10 vols. 12mo. N. York. 1809.
———, ———. Guardian. 2 vols. 8vo. Lond. 1760.
———, ———. Battle of the Pigmies and Cranes, from the Latin, by Warburton. See Tracts by Warburton and a Warburtonian.
Address to the People of Massachusetts recommending Sullivan and Heath for Governor and Lieut. Governor. Feb. 1805. 8vo.
——— to the Electors of Massachusetts recommending the Same. 8vo.
——— to the Electors of Massachusetts recommending Sullivan and Lincoln. 8vo.
——— to the Christian World; or Religious Remembrancer. 12mo. 1757.
——— to Unlearned Christians. 12mo. 1772.
Adelung, Joh. Christoph. Geschichte der Cultur. 12mo. Leipzig.
———, ———. ———. Mithridates. 4 vols. Berlin. 1806—16.
———, ———. ———. Three Philological Essays, from the German. Vide Kant. Elements of Crit. Philos
———, ———. ———. Geschichte von Californien. 4to. Lemgo. 1769.
Adet. Notes as Minister of the French Republic to the Secretary of State of the United States. French and English. 1796. 8vo. Phil. 1796.
———. Nomenclature Chimique. See Lavoisier.
Adler, J. G. C. Nov. Test. Versiones Syriacæ. 4to. Hafniæ. 1789.
———, ———. Reise nach Rom. 8vo. Altona. 1783.
Admiralty. Laws, Ordinances, and Institutions of the Admiralty of Great Britain, Civil and Military. 2 vols. 8vo. Lond. 1746.
———. Decisions in the High Court of Admiralty, from 1776 to 1779. 8vo. Lond. 1801.
——— Reports, Robinson's, from 1798 to 1808. 3d ed. 6 vols. 8vo. Lond. 1806, et seqq.
——— ———, Edwards', from 1808 to 1812. Lond. 1810—2.
———. Decisions in the District Court of Pennsylvania. See Peters.
Adolphus, John. History of France from 1790 to the Peace of Amiens. 2 vols. 8vo. Lond. 1803.

Adrichomius, Christian. Theatrum Terræ Sanctæ et Biblicarum Historiarum. fol. 1589.
Aduarte, Diego. Historia del S. Rosario de Filipinas, Japon, y China. 2 vol. fol. Zaragoça. 1693.
Advice, Friendly, to the Gentlemen Planters of the East and West Indies. 16mo.
——— of a Mother to her Son and Daughter. From the French of the Marchioness de Lambert. 16mo. Haverhill, Mass. 1814.
———, Dutifull, of a Loving Sonne, to his Aged Father. 12mo. Lond. 1632.
———, Friendly and Honest, of an Old Tory to the Vice-Chancellor of Cambridge. 8vo. Lond. 1751.
Ægineta, Paulus. Opus de Re Medica, Latine, per J. Guinterium. 4to. Paris. 1532.
Ægyptiaca, seu Veterum Scriptorum de Rebus Ægypti Commentarii et Fragmenta. Collegit F. A. Stroth. 12mo. Gothæ. 1782—4.
Ælfric. Testimony of the Ancient Church concerning the Sacrament, with a Sermon on the Sacrament.
Ælianus, Claudius. Varia Historia, a Coray. 8vo. Paris. 1805.
———, ————. Varia Historia et Fragmenta, a Kühnio. 2 tom. 8vo. Lips. 1780.
———, ————. Tactica, Latine, a Gaza. Vide Scriptores de Re Militari.
———, ————. De Natura Animalium, Gr. et Lat. a Gronovio. 2 tom. 4to. Lond. 1744.
———, ————. Idem, a Schneidero. 8vo. Lips. 1784.
———, ————. Observationes in Ælianum. Vide Jacobs.
Æneas Tacticus. De Toleranda Obsidione Commentarius. Vide Polybius.
Æpinus, F. M. U. T. Tentamen Theoriæ Electricitatis et Magnetismi. 4to. Petrop. 1760.
———, ————. De Distributione Caloris per Tellurem. 4to. Petropoli. 1761.
Æs Redivivum, sive Tabula Ærea, e Terræ Visceribus Eruta. (Græv. Thes. Ital.)
Æschines, Orator. Opera, a Wolfio. fol. Aurel. Allob. 1607.
———, ———. Idem, a J. Taylor. 8vo. Cant. 1769.
———, ———. Vide Oratores Græci, a Reiskio.
Æschines, Socraticus. Dialogi tres, Gr. and Lat. curante Clerico. 8vo. Amst. 1711.
———, ————. Dialogi Tres in usum Scholarum, cura J. F. Fischeri. 12mo. Lips. 1753. (2 copies.)
Æschylus. Tragœdiæ Septem et Fragmenta, Gr. et Lat. cum Comment. cura Stanleii. fol. Lond. 1663.
———. Idem. C. G. Schützii. 3 tom. 8vo. Halæ. 1782—94.
———. Idem. ————. 4 tom. 8vo. Halæ. 1808—21.
———. Tragœdiæ Septem, Gr. et Lat. 2 tom. in 1 vol. 8vo. Halæ. 1800.
———. Idem. 2 tom. 12mo. Glasguæ. 1806.
———. Choephoræ. 12mo. Oxon. 1729.

Æschylus. Tragedies, translated by Potter. 2 vols. 8vo. Lond. 1779.
————. Agamemnon, übers. von Humboldt. 4to. Leip. 1816.
Æsopus. Fabulæ, Gr. et Lat. per J. Hudson. 8vo. Oxon. 1718.
————. Fabulæ, a Coray. 8vo. Paris. 1810.
————. Idem, a Klotzio. 12mo. Lips. 1810.
————. Vida y Fabulas, por Mendes. 12mo. Lisboa. 1673.
Aetius. Amidenus. Specimen. Vide Weigel.
Affairs, Foreign and Domestic. Miscellaneous Thoughts upon them. 8vo. Lond. 1742.
———, ————————. Observations on the above. 8vo. Lond.
———, ————————. Brief Representation of the Posture of Affairs, Foreign and Domestic. 8vo. Lond. 1745.
Affaires de l'Angleterre et de l'Amérique. 15 vol. 8vo. Anvers 1775—9.
Affinati, Giacomo d'Acuto. Dumbe Divine Speaker, a Treatise in Praise of Silence, tr. from the Italian. 4to. Lond. 1605.
Africa. Account of that Part inhabited by the Negroes. 12mo. Philad. 1762.
Agapetus, (Diaconus.) Capita Admonitoria ad Justinianum Imperatorem. (Banduri, Imp. Orient. vol. 1.)
Agar, Wm. Sermons on Military Devotion. 8vo. Lond. 1757
Agard, Arthur. Antiquarian Papers. See Hearne.
Agathias. De Rebus Gestis Imper. Justiniani. (Script. Byz.)
Agius de Soldanis, G. P. F. Della Lingua Punica presentement usata da' Maltesi, etc. 8vo. Roma. 1750. (2 copies.)
Agocchi, J. B. De Bononia. (Grævius, Thes. Ital.)
Agostino, Ant. Dialoghi intorno alle Medaglie, Inscrittioni, et altre Antichità. fol. Rom. 1592.
Agricultural Society of Massachusetts, Papers and Journal. 4 pamphlets. 8vo. Bost. 1804, 1806, 1815, 1817.
———— ——— of New York. Transactions. Part II. 4to. 1794.
Agricultural Museum. vol. 1. 8vo. Georgetown, Ca. 1811.
Agriculture. See Philadelphia.
Agrippa, H. C. De Libro suo de Incertitudine et Vanitate omnium Scientiarum et Artium. (Shelhorn, vol. 2.)
————, ———. De Vita, Fatis, Moribus, et Scriptis suis. (Shelhorn, vol. 2.)
Agrœtius. De Orthographia et Proprietate et Differentia Sermonis. Vide Grammatici Veteres Latini.
Aguesseau, H. F. d'. Œuvres, avec un Discours sur sa Vie et sa Mort, par son Fils. 13 vol. 4to. Paris. 1787—9.
Aguirre, Manuel de. Sistema de Sociedades Patrióticas y de Seminarios ó Casas Públicas de Educacion. 4to. Madrid. 1785.
Ahmed, Arabsiades. Historia Timuri, Arabice, cura J. Golii. 4to. Lug. Bat. 1636.
Aignan, M. De l'Etat des Protestans en France depuis le XVIe. siècle jusq' à nos jours. 8vo. Paris. 1818.
Aikin, A. & C. R. Dictionary of Chemistry and Mineralogy. 2 vols. 4to. Lond. 1807.

Aikin, John. Vocal Poetry. 16mo. N. York. 1811. (3 copies.)
——, ——. Letters to a Young Lady on English Poetry. 12mo. Lond. 1807. (2 copies.)
——, ——. Biographical Memoirs of Medicine in Great Britain. 8vo. Lond. 1780.
——, ——. Letters from a Father to his Son. 2 vols. 8vo. Lond. 1794—1800.
——, ——. Life of Howard. 8vo. Lond. 1792.
Aikin, Lucy. Memoirs of Queen Elizabeth. 2 vols. 8vo. Bost. 1821.
——, ——. ———— James I. 2 vols. 8vo. Bost. 1822.
Ailredus, Abbas, Rievallensis. Historia, de Bello Standardii tempore Stephani Regis, Genealogia Regum Anglorum, Vita et Miraculis Edwardi Regis. (Twysden, Scrip. X.)
Ainsworth, Henry. Annotations upon the Books of Moses, Psalms, and Canticles. 2 vols. 4to. Lond. 1622. (2 copies.)
——, ——. The Same. fol. Lond. 1627. (2 copies.)
——, ——. Book of Psalms in Prose and Metre. 12mo. Amst. 1664.
Ainsworth, Rob. Dictionary, English and Latin. 2 vols. fol. London. 1752.
——, ——. The Same, by Morell. 2 vols. 4to. Lond. 1773.
——, ——. The Same, ————. 2 vols. 4to. Lond. 1783.
——, ——. Abridgement. ————. 8vo. Phil. 1812.
——, ——. Institutions of Domestic Education. 8vo. Lond. 1736.
——, ——. Monumenta Vetustatis Kempiana. 8vo. Lond. 1720.
——, ——. De Clypeo Camilli Antiquo. 4to. Lond. 1734.
Aislabie, John. His Case stated respecting the South Sea Company. 4to. Lond. 1721.
——, ——. Speech in the House of Lords. 4to. Lond. 1721.
——, ——. Second Speech ————. 4to. Lond. 1721.
——, ——. Speech upon the Consolidated Bill. 4to. 1721.
Aitchison, Alex. Encyclopædia Perthensis, or Universal Dictionary of Knowledge. 23 vols. 8vo. Perth.
Aitken, John. Theory and Practice of Physic and Surgery. 2 vols. 8vo. Lond. 1782.
——, ——. The Same. 2 vols. 8vo. Lond. 1783.
——, ——. Principles of Anatomy and Physiology. 2 vols. 8vo. Lond. 1786.
——, ——. On Fracture and Luxations.
Akber. Ayeen Akbery, or Institutes of the Emperor Akber, from the Persian, by F. Gladwin. Vol. I. and II. 4to. Calcutta. 1783—4.
Akenside, Mark. Ode to the Earl of Huntington. 4to. Lond. 1748.
——, ——. Ode to Thomas Edwards. fol. Lond. 1766.
——, ——. Ode to the Country Gentlemen of England. 4to. Lond. 1758.
——, ——. Odes on Several Subjects. 4to. Lond. 1760.
——, ——. Pleasures of the Imagination. 8th ed. 12mo. Lond. 1769.

Akenside, Mark. Pleasures of the Imagination, with Mrs. Barbauld's Critical Essay. 16mo. N. York. 1813.
———, ———. De Dysenteria. 8vo. Lond. 1764.
Alamanni, Luigi. Opere Toscane. 12mo. Vinegia. 1533.
———, ———. La Coltivazione. 8vo. Milano. 1804.
Alanson, Edw. On Amputation. 8vo. Lond. 1782. (2 copies.)
Albemarle, (Monk, Geo.) Duke of. Observations on Military and Political Affairs. Published by Heath. fol. Lond. 1671.
Albers, J. A. Americanische Annalen, Th. I, II, und III. 8vo. Bremen. 1802—3.
Albert, Jacques. Estat de l'Ægypte. 4to. Paris. 1651.
Alberti, Joannes. Observationes Philologicæ in Sacros Nov. Fœd. Libros. 8vo. Lug. Bat 1725.
Alberti, Leandro. Descrittione d' Italia. 4to. Venetia. 1577.
Alberti, Leonbatista. Della Pittura e della Statua. 8vo. Milano. 1804.
Alberti, Paulus Martinus. Lexicon Hebræo-Latino-Biblicum. 4to. Budissæ. 1704.
Albertus Magnus. Opera quæ hactenus haberi potuerunt, cura P. Jammy. 21 vol. fol. Lugd. 1651.
Albinus, B. S. (Weiss.) Icones Ossium Fœtus Humani. 4to. Leidæ. 1737.
———, ———. Annotationes Acad. 2 vol. 4to. Leidæ. 1754.
———, ———. Tables of the Skeleton and Muscles, from the Latin. fol. Lond. 1749.
———, ———. Tabulæ Sceleti et Musculorum Corporis Humani. fol. Lond. 1749.
———, ———. Explicatio Tabularum Anatomicarum Eustachii. fol. Leidæ. 1761.
———, ———. Anatomical Figures explained. 4to. Lond. 1754.
Albinus, J. E. (Weiss.) De Christi Hominis 'Αναμαρτησία. 4to. Wittenbergæ. 1690.
Albrecht, J. H. Dissertatio de Traditionibus Pontificiis Modestioribus. 4to. Jenæ. 1686.
Albricus. De Deorum Imaginibus. Vide Mythographi Latini.
Alcæus. Fragmenta, a Stange. 12mo. Halæ. 1810.
Alcazar, Baltasar de. Rimas. Vide Rioja.
Alcedo, Antonio Diccionario Geográfico-Hist. de América. 3 vol. 4to. Madrid. 1786.
Alcedo y Herrera, Dionysio de. Compendio Historico de Guayaquil. 4to Madrid. 1741.
———, ———. Aviso con las Noticias de Peru, etc. 4to. Madrid. 1740.
Alciatus, And. De Magistratibus, etc. Vide Rom. Hist. Script. vol. 3, et Sallengre, vol. 1.
———, ———. Rerum Patriæ, seu Historiæ Mediolanensis Libri IV. (Grævius. Thes. Ital.)
Alcidamas. Orationes. Vide Oratores Græci, a Reiskio.
Alciphron. Epistolæ. Gr. et Lat. ad editionem S. Bergleri. 8vo. Traj. ad Rhen. 1791.

Alciphron. Epistolæ, Gr. et Lat. a Wagner. 2 tom. 8vo. Lips. 1798.
Alcman. Fragmenta, a F. T. Welckero. 4to. 1815.
Alcoran. See Bibliander. See Sale.
Alcwinus, F. De Pontificibus. (Gale, Scriptores XV.)
Alden, Ebenezer. Address to Dart. Med. Society, Dec. 28, 1819. 8vo. Bost. 1820.
Alden, Timothy. Sermon at the Opening of the New Meeting House in Yarmouth, Jan. 1, 1795. 8vo. Bost. 1795.
Alden, Timothy. New Jersey Register. 12mo. Newark. 1811.
——, ——. Collection of Epitaphs. 5 vols. 12mo. N. York. 1814.
——, ——. Century Sermon. 8vo. Portsmouth. 1801.
——, ——. Alleghany Magazine. Nos. 1 and 10 of vol. 1. 8vo. Meadville. 1816.
——, ——. Sermon on the Death of Washington. 8vo. Portsmouth. 1800.
Aldini, John. Account of Improvements in Galvanism. 4to. Lond. 1803.
Aldobrandina Villa Tusculana. fol. Romæ. 1647.
Aldrete, Bern. Varias Antiquedades de España, Africa, &c. 4to. Amb. 1614.
——, ——. Del Origen y Principio de la Lengua Castellana. 4to. Roma. 1606.
Aldrich, Henry. Reply to Two Discourses concerning the Eucharist. 4to. Oxford. 1687.
Aldridge, Wm. Short Hand. See Holdsworth.
Aldrovandi, Ulysses. Hist. Quadrupedum Bisulcorum. fol. Bon. 1621.
Aldus Manutius, P. Fil. De Cælatura et Pictura Veterum. (Gronovius, vol. 9.)
——, ——. De Tibiis Veterum. (Ugolinus, vol. 32.)
Aleander, Hier. jun. Tabulæ Heliacæ Explicatio. (Græv. vol. 5.)
Alehouses. Thoughts on the great Circumspection necessary in Licencing them. 8vo.
Aleman, Mateo. Vida y Hechos del Picaro Guzman de Alfarache. 2 vol. 12mo. Valencia. 1787.
Alemann, Nic. De Lateranensibus Parietinis. (Grævius, Thes. Ital.)
Alembert, J. le Rond d'. Account of the Destruction of the Jesuits in France. From the French. 12mo. Lond. 1766.
——, ——. Œuvres Phil. Hist. et Lit. 18 vol. 8vo. Paris. 1805.
——, ——. Mélanges de Littérature, d'Histoire, et de Philosophie. 4 vol. 12mo. Amst. 1764.
——, ——. Miscellaneous Pieces in Literature, History, and Philosophy. From the French. 12mo. Lond. 1764.
——, ——. Lettre sur les Aveugles, à l'usage de ceux qui voyent. 12mo. Lond. 1749.
——, ——. Vide Diderot.
A Lent. Joh. De Judæorum Pseudo-Messiis. (Ugol. vol. 23.)
Alexander, A. Prophetæ XV Posteriores, Hebr. 8vo. 1814.

Alexander, A. Pentateuch, Heb. and Eng. 5 vols. 8vo. Lond. 1785.
Alexander, Dan. Tnangam, (a converted Jew.) Call to the Jews. 4to. London.
Alexander, John. Essay on Irenæus. 8vo. Lond. 1727.
Alexander, John. Paraphrase on the xvth Chapter of 1 Cor. with a Commentary on Rom. vi. vii. and viii. and a Sermon composed by him the day preceding his death. 4to. Lond. 1766.
Alexander Natalis. Theologia Dogmatica et Moralis. 2 vol. fol. Col. Agrip. 1698.
Alexander VII. Pope. Life and Death of. (Somer's Tracts, vol. 7.)
Alexander Trallianus. De Re Medica. Vide Haller, Art. Med. Principes.
Alexander, Wm. History of Women. 2 vols. 8vo. Lond. 1782.
Alexandre e Silva, Elias. Relaçao da infeliz Viajem da Nao Nossa Senhora da Ajuda, e S. Pedro de Alcantara. 4to. Lisb. 1778.
Alexandrinus Codex. Vide Woide.
Alfieri, Vittorio. Opere. 22 tom. 4to. Italia. 1805—15.
Alfonso el Noble. Memorias Historicas de su Vida, por el Marques de Mondexar, con Notas y Apendices. 4to. Madrid. 1783.
Alfonso el Sabio. Cronica de España. fol. Zamora. 1541.
———, ———. Siete Partidas, por la Real Acad. de la Hist. 3 tom. 4to. Madrid. 1807.
Alfonso el Oncéno. Cronica. fol. Valladolid. 1551.
———, ———. Idem, por D. F. Cerdá y Rico. 4to. Madrid. 1787.
Algarotti, Francesco. Opere. 17 tom. 8vo. Venez. 1792—4.
———, ———. Idem. 8 tom. 12mo. Livorno. 1764.
———, ———. Essay on the Opera, from the Italian. 12mo. Lond. 1767.
Ali Bey. Travels in Morocco, &c. 2 vols. 8vo. Phil. 1816.
Alison, Arch. Essays on Taste. 4to. Edin. 1790.
———, ——. The Same. 2 vols. 8vo. Edin. 1811.
———, ——. The Same. 8vo. Bost. 1812.
Allan, James. Letter concerning him to the General Assembly, by a Presb. Minister of the Church of Scotland. 4to. 1707.
Allard, Charles. Atlas Minor, sive Tab. Geograph. fol. Amst.
———, ———. Idem, 138 Mappas continens. fol. Amst.
Allatius, Leo. De Patria Homeri, ejusque Natales. (Gronov. vol. 10.)
———, ——. Confutatio Fabulæ de Joanna Papissa. (Shelhorn, 9.)
Allegiance. Essay on Naturalization and Allegiance. 8vo. Washington City. 1816.
Alleine, Joseph. Sure Guide to Heaven. 12mo. Lond. 1704.
Allen, Ethan. Narrative of his Voyages, Travels, and Captivity. 12mo. Phil. 1779.
Allen, Ira. History of Vermont. 8vo. Lond. 1798. (2 copies.)
Allen, James. Election Sermon. 4to. Bost. 1679.
Allen, James. Two Practical Discourses. 12mo. Bost. 1727.
——, ———. Sermon on Mans' Self-reflection. 12mo.
——, ———. Election Sermon. 8vo. Bost. 1744.
Allen, John, Rev. Trial of, for Forgery. 12mo. Bost. 1773.
Allen, John, M. D. Charity Sermon. 8vo. Lond. 1740.

Allen, John, M. D. Sermon on occasion of the Earthquakes. 8vo. Lond. 1750.

——, ————. Fast Sermon. 8vo. Lond. 1756.

——, ————. Thanksgiving Sermon on the Suppression of the Rebellion. 8vo. Lond. 1746.

Allen, John Associations against the Established Church Indefensible, a Sermon before the Univ. of Oxford. 8vo. Oxford. 1773.

Allen, Jonathan. Sermon at the Ordination of Rev. David T. Kimball. 8vo. Newburyport. 1806.

Allen, Robert. Vindiciæ Pietatis; or Vindication of Godliness. 12mo. Lond. 1664.

——, ———. The Godly Man's Portion, in two Sermons. 12mo. Lond. 1668.

Allen, S. C. Eulogy on the Hon. John Wheelock, Pres. of Dart. Univ. 8vo. Hanover. 1817.

Allen, Silas. Review of Doct. Freeman's Sermons. 8vo. Camb. 1821.

——, ——. Review of the Review, (by T. Keating.) 8vo. Camb. 1821.

Allen, Thomas. Chain of Scripture Chronology. 4to. Lond. 1659.

Allen, Thomas. Sermon on the Death of Mrs. Eliz. White. 8vo. Pittsfield. 1798.

——, ———. Sermon on the Death of Mr. Moses Allen. 8vo. Pittsfield. 1801.

——, ———. Sermon on the Death of Thomas Allen jr. Esq. 8vo. Bost. 1806.

——, ———. Election Sermon. 8vo. Bost. 1808.

Allen, Tim. Sermon at his own Installation at Ashford. 8vo. N. Haven. 1761.

Allen, Wilkes. Thanksgiving Sermon. 8vo. Camb. 1811.

Allen, Wm. American Biographical and Historical Dictionary. 8vo. Camb. 1809.

——, ——. Account of the Separation in the Church and Town of Pittsfield, Mass. 8vo. Pittsfield. 1809.

Allen, Wm. Collectanea Latina. 12mo. 1815.

Alleyne, James. Dispensatory. 8vo. Lond. 1733.

Alleyne, John. Assize Sermon. 4to. Camb. 1707.

Allies. Conduct of the Allies and of the Ministry. Remarks on the above. Defence of the Allies. Allies and late Ministry Defended. Full Account of the Conduct of the Allies. 8vo. Lond. 1712.

Allinga, Peter. Satisfaction of Christ stated and defended; also, Articles of Ayr contrasted with the Oracles of Truth, tr. by Rev. Thomas Bill. 8vo. Glasg. 1790.

Allionius, Car. Flora Pedemontana. 2 tom. in 1. fol. Aug. Taur. 1785. (2 copies.)

Allix, Peter. Two Treatises. 1. Confutation of the Hopes of the Jews. 2. Answer to Whiston on the Prophecies concerning the Messiah. 8vo Lond. 1707.

——, ——. Remarks on the Ecclesiastical History of the Ancient Churches of Piedmont. 4to. Lond. 1690.

Allix, Peter. Reflections on the Books of the Holy Scriptures. 2 vols. in 1. 8vo. Lond. 1738.
——, ——. The Same. (Watson's Tracts.)
——, ——. Book of Psalms, with the Argument. 8vo. Lond. 1701
——, ——. Discourse concerning Penance. fol. 1738.
——, ——. Theses Theologicæ de Justitia Christi Fidelibus Imputata. 4to. Sedani. 1662.
——, ——. Historical Discourse on the Sacraments. 4to. Lond. 1688.
——, ——. Judgment of the Ancient Jewish Church against the Unitarians. 4to. Lond. 1699.
——, ——. Preparation for the Lord's Supper, tr. from the French. 12mo. 1688.
——, ——. Discourse concerning the Merit of Good Works. 4to. Lond. 1688.
Allston, Washington. Sylphs of the Seasons, and other Poems. 12mo. Bost. 1813.
Allyn, John. Election Sermon. 8vo. Bost. 1805.
Almanac. See Nautical.
Almanach des Colonies, 1788. 16mo. Paris.
———— Américain. 12mo. Paris. 1783.
———— Américain, Asiatique, et Africain. Vide Rochetillac.
———— des Négocians. 12mo. Bruxelles. 1762.
Almanack, the New Jamaica, for 1799. 12mo. Kingston.
Almeida, Gius. de. Grammatica Punica. 8vo. Rom. 1750.
Almon, John. The Remembrancer, or Repository of Public Events. 17 vols. 8vo. London. 1775—84.
Alphonsus, G. Metamoros Hispalensis, &c. 12mo. Matri. 1736.
Alpinus, Prosper. De Medicina Methodica. 4to. Lug. Bat. 1719. (2 copies.)
———, ———. De Præsagienda Vita et Morte Ægrotantium. 4to. Lug. Bat. 1733. (2 copies.)
———, ———. Medicina Ægyptiorum. De Balsamo et Rhapontico. Jac. Bontii Medicina Indorum. 4to. Lug. Bat. 1719.
———, ———. Idem. 4to. Lug. Bat. 1745.
———, ———. Res Ægyptiacæ, sive Hist. Nat. Ægypti. 4to. Lug. Bat. 1735. (2 copies.)
———, ———. De Plantis Ægypti, et De Rebus Ægyptiacis. 2 tom. 4to. Lug. Bat. 1735. (2 copies.)
———, ———. De Balsamo. (Ugolinus, vol. 11.)
Alsarius, Vinc. De Invidia et Fascino Veterum. (Græv. vol. 12.)
Alsop, Anton. Odæ. 4to. Lond. 1752.
Alsop, Vincent. Speech to the King on presenting a Petition. fol.
——, ———. Sermon to the Society for the Reformation of Manners. 12mo. Lond 1698.
——, ———. Melius Inquirendum; or a Sober Inquiry in Defence of Non-Conformists.
Alstedius, Joh. Hen. Encyclopædia. 7 tom. in 4 vol. fol. Herbornæ Nassov. 1630.
Alston, Ch. Lectures on the Materia Medica, with an Appendix on Prescribing. 2 vols. 4to. Lond. 1770.

Alter, F. C. Novum Testamentum Græcum. 2 vol. 8vo. Viennæ. 1787—6.
Altham, Arthur. (or perhaps Michael. Vide Watt. Bib.) Queries to Protestants Answered, &c. 4to. Lond. 1687.
———, ———. Vindication of the Church of England. 4to. Lond. 1687.
———, ———. Creed of Pope Pius IV. or a Prospect of Popery, with Notes. 4to. Lond. 1687.
———, ———. Additional Articles in Pope Pius's Creed. 4to. Lond. 1688.
Altham, R. Sermon on the Election of the Lord Mayor. 4to. Lond. 1702.
———, —. Sermon, January 30th. 4to. Lond. 1702.
Altilius, Gab. Epithalamium, etc. 4to. Patav. 1731.
Alting, Jac. Synopsis Institutionum Chaldæarum et Syrarum. Vide Otho.
———, —. Hist. Acad. in Populo Hebræorum. 12mo. Amst. 1652.
Altmannus, J. G. De Gallicinio Hierosolymis in Ædibus Pontificis audito. (Ugol. vol. 27.)
———, ——. De Lydia Thyatirensi. (Ugol. vol. 29.)
Alvarez, Francisco. Noticia de las Colonias Inglesas en la America Septentrional. 4to. Madrid. 1778.
Alypius. Introductio Musica. Vide Musicæ Auctores.
Alzedo, Mauricio de. Jerusalen Cautiva. 4to. Madrid. 1642.
Amaltheus, Hieron. Odæ et Sylvæ. Vide Poemata Italorum.
Amaltheus, Joh. Bap. Eclogæ et Odæ. Vide Poemata Italorum.
Amama, Sixtinus. Grammatica Ebræa Martinio-Buxtorfiana. 12mo. Amst. 1625.
———, ———. Coronis ad Grammat. Buxtorf. 12mo. Amst. 1625.
———, ———. Antibarbarus Biblicus, seu Censura Versionis Vulgatæ Latinæ certorum Vet. Test. Librorum. 8vo. Amst. 1628.
Ambrose, Isaac. Complete Works. fol. Lond. 1674.
———, ——. Looking unto Jesus. 4to. Edin. 1723.
Ambrosius, Sanctus. Opera, a Monachis S. Mauri. 2 vol. fol. Paris. 1686—90.
———, ————. De Moribus Brachmanorum, a Bissæo. fol. Lond. 1665.
Ameilhon. Sur les Couleurs des Anciens. (Instit. Lit. vol. 1.)
———. Projet sur quelques Changemens qu' on pourroit faire à nos Catalogues de Bibliothèques. (Id. vol. 2.)
———. Sur le Sparte des Auteurs Anc. (Id. vol. 2.)
———. Sur la Péche des Anciens. (Id. vol. 5.)
America, or an Exact Description of the West Indies, by N. N. Gent. 16mo. Lond. 1655. (2 copies.)
———. De l'Amérique et des Américains. 12mo. Berlin. 1771.
———. Différentes Races de l'Amérique, par M. de la Cruz. (Planches.) fol. 1784.
———, Amerika in alle Byzonderheden. 4 vol. 12mo. Amst. 1780.
———, Staat van Amerika. 3 vols. 8vo. Amst. 1766.
———, Staat von America. 12mo.

America, European Settlements in. See Burke.

———, Geografico-Storico-Politica. 3 tom. in 1. 8vo. Venezia. 1785.

———, Sitten und Meinungen der Wilden in America. 4 vol. 12mo. Frank. am Mayn. 1777—81.

———, Neueste Kunde von. 2 vol. 8vo. Weimar. 1815.

———, Vide Roman Politique. Vide Researches. V. Public Lands. V. North America. V. South America.

American Academy of Arts and Sciences. Memoirs. 4 vols. 4to. Bost. 1785—1818.

American Academy of the Fine Arts. Charter and By-Laws, with an Account of its Statues, Paintings, and other property. 8vo. N. York. 1817.

American Glory. The Victories of Hull, Jones, Decatur, Bainbridge, &c. 8vo. Phil. 1813.

American Husbandry, containing an Account of the Soil, Climate, Productions, and Agriculture of the British Colonies in N. America and W. Indies. 2 vols. 8vo. Lond. 1775.

American Independence, the Interest and Glory of Great Britain, a new edition, with an Appendix. 8vo. Lond. 1775.

——— ————. Collection of State Papers relative to Holland's acknowledging the Sovereignty of the U. States. 8vo. The Hague. 1782.

——— ————. Réponse sur la Question; L'Indépendence de l'Amérique est elle à désirer? 8vo.

——— ————, Consolatory Thoughts on. 8vo. Edin. 1782.

——— ————, Account of the Grand Federal Procession in Philadelphia, July 4th, 1788, with Mr. Wilson's Oration, &c. 8vo. Phil. 1788.

——— ————. Thoughts on the Consequences of it to Great Britain.

——— ————. Biography of the Signers of the Declaration of Independence. 9 vols. 8vo. Phil. 1823—7.

American Law Journal, by Hall. 6 vols. 8vo. Phil. 1800—17.

American Medical and Philosophical Register, by Drs. Hosack and Francis. 4 vols. 8vo. N. York. 1814.

American Nepos; a Collection of the Lives of Eminent Men, who have contributed to the Discovery, Settlement, and Independence of America. 12mo. Baltimore. 1805.

American Philosophical Society. Transactions. 6 vols. 4to. Phil. 1786—1809.

————————. ————. New Series. 2 vols. 4to. 1818—1825.

————————. ————. Of the Hist. and Lit. Committee. vol. 1. 8vo. Phil. 1819.

American Plants. See Synopsis.

American Preacher. 8vo. N. Haven. 1793.

American Precedents of Declarations. 8vo. Bost. 1802.

——— ——————————. Anthon's. 8vo. N. York. 1810. Also Brookfield, 1821.

American Revolution. Detail and Conduct of the War under Generals Gage, Howe, and Burgoyne, and Admiral Howe.
——— ———. Shall I go to War with my American Brethren? a Discourse. 8vo. Lond. 1769.
——— ———. Reflections on the American Contest, by A. M. 8vo. Lond. 1776.
——— ———. View of the Evidence relative to the conduct of the War under Sir William Howe, Lord Howe, and Gen. Burgoyne. 2d ed. 8vo. Lond. 1779.
——— ———. Dispassionate Thoughts on the American War. 8vo. Lond. 1780.
——— ———. Considerations upon the American Enquiry. 8vo. Lond. 1779.
——— ———. Account of it.
——— ———. Collection of Interesting, Authentic Papers relative to the Dispute between Great Britain and America. (Prior Documents.) 8vo. Lond. 1777.
——— ———. Case of Great Britain and America. 2d ed. 8vo. Lond. 1769.
——— ———. The Same. 3d ed. 4to. Boston.
——— ———. Appeal to the Justice and Interests of the People of Great Britain in the present Disputes with America. 8vo. Lond. 1774.
——— ———. The Same. 4th ed. 8vo. Lond. 1776.
——— ———. Second Appeal. 8vo. Lond. 1775.
——— ———. Authentic Papers from America. 8vo. Lond. 1775.
——— ———. Vide Bericht. V. Briefe. V. Geschichte. V. American Independence. V. British Colonies.
American Spelling Book. 12mo. Worcester. 1785.
American Star, being a Choice Collection of Patriotic and other Songs. 2d ed. 16mo. Richmond. 1817.
American Traveller. See Cluny.
Ames, Fisher. Works; with his Life (by J. T. Kirkland.) 8vo. Bost. 1809.
———. Speech on the British Treaty. 8vo. Bost. 1796.
Ames, Jos. Typographical Antiquities of Great Britain and Ireland. 4to. Lond. 1749.
———, —. Catalogue of English Heads; or an Account of about 2000 prints. 8vo. Lond. 1748.
Amesius, Gul. Explicatio utriusque Epistolæ Divi Petri, et Conciones; item Christianæ Catecheseos Sciagraphia. 12mo. Amst. 1650—60.
———, —. Lectiones in Psalmos Davidis. 12mo. Amst. 1658.
———, —. De Conscientia et ejus Jure vel Casibus. 16mo. Amst. 1635.
———, —. Idem. 16mo. Amst. 1660.
———, —. Power and Cases of Conscience. Marrow of Sacred Divinity. Exposition of Peter. 4to. Lond. 1641—43.
———, —. Medulla Theologiæ. 12mo. Amst. 1628. Item 24to. Amst. 1628, et 1656.

Amesius, Gul. Bellarminus Enervatus. 4 vol. in 2. 12mo. Oxon. 1629.
———, —. De Origine Sabbati, et Die Dominico; item Puritanismus Anglicanus. 16mo. Amst. 1658.
———, —. Anti-Synodalia Scripta. 16mo. Amst. 1661.
———, —. Coronis ad Collationem Hagiensem. 16mo. Amst. 1664.
———, —. Rescriptio ad Grevinchovii Responsum de Redemptione, etc. 16mo. Harderv 1645. Item Amst. 1658.
———, —. Philosophemata, etc. 16mo. Amst. 1651.
Amico, Ant. de. De Urbis Syracusarum Antiquo Archiepiscopatu, ac de ejusdem in universa Sicilia Metropolitico Jure. (Græv. Thes. Ital.)
Amiot. Vie de Confucius. (Mémoires sur les Chinois.)
Ammendorf. De Situ Gosen.
Ammianus Marcellinus. Res Gestæ, cum Notis J. Gronovii. 4to. Lug. Bat. 1693.
———, ———. Idem. fol. Lug. Bat. 1693.
———, ———. Idem. Vide Rom. Hist. Script.
Ammon, C. F. Summa Theologiæ Christianæ. 8vo. Erlangæ. 1808.
———, —. Biblische Theologie. 3 vol. 8vo. Erlangen. 1801—2.
———, —. Pentateuchi Nova Versio Græca. 3 vol. 8vo. Erlangæ. 1790—1.
———, —. Predigten. 2 vol. 8vo. Nürnberg. 1814.
———, —. Idem. 2 vol. 8vo. Dresden. 1819.
———, —. Vorträge. 3 vol. 8vo. Götting. 1804—9.
Ammonius. De Adfinium Vocabulorum Differentia, a Valcknaer. 4to. Lug. Bat. 1739.
———. Idem; ab Ammon. 8vo. Erlangæ. 1787.
Amœnitates Literariæ. Vide Schelhorn.
Amort, Eusebius. Dictionarium Casuum Conscientiæ. 2 tom. 4to. Aug. Vin. 1762.
Amory, Thomas. Sermons on Daily Devotion. 8vo. Lond. 1747.
———, ———. Eight Sermons on a Future Judgment. 8vo. Lond. 1648.
———, ———. Sermons. 2 vols. 8vo. Lond. 1758—66.
———, ———. Charity Sermon. 8vo. Lond. 1760.
———, ———. Sermon at the Young Men's Lecture. 8vo. Lond. 1735.
———, ———. Sermon at the Ordination of the Rev. Wm. Richards. 8vo. Lond. 1751.
———, ———. Fast Sermon. 8vo. Lond. 1745.
———, ———. Sermon on the Death of the Rev. James Strong. 8vo. Lond. 1733.
———, ———. Sermon on the Death of the Rev. John Moore. 8vo. Lond. 1749.
———, ———. Dialogue on Devotion after the Manner of Xenophon. 8vo. Lond.
———, ———. The Same, with a Conversation of Socrates, from the Greek of Xenophon. 8vo. Lond. 1733.

Ampelius, L. Liber Memorialis. Vide Florus.
———, —. Liber Memorialis in usum Scholarum. 16mo. Lips. 1793.
Amphilochius Iconiensis. Opera; item Methodii Patarensis, et Andreæ Cretensis. Gr. et Lat. fol. Paris. 1644.
Amphlett, Wm. Emigrant's Directory to the Western States of North America, &c. 8vo. Lond. 1819.
Amralkeisi Moallakah. Vide Caab Ben Zohier.
Amyot, Jacques. Daphnis et Chloé, escrit en Grec par Longus, trad. par J. A. 12mo. London. 1780.
Ana, ou Collection des Bons Mots, Contes, Anecdotes, etc. des Hommes Célèbres parmi les Modernes. 10 vol. Amst. 1799.
Anabaptists, Short History of. 4to.
Anacreon. Odæ. Gr. et Lat. cum Notis, ex editione Josuæ Barnes. 12mo. Cant. 1721.
———. Idem, per J. Trapp. 2d ed. 12mo. Lond. 1742.
———. Convivialia Semiambia, Gr. et Lat. cum Tabulis Æneis fol. Romæ. 1781.
———. Carmina, Gr. cum Notis Baxteri et Fischeri. 8vo. Lips. 1793.
———. Odes, Greek and English, by John Addison. 12mo. Lond. 1735.
Analecta Vet. Poet. Græc. a R. F. P. Brunck. 3 vol. 8vo. Argent. 1772—6.
Analecta Hellenica. Vide Collectanea.
Analysis of the late Correspondence between our Administration and Great Britain and France. (By J. Lowell.) 8vo. Boston.
———, Supplement to. (By the Same.) 8vo.
Anastasius. Historia Ecclesiastica. (Script. Byz. et Sirmondi Opera.)
Anatomical Dialogues. 8vo. Lond. 1796. (6 copies.)
Anburey, Thomas. Travels through the Interior Parts of America. 2 vols. 8vo. Lond. 1789.
Ancient Languages. Inquiry whether the Study of them be a Necessary Branch of Modern Education. 8vo. Edin. 1769.
Ancillon, Charles. Histoire de l'Etablissement des François Refugiéz en Brandebourg. 8vo. Berlin. 1690.
Ancora, G. d'. Scavi di Ercolano e di Pompei, etc. 8vo. Napoli. 1803.
Anderson, Adam. Historical and Chronological Deduction of the Origin of Commerce from the earliest accounts. 2 vols. fol. Lond. 1764.
———, —. The Same, with an Appendix by Mr. Coombe. 6 vols. 8vo. Dublin. 1790.
Anderson, Andrew. Inaugural Dissertation on the Eupatorium Perfol. of Linnæus. 8vo. N. York. 1813.
Anderson, David. Canada, or a View of the Importance of the British American Colonies. 8vo. Lond. 1814.
Anderson, James. Royal Genealogies from Adam to the present time. 2d. ed. fol. Lond. 1736.

Anderson, James. Interest of Great Britain with regard to her American Colonies. 8vo. Lond. 1782.

———, —. Further Description of Ancient Fortifications in Scotland. (Archæol. vol. 6.)

Anderson, John. Defence of Presbyterianism. 4to. Glasg. 1714.

Anderson, John. Nouvelle Description de l'Islande. Vide Horrebows.

Anderson, Robert. Life of Smollett. 8vo. Edinburgh. 1806.

Anderson, Walter. History of France during the Reigns of Francis II. and Charles IX. 2 vols. 4to. Lond. 1769.

———, ———. Philosophy of Ancient Greece investigated. 4to. Edinburgh. 1795.

Andocides. Orationes. Vide Oratores Gr. a Reiskio.

Andover. Constitution and Associate Statutes of the Theological Seminary in Andover, with a Sketch of its Rise and Progress. 4to. Boston. 1808.

———. Laws of the Theological Institution in Andover. 8vo. 1817.

André, J. (Major.) The Cow Chace; an Heroick Poem, in Three Cantos. 4to. Lond. 1781.

———, ———. Letters to Miss Seward, when in his 18th year. 12mo. N. York. 1792.

———, ———. Proceedings and Letters respecting him. 8vo. Philadelphia. 1780.

———, ———. Vindication of his Captors. 12mo. N. York. 1817.

Andreas Cretensis. Vide Amphilochius.

Andreas, Tob. Brevis Replicatio pro Notis Cartesii. 12mo. Amst. 1653.

Andres, Giovanni. Origine, Progressi et Stato Attuale di Ogni Letteratura. 8 tom. 4to. Roma. 1808—17.

———, ———. Elogio Storico del Padre G. Andres. 8vo. Napoli. 1817.

Andrew, Dr. Examination of the Scheme of Church-Power laid down in the Codex Juris Ecclesiastici Anglicani. 8vo. London. 1735.

———, —. Answer to the Above, by the Author of the Parallel. 8vo. Lond. 1735.

Andrews, George. Reports in K. B. 11 and 12, Geo. II., by G. W. Vernon. 8vo. Dublin. 1791.

Andrews, John. The Kebla; Defence of Eastward Adoration. 8vo. Lond. 1728.

———, —. ———; Further Defence, Part II. 8vo. Lond. 1729.

Andrews, John. History of the War with America, France, Spain, and Holland, from 1775 to 1783. 4 vols. 8vo. Lond. 1785.

Andrews, John. Scripture Doctrine of Divine Grace, in Answer to Warburton. 2d edition. 12mo. Lond. 1769.

Andrews, John. Sermon at the Interment of the Rev. Thomas Cary. 8vo. Newburyport. 1808.

———, —. Dedication Sermon. Newburyport. 1801.

Andrews, John. Thanksgiving Sermon. 8vo. Newburyport. 1795.
———, ——. Anniversary Discourse before the Merrimack Humane Society. 8vo. Newburyport. 1812.
Andrews, Launcelot, (Bp.) Summarie View of the Government both of the Old and New Testament, whereby the Episcopall Government of Christ's Church is vindicated. 4to. Oxford. 1641.
———, —————. Exposition of the Moral Law; and Sermons. fol. Lond. 1642.
———, —————. XCVI. Sermons. fol. Lond. 1629.
Andrieux. Dialogue sur les Mots, *Monsieur* et *Citoyen*. (Instit. Lit. 4.)
———. Sur la Continuation du Dictionnaire de la Langue Française. (Id. 5.)
Andronicus Rhodius. Ethicorum Aristot. Paraphrasis. Gr. et Lat. cum Notis Variorum, curante D. Heinsio. 8vo. Cant. 1679.
Andry, Nicolas. Orthopædia, from the French. vol. 1. 12mo. Lond. 1743.
Anecdota Græca, a Villoison. 2 tom. in 1. 4to. Venet. 1781.
——— ———, a Wolfio. 4 tom. in 2. 12mo. Hamb. 1722—4.
——— ———, a Bekkero. 3 tom. in 2. 8vo. Berol. 1814—21.
Anecdotes Ecclesiastiques. 12mo. Amst. 1738.
Anecdotes, Historical, in a Series of Letters written from America in 1777 and 1778. 8vo. Lond. 1779.
———, Anglaises et Américaines, Années 1776—1783. 2 vol. in 1. 8vo. Paris. 1813.
Anekdoten, Amerikanische, aus den neuesten Zeiten. 12mo. Leips. 1789.
Angelerius, Hippol. De Antiquitate Urbis Atestinæ. (Græv. Thes. Ital.)
Angelita, J. F. Urbis Recineti Historia et Descriptio. (Græv. Thes. Ital.)
Angelius, Jo Psychologia Vera. 24to. Amst. 1632.
Angeloni, Batista. Letters on the English Nation. See Shebbeare.
Angelottus, Pomp. Descriptio et Antiquitates Urbis Reate, etc. (Græv. Thes. Ital.)
Angelus, Dom. De Deprædatione Castrensium, et suæ Patriæ Historia (Græv. Thes. Ital.)
Angelus à S. Joseph. Gazophylacium Linguæ Persarum, cum Clavi fol. Amst. 1684.
Angleterre et Colonies, (Miscellaneous Tracts entered under their respective Authors or Titles.) 6 vols. 8vo.
Angleterre et l'Amérique. Vide Affaires.
Anglia. Ratio constitutæ nuper Reipublicæ Angliæ, Scotiæ, et Hiberniæ. 16mo. Hagæ Com. 1651.
Anguillara, G. A. dell'. Le Metamorfosi d'Ovidio. 3 vol. 8vo. Milano. 1805.
Animal Creation. Philosophical Survey of it, from the French. 12mo. 1768.
Anna Comnena. Alexias. (Script. Byz.)

Annales du Muséum d'Histoire Naturelle. 10 vol. 4to. Paris. 1802—7.
Annales de Mathématiques, Pures et Appliquées ; Recueil Periodique rédigé par J. D. Gergonne et J. E. Thomas-Lavernède. 11 vol. 4to. Paris. 1810—21.
Annales Protestantes. vol. 1. 8vo. Paris.
Annals of Philosophy. 27 vols. 8vo. Lond. 1813—26.
Anne. Good Queen Anne Vindicated 2d. ed. 8vo. Lond. 1748.
——. Tracts on the War in her time. See Allies.
Annesley, Arthur, (Earl of Anglesey.) The King's Right of Indulgence in Spiritual Matters.
——, ——, ——. Memoirs, in a Letter to Sir P. Pett. 8vo. Lond. 1693.
Annesley, Samuel. Sermons at Cripple-Gate. See Morning Exercises.
Annett, Peter. Resurrection of Jesus considered, in Answer to the Trial of the Witnesses. 8vo. Lond. 1743.
Annio, Gio. Libri delle Antichità di Beroso Caldeo. 12mo. Venezia. 1550.
Anonymus. De Origine Urbis Romæ. Vide Rom. Hist. Script.
——. De Rebus Bellicis. Vide Script. de Re Militari.
Anonymus Sophista. De Rhetorica. Vide Rhetores Selecti.
—— ——. De Incredibilibus. Vide Opuscula Mythologica.
Anquetil, L. P. Histoire de France. 14 vol. 12mo. Paris. 1805.
——, ——. Esprit de la Ligue. 3 vol. 12mo. Paris. 1783.
——, ——. Intrigue du Cabinet sous Henry IV. et Louis XIII. 4 vol. 12mo. Paris. 1783.
——, ——. Louis XIV, sa Cour, et le Régent. 4 vol. 12mo. Paris. 1789.
——, ——. Universal History, from the French. 9 vols. 8vo. Lond. 1800.
Anquetil du Perron, A. H. Recherches sur Zoroastre. (Acad. des Inscriptions, vol. 37.)
——, ——. Sur les Livres Zends. (Id. 38.)
——, ——. Sur les Anciennes Langues de la Perse. (Id. 31.)
——, ——. Système des Mages, selon Plutarque. (Id. 34.)
——, ——. Exposition du Système Théologique des Perses. (Id. 37.)
Ansaldus, Cast. Inn. De Forensi Judæorum Buccina. (Ugol. vol. 27.)
Anselme, M. l'Abbé. Sur l'Opinion des Sages du Paganisme touchant la Félicité de l'Homme. (Acad. des Inscriptions, vol. 5.)
——, ——. Sur les Monuments qui ont servi de Mémoires aux premiers Historiens. (Id. 4.)
Anselmus, (Archiep. Cant.) Opera, cum Vita. fol. Paris. 1721.
Anson, (Lord George.) Voyage round the World. 8vo. Lond. 1748.
——, ——. The Same. 4to. Lond. 1756.
——, ——. The Same. 4to. Lond. 1767.

Anson, (Lord George.) Voyage autour du Monde, traduit de l'Anglois. 4to. Genève. 1750.
———, ————. Idem. 4 vol. 12mo. Paris. 1764.
Anstis, John. Register of the most noble Order of the Garter. 2 vols. fol. Lond. 1724.
Anthologia Græca, a Jacobs. 13 tom. 8vo. Lips. 1794—1814.
———— ————, a Cephala. 12mo. Lips. 1754.
———— Secunda; sive Gr. Epigram. Flor. Nov. in usum Scholæ Westm. 12mo. Lond. 1711.
———— Secunda; sive Poem. Græc. Min. Delectus, in usum Scholæ Westm. 12mo. Oxon. 1725.
———— Persica, seu Selecta e diversis Persis Auctoribus Exempla, Pers. et Lat. 4to. Viennæ. 1778.
Anthology, Monthly. 10 vols. 8vo. Boston. 1804—11.
Anticipation, containing the Substance of His M——Y's most gracious Speech to both H——S of P——L——T, &c. 8vo. Lond. 1778.
Anti-Gallican, by a Citizen of New England. 8vo. Phil. 1797.
Antilles. Description des Isles possédées par les Anglois. 4to. Paris. 1758.
————. Derrotero de las Antillas, &c. 4to. Madrid. 1810.
————. Histoire et Commerce des Antilles Angloises. 12mo. 1758.
————. Beschreibung der Antillischen Inseln. 12mo. Stutgart. 1762.
Antimachus Coloph. Reliquiæ, a Schellenburg. Accessit Epistola F. A. Wolfii. 8vo. Hal. 1786.
Antiphon. Orationes. Vide Oratores Græci, a Reiskio.
Antiquæ Inscriptionis, qua L. Scipionis Barbati F. expressum est Elogium, Explanatio. (Græv. vol. 4.)
Antiquæ Literaturæ Septentrionalis Libri Duo, ab Hickesio, Fountaine, et Wanleio. 3 vol. fol. Oxon. 1703—5.
Antiquarian Society, American, Account of. 8vo. Boston. 1813.
————, ————. List of Officers and other Members. 8vo. Boston. 1814.
————, ————. Address to the Members. 8vo. Worcester. 1819.
————, ————. Transactions and Collections, or Archæologia Americana. vol. 1. 8vo. Worcester, Mass. 1820.
Antiquaries, Society of. Archæologia; or Miscellaneous Tracts relating to Antiquity. Vols. 1, 2, 3, 4, 5, 6, 7. 4to. Lond. 1773—85. Also vols. 20, 21. 4to. Lond. 1824—7.
Antiquities of Great Britain and Ireland, Essay on the. 8vo. Edin. 1738.
Antiromanus, oder die Kirchengescichte. 8vo. Leipz. 1823.
Antisthenes. Orationes. Vide Oratores Græci, a Reiskio.
Antoine, Paul. Gab. Theol. Moralis Univ. 4to. Aug. Vin. 1774.
Antoninus Liberalis. Transformationes, a Xylandro. Vide Hist. Poet. Scriptores.
———— ————. ————, a Verheyk. 8vo. Lug. Bat. 1774.

Antoninus, Marcus, (Imp.) De Rebus suis, Gr. et Lat. cum Comment. a G. Stanhope. 4to. Lond. 1697.

———, ———. Idem. Gr. et Lat. inter Opera Critica Gattakeri.

———, ———. Idem. Gr. et Lat. cum Notis. 8vo. Oxon. 1704.

———, ———. Idem. Gr. et Lat. a Moro. 8vo. Lips. 1775.

———, ———. Diall of Princes, or Golden Booke of M. Antoninus, tr. out of French by T. North. fol. Lond. 1619.

———, ———. Meditations, with the Picture of Cebes, &c. by Collier. 8vo. Lond. 1708.

———, ———. Meditations, with his Life. 2 vols. 12mo. Glasgow. 1749.

———, ———. Pensées, par M. de Joly. 24to. Paris. 1803.

———, ———. Commentarii, Gr. et Lat. 8vo. Lips. 1775.

Antoninus, Phil. Descriptio Urbis Umbrorum, Sassina olim, nunc Sarsina, dictæ. (Græv. Thes. Ital.)

Antoninus, Placent. Itinerarium. (Ugol. vol. 7.)

Antonio, Juan Francisco de S. Chronicas de la Provincia de S. Gregorio. 3 vol. fol. Manila. 1738.

Antonio, Nicolas. Bibliotheca Hispana Vetus. 2 vol. fol. Matriti. 1788.

———, ———. ——— Nova. 2 vol. fol. Matriti. 1783—8.

Anvers, Caleb. Craftsman. 14 vols. 12mo. Lond. 1731—7.

———, ———. Craftsman Extraordinary. 8vo. Lond. 1729.

———, ———. Observations on the Writings of the Craftsman. 8vo. Lond. 1730.

———, ———. Final Answer to Remarks on the Craftsman's Vindication, &c. 8vo. Lond. 1731.

Anvers, Knightley d'. Abridgment of the Common Law. 3 vols. fol. Lond. 1725—37.

Anville, J. B. B. d'. Ancient Geography, from the French. 2 vols. 8vo. Lond. 1791.

———, ———. Atlas of Anc. Geog. fol. Lond. 1802. (2 copies.)

———, ———. Extent of the Ancient Jerusalem.

———, ———. Mémoire sur les Gètes. (Acad. des Inscrip. 25.)

———, ———. ———, Sur le Pays d'Ophir, et sur l'Etendue de l'Ancienne Rome. (Id. 30.)

———, ———. ———, sur le Golfe d'Ambracie—sur l'Isle de Cypre—sur l'Expédition de l'Empereur Héraclius en Perse—sur la Sérique des Anciens—sur les Limites du Monde connu aux Anciens. (Id. 32.)

———, ———. ———, sur la Navigation de Pythéas à Thulé, et Observations sur l'Islande. (Id. 37.)

Anyta. Epigrammata. Vide Poetriæ Octo.

Apel, August. Metrik. 2 vol. 8vo. Leips. 1814—6.

Aphthonius Sophista. Progymnasmata, Lat. 16mo. Lond. 1655.
Apicius, Cœlius. De Opsoniis et Condimentis, a J. M. Bernhold. 12mo.
Apocalypse de Chiokouhikou, Chef des Iroquois, Peuple Sauvage du Nord de l'Amérique. 8vo.
Apocrypha. Essay concerning the Books commonly called Apocrypha, and the public Reading of them in the Church. 8vo. Lond. 1740.
———. Libri Apocryphi Vet. Test. Græci. 12mo. Hal. Magd. 1749.
———. Vide Fabricius.
Apollo, American. 8vo. Boston. 1792.
Apollodorus. Bibliotheca, Gr. et Lat. Vide Historiæ Poeticæ Scriptores.
———. Bibliotheca, cum Notis amplissimis, curante C. G. Heyne. 4 tom. 12mo. Götting. 1782—3.
Apollonius Dyscolus. Historiæ Commentitiæ, Gr. et Lat., a Teuchero. 8vo. Lips. 1792.
Apollonius, Gul. Disputationes Theologicæ in Schola Medioburgensi. 12mo. Mediob. Zel. 1655.
Apollonius, Pergæus. Conica, Gr. et Lat. ab E. Halleio. fol. Oxon. 1710.
———, ———. De Sectione Rationis, etc., Halleii. 8vo. Oxon. 1706.
Apollonius Rhodius. Argonautica, Gr. et Lat., cum Comment. et Notis, cura Hoelzlini. 8vo. Lug. Bat. 1641.
———, ———. Idem, cum Annotationibus H. Stephani. 4to. 1574.
———, ———. Idem, ex Recensione et cum Notis R. F. P. Brunckii. 2 tom. 8vo. Lips. 1810—3.
———, ———. Idem, cum Notis Variorum, a J. Shaw. 2 vol. 8vo. Oxon. 1779.
Apollonius Sophista. Lexicon Græcum Iliad. et Odys. cum Versione Latina, a Villoison. 2 tom. in 1. 4to. Paris. 1773.
Apology for the Conduct of a late celebrated second-rate Minister from 1729 to 1746. 8vo. Lond.
——— for a late Resignation in a Letter from an English Gentleman to his Friend at the Hague. 8vo. Lond.
Appeal to the Old Whigs of Massachusetts. 8vo. 1806.
——— to the Good Sense of the Democrats and the Public Spirit of the Federalists. (By Willard Phillips.) 8vo. Bost. 1814.
Appetites. Origin of the Human Appetites and Affections. 8vo. Lincoln. 1747.
Appianus Alexandrinus. Historiæ Romanæ Gr. et Lat. cum Notis Variorum, a Tollio. 2 vol. 8vo. Amst. 1670.
———, ———. Idem. Gr. et Lat. a Schweighæusero. 3 vol. 8vo. Lips. 1782—5.
———, ———. Historia delle Guerre de' Romani, trad. da Braccio e Dolce. 2 vol. 4to. Verona. 1730.
———, ———. Historia delle Guerre di Spagna. 12mo. 1551. (Aldine edition.)

Appianus Alexandrinus. History, made English by Davies. fol. Lond. 1690.

Appleton, Jesse. Sermon at the Ordination of the Rev. James A. Neal. 8vo. Portsm. 1805.

———, ——. General Election Sermon. 8vo. Bost. 1814.

———, ——. Address on the Suppression of Intemperance. 8vo. Boston. 1816.

———, ——. Addresses to Students in Bowdoin College. 8vo. Brunsw. 1820.

———, ——. Lectures and Sermons. 8vo. Brunsw. 1822.

Appleton, Jos. Reply to the Enquiry, "What must I do to be saved?" &c. 8vo. Worcester. 1779.

Appleton, Nathaniel. Sermon on the Death of the Rev. John Leverett, Pres. of Harv. College. 16mo. Bost. 1724.

———, ———. Sermon on the Death of the Hon. Francis Foxcroft, with a Preface by H. Flynt. 12mo. Bost. 1728.

———, ———. Sermon on the Death of the Rev. Benjamin Wadsworth, Pres. of Harv. College. 8vo. Bost. 1737.

———, ———. Two Discourses on the sudden Death of the Rev. John Hancock. 8vo. Bost. 1752.

———, ———. Sermon on the Death of the Hon. Spencer Phips. 8vo. Bost. 1757.

———, ———. Sermon on the Death of Henry Flynt, Esq. 8vo. Bost. 1760.

———, ———. Sermon on the Death of the Rev. Edward Wigglesworth, Hollis Prof. of Divinity in Harv. College. 8vo. Bost. 1765.

———, ———. Two Discourses on the Death of the Rev. Edward Holyoke, Pres. of Harv. College. 8vo. Bost. 1769.

———, ———. Sermon at the Ordination of the Rev. Josiah Cotton. 8vo. Bost. 1728.

———, ———. Sermon at the Ordination of Mr. John Sargeant, as Missionary to the Indians. 8vo. Bost. 1735.

———, ———. Sermon at the Ordination of the Rev. John Sparhawk. 12mo. Bost. 1737.

———, ———. Sermon at the Ordination of the Rev. M. Bridge. 8vo. Bost. 1746.

———, ———. Sermon at the Ordination of the Rev. Oliver Peabody. 8vo. Bost. 1751.

———, ———. Sermon at the Ordination of Stephen Badger, as Missionary to the Indians. 8vo. Bost. 1753.

———, ———. Two Fast Sermons. 12mo. Bost. 1748.

———, ———. Thanksgiving Sermon for the Surrender of Canada. 8vo. Bost. 1760.

———, ———. Thanksgiving Sermon on the Repeal of the Stamp Act. 8vo. Bost. 1766.

———, ———. Election Sermon. 8vo. Bost. 1742.

———, ———. Wisdom of God in the Redemption of Man. 12mo. Bost. 1728.

———, ———. Discourses on Romans viii. 14. 12mo. Bost. 1743.

Appleton, Nathaniel. Difference between a Legal and Evangelical Righteousness. 8vo. Bost. 1749.
———, ———. Boston Lecture Sermon. 8vo. Bost. 1763.
———, ———. Substance of several Discourses from James v. 12. 8vo. Bost. 1765.
———, ———. Artillery Election Sermon. 8vo. Boston. 1733.
———, ———. Convention Sermon. 8vo. Bost. 1743.
Apthorp, East. Sermon at the Opening of Christ Church at Cambridge, N. E. 4to. Bost. 1761.
———, ———. Sermon on the Death of Mrs. Anne Wheelwright. 4to. Bost. 1764.
———, ———. Thanksgiving Sermon on the Peace of 1763. 4to. Bost. 1763.
———, ———. Considerations respecting the Society for the Propagation of the Gospel in Foreign Parts. 8vo. Lond. 1763.
———. ———. Review of Mayhew's Remarks on the Answer to his Observations on the Conduct of the Society for Propagating the Gospel. 8vo. Lond. 1765.
Apuleius, Lucius. Opera, in usum Delphini, a J. Florido. 4to. Paris. 1688.
———, ———. Metamorphosis, cum Annotationibus J. Pricæi. 8vo. Goudæ. 1650.
———, ———. Asino d' Oro, trad. en Ital. Vide Firenzuola.
Aquinas, Thomas, Sanctus. Summa Totius Theologiæ, cum Aug. Hunnæi de Sacramentis Axiomatibus. fol. Colon. 1622.
———, ———, ———. Idem. fol. Lugd. 1677.
———, ———, ———. Super Quarto Libro Sententiarum. fol. Venet. 1481.
———. ———, ———. De Incarnatione, MS.
Aquino, Carolus de. Lexicon Militare. 2 vol. fol. Romæ. 1724.
Aquinus, Phil. Veterum Rabbinorum in exponendo Pentateucho Modi Tredecim, etc. 4to. Paris. 1620.
Arabian Nights, tr. by Edw. Forster. 5 vols. 8vo. Lond. 1802.
——— ———, in Modern Greek. vol. 1. 12mo.
——— ———. Remarks on the Arabian Nights. See Hole.
Arama, R. Isaac. Dissertatio Rabbinica de Usu Linguæ in Commentario in Pentateuchum, cum Versione Latina, curante von der Hardt. 4to. Helmest. 1729.
Arantius, Jul. C. De Humano Fœtu. 16mo. Lug. Bat. 1664.
Aratus, T. Phænomena, Germanico Cæsare Interprete, cum Commentariis et Imaginibus. Phænomenon Fragmentum. Phænomena, Ruffo Avienio Paraphraste. Phænomena, Græce. Theonis Commentaria in Arati Phænom. Græce. fol. Venetiis. 1499.
———, —. Diosemea cum Notis, a T. Forster. 8vo. Lond. 1815.
———, —. Phænomena et Diosemea, Gr. et Lat. cum Notis, curante J. T. Buhle. 2 vol. 8vo. Lips. 1793—1801.
Arbuthnot, John. On the Effects of Air on Human Bodies. 8vo. Lond. 1751.

Arbuthnot, John. On the Nature of Aliments, with Rules of Diet. 8vo. Lond. 1756.

———, ——. Tables of Ancient Coins, Weights, and Measures explained. 4to. Lond. 1727.

Archæologia. Vide Antiquaries.

Archenholtz, J. W. d'. Histoire des Flibustiers, traduite de l'Allemand. 8vo. Paris. 1804.

Archer, John. Every Man his own Doctor. 12mo. Lond. 1671.

Archer, John. Accession Sermon. 8vo. Lond. 1720.

———, ——. Essay on Prayer. 8vo. Lond. 1730.

Archias, Nicolaus. Odæ. Vide Poemata Italorum.

Archimedes. Opera, cum Eutocii Comment. fol. Basil. 1544.

———. Idem. Gr. et Lat. a D. Rivalto. fol. Paris. 1615.

———. Circuli Dimensio. Vide Horsley.

———. Lemmata quædam, e Codice Arabico.

Archives du Christianisme du Dix-Neuvième Siècle. vol. 1 et 2. 8vo. Paris.

Arckenholtz, John. Mémoires concernant Christine, Reine de Suède. 4 vol. 4to. Amst. et Leips. 1751—60.

Aretæus Cappadox. De Causis, Signis, et Curatione Morborum. Gr. et Lat. cum Comment. a Boerhaave. fol. Lug. Bat. 1735.

———, ———. Idem. Vide Halleri Art. Med. Principes.

———, ———. De Pulmonum Inflammatione, Gr. et. Lat. a C. Weigel. 4to. Lips. 1790.

———, ———. Comment. P. Petiti in tres priores Libros. 4to. Lond. 1726.

———, ———. De Acutis et Diuturnis Morbis, a Wigan. fol. Oxon. 1723.

Aretin, J. Chr. Freyherrn. Ueber die frühesten universalhistorischen Folgen der Erfindung der Buchdruckerkunst. 4to. München. 1808.

Aretino, Pietro. Vita di S. Caterina Vergine. 16mo. Venet. 1628.

———, ——. Vita di S. Tomaso d' Aquino. 16mo. Venet. 1636.

Aretinus, Leon. Commentaria Rerum Græcarum. (Gronov. vol. 6.)

Aretius, Bened. Comment. in Epistolam Pauli ad Ephesios. 12mo. Lausan. 1579.

———, ——. Comment. in quatuor Evangelistas, et in Acta Apostolorum. fol. Morgiis. 1580.

Aretius, C. M. Siciliæ Chorographia. (Græv. Thes. Ital.)

Argens, J. B. de Boyer, (Marquis d'.) Chinese Letters, tr. from the French. 12mo. Lond. 1741.

———, ———————. Impartial Philosopher, tr. from the French. 2 vols. 12mo. Lond. 1749.

———, ———————. Jewish Spy, tr. from the French. 5 vols. 12mo. Lond. 1766.

Argensola, B. L. de. Conquista de las Islas Malucas. fol. Madrid. 1609.

———, ———. Discovery and Conquest of the Molucco and Philippine Islands, tr. from the Spanish. 4to. Lond. 1708.

Argensola, B. L. y L. L. de. Rimas. 4to. Zaragoza. 1634.
———, ————. Idem. 8vo. Madrid. 1804.
Argenson, (Marquis d'.) Sur les Historiens François. (Acad. des Inscrip. 28.)
Argonautica Gustaviana, oder Nachricht der Schwedischen Handel Compagnie. fol. 1633.
Argote de Molina, Gonzalo. Historia del Gran Tamorlan. 4to. Madrid. 1782.
Arguijo, Juan de. Versos. Vide Rioja.
Arianism. Caution against the Diabolism of Arianism. 8vo. Exon.
———. The Innocent Vindicated, or Arians Defended by a few plain Texts of Scripture. 2d. ed. 8vo. Lond. 1719.
———, Remarks on the above. 12mo. Lond. 1718.
———. Arius Detected and Confuted. 8vo. Exon. 1719.
———. Plain Christianity Defended, in answer to the preceding. Parts 1, 2, 3, 4. 8vo. Lond. 1719—20.
———. Answer to some Queries printed at Exeter concerning the Arian Controversy. 8vo. Lond. 1721.
———. Scripture and the Arians compared in their Accounts of God the Father and God the Son. 8vo. Lond. 1722.
———. Sovereign Antidote to expel it, by G. T. 8vo. Exon.
Arians. Letters concerning their Doctrine, proving Christ to be of the same Essence with God. 3d ed. 8vo. Boston. 1756.
Arie, (Abraham ben David R.) De Templo, etc. (Ugol. vol. 9.)
———, ————. De Suffitu, etc. (Id. 11.)
———, ————. De Vestitu Heb. Sacerdot. (Id. 13.)
Aringhus, Paulus. Roma Subterranea, post Bosium et alios. 2 vol. fol. Romæ. 1651. (2 sets.)
Ariosto, Lodovico. Opere. 2 tom. fol. Venezia. 1731.
———, ————. Opere, con Dichiarazioni. 5 tom. 12mo. Venez. 1783.
———, ————. Orlando Furioso. 5 tom. fol. Pisa. 1809.
———, ————. Idem. 5 tom. 8vo. Milano. 1812.
———, ————. Orlando Furioso, tr. by Hoole. 6 vols. 12mo. Lond. 1807.
———, ————. Elegiæ et Odæ. Vide Poem. Ital.
Arispe, M. R. de. Memorial on the State of the Province of Cohauila in Mexico, from the Spanish. 8vo. Phil. 1814.
Aristænetus. Epistolæ, cum Emend. ac Conject. Variorum, curante F. L. Abresch. 12mo. Zwollæ. 1749.
Aristarchus Samius. De Magnitud. et Dist. Solis et Lunæ, Gr. et Lat.; accedit Pappi Fragment. a J. Wallis. 8vo. Oxon. 1688.
Aristeas. Historia LXXII Interpretum, Gr. et Lat. cum Dissertatione Ant. Van Dale. 4to. Amst. 1705.
———. Dissertatio contra Historiam, per H. Hody. 8vo. Oxon. 1684.
———. Dissertatio contra Historiam; præmittitur Historia, Gr. et Lat.; per Hodium. fol. Oxon. 1705.
———. Vindication of his History. 8vo. Lond. 1736.
———. See also Whiston's Authentic Records.

Aristides Ælius. Orationes. fol. Florentiae. 1517.
Aristides, Quintilianus. De Musica Lib. III. Vide Musicæ Auctores Antiquæ.
Aristocracy, an Epic Poem. 8vo. Philadelphia. 1795.
Aristophanes. Comœdiæ, Gr. et Lat. cum Notis Variorum, a Kustero. fol. Amst. 1710.
———. Idem, Gr. et Lat., a Brunck. 4 vol. 8vo. Argent. 1781—3.
———. Idem, Gr. cum Notis Variorum, cura Invernizii et Beckii. 5 vol. 8vo. Lips. 1794—1811.
———. Nubes, Hermanni. 8vo. Lips. 1799.
———. Ranæ, Höpfner. 8vo. Hal. Sax. 1797.
———. Plutus, Hemsterhusii. 8vo. Harlingæ. 1744.
———. Comedies translated by T. Mitchell. vol. 1 and 2. 8vo. Lond. 1820.
———. Observationes Ernesti in Nubes. 8vo. Lips. 1795.
———. Conject. C. Reisigii in Aristoph. 8vo. Lips. 1816.
Aristoteles. Opera, Gr. et Lat. a Gul. Duval. 2 vol. fol. Paris. 1619.
———. Idem. 2 vol. fol. Paris. 1629.
———. Opera, Gr. et Lat. cum Annotatione Critica, a Buhle. 5 vol. 8vo. Biponti et Argent. 1791—1800.
———. Politica. fol. Paris. 1510.
———. ———. 4to. Paris. 1556.
———. ———, cum Comment. Schneideri. 2 vol. 8vo. Francof. ad Viad. 1809.
———. De Arte Poetica, Gr. et Lat. cum Notis, a Gul. Cooke. 8vo. Cant. 1785.
———. Idem, cum Comment. G. Hermanni. 8vo. Lips. 1802.
———. Treatise on Poetry, with Notes, &c., by T. Twining. 4to. Lond. 1789.
———. The Same, with a Commentary, by H. J. Pye. 4to. Lond. 1792.
———. La Poëtique trad. en François, avec des Remarques Critiques, par M. Dacier. 12mo. Amst. 1733.
———. Politiques tr. out of French into English. fol. Lond. 1598.
———. Ethica, Latine, per S. Heilandum. 12mo. Tubingæ. 1605.
———. Ethics and Politics, with Notes, and Life of Aristotle, &c. by J. Gillies. 2 vols. 4to. Lond. 1797.
———. De Virtutibus et Vitiis. Vide Golium.
———. Histoire des Animaux en Grec et Français, avec Notes, par Camus. 2 vol. 4to. Paris. 1783.
———. In Libris de Anima Comment. Soc. Jesu Conimbricensis. 4to. Colon. 1617.
———. In Libros de Cœlo, etc. Comment. Soc. Jesu Conimbricensis. 4to. Colon. 1603.
———. Ethica, Gr. et Lat. cum Comment. Magiri. 12mo. Francof. 1628.

Aristoteles. Ethicorum Paraphrasis, Gr. et Lat. a D. Heinsio. 4to. Lug. Bat. 1607.

——————. Politica, Rhetorica, et Magna Moralia, Latine. MS. (Black letter, on parchment; it belonged originally to Petrus Victorius.)

——————. Ignorance of the Moderns concerning his Philosophy. (Class. Journ. vols. 16, 17, 18, and 19.)

Aristoxenus. Harmonicorum Elem. Lib. III. Vide Musicæ Auct.

Arkevolti, Sam. Hebrew Grammar, (in Hebrew.) 4to. Venice. 1602.

Arlunus, Bern. De Bello Veneto, etc. (Græv. Thes. Ital.)

Armerius, Aloysius. De Golleta et Tuneto expugnatis. (Clauser de Rebus Turc.)

Arminianism. Anatome Arminianismi. 4to. Lug. Bat. 1619.

Arminius, Jac. Opera Theologica. 4to. Francof. 1635. (2 copies.)

Armstrong, Geo. Account of Diseases incident to Children; Essay on Nursing; and Account of the Dispensary for the Infant Poor. 8vo. Lond. 1783.

——————, ——. The Same. 8vo. Lond. 1808.

Armstrong, John. History of the Island of Minorca. 8vo. Lond. 1756.

Armstrong, John. Synopsis of the History and Cure of Venereal Diseases. 8vo. Lond. 1737.

Armstrong, John, M. D. On Scarlet Fever, Measles, and Consumption. 8vo. Lond. 1818.

Army. Act respecting the Army, Anno 28 Geo. II. with Rules and Articles of War. 12mo. Lond. 1755.

——. See Standing Armies.

Arnald, Richard. Critical Commentary on the Apocrypha. 2d. ed. fol. Lond. 1760.

Arnaud, Ant. L'Esprit de M. Arnaud tiré de sa Conduite, etc. 2 vol. 12mo. Deventer. 1684.

Arnaud, F. T. M. de Barnlard d'. Œuvres. 12 vol. 8vo. Paris. 1783.

Arnaud, M. l'Abbé François. Dissertations dans les Mémoires de l'Académie des Inscriptions.

Arnaud, Geo. d'. Animadversiones Criticæ ad aliquot Scriptores Græcos. 8vo. Harlingæ. 1728.

——————, ——————. De Diis Παρέδροις, etc. 8vo. Hagæ Com. 1732.

Arnaud, G. de Ronsil. Mémoires de Chirurgie. 4to. Paris. 1768.

Arnay, M. d'. Private Life of the Romans; from the French. 12mo. Lond. 1764.

Arndt, John. Garden of Paradise, or Holy Prayers and Exercises; from the German. 8vo. Lond. 1716.

——, ——. True Christianity; from the German. 2 vols. 8vo. Lond. 1720.

——, ——. De Vero Christianismo, cum Adnot. Dorschei, a Pritio. 12mo. Lips. 1704.

Arnobius Afer. Adversus Gentes Lib. VII. 4to. Lug. Bat. 1651.

Arnold, Charles Hen. History of N. and S. America. 12mo. Lond.
Arnold, Sam. New Plymouth Election Sermon. 4to. Camb. 1674.
Arnold, Theod. Britische Reich in America; aus dem Eng. 4to. Lemgo. 1744.
Arnoldus, N. Religio Sociniana, seu Catechesis Racoviana Refutata. 4to. Franeg. 1654.
Arnot, Hugo. History of Edinburgh to the Year 1780. 8vo. Edin. 1816.
Arnulphus. Historia Mediolanensis, qua continentur Gesta quorundam Italiæ Regum, ab An. DCCCCXXV. usque ad MLXXVI. (Græv. Thes. Ital.)
Aron Afia. Definiciones de la Alma. 4to. Venet. 1568.
Arpe, Pet. Fr. Apologia pro J. C. Vanino. 8vo. Cosmop. 1712.
Arrianus. De Alexandri Expeditione. 12mo. Basil. 1539.
———. Idem, cum Notis, a F. Schmieder. 8vo. Lips. 1788.
———. Historia Indica, Gr. et Lat. cum Notis, a F. Schmieder. 8vo. Hal. Magd. 1798.
———. De Alexandri Expeditione; et De Rebus Indicis, Gr. et Lat. a N. Blancardo. 8vo. Amst. 1668.
———. History of Alexander's Expedition; from the Greek, with Notes, by Rooke. 2 vols. 8vo. Lond. 1729.
———. Idem, Italice, a Lauro. 4to. Verona. 1730.
———. Ars Tactica; Acies contra Alanos; Periplus Ponti Euxini et Maris Erythræi; et De Venatione; Gr. et Lat. cum Notis; a N. Blancardo. 8vo. Amst. et Lips. 1750.
———. Voyage of Nearchus, and Periplus of the Erythræan Sea, Gr. and Eng. by Vincent. 4to. Oxford. 1809.
———. Comment. de Epicteti Disputationibus, Gr. et Lat. cura H. Wolfii. 8vo. Cant. 1655.
Arrowsmith, John. Armilla Catechetica. 4to. Cant. 1659.
Arroyal, Leon de. Las Odas. 12mo. Madrid. 1784.
Arscott, Alex. Present State of the Christian Religion. 8vo. Lond. 1732, 1734, 1735.
Arsillus, Franc. De Poetis Urbanis. (Tirab. vol. VII. par. 4.)
Art of Speaking. 8vo. Lond. 1761. See Burgh.
Art of Making Sugar. 4to. Lond. 1752.
Art de Voyager Utilement. 12mo. Amst. 1698.
— de Bien Parler François. 12mo. Amst. 1710.
— de Vérifier les Dates. 4to. Paris. 1750.
Arteaga, Felix de. Obras Postumas. 12mo. Alcalá. 1650.
Artedi, Petrus. Ichthyologia. 8vo. Lug. Bat. 1738.
———, ———. Synonymia Piscium, Gr. et Lat.; sive Historia Piscium. 4to. Lips. 1789.
Artemonius, L. M. Vide Crellius.
Arthur, M. Repository of Knowledge, No. I. 8vo. Phil. 1801.
Articles of Religion. Exposition of the 34th Article of the Church. 8vo. Lond. 1718.
———————. Hist. and Crit. Essay on the 39 Articles, by Collins. 8vo. Lond. 1724.

Articles of Religion. View of the Articles of the Protestant and Popish Faith. 12mo. Lond. 1735.

———. Queries recommended to the Consideration of the Public, with regard to the 39 Articles. 8vo. Lond. 1772.

———. Essay to illustrate necessary Articles of the Christian Faith. 8vo. Bath. 1763.

———. Catholic Doctrine of the Church of England analysed. 4to. Lond. 1625.

———. Vide Subscription. V. Creeds. V. Confession of Faith. V. Church.

Artieda, Andres Rey de. Discursos, Epistolas, y Epigramas de Artemidoro. 4to. Caragoça. 1605.

Arts and Sciences, Universal History of. 2 vols. 4to. Lond. 1759.

———, Complete Dictionary of. (Owen's.) 4 vols. 8vo. Lond. 1763—4.

———. History of First Inventers and Instituters of Arts. 24to. Lond. 1686.

———. Transactions of the Society at London for the Encouragement of Arts, Manufactures, and Commerce. 4 vols. i. e. 7—10. 8vo. Lond. 1789—92.

———. List of Members of the Soc. at Lond.; Rules and Orders; and Premiums offered for the Years 1760, -1, -3, -6, -8, and 9.

Arts et Métiers. Déscriptions faites ou approuvées par MM. de l'Académie Royale des Sciences, avec figures. 18 vols. fol. Paris. 1761—78.

Artus III. Duc de Bretagne. Mémoires. (Mém. de France, vol. 7.)

Aruch. Liber Aruch, sive Lexicon Talmudicum, Hebr. 4to. Venetiis.

Arvieux, Laurence d'. Travels in Arabia the Desart; from the French. 12mo. Lond. 1732.

As. Commentarius de Asse et ejus Partibus. 8vo. Lond. 1719.

Ascham, Ant. Discourse on what is Lawful during the Confusions and Revolutions of Government. 12mo. Lond. 1648.

———, ——. Enquiry how far a Man may conform to the Ruling Powers in Civil and Foreign Wars. 12mo. Lond. 1649.

Ascham, Roger. English Works, with Notes and Life, by Bennet. 4to. Lond. 1761.

———, ———. The Schoolmaster; a Plain Way of Teaching Children Latin. 4to. Lond. 1571.

———, ———. On Double Translations. Vide Phillips's Treatises.

———, ———. Toxophilus. The Schole of Shootinge. 4to. Lond. 1571.

———, ———. Idem. 4to. Lond. 1589.

———, ———. Affaires and State of Germany. 4to. Lond. 1552.

Asgill, John. Abstract of Woolston's Discourses against the Miracles of Christ, and a Ridicule thereof. 8vo. Lond. 1730.

—, ——. De Jure Divino. 8vo. Lond. 1710.

Asgill, John. Essay on the Liberty of the Press, chiefly as it respects Personal Slander. 8vo. Lond. 1712.
——, ——. The Same. 8vo. Lond. 1753.
——, ——. Extract of Acts of Parliament relating to the Hanover Succession. 8vo. Lond. 1714.
——, ——. Argument to prove that Man may be Translated into Eternal Life without seeing Death. 8vo. Lond. 1700.
——, ——. Metamorphosis of Man by Christ's Death, &c. 8vo. Lond. 1727.
——, ——. Abstract of Woolston on Miracles. 8vo. Lond. 1730.
——, ——. Defence upon his Expulsion from the House of Commons. 8vo. Lond. 1712.
——, ——. Pretender's Declaration, abstracted from Two Anonymous Pamphlets. 8vo. Lond. 1713.
——, ——. Succession of the House of Hanover vindicated against the Pretender's Second Declaration. 8vo. Lond. 1714.
——, ——. Pretender's Declaration Englished, with a P. S. before it. 8vo. Lond. 1715.
——, ——. Pretender's Declaration transposed. 8vo. Lond. 1716.
——, ——. Several Assertions proved in order to create another Species of Money than Gold and Silver. 12mo. Lond. 1696.
Ash, John. Introduction to Lowth's English Grammar. 24to. Lond. 1772.
Ash, St. George, (Bp.) Reformation of Manners Sermon. 8vo. Lond. 1717.
Ashburnham, John. Letter to a Friend concerning King Charles I. 8vo. Lond. 1764.
Ashe, Simeon. Sermon on the Death of the Rev. Jer. Whitaker, &c. 3d ed. 4to. Lond. 1656.
Ashe, Tho. Travels in America performed in 1806. 12mo. Newburyport. 1808.
Asher, R. Jacob Ben. Ordo Semitæ Vitæ, etc. Hebr. 4 vol. fol. Berol. 1764.
Ashley, James. His Case and Appeal to the Public in Relation to H. Simon's Apprehension and Trial. 8vo. Lond. 1753.
Ashley, John. Memoirs on British America. 8vo.
——, ——. Memoirs on the Trade and Revenues of the British Colonies in America. 2 vols. 8vo. Lond. 1740.
Ashley, Jona. Great Duty of Charity, a Sermon. 8vo. Boston. 1742.
——, ——. Remarks on Objections to it, by J. F. See Cooper.
Ashley, Maurice. Institution of Cyrus; from the Greek. 2 vols. 8vo. Lond. 1728.
——, ——. The Same. 3d ed. 2 vols. 8vo. Lond. 1770.
Ashmole, Elias. Institution, Laws, and Ceremonies of the Most Noble Order of the Garter. fol. Lond. 1672.

Ashworth, C. Sermon on the Death of the Rev. Isaac Watts. 8vo. Lond. 1749.
Asiæ Descriptio. fol. Lut. Par. 1656.
Asiatic Miscellany. vol. 1. 4to. Calcutta. 1785.
——— Researches. 12 vols. i. e. vols. 1—12. 8vo. Lond. 1801—18.
Asper Junior. Ars Grammatica. Vide Grammatici Veteres Latini.
Asplin, Wm. Alkibla; a Disquisition on Worshipping toward the East. 8vo. Lond. 1728.
———, ———. Anatomy of the Kebla. 8vo. Lond. 1729.
———, ———. Letter to the Bishop of London in Defence of the Anatomy. 8vo. Lond. 1730.
Assemanus, Jos. Simon. Bibliotheca Orientalis Clementino-Vaticana. 3 tom. in 4 vol. fol. Romæ. 1719—28. (2 copies.)
Assemanus, Steph. Evodius. Bibliothecæ Mediceæ Laurentianæ et Palatinæ Codicum MSS. Orient. Catalogus. fol. Flor. 1742.
Asser, Rabbi. Talmud Babylonicum. 12 vol. fol. Berol. et Francof.
Asserius Menevensis. Annales Rerum Gestarum Ælfredi Regis. 8vo. Oxon. 1722.
———, ———. Annales. Vide Gale, Scri tores XV.
Assiento Trade. Observations on it, as exercisedpby the South Sea Company; its Damage to Jamaica, &c. 8vo. Lond. 1728.
——— ———. Remarks upon the Above. 8vo. Lond. 1728.
——— ———. Defence of the Observations. 8vo. Lond. 1728.
——— ———. Occasional Papers. See Wood.
Ast, Fried. Platon's Leben und Schriften. 8vo. Leipz. 1816.
Aster, Gottlieb Ludov. Eleemosynæ Judæorum ex Antiquitate Judaica delineatæ. 4to. Lips. 1728.
Astle, Thomas. Origin and Progress of Writing. 2d ed. 4to. Lond. 1803.
———, ———. On the Grant of Sicily to Prince Edmund. (Archæologia, vol. 4.)
———, ———. On the Radical Letters of the Pelasgians. (Idem, vol. 7.)
———, ———. Catalogue of the Harleian MSS. in the Brit. Mus. 2 vols. fol. 1759—63.
Astorius, Joh. Ant. De Deo Brotonte. (Sallengre, vol. 2.)
———, ———. In antiquum Alcmanis Poetæ Laconis Monumentum. (Idem.)
Astronomici Veteres Græci. Uranologion, cura Dion. Petavii. fol. Paris. 1630.
——— ——— Latini. fol. Rhegii. 1503.
Astruc, J. Traité des Maladies des Femmes. 6 vol. 12mo. Paris. 1761—5.
———, —. On the Diseases of Women; from the French. 3 vols. 8vo. Lond. 1762—7.
———, —. Traité des Maladies Vénériennes, trad. du Latin. 4 vol. 12mo. Paris. 1755.
———. On the Diseases of Children; from the French. 8vo. Lond. 1746.

Atavantus, Paullus. De Origine Ordinis Servorum B. Mariæ. 12mo. Florent. 1741.

Athanasianism. Acts of Athanasius, with Remarks on his Creed. 4to. 1690.

——————. True History of Athanasius and his Creed. 8vo. Lond. 1719.

——————. Scriptures and the Athanasians compared. 8vo. Lond. 1722.

——————. Athanasian Forgeries, Impositions, and Interpolations. 8vo. Lond. 1736.

——————. Remarks on the Athanasian Creed, by a Lady. 8vo. Lond. 1752.

Athanasius, Sanctus. Opera. fol. Basil. 1556.

——————, ————. Opera, Gr. et Lat. a B. de Montfaucon. 3 tom. fol. Paris. 1698.

——————, ————. Acts, with Remarks on his Creed. 4to. 1690.

——————, ————. Symbolum. Vide Usserius de Rom. Eccles. Symb.

——————, ————. Opuscula. Vide Montfaucon.

Athenæus. Deipnosophistarum Lib. XV. Gr. et Lat. cum Notis Dalechampii et Casauboni. fol. Lugd. 1612.

————. Idem. 2 vol. fol. Lugd. 1657—64.

————. ———, cum Notis Variorum, cura J. Schweighaeuseri. 5 tom. 8vo. Argent. 1801—5.

————. Banquet des Savans, traduit par Villebrune. 5 vol. 4to. Paris. 1789—91.

————. Animadversiones in Athenæum. Vide Casaubon.

————. Idem. Vide Schweighæuser.

————. ———. Vide Jacobs.

Athenagoras. Legatio pro Christianis; item de Mortuum Resurrectione, Gr. et Lat. accedunt Notæ, etc. 8vo. Oxon. 1706.

——————. Apologeticks; 1st. For the Christian Religion; 2d. For the Truth of the Ressurrection, &c. done into English. By D. Humphreys. 8vo. Lond. 1714.

Atheneum, or Spirit of the English Magazines. 10 vols. i. e. vols. 1—10. 8vo. Boston. 1817—22.

Atheniensische Briefe. (Athenian Letters, tr. into German.) 2 vol. 8vo. Leipz. 1799—1800.

Atkey, Ant. Christianity as Old as Creation, examined. 8vo. Lond. 1733.

———, ——. Sermon on the Death of the Rev. Simon Browne. 8vo. Lond. 1733.

———, ——. Letters written in 1725 to the Rev. Dr. Samuel Clarke, on the Being and Attributes of God, with the Doctor's Answers. 8vo. Lond. 1745.

Atkins, John. Navy Surgeon, with Observations on the Coast of Guiney. 12mo. Lond 1737.

———, ———. Voyage to Guinea, Brasil, and the W. Indies. 8vo. Lond. 1735.

Atkins, John. See Atkyns.
Atkinson, Benj. Scripture History, Precepts, and Prophecy vindicated. 8vo. Lond. 1731.
———, ——. Sermon on the 5th Nov. Lond. 8vo. 1739.
Atkinson, James. Epitome of Navigation revised. 8vo. Lond. 1749.
———, ——. The Same. 8vo. Lond. 1778.
Atkyns, J. T. Reports in Chancery, in the time of Hardwicke. 3 vols. fol. Lond. 1765.
Atkyns, Sir Rob. Parliamentary and Political Tracts. 8vo. Lond. 1741.
Atlas, General. fol. Lond. 1721.
—— of Ancient Geography. 4to. Philadelphia. 1814.
——, Ancient and Modern, by J. A. Cummings. 4to. Boston.
——, Moderne, par plusieurs Auteurs. fol. Paris. 1771.
——. Atlante Novissimo (Italia.) tom. 3. fol. Venez. 1782.
—— of the British West Indies. 4to. Charlestown. 1810.
——, para el Viage de las Goletas Sutil y Mexicana al Reconocimiento del Estrecho de Juan de Fuca en 1792. 4to. 1802.
Atonement. Defence of the Doctrine. 8vo. Edin. 1789.
Atterbury, Fr. (Bp.) Sermon on Easter Tuesday. 8vo. London. 1707.
———, ———. Sermons and Discourses. 4 vols. 8vo. Lond. 1761.
———, ———. Epistolary Correspondence and Miscellany. 4 vols. 8vo. Lond. 1783.
———, ———. Answer to Considerations on "The Spirit of Martin Luther," &c. 4to. Oxford. 1687.
Attersoll, Wm. Commentary on the Epistle of Paul to Philemon. 2d ed. fol. Lond. 1633.
Attorney. Observations on the Duty of an Attorney and Solicitor. 8vo. Lond. 1759. (2 copies.)
Attributes of God, a Moral Discourse on; or a Short Review of the Christian Religion on the Principles of Reason. By a Layman. 8vo. Lond. 1754.
Atwater, Jesse. Considerations on the Approaching Dissolution of the U. S. Bank. 8vo. New Haven. 1810.
Atwood, Tho. Observations on the True Methods of Treatment and Usage of the Negro Slaves. 8vo. Lond. 1789.
———, ——. History of Dominica. 8vo. Lond. 1791.
Atwood, Wm. Argumentum Anti-Normanicum. 8vo. Lond. 1682.
———, ——. Jani Anglorum Facies Nova. 8vo. Lond. 1680.
———, ——. Jus Anglorum ab antiquo. 8vo. Lond. 1681.
Aubert de Verse Natalis. Theses Theologicæ. Sedani. 1664.
Aucher, John. Arraignment of Rebellion. 8vo. Lond. 1718.
Aucher, Paschal. English and Armenian Grammar. 12mo. Ven. 1817.
———, ———. Dictionnaire Français-Arménien et Arménien-Français. 2 vol. 8vo. Ven. 1812—7.

Audley, Math. Sermon before the Society of Anti-Gallicans. 4to. Lond. 1752.
Augurello, Jo. Aurelius. Odæ. Vide Poemata Italorum.
Auguspurgische Confession. fol. Franck. 1572.
Augusti, J. C. W. und Wette, W. M. L. de. Die Schriften des Alt. Test. neu übersetzt. 5 vol. 8vo. Heidleb. 1809—11.
———, ———————————. Die Schriften des Neu. Test. neu übersetzt. 8vo. Heidleb. 1814.
Augustinus, Ant. De Legibus Romanis, cum Notis Fulvii Ursini. (Græv. vol. 2.)
———, ———. De Hæresibus. 12mo. Genevæ. 1595.
Augustinus, Leon. Gemmæ et Sculpturæ Antiquæ, Lat. a Gronovio. 4to. Franeq. 1694.
Augustinus, Sanctus. Opera. 10 vol. in 5. fol. Bazil. 1556.
———, ———. ———. 10 vol. in 6. fol. Basil. 1569.
———, ———. De Gestis Pelagii. 12mo. Aug. Vind. 1611.
———, ———. Of the Citie of God with the Comments of J. L. Vives. fol. Lond. 1620.
————, — . De Familiis Romanorum. (Id. 7.)
Augustus; or an Essay on the Means whereby the Commonwealth of Rome was reduced to a Monarchy. 8vo. Lond.
Aulisius, Dom. De Gymnasii Constructione et Mausolei Architectura. (Salengre, vol. 3.)
———, ——. De Colo Mayerano Epistola ad D. D. Did. Vincentium a Vidania. (Idem.)
Aurelianus, Cælius. De Morbis Acutis et Chronicis, cum Notis, a J. C. Amman. 4to. Amst. 1709.
————, ———. Idem. 4to. Amst. 1722.
————, ———. ——. 4to. Amst. 1755.
Auria, J. V. Notitia Historica Originis ct Antiquitatis Cephaledis, Urbis Placentissimæ Siciliæ. (Græv. Thes. Ital.)
Ausonius, D. Magnus. Opera, cum Notis Variorum, a Tollio.
———, ————. ——. Vide Corpus Poet. Lat.
Austin, Benj. Constitutional. Republicanism, &c., as published under the signature of Old South. 8vo. Bost. 1803.
Austin and the Monks of Bangor. fol. Lond. 1718.
Austin, Wm. Oration, June 17th, being the Anniversary of the Battle of Bunker Hill. 8vo. Charlestown. 1801.
Austin, Wm. M. D. On the Stone. 8vo. Lond. 1791.
Avalle. Tableau Comparatif des Productions des Colonies Françaises aux Antilles, etc. 4to. Paris. (2 copies.)
Avellaneda, A. F. de. Vida y Hechos del D. Quixote. 2 tom. 12mo. Madrid. 1805.
Averanus, Nicol. De Mensibus Ægyptiorum. 4to. Flor. 1737.
Avery, Benj. Sermon, preached Nov. 4, 1713. 8vo. Lond. 1714.
Avicenna, Abou-Ali-Alussein-Ben-Abdoullah, Ebn- Sina. Canonis Avicennæ Liber Secundus, Arab. et Lat. a Kirstenio. fol. Breslæ. 1608.
Avis aux Hessois et autres Peuples de l'Allemagne, etc. 8vo. Cleves. 1777.

Ayala, Pedro Lopez de. Coleccion de las Cronicas de los Reyes de Castilla, Don Pedro, Don Enrique II., Don Juan I., Don Enrique III. 2 tom. 4to. Madrid. 1780.

Ayliffe, John. Ancient and Present State of the University of Oxford. 2 vols. 8vo. Lond. 1714.

———, ——. The Same. 2 vols. 8vo. Lond. 1723.

———, ——. Parergon Jur. Can. Ang. 2d ed. fol. Lond. 1784.

Ayray, James. Sermon on the Third Sunday of Advent in the Spanish Ambassador's Chapel. 12mo. Lond. 1686.

Ayres, John. Tradesman's Copy Book.

——, ——. Tutor to Penmanship.

Azpilcueta, Martinus, (Doct. Navarrus.) Opera. 3 vol. fol. Lugd. 1589.

Azumi, M. D. Maritime Law of Europe; from the French. 2 vols. 8vo. N. York. 1806.

B

Babington, Humfrey. Assize Sermon. 4to. Cambridge. 1678.
Bacchinus, Benedictus. De Sistris. (Grævius, vol. 6.)
Bacchius Senior. Introductio Artis Musicæ. Vide Musicæ Auct.
Baccius, And. De Thermis Veterum. (Grævius, vol. 12.)
———, ——. De Conviviis Antiquorum. (Gronovius, vol. 9.)
Baccus, Henr. Descriptio Regni Neapolitani. (Græv. Thes. Ital.)
Back, J. de. De Corde. Vide Harveius.
Backus, Isaac. History of New England, with particular Reference to the Baptists. 3 vols. 8vo. Bost. 1777—96.
———, ———. True Faith will produce Good Works; a Discourse. 8vo. Bost. 1767.
Bacmeisterus, J. Acta Philippica: sive Pacificatio frustra tentata inter Melancthonem et Flacium Illyricum. 4to. Tubingæ. 1719.
Bacon, John. Sermon on the Lord's Day after his Installation. 8vo. Bost. 1772.
Bacon, John. Speech on the Organization of the Courts of the United States. 8vo. Bost. 1802.
Bacon, Fr. (Lord.) Opera Omnia. fol. Francof. ad Mœnum. 1665.
———, ————. Philosophical Works, by Shaw. 3 vols. 4to. Lond. 1737.
———, ————. Works; with his Life, by Mallet. 3 vols. fol. Lond. 1753.
———, ————. The Same. 5 vols. 4to. Lond. 1778.
———, ————. ————. 12 vols. 12mo. Lond. 1807.
———, ————. Advancement of Learning; from the Latin, by Wats. fol. Oxford. 1640.
———, ————. Sermones Fideles, Ethici, etc. 16mo. Amst. 1662.
———, ————. Life of Henry VII. (Kennet, Hist. of Eng. vol. 1.)
———, ————. Elements of the Common Law. 8vo. Lond. 1630.
———, ————. Cases of Treason. 4to. Lond. 1641.
———, ————. Office of Constables. See Parish Officer.
Bacon, Matthew. Abridgement of the Law. 5 vols. fol. Lond. 1768.
———, ————. The Same, by H. Gwillim. 1st Am. ed. by Bird Wilson. 7 vols. 8vo. Phil. 1813.
Bacon, Nathaniel. Historicall Discourse of the Uniformity of the Government of England. 4to. Lond. 1647.
Bacon, Roger. Frier Bacon his Discovery of the Miracles of Art, Nature, and Magick. 16mo. Lond. 1659.

Baculus Mosis, ubi agitur de Benedictionibus et Precibus, de Sabbato, Festis, etc. 4to. Cracow. 1591.
Badham, Charles. On Bronchitis, etc. 12mo. Lond. 1814.
Baglivus, Geo. De Praxi Medica ad Priscam Observandi Rationem revocanda. 8vo. Lugd. 1699.
———, ——. Tractatus de Fibra Motrice et Morbosa. 8vo. Lugd. 1703.
———, ——. Opera Omnia. 4to. Lugd. 1714.
Bahrdt, D. C. F. Apparatus Criticus ad formandum Interpretem Veteris Testamenti. 8vo. Lips. 1775.
———, ———. Hexapla Origenis. Vide Origen.
Baierlino, J. C. De Servo Dei Justificante. 4to. 1692.
Bail, Lud. Summa Conciliorum Omnium. 2 tom. fol. Paris. 1672.
Bailey, Winthrop. Sermons on the Unity of God, and the Character of Jesus Christ. 8vo. Springfield. 1822.
Baillet, Adrien. Vies des Saints. 4 vol. fol. Paris. 1701—3.
———, ———. Jugemens des Savans sur les Principaux Ouvrages des Auteurs. 8 vol. in 3. 4to. Amst. 1725.
Baillie, (Dr.) Essay on the Sublime. 8vo. Lond. 1747.
Baillie, Hugh. Letter to Dr. Shebbear, refuting his Arguments concerning the Boston and Quebec Acts. 8vo. Lond. 1775.
Baillie, Joanna. Series of Plays on the Passions. 2d ed. 8vo. Lond. 1799.
Baillie, Marianne. Tour upon the Continent in 1818. 8vo. Lond. 1819.
Baillie, Matthew. Morbid Anatomy. 8vo. Albany. 1795.
———, ———. The Same. 8vo. Lond. 1797.
Baillie, Robert. See Baylie.
Bailly, J. S. Histoire de l'Astronomie. 4 vol. 4to. Paris. 1781—5.
Baily, Lewis, (Bp.) Practice of Piety. 4th ed. 12mo. Lond. 1699.
——, ————. The Same. 71st ed. 12mo. 1792.
——, ————. Pratique de Piété, trad. de l'Anglois. 8vo. Saumur. 1675.
Bajon. Mémoires pour servir à l'Histoire de Cayenne et de la Guiane Françoise. 2 vol. 8vo. Paris. 1777.
——. Nachrichten von Cayenne, etc. 8vo. Erfurt. 1780.
Baker, D. E. Companion to the Play-House. 2 vols. 12mo. Lond. 1764.
Baker, Geo. History of Rome; from the Latin of Livy. 6 vols. 8vo. Lond. 1797.
Baker, Sir Geo. Enquiry respecting the Method of Inoculation practised in England. 8vo. Lond. 1761.
Baker, Henry. Employment for the Microscope. 8vo. Lond. 1753.
——, ——. Microscope made Easy. 8vo. Lond. 1754.
Baker, Humfrey. Worke and Practise of Arithmetick. 16mo. Lond. 1646.
Baker, Sir James. Admonition merry and wise to Mr. Tr——p, on his Encomiums upon the Bp. of Bangor. 8vo. Lond. 1717.
Baker, John. Sermons. 2 vols. 8vo. Lond. 1763—4.
Baker, Sir Rich. Chronicle of the Kings of England. fol. Lond. 1684.

Baker, Samuel. Thanksgiving Sermon. 8vo. Lond. 1710.
Baker, Wm. (Bp.) Authority of the Church in Controversies of Faith. 8vo. Lond. 1716.
——, ——. Sermon on the 30th January. 8vo. Lond. 1720.
——, ——. Another. 8vo. Lond. 1724.
Balbec, Ruins of. See Wood.
Balbuena, Bernardo de. El Bernardo, Poema Heroyco. 3 tom. 12mo. Madrid. 1808.
Balch, Tho. Sermon at the Ordination of the Rev. William Patten. 8vo. Bost. 1757.
——, ——. Artillery Election Sermon. 12mo. and 8vo. Bost. 1763.
Balch, Wm. Sermon at the Lecture in Bradford. 8vo. Bost. 1743.
——, ——. Account of the Proceedings in the Second Church of Bradford. 18mo. Bost. 1746.
——, ——. Election Sermon. 8vo. Bost. 1749.
——, ——. Convention Sermon. 8vo. Bost. 1760.
Balch, Wm. Address on Music. 8vo. Newburyport. 1812.
Baldelli, Gio. Batista. Vita di Gio. Boccacci. 8vo. Firenze. 1806.
Baldelli, Fr. Commentari di C. Giulio Cesare, con le Figure in Rame fatti da Palladio. 4to. Venetia. 1575.
——, —. Flavio Giuseppe dell' Antichita' de' Giudei, etc. 4to. Vinegia. 1583.
Baldinger, G. R. Medicinisches und Physisches Journal. 8vo. Göttingen. 1793.
Baldinucci, Filippo. Opere. 14 vol. 8vo. Milano. 1808—12.
Balduinus, Frid. De Casibus Conscientiæ. 4to. Francof. 1654.
——, ——. Commentarius in Epistolas Pauli. fol. Witteb. 1655.
Baldwin, L. On the Study of Political Economy. 8vo. Camb. 1809.
Baldwin, Tho. Sermon on the Death of Lieut. Gov. Phillips. 8vo. Bost. 1802.
——, ——. Election Sermon. 8vo. Bost. 1802.
——, ——. Baptism of Believers Only. 12mo. Bost. 1806.
——, ——. Quarterly Sermon. 8vo. Bost. 1799.
——, ——. Thanksgiving Sermon. 8vo. Bost. 1795.
——, ——. Account of Revivals of Religion. 8vo. Bost. 1799.
——, ——. Artillery Election Sermon. 8vo. Bost. 1807.
Bale, John, (Bp.) Yet a Course at the Romyshe Foxe. 12mo. 1543.
Baleus, Joh. Acta Romanorum Pontificum. 16mo. 1559.
Balfour, Fr. On Sol-Lunar Influence in Fevers, &c. vol. 1. 8vo. Lond. 1795.
——, —. Forms of Herkern, in Persian and English, &c. 4to. Calcutta. 1781.
Balfour, Walter. On the Words translated Hell. 8vo. Charlestown. 1824.
Balguy, John. Divine Rectitude; or an Enquiry concerning the Moral Perfections of the Deity. 8vo. Lond. 1730.
——, ——. Law of Truth. 8vo. Lond. 1733.
——, ——. Second Letter to a Deist concerning "Christianity as Old as Creation." 8vo. Lond. 1731.

Balguy, John. Examination of certain Doctrines of Mr. Stebbing. 8vo. Lond. 1718.

———, ———. Letter to Dr. Sherlock. 8vo. Lond. 1720.

———, ———. Answer to Mr. Stebbing on Popery. 8vo. Lond. 1720.

———, ———. On Redemption. 8vo. Lond. 1785.

———, ———. Remarks on his Consecration Sermon. 8vo. Lond. 1775.

———, ———. Five Sermons on Atheism, God's Government, Human Nature, and a Future State. 8vo. Lond. 1738.

———, ———. Letter to a Deist on Moral Virtue. 8vo. Lond. 1730.

———, ———. Foundation of Moral Goodness. 8vo. Lond. 1733.

———, ———. Sermons on Various Subjects. 2 vols. 8vo. Lond. 1760.

Ball, J. Treatise on Faith. 4to. Lond. 1632.

Ball, Jacob. On the Death of John Fryer, Esq. 8vo. Lond. 1725.

———, ———. Sermon on the Death of Mr. Wm. Drew. 8vo. Lond. 1727.

Ball, John. Importance of Right Apprehensions of God with respect to Religion and Virtue. 8vo. Lond. 1736.

Ball, John. On Fevers. 8vo. Lond. 1758.

Ball, Nathaniel. Visitation Sermon. 8vo. Lond. 1755.

Ball, Wm. Power of Kings discussed. (Som. Tr. vol. 4.)

Ballou, Hosea. Divine Benevolence vindicated, in Reply to Kelly. 8vo. Bost. 1815.

———, ———. ——————— further vindicated. 8vo. Salem. 1816.

Balmerino (Lord.) Reflections on his Dying Words and Deportment. 8vo. Lond. 1746.

Balmis, Abraham de. Grammatica Hebræa. 4to. Venet. 1523.

Baltus, J. F. Défense des Pères accusez de Platonisme. 4to. Paris. 1711.

———, ———. Answer to Fontenelle's History of Oracles; from the French. 2 vols. 8vo. 1709—10.

Balzac, J. L. G. de. Œuvres Diverses. 12mo. Leide. 1651.

Bamba. Rhetorica. (Mod. Greek.) 8vo. Paris. 1813.

Bampfield, Tho. Reply to Dr. Wallis on the Christian Sabbath. 4to. 1693.

Bampton Lecture Sermons. 40 vols. 8vo. Lond. 1780—1819.

Bancroft, Aaron. Sermon on the Nature and Worth of Christian Liberty. 1st and 2d ed. 8vo. Worcester. 1816.

———, ———. Election Sermon. 8vo. Bost. 1801.

———, ———. Discourse on the Fourth Commandment. 8vo. Worcester. 1817.

———, ———. Convention Sermon. 8vo. Bost. 1820.

———, ———. Discourse on Conversion. 8vo. Worcester. 1818.

———, ———. Sermon at the Installation of the Rev. Mr. Willson. 8vo. Worcester. 1819.

Bancroft, Aaron. A Christmas Sermon. 8vo. Worcester. 1819.
———, ——. Vindication of the Mutual Council at Princeton. 8vo. Worcester. 1817.
———, ——. Sermon on the Benefits of Christ's Mediation. 8vo. Worcester. 1821.
———, ——. Life of Washington. 8vo. Worcester. 1807.
———, ——. Sermons on the Doctrines of the Gospel. 8vo. Worcester. 1822.
Bancroft, Edw. Naturgeschichte von Guiana; aus dem Englischen. 8vo. Frank. und Leipz. 1769.
———, ——. Natural History of Guiana. 8vo. Lond. 1769.
Bancroft, Edw. N. Sequel to an Essay on Yellow Fever. 8vo. Lond. 1817.
Bandello, Mat. Novelle. 9 vol. 8vo. Lond. 1791—3.
Bandinius, Ang. Mar. Vita e Lettere di Amerigo Vespucci. 4to. Firenze. 1745.
———, ———. Americus Vespucci Leben; aus dem Italienischen. 12mo. Hamb. 1748.
———, ———. Catalogus Codicum MSS. Bibliothecæ Mediceæ Laurentianæ. 8 vol. fol. Florentiæ. 1764—78.
Banduri, Anselmus. Imperium Orientale. 2 vol. fol. Paris. 1711.
———, ———. Numismata Imperatorum Romanorum. 2 vol. fol. Lut. Paris. 1718.
Bangs, Edw. Oration, July 4th. 8vo. Worcester. 1800.
Banier, Antoine. Mythology and Fables of the Ancients explained; from the French. 4 vols. 8vo. Lond. 1739—40.
———, ———. Sur l'Origine du Culte que les Egyptiens rendoient aux Animaux. Sur le Culte d' Adonis. Sur Typhon. (Acad. des Inscrip. vol. 3.)
———, ———, Sur les Argonautes. (Id. 9 et 12).
Banister, James. Translation of Pindar. 8vo. Salisbury. 1791.
Banister, John. Plants found in Virginia. (Phil. Trans. 1693.)
———, ——. Insects in Virginia. (Id. 1700.)
Bank of England defended from the Aspersions in "A Review of the Universal Remedy for all Diseases incident to Coin." 12mo. Lond. 1697.
Bank of N. America. Remarks on "Considerations on the Bank of N. America. 12mo. Phil. 1785.
Banks, John. Life of J. Banks, Executed for the Murder of his Wife. 8vo. N. York. 1806.
Banks, Sir Joseph. Voyage in the Endeavour, in 1768—71. See Hawkesworth.
——, ———. Horticultural Papers.
Banneker, Benj. Copy of a Letter to the Secretary of State, with his Answer. 4to. Phil. 1792.
Bannerman, Anne. Poems. 4to. Edinburgh. 1807.
Baptism. Lay-Baptism Invalid; to which is prefixed a Letter to the Author, by Geo. Hickes D. D. 8vo. Lond. 1712.
———. Letter to the Rev. Mr. C—stl—n on his Rebaptising those who had been Baptised in Infancy. 12mo.

Baraterius, J. P. Anti-Artemonius. 12mo. Norimb. 1735.
Barba, Alvarez Alphonso. Métallurgie, trad. de l'Espagnol. 2 tom. 12mo. Paris. 1751.
Barbados. Acts of Assembly from 1648 to 1718. fol. Lond. 1721.
————. Short History of Barbados. 12mo. Lond. 1768.
————. Remarks upon "A Short History of Barbados." 12mo. Barbados. 1768.
Barbary. History of the Piratical States. 8vo. Lond. 1750.
Barbauld, Anna L. Remarks on Wakefield's Enquiry concerning Public Worship. 8vo. Lond. 1792.
————, ————. Works, with a Memoir by Lucy Aikin. 3 vols. 12mo. Bost. 1826.
Barbault, M. Les plus beaux Monumens de Rome Ancienne. fol. Rome. 1761.
————, —. Les plus beaux Edifices de Rome Moderne. fol. Rome. 1763.
Barberini. Dichiaratione delle Pitture della Sala de' Signori Barberini. 4to. Roma. 1640.
Barberinus, Maph. (Urbanus VIII.) Poemata. 4to. Romæ. 1631.
————, ————————. Poemata, cum Notis Dormalii. 4to. Romæ. 1643.
Barberius, Jos. De Miseria Poetarum Græcorum. (Gronov. vol. 10.)
Barbeyrac, Jean. La Morale des Pères de l'Eglise. 4to. Amst. 1728.
————, ————. Supplément au Corps Universel Diplomatique du Droit des Gens. 5 vol. fol. Amst. et La Haye. 1739.
————, ————. Spirit of Ecclesiastics as to the Doctrines of Morality. 8vo. Lond. 1722.
Barcia, And. Gonz. Historiadores Primitivos de las Indias Occidentales. 3 tom. fol. Madrid. 1749.
Barclaius, Joh. Argenis. 16mo. Venet. 1656.
————, —. ————. 16mo. Amst. 1671.
————, —. Argenis, translated out of Latin into English, by K. Long. 4to. Lond. 1636.
————, —. Satyricon, ct Conspiratio Anglicana. 4to. Lug. Bat. 1674.
————, —. Defence of the Eucharist, Englished by a Person of Quality. 4to. Lond. 1688.
Barclay, John. Anatomical Nomenclature. 8vo. Edin. 1803.
Barclay, P. Ruling and Ordaining Power of Presbyters Defended against him. 12mo. Bost. 1724.
Barclay, Robert. Apology for the True Christian Divinity, preached by the Quakers. 8vo. Lond. 1736.
————, ————. The Same. 8vo. Lond. 1765.
————, ————. The Same. 8th ed. (Baskerville's.) 4to. Birmingham. 1765.
Bards. American Bards; a Satire. 8vo. Phil. 1820.
Bardsley, Sam. A. Medical Reports, and Hydrophobia. 8vo. Lond. 1807.

Baretti, Joseph. Dictionary and Grammar of the English and Italian Languages. 2 vols. 4to. Lond. 1760.
——, ——. The Same. 6th ed. 2 vols. 8vo. Lond. 1820.
——, ——. Appendix to his Account of Italy. 8vo. Lond. 1768.
Bargæus, P. A. De Ædificiorum Urbis Romæ Eversoribus. Commentarius de Obelisco. (Græviu, vol. 4.)
Bariffe, Wm. Militarie Discipline; with Mars his Triumph. 4to. Lond. 1645—7.
Barker, John. Charity Sermon. 8vo. Lond. 1721.
——, ——. Sermon to a Society of Young Persons. 8vo. Lond. 1723.
——, ——. Sermon against Popery. 8vo. Lond. 1735.
——, ——. Sermon before the Society for the Relief of Widows and Children of Dissenting Ministers. 8vo. Lond. 1740.
——, ——. Sermon on the Victory over the Rebels in Scotland. 8vo. Lond. 1746.
——, ——. Sermon on Reformation of Manners. 12mo. Lond. 1721.
——, ——. Sermons on Various Subjects. 2 vols. 8vo. Lond. 1764.
——, ——. Sermon on the Death of John Jacob, Esq. 8vo. Lond. 1738.
——, ——. Sermon on the Death of the Rev. Benjamin Grosvenor. 8vo. Lond. 1758.
——, ——. Fast Sermon. 8vo. Lond. 1720.
Barker, Samuelis. Poesis Vetus Hebraica Restituta, etc. 4to. Lond. 1761.
Barker, Tho. Vindication of Dissenters. 12mo. Lond. 1707.
Barkey, Nic. Museum Haganum Historico-Philologico-Theologicum. 4 tom. 12mo. Hagæ Com. 1774—80.
——, ——. Symbolæ Litterariæ Haganæ. 2 tom. Hagæ Com. 1777—9.
——, ——. Bibliotheca Bremensis. Vide Bibliotheca.
Barlæus, Caspar. Rerum in Brazilia Gestarum Historia. fol. Amst. 1647.
——, ——. Idem. 12mo. Clivis. 1660.
——, ——. Brasilianische Geschichte. 12mo. Cleve. 1659.
——, ——. Poemata. 2 tom. 16mo. Amst. 1645.
——, ——. Vide Herrera.
Barletius, Marinus. De Scodrensi Urbe a Turca expugnata. (Clauser.)
Barlow, Joel. Vision of Columbus. 8vo. Hartford. 1787.
——, ——. The Same. 8vo. Paris. 1793.
——, ——. Conspiracy of Kings; a Poem. 8vo. Paris. 1793.
——, ——. Political Writings. 12mo. New York. 1796.
——, ——. Advice to the Privileged Orders. 8vo. Lond. 1792.
——, ——. Hasty Pudding; a Poem. 12mo. Salem. 1799.
——, ——. Letter to his Fellow Citizens, 4th March. 1799.
——, ——. Another. 20th Dec. 1799.

Barlow, Joel. Letter to the People of Piedmont on the French Revolution. 12mo. N. York. 1795.

———, ———. The Columbiad. 4to. Phil. 1807.

———, ———. —————. 8vo. Paris. 1813.

———, ———. —————. 4to. Paris. 1813.

———, ———. Prospectus of a National Institution. 8vo. Washington City. 1806.

———, ———. Oration, July 4th. 8vo. Washington City. 1809.

———, ———. Notice sur sa Vie et ses Ecrits, (par Dupont de Nemours.) 4to. 1813.

Barlow, Peter. Mathematical Dictionary. 8vo. Lond. 1814.

Barlow, Tho. (Bp.) Genuine Remains. 8vo. Lond. 1693.

———, ———. Letter concerning Invocation of Saints. 4to. Lond. 1679.

———, ———. Cases of Conscience Resolved. 8vo. Lond. 1692.

———, ———. Few plain Reasons why a Protestant of the Church of England should not turn Roman Catholick. 4to. Lond. 1688.

Barlow, Wm. Conference between James I. and the Bishops, &c. 4to. Lond. 1604.

Barnabas, Sanctus. Epistola Catholica, Gr. et Lat.; accessit Sancti Hermæ Pastor. 12mo. Oxon. 1685.

———, ———. Epistola Catholica. Vide Ignatius. Vide Cotelerius.

———, ———. Catholick Epistle. See Wake.

Barnard, Edw. Election Sermon. 8vo. Bost. 1766.

———, ———. Sermon at the Ordination of the Rev. Tho. Cary. 8vo. Bost. 1768.

———, ———. Convention Sermon. 4to. Bost. 1773.

Barnard, James. Divinity of Christ demonstrated in Letters to Dr. Priestley 12mo. Lond. 1789.

Barnard, John. Short View of the Prelatical Church of England. 4to. Lond. 1661.

Barnard, John. Sermon on the Death of the Rev. George Curwin. 8vo. Bost. 1717.

———, ———. History of the Strange Adventures &c. of Philip Ashton. 8vo. Bost. 1725.

———, ———. Two Discourses to Young Persons, &c. 12mo. Bost. 1727.

———, ———. Sermon on the Death of the Rev. S. Cheever. 8vo. Bost. 1724.

———, ———. Sermon on the Weightier Matters of the Law. 8vo. Bost. 1729.

———, ———. Zeal for Good Works excited and directed; a Sermon. 8vo. Bost. 1742.

———, ———. Call to Parents and Children; a Sermon. 8vo. Bost. 1737.

———, ———. True Divinity of Christ; a Sermon. 8vo. Bost. 1761.

———, ———. Discourses on Acts XVI. 30. 8vo. Bost. 1750.

Barnard, John. Imperfection of the Creature and the Excellency of the Divine Government, in nine Sermons. 8vo. Bost. 1747.
———, ———. Convention Sermon. 4to. Bost. 1738.
———, ———. Dudleian Lecture. 8vo. Bost. 1756.
———, ———. Version of the Psalms. 12mo. Bost. 1752.
———, ———. Election Sermon. 8vo. Bost. 1734.
———, ———. Election Sermon. 8vo. Bost. 1746.
Barnard, Sir John. Defence of the Proposals for raising Three Millions for the Service of the Government. 8vo. Lond. 1746.
Barnard, Tho. Sermon at the Ordination of Edward Barnard. 8vo Bost. 1743.
———, ———. Sermon at the Ordination of the Rev. William Whitwell. 8vo. Bost. 1762
———, ——— Artillery Election Sermon. 8vo. Bost. 1758.
———, ———. Sermon in Boston to the Society for Encouraging Industry. 8vo. Bost. 1758.
———, ———. Dudleian Lecture. 8vo. Salem. 1768.
———, ———. Election Sermon. 8vo. Bost. 1763.
———, ———. Discourse at the Funeral of the Rev. P. Clarke. 8vo Salem. 1768.
Barnard, Tho. Sermon before the Salem Female Charitable Society. 8vo. Salem. 1803.
———, ———. Discourse before the Society for Propagating the Gospel among the Indians. 8vo. Charlestown. 1806.
———, ———. Thanksgiving Sermon. 8vo. Salem. 1795.
———, ———. Another. 8vo. Salem. 1796.
———, ———. Dudleian Lecture 8vo. Bost. 1795.
———, ———. Sermon at the Ordination of the Rev. Ichabod Nichols. 8vo. Portland. 1809.
———, ———. Anniversary Discourse before the Humane Society of Massachusetts. 8vo. Bost. 1794.
———, ———. Election Sermon. 8vo. Bost. 1789.
———, ———. Convention Sermon. 4to. Bost. 1793.
———, ———. Sermon at the Ordination of the Rev. Aaron Bancroft. 8vo. Worcester. 1786.
Barnard, Wm. (Bp.) Sermon before the Society for Promoting English Protestant Schools in Ireland. 4to. Dublin. 1752.
Barnes, David. Sermon on the Love of Life and Fear of Death. 8vo. Bost. 1795.
———, ———. Sermon on the Death of the Rev. James Hawley. 8vo. Bost. 1801.
———, ———. Discourse on Education. 8vo. Bost. 1803.
Barnes, Henry. Notes of Cases. 2d ed. 8vo. Dublin. 1788.
Barnes, Josua. Estheræ Historia. 8vo. Lond. 1679.
———. ———. History of Edward III. and the Black Prince. fol. Camb. 1688
———, ———. Vide Homerus.
Barnuevo, Fr. Mosquera de La Numantina. 4to. Sevilla. 1612.
Barnuevo, Pedro de Peralta. Lima Fundada, o Conquista del Peru, Poema Heroico. 4to. Lima. 1732.

Baro, Roulox. Relation du Voyage au Pays des Tapuies dans la Terre Ferme du Brazil, trad. d'Hollandois. 4to. Paris. 1651.
Baron, Rich. Pillars of Priestcraft and Orthodoxy Shaken. 2 vols. 12mo. Lond. 1752.
——, ——. The Same. 4 vols. 12mo. Lond. 1768.
——, ——. Cordial for Low Spirits. See Gordon.
Baronius, Cæs. De Monarchia Siciliæ. (Græv. Thes. Ital.)
——, ——. Annales Ecclesiastici. 19 vol. fol. Col. Agrip. 1610—30.
Baronius, Fr. De Panormitana Majestate. (Græv. Thes. Ital.)
Baronius, Rob. Apologia pro Disputatione de Formali Objecto Fidei, ad G. Turnebullum. 12mo. Lond. 1657.
Barozzio, Jacomo da Vignola. Regola delli Cinque Ordini d'Architettura. fol. Roma. 1617.
Barre, M. de la. Dissertations sur le Poëme Epique. (Acad. des Inscrip. vol. 9.)
——, ——. Mémoires pour servir à l'Histoire de la Religion de la Grèce. (Id. 16 et 18.)
Barrère, Pierre. Essai sur l'Histoire Naturelle de la France Equinoxiale. 12mo. Paris. 1741.
——, ——. Idem. 12mo. Paris. 1749.
——, ——. Nouvelle Relation de la France Equinoxiale. 12mo Paris. 1743.
Barrère, Bouguer, und de la Condamine. Neue Reisen nach Guiana, Peru, etc. aus dem Französischen. 8vo. Göttingen. 1751.
Barrett, John. Enquiry into the Origin of the Constellations of the Zodiac. 8vo. Dublin. 1800.
——, ——. Essay on the Earlier Part of Swift's Life. 8vo. Lond. 1808.
——, ——. Evangelium secundum Matthæum, ex Codice Rescripto. 4to. Dublinii. 1801.
Barrington, Daines. Observations on the Statutes. 4to. Lond. 1766. (2 copies)
——, ——. The Same. 4to. Lond. 1769.
——, ——. Miscellanies. 4to. Lond. 1781.
——, ——. Papers in the Antiquarian and Philosophical Transactions.
Barrington, Geo. Voyage to New South Wales. 8vo. Lond. 1810.
——, ——. History of New South Wales. 8vo. Lond 1810.
Barrington, J. Shute, Ld. Miscellanea Sacra. 2 vol. 8vo. Lond. 1725
——, ——. Letter to the Lord Bishop of —— &c. 4to. Lond. 1714.
——, ——. Another Copy. 2d ed. 3 vols. 8vo. Lond. 1770.
——, ——. Peace without Union. 12mo. Lond. 1704.
——, ——. On the Dispensations of God to Man. 8vo. Lond. 1728.
——, ——. On Natural and Revealed Religion. 8vo. Lond. 1732.

Barrington, Sir Jonah. Personal Sketches of his Own Times. 2 vols. Phil. 1827.
Barrios, Miguel de. Flor de Apolo, y Comedias. 4to. Bruselas. 1665.
Barrius, Gab. De Laudibus Italiæ. De Calabriæ Antiquitate et Situ. (Græv. Thes. Ital.)
Barrow, Isaac. Theological Works, 3 vols., with a 4th on Other Subjects. fol. Lond. 1687.
——, ——. Theological Works, by Tillotson. 3 vols. in 2. fol. Lond. 1716.
——, ——. On the Pope's Supremacy; also, On the Unity of the Church. 4to. Lond. 1680.
——, ——. Euclidis Elementa. Vide Euclid.
——, ——. Lectiones Geometricæ. 4to. Lond. 1670.
——, ——. Euclide's Elements. 8vo. Lond. 1732.
——, ——. Twenty-Two Sermons. 8vo. Oxford. 1798.
Barrow, J. Abrégé Chronologique; ou Histoire des Découvertes faites par les Européens dans les différentes parties du Monde, trad. de l'Anglois par M. Targe. 12 tom. 12mo. Paris. 1766.
Barrow, James. His Wonderful Deliverance from Evil Spirits. 4to. Lond. 1664.
Barrow, John. Travels in China. 8vo. Phil. 1805.
——, ——. Travels in Africa. 4to. Lond. 1801.
——, ——. ————. 8vo. N. York. 1802.
——, ——. Voyage to Cochinchina. 4to. Lond. 1806.
Barrow, Wm. Eight Sermons at the Bampton Lecture. 8vo. Lond. 1799.
Barruel, l'Abbé. Histoire du Clergé pendant la Révolution Françoise. 8vo. Lond. 1793.
——, ——. Mémoires pour servir à l'Histoire du Jacobinisme. 4 vol. 8vo. Lond. 1797—8.
——, ——. Memoirs of Jacobinism; from the French. 3 vols. 8vo. Hartford and N. York. 1799.
Barry, Sir Edward. On the Wines of the Ancients. 4to. Lond. 1775.
Bartenora, R. Obadias. Mischna: Ordo Seminum, cum Comment. 4to. (Hebrew.)
Barthel, Sam. De Sadducæis. (Ugol. vol. 22.)
Barthélemy, J. J. Voyage du Jeune Anacharsis en Grèce. 5 vol. 4to. Paris. 1788.
————, ——. Idem. 7 vol. 8vo. et 1 vol. 4to. Atlas. Paris. 1790.
————, ——. Idem. 7 vol. 4to. et 1 vol. fol. Atlas. Paris. 1799.
————, ——. Travels of Anacharsis. 4 vols. 8vo. Phil. 1804.
————, ——. The Same. 7 vols. 8vo. and 1 vol. 4to. Atlas. Lond. 1806.
————, ——. Sur les Rapports des Langues Egyp. Phénic. et Grecque. (Acad. des Inscrip. vol. 32.)
————, ——. Sur le Nombre de Pièces qu'on représentoit dans un même jour sur le Théatre d'Athènes. (Id. 39.)

Barthélemy, J. J. Sur les Médailles Arabes.—Sur l'Alphabet et la Langue de Palmyre. (Id. 26.)

————, ——. On the Ancient Alphabet and Language of Palmyra; from the French. fol. Lond. 1755.

Bartholinus, Caspar. De Ovariis Mulierum, et Generationis Historia. 16mo. Amst. 1679.

————, ———. De Inauribus Veterum. 16mo. Amst. 1676.

Bartholinus, Tho. Anatomia Reformata. 8vo. Hagæ Com. 1666.

————, ——. De Armillis Veterum.—De Annulis Narium.—De Puerperio Veterum. 16mo. Amst. 1676.

————, ——. Hist. Anatom. et Med. Rar. 16mo. Hafniæ. 1661.

————, ——. Paralytici Nov. Test.—De Morbis Biblicis. (Ugol. vol. 30.)

Bartholoccius, J. De Musicis Instrumentis Hebræorum.—De voce Selah. (Ugol. vol. 32.)

Bartlett, Israel. Oration on Masonry. 8vo. Portsm. 1801.

Bartlett, John. Anniversary Discourse before the Humane Society of Massachusetts. 4to. Boston. 1792.

Bartlett, Joseph. Physiognomy, a Poem delivered before the Phi Beta Kappa Society. 4to. Boston. 1799.

Bartlett, Josiah. Address to Free Masons. 8vo. Charlestown. 1797.

———, ———. Oration on the Death of Dr. John Warren. 8vo. Bost. 1815.

———, ———. Progress of Medical Science in Massachusetts. 8vo. Bost. 1810.

———, ———. Historical Sketch of Charlestown, Mass. 8vo. Bost. 1814.

Bartlett, Oliver C. Vindication of Baptism and the Lord's Supper. 12mo. Nantucket. 1817.

Bartoli, P. S. Antichi Sepolcri, ovvero Mausolei Romani ed Etruschi. fol. Roma. 1727.

———, —. Antiche Lucerne Sepolcrali di Roma. fol. Roma. 1729.

———, —. Veterum Sepulcra, seu Mausolea Romanorum et Etruscorum.—Veterum Lucernæ Sepulcrales. (Gronov. vol. 12).

———, —. Admiranda Rom. Antiq. etc. Vide Bellori.

Bartolini, G. F. Della Futura Rinnovazione de' Cieli e della Terra, etc. 4to. 1780.

Bartoloccius de Celleno, J. Bibliotheca Magna Rabbinica. 4 vol. fol. Romæ. 1675—93.

Bartolomei, Girolamo. L'America, Poema Eroico. fol. Roma. 1650.

Bartolommeo, F. Ammaestramenti degli Antichi. 8vo. Milano. 1808.

Bartolozzi, Fr. Ricerche Istorico-Critiche circa alle Scoperte d' Amerigo Vespucci. 12mo. Firenze. 1789.

————, —. Apologia delle Ricerche. 12mo. Firenze. 1789.

Barton, Benj. S. New Views of the Origin of the Tribes and Nations of America. 8vo. Phil. 1797.

Barton, Benj. S. The Same. 8vo. Phil. 1798.
——, ——. Observations on the Opossum. 8vo. Phil. 1813.
——, ——. Philadelphia Medical and Physical Journal. vol. 2. 8vo. Phil. 1806.
——, ——. Observations on Natural History. 8vo. Lond.
——, ——. Collections towards a Materia Medica of the U. States. 8vo. Phil. 1798.
——, ——. Elements of Botany. 8vo. Lond. 1804.
——, ——. Materia Medica. See Cullen.
——, ——. Remedy for the Bite of the Rattle-Snake; Enquiry relative to the Honey Bee; On the Native Country of the Potatoe; and other papers in the American Philosophical Transactions.
——, ——. On the Facinating Faculty ascribed to the Rattle-Snake, &c. 8vo. Phil. 1796.
Barton, Charles. History of a Suit in Equity. 8vo. Dublin. 1796.
Barton, Phil. Consecration Sermon. 4to. Lond. 1766.
Barton, Tho. Sermon on Braddock's Defeat 8vo.
Barton, Wm. Book of Psalms, in Metre. 12mo. Lond. 1615.
Barton, Wm. P. C. Plan for Marine Hospitals in the U. States. 8vo. Phil. 1817.
——, ——. Biographical Sketch of B. S. Barton. 8vo. Phil. 1816.
——, ——. Remarks on Holcus Bicolor. 8vo. Phil. 1816.
——, ——. Floræ Philadelphicæ Prodromus. 4to. Phil. 1815.
Bartram, John. Observations made in his Travels from Pennsylvania to Canada. 8vo Lond. 1751.
——, ——. Description of East Florida, with a Journal. 4th ed. 4to. Lond. 1774.
——, ——. Papers in the Philosophical Transactions.
Bartram, Wm. Travels through North and South Carolina, Georgia, &c. 8vo Phil. 1791.
——, ——. The Same. 8vo. Lond. 1792.
——, ——. Voyage dans les Parties Sud de l'Amérique Septentrionale, trad. de l'Anglois, par P. V. Benoist. 2 vol. 8vo. Paris. 1801.
Baruffaldus, Hier. De Armis Convivalibus.—De Præficis, ad Illustrationem Urnæ Sepulcralis Fl. Quartillæ Præficæ. (Sallengre, vol. 3.)
Barwick, John. Sermon on the Death of Thomas, L. Bishop of Duresme; with his Life. 4to. Lond. 1660.
Barwick, Peter. Life of Dr John Barwick, from the Latin; with Letters of Charles I. and II., and the Earl of Clarendon. 8vo. Lond. 1724.
Basilius, Sanctus. Opera, Græce. fol. Basileæ. 1551.
Basilius, Seleuciensis. Vide Gregorius Neocæsariensis.
Basnage, J. de Franquener. Annales des Provinces-Unies. 2 vol. fol. La Haye. 1726.
——, ——. History of the Jews; from the French. fol. Lond. 1708.
Bassano, L. da. Concetti della Lingua Latina. 12mo. Venet. 62.

Basset, John. Herm'elogium; or an Essay at the Rationality of the Art of Speaking. 16mo. Lond. 1659.
Bassnett, Chr. Sermon at a Public Ordination. 8vo. Lond. 1717.
———, ——. Seaman's Character and Calling considered and improved. 8vo. 1712.
Baster, Job. Opuscula Subseciva. 4to. Harlemi. 1762.
Bastide, Martin de la. Mémoire sur un Nouveau Passage de la Mer du Nord à la Mer du Sud. 8vo. Paris. 1791.
Bastie, (M. le Baron de la.) Vie de Pétrarque. (Acad. des Inscrip. vol. 17.)
Bastius, Frider. Jac. Commentatio Palæographica. Vide Gregorius.
Baston, Rob. Metra de Illustri Bello de Bannockburn. (Fordun, Scotichronicon.)
Bastwick, John. Third and Fourth Parts of his Litany. 4to. 1637.
———, ——. Flagellum Pontificis, etc. 16mo. 1635
———, ——. Idem, cum Tribus Epistolis. 16mo. Lond. 1641.
———, ——. Independency not God's Ordinance. 4to. Lond. 1646.
———. ——. Apologeticus ad Præsules Anglicanos. 12mo. 1636.
———, ——. Relation of Certain Passages and Speeches in the Star-Chamber.
———, ——. Defence of himself against Lilbourn.
Bate, Geo. Pharmacopœia Bateana. Vide Salmon.
——, ——. Elenchus Motuum Nuperorum in Anglia. 12mo. Lond. 1676.
Bate, James. Infidelity Scourged. 8vo. 1746.
Bate, Julius. Remarks on Dr. Benson's Sermon on Justification. 8vo. Lond.
——, ——. Pentateuch, &c.; from the Hebrew. 4to. Lond. 1773.
Bateman, Tho. Synopsis of Cutaneous Diseases. 4th ed. 8vo. Lond. 1817.
———, ——. Delineations of Cutaneous Diseases. 4to. Lond. 1817.
———, ——. On Contagious Fever. 8vo. Lond. 1818.
Bates, Ely. Rural Philosophy. 8vo. Lond. 1804.
———, ——. The Same. 12mo. Phil. 1807.
Bates, John. Sermon on the Present Mortality of Cattle. 8vo. Lond. 1714.
Bates, Wm. Life of the Rev. Philip Henry. 12mo. Lond. 1698.
——, ——. Harmony of the Divine Attributes. 4to. Lond. 1675.
——, ——. Works. fol. Lond. 1700.
——, ——. ———. fol. Lond. 1723.
Batsch, A. J. G. C. Synopsis Univ. Analytica Generum Plantarum. pars I. 4to. Jenæ. 1793.
———, —————. Dispositio Generum Plantarum Jenensium. 4to. Jenæ.
Batteux, (L'Abbé le.) Sur l'Etude de la Philosophie Ancienne. Sur le Principe Actif de l'Univers. (Acad. des Inscrip. vol. 27 et 32.)

Batteux, (L'Abbé le.) Sur la Poëtique d'Aristote. Sur la Tragédie. Sur la Comédie. (Id. 39 et 41.)
Baudius, Dom. Epistolæ, Orationes, etc. 16mo. Amst. 1660.
Baudry, Des Lozières. Voyage à la Louisiane. 8vo. Paris. 1802.
Bauern, C. F. Die Vernünfftige Gewiskheit der Hebraischen Accentuation. 8vo. Leipz. 1730.
Bauhin, Casp. Pinax Plantarum. 4to. Basil. 1671.
Bauhin, J. J. H. Historia Plantarum. 3 vol. fol. Ebrod. 1650.
Baumeister, F. C. Elementa Philosophiæ. 12mo. Lips. 1755.
Baumgarten, Sig. Jac. Dissertatio, qua Hardtii Hypothesis de Linguæ Hebraicæ Derivatione expenditur. 4to. Hal. Magd. 1726.
———, ———. Beschreibung von Amerika. 2 theil. 4to. Halle. 1752—3.
Bavermeister, J. P. Observationum in Hesiodi Carmina Specimen Primum. 4to. Gottingæ.
Baxter, Andrew. Enquiry into the Nature of the Human Soul. 2 vols. 8vo. Lond. 1745.
———, ———. Appendix to the First Part of the Enquiry. 8vo. Lond. 1750.
———, ———. Remarks on the Enquiry. 8vo. Lond. 1741.
———, ———. Letter to the Author of the Enquiry. 8vo. Lond. 1741.
———, ———. Letter to J. Wilkes. 12mo. 1753.
———, ———. Matho, or Astronomy and Natural Philosophy for Young Persons. 2 vols. 8vo. Lond. 1745.
———, ———. Matho; sive Cosmotheoria Puerilis. 8vo. Lond. 1746.
Baxter, Gul. Glossarium Antiquitatum Britannicarum; cum Luidio de Nominibus Fluviorum, etc. 8vo. Lond. 1719.
———, —. Glossarium Antiquitatum Romanarum. 8vo. Lond. 1726.
———, —. De Analogia Ling. Lat. 12mo. Lond. 1679.
———, —. Philological Letters to Dr. Geeky. (Archæol. vol. 1.)
Baxter, Joseph. Election Sermon. 16mo. Boston. 1727.
Baxter, R. Important Tenets of the Roman Catholic Church fairly explained. 8vo. Washington, D. C. 1820.
Baxter, Richard. Gildas Salvianus; The Reformed Pastor. 8vo. Lond. 1656.
———, ———. The Same, abridged by S. Palmer. 12mo. Lond. 1766.
———, ———. Right Method for a Peaceful Conscience, &c. 8vo. Lond. 1657.
———, ———. Treatise of Conversion. 4to. Lond. 1657.
———, ———. A Saint or a Brute. 4to. Lond. 1662.
———, ———. Quaker's Catechism. 4to. Lond. 1656.
———, ———. Now or Never. 16mo. Edinburgh. 1672.
———, ———. Christian's Directory. fol. Lond. 1678.
———, ———. Full and Easie Satisfaction. 8vo. Lond. 1674.
———, ———. Catholick Theologie; Plain, Pure, Peaceable. fol. Lond. 1675.

Baxter, Richard. Moral Prognostication of what shall befall the Churches. 4to. Lond. 1680.
——, ——. Methodus Theologiæ Christianæ. fol. Lond. 1681.
——, ——. Call to the Unconverted, (translated into the Massachusetts language by Eliot.) 12mo. Camb. 1685.
——, ——. Account of the Irish Massacre Confuted.
——, ——. Practical Works. 4 vols. fol. Lond. 1707.
——, ——. Converse with God in Solitude.—Dying Thoughts, abridged by B. Fawcett. 12mo. Salop. 1761.
——, ——. Life of Faith, abridged by B. Fawcett. 12mo. Salop. 1764.
——, ——. Life and Times, written by himself. fol. Lond. 1696.
Bay, E. H. Reports of Cases in the Superior Courts in South Carolina. 2 vols. 8vo. N. York. 1809.
Bay, Wm. Inaugural Dissertation on the Dysentery. 8vo. New York. 1797.
Bayard, Chevalier. Mémoires. (Mémoires de France, vol. 14 et 15.)
Bayard, F. M. Voyage dans l'Intérieur des Etats Unis. 8vo. Paris. 1797.
——, ——. Idem. 8vo. Paris. 1798.
Bayard, James A. Speech on the Foreign Intercourse Bill. 8vo. 1798.
——, ——. Speech on the Organization of the Courts of the United States. 8vo. Bost. 1802.
Bayers, H. P. W. Reise nach Peru. 12mo. Nürnberg. 1776.
Bayes, Joshua. Sermon against Popery. 8vo. Lond. 1735.
——, ——. Reformation of Manners Sermon. 8vo. Lond. 1723.
——, ——. Sermon on the Death of the Rev. C. Taylor. 8vo. Lond. 1723.
——, ——. Divine Benevolence. 8vo. Lond. 1731.
Bayfius, Laz. de. De Re Vestiaria, Vascularia, et Navali. 12mo. Lutetiæ. 1553.
——, ——. Idem. (Grævius, vol. 6; item, Gronov. v. 9 et 11.)
Bayle, Pierre. Dictionaire Historique et Critique. 3me ed. 4 vol. fol. Rotter. 1720.
——, ——. Dictionary, Historical and Critical; from the French, with the Life of the Author, by Des Maizeaux. 5 vols. fol. Lond. 1734—8.
——, ——. See Bernard.
——, ——. Œuvres Diverses. 4 vol. fol. La Haye. 1727—31.
——, ——. Philosophical Commentary on the words, "Compel them to come in;" from the French. 2 vols. 12mo. Lond. 1708.
——, ——. Pensées Diverses sur la Comète de 1680. 4 vol. 12mo. Amst. 1749.
——, ——. Reflections on the Comet of 1680; from the French; with the Author's Life. 2 vols. 12mo. Lond. 1708.
Baylie, Robert. Sermon on Errours and Induration. 4to. Lond. 1645.

Baylie, Robert. Dissuasive from the Errours of the Times. 4to. Lond. 1645.
——, ——. Vindication of the Government of the Church of Scotland. 4to. Lond. 1646.
——, ——. Fast Sermon. 4to. Lond. 1643.
——, ——. Comparison of the Liturgie with the Masse-Book. 4to. Lond. 1641.
——, ——. The Canterburians Self-Conviction, &c. 4to. Lond. 1640.
——, ——. The Same. 4to. Lond. 1641.
——, ——. Supplement of the Canterburian Self-Conviction. 4to. Lond. 1641.
——, ——. Life of Laud examined. 4to. Lond. 1643.
——, ——. Opus Historicum et Chronologicum. fol. Amst. 1668.
——, ——. Transactions in England and Scotland from 1637 to 1662. 2 vols. 8vo. Edin. 1775.
Baylies, Wm. On the Proceedings of Congress in relation to the Plymouth Election. 8vo. Bost. 1809.
Bayly, Anselm. Introduction to Languages. 8vo. Lond. 1758.
Bayly, Lewis, (Bp.) See Baily.
Baynes, Paul. Diocesans Tryall. 4to. 1621.
Beacon, Joseph. Miscellanies. MS. 8vo. Bost. 1688.
——, ——. Private Thoughts. MS. 8vo. Bost. 1689.
Beasts. Congress of the Beasts, a Comedy. 8vo. Lond. 1748.
Beatinus, August. Verona. Vide Sannazarius.
Beatson, Rob. Political Index to the Histories of Great Britain and Ireland. 3d ed. 3 vols. 8vo. Lond. 1806.
Beattie, James. Works; with the Miscellanies and Life of James Hay Beattie. 10 vols. 16mo. Phil. 1809.
——, ——. Dissertations, Moral and Critical. 4to. Lond. 1783.
——, ——. On the Nature and Immutability of Truth. 8vo. Edin. 1770.
——, ——. The Same. 12mo. Dublin. 1773.
——, ——. ————. 8vo. Lond. 1773.
——, ——. Evidences of the Christian Religion. 12mo. Lond. 1786.
——, ——. Poems. 12mo. Lond. 1766.
——, ——. ——. See Chalmers.
Beatty, Charles. Journal of a Tour to promote Religion among the Frontier Inhabitants of Pennsylvania. 8vo. Lond. 1768.
Beau, C. le. Avantures; ou Voyage parmi les Sauvages de l'Amériqne Septentrionale. 2 vol. 12mo. Amst. 1738.
Beau, M. le, (l'Ainé.) Sur la Légion Romaine. (Acad. des Inscrip. vol. 29, 32, 37, 39, et 41.)
Beau, M. le, (le Cadet.) Sur le Plutus d' Aristophane, etc. (Acad. des Inscrip. vol. 30.)
Beaujour, Félix de. Traité d'Amiens. 8vo. Paris. 1802.
——, ——. Aperçu des Etats Unis depuis 1800 jusq'en 1810. 8vo. Paris. 1814.

Beaujour, Felix de. Sketch of the United States from 1800 to 1810; from the French. 8vo. Lond. 1814.
Beaumont, C. G. L. A. C. A. T. d'Eon de. Mémoires pour servir à l'Histoire Générale des Finances. 2 vol. 12mo. Lond. 1764.
Beaumont, Fr. Poems. See Chalmers.
———, —. and John Fletcher. Dramatic Works. 10 vols. 8vo. Lond. 1778.
Beaumont, Sir John. Poems. See Chalmers.
Beauregard, F. de. Sur la Fièvre Jaune. 8vo. Paris. 1826.
Beausobre, Isaac de. Introduction to the Reading of the Scriptures, with a New Version of St. Matthew; from the French of Beausobre and L'Enfant. 4to. Lond. 1727—34.
———, ———. Sermons. 4 vol. 8vo. Lausanne. 1755.
———, ———. Histoire de Manichée et du Manichéisme. 2 vol. 4to. Amst. 1734—9.
———, ———. Thorn Affligée. Vide Jablonski.
———, ———. Remarques Hist. Crit. et Phil. sur le Nouveau Testament. 4to. La Haye. 1742.
———, ———. Nouveau Testament, trad. du Grec, avec des Notes, par MM. de Beausobre et Lenfant. 2 vol. 4to. Amst. 1741.
Beausobre, L. Introduction à l'Etude de la Politique, des Finances, et du Commerce. 12mo. Amst. 1765.
Beauwes, Wynd. Lex Mercatoria. 4th ed. fol. Lond. 1813.
Bebelius, Hen. De Sacerdotiis et Magistratibus Romanorum. (Sallengre, vol. 3.)
Beccaria, C. Dei Delitti e delle Pene. 12mo. Harlem. 1766.
———, —. On Crimes and Punishments, &c.; from the Italian; with Voltaire's Commentary. 8vo. Lond. 1770.
———, —. The Same. 8vo. Phil. 1778.
———, —. Traité des Délits et des Peines; de l'Italien. 12mo. Lausanne. 1766.
———, —. On Public Economy and Commerce; from the Italian. 12mo. Lond. 1769.
———, —. Ricerche intorno alla Natura dello Stile. 8vo. Milano. 1809.
Beccaria, Joh. Refutatio Libelli de Jure Magistratuum in Subditos, et Officio Subditorum erga Magistratus. 12mo. 1590.
Becelli, G. C. Erodoto, con la Vita d' Omero. Vide Herodotus.
Becherus, J. J. Experimentum Chymicum. 12mo. Francof. 1671.
Becker, Clemens. Kirchengeschichte. 12mo. Münster. 1791.
Beckett, Wm. Attempt to prove the Antiquity of the Venereal before the Discovery of the West Indies. (Phil. Trans. 1718.)
———, ———. On the Difference in the Height of the Human Body, Morning and Evening. (Id. 1724.)
Beckford, Wm. Remarks upon the Situation of Negroes in Jamaica. 8vo. Lond. 1788.
———, ———. History of the Caliph Vathek.
———, ———, Bee Revived, or Prisoners Magazine. No. I. 8vo. Lond. 1750.

Beckhaus, M. J. H. Integrität der Prophetischen Schriften. 12mo. Halle. 1796.
Beckius, C. D. Commentationes de Interpretatione Veterum Scriptorum. 8vo. Lips. 1791.
———, ———. Commentarii Historici Decretorum Religionis Christianæ et Formulæ Lutheriæ. 8vo. Lips. 1801.
———, ———. Anleitung zur genauern Kenntniss der Allgemeinen Geschichte. 4 vol. 8vo. Leipz. 1807—13.
———, ———. Vide Commentarii.
Beckius, M. F. Monumenta Antiqua Judaica. (Ugol. vol. 33.)
Beckmann, John. History of Inventions and Discoveries, translated from the German by Wm. Johnston. 4 vols. 8vo. Lond. 1814.
Beckmannus, D. H. Utrum Libri Symbolici vere an æquivoce dicantur Divini, Disputatio. 4to. Rostochii. 1705.
Beckwith, Geo. Connecticut Election Sermon. 12mo. N. Lond. 1756.
Becmanus, Christianus. Exercitationes Theologicæ. fol. Amst. 1643.
Beda, Venerabilis. Historiæ Ecclesiasticæ Gentis Anglorum Libri V. cum Reliquis ejus Operibus Historicis, cura J. Smith. fol. Cantab. 1722.
——, ————. Idem, cum Continuatione. Vide Rerum Britannicarum Scriptores.
——, ————. Axiomata Philosophica. 12mo. Coloniæ, 1609.
Beddoes, Thomas. On Consumption. 8vo. Lond. 1799.
———, ———. Hygeia. 3 vols. 8vo. Bristol. 1802—3.
———, ———. Contributions to Phys. and Med. Knowledge. 8vo. Bristol. 1799.
———, ———. Tracts on Calculus, Sea Scurvy, Consumption, Catarrh, and Fever. 8vo. Lond. 1793.
———, ———. Letter to Dr. Darwin on Consumption. 8vo. Bristol. 1793.
———, ———. Treatment of the Venereal Disease by Nitrous Acid. 8vo. Lond. 1799.
———, ———. On the Management of the Consumptive; on Digitalis Purpurea; and on Scrophula. 8vo. Lond. 1801.
———, ———. Elements of Medicine. See Brown.
———, ———, and J. Watt. On Factitious Airs. 2 vols. 8vo. Bristol. 1795—6.
Bedell, Wm. (Bp.) Letters between him and J. Waddesworth concerning the Motives to the Roman Obedience. 8vo. Lond. 1685.
———, ———. Sermon on Rev. xviii. 4. 12mo. Lond. 1658.
———, ———. Character of Bishop Bedell. 12mo. Lond. 1658.
Bedford, Arthur. Scripture Chronology. fol. Lond. 1730.
Beecher, Lyman. Sermon at the Installation of the Rev. John Keyes. 8vo. Andover. 1815.
———, ———. Sermon at the Ordination of the Rev. S. E.

Dwight, as Pastor of Park Street Church, Boston; and of Elisha P. Swift and others, as Missionaries. 8vo. Andover. 1818.
———, ———. Sermon on Reformation of Morals. 8vo. Andover. 1814.
Beede, Tho. Allegory of the Olive Tree; a Discourse. 8vo. Amherst. 1817.
Beere, (Major.) Relation of the Defeat of the Enemies Horse near Cambden. 4to. 1644.
Beerensprung, M. S. An Fidelibus Gratia Divina et Remissio Peccatorum iterum a Ministro Ecclesiæ conferri possit et debeat? 4to. Halæ Magd. 1704.
Beers, Wm. P. Oration on the Death of Washington. 4to. Albany. 1800.
Beesly, Henry. The Soule's Conflict, in Eight Severall Sermons. 12mo. Lond. 1657.
Begerus, Laur. Gemmarum et Numismatum Græcorum Series. 3 vol. fol. Col. Mar. 1696.
———, ———. Numismata Pontificum Romanorum, etc. fol. Col. Brand. 1704.
Behlcke, M. S. De Nummo Aureo Theodosii II. et Valentiniani III. 4to. Sedini. 1727.
Behrens, H. Natural History of Hartz-Forest; from the German. 8vo. Lond. 1730.
Behrens, Phil. De Felicitate Ecclesiæ Externa, Internæ plerumque Noxia. 4to. Helmstadii. 1726.
Beiger, J. S. De Malis Ecclesiæ Admixtis. 4to. Argent. 1708.
Bekker, Immanuel. Vide Anecdota Græca.
Belcher, Jonathan. Conference with the Indians. 4to. 1732.
Belcher, Joseph. Election Sermon. 16mo. Boston. 1701.
Belcher, Sam. Election Sermon. 8vo. Boston. 1707.
———, ———. Assize Sermon at Ipswich. 12mo. Bost. 1707.
Belgii Urbium Ichnographiæ.
Belidor, B. F. de. New Method of Mining. See Muller.
Belisario, A. M. Report of the Trial of Arthur Hodge, Esq. at Tortola, for the Murder of his Negro-Man. 12mo. Middletown. 1812.
Belknap, Jeremy. Dissertations on Christianity, with Remarks on "The Age of Reason." 8vo. Bost. 1795.
———, ———. Fast Sermon. 8vo. Bost. 1798.
———, ———. Sermon at the Installation of the Rev. J. Morse. Bost. 1789.
———, ———. Convention Sermon. 4to. Bost. 1796.
———, ———. Sermon on Military Duty. Salem. 1773.
———, ———. Discourse on the Discovery of America, &c. 8vo. Bost. 1792.
———, ———. American Biography. 2 vols. 8vo. Boston. 1794—8.
———, ———. History of New Hampshire. 3 vols. 8vo. Phil. and Bost. 1784—92.
———, ———. The Same. 2d ed. 3 vols. 8vo. Bost. 1813.

Belknap, Jeremy. Selection of Psalms and Hymns. 12mo. Bost. 1795.

———, ———. The Same. 12mo. Bost. 1820.

Bell, Andrew. Anatomia Britannica. 2 vol. fol. Edin. 1798.

Bell, Benj. Theory and Management of Ulcers. 8vo. Edin. 1784.

——, ——. System of Surgery. 3 vols. 8vo. Edin. 1783—5.

——, ——. The Same. 6th ed. 7 vols. 8vo. Edin. 1796.

Bell, Charles. Engravings explaining the Course of the Nerves. 4to. Lond. 1803.

——, ———. Anatomy of the Brain. 4to. Lond. 1802.

——, ———. Engravings of the Arteries. 4to. Lond. 1801.

——, ———. Operative Surgery. 2 vols. 8vo. Hartford. 1812.

——, ———. System of Dissections with Plates. 2 vols. fol. Edin. 1798—1801.

——, ———. Surgical Observations. 2 vols. 8vo. Lond. 1816—18.

Bell, John. Common-Place Book on the Principles of Locke. fol. Lond. 1770.

Bell, John, of Antermony. Travels from St. Petersburgh to various parts of Asia. 2 vols. 8vo. Edin. 1788.

Bell, John. Anatomy of the Bones, Muscles, and Joints. 4to. and 8vo.

——, ——. Principles of Surgery. 3 vols. 4to. Edin. and Lond. 1801—8.

——, ——. Principles of Surgery, abridged by J. A. Smith. 8vo. N. York. 1810.

——, ——. On the Nature and Cure of Wounds. 2 vols. 8vo. Edin. 1800.

Bell, John, and Charles. Anatomy of the Human Body. 4 vols. 8vo. Edin. and Lond. 1797—1804.

Bell, Robert. Address concerning an Embargo laid on the Free Sale of Books by Auction. 8vo. Phil. 1784.

Bell, Tho. Articles of Ayr compared with Scripture. See Allinga.

Bell, Wm. Divine Missions of John the Baptist and Jesus Christ. 8vo. Lond. 1761.

——, ——. The Same; with Arguments in proof of the Miraculous Conception. 8vo. Lond. 1795.

——, ——. Practical Enquiry into the Authority, &c. of the Lord's Supper. 8vo. Bost. 1781.

——, ——. The Same. 8vo. Camb. 1809.

Bellamy, Joseph. Sermons on the Divinity of Jesus Christ, the Millennium, and Wisdom of God in the Permission of Sin. 8vo. Bost. 1758.

———, ———. Essay on the Nature and Glory of the Gospel. 12mo. Lond. 1784.

———, ———. True Religion Delineated. 12mo. Edin. 1788.

———, ———. Half-way Covenant; a Dialogue. 8vo. Bost. 1769.

Bellarmino, Rob. (Card.) Dichiarazione della Dottrina Cristiana. 16mo. Lucca.

Bellarmino, Rob. (Card.) Examination of his Fifteen Notes of the Church, by Sherlock and others. 4to. Lond. 1687.
———, ———. Advice to his Confuter, with Considerations on the Antiquity of the Church of England. 4to. Lond. 1687.
———, ———. De Scriptoribus Ecclesiasticis.
Belleisle, (Le Marèchal Duc de.) Lettres à M. le Marêchal de Contades. fol. 1759.
Bellendenus, Guil. De Tribus Luminibus Romanorum Libri xvi. fol. Paris. 1634.
———, ——. De Statu Libri iii. 8vo. Lond. 1787. V. Parr.
Bellers, Fettiplace. Delineation of Universal Law. 4to. Lond. 1754.
Belleval, P. Démonstration des Plantes. 2 vol. 4to. Lyons. 1796.
Belley, (L'Abbé.) Sur l'Histoire et les Monumens des Villes de Cyrène, de Tarse, et d'Ancyre en Galatie.—Sur le Titre d'Eleuthère, etc. (Acad. des Inscrip. vol. 37.)
———, ———. Sur deux Voies Romaines. (Id. 41.)
Bellin, N. Description des Isles Antilles possédées par les Anglois. 4to. Paris. 1758.
——, —. Remarques sur le Détroit de Belle-Isle, etc. 4to. 1758.
——, —. Description des Débouquemens de Saint Domingue. 4to. Paris. 1773.
——, —. Description de la Guyane. 4to. Paris. 1763.
Bellini, Laurent. De Motu Cordis et Bilis, etc. 4to. Lug. Bat. 1696.
———, ———. De Urinis et Pulsibus; De Missione Sanguinis; De Febribus; De Morbis Capitis et Pectoris. 4to. Lug. Bat. 1717.
———, ———. Idem; cum Præfatione H. Boerhaave. 4to. Lips. 1731.
Bellonius, Pet. Rerum in Græcia, Asia, etc. conspectarum Observationes. Vide Clusius.
———, —. De Neglecta Plantarum Cultura. Vide Clusius.
———, —. De Operum Antiquorum Præstantia. (Gronov. v. 8.)
Bellori, G. P. Scelta de' Medaglioni di Cardinale Gasparo Carpegna. 4to. Roma. 1679.
———, ——. Veteres Arcus Augustorum Triumphis Insignes. fol. Romæ. 1690.
———, ——. Admiranda Romanorum Antiquitatum Vestigia. fol. Romæ. 1693.
———, ——. Picturæ Antiquæ Cryptarum Romanarum et Sepulchri Nasonum. fol. Romæ. 1750.
———, ——. Notæ in Numismata tum Ephesia, tum aliarum Urbium Apibus insignita. (Gronov. vol. 7.)
———, ——. Expositio Symbolici Deæ Syriæ Simulacri. (Idem.)
Bellus, J. B. Diatriba de Partibus Templi Auguralis. Græv. v. 5.)
——, ——. Diatriba de Pharsalici Conflictus Mense et Die. (Id. 8.)
Bellus, Tho. Roma Restituta. 12mo. Lond. 1677.
Beloe, Wm. History of Herodotus; from the Greek, with Notes 4 vols. 8vo. Lond. 1791.

Beloe, Wm. Anecdotes of Literature and Scarce Books. 6 vols. Lond. 1807—12.
——, ——. Sexagenarian; or Recollections of a Literary Life. 2 vols. 8vo. Lond. 1818.
Belon du Mans, P. Histoire des Oyseaux. fol. Paris. 1555.
——————, —. Singularitez en Grèce, etc. 4to. Paris. 1555.
Belsham, Tho. Memoirs of the Rev. Theophilus Lindsey. 8vo. Lond. 1812.
———, ——. Elements of the Philosophy of the Mind and of Moral Philosophy, &c. 8vo. Lond. 1801.
———, ——. Review of Wilberforce's Practical View. 8vo. Lond. 1798.
———. ——. The Same. 12mo. Lond. 1800.
———, ——. Calm Inquiry into the Scripture Doctrine concerning the Person of Christ, &c. 8vo. Lond. 1811.
———, ——. American Unitarianism. 8vo. Bost. 1815.
———, ——. Epistles of Paul translated, with Notes, &c. 2 vols. 4to. Lond. 1822.
———, ——. The Same. 4 vols. 8vo. Lond. 1822.
Belsham, Wm. Memoirs of the Reign of George III. 4 vols. 8vo. Lond. 1795.
————, ——. History of Great Britain. 5 vols. 4to. Lond. 1798—1805.
Belu, C. Des Colonies et de la Traite des Nègres. 8vo. Paris. 1800.
Belzoni, G. Narrative of the Operations and Recent Discoveries in Egypt, Nubia, &c. 3d ed. 2 vols. 8vo. Lond. 1822.
———, —. Plates illustrative of the above. fol. Lond. 1822.
———, —. Remarks on the Pyramid opened by him. (Class. Journ. vol. 21.)
Bembo, P. (Card.) Opere. 12 vol. 8vo. Milano. 1808—10.
———, —————. Benacus, Poema. Vide Sannazarius, Fracastorius, et Poemata Italorum.
———, —————. Historiæ Venetæ Libri XII. (Græv. Thes. Ital.)
Bembridge, Dr. Answer to a Book entitled "Reason and Authority." 4to. Lond. 1687.
Benaduci, L. B. Idea de una Historia de la America Septentrional. 4to. Madrid. 1746.
Benaglia, J. Reisz-Beschreibung von Wiennach Constantinopel. 12mo. Franckf. 1687.
Benedict, David. General History of the Baptist Denomination. 2 vols. 8vo. Bost. 1813.
Benedictus, Abbas. De Vita et Gestis Henrici II. et Ricardi I. Vide Hearne.
Beneventum. Thesaurus Antiquitatum Beneventanarum. fol. Romæ. 1754.
Benezet, Ant. Account of Guinea, and the Slave Trade. 8vo. Lond. 1788.
————, ——. Observations sur l'Origine, les Principes, etc. de la Société de Quakers, ou Trembleurs. 8vo. Phil. 1780.
————, ——. Idem. 12mo. Lond. 1783.

Bengalee Vocabulary by Mohunpersand Takoor. 8vo. Calcutta. 1810.

Bengelius, J. A. Gnomon Novi Testamenti. 4to. Tubingæ. 1742.

———, ——. Introduction to his Exposition of the Apocalypse; from the high Dutch by Robertson. 8vo. Lond. 1757.

———, ——. Apparatus Criticus ad Novum Testamentum, a Burkio. 4to. Tubingæ. 1763.

———, ——. Novum Testamentum Gr. 4to. Tubin. 1734.

Benger, Eliz. O. Memoirs of Anne Boleyn. 8vo. Phil. 1822.

———, ——. Memoirs of Mary Queen of Scots. 2 vols. 8vo. Lond. 1823.

Benkowitz, C. F. Der Messias von Klopstock beurtheilt, etc. 8vo. Breslau. 1797.

Benloe, Wm., and Wm. Dalison. Reports in the time of Henry VII. and VIII., Edward VI., Philip and Mary, Eliz., James I., and Charles I. fol. Lond. 1689.

Benlow. Animadversions upon an Essay on Religious Establishments. 8vo. Lond. 1769.

———. Enquiry into the Cause which obstructed the Reformation. 8vo. Lond. 1768.

Benlowes, Edw. Theophila, or Loves Sacrifice; a Divine Poem. 4to. Lond. 1652.

Bennet, Benj. Memorial of the Reformation. 8vo. Lond. 1721.

———, ——. Defence of the Memorial. 8vo. Lond. 1723.

———, ——. Truth, Inspiration, and Usefulness of the Scripture. 8vo. Lond. 1730.

———, ——. Christian Oratory. 2 vols. 8vo. Lond. 1757.

———, ——. Irenicum: or a Review of Controversies about the Trinity. 8vo Lond. 1722.

Bennet, Christ. Tabidorum Theatrum. 16mo. Lug. Bat. 1714.

Bennet, J. E. Réponse aux Principales Questions, qui peuvent être faites sur les Etats Unis de l'Amérique. 2 vol. 8vo. Lausanne. 1795.

———, ——. Two Letters, &c. on the Sugar Colonies. 8vo. Lond. 1738.

Bennet, Tho. Grammatica Hebræa. 8vo. Lond. 1728.

———, ——. Non-Jurors Separation proved Schismatical. 8vo. Lond. 1716.

———, ——. Letter to B. Robinson occasioned by his Review of the Case of Liturgies, &c. Lond. 1710.

———, ——. Second Letter. Camb. 1710.

———, ——. Confutation of Popery. 8vo. Camb. 1701.

———, ——. Confutation of Quakerism. 8vo. Camb. 1709.

———, ——. His Concessions to Non-Jurors Destructive to the Cause he defends. 8vo. Lond. 1717.

———, ——. Answer to the Dissenter's Pleas. 8vo. Camb. 1701.

———, ——. Brief History of the Joint Use of Set Forms of Prayer. 8vo. Camb. 1708.

———, ——. Remarks on the Brief History.

———, ——. Discourse of Schism; with Defences of the Discourse. 8vo. Camb. 1704.

Bennet, Tho. Considerations on his Discourse of the Everblessed Trinity in Unity, &c. 8vo. Lond. 1718.
Bennett, James. See Bogue.
Benoit, Elias. Histoire de l'Edit de Nantes. 5 vol. 4to. Delft. 1693—5.
Benschlag, G. W. Theses de Morte Æterna. 4to. Argent. 1702.
Benson, Egbert. Remarks on "The Wife" of Washington Irving. 8vo. N. York. 1819.
Benson, Geo. Paraphrase and Notes on the Epistles. 2 vols. 4to. Lond. 1752—6.
———, ——. Reasonableness of the Christian Religion. 2 vols. 8vo. Lond. 1759.
———, ——. Appendix to the Reasonableness. 8vo. Lond. 1746.
———, ——. View of the Evidences of Christ's Resurrection. 8vo. Lond. 1754.
———, ——. Supplement to some Tracts respecting Calvin's causing Servetus to be burned; Laud's Treatment of Leighton; and Belief of Things above Reason. 8vo. Lond. 1748.
———, ——. Dissertation concerning the Man of Sin. 2d ed. 8vo. Lond.
———, ——. The Same. 3d ed. 8vo. Lond. 1743.
———, ——. Charity Sermon. 8vo. Lond. 1744.
———, ——. Sermons on Various Subjects. 8vo. Lond. 1748.
———, ——. Charity Sermon. 8vo. Lond. 1758.
———, ——. Fast Sermon. 8vo. Lond. 1745.
———, ——. Accession Sermon. 8vo. Lond. 1742.
———, ——. Another. 8vo. Lond. 1758.
———, ——. Collection of Ten Tracts. 8vo. Lond. 1748.
———, ——. On the Death of the Rev. James Read. 8vo. Lond. 1755.
———, ——. First Planting of the Christian Religion. 3 vols. in 1. 4to. Lond. 1756.
———, ——. History of the Life of Christ. 4to Lond. 1764.
———, ——. Letters on Prayer and Predestination. 8vo. Lond. 1737.
Benson, Martin, (Bp.) Sermon in Easter-Week. 4to. Lond. 1736.
Benson, Tho. Vocabularium Anglo-Saxonicum. 8vo. Oxon. 1701.
Bentham, Edw. Letter to a Young Gentleman of Oxford. 8vo. Lond. 1748.
———, ——. Funeral Eulogies, from Thucydides, Plato, Lysias, and Xenophon, in the Original Greek, &c. 8vo. Oxford. 1768.
———, ——. De Vita et Moribus Joh. Burtoni.
———, ——. Epistola ad Rob. Lowth.
Bentham, Jeremy. Defence of Usury. 16mo. Phil. 1796.
———, ——. On Codification and Public Instruction. 8vo. Lond. 1817.
Bentivoglio, G. (Card.) Relatione delle Provincie Unite di Fiandra, etc. 2 vol. in 1. fol. Anversa. 1629.
———, ———. Opere Storiche. 5 vol. 8vo. Milano. 1806—7.

Bentley, Rich. Eight Sermons at Boyle's Lecture, on the Folly of Atheism, preached in 1692, being the First on that Foundation. fol. Lond. 1699.

——, ——. The Same. 4to. Lond. 1699.

——, ——. Account of his Humanity and Justice to the Authors who have written before him. 8vo. Lond. 1699.

——, ——. Present State of Trinity College. 8vo. Lond. 1710.

——, ——. Dissertation on the Epistles of Phalaris. 8vo. Lond. 1699.

——, ——. Opuscula Philologica. 8vo. Lips. 1781.

——, ——. See Boyle, Milner, Wotton, Milton, Horatius, Lucan.

——, ——. Remarks upon a late Discourse of Freethinking. 8vo. Lond. 1714.

——, ——. The Same. 8vo. Camb. 1743.

——, ——. Second Part of the Remarks. 8vo. Lond. 1715.

——, ——. Address to the University of Oxford on the Divine Institution of the Ministry. 8vo. Lond. 1730.

——, ——. Proposals for Printing the Greek Testament with St. Hierom's Latin Version. 4to. Lond. 1721.

——, ——. Remarks on his Sermon on Popery. 8vo. Lond. 1716.

——, ——. His Life. (Classical Journal, vol. 5)

Bentley, Wm. Fast Sermon. 8vo.

Bentley, Wm. Sermon on the Death of Benj. Hodges. 12mo. Salem. 1804.

——, ——. Sermon on the Death of Gen. Fiske. 8vo. Salem. 1797.

——, ——. Sermon before the Female Charitable Society. 8vo Salem. 1807.

——, ——. Sermon at the Ordination of the Rev. J. Richardson. 8vo. Bost. 1806.

——, ——. Election Sermon. 8vo. Bost. 1807.

——, ——. Artillery Election Sermon. 8vo. Bost. 1796.

——, ——. Sermon on Matthew vii. 21 8vo. Bost. 1790.

——, ——. Sermon on the Death of J. Gardner. 8vo. Salem. 1791.

——, ——. Masonic Address. 8vo. Salem. 1799.

——, ——. Masonic Address. 8vo. Salem. 1797.

——, ——. Masonic Address. 8vo. Bost. 1797.

——, ——. Masonic Charge. 8vo. Worcester. A. L. 5798.

——, ——. Collection of Psalms and Hymns. 16mo. Salem. 1795.

Benzoni, Hieron. Historia Novi Orbis, ex Ital. Serm. 12mo.

Berbice, Beschryvinge van de Colonie de. 4to. Amst. 1763.

Berchetus, T. Elementaria Traditio Christianorum Fidei. 8vo Hanoviæ. 1628.

Bercy, Drouin de. L'Europe et l'Amérique Comparées. 2 vol. 8vo. Paris. 1818

Berger, Imman. Praktische Einleitung in 's Alte Testament. 4 Th. 8vo. Leips. 1799—1808.

Berger, Imman. Moralischen Einleitung in das Neue Test. 4 Th. 8vo. Lemgo. 1797—1801.
Berger, J. G. Physiologia Medica. 4to. Vitemb 1702.
Bergier, Nicolas. Le Dessein de l'Histoire de Reims. 4to. Reims. 1635.
——, ——. De Publicis et Militaribus Imp. Rom. Viis. (Græv. vol. 10.)
Bergius, C. De Sufficientia et Efficacia Mortis Christi. 4to. Colon. ad Suev. 1668.
Bergius, P. J. Materia Medica. 2 vol. 8vo. Stockholmiæ. 1778.
Bergk, J. A. Reise in Brasilien, Peru, und Caracas. 8vo. Leipz. 1808.
Bergman, Torbern. Physical and Chemical Essays, tr. by Cullen. 2 vols. 8vo. Lond. 1784.
——, ——. On Elective Attractions; from the Latin. 8vo. Lond. 1785.
Bericht eines Englischen Americaners von Philadelphia an seinen Freund in England, nach dem Englischen Original. 12mo. Frank. und Leipz. 1777.
Berington, Joseph. Lives of Abeillard and Heloisa. 8vo. Phil. 1819.
Berington, S. Dissertations on the Mosaical Creation, Deluge, and Building of Babel. 8vo. Lond. 1750.
Berkauf von Ländereyen in Amerika. 12mo. Hamb. 1793.
Berkeley, Geo. (Bp.) On Human Knowledge. 8vo. Dublin. 1710.
——, ——. The Same, with Three Dialogues against Sceptics and Atheists. 8vo. Lond. 1734.
——, ——. The Same. 8vo. Lond. 1776.
——, ——. Alciphron, or the Minute Philosopher; with his Essay towards a New Theory of Vision. 2 vols. 8vo. Lond. 1732.
——, ——. Siris, or the Virtues of Tar-Water. 8vo. Lond. 1744.
——, ——. Tracts on Various Subjects. 8vo. Lond. 1752.
——, ——. Essay towards a New Theory of Vision. 8vo. Dublin. 1709.
——, ——. The Same. 8vo. Lond. 1733.
——, ——. Analyst; or a Discourse addressed to an Infidel Mathematician. 8vo. Lond. 1754.
Berkenhout, John. Symptomatology. 8vo. Lond. 1784.
——, ——. Pharmacopœia Medici. 8vo. Lond. 1782.
Berkenmeyer, W. C. Consilium in Arena, oder Mitleidens volle Antwort auf das Bitt-Schreiben der Hoch-Teutsch-Luthrischen Gemeinde im Camp. 4to. Nieuw-York.
——, ——. Getrouwe Herder-en Wachter-stem. 4to. Nieuw-Jork. 1728.
Bermuda. Acts of Assembly in the Bermuda or Summer-Islands, from 1690 to 1713—14. fol. Lond. 1719.
Bernard, Sir Fr. (Gov.) Letters to the Ministry from Gov. Bernard, Gen. Gage and Commodore Hood, with Memorials, &c. 8vo. Lond. 1769.

Bernard, Sir Fr. (Gov.) Letters to the Earl of Hillsborough. See Massachusetts.

——–, ————. Select Letters on the Trade and Government of America; and the Principles of Law and Polity applied to the American Colonies. 8vo. Lond. 1774.

———, ————. Papers relating to the supposed Libel on him. 8vo.

Bernard, J. P. General Dictionary, including a New Translation of Bayle's Dictionary, by J. P. Bernard, T. Birch, J. Lockman, and others; the Articles relating to Oriental History by Geo. Sale. 10 vols. fol. Lond. 1734—41.

Bernard, Nicholas. Character of Bp. Bedell, with an Answer to Mr. Pierce on the late Judgment of the Primate of Ireland. See Usher on the Church of Rome.

Benardus, Edw. Inscriptiones Græcæ Palmyrenorum, cum Scholiis Bernardi et Smithi. 8vo. Traj. ad Rhen. 1698.

————, ——. Etymologicon Britannicum. Vide Hickes.

————, ——. Veterum Mathematicorum Gr., Lat., et Arab., Synopsis. Vide Smith.

————, ——. Chronologiæ Samaritanæ Synopsis. (Acta Eruditorum, An. 1691.)

————, ——. De Ponderibus et Mensuris Antiq. Vide Pococke on Hosea.

————, ——. Annotationes in Patres Apostolicos. Vide Cotelerius.

————, ——. Veterum Testimonia de Versione LXXII Interpretum.

————, ——. Adnotationes in Epistolam S. Barnabæ. Vide Barnabas.

Bernardus, Sanctus. Opera. fol. Antverpiæ. 1576.

————, ————. ————. 2 vol. fol. Paris. 1719.

Bernberch, Paulus. Tyrannus Delineatus. 4to. Jenæ. 1675.

Berni, Fr. Opere. 5 vol. 8vo. Milano. 1806.

——, —. The Enchanted Lake of the Fairy Morgana; from the Italian. 8vo. N. York. 1806.

Bernis, F. J. de Pierres, (Cardinal.) La Religion Vengée. 8vo. Paris. 1805.

Bernoulli, Jac. Opera. 2 vol. 4to. Genevæ, 1744. Basil. 1692.

Bernoulli, Joh. Opera Omnia. 4 vol. 4to. Lausannæ et Genevæ. 1742—3.

————, ——. Recueil pour les Astronomes. 3 vol. 8vo. Berlin. 1771—6.

Bernstorffius, H. Phil. De Paupertate Christi Homines ditante. 4to. Rintellii.

Berosus. Vide Annio.

Berquin, Arnaud. Œuvres Complètes. 10 vol. 12mo. Paris. 1802.

Berriman, John. Critical Dissertation on 1 Tim. iii. 16, giving an account of more than 100 Greek MSS. of St. Paul's Epistles. 8vo. Lond. 1741.

Berriman, Wm. Twenty-Four Sermons at Boyle's Lecture. 2 vols. 8vo. Lond. 1733.

Berriman, Wm. The Same. fol. Lond. 1739.
———, ——. True Narrative of the Controversy concerning the Trinity in Reply to Berriman. 8vo. Lond. 1725.
———, ——. Remarks on his Sermon on the 30th of January. 12mo. Lond. 1733.
Berry Street. See Sermons.
Berthaldus, P. De Ara. (Grævius, vol. 6.)
Bertholdt, Leonhard. Einleitung in die Schriften des Alten und Neuen Test. 6 vol. 8vo. 1812—6.
———, ————. Daniel, aus dem Hebräisch-Aramäischen neu übersetzt, und erklärt. etc. 2 vol. 8vo. Erlangen. 1806—8.
———, ————. Kritisches Journal der Neuesten Theologischen Literatur. Bände 1, 2, 3, 4, 5, 8, 9; und B. 10, St. 1, 2, 3. 12mo. Nürnberg und Sulz. 1813—20.
Berthollet, C. L. et A. B. Elémens de l'Art de Teinture. 2 vol. 8vo. Paris. 1804.
Berti, J. L. Ecclesiasticæ Historiæ Breviarium. 12mo. 1762.
Bertie, Willoughby. See Abingdon, Earl of.
Bertius, P. Theatrum Geographiæ Veteris. 2 tom. in 1. fol. Amst. 1619.
———, —. De Aggeribus et Pontibus. (Sallengre, vol. 2.)
———, —. Brevis Americæ Descriptio, excerpta e Tab. Geog. P. Bertii. fol. Amst. 1622.
Bertoli, Giandom. Antichità d' Aquileja. fol. Venezia. 1739.
Bertramus, Bonav. Corn. De Republica Hebræorum. (Ugol. v. 4.)
———, ————. Idem. 24to. Lug. Bat. 1641.
———, ————. De Politia Judaica. 12mo. Genevæ. 1680.
Bertramus, Car. Historiæ Britannicæ Scriptores Tres: Ricardus Corinensis, Gildas Badonicus, Nennius Banchorensis. 8vo. Havniæ. 1757.
Bertrand de Moleville, F. A. Annals of the French Revolution, translated from the French, by R. C. Dallas. 9 vols. 8vo. Lond. 1800—2.
Besantinous, Helladius. Chrestomathiæ. (Gronov. vol. 10.)
Beschster, John. W. Luther Pourtrayed. 8vo. Phil. 1818.
Besenbeck, C. J. De Ingenio Sophoclis. 4to. Erlangæ.
Besoldus, Chr. De Arcanis Rerumpublicarum. Vide Clapmarius.
Besse, Joseph. Sufferings of the Quakers. 2 vols. fol. Lond. 1753.
Bessel, Fr. W. Fundamenta Astronomiæ pro Anno 1755. fol. Regiomonti. 1818.
Besseldt, Karl. Einleitung zu Homers Odyssee, etc. 12mo. Königs. 1816.
Betham, John. Sermon before the King and Queen on the Annunciation of the Blessed Virgin. 4to. Lond. 1686.
Bethel, S. The World's Mistake in Oliver Cromwell. 4to. Lond. 1668.
Betz, Joh. Phil. De Legum Ebræorum Forensium contra Idololatriam Usu Politico in Republica. 4to. Argent. 1693.
Beveridge, Wm. (Bp.) Sermons. 6 vols. 8vo. Lond. 1709.

Beveridge, Wm. (Bp.) Sermons. fol. Lond. 1720.
———, ——. Institutiones Chron. et Arith. 4to. Lond. 1705.
———, ——. Concio ad Clerum. 4to. Lond. 1689.
———, ——. Private Thoughts upon Religion. 8vo. Lond. 1709.
———, ——. Thesaurus Theologicus. 4 vol. 8vo. Lond. 1711.
———, ——. Sermon on the Fifth of Nov. 4to. Lond. 1704.
———, ——. Grammatica Syriaca. 12mo. Lond. 1658.
———, ——. Idem. 12mo. Lond. 1664.
———, ——. Codex Canonum Ecclesiæ Primitivæ. Vide Cotelerius.
———, ——. Pandectæ Canonum SS. Apostolorum et Conciliorum ab Ecclesia Gr. receptorum, etc. 2 vol. fol. Oxon. 1672.
———, ——. De Linguarum Orientalium Præstantia, Necessitate, et Utilitate. 12mo. Lond. 1658.
———, ——. Idem. 12mo. Lond. 1664.
Beverinus, Barth. De Ponderibus et Mensuris. (Ugol. vol. 28.)
Beverley, J. Unio Reformantium, contra Hoornbeckium. 16mo. Lond. 1659.
Beverly, Rob. History of Virginia. 2d. ed. 8vo. Lond. 1722.
———, ——. Histoire de la Virginie, trad. de l'Anglois. 12mo. Paris. 1707.
Bexon, Scipion. Parallèle du Code Pénal d'Angleterre avec les Loix Pénales Françoises. 8vo. Paris. 1800.
Beyerlinck, Laurentius. Magnum Theatrum Vitæ Humanæ. 8 vol. fol. Col. Agrip. 1631.
Beyerus, And. De Diis Syris.—Mythologia Deorum et Heroum. (Ugol. vol. 23.)
———, ——. Siclus Sacer et Regius Appensus. (Id. 28.)
Beyschlag, Geo. W. De Morte Æterna. 4to. Argent. 1702.
Beza, Theod. Observationes et Paraphrasis in Jobum. 12mo. Lond. 1589.
——, ———. Tractatus de Vera Excommunicatione, et Christiano Presbyterio. 4to. Genevæ. 1590.
——, ———. De Hæreticis a Civili Magistratu Puniendis. Vide Celsus.
——, ———. De Polygamia et Divortiis. 12mo. Genevæ. 1568.
——, ———. Poemata Juvenilia. 12mo.
——, ———. Epistolæ Theologicæ. 12mo. Genevæ. 1575.
——, ———. Nov. Test. Lat. (R. Stephani.) fol. 1556.
——, ———. Idem. fol. Genevæ. 1598.
——, ———. De Prædestinatione. 12mo. Genevæ. 1582.
——, ———. Codex. Vide Kipling.
Bezius, J. P. De Electione secundum Prævisionem Fidei facta. 4to. Argent. 1697.
Bianchi, A. Eloge Historique de P. P. Celesia.
Bibel, oder die ganze Heilige Schrift, nach der deutschen Uebersetzung D. Martin Luthers, (Abgedruckt nach der Hallischen Ausgabe 1813.) 8vo. Lond.
Bibell, durch Dietenburger. fol. 1610.
Bibl Cyssegr-lan. (Welch Bible.) 8vo. Llundain. 1804.

Bible. Annotations (without the Text) upon all the Books of the Old and New Testament, by several Divines. fol. Lond. 1645.
——. The Same. 3d ed. 2 vols. fol. Lond. 1657.
——. Discourse concerning the Oriental Translations. 8vo. Lond. 1735.
——. The Bible needs no Apology; or Watson's System of Religion refuted. 8vo. Portsmouth. 1796.
Bible, English, Cranmer's. fol. Lond. 1539.
——————, ————. 4to. Lond. 1541.
——————, Barker's. fol. Lond. 1578.
——————, Geneva Version. 4to. Lond. 1584.
——————, ——————. 4to. Lond. 1606.
——————, King James's. 4to. Lond. 1638.
——————, ——————. fol. Oxford. 1701.
——————, ——————. Baskerville's ed. fol. Camb. 1763.
——————, ——————. 12mo. Edin. 1782.
——————, ——————. Thomas's ed. 2 vols. fol. Worcester, Mass. 1791.
——————, ——————. 2 vols. 8vo. Oxford. 1773.
——————, ——————. By Reeves. 9 vols. 8vo. Lond. 1802.
——————, ——————. ——————. 4 vols. 4to. Lond. 1802.
——————, ——————. 4 vols. 8vo. Phil. 1804.
——————, ——————. 8vo. Bost. 1812.
——————, ——————. 8vo. Lond. 1817.
——————, Clark's. fol. Lond. 1690.
——————, Nelson's. 2 vols. fol. Lond. 1758.
——————, Purver's. 2 vols. fol. Lond. 1764.
——————, Wilson's. 3 vols. 4to. Bath. 1785.
——————, Geddes's. 2 vols. 4to. Lond. 1792—7.
——————, Thompson's. (From the Septuagint, &c.) 4 vols. 8vo. Phil. 1808.
——————, Scott's. 6 vols. 8vo. Bost. 1816—7.
——————, Bagster's. 8vo. Lond. 1826.
——————, See Concordance. See Commonplace Book to the Bible.
Bible, in the Gaelic Language. 12mo. Edin. 1807.
————— Malay Language. 4to. Amst. 1733.
————— Orissa Language. (Hagiographia.) 8vo.
————— Indian Language, Eliot's. 4to. Camb. N. E. 1663.
————— ——————, ————. 4to. Camb. N. E. 1685.
Bible, La Sainte, par D. Martin. fol. Amst. 1707.
——, ————, ——————. 4to. Amst. 1722.
——, ————, trad. par les Pasteurs etc. de Genève. 2 vol. fol. Genève. 1805.
——, ————, sur l'Edition de Paris de l'année 1805. 12mo. à Londres. 1817.
——, ————, Expliquée. 12mo. Genève. 1776.
Bible Society, British. Summary Account of it. 8vo. Lond. 1810.
——————, ————. Sixth Report. 8vo. Lond. 1810.
——————, ————. Sixteenth Report. 8vo. Lond. 1820.

Bible Society, American. Constitution, &c. N. York. 1816.
———, ———. First Annual Report. 8vo. N. York. 1817.
———, New York. First Annual Report. 8vo. N. York. 1817.
———, Massachusetts. Report. 8vo. Bost. 1810.
———, ———. ———. 8vo. Bost. 1816.
———, ———. ———. 8vo. Bost. 1820.
———, Middlesex, Mass. First Report. 8vo. Camb. 1816.
———, ———. Second Report. 8vo. 1817.
———, ———. Third Report. 8vo. Camb. 1818.
———, ———. Fourth Report. 8vo. Camb. 1819.
———, New Hampshire. Sixth Report. 8vo. Concord. 1817.
———. Rapports de la Société de Bible du Canton de Vaud. 1—4. 8vo. Lausanne. 1816—19.
———. Rapports de la Société Biblique Protestante de Paris, 1—3. 8vo. Paris. 1819—22.
———. Notice of Bible Societies. See Porter.
Biblia; dat is, De Gantsche Heylighe Schrift. 4to. Delft. 1581.
——; dat is, De Gansche H. Schriftuur. 8vo. Lond. 1817.
Biblia Española, por Cypriano de Valera. fol. Amst. 1602.
—— ———, y Latina, por P. S. de San Miguel. 10 vol. 4to. Valencia. 1790—3.
Biblia Hebraica, Plantini. 16mo. Antwerp. 1610.
—— ———, Cephas Elon, (vulgo Petri de la Rouvière.) 4to. Genevæ. 1618.
—— ———, Nisselii. 8vo. Lug. Bat. 1662.
—— ———, Leusden, typis Athiæ. 2 vol. 8vo. Amst. 1667.
—— ———, Vander Hooght. 2 vol. 8vo. Amst. 1705.
—— ———, ———. 2 vol. 8vo. Phil. 1814.
—— ———, Michaelis. 3 vol. 8vo. Halæ Mag. 1720.
—— ———, Fosteri. 2 vol. 4to. Oxon. 1750.
—— ———, Houbigant. 4 vol. fol. Lut. Paris. 1753.
—— ———, Kennicott. 2 vol. fol. Oxon. 1776—80.
—— ———, Doederlein et Meisner. 4 vol. 12mo. Lips. 1793.
—— ———, Frey. 2 vol. 8vo. Lond. 1812—14.
—— Hebr. et Gr. cum duplici Interpretatione Latina, et Annot. Vatabli, etc. (Vet. Test. solum.) fol. ex Off. Commel. 1599.
——, Hebr. cum Nov. Test. Gr. et Interpret. Interlin. fol. Genevæ. 1619. Vide etiam Bib. Polyg. Ariæ Mont. tom. 6.
——, Hebr. et Chald., Buxtorfii. 2 vol. fol. Basil. 1618.
——, Hebr. Gr., et Lat. Vatabli. fol. ex Off. Sanctand. 1586.
Biblia, Italiana, per Brucioli. fol. Vinetia. 1541.
—— ———, Volgare. fol. Vinegia. 1567.
—— ———, da Diodati. 4to. Geneva. 1607.
—— ———, da Mattia d' Erberg. fol. Norimb. 1711.
Biblia Latina, S. Hieronymi. fol. Nuremb. 1501.
—— ———, ———. fol. Lugd. 1515.
—— ———, Munsteri et Erasmi. 8vo. Tiguri. 1539.
—— ———, L. Judae et Al. fol. Tiguri. 1543.

Biblia Latina, L. Judæ et Al. 4to. Tiguri. 1544.
—— ——, Vulg. et Tigur. ex Off. R. Stephani. 8vo. Lut. 1545.
—— ——, ————. 4to. Hanoviæ. 1605.
—— ——, Vulg. Ed., a R. Stephano. 8vo. 1555.
—— ——, ————. 8vo. Basil. 1562.
—— ——, ————. 4to. Basil. 1590.
—— ——, ————. 4to. Antv. 1631.
—— ——, ————. 8vo. Lugd. 1685.
—— ——, ————. 4to. Bamb. 1693.
—— ——. 4to. Norimb. 1522.
—— ——. 4to. Lugd. 1522.
—— ——, Ex Off. R. Stephani. 8vo. 1573.
—— ——, Pagnini et Vatabli. fol. Basil. 1564.
—— ——, Tremellii et Junii. 4to. Lond. 1579—80.
—— ——, ————. fol. Lond. 1593.
—— ——, ————. fol. Hanoviæ. 1603.
—— ——, ————. fol. Hanoviæ. 1624.
—— ——, Castellionis. fol. Francof. 1697.
—— ——, ————. 4 vol. 12mo. Lond. 1726.
—— ——, Osiandri. fol. Tubingæ. 1600.
—— ——. 4to. Tubingæ. 1593.
—— ——, Schmidt. 4to. Argent. 1696.
—— ——, MS.
—— Latino-Germanica, Erhard. 2 vol. fol. Augs. 1730.
—— Polyglotta. 5 vol. fol. Compluti. 1514—17.
—— ——, Le Jay. 10 vol. fol. Paris. 1628—45.
—— ——, Waltoni. (Republican copy.) 6 vol. fol. Lond. 1653—57.
—— —— ——. (Loyal copy; Large paper; with a Dedication to Charles II. "A gift originally of the author to the Earl of Clarendon") 12 vol. fol. Lond. 1653—57.
—— —— Montani. 8 vol. fol. Antverpiæ. 1569—72.
——. Vide Testamentum. Vide Concordantia. Vide Biobla. Vide Apocrypha.
Bibliander, Theod. (Buchman.) Machumetis, ejusque Successorum Vitæ ac Doctrina; ipseque Alcoran, secundum Versionem Cluniacensem. His adjunctæ sunt Confutationes Legis Machumeticæ; item Historiæ Saracenorum Origine, Moribus, etc. fol. Basil. 1543.
Bibliografia de' Classici Italiani. 8vo. Milano. 1814.
Bibliotheca Americana, (by A. Homer.) 4to. Lond. 1789.
—— Bernensis. 2 vol. 8vo. Bernæ. 1764.
—— Bremensis, Hist. Philol. Theol. 16 vol. 12mo. Bremæ. 1719—26.
—— ——. Nova. 6 vol. 12mo. Bremæ et Amst. 1760—6.
—— Britannica. See Watt.
—— Coisliniana, opera Montfaucon. fol. Paris. 1715.
—— Critica. 3 vol. 8vo. Amst. 1777—87.
—— Græca, a Coray. 10 vol. 8vo. Paris. 1805—13.
—— Literaria. 4to. Lond. 1722—4.
—— Pinelliana. 8vo. Lond. 1789.

Bibliotheca. See Catalogue.
Bibliothek der schönen Wissenschaften und der freyen Künste, 13 Bände. 12mo. Leipz. 1757—65.
———, Neue, der Schönen Wissenschaften, etc. 36 Bände. 12mo. Leipz. 1765—88.
———. Register über die zwölf ersten Bände der Neuen Bibliothek, etc. 12mo, Leipz. 1772.
Bibliothèque Américaine, (par H. Caritat.) 2 vol. 8vo. Paris. 1807.
——— des Voyages. Vide Boucher de la Richarderie.
——— Raisonnée des Ouvrages des Savans de l'Europe (par Massuet, s'Gravesande, de Jaucourt, Armand de la Chapelle, Barbeyrac, et Desmaiseaux.) 52 vol. 12mo. Amst. 1728—53.
Bichat, M. F. X. Anatomie Générale. 4 vol. 8vo. Paris. 1801.
———, ———. Anatomie Descriptive. 5 vol. 8vo. Paris. 1801.
———, ———. Recherches Physiologiques. 8vo. Paris. 1805.
Bickham, George. Universal Penman. fol. Lond. 1743.
———, ———. Penmanship, 5 parts. Lond. 1731.
Biddle, C. Philadelphia Directory. 8vo. Phil. 1791.
Biddle, Owen. Account of the Transit of Venus, June 1769. (Amer. Phil Trans., vol. 1.)
Bidembachius, Felix. De Causis Matrimonialibus. 12mo. Francof. 1608.
Biel, J. C. De Purpura Lydia, ad Act. xvi. (Ugol. vol. 13 et 29.)
———, ———. De Gallicinio Altmanni, etc. (Id. 27.)
———, ———. De Lydia Thyatirensi Altmanni. (Id. 29.)
———, ———. Novus Thesaurus Philologicus, sive Lexicon in LXX. et alios Interpretes Vet. Test. 3 vol. 8vo. Hagæ Com. 1779—80.
Bielfield, J. F. (Baron de.) Institutions Politiques. 2 vol. 4to. La Haye. 1760.
———, ———. Anecdotes of the Russian Court; from the German. 2 vols. 12mo. Lond. 1768.
Bierling, Fr. Wil. De Veterum Hebræorum circa Vitulam decollandam Ritibus.
Biet, Ant. Voyage de la France Equinoxiale. 4to. Paris. 1664.
Bifield, Nic. Exposition of the Epistle to the Colossians. fol. Lond. 1627.
———, ———. Exposition of the Apostles Creed. 4to. Lond. 1626.
Bigelow, Andrew. Oration before the Washington Benevolent Society. 8vo. Camb. 1815.
———, ———. Sermon at Eastport. 8vo. Eastport. 1820.
Bigelow, Jacob. American Medical Botany. 3 vols. 4to. Bost. 1817—20.
———, ———. Florula Bostoniensis. 8vo. Bost. 1814.
———, ———. Inaugural Address. 8vo. Bost. 1817.
Bigelow, Lewis. Digest of the twelve first vols. of Massachusetts Reports. 8vo. Camb. 1818.
———, ———. Digest of the Cases argued in the Supreme Court of Massachusetts. 8vo. Bost. 1825.
Bigelow, Timothy. Phi Beta Kappa Oration. 8vo. Bost. 1797.
Bigland, John. History of England. 2 vols. 8vo. Bost. 1812.

Bigland, John. The Same, with an Appendix. 2 vols. 8vo. Bost. and N. York. 1815.
———, ——. Letters on History. 8vo. Lond. 1808.
Biglow, Wm. Select Odes of Anacreon; from the Greek. 16mo. Camb. 1817.
———, ——. Poem on Education, delivered before the Phi Beta Kappa Society. 8vo. Salem. 1799.
Bigne, M. de la. Bibliotheca Sanctorum Patrum. 8 tom. in 3 vol. fol. Paris. 1575.
Bigot, Fr. Mémoire pour M. Fr. Bigot, ci-devant Intendant de Justice en Canada, accusé, etc. 2 parties. 4to. Paris. 1763.
Billardierus, J. J. Plantæ Novæ Hollandiæ [incomplete.] 4to. Paris. 1804.
Billerbeck, Jul. De Locis nonnullis difficilioribus Aristotelis Hist. Animalium. 12mo. Hildesiæ.
———, ——. De Strigibus ab Aristotele, Plinioque, etc. commemoratis. 4to. Hild.
———, ——. De Avibus ab Aristotele Plinioque commemoratis. 4to. Hild.
Billinghurst, Geo. Bankrupt Law. 12mo. Lond. 1676.
Billings, Wm. Anthem for Thanksgiving.
———, ——. Anthem for Easter.
———, ——. Suffolk Harmony. Bost. 1786.
Billingsley, John. Sermons against Popery. 8vo. Lond. 1723.
———, ——. Sermon on Reformation of Manners. 12mo. Lond. 1706.
Billingsley, Nich. Sermon on the Death of the Rev. H. Stogdon. 8vo. Lond. 1728.
———, ——. Sermon at the Ordination of T. Morgan. 8vo. Lond. 1717.
Billingsley, Sam. Sermon at the Ordination of the Rev. William Harris. 8vo. Lond. 1741.
———, ——. Exhortation at the Ordination of the Rev. Mr. Richards. 8vo. Lond. 1751.
———, ——. Charity Sermon. 8vo. Lond. 1759.
Bilson, Thomas, (Bp.) True Difference between Christian Subjection and Unchristian Rebellion. 4to. Oxford. 1585.
Bilstone, John. Sermon before the University of Oxford. 8vo. Oxford. 1763.
Binchius. Johannes. Mellificium Theologicum. 4to. Amst. 1658.
Bindrim, Joh. Geo. De Gradibus Excommunicationis apud Hebræos. (Ugol. vol. 26.)
Bingham, Caleb. Young Lady's Accidence. 16mo. Bost. 1789.
Bingham, Joseph. Works. 2 vols. fol. Lond. 1726.
———, ——. French Churches Apology for the Church of England. 8vo. Lond. 1706.
———, ——. Antiquities of the Church. 3 vols. 8vo. Lond. 1710—11.
Bingham, Wm. On American Commerce. 8vo. Phil. 1784.
Bini, Pietro di Lorenzo. Memorie del Calcio Fiorentino, tratte da Diverse Scritture. 4to. Firenze. 1688.

Binius, Sev. Concilia Generalia et Provincialia, etc. 4 vol. fol. Col. Agrip. 1606.
Binney, Barnabas. Oration at the Commencement in Rhode-Island College. fol. Bost. 1774.
Binney, Hor. Reports in the Supreme Court of Pennsylvania. 6 vols. 8vo. Phil. 1809 et seqq.
Biobla Naomhtha. (Irish Bible.) 8vo. Lond. 1817.
Biographia Britannica. 6 vol. fol. Lond. 1747—66.
——— Classica. Vide Harwood.
Biographical Dictionary of Living Authors. 8vo. Lond. 1816.
Biography and Obituary, Annual. 5 vols. 8vo. Lond. 1817—21.
——— of the Signers of the Declaration of Independence. See American Independence.
Bion. Idyllia. Vide Theocritus. Vide Poetæ Græci Minores.
Bion, M. On Mathematical Instruments; from the French, by E. Stone. fol. Lond. 1758.
Birch, John. On Medical Electricity. 8vo. Lond. 1803.
——, ——. On Cow-Pox. 8vo. Lond. 1805.
Birch, P. Sermon on the Fifth of Nov. 4to. In the Savoy. 1689.
Birch, Tho. Negotiations between the Courts of England, France, and Brussels. 8vo. Lond. 1749.
——, ——. Memoirs of the Reign of Queen Elizabeth. 2 vols. 4to. Lond. 1754.
——, ——. Inquiry into the Share King Charles I. had in the Transactions of the Earl of Glamorgan. 8vo. Lond. 1756.
——, ——. Life of Archbishop Tillotson. 8vo. Lond. 1753.
——, ——. Letters between Col. Hammond and others, relating to Charles I., &c. 8vo. Lond. 1764.
——, ——. Heads of Illustrious Persons, with their Lives and Characters. fol. Lond. 1756.
——, ——. Life of Dr. John Ward. 8vo. Lond. 1766.
——, ——. History of the Royal Society. 4 vols. in 2. 4to. Lond. 1756.
——, ——. General Dictionary. See Bernard.
Bircherodius, J. Lumen Historiæ Sacræ. fol. Hafniæ. 1687.
Biringuccio, Vanoccio. Pirotechnia. 4to. Venetia. 1540.
Birkbeck, Morris. Notes on a Journey from Virginia to Illinois. 8vo. Lond. 1818.
———, ———. Letters from Illinois. 12mo. Phil. 1818.
Bischoff, Ch. Fr. Stricturæ Anti-Becanianæ. 4to. Altdorfi. 1708.
Biscionius, Ant. Mar. Catalogus Bib. Med. Laurent. Codices Orientales et Græcos complectens. 2 vol. in 1. fol. Florentiæ. 1752.
Biscoe, Richard. History of the Acts of the Apostles, being Twenty-four Sermons at Boyle's Lecture. 2 vols. 8vo. Lond. 1742.
Bishop, Abr. Georgia Speculation Unveiled. 8vo. Hartford. 1797.
———, ——. Connecticut Republicanism; an Oration delivered in N. Haven. 8vo. 1800.
———, ——. Oration in Wallingford, March 11, 1801. 8vo. N. Haven. 1801.
Bishop, Rob. Instructions and Observations relative to the Navigation of the Windward and Gulph Passages. 8vo. Lond. 1761.

Bishops and Metropolitans. Their Origin briefly laid down. 4to. 1641.

——— ————————. Inquiry into the Necessity of an uninterrupted Succession of Diocesan Bishops. 8vo. Lond. 1719.

——— ————————. Pastoral Letter from the Four Catholic Bishops to the Lay-Catholics of England. 4to. Lond. 1688.

Bisse, Thomas. Sermon before the Sons of the Clergy. 8vo. Lond. 1717.

——, ———. Sermon on Musick. 8vo. Lond. 1726.

——, ———. Beauty of Holiness in the Common Prayer; in Four Sermons. 8vo. Lond. 1720.

——, ———. The Same. 8vo. Lond. 1744.

——, ———. Assize Sermon. 8vo. Oxford. 1711.

——, ———. Visitation Sermon. 8vo. Lond. 1716.

Bisselius, Joannes. Icaria. 16mo. Ingolstadii. 1637.

———, ———. Æstas. 16mo. 1644.

Bisset, Geo. Sermon at the Funeral of Mrs. A. Wanton. 4to. Newport. 1771.

Bisset, J. Remarks upon a late Apology for the Presbyterians in Scotland, who keep Communion with Mr. Whitfield. 2d ed. 16mo. Glasgow. 1743.

Bisset, Rob. History of the Reign of George III. 7 vols. 8vo. Lond. 1803—20.

——, ——. The Same. 4 vols. 8vo. Phil. and Balt. 1810—1.

——, ——. Life of Burke. 2 vols. 8vo. Lond. 1800.

——, ——. Sketch of Democracy. 8vo. Lond. 1796.

Bisset, W. Reformation of Manners Sermon. 5th ed. 12mo. Edin. 1746.

Bitaubé, P. J. Sur l'Etude des Anciens.—Sur l'Eutyphron de Platon. (Instit. Lit. vol. I.)

———, ——. Sur les Deux Premiers Livres de la Politique d'Aristote. (Id. 2.)

———, ——. Sur les Républiques Anciennes. (Id. 3.)

———, ——. Réflexions sur Pindare, etc. (Id. 4.)

Bizarus, P. De Reipub. Genuensis Statu et Administratione.—Reipub. Gen. Novæ Leges. (Græv. Thes. Ital.)

Bizot. Histoire Métallique de la Hollande. 2 vol. 4to. Amst. 1688.

Björnsen, Steph. Rymbegla; i. e. Computistica et Chronologica Veterum Islandorum. 4to. Haf. 1801.

Black, Joseph. Experiments on Magnesia Alba, Quicklime, &c. 16mo. Edin. 1777.

——, ———. Elements of Chemistry. 2 vols. 4to. Edin. 1803.

——, ———. The Same. 3 vols. 8vo. Phil. 1807.

Black, Wm. Observations Medical and Political on the Small Pox and Inoculation. 8vo. Lond. 1781.

——, ——. Historical Sketch of Medicine and Surgery. 8vo. Lond 1782.

Blackall, Ofspring, (Bp.) Works. 2 vols. fol. Lond. 1723.

———, ————. Accession Sermon. 8vo. Lond. 1708.

———, ————. Christmas Sermon. 4to. Lond. 1705.

———, ————. Sermon, January 30th. 8vo. Lond. 1708.

Blackall, Ofspring, (Bp.) Another. 12mo. Lond. 1709.
———, ————. Sermon to promote Charity Schools. 8vo. Lond. 1709.
———, ————. Fast Sermon. 8vo. Lond. 1708.
———, ————. Sermon on John IV. 1. 4to. Lond. 1707.
———. ————. Sermon on 1 John IV. 1. 8vo. Lond. 1707.
———, ————. Visitation Sermon. 4to. Lond. 1694.
———. ————. The Same. 3d ed. 4to. Lond. 1704.
———, ————. Sermon to the University of Cambridge. 8vo. Lond. 1708.
———, ————. Eight Sermons at Boyle's Lecture. fol. Lond. 1739.
Blackburn, J. Peace Sermon. 8vo. Lond. 1749.
Blackburne, Fr. Works, Theological and Miscellaneous. 7 vols. 8vo. Camb. 1804.
————, —. On the Use and Importance of External Religion. 8vo. Lond. 1752.
————, —. View of the Controversy concerning an Intermediate State. 8vo. Lond. 1765.
————, —. Confessional; or Inquiry on Confessions of Faith in Protestant Churches. 8vo. Lond. 1766.
————, —. The Same. 8vo. Lond. 1767.
————, —. Remarks on Strictures on the Confessional. Parts 1 and 2. 8vo. Lond. 1768—9.
————, —. Dialogue between I. Walton and Homologistes. 8vo. Lond. 1768.
————, —. Doubts addressed to him concerning the Authenticity of the last Publication of the Confessional, and Defence of them. 8vo. Lond. 1767—8.
————, —. Remarks on Three Letters (by Ridley) against the Confessional. 8vo. Lond. 1768.
————, —. Short View of the Controversy concerning the Confessional. 8vo. Lond. 1773.
————, —. Considerations on the Present State of Popery in Great Britain and Ireland. 8vo. Lond. 1768.
————, —. Commentary on Abp. Secker's Letter concerning Bishops in America 8vo. Lond. 1770.
Blackburne, Lancelot, (Abp.) Mystery of Godliness; a Sermon. 4to. Lond. 1705.
Blacklock, Tho. Poems. 8vo. Lond. 1756.
———, ——. ——. See Chalmers.
Blackmore, Sir Rich. Prince Arthur. 3d ed. fol. Lond. 1696.
————, ————. On Consumptions. 8vo. Lond. 1725.
————, ————. Just Prejudices against the Arian Hypothesis. 8vo. Lond. 1721.
————, ————. Poems. See Chalmers.
Blackrie, Alex. On the Stone. 8vo. Lond. 1771.
Blackstone, Henry. Reports in C. B. and Excheq. from East, 28 Geo. III., to Trin. 31 Geo. III. 1791. 3d ed. 2 vols. 8vo. Lond. 1801.

Blackstone, Sir Wm. Law Tracts. 2 vols. 8vo. Lond. 1762.
———, ———. Analysis of the Laws of England. 8vo. Oxford. 1762.
———, ———. Commentaries on the Laws of England. 4 vols. 4to. Oxford. 1768.
———, ———. The Same. 4 vols. 8vo. Portland, Mass. 1805—7.
———, ———. The Same. 6 copies, various editions, with Notes by Christian, Archbold, Tucker, &c.
———, ———. Reply to Dr. Priestley's Remarks on the Commentaries. 8vo. Lond. 1769.
———, ———. Objection drawn from the Act of Union against a Review of the Liturgy, submitted to his After-Thoughts. 8vo. Lond. 1770.
Blacow, Rich. Letter to Wm. King concerning the Riot at Oxford in 1747. 8vo. Lond. 1755.
Blackwall, Anth. Introduction to the Classics. 6th ed. 12mo. Lond. 1746.
———, ———. Sacred Classics Defended and Illustrated. 2d ed. 2 vols. 8vo. Lond. 1727.
———, ———. The Same. 3d ed. 2 vols. 12mo. Lond. 1737.
Blackwell, Tho. Letters on Mythology. 8vo. Lond. 1748.
———, ———. Memoirs of the Court of Augustus. 3 vols. 4to. Edin. 1753—63.
———, ———. Enquiry into the Life and Writings of Homer. 8vo. Lond. 1735.
———, ———. The Same, with Translations of the Proofs. 8vo. Lond. 1736.
Blackwood, Wm. See Magazine.
Bladen, Martin. Cæsar's Commentaries, made English from the Latin. 8vo. Lond. 1706.
Bladensburg, Narrative of the Battle of. By an Officer of Gen. Smith's Staff. 8vo.
Blaeu, Joannes. Atlas Major. Vol. 1, 4, 5, 7, 8, 9, 10, 11. fol. Amst. 1662.
———, ———. Vyfde Stuck der Aerdryckxbeschryving, welck vervat Schotlandt en Yrlandt. fol. Amst. 1662.
———, ——— et Guil. Nieuwe Atlas. 2 fol. fol. Amst. 1635.
———, ———. Novus Atlas. 4 vol. fol. Amst. 1646—9.
Blaine, D. P. Veterinary Art. 8vo. Lond. 1816.
Blair, Hugh. Lectures on Rhetoric and Belles Lettres. 2 vols. 4to. Lond. 1783.
———, ———. The Same. 4th ed. 3 vols. 8vo. Lond. 1790.
———, ———. ———. 6th Amer. ed. 8vo. N. York. 1815.
———, ———. Sermons. 2 vols. 8vo. Lond. 1785.
———, ———. ———. 2 vols. 8vo. Lond. 1786.
———, ———. Sermons; with his Life, by Finlayson. 5 vols. 8vo. Lond. 1802.
——— ———. Dissertation on the Poems of Ossian. 4to. Lond. 1763.
———, ———. Sermon before the Society for propagating Religious Knowledge. 8vo. Edin. 1750.

Blair, John. Chronology and History of the World. fol. Lond. 1756.
——, ——. The Same. fol. Lond. 1779.
——, ——. Lectures on the Canon of the Scriptures. 4to. Lond. 1785.
Blair, Rob. The Grave, with Gray's Elegy. 8vo. Lond. 1790.
——, ——. The Grave, altered into Rhime from Blank Verse, by H. Lemoine. 8vo. Lond. 1790.
——, ——. The Grave. See Chalmers.
Blair, Wm. On the Venereal. 2 vols. 8vo. Lond. 1798—1800.
——, ——. Anthropology. 8vo. Lond. 1803.
Blaise de Montluc. Mémoires. (Mem. de France, vol. 22—26.)
Blake, George. Eulogy on Washington. 8vo. Bost. 1800.
Blake, James, jr. Memoirs of Capt. Roger Clap. 16mo. Bost. 1731.
Blakeway, Robert. Two Sermons recommending Obedience to King George. 8vo. Lond. 1716.
Blanc, Ludov. le. Theses Theologicæ. fol. Lond. 1675.
Blancardus, Steph. Lexicon Medicum Græco-Latinum, cum Interpretatione Belgica, Germanica, Gallica, Anglica, etc. 8vo. Lug. Bat. 1702.
Blanchinus, J. Evangeliarium Quadruplex. 2 vol. fol. Romæ. 1749.
Bland, Miles. Algebraical Problems. 8vo. Camb. (Eng.) 1824.
Blane, Sir Gilb. On the Diseases of Seamen. 8vo. Lond. 1803.
Blaquiere, Edw. Narrative of a Second Visit to Greece, &c. 8vo. Lond. 1825.
Blasius, G. L. Anatome Animalium. 4to. Amst. 1681.
Blayney, Benj. Translation of Jeremiah and Zechariah, with Notes; also Dissertation on Daniel. 4to. Oxford. 1784.
Blebelius, Tho. Grammatica Hebræa. 12mo. Witebergæ. 1587.
Blechschmidius, Christ. De Theocratia. (Ugol. vol. 24.)
Bleecker, Ann E. Pothumous Works. 12mo. N. York. 1793.
Blennerhaysett, Tho. Thanksgiving Sermon on the Accession of George I. 8vo. Lond. 1715.
Blesdikius, Nic. Historia Davidis Georgii Hæresiarchæ. 16mo. Davent. 1642.
Blesensis, P. Continuatio ad Hist. Ingulphi. (Script. Rer. Angl.)
Bleterie, J. P. R. de la. Vie de l'Empereur Julien. 12mo. Paris. 1746.
———, —————. Sur l'Empereur Romain dans le Sénat. (Acad. des Inscrip. vol. 27.)
Bliss, George. Address to the Bar of Hampshire, &c. 8vo. Springfield. 1827.
Blizard, Sir Wm. On the Large Blood Vessels. 4th ed. 12mo. Lond. 1803.
Block, A. S. Die Bürger Athens. 8vo. Leipz. 1817.
Blodget, Sam. Economy. 8vo.
———, ——. Economica: a Statistical Manual for the United States of America. 8vo. Washington. 1810.
Blom, Anthony. Verhandeling over den Landbouw in de Colonie Suriname. 8vo. Haarlem. 1786.

Blome, Rich. Description of Jamaica, &c., from the Notes of Sir Thomas Linch. 16mo. Lond. 1672.
———, ——. Geography. fol. Lond. 1670.
———, ——. Description des Isles et Terres du Roi d'Angleterre dans l'Amérique, trad. de l'Anglois. 12mo. Amst. 1688.
———, ——. Idem. 12mo. Amst. 1715.
———, ——. History of the Bible. fol. Lond.
———, ——. Gentleman's Recreations. fol. Lond. 1710.
Blomer, Tho. View of Dr. Bentley's Letter to the Bishop of Ely. 8vo. Lond. 1710.
Blomfield, E. V. Greek Grammar. See Matthias.
Blondus, Flavius. De Origine et Gestis Venetorum. (Græv. Thes. Ital.)
Blos, Balthazar. De Transfiguratione Christi in Monte. 4to. 1717.
Blosius, Ludov. Opera. fol. Ingolstadii. 1727.
Blount, Charles. Miscellaneous Works. 12mo. Lond. 1693.
Blount, Tho. Law Dictionary and Glossary. fol. Lond. 1717.
Blount, Sir Tho. Pope. Censura Celebriorum Authorum. fol. Lond. 1690.
———, ————. Remarks upon Poetry. 4to. Lond. 1694.
Blount, Wm. Proceedings on the Impeachment of Wm. Blount, a Senator of the U. States from Tennessee. 8vo. Phil. 1799.
Blumenbach, J. F. Handbuch der Naturgeschichte. 8vo. Göttingen. 1818.
—————, ——. Handbuch der Vergleichenden Anatomie. 8vo. Göttingen. 1815.
————— ——. Institutiones Physiologicæ. 8vo. Gottingæ. 1810.
—————, ——. Ueber den Bildungstrieb und das Zeugungsgeschäfte. 12mo. Göttingen. 1781.
—————, ——. Institutions of Physiology, tr. from the Latin by J. Elliotson. 8vo. Lond. 1817.
Blümner, H. Ueber die Idee des Schicksals in den Tragödien des Aischylos. 8vo. Leipz. 1814.
————, —. De Sophoclis Œdipo Rege. 4to. Lips. 1788.
Blunt, E. M. Stranger's Guide to the City of N. York. 16mo. N. York. 1817.
Bobovius, Albertus, (Ali-Bey.) Concerning the Turkish Liturgy, &c. 8vo. Lond. 1712.
Boccaccio, Gio. Il Decamerone. 4to. Firenze. 1761.
————, —. Idem. 4 vol. 8vo. Lond. 1790.
————, —. Decameron, Lettere, e Vita di Dante. 4 vol. 8vo. Milano. 1803.
————, —. Le Décameron, trad. de l'Italien. 5 vol. 8vo. Lond. 1757—61.
————, —. Delle Donne Illustri, con la Vita del Boccaccio, etc. 12mo. Vinegia. 1545.
————, —. Novelle Scelte dal Decamerone. 8vo. Prato. 1818.
————, —. Novelle Scelte, etc. 16mo. Firenze. 1820.

Boccage, Marie-Anne du. La Columbiade ; ou La Foi portée au Nouveau Monde. 8vo. Paris. 1756.
———, ————. La Colombiade, trad. dal Francese. 8vo. Milano. 1771.
Bochartus, Sam. De Situ Paradisi. (Ugol. vol. 7.)
———, ——. De Quæstione, num Æneas unquam fuerit in Italia. 16mo. Hamb. 1672.
———, ——. Opera Omnia. 3 vol. fol. Lug. Bat. 1707—12.
———, ——. Hierozoicon. fol. Franc. 1675.
Böckhius, Aug. Specimen Editionis Timæi Platonis. 4to. Heidelbergæ. 1807.
———, ——. In Græcas Tragœdias. 8vo. Heidelb. 1808.
———, ——. In Platonis Minoem, etc. 8vo. Hal. Sax. 1806.
Bocrisius, J. H. De Musica Hebræorum, etc. (Ugol. vol. 32.)
Bode, Chr. Aug. Pseudocritica Millio-Bengeliana. 2 vol. Halæ Magd. 1767—9.
Bode, G. H. Orpheus Poetarum Græcorum Antiquissimus. 4to. Gottingæ. 1824.
Bodenham, John. Politeuphia, or Wit's Commonwealth.
Boderianus, G. F. Dictionarium Syro-Chaldaicum. fol. Antv. 1573.
Bodin, J. Six Livres de la République. fol. Paris. 1577.
Bodius, Rob. (Boyd.) Hecatombe ad Christum.
———, ————. Prælectiones in Epistolam Pauli ad Ephesios. fol. Genevæ. 1660.
Boeclerus, J. H. De Legione Romana. (Grævius, vol. 10.)
———, ——. De Scriptoribus Græcis et Latinis. (Gonov. vol. 10.)
Boehm, A. W. Discourses and Tracts. 8vo. Lond. 1717.
Boehmerus, G. L. Electa Juris Civilis. 2 vol. 4to. Goett. 1767.
Boemus, Jo. Mores, Leges, et Ritus Omnium Gentium. 16mo. Lugd. 1576.
———, —. Idem. Accedit Damiani à Goës Tractatus de Moribus Æthiopum ; cum ejusdem Deploratione Lappianæ Gentis.
Boerhaave, Herm. De Materia Medica et Remediorum Formulis. 12mo. Lug. Bat. 1727.
———, ———. Materia Medica ; from the Latin. 8vo. Lond. 1741.
———, ———. Praxis Medica. 5 vol. 12mo. Petavii. 1728.
———, ———. Prælectiones Academicæ in Proprias Institutiones Rei Medicæ. 6 vol. 12mo. Gottingæ. 1741—5.
———, ———. Practical Aphorisms ; from the Latin. 8vo. Lond. 1742.
———, ———. The Same. 8vo. Lond. 1755.
———, ———. Academical Lectures on the Theory of Physic ; from the Latin. 6 vols. 8vo. Lond. 1743—66.
———, ———. Aphrodisiacus. Vide Luisinus.
———, ———. Medical Correspondence. 8vo. Lond. 1745.
———, ———. De Viribus Medicamentorum. 2 vol. 12mo. Jenæ. 1750—2.
———, ———. Chemistry, tr. by Shaw. 2 vols. 4to. Lond. 1753.

Boerhaave, Herm. Hortus Lugduno-Batavus. 2 vol. 4to. Lug. Bat. 1727.
———, ———. Elementa Chemiæ. 2 tom. 4to. Paris. 1733.
———, ———. Methodus Studii Medici. 2 tom. 4to. Amst. 1751.
———, ———. Vide Bellini.
Boernerus, C. F. et J. D. Acta Pauli et Barnabæ Lycaonica. 4to. Lipsiæ. 1714.
———, ———. De Fide Jacobi in Utero. 4to. Lipsiæ. 1708.
Boers, Car. Oratio de Difficultatibus Disciplinæ Theologicæ Professionem prementibus. 4to. Lug. Bat. 1779.
Boethie, Steph. de la. On Voluntary Servitude; from the French. 12mo. Lond. 1735.
Boethius. De Consolatione Philosophiæ. 12mo. Florentiæ. 1513.
———. Idem, cum Notis Variorum. 12mo. Lug. Bat. 1671.
———. ——, cum Vita, etc. 12mo. Patavii. 1744.
———. ——, cura J. Eremitæ. 12mo. Paris. 1783.
———. Consolations of Philosophy, 1st B.
———. Speech to the Emperor. (Harl. Miscel. vol. 7.)
———. Los Cinco Libros de la Consolacion. Vide Villegas.
Boetius, Hector. Description of Scotland; from the Latin. fol. 1585.
Bogermannus, J. Annotationes in Grotii Scripta. 4to. Franek. 1614.
Bogue, David. Divine Authority of the New Testament. 12mo. Lond. 1804.
———, and J. Bennett. History of the Dissenters from 1688 to 1808. 4 vols. 8vo. Lond. 1808—12.
Bohemia. Consideratio Causarum Belli quod anno 1618 et postea in Bohemia grassebatur. 4to. Libert. 1647.
Bohnius, J. G. De Igne Gentilium Sacro. (Ugol. vol. 10.)
Bohun, Edmund. Vindication of Filmer. See Filmer.
———, ———. Method of Reading History. See Wheare.
Bohun, W. Brief View of Ecclesiastical Jurisdiction. 8vo. Lond. 1733.
———, —. The Same. 4to. Bost. 1765.
Boiardo, M. M. Orlando Innamorato. 2 vol. 4to. Venetia. 1611.
Boileau, D. Introduction to Political Economy. 8vo. Lond. 1811.
Boileau, James. Protestants on the Safer Side. 4to. Lond. 1687
———, ———. History of the Flagellants, tr. by De Lolme. 8vo. Lond. 1783.
Boileau, Nicolas. Œuvres, avec des Eclaircissemens Historiques, par lui-même. 2 vol. 4to. Genève. 1716.
———, ———. Œuvres, par M. de Saint-Marc. 5 vol. 8vo. Paris. 1772.
———, ———. Œuvres Poétiques. 16mo. Paris. 1781.
———, ———. ———. 8vo. Paris. 1814.
Boindin, N. Sur la Forme etc. du Théatre des Anciens. (Acad. des Inscrip. vol. 1.)
———, —. Sur les Tribus Romaines. (Id. 4.)

Boisrond-Tonnerre, (Gen.) Mémoires pour servir á l'Histoire d'Hayti. 8vo. Dessalines. 1804.
Boivin, Fr. de. Baron de Villars. Mémoires. (Mém. de France, vol. 33—37.)
Boivin, J. Système d' Homère sur l'Olympe. (Acad. des Inscrip. vol. 7.)
——, —. Carmina. (Poetæ Recentiores Gr. et Lat.)
Boke of Presidentes. 12mo. Lond.
Bolde, Sam. Tracts in Vindication of Locke's Reasonableness of Christianity, and of his Essay on Human Understanding. 12mo. Lond. 1706.
——, ——. Accession Sermon. 8vo. Lond. 1716.
——, ——. Sermon against Persecution. 8vo. Lond. 1720.
——, ——. On Church Authority. 8vo. Lond. 1724.
Boldich, E. C. Pontifex Maximus Hebræorum. (Ugol. vol. 12.)
Bolingbroke, H. Reise nach dem Demerary; aus dem Englischen. 8vo. Leipz. 1812.
Bolingbroke, Hen. St. John, Ld. Works Complete. 5 vols. 4to. Lond. 1754.
——————, ——————. On Patriotism, a Patriotic King, and the State of Parties at the Accession of Geo. I. 8vo. Lond. 1749.
——————, ——————. Dissertation on Parties. 8vo. Lond. 1771.
——————, ——————. Remarks on the History of England; from the Minutes of Humphry Oldcastle. 8vo. Lond. 1747.
——————, ——————. Letter to Sir Wm. Windham.—Reflections on the State of the Nation.—Letter to Mr. Pope. 8vo. Lond. 1753.
——————, ——————. Letters on History. 8vo. Lond. 1779.
——————, ——————. Examen important des Livres de Moïse et des Dogmes des Chrétiens.
Bollan. Coloniæ Anglicanæ Illustratæ; or the Acquest of Dominion, and the Plantation of Colonies made by the English in America, with the Rights of the Colonists, Examined. 4to. Lond. 1762.
———. Continued Corruption; Standing Armies, &c., considered. 4to. Lond. 1768.
———. Free Briton's Memorial on the Right of Election. 4to. Lond. 1769.
———. Supplemental Memorial on the Origin of Parliaments, &c. 4to. Lond. 1770.
———. Freedom of Speech and Writing considered. 4to. Lond. 1766.
———. Right of the English Nation to the American Fisheries. 4to. Lond. 1764.
Bolletti, Giuseppe G. Dell' Origine e de' Progressi dell' Instituto delle Scienze di Bologna. 8vo. Bologna. 1751.

Bolleville. Réponse au Sentimens de quelques Théologiens de Hollande sur l'Hist. Crit. du V. T. 4to. Rotterdam. 1686.
Bolognesi. Vide Lettere.
Bolron, Rob. The Papist's Bloody Oath of Secrecy. 4to. 1686.
Bolton, Edm. Hypercritica; or a Rule of Judgment for writing or reading our Histories. Vide Trivetus.
Bolton, G. On the present Defective State of Fire Arms, &c. 8vo. Lond. 1795.
Bolton, Rob. Instruction for a right Comforting afflicted Consciences. 4to. Lond. 1631.
———, ———. The Same; with his Foure Last Things. 4to. Lond. 1640.
———, ———. Saints Sure Guide. 4to. Lond. 1634.
———, ———. A Treatise of Faith. 4to. Lond. 1632.
Bolton, Rob. On the Employment of Time. 8vo. Lond. 1750.
———, ———. The Same. 8vo. Lond. 1754.
Bolton, Theophilus, (Abp.) Sermon on the Irish Rebellion. 8vo. Lond. 1721.
Bomare, Valmont de. Dictionnaire Raisonné Universel d' Histoire Naturelle. 9 vol. 8vo. Paris. 1775.
Bonacina, Martinus. Opera Omnia. 3 tom. fol. Antv. 1643.
Bonamicus, Castr. De Bello Italico Commentarii. 3 vol. 4to. Lug. Bat. 1750—1.
———, ———. Commentaries of the late War in Italy; from the Latin. 8vo. Lond. 1753.
Bonamy. Sentiments des Anciens Philosophes sur la Pluralité des Mondes.—Dissertation Hist. sur la Bibliothèque d'Alexandrie. (Acad. des Inscrip. vol. 9.)
———. Sur les Loix des XII Tables. (Id. 12.)
———. Sur l'Introduction de la Langue Lat. dans les Gaules.—Réflexions sur la Langue Lat. vulgaire, etc.—Dissertations sur les Causes de la Cessation de la Langue Tudesque en France, etc. (Id. 24.)
Bonannus, Phil. Numismata Pontificum Romanorum. 3 tom. fol. Romæ. 1699—1715.
———, ———. Museum Kircherianum. fol. Romæ. 1773.
Bonannus et Columna. Syracusarum Antiquarum Illustratarum Libri Duo. (Græv. Thes. Ital.)
Bonaparte, C. L. American Ornithology. vol. 1. 4to. Phil. 1825.
Bonaparte, Louis. Maria, or the Hollanders; from the French. 2 vols. 16mo. Bost. 1815.
Bonaparte, Lucien. Charlemagne, ou l'Eglise Délivrée. 2 vol. 4to. Rom. 1814.
Bonaparte. See Napoleon.
Bonar, Arch. Genuine Religion the Best Friend of the People. 12mo. 1807.
Bonefonius, Johannes. Carmina. 16mo. Lond. 1720.
Bonetus, Theoph. Sepulchretum; sive Anatomia Practica, ex Cadaveribus Morbo Denatis. 2 tom. in 1 vol. fol. Genevæ. 1679.

Bonetus, Theoph. Mercurius Compitalitius; or a Guide to the Practical Physician; from the Latin. fol. Lond. 1684.
Bonfadius, J. Annales Genuenses. (Græv. Thes. Ital.)
———, –. Carmina. Vide Fracastorius.
Bonfilius et Constantius. Messanæ Urbis Descriptio. (Græv. Thes. Ital.)
Bonfrerius, Jac. Annotationes in Promissæ Terræ Chorographicam Tabulam. (Ugol. vol. 5.)
Bongiovanni, Ant. Græca Scholia Scriptoris Anonymi in Homeri Iliados Lib. I. Gr. et Lat. 4to. Venet. 1740.
Bonicelli, A. Dua Nauka Mnogho Koristna, etc. (Sclavonic.) 16mo. U'Mlecih. 1762.
Bonnaterre. Ornithologie et Ichthyologie. (Encyclopédie Méthodique.)
Bonnemain, A. Régénération des Colonies. 8vo. Paris. 1792.
Bonner, Edm. (Bp.) Letters, Declarations, &c. (Fox, Martyrs.)
———, ———, Epitaph upon. (Harl. Misc. vol. 1.)
Bonnet, Charles. Philosophical Enquiries concerning Christianity. 8vo. Lond. 1787.
———, ———. Contemplation de la Nature. 2 vol. 8vo. Amst. 1769.
———, ———. Œuvres Physiques. 18 vol. 8vo. Neufchatel. 1779—83.
———, ———. Interesting Views of Christianity. 12mo. Bost. 1813.
Bonnet, E. Tableau des Etats-Unis de l'Amérique. 8vo. Paris. 1816.
Bonnet, Gisb. Orationes Duæ; I. In Religionis Contemptores. II. De Vaticiniis Christi Fata præsignificantibus. 4to. Traj. ad Rhen. 1793.
Bonneval, Bashaw Count. Memoirs. 8vo. Lond. 1750.
Bonnycastle, John. Introduction to Mensuration and Practical Geometry. 12mo. Lond. 1782.
———, ———. Introduction to Algebra. 12mo. Lond. 1782.
Bonnycastle, R. H. Account of the Dominions of Spain in the Western Hemisphere. 2 vols. 8vo. Lond. 1818.
Bonpland, Alex. Vide Annales du Mus. d'Hist. Nat.—V. Humboldt.
Bons, L. de. Sermons sur le Chapitre VIII. de l'Epître aux Romains. 3 vol. 8vo. Lausanne. 1774—6.
Bontius, Jac. Medicina Indorum. Vide Alpinus.
Booth, Abr. Glad Tidings to Perishing Sinners. 12mo. Lond. 1796.
Booth, Geo. The Historical Library of Diodorus the Sicilian, made English. fol. Lond. 1700.
———, ———. Real Actions. fol. Lond. 1701.
———, ———. ———. 8vo. N. York. 1808.
Booth, Peniston. Sermon on Baptism. 8vo. Lond. 1718.
Boothby, Sir Brooke. Fables and Satires. 2 vols. 12mo. Edin. 1809.
Borda, Ch. de. Description et Usage du Cercle de Réflexion. 4to. Paris. 1816.

Bordan, G. Theosebia Christ. et Evang. 4to. Vitemb. 1722.
Borde, H. la. Grausamkeit der Neger auf der Insel St. Domingo; aus dem Französischen. 12mo. Leipz. 1792.
Borde, J. B. de la. Tableaux de la Suisse; ou Voyage Pittoresque fait dans les Treize Cantons et Etats Alliés du Corps Helvétique. 4 vol. fol. Paris. 1780—6.
Borellus, Joh. Alph. De Motu Animalium. 4to. Lug. Bat. 1685.
Borgeest, J. B. De Differentiis Vocum Hebraicarum. 4to. Vitembergæ. 4to. 1718.
Borghini, Raffaello. Il Riposo. 3 vol. 8vo. Milan. 1807.
Borghini, Vinc. Discorsi dell' Origine di Firenze, etc. 4 vol. 8vo. Milano. 1808—9.
Borgnis, J. A. Théorie de la Mécanique Usuelle. 4to. Paris. 1821.
Borhöck, Aug. Chr. Apparatus ad Herodotum. 5 vol. 8vo. Lemgov. 1795—8.
Borlase, Wm. Antiquities of Cornwall. fol. Oxford. 1754.
———, ——. Natural History of Cornwall. fol. Oxford. 1758.
Born, Baron Inigo. Sur l'Extrait des Métaux. 4to. Vienne. 1788.
Bornitius, Christ. De Synagogis Vet. Hebr. (Ugol. vol. 21.)
Borrichius, Olaus. Cogitationes de Variis Latinæ Linguæ Ætatibus, etc. 4to. Hafniæ. 1675.
————, ——. Analecta ad Cogitationes. 4to. Hafniæ. 1682.
————, ——. De Antiqua Urbis Romæ Facie. (Gronov. v. 4.)
Borromeo, Anton-Maria. Notizia de' Novellieri Italiani. 8vo. Bassano. 1794.
Bos, Lambertus. Observationes Miscellaneæ ad Loca quædam Nov. Test. etc. Accedit Vitringæ Animadversionum ad J. Vorstii Philologiam Sacram Specimen. 8vo. Franeq. 1707.
—, ————. Exercitationes Philologicæ. 8vo. Franeq. 1713.
—, ————. Ellipses Græcæ. 8vo. Norimb. 1763.
—, ————. Idem. 12mo. Halæ. 1765.
—, ————. ——, Schæferi. 8vo. Lips. 1808.
—, ————. Animadversiones ad Scriptores quosdam Græcos; item Specimen Animadversionum Latinarum. 8vo. Franek. 1715.
—, ————. Vet. Test. Græc. 4to Franeq. 1709.
—, ————. Antiquities of Greece, with Leisner's Notes; from the Latin by P. Stockdale. 8vo. Lond. 1772.
Bosanquet and Puller. Reports in C. B. and H. of Lords, from 1796 to 1804. 3 vols. Phil. 1805.
———— ————. New Reports, from East. 44 Geo. III. to Trin. 47 Geo. III. 2 vols. 8vo. Phil. 1807—9.
Boscan, J. A. Obras de Boscan y Garcilaso. 4to. Medina. 1544.
Boscawen, Wm. Poems. 12mo. Lond. 1801.
Boschius, De Patriarchis Antiochenis. (Script. Byz.)
Boscovich, R. J. Opera pertinentia ad Opticam et Astronomiam, etc. 5 vol. 4to. Bassani. 1785.
————, ——. Theoria Philosophiæ Naturalis. 4to. Venet. 1763.
————, ——. De Solis ac Lunæ Defectibus. 4to. Lond. 1760.

Bose, Ram Ram. History of King Pritapadityo, in the Bengalee Language. 8vo. Calcutta.

Bosius, J. A. De Pontifice Maximo Romæ Veteris Exercitatio Historica.—De Pontificatu Max. Imperatorum Roman. Exercitatio Hist. Altera. (Græv. vol. 5.)

Bosius, J. J. De Verbo, Σαάλλω. Mar. v. 35, etc. 4to. Lips. 1734.

Bosman, Wm. Description of the Coast of Guinea; from the Dutch. 8vo. Lond. 1721.

Bosse, Abraham. Sentimens sur la Distinction des Manières de Peinture, Dessein, et Graveure. 12mo. Paris. 1649.

Bossi, Luigi. Vita di Colombo. 8vo. Milano. 1818.

Bossius, Hieron. De Toga Romana.—De Senatorum Lato Clavo.—De Sistro.—De Strena. (Sallengre, vol. 2.)

Bossu. Travels through that Part of North America formerly called Louisiana; from the French. 2 vols. 8vo. Lond. 1771.

——. Nouveaux Voyages aux Indes Occidentales. 2 vol. 12mo. Paris. 1768.

——. Nouveaux Voyages dans l'Amérique Septentrionale. 8vo. Amst. 1777.

——. Neue Reisen nach West-Indien; aus dem Französischen. 12mo. Helmst. 1776.

Bossu, René le. Treatise upon the Epick Poem, made English, from the French. 2 vols. 12mo. Lond. 1719.

Bossuet, J. B. (Evêque de Meaux.) Œuvres. 43 vol. 8vo. Versailles. 1815—9.

——, ——. Œuvres Choisies. 8 vol. 8vo. Nismes. 1784—8.

——, ——. Pastoral Letter to his New Catholics; from the French. 4to. Lond. 1686.

——, ——. Discours sur l'Histoire Universelle. 2 vol. 12mo. Paris. 1752.

——, ——. Exposition of the Doctrine of the Catholick Church. 4to. Lond. 1686.

——, ——. Vindication of the Bishop of Condom's Exposition. 4to. Lond. 1686.

——, ——. Letter from the Vindicator of the Bishop of Condom. 4to. Lond. 1687.

——, ——. Conference with Mr. Claude. 4to. Lond. 1687.

——, ——. Account of the Education of the Dauphine.

Bossut, Jean. Cours de Mathématiques. 2 vol. 8vo. Paris. 1782—8.

——, ——. Traité d'Hydrodynamique. 2 vol. 4to. Paris. 1786—7.

——, ——. General History of Mathematics; from the French. 8vo. Lond. 1803.

Boston, (Mass.) State of Importations into the Town from Great Britain in 1770. 8vo. Bost. 1770.

——, ——. Narrative of the Massacre, March 5th, 1770, with Depositions, &c. 8vo. Bost. 1770.

——, ——. Observations of its Merchants upon Several Acts of Parliament. 8vo. 1770.

Boston, (Mass.) Appeal to the World; or a Vindication of Boston against the Letters of Gov. Barnard, Gen. Gage, &c. 8vo. Lond. 1770.

——, ——. Votes and Proceedings in Town Meeting, Oct. 28th, 1772. 8vo. Bost.

——, ——. Votes and Proceedings of the Inhabitants in 1772 and 1773. 8vo. Bost.

——, ——. Letter to a Friend on the Sufferings of the Town in consequence of the Port-Bill, by T. W. 8vo. Bost. 1774.

——, ——. Two Plans for forming it into a City in 1784. 8vo. Bost.

——, ——. By-Laws and Orders in force in 1758. 8vo. Bost.

——, ——. ———————— in 1785—6. 8vo. Bost.

——, ——. ———————— in 1801, &c. 8vo. Bost.

——, ——. Report of the Town Convention in 1804. 8vo. Bost.

——, ——. Facts and Documents relative to the Project of a Bridge from South Street to Dorchester Neck. 8vo. Bost. 1805.

——, ——. Considerations on the Expediency of a Bridge from One part of Boston to the Other. 8vo. Bost. 1806.

——, ——. Answer to the above. 8vo. Bost. 1806.

——, ——. System of Public Education. 8vo. Bost.

——, ——. Report on its Pecuniary Concerns in 1811. 8vo.

——, ——. ———————— in 1812. 8vo.

——, ——. Orations commemorating the Massacre of the Fifth of March, 1770. 2d ed. 12mo. Bost. 1807.

——, ——. Sketch of the Church Solemnities, &c. in Honour of the Russian Achievements over the French Invaders. 16mo. Bost. 1813.

——, ——. Miscellaneous Remarks on its Police. 8vo. Bost. 1814.

Boston Medical Police. 8vo. Bost. 1820.

—— Exchange Office. See Changery.

—— News Letter and City Record. See Bowen. See Smith.

Boston, Tho. Human Nature in its Fourfold State. 12mo. Edin. 1763.

Bostonus, Joannes. Speculum Cœnobitarum. Vide Trivetus.

Bostwick, David. Right of Infants to Baptism. 8vo. Lond. 1765.

Boswell, James. Tour to the Hebrides. 8vo. Phil. 1810.

——, ——. Life of Sam. Johnson. 2 vols. 4to. Lond. 1791.

——, ——. ————————. 4 vols. 8vo. Lond. 1799.

——, ——. ————————. 3 vols. 8vo. Bost. 1807.

——, ——. Account of Corsica, with Memoirs of Paoli. 8vo. Lond. 1768.

Boswell, John. Method of Study. 2 vols. 8vo. Lond. 1738.

Bosworth, Newton. Accidents of Human Life, with Hints for their Prevention. 16mo. N. York. 1814.

Bott, Tho. Simplicity and Reasonableness of the Christian Institution. 8vo. Lond. 1727.

——, ——. Answer to Warburton's Divine Legation of Moses. 8vo. Lond. 1743.

——, ——. Discourse on Luke ix. 56. 8vo. Lond. 1724.

Botta, Carlo. Storia della Guerra dell' Independenza degli Stati Uniti d' America. 4 vol. 8vo. Parigi. 1809.

——, ——. Idem. 4 vol. 8vo. Milano. 1819.

——, ——. History of the War of the Independence of the U. States of America, tr. by G. A. Otis. 2 vols. 8vo. Phil. 1820.

——, ——. Histoire de la Guerre de l'Indépendence des Etats-Unis d'Amérique, trad. de l'Italien et précédée d'une Introduction, par L. de Sevelinges. 4 vol. 8vo. Paris. 1812.

Böttiger, C. A. Ideen zur Archäologie der Malerei. 8vo. Dresden. 1811.

———, ——. Griechische Vasengemälde. 8vo. Weimar. 1797.

———, ——. Die Furienmaske. 8vo. Weimar. 1801.

———, ——. Sabina oder Morgenszenen im Putzzimmer einer Reichen Römerin. 2 vol. 12mo. Leipz. 1806.

Bouchard. Sur les Edits des Magistrats Romains. (Acad. des Inscrip. vol. 41.)

Boucharlat, J. L. Elémens de Calcul Différentiel et de Calcul Intégral. 8vo. Paris. 1826.

Boucher. Histoire de la dernière Guerre entre la Grande-Bretagne et les Etats-Unis de l'Amérique, etc. fol. Paris. 1787.

———. Institution au Droit Maritime. 4to. Paris. 1803.

Boucher, Jona. View of the Causes and Consequences of the American Revolution. 8vo. Lond. 1797.

Boucher, Pierre. Histoire de la Nouvelle France, vulgairement dite le Canada. 24to. Paris. 1664.

Boucher de la Richarderie, G. Bibliothèque Universelle des Voyages. 6 vol. 8vo. Paris. 1808.

Boudinot, Elias. Age of Revelation. 8vo. Phil. 1801.

———, ——. Second Advent, or Coming of the Messiah. 8vo. Trenton. 1815.

———, ——. Star in the West. 8vo. Trenton. 1816.

Bougainville, J. P. de. Sur la Vie et sur les Voyages de Pythéas de Marseille. (Acad. des Inscrip. vol. 19.)

————, ———. Recherches sur l'Origine des Mystères célébrés à Eleusis. (Id. 21.)

————, ———. Sur les Découvertes et les Etablissemens faits par Hannon. (Id. 26 et 28.)

————, ———. Antiquités Grecques du Premier Age. (Id. 29.)

Bougainville, L. de. Voyage round the World, translated from the French by J. R. Forster. 4to. Lond. 1772.

Bouguer, Pierre. Traité d' Optique sur la Gradation de la Lumière. 4to. Paris. 1760.

———, ———. Reisen nach Peru, Acadien und Egypten; aus dem Französischen. 8vo. Göttin. 1751.

Bouguer, Pierre. Neue Reisen nach Guiana, etc. Vide Barrère.
Bouillon, Henri, Duc de. Mémoires. (Mém. de France, vol. 47.)
Boulainvilliers, Henry, Count of. Life of Mahomet; from the French. 12mo. Lond. 1752.
Boulanger. Recherches sur l'Origine du Despotisme Oriental. 12mo. 1763.
———. Idem. 12mo. 1766.
———. Origin and Progress of Despotism; from the French. 8vo. Amst. 1764.
———. Antiquité Dévoilée par ses Usages. 3 vol. 12mo. Amst. 1766.
———. Dissertations sur Elie et Enoch, et sur Esope; et Traité Mathématique sur le Bonheur. 12mo. 1764.
Boullier, D. R. Sur l'Ame des Bêtes. 2 vol. 12mo. Amst. 1737.
Boulter, Hugh, (Abp. Farewell Sermon. 8vo. Lond. 1722.
———, ———. Assize Sermon. 8vo. Lond. 1716.
———, ———. Letter to Ministers of State. 2 vols. 8vo. Oxford. 1769.
———, ———. Fast Sermon. 8vo. Lond. 1720.
———, ———. Sermon before the Society for Propagating the Gospel. Lond. 1722.
———, ———. Three Essays on the Employment of Time. 3d ed. 8vo. Lond. 1754.
Bouquet, Henry. Historical Account of his Expedition against the Ohio Indians in 1764, &c. 4to. Phil. 1766.
———, ———. Rélation Historique de son Expédition contre les Indiens de l'Ohio en 1764, avec des Réflexions sur la Guerre avec les Sauvages, etc. trad. de l'Anglois par C. G. F. Dumas. 8vo. Amst. 1769.
Bourdaloue, Louis. Œuvres. 16 vol. 12mo. 1708—35.
———, ———. Exhortations et Instructions Chrétiennes. 4 vol. 12mo. Paris. 1716.
Bourdon, Elémens d' Arithmétique. 4me. ed. 8vo. Paris. 1826.
Bourdonnais, Mahé de la. Mémoire pour le Sieur de la Bourdonnais. 3 tom. 12mo. Paris. 1751.
Bourgoanne. Travels in Spain. (Pinkerton, vol. 5.)
Bourn, Dan. On Wheel Carriages. 8vo. Lond. 1763.
Bourne, Sam. Discourses on Natural Religion and the Christian Revelation. 2 vols. 8vo. Lond. 1760.
———, ———. The Same, with Discourses on the Parables. 4 vols. 8vo. Lond. 1763.
———, ———. Sermon before an Assembly of Ministers. 4to. Lond. 1753.
Bourne, Vincent. Poems. 4to. Lond. 1772.
Boussole Politique, Administrative, et Littéraire. Livraisons 1—32. 8vo. Paris. 1818—9.
Bouterwek, Fried. Geschichte der Poesie und Beredsamkeit, etc. 10 bände. 8vo. Gött. 1801—17.
———, ———. Aesthetik. 2 vol. 8vo. Göttin. 1815.
Bowchier, Joshua. Hæreticus Triumphatus. 8vo. Exon. 1719.

Bowden, John. Sermon on the Death of King George I. 8vo. Lond. 1727.

———, ——. Sermon on the Death of Mr. J. Blunt. 8vo. Bristol. 1749.

———, ——. Sermon at the Ordination of Samuel Billingsley. 8vo. Lond. 1725.

Bowditch, Nathaniel. New American Practical Navigator. 8vo. Newburyport. 1807.

———, ———. The Same. 8vo. N. York. 1811.

———, ———. Directions for Sailing into the Harbours of Salem, Marblehead, &c. 8vo. Newburyport. 1806.

———, ———. Estimate of the Meteor at Weston. 4to.

———, ———. Papers in the Memoirs of the American Academy, vols. 2, 3, and 4.

Bowdler, H. M. Fragments by Elizabeth Smith, &c. See Smith.

Bowdler, Tho. Family Shakspeare. 2d ed. 10 vols. 12mo. Lond. 1820.

Bowdoin, James. Inaugural Discourse before the American Academy of Arts and Sciences. 8vo. Bost. 1780.

Bowen, Abel. Naval Monument. 8vo. Bost. 1816.

———, ——. Boston News-Letter and City Record. See Smith.

Bowen, Emanuel. Geography. 3 vols. fol. Lond. 1747. (3d vol. Maps.)

Bowen, Penuel. Sermon on the Death of the Rev. Samuel Checkley. 12mo. Bost. 1770.

Bower, Archibald. Faithful Account of his Leaving the Office of Secretary to the Court of Inquisition. 8vo. Lond. 1751.

———, ———. Six Letters to Father Sheldon. 8vo. Lond. 1756.

———, ———. Answer to the above. 8vo. Lond. 1757.

———, ———. Bower and Tillemont compared. 8vo. Lond. 1757.

———, ———. Answer to the above. 8vo. Lond. 1757.

———, ———. Confutation of his Three Defences. 8vo. Lond. 1757.

———, ———. Reply to the Confutation. 8vo. Lond. 1757.

———, ———. One very remarkable Fact more relating to the Conduct of the Jesuits, &c. 8vo. Lond. 1758.

———, ———. History of the Popes; with a Summary View of his Controversy with the Papists. 5 vols. 4to. Lond. 1750—61.

Bowman, Tho. Principles of Christianity as taught in Scripture. 12mo. Lond. 1766.

———, ——. The Same. 12mo. Lond. 1769.

———, ——. Review of the Doctrines of the Reformation. 8vo. Norwich. 1768.

Bowman, Wm. Defence of our Saviour's Miracle in Cursing the Fig-Tree. 8vo. Lond. 1721.

———, ——. Visitation Sermon. 8vo. Lond. 1731.

Bowring, John. Specimens of the Russian Poets. 16mo. Lond. 1821.

Bowring, John. The Same. 12mo. Bost. 1822.
Bowyer, Wm. Conjectures on the New Testament. 8vo. Lond. 1772.
———, ——. The Same. 4to. Lond. 1812.
———, ——. Nov. Test. Gr. cum Emend. Conjec. 2 vol. 12mo. Lond. 1763.
Boxhornius, Marc. Z. De Majestate et Prærogativa Regum. 4to. Lug. Bat. 1649.
————, ———. Cogitationes Subitaneæ ad Boxhornii Dissertationem. 4to. Gedani. 1649.
————, ———. Quæstiones Romanæ. (Græv. vol. 5.)
Boy of Bilson. See Fowles.
Boyd, J. P. (Gen.) Documents and Facts relative to Military Events during the late War. 8vo. 1816.
Boyer, Abel. Dictionnaire François-Anglois et Anglois-François. 2 vol. 4to. Lond. 1773.
——, ——. Idem, par Garner. 2 vol. 4to. Rouen. 1802.
——, ——. Dictionary Abridged. 8vo. Lond. 1715.
——, ——. French Dictionary, with Tardy's Pronunciation, &c. 8vo. Bost. 1822.
——, ——. Annals of Queen Anne's Reign. 11 vols. 8vo. Lond. 1703—13.
——, ——. Annals of King George I. 6 vols. 8vo. Lond. 1716—21.
——, ——. Political State of G. Britain. 16 vols. 8vo. Lond. 1722—40.
Boyer, J. B. N. On Diseases of the Bones, translated from the French by M. Farrel. 2 vols. 8vo. Lond. 1804.
Boyer, Paul. Véritable Rélation du Voyage de M. de Bretign à l'Amérique Occidentale. 8vo. Paris. 1654.
Boyle, Charles. Dr. Bentley's Dissertations on the Epistles of Phalaris, and the Fables of Æsop, Examined. 12mo. Lond. 1698.
——, ———. Review of the Controversy between Boyle and Bentley. 8vo. Lond. 1701.
——, ———. See Bentley.
Boyle, John, (Earl of Cork and Orrery.) Remarks on the Life and Writings of Swift. 8vo. Lond. 1752.
Boyle, Rob. On Effluviums, with Experiments to make Fire and Flame Ponderable. 16mo. Lond. 1673.
——, ——. Experimenta, Observationes, etc. 12mo. Lond. 1692.
——, ——. Usefulness of Experimental Natural Philosophy. 4to. Lond. 1664.
——, ——. Exercitationes de Utilitate Philosophiæ Naturalis Experimentalis, et Medicina Hydrostatica. 4to. Lind. et Genev. 1693.
——, ——. Works; with his Life. 5 vols. fol. Lond. 1744.
——, ——. Opera Varia. 4to. Genevæ. 1680.
——, ——. On the Style of the Scriptures. 12mo. Lond. 1668.
——, ——. The Same. 12mo. Lond. 1675.
——, ——. Seraphic Love. 12mo. Lond. 1663.

Boyle, Rob. On the high Veneration Man's Intellect owes to God. 12mo. Lond. 1685.

——, ——. Physico-Theological Considerations about the Possibility of the Resurrection. 12mo. Lond. 1675.

Boyle's Lecture Sermons, in Defence of Natural and Revealed Religion. 3 vols. fol. Lond. 1739.

Boylston, Zabdiel. Abridgement of Two Accounts in the Philosophical Transactions of Inoculating or Transplanting the Small Pox. 16mo. Bost. 1721.

———, ———. Historical Account of the Small-Pox Inoculated in N. England. 12mo. Bost. 1730.

Boyse, Joseph. Works. fol. Lond. 1728.

——, ———. Accession Sermon. 8vo. Lond. 1714.

Boyse, Samuel. Poems. See Chalmers.

Boze, C. Gros de. Inscription Taurobolique trouvée à Lyon. 8vo. Paris. 1705.

Bozius, Tho. De Jure Status; sive de Jure Divino et Naturali Ecclesiasticæ Libertatis et Potestatis. 4to. Romæ. 1600.

Bozman, J. L. Sketch of the History of Maryland during the First Three Years after its Settlement. 8vo. Baltimore. 1811.

Braam, A. E. Van. Embassy to China. See Saint-Mery.

Bracciolini, Fr. Scherno degli Dei. 8vo. Milano. 1804.

Bracellius, J. Oræ Ligusticæ Descriptio.—De Claris Genuensibus.—De Bello inter Hispanos et Genuenses seculo suo.—Diploma Miræ Antiq. Tabel. in Agro Genuensi repert. (Græv. Thes. Ital.)

Brachmani. Vide Palladius.

Brackenridge, H. H. Incidents of the Insurrection in the Western Parts of Pennsylvania, in 1794. 8vo. Phil. 1795.

—————, ——. Law Miscellany. 8vo. Phil. 1814.

Brackenridge, H. M. Lobrede aus diejenigen Männer welche gefallen den 5ten July, 1779. 16mo.

Brackenridge, H. M. Views of Louisiana, with a Journal of a Voyage up the Missouri in 1811. 8vo. Pittsburgh. 1814.

—————, ——. Journal of a Voyage up the Missouri in 1811. 12mo. Baltimore. 1815.

—————, ——. Views of Louisiana. 12mo. Baltimore. 1817.

Bracton, H. de. De Legibus et Consuetudinibus Angliæ. 4to. Lond. 1640.

—————, ——. Idem. fol. Lond. 1659.

Bradbury, John. Travels in the Interior of America, in 1809, 1810, and 1811. 8vo. Liverpool. 1817.

Bradbury, Tho. Sermon on the French Invasion in Favour of the Pretender. 12mo. Lond. 1708.

———, ——, Character of, from his own Pen. 8vo. Lond. 1749.

———, ——. Sermon on the Lawfulness of Resisting Tyrants. 8vo. Lond. 1714.

———, ——. Restoration Sermon. 8vo. Lond. 1715.

———, ——. Sermon on the Death of Mr. Salisbury. 12mo. Lond. 1709.

Bradbury, Tho. Sermon on the Death of King George I. 8vo. Lond. 1727.

———, ——. Sermons on June 7th and 10th. 8vo. Lond. 1716.

———, ——. Sermons on the Fifth of November, 1814, —16, —17, —21. 8vo. Lond. 1814—21.

———, ——. Answer to the Reproaches cast on the Dissenting Ministers, who believe in the Trinity. 8vo. Lond. 1719.

Bradby, James. Law of Distresses. 1st Am. ed. N. York. 1808.

Bradford, Alden. Two Sermons on the Doctrines, Character, and Kingdom of Christ. 8vo. Bost. 1795.

———, ——. History of Massachusetts from 1764 to 1789. 2 vols. 8vo. Bost. 1722—5.

Bradford, Ebenezer. Thanksgiving Sermon. Bost. 1795.

———, ———. Fast Sermon, with an Answer to Dr. Tappan's Remarks on his Thanksgiving Sermon. 1795.

Bradford, Gam. Address to the Massachusetts Society for the Suppression of Intemperance. 12mo. Bost. 1826.

Bradford, John. Epistle to a Faithful Christian in Coventry. 4to.

Bradford, Sam. (Bp.) Eight Sermons at Boyle's Lecture on the Intrinsick Evidence of Christianity. fol. Lond. 1699.

———, ———. Sermon before the King on the Nature of Christian Union. 8vo. Lond. 1708.

———, ———. Charity Sermon. 4to. Lond. 1709.

———, ———. Sermon on Purity and Peace. 8vo. Lond. 1710.

———, ———. Consecration Sermon. 12mo. Lond. 1708.

———, ———. Reformation of Manners Sermon. 12mo. Lond. 1697.

Bradford, Wm. Inquiry how far the Punishment of Death is Necessary in Pennsylvania. 8vo Phil. 1793.

Bradley, James. Astronomical Observations at Greenwich. 2 vols. fol. Oxford. 1798.

Bradley, Rich. Philosophical Account of the Works of Nature 4to. Lond. 1721.

———, ——. Husbandry and Trade Improved. vol. 1. 8vo. Lond. 1727.

Bradley, T. (and others.) Medical and Physical Journal. 40 vols. 8vo. Lond. 1799—1818.

Bradshaw, Gul. De Justificatione. 12mo. Lug. Bat. 1618.

Bradstreet, Simon. Sermon on the Death of Mr. Samuel Bradstreet. 4to. Bost. 1755.

Bradwardinus, Tho. (Archiepisc.) De Causa Deicontra Pelagium et de Virtute Causarum. fol. Lond. 1618.

Brady, J. On the Burning of the Holy Bible, by order of the Rev. Mr. Edelin. 12mo. 1819.

Brady, John. Clavis Calendaria. 2 vols. 8vo. Lond. 1812.

Brady, Nich. Sermon before the Queen on Luke x. 41, 42. 8vo. Lond. 1707.

——, ——. Version of the Psalms. See Tate.

Brady, Robert. Answer to Wm. Petit on Representation in Parliament. 8vo. Lond. 1681.

Brady, Robert. Letter to Sydenham on Air. See Sydenham.
Bragge, Fr. Sermons on Undissembled and Persevering Religion. 8vo. Lond. 1713.
———, —. On the Regulation of the Passions. 8vo. Lond. 1708.
Bragge, Rob. On the Soul of Man, with an Answer to the Enquiry "Watchmen, What of the Night?" 8vo. Lond. 1725.
Brahe, Tycho. Historia Cœlestis, etc. fol. Ratisb. 1672.
Brainerd, David. Work of Grace among the Indians of New-Jersey and Pennsylvania. 8vo. Phil. 1746.
Bramhall, John, (Abp.) Works, with his Life. fol. Dublin. 1677.
Bramston, James. Art of Politicks, in imitation of Horace's Art of Poetry. 8vo. Lond. 1729.
Bramston, John. Texts examined, which Papists cite on Purgatory. 4to. 1688.
Bramston, Sir John, and others, Articles of Accusation against. 4to. 1641.
Brancas, H. I. de, (Bp.) Love and Charity the Basis of Religion; a Sermon, translated by J. Vailiant. 8vo. Lond. 1754.
Brancker, Tho. Introduction to Algebra, from Rhonius. 4to. Lond. 1668.
Brand, John. Description of Orkney, &c. (Pinkerton, vol. 3.)
Brand, T. On Ruptures. 8vo. Lond. 1782.
Brande, W. T. Manual of Chymistry. 3 vols. in 1. 8vo. N. York. 1821.
———, ———. Journal of Science and the Arts. 21 vols. 8vo. N. York and Lond. 1817—26.
———, ———. Dissertation on the Progress of Chemical Science. 8vo. Bost. 1818.
Brandt, Gerard. History of the Reformation in the Low Countries; from the Low-Dutch. 4 vols. fol. Lond. 1720—3.
———, ———. The Same, Abridged. 2 vols. 8vo. Lond. 1725.
Brant, Joseph. Nene Karighwiyoston tsinihorighhoten ne Saint John: (The Gospel according to St. John, Mohawk and English.) 12mo. Lond.
———, ———. The Book of Common Prayer, and the Gospel of St. Mark, in the Mohawk and English Languages. 8vo. Lond. 1787.
Brasil. Vertooch van de Verradersche en Vyantlijcke Acten en Proceduren van Poortugaal in Brasil. 4to. Amst. 1647.
Braun, Placidus. Notitia de Codicibus MSS. in Bibliotheca Monasterii S. Benedicti ad SS. Udalricum et Afram Augustæ extantibus. 3 vol. in 1. Aug. Vind. 1791—3.
Braunius, J. A. De Admirando Frigore Artificiali, quo Mercurius est congelatus. 4to. Petropol. 1760.
———, —. Idem. (Phil. Trans. vol. 52.)
Braunius, Joh. De Adolitione Suffitus. (Ugol. vol. 11.)
———, ——. De Sanctitate Pontif. Max. (Id. 12.)
———, ——. Comment. in Epistolam ad Hebræos. 4to. Amst. 1705.
———, ——. De Vestitus Sacerdotum Hebræorum. 4to. Amst. 1680.

Bray, (Rev. Dr.) Memorial concerning the Erecting of a Hospital for Foundlings in London. 12mo.
Bray, Tho. Papal Usurpation and Persecution. fol. Lond. 1712.
——, ——. Sermon on Reformation of Manners. 4to. Lond. 1709.
——, ——. Discourse upon the Baptismal Covenant. 12mo. Lond. 1698.
Bray, Wm. Tour into Derbyshire, &c. (Pinkerton, vol. 2.)
——, ——. Memoirs of Evelyn. See Evelyn.
Brazer, John. Discourse before the Society for the Promotion of Christian Education in Harv. University. 8vo. Bost. 1825.
Breck, Rob. Election Sermon. 16mo. Bost. 1728.
——, ——. Century Sermon. 8vo. Hartford. 1784.
Breck, Sam. Sketch of the Internal Improvements in Pennsylvania. 8vo. Phil. 1818.
Bredow, G. G. Geographiæ et Uranologiæ Herodoteæ Specimina. 4to. Helmst. 1804.
Bree, Rob. On Convulsive Asthma.
Breirly, Roger. Bundle of Soul-Convincing, Directing, and Comforting Truths. 12mo. Edinburgh. 1670.
Breislak, Scip. Introduzione alla Geologia. 8vo. Milano. 1811.
Breitingerus, J. J. Vetus Testamentum Gr. cum Lectionibus Var. et Criticis Dissertationibus. 4 vol. 4to. Tiguri Helvet. 1730—2.
——, ——. Brevis de Idiotismis Sermonis Hebræi Commentarius, etc. 8vo. Tiguri. 1737.
——, ——. Exercitatio in Vitam Persii. (Schelhorn, v. 10.)
——, ——. Eclogæ ex optimis Græcis Scriptoribus. 12mo. Turici. 1749.
Brekell, John. Christian Warfare, a Discourse. 8vo. Lond. 1742.
——, ——. Grounds and Principles of the Christian Revelation. 8vo. Lond. 1765.
Bremisch-Niedersächsisches Wörterbuch. 5 vol. 8vo. Bremen. 1767—71.
Brencmannus, H. Gemina Dissertatio; Altera de Republica Amalphitana; Altera de Amalphi a Pisanis direpta. (Græv. Thes. Ital.)
Brent, Charles. Sermon before the Guardians of the Poor in Bristol. 4to. Lond. 1704.
Brequigny, L. G. Sur l'Etablissement de la Religion et de l'Empire de Mahomet. (Acad. des Inscrip. vol. 32.)
——, —. Sur les Recherches relatives à l'Histoire de France faites à Londres. (Id. 37.)
Brera, V. L. On Verminous Diseases; translated from the Italian into French by Bartoli and Calvert, and from the French by J. G. Coffin, with Additions. 8vo. Bost. 1817.
Brerewood, Edw. De Ponderibus et Pretiis Veterum Nummorum. 4to. Lond. 1614.
——, ——. Enquiries touching the Diversities of Languages and Religions. 8vo. Lond. 1674.
——, ——. Tractatus Logici, et Alii. 12mo. Oxon. 1631.

Brerewood, Edw. Patriarchicall Government of the Ancient Church. 4to. Oxford. 1641.
Breton. See Cape Breton.
Bretschneider, C. G. Lexicon in Interpretes Græcos Vet. Test. 8vo. Lips. 1805.
——————, ——. Liber Jesu Siracidæ, Græce. 8vo. Ratisb. 1806.
Bretus, Carolus. De Ordine Antiquo Judiciorum Civilium apud Romanos. (Sallengre, vol. 2.)
Breviarium Monasticum. 4 vol. 8vo. 1756.
—————. Vide Romanum.
Brevint, Dan. Missale Romanum, or Depth and Mystery of the Roman Mass laid open. 8vo. Oxford. 1672.
———, ——. Idem. 12mo. Oxford. 1673.
———, ——. Saul and Samuel at Endor. 8vo. Oxford. 1674.
Brewster, David. Encyclopædia. 15 vols. Nos. 1—30 (15 vols.), and No. 31. 4to.
—————, ——— and Jameson. Edinburgh Philosophical Journal. Nos. 1 and 2 (vol. 1.), and No. 3. 8vo. Edin. 1819—20.
Brewster, Martha. Poems on divers Subjects. 8vo. Bost. 1757.
Brez, J. Flore des Insectophiles.
Briant, J. O. Nehiro-Iriniui Aiamihe Massinahigan, etc. 8vo. Uabistiguiatsh. 1767.
Briant, Lem. Friendly Remarks on the Rev. Mr. Porter's Sermon from Isaiah lxiv. 6. 8vo. Bost. 1750.
Brice, Andrew. Grand Gazetteer. fol. Exeter. 1760.
Brickell, John. Natural History of North Carolina. 8vo. Dublin. 1737.
Bridel, Louis. Le Pour et le Contre, ou Avis à ceux qui se proposent de passer dans les Etats-Unis d'Amérique. 12mo. Paris. 1803.
Bridge, Eben. Artillery Election Sermon. 8vo. Bost. 1752.
———, ——. Election Sermon. 8vo. Bost. 1767.
Bridge, Josiah. Election Sermon. 8vo. Bost. 1789.
Bridge, Tho. Discourse on the Choice of Town Officers. 16mo. Bost. 1710.
———, ——. Sermon on Faith. 16mo. Bost. 1713.
———, ——. Artillery Election Sermon. 16mo. Bost. 1705.
Bridges, Geo. Method of Wool Smuggling clearly Discovered.
Bridges, John. Catalogue of his Library. 8vo. Lond. 1725.
Bridgman, Sir John. Reports from 12 to 19 Jac. I. fol. Lond. 1659.
Bridgman, Sir Orlando. Conveyances. 3d ed. fol. Lond. 1699.
Bridoul, F. T. School of the Eucharist Established. 4to. Lond. 1687.
Briefe den gegenwärtigen Zustand von Nord America betreffend. 12mo. Göttingen. 1777.
——— über die jetzige uneinigkeit zwischen den Amerikanischen Colonien und dem Englischen Parlament; aus dem Englischen. 12mo. Hannover. 1776.
——— aus Amerika. 12mo. Arau und Basel. 1806.

Briefe von Personen in Paris an Doctor Priestley in America geschrieben, etc. 8vo. Lond. 1798.
———. Vide Brieven.
Brietius, Philip. Parallela Geographiæ Vet. et Nov. 3 vol. 4to. Paris. 1648—9.
Brieven gewisselt tusschen den Engelschen Vice-Admiraal Joung. 8vo.
——— Brieven over Essequebo en Demerary. 4 vol. 8vo. Amst. 1785—7.
Briggs, Guil. Ophthalmo-graphia. 12mo. Lond. 1685.
Briggs, James. On the Diseases of the Eyes. See Scarpa.
Bright, Rich. Travels through Lower Hungary. 4to. Edin. 1818.
Brightman, Tho. Workes; on the Apocalyps, &c. 4to. Lond. 1644.
Brightus, Tim. Hygieina, et Therapeutica. 12mo. Lond.
Brine, John. Defence of the Superlapsarian Scheme. 8vo. Lond. 1736.
Brinsley, John. Healing of Israel's Breaches, in Six Sermons. 4to. Lond. 1642.
———, ———. Stand-Still; or a Bridle for the Times; a Discourse. 4to. Lond. 1647.
Brion, M. Almanach Intéressant; Déscription abrégée des Etats-Unis. 18mo. Paris.
Brisson, M. J. Règne Animal. 4to. Paris. 1756.
———, —. Ornithologie. 6 vol. 4to. Paris. 1760.
Brissonius, Barn. Opera Minora Varii Argumenti, cum Notis Trekelli. fol. Lug. Bat. 1749.
———, ———. De Ritu Nuptiarum et Jure Connubiorum. (Græv. vol. 8.)
———, ———. De Adulteriis.—De Spectaculis. (Gronov. v. 8.)
Brissot, J. P. de Warville. Nouveau Voyage dans les Etats-Unis de l'Amérique Septentrionale, fait en 1788. 3 vol. 8vo. Paris. 1791.
———, ———. Examen des Voyages dans l'Amérique Sept. de M. le Marquis de Chastellux. 8vo. Lond. 1786.
———, ———. L'Indépendence des Anglo-Américains Utile à la Grande-Bretagne. 12mo.
———, ———. De la France et des Etats-Unis, par Brissot et Clavière. 8vo. Lond. 1787.
———, ———. Considerations on the Relative Situation of France and the United States; from the French of Clavière and Brissot. 8vo. Lond. 1788.
———, ———. Théorie des Loix Criminelles. 2 vol. 8vo. Berlin. 1781.
———, ———. Bibliothèque du Législateur. 10 vol. 8vo. Berlin. 1782—5.
———, ———. De la Vérité. 8vo. Neuchatel. 1780.
———, ———. Lettre à M. Barnave. 8vo. Paris. 1790.
———, ———. Réflexions sur le nouveau Décret rendu pour les Colonies. 8vo. 1790.

Brissot, J. P. de Warville. Discours sur la Question, si le Roi peut être jugé.

———, —————. Discourse upon the Question, "Whether the King shall be tried?" translated by J. G. de Nancrede. 12mo. Bost. 1791.

———, ——— ———. Réplique à M. Gouy, Défenseur de l'Esclavage. 8vo. Paris. 1791.

Bristed, John. Resources of the United States. 8vo. N. York. 1818.

Bristol, Electors of. Answer to Edmund Burke. 8vo. Lond. 1778.

Britain. Rerum Britannicarum Scriptores Vet. ac Præcipui. fol. Heidelb. 1687.

———. The Golden Fleece; or the Interest of G. Britain considered, &c. fol.

———. Excidium Angliæ; or the Fatal Consequences of Smuggling Wool. 4to. Lond. 1727.

———. Anglia Restaurata; or the Advantages of Preventing the Smuggling of Wool. 4to. Lond. 1727.

———. Enquiry into the Reasons of the Conduct of G. Britain, &c. 8vo. Lond. 1727.

———. Defence of the Enquiry. 8vo. Lond. 1729.

———. Observations on the Conduct of G. Britain. 8vo. Lond. 1729.

———. Importance of the British Plantations in America to this Kingdom. 8vo. Lond. 1731.

———. Britannia Major; the New Scheme for Discharging the Debts, &c. of the British Dominions. 8vo. Lond. 1732.

———. Britain's Memorial against the Pretender and Popery. 8th ed. 8vo. Lond.

———. Laws, Ordinances, and Institutions of the Admiralty of G. Britain. 2 vols. 8vo. Lond. 1746.

———. Danger of G. Britain and Ireland becoming Provinces to France. 8vo. Lond. 1745.

———. Interest of G. Britain with regard to her Colonies. 8vo. Lond.

———. Thoughts, whether the Immense Territory acquired at the late Peace will be advantageous to Great Britain. 8vo. Lond. 1765.

———. British Liberties. 8vo. Lond. 1766.

———. Application of some general Political Rules to the Present State of G. Britain, Ireland, and America. 8vo. Lond. 1766.

———. Collection of Tracts on Taxing the American Colonies and Regulating their Trade. 3 vols. 8vo. Lond. 1766—7.

———. Present State of Liberty in G. Britain and her Colonies. 12mo. Lond. 1769.

———. Substance of the Evidence before a Committee of the House of Commons, 8vo. Lond. 1774.

———. Description of the British Possessions in N. America. 8vo

———. Vide England. V. Scotland. V. Ireland. V. British Colonies. V. American Revolution. V. Parliament, &c.

Britain's Remembrancer; or the Danger not Over. 8vo. Lond. 1746.

British Colonies. Histoire et Commerce des Colonies Angloises dans l'Amérique Septentrionale. 12mo. Lond. 1755.

—— ——. Coloniæ Anglicanæ Illustratæ; or the Rights of the English Colonies Displayed. 4to. Lond. 1762. (By Bollan.)

—— ——. Essay on the Trade of the Northern Colonies in N. America. 8vo. Lond. 1764.

—— ——. Their Claim to an Exemption from Internal Taxes imposed by Parliament. 8vo. Lond. 1765.

—— ——. Letter from a Merchant in London to his Nephew in N. America relative to Affairs in the Colonies. 8vo. Lond. 1776.

—— ——. Late Occurrences in N. America and Policy of G. Britain considered. 8vo. Lond. 1766.

—— ——. Importance of the Colonies of N. America considered. 4to. Lond. 1766.

—— ——. True Interest of G. Britain with respect to them stated. 8vo. Lond. 1766.

—— ——. Considerations relative to the N. American Colonies. 8vo. Lond. 1765.

—— ——. Grievances of the American Colonies examined. 8vo. Lond. 1766.

—— ——. Considerations on the Propriety of Imposing Taxes on them. 2d ed. 8vo. Lond. 1766.

—— ——. Late Regulations respecting them considered, in a Letter from a Gentleman in Philadelphia. 8vo. Lond. 1765.

—— ——. Considerations on the Power of Parliament to Tax the N. American Colonies. 4to. Lond. 1766.

—— ——. Examination of their Rights upon Principles of Law. 8vo. Lond. 1766.

—— ——. Account of a late Conference on the Occurrences in N. America, in a Letter to a Friend. 8vo. Lond. 1766.

—— ——. Regulations lately made concerning them, &c. considered. 8vo. Lond. 1765.

—— ——. Their Rights Considered.—The Administration and Regulation of them Exploded. 8vo. Lond.

—— ——. Objections to the Taxation of them considered. 2d ed. 8vo. Lond. 1765.

—— ——. Considerations on behalf of the Colonists, in a Letter to a Noble Lord. 8vo. Lond. 1765.

—— ——. The Same. 2d ed. 8vo. Lond. 1765.

—— ——. Justice and Necessity of Taxing them considered. 8vo. Lond. 1766.

—— ——. Considerations on the Dependencies of G. Britain; with Observations on "The Present State of the Nation." 8vo. Lond. 1769.

—— ——. Strictures on the late Occurrences in N. America. 8vo. Lond. 1766.

—— ——. Short and Friendly Caution to the Good People of England. 8vo. Lond. 1766.

British Colonies. Plain and Seasonable Address to the Freeholders of G. Britain on the Present Posture of Affairs in America. 8vo. Lond. 1766.

——— ———. Letter to a Member of Parliament on the Power of the British Legislature, and the Case of the Colonists. 8vo. Lond. 1765.

——— ———. Legislative Authority of the British Parliament with respect to N. America, &c. considered. 8vo. Lond. 1766.

——— ———. True Interest of G. Britain in regard to the Trade and Government of Canada, Newfoundland, and Labrador. 8vo. Lond. 1767.

——— ———. Thoughts on the Origin and Nature of Government, occasioned by the Disputes between G. Britain and her American Colonies. 8vo. Lond. 1769.

——— ———. Importance of the British Dominion in India compared with that in America. 12mo. Lond. 1770.

——— ———. Constitutional Right of G. Britain to Tax them, stated. 8vo. Lond. 1768.

——— ———. Rights of the Colonies and the Extent of the Legislative Authority of G. Britain stated and considered. 8vo. Lond. 1769.

——— ———. True Constitutional Means for putting an end to the Disputes between G. Britain and the American Colonies. 8vo. Lond. 1769.

——— ———. Controversy between G. Britain and her Colonies Reviewed (by Mauduit.) 8vo. Lond. 1769.

——— ———. Inquiry into the Nature and Causes of the Present Disputes. 8vo. Lond. 1769.

——— ———. Letter to the Earl of Hilsborough on the Situation of Affairs in America. 8vo. Lond. 1769.

——— ———. Observations on the Review of the Controversy between G. Britain and her Colonies. 8vo. Lond. 1769.

——— ———. Remarks on the above "Review." 8vo. Lond. 1769.

——— ———. Humble Enquiry into the Nature of the Dependency of the American Colonies upon the Parliament of G. Britain, &c. by a Freeholder of S. Carolina. 8vo. 1769.

——— ———. Brittische Reich in America. 4to. Sorau. 1771.

——— ———. Britische Reich in America. Vide Arnold.

——— ———. Considerations on the Measures carrying on with respect to the Colonies in N. America. 8vo. Bost. 1774.

——— ———. Argument in Defence of their Exclusive Right to Tax themselves, &c. 8vo. Lond. 1774.

——— ———. The Other Side of the Question; or a Defence of the Liberties of N. America. 8vo. N. York. 1774.

——— ———. American Querist; or Questions relative to the present Disputes. 8vo. N. York. 1774.

——— ———. Interest of the Merchants and Manufacturers of G. Britain in the present Contest, considered. 8vo. Lond. 1774.

——— ———. Notiz der Grossbrittannischen Colonien in America. 12mo. Frank. und Leipz. 1776.

British Colonies. Beschryving der voornaamste Engelsche Volkplantingen in Noord-Amerika. 8vo. Amst. 1776.

——— ———. Further Examination of our present American Measures. 8vo. Bath. 1776.

——— ———. Conciliatory Address to the People of G. Britain and of the Colonies, on the present Important Crisis. 8vo. Lond. 1775.

——— ———. Historical Account of all the British Colonies in N. America. 8vo. Lond. 1775.

——— ———. Address of the People of G. Britain to the Inhabitants of America. 8vo. Lond. 1775.

——— ———. Crisis Extraordinary. 8vo. Phil.

——— ———. Beskrifning öfver de Engelska Colonierne i Nord-America. 8vo. Stockholm. 1777.

——— ———. Mutual Interest of G. Britain and the American Colonies considered.

——— ———. Letter to Lord Geo. Germaine, giving an Account of the Origin of the Dispute between G. Britain and the Colonies, &c. 8vo. Lond. 1778.

——— ———. Letter to the People of America. 8vo. Lond. 1778.

——— ———. History of the War in America between G. Britain and her Colonies to 1779.

——— ———. Letters to a Nobleman on the Conduct of the War in the Middle Colonies. 8vo. Lond. 1779.

——— ———. Rêveries d'un Suisse, ayant pour but la Réconciliation entre l'Angleterre et ses Colonies. 8vo. Lond. 1781.

——— ———. Reflexions sur l'Amérique, trad. de l'Anglois. 8vo. Amst. 1781.

——— ———. Essay on the Interests of G. Britain in regard to America. 8vo. Lond. 1780.

——— ———. Reflexions on the Conduct of the late Administration and Opposition, and of the American Congress. 8vo. Lond.

——— ———. Observations from a Gentleman in Town to his Friend in the Country relative to the Sugar Colonies. 8vo. Lond. 1781.

——— ———. Political Reflections on the late Colonial Governments. 8vo. Lond. 1783.

——— ———. Crisis of the Colonies considered. 8vo. Lond. 1785.

——— ———. Vide American Husbandry. V. American Revolution. V. Stamp-Act. V. Britain. V. Colonies. V. Canada. V. Indies. V. Congress. V. Massachusetts. V. Jamaica, etc.

British Drama, Ancient. 3 vols. 8vo. Lond. 1810.

——— ———, Modern. 5 vols. 8vo. Lond. 1811.

British Honour and Humanity, or the Wonders of American Patience. 8vo. Phil. 1796.

——— Liberties, or the Freeborn Subject's Inheritance, &c. 8vo. Lond. 1766.

——— Librarian, or Review of Books. 8vo. Lond. 1738.

British Museum. See Museum.
Britton, by Wingate. 12mo. Lond. 1640.
Broadfoot, Alex. Case of the King against. 4to. Oxford. 1758.
Brochant, A. J. M. Traité de Minéralogie. 2 vol. 8vo. Paris. 1801.
Brochardus, (Monachus.) Descriptio Terræ Sanctæ. (Ugol. v. 6.)
Brochmand, C. E. Systema Universæ Theologiæ, cum Commentario in Epistolam Jacobi. fol. Francof. 1658.
Bröder, Chr. Gott. Practische Grammatik der Lat. Sprache. 8vo. Leipz. 1815.
———, ———. Kleine Lat. Grammatik. 8vo. Leipz. 1815.
Brodie, B. C. On Diseases of the Joints. 8vo. Lond. 1818.
Brodie, Geo. History of the British Empire from the Accession of Charles I. to the Restoration, &c. 4 vols. 8vo. Edin. 1822.
Broes, B. Oratio de Literarum Sacrarum Studio. 4to. Lug. Bat. 1784.
Brograve, Rob. Sermon before the King and Queen. 4to. Lond. 1689.
Broke, George, Ld. Willoughby de. Charity Sermon. 4to. Lond. 1712.
Brome, Alex. Poems. See Chalmers.
Bromfield, Wm. Chirurgical Observations and Cases. 2 vols. 8vo. Lond. 1773.
Bromton, Johannes. Chronicon. (Twysden, Script. X.)
Broocks, Fr. Unglückiche Schiffarth in die Barbarey ; aus dem Französischen. 8vo. Stutt. 1748.
Brook, A. On Electricity, the Air-Pump, and Barometer. 8vo. Norwich. 1789.
Brook, Marie. Preuves de la Nécessité de s' attendre en Silence pour rendre un Hommage Solemnel à Dieu. 12mo. Lond. 1792.
Brooke, Edw. Bibliotheca Legum Angliæ. 2 vol. 12mo. Lond. 1788.
Brooke, Fulke Greville, Lord. Certaine Learned and Elegant Workes. 8vo. Lond. 1633.
———, ———. Five Years of King James. (Harl. Miscel. vol. 7.)
Brooke, Henry. Poems. See Chalmers.
Brooke, Rob. Reading on Magna Charta. Lond. 1641.
Brooke, Z. Examination of Middleton's Free Enquiry. 8vo. Camb. 1756.
Brookes, Richard. Introduction to Physic and Surgery. 8vo. Lond. 1754.
———, ———. Practice of Physic. 7th ed. 2 vols. 8vo. Lond. 1777.
———, ———. General Gazetteer. 8vo. Lond. 1791.
Brooks, Charles. Address to the Hingham Peace Society. 8vo. Bost. 1821.
Brooks, John. Anniversary Discourse before the Humane Society of Massachusetts. 4to. Bost. 1795.
Brooks, Tho. Golden Key to open Hidden Treasures. 4to. Lond. 1675.

Brooks, Wm. Penmanship. London.
Broome, Wm. Poems. See Chalmers.
Brosius, F. X. New Method of Finding the Latitude by Double Altitudes. 8vo. Cambridge. 1815.
Brosses, Charles de. Traité de la Formation Méchanique des Langues. 2 vol. 12mo. Paris. 1801.
———, ———. Histoire de la République Romaine, par Salluste, en partie trad. du Latin, etc. 3 vol. 4to. Dijon. 1777.
Broterus, F. A. Flora Lusitanica. 2 vol. 8vo. Olissiponæ. 1804.
Brougham, Henry. Inquiry into the Colonial Policy of the European Powers. 2 vols. 8vo. Edin. 1803.
Broughton, Hugh. Works; Scripture Chronology, Expositions, Controversy, &c. fol. Lond. 1662.
Broughton, Tho. Historical Dictionary of all Religions. fol. Lond. 1742.
———, ——. Defence of the Doctrine of the Human Soul as an Immaterial Principle. 8vo. Bristol. 1766.
———, ——. Prospect of Futurity. 8vo. Lond. 1768.
Brower, J. V. Popular Treatise on the Yellow Fever. 8vo. N. York. 1805.
Brown, And. Sermon on a Sea-faring Life. 8vo. Bost. 1793.
Brown, A. C. Colony Commerce. 8vo. Lond.
Brown, Charles Brockden. Novels. 6 vols. 12mo. Bost. 1827.
———, ———————. See Volney.
Brown, J. Letter to the Rev. W. E. Channing on his Sermon at Mr. Sparks's Ordination. 8vo.
Brown, John. Sermon on the Death of the Rev. Tho. Symmes. 12mo. Bost. 1726.
Brown, John. Sermon at Bath to aid the General Hospital. 8vo. Bath. 1750.
———, ——. Dissertation on Poetry and Music; with The Cure of Saul, an Ode. 4to. Lond. 1763.
——— ——. On Shaftesbury's Characteristics. 8vo. Lond. 1751.
——— ——. The Same. 8vo. Lond. 1752.
——— ——. Estimate of the Manners and Principles of the Times. 2 vols. 8vo. Lond. 1757.
——— ——. The Same, with Defence of it. 2 vols. 8vo. Lond. 1758.
——— ——. On Civil Liberty, Licentiousness, and Faction. 8vo. Lond. 1765.
Brown, John. Elements of Medicine, by Beddoes. 2 vols. 8vo. Lond. 1795.
Brown, Josiah. Cases in Parliament. 8 vols. 8vo. Dublin. 1784—9.
Brown, Sam. R. Western Gazetteer, or Emigrant's Directory. 8vo. Auburn, N. Y. 1817.
———, ———. Campaigns of the North Western Army, &c. 12mo. Troy, N. Y. 1814.
Brown, Tho. Lectures on the Philosophy of the Human Mind. 4 vols. 8vo. Edin. 1820.
———, ——. The Same. 3 vols. 8vo. Andover. 1822.

Brown, Tho. Inquiry into the Relation of Cause and Effect. 8vo. Edin. 1818.
———, ———. The Same. 8vo. Andover. 1822.
———, ———. Observations on Darwin's Zoonomia. 8vo. Edin. 1798.
———, ———. Renovation of India, a Poem; &c. 12mo. Edin. 1808.
———, ———. Treatise on the Philosophy of the Human Mind, abridged by L. Hedge. 2 vols. 8vo. Camb. 1827.
Brown, Wm. Formularum bene Placitandi Pars Secunda. fol. Lond. 1674.
Brown, Wm. Benefit and Comfort of the Christian Revelation, a Sermon. 8vo. Edin. 1736.
Brown, Wm. Cases in Chancery in the time of Thurlow, Commissioners, and Ld. Loughborough, from 1778 to 1794. 4 vols. 8vo. Dublin. 1786—94.
Brown, Wm. Oration, July 4th. 8vo. Hartford. 1799.
Brown, W. G. Travels in Africa, Egypt, and Syria. 2d ed. 4to. Lond. 1806.
Brown, Wm. Lawrence. On the Existence of a Supreme Creator possessed of Infinite Power, Wisdom, and Goodness. 2 vols. 8vo. Aberdeen. 1816.
———, ———. Sermons. 8vo. Edin. 1803.
———, ———. On the Natural Equality of Men, &c. 12mo. Lond. 1794.
———, ———. Philemon, or the Progress of Virtue. 2 vols. 12mo. Edin. 1809.
Browne, Arthur. Sermon on the Excellency of the Christian Religion. 8vo. Bost. 1738.
Browne, Isaac H. Poems, Latin and English. 4to. Lond. 1768.
———, ———. Pipe of Tobacco. 8vo. Lond. 1744.
———, ———. De Animi Immortalitate. 4to. Lond. 1754.
Browne, John. Sermon on the Death of the Rev. Dr. Mayhew. 8vo. Bost. 1766.
Browne, Patrick. Civil and Natural History of Jamaica. fol. Lond. 1789.
Browne, Peter, (Bp.) On the Human Understanding. 8vo. Lond. 1737.
———, ———. Things Divine and Supernatural conceived by Analogy with Things Natural and Human. 8vo. Lond. 1733.
———, ———. Answer to the above, by a Presbyter of the Church of England. 8vo. Lond. 1733.
Browne, Rich. De Principiis. 12mo. Lond. 1678.
Browne, Simon. Sermon on the King's Nativity. 8vo. Lond. 1721.
———, ———. Sermons on Several Subjects. 8vo. Lond. 1722.
———, ———. Sermon on Reformation of Manners. 8vo. Lond. 1718.
———, ———. Accession Sermon. 8vo. Lond. 1715.
———, ———. Another. 8vo. Lond. 1719.
———, ———. Sermons on the 5th of Nov. 8vo. Lond. 1715—6.

Browne, Simon. Sermon, January 30th. 8vo. Lond. 1716.
———, ———. Regulations of Diversions, on the Fifth of November. Lond. 1712.
———, ———. Fit Rebuke to a Ludicrous Infidel; in some Remarks on Mr. Woolston's Fifth Discourse. 8vo. Lond. 1732.
———, ———. Defence of the Religion of Nature, and the Christian Revelation. 8vo. Lond. 1732.
———, ———. Close of the Defence. 8vo. Lond. 1733.
———, ———. Disquisition concerning the Trinity. 8vo. Lond. 1732.
———, ———. Letter to the Rev. Th. Reynolds, occasioned by a Passage in his Sermon on Mr. Pomfret. 8vo. Lond. 1723.
———, ———. Letter to him on the Faith of Ministers. 8vo. Lond. 1723.
Browne, T. Concio ad Clerum. 4to. Cantab. 1688.
———, —. Concio coram Acad. Cantab. 4to. Cantab. 1688.
Browne, Tho. British Cicero. 3 vols. 8vo. Phil. 1810.
Browne, Sir Tho. Pseudodoxia Epidemica; or Enquiries into Vulgar Errors. fol. Lond. 1686.
———, ———. Works. fol. Lond. 1686.
———, ———. Christian Morals, with his Life, by Johnson. 16mo. Lond. 1756.
Browne, Wm. Poems. See Chalmers.
Brownell, T. C. Family Prayer-Book, or Book of Common Prayer. 4to. 1823.
Brownlow, Richard. Declarations and Pleadings. 2 vols. 4to. Lond. 1653.
———, ———. Entries. fol. Lond. 1693.
———, ———. Brevia Judicialia. fol. Lond. 1662.
Browlow and Goldsborough. Reports in C. B. temp. Eliz. et Jac. I. 4to. Lond. 1652—4.
Brownrig, Ralph, (Bp.) Sixty-five Sermons. fol. Lond. 1674.
Bruce, A. Lectures for Young Men intended for the Ministry. 8vo. Whitburn. 1797.
Bruce, Archibald. American Mineralogical Journal. Nos. 1—3 of vol. 1. 8vo. N. York. 1810.
Bruce, James. Travels to Discover the Source of the Nile. 5 vols. 4to. Edin. 1790.
———, ———. Travels abridged. 12mo. Bost. 1798.
Brucioli, Ant. La Biblia, trad. de la Heb. e Gr. in Lingua Toscana. fol. Vinetia. 1541.
Bruckerus, Jac. Institutiones Historiæ Philosophicæ. 8vo. Lips. 1747.
———, —. Historia Critica Philosophiæ. 6 vol. 4to. Lips. 1766—7.
———, —. Notitia Rarissimæ Versionis Germanicæ Libri Psalmorum. (Schelhorn, vol. 6.)
———, —. See Enfield.
Bruell, Walter. Praxis Medicinæ. 4to. Lond. 1648.
Bruguières. Histoire des Vers (Encyclopédie Méthodique.)

Brumoy, P. Greek Theatre, tr. by Mrs. Lennox. 3 vols. 4to. Lond. 1759.

Brun, Jean B. Le Triomphe du Nouveau Monde. 2 vol. 8vo. Paris. 1785.

Brunck, R. F. P. Vide Analecta.

———, ———. Index to the Analecta. (Class. Journ. vol. 10.)

Brunet, J. C. Manuel du Libraire. 3 vol. 8vo. Paris. 1810.

Brunn, J. C. Glandulæ Duodeni. 4to. Francof. et Heidel. 1715.

Brunne, Robert of. Peter Langtoft's Chronicle Illustrated and Improved. Vide Hearne, Langtoft.

Brunst, Aug. Chr. De Monothelismo Honorii Papæ. 4to. Vitembergæ. 1710.

Brunton, Alex. Sermons and Lectures. 8vo.

Brunus, Jordanus. Cantus Circæus. 16mo. Paris. 1577.

Brush. Speech in the General Assembly of N. York against sending Delegates to the General Congress. 8vo. N York. 1775.

Brutes. Clemency to Brutes; the Substance of Two Sermons. 8vo. Dublin. 1769.

Brutus, J. M. Historia Florentina. (Græv. Thes. Ital.)

Brutus, Steph. Junius. Vide Languet.

Bruycker, Jac. de. De Peccatis Typicis. 4to. Jenæ. 1706.

Bruyère, J. de la. Les Caractères de Theophraste, avec les Caractères de ce Siècle. 12mo.

———, ———. Idem. 2 vol. 12mo. Amst. 1743.

Bruyn, Corn. le. Voyages au Levant. 5 vol. 4to. La Haye. 1732.

———, ———. Travels into Muscovy, Persia, &c. from the French. 2 vols. fol. Lond. 1737.

Bry, Theod. de. America. Partes 1—5, et 9. 2 vol. fol. Francof. 1590—1602.

———, ———. Idem. Partes 1—9. 10 tom. fol. Francof. 1590—1625.

———, ———. Africa et India Orientalis. Partes 1—9. 9 tom. fol. Francof. 1601—29.

———, ———. America, ins Deutsche übersetzung. Theile 1—7. fol. Franck. 1590—7.

Bryan, Augustin. Sermon at the Election of Lord Mayor. 8vo. Lond. 1718.

Bryant, C. History of Esculent Plants.

Bryant, Jacob. Observations and Enquiries relating to Ancient History. 4to. Camb. 1767.

———, ———. Analysis of Ancient Mythology. 3 vols. 4to. Lond. 1775—6.

———, ———. Sentiments of Philo Judeus concerning the Logos. 8vo. Camb. 1797.

———, ———. Vocabulary of the Gypsey Language. (Archæol. vol. 7.)

———, ———. Observations on some Passages in Scripture. 4to. Lond. 1803.

Bryant, Wm. Cullen. Embargo. 12mo. Bost. 1808.

Bryant, Wm. Cullen. The Same, with other Poems. 12mo. Bost. 1809.

——, ————. Poems. 12mo. Camb. 1821.

Brydges, Henry. Speech to the Clergy of the Diocese of Rochester. 4to. Lond. 1721.

——, ——. Sermon, January 30th. 12mo. Lond. 1709.

Brydone, P. Tour through Sicily and Malta. 2 vols. 8vo. Lond. 1776.

——, —. The Same. 2 vols. 8vo. Lond. 1790.

Buache, Phil. Considérations Géographiques et Physiques sur les Nouvelles Découvertes au Nord de la Grande Mer. 4to. Paris. 1753.

Buc, Sir Geo. Life and Reign of Richard III.

—, ———. Treatise of the Schools in London.

Bucaniers. Historie der Boecaniers of Vrybuyters van America. 4to. Amst. 1700.

Bucanus, Gul. Intitutiones Theologicæ. 12mo. Genevæ. 1617.

——, —. ————————. 12mo. Genevæ. 1630.

Bucer, Martin. Psalterium Davidis cum Familiari Explanatione. fol. Basil. 1547.

——, ———. Originall of Bishops and Metropolitans. See Usher.

Buch, Léopold de. Essai d'une Déscription Minéralogique des Environs de Landeck, trad. de l'Allemand. 8vo. Paris. 1805.

Buchan, A. P. On Sea Bathing, &c. 12mo. Lond. 1810.

Buchan, Wm. Domestic Medicine. 8vo. Lond. 1772.

Buchanan, Claudius. On the Expediency of an Ecclesiastical Establishment for British India. 8vo. Camb. 1811.

————, ————. Works; Researches in Asia, &c. 12mo. Albany. 1812.

————, ————. Star in the East, a Sermon on Oriental Missions. 8vo. Bost. 1811.

Buchanan, Francis. Journey through Mysore, Canara, and Malabar. 3 vols. 4to. Lond. 1807.

Buchanan, James. Plan for an English Grammar-School Education. 12mo. Lond. 1770.

Buchanan, Joseph. Philosophy of Human Nature. 8vo. Richmond, Ky. 1812.

Buchananus, Geo. Opera Omnia, cura Ruddimanni, cum Præfatione Burmanni. 2 vol. 4to. Lug. Bat. 1725.

——————, —. Rerum Scoticarum Historia. fol. Edin. 1582.

——————, —. Due Priviledge of the Scotch Government; from the Latin. 4to. Lond. 1689.

——————, —. The Same. 8vo. 1721.

——————, —. Detection of Mary, Queen of Scots; from the Latin.—Geneologie of the Kings of Scotland. 8vo. 1721.

——————, —. Psalmorum Davidis Paraphrasis Poetica. 8vo. apud H. Stephanum.

——————, —. Odæ. Vide Poemata Italorum.

Bucherus, Sam. Frid. Synedrium Magnum. (Ugol. vol. 25.)

————, ————. De Velato Hebr. Gynæceo. (Id. 29.)

————, ————. De Unctione in Bethania. (Id. 30.)

Bucherus, Sam. Frid. Antiquitates Biblicæ ex Nov. Test. Selectæ. 4to. Vitemb. et Lips. 1729.
Buchlerus, Jo. Thesaurus Poeticus. ed. 13tia. 16mo. Lond. 1642.
———, —. Idem. ed. 18va. 16mo. Lond. 1679.
Buchoz, P. J. Figures des Animaux, etc. fol. Paris. 1778.
Buchwaldus, J. S. De Atheismo. 4to. Vitembergæ. 1716.
Bucke, Charles. On the Beauties, Harmonies, and Sublimities of Nature, &c. 4 vols. 8vo. Lond. 1823.
Buckfisch, Fr. Geo. De Apostolis Uxoratis. 4to. Vitemb. 1734.
Buckingham, Geo. Villiers, Duke of. Discourse on Religion. (Som. Tr. vol. 7.)
Buckingham, Tho. Connecticut Election Sermon. 16mo. N. Lond. 1729.
Buckler, Benj. Vindication of the Mallard of All-Souls College. 8vo. Lond. 1750.
Buckley, Sam. Letter to Dr. Mead concerning a New Edition of Thuanus's History. 8vo. Lond. 1728.
Buckminster, Joseph. Two Discourses on Family Religion. 16mo. Bost. 1759.
———, ———. Discourse at the Interment of the Rev. S. Haven and his Wife. 8vo. Portsmouth. 1806.
Buckminster, Jos. S. Catalogue of his Library. 8vo. Bost. 1812.
———, ———. Sermons, with his Life (by S. C. Thacher.) 8vo. Bost. 1814.
———, ———. The Same. 2d ed. 8vo. Bost. 1815.
———, ———. Sermon at the Funeral of the Rev. Wm. Emerson. 8vo. Bost. 1811.
———, ———. Sermon on the Death of Gov. Sullivan. 8vo. Bost. 1809.
———, ———. Address to the Phi Beta Kappa Society. (Monthly Anthology, vol. 7.)
Budæus, Gul. Commentarii Linguæ Græcæ. fol. Paris. 1548.
Buddeus, Jo. Franc. Theses Theologicæ de Atheismo et Superstitione. 8vo. Traj. ad Rhen. 1737.
———, ———. Institutiones Theologiæ Dogmaticæ. 4to. Francof. et Lips. 1741.
———, ———. Miscellanea Sacra. 3 vol. 4to. Jenæ. 1727.
———, ———. Dissertatio Moralis de Cultura Ingenii. 4to. Halæ, Magd. 1699.
———, ———. De Jure Zelotarum in Gente Ebræa. (Oelrichs, Col. Opusculorum.)
———, ———. De Pelagianismo in Ecclesia Romana. 4to. Jenæ. 1719.
———, ———. De Concordia Religionis Christianæ, Statusque Civilis, etc. 12mo. Halæ. 1712.
———, ———. Introductio ad Hist. Philos. Ebræorum; cum Dissertatione de Hæresi Valent. 12mo. Halæ. 1702.
———, ———. Analecta Historiæ Philosophicæ. 12mo. Halæ. 1724.
Budgell, Eustace. Memoirs of the Boyles. 8vo. Lond. 1737.
———, ———. Papers in the Spectator.

Buenos Ayres. Relation of R. M's Voyage to Buenos Ayres, and thence by land to Potosi. 12mo. Lond. 1716.

Buffon, G. L. le Clerc, Comte de. Histoire Naturelle. 24 vol. 4to. Paris. 1749—83.

——, ————. Supplément. 6 vol. 4to. Paris. 1774—82.

——, ————. Natural History, tr. by Kenrick and others. 6 vols. 8vo. Lond. 1775.

——, ————. Histoire Naturelle des Minéraux. 3 vol. 4to. Paris. 1783—5.

——, ————. Histoire Naturelle des Oiseaux. 10 vol. fol. Paris. 1771—86.

Bugg, Fr. Pilgrim's Progress from Quakerism to Christianity. 8vo. Lond. 1700.

Buisson, P. U. du. Abrégé de la Révolution de l'Amérique Angloise, jusqu'au premier Janvier, 1778. 12mo. Paris. 1778.

——, ——. Nouvelles Considérations sur St. Domingue. 8vo. Paris. 1780.

Bulengerus, J. C. De Oraculis et Vatibus.—De Templis Ethnicorum.—De Ludis Veterum. (Gronov. vol. 7.)

——, —. De Pictura, Plastice, etc. (Id. 9.)

——, —. De Triumphis, Spoliis Bellicis, etc. (Id. 11.)

——, —. De Sortibus.—De Auguriis et Auspiciis.—De Ominibus.—De Prodigiis.—De Terræ Motu et Fulminibus. (Græv. vol. 5.)

——, —. De Tributis ac Vectigalibus Pop. Rom. (Id. 8.)

——, —. De Circo Romano, Ludisque Circensibus; de Venatione Circi, etc. (Id. 9.)

——, —. De Conviviis. (Id. 12.)

Bulifon, Ant. Lettere. 4 vol. 12mo. Napoli. 1698.

——, —. Dell' Assedio di Vienna. 16mo. Napoli. 1684.

——, —. Descrizione dello Stendardo Regale del Gran Turco. 16mo. Nap. 1684.

Bulkeley, Benj. Sermon at Bridgwater at the Mayor's Entrance into Office. 4to. Lond. 1722.

Bulkeley, Peter. The Gospel Covenant. 4to. Lond. 1651.

Bulkley, Charles. Discourses. 8vo. Lond. 1752.

——, ——. Œconomy of the Gospel. 4to. Lond. 1764.

——, ——. Two Discourses on Catholic Communion. 8vo. Lond. 1754.

——, ——. Discourses on the Parables and Miracles of our Saviour. 4 vols. 8vo. Lond. 1771.

——, ——. Observations on Natural Religion and Christianity. 8vo. Lond. 1757.

——, ——. Vindication of Lord Shaftesbury's Writings.

Bulkley, John. Sermon before the Connecticut General Assembly. 16mo. 1713.

Bull. The famous Bull, in Cœna Domini. 4to. 1688.

Bull, Geo. (Bp.) Opera Omnia, Latine conscripta, cura Grabii. fol. Lond. 1703.

——, ——. Idem. fol. Lond. 1721.

Bull, Geo. (Bp.) Works; with his Life, by Nelson. 4 vols. 8vo. Lond. 1713.
——, ———. Defensio Fidei Nicænæ ex Veterum Scriptis. 4to. Oxon. 1688.
——, ———. Judgment of the Fathers concerning the Trinity opposed to Bp. Bull. Part. I. 4to. Lond. 1695.
Bullard, John. Discourse on Agriculture. 8vo.
Bullarium Magnum Romanum. 10 vol. fol. Lugduni et Luxemburgi. 1655—1758.
Bullet, J. B. Mémoires sur la Langue Celtique. 3 vol. fol. Besançon. 1754—60.
——, ——. History of the Establishment of Christianity; from the French, with Notes, by Wm. Salisbury. 8vo. Lond. 1771.
Bulletin Météorologique, Oct. 1817. 8vo. Paris.
——— Universelle. Vide Férussac.
Bullialdus, Ism. (Boulliau.) Astronomia Philolaica. fol. Paris. 1645.
Bulliard. Herbier de la France. 12 tom. fol. Paris. 1780—93.
———. Histoire des Plantes Vénéneuses et Suspectes de la France. fol. Paris. 1784.
———. Histoire des Champignons de la France. fol. Paris. 1791.
———. Dictionnaire Elémentaire de Botanique. fol. Paris. 1783.
———. Idem. fol. Paris. 1797.
Bullingerus, Heinr. In Omnes Apostolicas Epistolas; item de Testamento Dei unico et æterno; et de Utraque in Christo Natura. fol. Tiguri. 1539.
————, ——. Archetypi Homiliarum in Apocalypsin Johannis, etc. 12mo. Tiguri. 1602.
Bullock, Thomas. The Reasoning of Christ and his Apostles considered in Seven Sermons. 8vo. Lond. 1725.
———, ————. The Same vindicated. 8vo. Lond. 1728.
———, ————. The Gospel a Reinforcement of the Law of Nature; a Sermon. 8vo. Lond. 1730.
———, ————. Remarks upon a Letter to the Archbishop of York. 4to. Norwich. 1756.
Bullock, Wm. Virginia Impartially Examined. 4to. Lond. 1649.
Bülow, D. Von. Der Freistaat von Nordamerika. 12mo. Berlin. 1797.
Bulstrode, Edw. Reports of Cases in the time of James I. and Charles I. fol. Lond. 1688.
Bulstrode, Sir Rich. Miscellaneous Essays. 8vo. Lond. 1715.
Bunbury, Wm. Reports in Exchq. from 1 Geo. I. to 14 Geo. II. 8vo. Dublin. 1793.
Buncle, John. Antiquarian Doctor's Sermon on an Antiquated Subject. 8vo. Lond. 1767.
Bundy, R. Roman History. See Catrou and Rouillé.
Bunon, M. Expériences et Démonstrations faites à l'Hôpital de la Salpêtrière, etc. 12mo. Paris. 1746.
Bunyan, John. Pilgrim's Progress. 22d ed. 8vo. Lond. 1728.

Bunyan, John. The Same. 30th ed. 12mo. Edin. 1755.
Buommattei, Bened. Della Lingua Toscana. 4to. Venezia. 1735.
———, ———. Idem. 2 vol. 8vo. Milano. 1807.
Buonaparte. Vide Bonaparte.
Buonarruoti, Filippo. Frammenti di Vasi Antichi di Vetro. fol. Firenze. 1716.
Buonarruoti, Michelagnolo, (il Giovane.) La Fiera, e la Tancia Commedia. fol. Firenze. 1721.
Burchiello del Bellincioni, Sonetti del, e d' altri Poeti Fiorentini alla Burchiellesca. 8vo. Lond. 1751.
Burckhardt, J. L. Travels in Nubia. 4to. Lond. 1819.
———, —. Travels in Syria and the Holy Lond. 4to. Lond. 1822.
Burder, George. The Welch Indians. 8vo. Lond. 1797.
Burder, Sam. Oriental Customs. 6th. ed. 2 vols. 8vo. Lond. 1822.
Burdick, Wm. Oration on Printing. 8vo. Bost. 1802.
Burette, P. J. Sur la Danse des Anciens.—Sur les Athlètes. (Acad. des Inscrip. vol. 1.)
———, ———. Sur la Lutte des Anciens.—Sur le Pugilat des Anciens.—Sur la Course des Anciens. (Id. 3.)
———, ———. Examen du Traité de Plutarque sur la Musique, etc. (Id. 8, 10, 13, 15, 17.)
———, ———. De Veterum Symphonia. (Ugol. vol. 32.)
Bürger, G. A. Akademie der Schönen Redekünste. 12mo.
Burgersdicius, Fr. Institutiones Metaphysicæ. 16mo. Lug. Bat. 1642.
———, —. Logica. 12mo. Lug. Bat. 1642.
———, —. ———. 12mo. Cantab. 1680.
———, —. Collegium Physicnm. 24to. Lug. Bat. 1642.
———, —. Idea Philosophiæ. 16mo. Oxon. 1631.
———, —. ———. 16mo. Oxon. 1667.
———, —. Abstract and Translation of his Logic. 12mo. Lond. 1697.
Burges, Barthol. On the Solar System. 12mo. Bost. 1789.
Burges, Corn. Concerning Bishops Lands. Lond. 1659.
Burges, John. Answer to a "Reply to Dr. Moreton's Defence of Three Nocent Ceremonies."—Lawfulnes of Kneeling at the Sacrament. 4to. Lond. 1631.
Burgess, Anthony. Spirituall Refinings, in CLXI Sermons. fol. Lond. 1658.
Burgess, Dan. Golden Snuffers; a Reformation of Manners Sermon. 12mo. Lond. 1697.
Burgh, James. Hymn to the Creator, &c. 8vo. Lond. 1750.
———, ———. Britain's Remembrancer. 8vo. Lond. 1746.
———, ———. Dignity of Human Nature. 8vo. Lond. 1767.
———, ———. Political Disquisitions. 3 vols. 8vo. Lond. 1774—5.
———, ———. The Same. 3 vols. 8vo. Phil. 1775.
———, ———. Art of Speaking. 8vo. Lond. 1761.
———, ———. Crito, or Essays on Various Subjects. 2 vols. 12mo. Lond. 1766—7.

Burgoyne, J. (Gen.) Letter to his Constituents upon his late Resignation, with the Correspondence relative to his Return to America. 5th ed. 8vo. Lond. 1779.

———, ———. Reply to his Letter to his Constituents. 8vo. Lond. 1779.

———, ———. State of the Expedition from Canada. 4to. Lond. 1780.

———, ———. Remarks on the "State of the Expedition." 8vo. Lond. 1780.

———, ———. Letter to him occasioned by a Second Edition of his "State of the Expedition." 8vo. Lond. 1780.

Burguillos, Tomé de. Rimas Humanas y Divinas. 12mo. Madrid. 1792.

Burigny, L'Evesque de. Life of Grotius; from the French. 8vo. Lond. 1754.

———, ———. Storia Generale di Sicilia, trad. dal Francese. 6 vol. 4to. Palermo. 1787—92.

Burius, Guil. Romanorum Pontificum Brevis Notitia. 12mo. Patavii. 1724.

Burk, John. History of Virginia. vol. 1. 8vo. Petersburg, Va. 1804.

Burke, Ædanus. Address to the Freemen of South Carolina. 8vo. Phil. 1783.

———, ———. Observations on his "Considerations upon the Order of the Cincinnati." 8vo. Phil. 1783.

Burke, Edmund. Works. 8 vols. 8vo. Lond. 1801.

———, ———. ———. 6 vols. 8vo. Boston and N. York. 1806—13.

———, ———. European Settlements in America. 2 vols. 8vo. Lond. 1760.

———, ———. The Same. 6th ed. 2 vols. 8vo. Lond. 1778.

———, ———. Storia degli Stabilimenti in America. 2 vol. 8vo. Venezia. 1763.

———, ———. Geschichte der Englischen Pflauzungen in Nord-Amerika; aus dem Englischen. 4 Theile. Danzig. 1777.

———, ———. Geschichte der Englischen Kolonien in Nord-America; aus dem Englischen. 12mo. 2 Thle. Leipz. 1775.

———, ———. On the Sublime and Beautiful. 8vo. Lond. 1760,

———, ———. The Same. 8vo. Lond. 1761.

———, ———. Life. See Bisset. See Prior.

———, ———. Speech on American Taxation. April 19, 1774. 8vo. Lond. 1775.

———, ———. Speech on Moving his Resolutions for Conciliation with the Colonies, March 22, 1775. 8vo. Lond. 1775.

———, ———. Letter to the Sheriffs of Bristol on the Affairs of America. 8vo. Lond. 1777.

———, ———. Answer to the Same. 8vo. Lond. 1777.

———, ———. Thoughts on the Same. See Abingdon.

———, ———. Appeal from the New to the Old Whigs. 8vo. Lond. 1791.

———, ———. The Same. 8vo. N. York. 1791.

Burke, Edmund. Speech on Mr. Fox's E. India Bill. 8vo. Lond. 1784.

——, ———. Letter to a noble Lord. 8vo. Lond. 1796.

——, ———. Reflections on the French Revolution. 8vo. Lond. 1790.

Burkitt, Wm. Expository Notes and Practical Observations on the New Testament. 5th ed. fol. Lond. 1712.

Burlamaqui, J. J. Principes du Droit Naturel. 12mo. Genève. 1748.

———, ——. Principles of Natural and Political Law, tr. by Nugent. 2 vols. 8vo. Lond. 1763.

———, ——. The Same. 2 vols. 8vo. Camb. 1807.

Burleigh, Lord. See Cecil.

Burmannus, Fr. Oratio de Theologi Docentis Officio. 4to. Traj. ad Rhen. 1743.

Burmannus, Joan. Thesaurus Zeylanicus, exhibens Plantas in Insula Zeylana nascentes. 4to. Amst. 1737.

———, ——. Rariorum Africanarum Plantarum Decades X. 4to. Amst. 1738.

Burmannus, Nic. Laur. Flora Indica, etc. 4to. Lug. Bat. 1768.

Burmannus, Pet. Vectigalia Populi Romani, et Jupiter Fulgerator. 4to. Leidæ. 1734.

———. ——. Sylloges Epistolarum a Viris Illustribus Scriptarum. 5 vol. 4to. Leidæ. 1727.

Burn, Rich. Ecclesiastical Law. 2 vols. 4to. Lond. 1763.

——, ——. History of the Poor Laws. 8vo. Lond. 1764.

——, ——. Justice of the Peace and Parish Officer. 10th ed. 4 vols. 8vo. Lond. 1766.

——, ——. The Same. 18th ed. 4 vols. 8vo. Lond. 1793.

——, ——. The Same, abridged. 4to. Bost. 1773.

Burnaby, And. Travels through the Middle Settlements in North America. 8vo. Lond. 1775.

——, ——. Reisen durch die Mittlern Kolonien der Engländer in Nord-Amerika; aus dem Englischen. 12mo. Hamb. und Kiel. 1776.

Burnap, Jacob. Discourse at the Funeral of R. M. Davidson. 8vo. Amherst. 1808.

Burnet, Geo. Specimens of English Prose Writers. 3 vols. 12mo. Lond. 1807.

Burnet, Gilb. (Bp.) Sermon on Peace and Union. 4to. Lond. 1689.

——, ———. Sermon before the King and Queen on Christmas Day. 4to. Lond. 1689.

——, ———. Sermon before the Lord Mayor. 8vo. Lond. 1711.

——, ———. Sermon before King George. 8vo. Lond. 1714.

——, ———. Abridgement of Sermons at Boyle's Lecture. 4 vols. 8vo. Lond. 1765.

——, ———. Charity Sermon. 8vo. Lond. 1714.

Burnet, Gilb. (Bp.) Sermons, with an Essay towards a New Book of Homilies. 8vo. Lond. 1713.

——, ————. Thanksgiving Sermon. 8vo. and 4to. Lond. 1707.

——, ————. Restoration Sermon. 8vo. Lond. 1710.

——, ————. Sermon, November 5th. 8vo. Lond. 1710.

——, ————. Sermon, November 7th. 8vo. Lond. 1710.

——, ————. Sermon, January 30th. 2d ed. 4to. Lond. 1681.

——, ————. History of the Reformation of the Church of England. 3 vols. fol. Lond. 1681—1715.

——, ————. The Same. 3 vols. fol. Lond. 1715.

——, ————. ————. 3 vols. fol. Dublin. 1730—3.

——, ————. Reflections on the Above. 4to. Amst. 1688.

——, ————. Abridgement of the History. 3 vols. 12mo. Lond. 1719.

——, ————. Sermon on the 29th of May. 8vo. Lond. 1710.

——, ————. Apology for the Church of England. 4to.

——, ————. Exposition of the Church Catechism. 8vo. Lond. 1710.

——, ————. Reasons against Repealing the Test Acts. 4to. 1687.

——, ————. Remarks on King Charles II.'s Papers concerning Religion. 4to. 1689.

——, ————. Vindication of the Ordinations of the Church of England. 4to. Lond. 1688.

——, ————. Exposition of the xxxix Articles. fol. Lond. 1720.

——, ————. Discourse concerning Transubstantiation and Idolatry. 4to. Lond. 1688.

——, ————. Letter to Mr. Trapp on the Nature of the Church of Christ. 8vo. Lond. 1717.

——, ————. Answer to Mr. Law's Letter to the Bp. of Bangor. 8vo. Lond. 1717.

——, ————. Opposition of the Doctrine &c. of the Roman Church to the Nature &c. of the Christian Faith. 4to. Lond. 1688.

——, ————. Discourse of the Pastoral Care. 8vo. Lond. 1692.

——, ————. The Same. 12mo. Lond. 1736.

——, ————. Collections of Papers against Popery and Arbitrary Government. 4to. Amst. 1689.

——, ————. Memoirs of James and William, Dukes of Hamilton, &c. fol. Lond. 1677.

——, ————. Life of Sir Matthew Hale. 12mo. Lond. 1682.

——. ————. Life of Bishop Bedell. 8vo. Lond. 1685.

——, ————. Essay on the Memory of the late Queen. 12mo. Lond. 1695.

——, ————. Life and Reign of William III. 8vo. Lond. 1702.

Burnet, Gilb. (Bp.) Life of John, Earl of Rochester. 12mo. Lond. 1782.

——, ———. Specimen of Dr. Burnet's Behaviour. 8vo. Lond.

——, ———. Vindication of himself against the Pamphlet entitled "Parliamentum Pacificum." 4to. Lond. 1688.

——, ———. Full Answer to the Conduct of the Allies. 8vo. Lond. 1712.

——, ———. Rights of Princes to Dispose of Benefices, &c. 8vo. Lond. 1682.

——, ———. Letters concerning Switzerland, &c. 8vo. Rotterdam. 1686.

——, ———. The Same. 8vo. Lond. 1724.

——, ———. Supplement to the Letters. 12mo. 1688.

——, ———. Travels through France, Italy, Germany, and Switzerland. 12mo. Lond. 1750.

——, ———. History of his Own Time. 2 vols. fol. Lond. 1724—34.

——, ———. The Same. 4 vols. 8vo. Lond. 1753.

——, ———. Remarks on the History of his Own Time.—Impartial Reflexions on the Same.—Review of it.—Vindication against Cockburn. 8vo. Lond. 1724.

——, ———. Remarks on Lord Landsdowne's Letter. 4to. Lond. 1732.

——, ———. Historical Remarks on the Second Volume of the History. 8vo. Lond. 1734.

——, ———. Letter to T. Burnet on the Castrations, &c. in the History.—Remarks on the Letter. 8vo. Lond. 1736.

Burnet, Thomas. Demonstration of True Religion, in XVI Sermons at Boyle's Lecture. 2 vols. 8vo. 1726.

——, ———. The Same. fol. Lond. 1739.

——, ———. Argument in "Christianity as old as the Creation" Confuted. 8vo. Lond. 1730.

——, ———. Essay on the Power of Human Reason. 8vo. Lond. 1732.

——, ———. De Fide et Officiis Christianorum. 4to. Lond. 1722.

——, ———. Idem. 8vo. Lond. 1733.

——, ———. Scripture-Trinity Explained. 8vo. Lond. 1720.

——, ———. Scripture Doctrine of Redemption Explained. 8vo. Lond. 1737.

——, ———. Sermon on Love and Unity. 8vo. Lond. 1722.

Burnet, Tho. Archæologiæ Philosophicæ. 8vo. Lond. 1733.

——, ———. Sacred Theory of the Earth. 2 vols. 8vo. Lond. 1759.

Burnett, Wm. On the Mediterranean Fever. 8vo. Lond. 1816.

Burney, C. Tentamen de Metris ab Æschylo in Choricis Cantibus adhibitis.

Burney, James. Chronological History of the Voyages and Discoveries in the South Sea and Pacific Ocean. 5 vols. 4to. Lond. 1803—17.

Burnham, Wm. Connecticut Election Sermon. 16mo. N. Lond. 1722.
Burns, John. Midwifery, by Buchanan. 8vo. N. York. 1810.
———, ———. On Inflammation. 2 vols. 8vo. Albany. 1812.
Burns, Rob. Works, with his Life, &c. 4 vols. 8vo. Lond. 1803.
Burr, Aaron. Sermon before the Synod of N. York. 8vo. N. York. 1757.
———, ———. Fast Sermon. 8vo. N. York. 1755.
———, ———. Supreme Deity of Christ maintained. 8vo. Bost. 1757.
Burr, Aaron, (Vice-Pres.) Examination of the Charges against him, by Aristides. 8vo. N. York. 1803.
———, ———————. The Same. 8vo. Virginia. 1804.
Burridge, Ezek. Historia Nuperæ Rerum Mutationis in Anglia. 8vo. Lond. 1697.
Burriel, And. Marc. Histoire Naturelle et Civile de la Californie, trad. de l'Anglois par M. E. (Eidous.) 3 vol. 12mo. Paris. 1767.
Burroughs, James. Occasional Sermons. 8vo. Lond. 1733.
Burroughs, Jer. Moses his Self-Denyall. 12mo. Lond. 1649.
———, ——. Rare Jewel of Christian Contentment. 4to. Lond. 1651.
———, ——. Saint's Duty in Time of Extremity. 4to. 1751.
———, ——. Sermon, Nov. 5th. 8vo. Lond. 1716.
———, ——. Exposition of Hosea. 4to.
Burroughs, Joseph. Sermons and Tracts. 2 vols. 8vo. Lond. 1713.
———, ———. Sermons, with an Oration de Locorum Sanctitate. 8vo. Lond. 1741.
———, ———. Sermon on the Death of Dr. John Gale. 8vo. Lond. 1722.
———, ———. Two Sermons on the Right Manner of Contending for the Faith, and on the Traditions of the Church of Rome. 8vo. Lond. 1732.
———, ———. Sermon on Auricular Confession and Priestly Absolution. 8vo. Lond. 1735.
———, ———. New Year's Sermon. 8vo. Lond. 1737.
———, ———. Sermon to the Society for Relieving Widows and Orphans of Dissenting Ministers. 8vo. Lond. 1743.
———, ———. Sermon at an Ordination of Deacons. 8vo. Lond. 1730.
———, ———. Sermon at the Ordination of the Rev. Richard Barron. 8vo. Lond. 1753.
———, ———. Sermon on the Death of the Rev. J. Kimber. 8vo. Lond. 1755.
———, ———. Sermon on the Death of the Rev. J. Norris. 8vo. Lond. 1755.
———, ———. Sermon on Reformation of Manners. 8vo. Lond. 1731.
———, ———. Thanksgiving Sermon. 8vo. Lond. 1713.
———, ———. Sermon against Popery. 8vo. Lond. 1735.
———, ———. Two Discourses on Positive Institutions. 8vo. Lond. 1742.

Burroughs, Joseph. Defence of the above. 8vo. 1743.

———, ———. Further Defence. 8vo. 1746.

———. ———. View of Popery. 8vo. Lond. 1737.

Burrow, E. J. Second Letter to the Rev. Wm. Marsh. 8vo. Lond. 1819.

Burrow, Sir James. Reports in B. R. from M. 30 Geo. II. to E. 12 Geo. III. 5 vols. 8vo. Lond. 1790.

Burrow, Rob. Sermon at the Election of the Lord Mayor. 8vo. Lond. 1723.

Burscough, Rob. Treatise of Church-Government. 8vo. Lond. 1692.

Burscough, Wm. Sermon, Nov. 5th. 8vo. Lond. 1722.

Burthogge, Richard. Divine Goodness Explicated and Vindicated. 12mo. Lond. 1671.

———, ———. Organum Vetus et Novum; or a Discourse of Reason and Truth. 12mo. Lond. 1678.

———, ———. Essay on Reason and the Nature of Spirits. 8vo. Lond. 1694.

———, ———. Of the Soul of the World and of Particular Souls. 8vo. Lond. 1699.

———, ———. Christianity a Revealed Mystery, &c. 8vo. Lond. 1755.

Burton, Edmund. Ancient Characters. 12mo. Lond. 1763.

Burton, Hezekiah. Sermon on calling no Man Master on Earth. 8vo. Lond. 1718.

Burton, John. Papists and Pharisees compared; a Discourse. 8vo. Lond. 1766.

———, ———. Commentariolus Thomæ Secker, Archiep. Cantuar. Memoriæ sacer. 8vo. Lond. 1768.

———, ———. Epistola Critica ad J. G. Thompson, Gr. Accedit Eulogium J. Rogers. Item, Epistola ad E. Bentham. 8vo. Lond. 1750.

Burton, Rob. Anatomy of Melancholy. 1st ed. 4to. Oxford. 1621.

———, ———. The Same. fol. Oxford. 1632.

———, ———. The Same, with an Account of the Author. 2 vols. 8vo. Lond. 1806.

Bury, Sam. Sermon on the Death of the Rev. S. Cradock. 8vo. Lond. 1707.

———, ———. Sermon on the Death of the Rev. R. Baker. 8vo. Lond. 1714.

Busæus, Joannes. De Statibus Hominum. 4to. Moguntiæ. 1613.

Busbequius, A. G. Itinera Constantinopol. et Amasianum; item de Acie contra Turcam instruenda Consilium. 12mo. Antv. 1681.

Busby, Richard. Rudimentum Grammaticæ Græco-Latinæ Metricum. 8vo. Lond. 1789.

Büsching, A. F. Geography; from the German. 6 vols. 4to. Lond. 1762.

———, ———. Nuova Geografia di America, trad. dall' Ab. G. Jagemann. 3 tom. 4to. Venez. 1780—1.

Bush, Wm. Fast Sermon. 8vo. Lond. 1747.

Bush, Wm. Friendly Reproof to the Rev. Wm. Bush, and D. Jennings in regard to the Trinity; with a Black List of the Clergy, who refused to sign the Declaration in Belief of the Trinity. 8vo. Lond. 1719.
Buskirk, L. N. Six Sermons. 12mo. N. York. 1797.
Bussières, J. de. Flosculi Historiarum. Ed. 5ta. 18mo. Oxon. 1663.
Butius, Vinc. De Calido, Frigido, et Temperato Antiquorum Potu. (Grævius, vol. 12.)
Butler, Car. Rhetorica. 16mo. Lond. 1684.
Butler, Charles. Horæ Juridicæ Subsecivæ. 8vo. Lond. 1807.
———, ———. Idem. 8vo. Phil. 1808.
———, ———. Life of Fenelon. 12mo. Phil. 1711.
———, ———. Horæ Biblicæ. 2 vols. 12mo. Oxford and Lond. 1799—1807.
———, ———. Idem. 2 vols. 8vo. Lond. 1807.
———, ———. Historical and Literary Account of Confessions of Faith, &c. 8vo. Lond. 1816.
———, ———. See Coke.
———, ———. Philological and Biographical Works. 5 vols. 8vo. Lond. 1817.
———, ———. Memoirs of the English, Irish, and Scotish Catholics. 3d ed. 4 vols. 8vo. Lond. 1822.
———, ———. Reminiscences. 4th ed. 8vo. Lond. 1824.
———, ———. Book of the Roman Catholic Church. 8vo. Lond. 1825.
Butler, Joseph, (Bp.) Analogy of Religion to the Constitution and Course of Nature. 4to. Lond. 1736.
———, ———. The Same. 8vo. Bost. 1793.
———. ———. ———. 8vo. Lond. 1798.
———, ———. ———. 8vo. Bost. 1809.
———, ———. Remarks on the vi Chapter of his Analogy. 8vo. Lond. 1737.
———, ———. Fifteen Sermons at the Rolls Chapel. 2d ed. 8vo. Lond. 1729.
———, ———. The Same; with Six others on Public Occasions. 4th ed. 8vo. Lond. 1749.
———, ———. The Same. 5th ed. 8vo. Lond.
———, ———. ———. 6th ed. 8vo. Lond. 1792.
Butler, Lilly. Eight Sermons at Boyle's Lecture. 8vo. Lond. 1711.
———, ———. The Same. fol. Lond. 1739.
———, ———. Sermon on Reformation of Manners. 12mo. Lond. 1697.
Butler, Sam. Hudibras. 12mo. Edin. 1775.
———, ———. ———, by Grey. 2 vols. 8vo. Lond. 1799.
———, ———. Poems. See Chalmers, A.
Butter, Wm. On the Infantile Remittent Fever. 8vo. Lond. 1806.
Buttig, And. De Verbo, Σπλαγχνίζομαι, Marc. viii. 2. 4to. Lips. 1712.

Buttmann, Philip. Griechische Grammatik. 7te Aufl. 12mo. Berlin. 1817.
———, ———. Greek Grammar, tr. by Edw. Everett. 8vo. Bost. 1822.
———, ———. Griechische Schul-Grammatik. 4te Aufl. 12mo. Berlin. 1817.
———, ———. Museum Antiquitatis Studiorum. Vide Wolfius, F. A.
Buxtorfius, Joh. (P.) De Abbreviaturis Hebraicis; item, Operis Talmudici Recensio brevis et Bibliotheca Rabbinica. 12mo. Basil. 1640.
———, ———. Grammatica Chaldaica et Syriaca. 12mo. Basil. 1615.
———, ———. Idem. 12mo. Basil. 1650.
———, ———. Thesaurus Grammaticus Linguæ Hebrææ. 12mo. Basil. 1629.
———, ———. Idem. Editio quinta. 12mo. Basil. 1651.
———, ———. Lexicon Hebraicum et Chaldaicum. 8vo. Basil. 1655.
———, ———. Idem. 12mo. Basil. 1663.
———, ———. ———. 8vo. Basil. 1735.
———, ———. Lexicon Chaldaicum, Talmudicum, et Rabbinicum. fol. Basil. 1639.
———, ———. Idem. fol. Basil. 1640.
———, ———. Concordantiæ Bibliorum Hebraicæ. fol. Basil. 1632.
———, ———. Biblia Hebraica et Chaldaica cum Masora. 2 vol. fol. Basil. 1618.
———, ———. Tiberias, sive Commentarius Masorethicus. 4to. Basil. 1620.
———, ———. Synagoga Judaica. 12mo. Basil. 1661.
———, ———. ———. 12mo. Basil. 1680.
———, ———. ———. (Ugol. vol. 4.)
———, ———. De Manna. (Ugol. vol. 8.)
———, ———. Historia Ignis Sacri. (Id. 10.)
———, ———. Historia Urim et Thummim. (Id. 12.)
———, ———. De Literarum Hebraicarum Genuina Antiquitate. (Id. 28.)
———, ———. De Sponsalibus et Divortiis. (Id. 30.)
———, ———. De Conviviis Veterum Hebræorum. (Id.)
———, ———. De Prosodia Metrica Hebræorum. (Id. 31.)
Buxtorfius, Joh. (Fil.) Lexicon Chaldaicum et Syriacum. 4to. Basil. 1622.
———, ———. Liber Cosri. Vide Jehudah.
———, ———. Historia Arcæ Fœderis.—Maimonidis Vita. (Ugol. vol. 8.)
———, ———. Versio Habarbanelis de Statu et Jure Regio.—Versio ejusdem de Judicum et Regum Differentia. (Id. 24.)
Buys, E. Dictionary of Terms of Art, English and Dutch. 4to.
Byfield, Nathanael. Account of the late Revolution in New England. 8vo. Lond. 1689.

Byfield, Nicolas. See Bifield.
Byles, Mather. Character of the Perfect Man; a Sermon. 12mo. Bost. 1729.
——, ——. Sermon on setting our Affections on Things Above. 8vo. Bost. 1740.
——, ——. Sermon before an Execution for Murder. 8vo. Bost. 1751.
——, ——. Sermon on the late Earthquake. 4to. Bost. 1755.
——, ——. Sermons; with Pious Remains of a Young Gentleman. 8vo. Bost. 1764—71.
——, ——. Sermon on Conversion. 3d ed. 8vo. Bost. 1771.
——, ——. Artillery Election Sermon. 8vo. Bost. 1740.
——, ——. The Same. 3d ed. 8vo. Bost. 1769.
——, ——. Thanksgiving Sermon. 16mo. N. Lond. 1760.
——, ——. Sermon on the Death of Lady Dummer. 8vo. Bost. 1752.
——, ——. Flourish of the Annual Spring; a Sermon. 2d ed. 8vo. Bost. 1769.
——, ——. Sermon on the Death of Wm. Dummer, Esq. 4to. Bost. 1761.
——, ——. Lines to Gov. Belcher on his Lady's Death. 4to. Bost. 1736.
——, ——. Discourse on the Glorious Change of the Vile Body. 2d ed. 8vo. Bost. 1771.
Bynæus, Ant. De Calceis Hebræorum. (Ugol. vol. 29.)
Byng, George, (Admiral.) Expedition of the British Fleet to Sicily, under his Command, in 1718, 1719, and 1720. 8vo. Bost. 1739.
Byng, John, (Admiral.) Proceedings of the Court Martial on his Trial, with his Defence. 4to. Bost. 1757.
Bynkershoek, Corn. Observationum Juris Romani Libri IV. 4to. Francof. et Lips. 1723.
——, ——. Treatise on the Law of War; being the First Book of his Questiones Juris Publici, tr. from the Latin, with Notes, by P. S. Du Ponceau. Phil. 1810.
Byrom, John. Poems. See Chalmers, A.
Byron, John. Narrative of Distresses on the Coast of Patagonia. 8vo. Lond. 1768.
Byron, (Lord.) Works, with his Life. 8vo. Paris. 1826.
Bytemeister, H. J. Delineatio Rei Numismaticæ. 4to. Helmst.
——, ——. De Selah. (Ugol. vol. 32.)
Bythner, Vict. Institutio Linguæ Sanctæ. 12mo. Oxon. 1638.
——, ——. Lyra Prophetica Davidis. 4to. Lond. 1664.
——, ——. Lyra Prophetica Davidis.—Item, Brevis Institutio Ling. Hebr. et Chald. 4to. Lond. 1679.
Byzantinæ Historiæ Scriptores. 24 tomi. fol. Venet. 1729.

C

Caab-Ben-Zohier. Carmen Panegyricum in Laudem Muhammedis; item Amralkeisi Moallakah, etc. Arab. et Lat. a G. J. Lette. 4to. Lug. Bat. 1748.
Cabala, sive Scrinia Sacra: Mysteries of State and Government. 3d ed. fol. Lond. 1691.
Cabeljavius, Petrus. Defensio Potestatis Ecclesiæ in Exercenda Disciplina. 16mo. Amst. 1642.
Cadálso, José. Cártas Marruécas y Poesías Seléctas, por F. Sales. 12mo. Bost. 1827.
Cadogan, Gul. Oratio Harveiana. 4to. Lond. 1764.
Cælius, Ludov. Lectionum Antiquarum Libri xxx. fol. Basil. 1542.
Cælius Secundus Curio. De Bello Melitensi Historia, etc. (Græv. Thes. Ital.)
Cæsalpinus, Andreas Aretinus. De Metallicis. 4to. Norib. 1602.
Cæsar, C. J. Quæ extant. Accedit Vetus Interpres Græcus Librorum vii. de Bello Gallico, cum Notis Variorum, opera G. Jungermanni. 4to. Francof. 1669.
——, —. De Bellis Gallico et Civili Pompeiano; nec non A. Hirtii Aliorumque Commentarii, cura Oudendorpii. 4to. Lug. Bat. 1737.
——, —. Idem, cura Oberlini. 8vo. Lips. 1805.
——, —. ——, —— T. Bentleii. 8vo. Lond. 1742.
——, —. ——, ex recensione J. Davisii, cum Notis Variorum; accessit Metaphrasis Græca Librorum vii. de Bello Gallico. 4to. Cantab. 1706.
——, —. Opera, cum Comment. A. Hirtii, cura S. Clarke. 8vo. Lond. 1720.
——, —. ——, in Usum Delphini. 8vo. Phil. 1813.
——, —. ——. Vide Rom. Hist. Scriptores.
——, —. ——, cum Versione Italica, curante Hermolao Albritio. 4to. Venet. 1737.
——, —. Commentaries, &c. made English by Martin Bladen. 8vo. Lond. 1706.
——, —. Commentari, trad. da Bandelli, con le Figure in Rame fatte da Palladio. 4to. Venet. 1575.
Cagnacinus, Alphonsus. Fragmentum Historicum Antiquitatis Urbis Ferrariæ. (Græv. Thes. Ital.)
Caille, N. L. de la. Vide Ephémérides.
——, ————. Elements of Astronomy, &c. tr. from the French by Robertson. 8vo. Lond. 1750.

Cailleau et Duclos. Dictionnaire Bibliographique, Historique, et Critique. 4 vol. 8vo. Paris. 1790—1802.

Cailliaud, Fr. Voyage à l'Oasis de Thèbes et dans les Déserts situés à l'Orient et à l'Occident de la Thébaïde, fait pendant les Années 1815—18; rédigé et publié par M. Jomard, accompagné de Cartes et de Planches, et d'un Recueil d'Inscriptions. 1ère. Livraison, Texte et Planches. fol. Paris. 1821.

Caines, Geo. Cases in Error in New York. 2 vols. 8vo. N. York. 1805—7.

———, —. Lex Mercatoria Americana. 8vo. N. York. 1802.

———, —. Practical Forms of the Supreme Court of New-York, taken from Tidd's Appendix of the Forms of the Court of King's Bench, &c. 8vo. N. York. 1808.

Cajetanus, Octavius. Isagoge ad Historiam Sacram Siculam. (Græv. Thes. Ital.)

Calaber. Vide Quintus Smyrnæus.

Calamy, Benj. Sermons. 4th ed. 8vo. Lond. 1704.

———, ——. Thanksgiving Sermon. 4to. Lond. 1683.

Calamy, Edmund. See Smectymnuus.

Calamy, Edm. Art of Divine Meditation. 12mo. Lond. 1680.

Calamy, Edm. Practical Discourse concerning Vows. 8vo. Lond. 1697.

———, ——. The Same. 12mo. Lond. 1704.

———, ——. Defence of Moderate Non-Conformity. 3 vols. 8vo. Lond. 1703—5.

———, ——. Church and Dissenters compared as to Persecution. 8vo. Lond. 1719.

———, ——. Sermon on Reformation of Manners. 12mo. Lond. 1699.

———, ——. Sermon at Salters-Hall on occasion of the many late Bankrupts. 12mo. & 8vo. Lond. 1709.

———, ——. Comfort and Counsel to Protestant Dissenters, in two Sermons. 8vo. Lond. 1712.

———, ——. Three Sermons at Salters-Hall. 8vo. Lond. 1815.

———, ——. Sermon to a Society of Catechumens. 8vo. Lond. 1717.

———, ——. Abridgement of Baxter's History of his Life and Times. 8vo. Lond. 1702.

———, ——. The Same. 2 vols. 8vo. Lond. 1713.

———, ——. Continuation of the Account of Ejected Ministers. 2 vols. 8vo. Lond. 1727.

———, ——. Memoirs of the Rev. J. Howe. 8vo. Lond. 1724.

———, ——. Sermon at the Ordination of Mr. John Munckley. 8vo. Lond. 1717.

———, ——. Ordination Sermon at Ailsbury. 8vo. Lond. 1724.

———, ——. Letter to Mr. Echard on his History of England. 8vo. Lond. 1718.

———, ——. Answer to the above. 8vo. Lond. 1718.

———, ——. Letter to him in defence of Echard's History. 8vo. Lond. 1718.

Calamy, Edm. Inspiration of the Writings of the Old and New Testaments in xiv. Sermons. 8vo. Lond. 1710.
———, ———. Sermon on the Death of Mrs. E. Williams. 12mo. Lond. 1698.
———, ———. Sermon on the Death of the Rev. Joseph Bennet. 8vo. Lond. 1726.
Calasio, F. M. de. Concordantiæ Bibliorum Hebraicorum. 4 vol. fol. Lond. 1747—9.
Calcagninus Cœlius. De Talorum ac Tesserarum et Calculorum Ludis. (Gronov. vol. 7.)
——— ———. De Re Nautica. (Id. vol. 11.)
Calchus, Trist. Historiæ Mediolanensis Libri xxii, Aliaque Opuscula de Nuptiis Principum Mediolanensium. (Græv. Thes. Ital.)
Calcutta. See Essays.
Calderon de la Barca, Pedro. Comedias. 11 tom. 4to. Madrid. 1760—3.
——— ———. Autos Sacramentales. 6 tom. 4to. Madrid. 1759—60.
Calderwood, David. History of the Church of Scotland, from 1560 to 1625. fol. 1680.
———, ———. Altare Damascenum. 4to. 1623.
———, ———. ———. 4to. Lug. Bat. 1708.
Caldwell, Charles. Oration, July 4th. 8vo. Phil. 1814.
Caldwell, J. Tour through Part of Virginia in the Summer of 1808; also some Account of the Azores. 12mo. Belfast. 1810.
Caldwell, John. Trial of the Present Spirit, a Sermon. 12mo. Bost. 1742.
———, ———. Scripture Characters or Marks of False Prophets, or Teachers; a Sermon. 8vo. Bost. 1742.
———, ———. Sermon against Uncharitable Judging. 8vo. Bost. 1742.
Calef, J. Siege of Penobscot by the Rebels. 8vo. Lond. 1781.
Calef, Rob. More Wonders of the Invisible World. 12mo. Salem. 1796.
———, ———. Remarks upon his Scandalous Book against the Government and Ministry of New England, by Obadiah Gill and others. 12mo. Bost. 1701.
Calepinus, Ambr. Dictionarium Linguæ Latinæ. fol. Haganoæ. 1531.
———, ———. Idem. fol. Basil. 1542.
———, ———. Dictionarium Decem Linguarum. fol. 1594.
California, Expeditions to the North of, in 1768—70. See Reveley, W.
———. Nachrichten von Californien. 12mo. Mannheim. 1772.
———. Hist. Nat. et Civ. de la Californie. Vide Burriel.
———. Viages de California, MS.
Calisto y Melibea. Vide Cota.
Callander, John. Voyages to the Southern Hemisphere. 3 vols. 8vo. Edin. 1766—8.
Callenbergius, J. H. Via Salutis, descripta a J. A. Freylinghausenio, Arabice exposita. 18mo. Halæ. 1731.

Callender, John. **Historical Discourse on Rhode-Island and Providence Plantations. 8vo. Bost. 1739.**
Callender, J. T. Sketches of the History of America. 8vo. Phil. 1798.
———, ——. Political Progress of Britain. 3d. ed. 8vo. Lond. 1795.
———, ——. Political Register. vol. 1. 8vo. Phil. 1795.
Callet, Fr. Tables de Logarithmes, etc. 8vo. Paris. 1795.
——, —. Tables of Logarithms. 8vo. Paris. 1800.
Calliachius, Nic. De Ludis Scenicis Mimorum et Pantomimorum. (Sallengre, vol. 2.)
Callimachus. Hymni, Epigrammata, et Fragmenta, Gr. et Lat. cum Notis Variorum, et E. Spanhemii Commentario, etc., cura J. A. Ernesti. 2 vol. 8vo. Lug. Bat. 1761.
———. Hymni et Epigrammata, Gr. et Lat. ex recensione J. A. Ernesti. 8vo. Lips. 1774.
———. Works in Verse, with Text and Notes, by Tyler. 4to. Lond. 1793.
———. Hymns, in Verse, with Notes, by Dodd. 4to. Lond. 1755.
Callis, Robert. On the Statute of Sewers. 8vo. Lond. 1647.
Callistratus. Expositiones Statuarum. Vide Philostratus.
Calmet, Aug. Great Dictionary of the Bible, translated from the French by D'Oyly and Colson. 3 vols. fol. Lond. 1732.
———, ——. The Same, in 2 vols., with a Third of Fragments, selected from voyages and Travels in the East, by C. Taylor. 3 vols. 4to. Lond. 1797—1801.
———, ——. The Same. 4 vols. 4to. Charlestown. 1812—14.
———, ——. ———. 5 vols. 4to. Lond. 1823.
———, ——. De Psalmis Graduum.—De Selah.—De Musica Veterum, præsertim Hebræorum.—De Musicis Instrumentis Hebræorum.—De Lamnazeach. (Ugol. vol. 32.)
———, ——. Histoire Universelle. 17 vol. 4to. Strasbourg et Nancy. 1735—71.
———, ——. Antiquities Sacred and Profane; or Critical Dissertations on the Old and New Testaments, done into English, with Notes, by N. Tindal. 4to. Lond. 1727.
Calovius, Abr. De Statu Judæorum Ecclesiastico et Politico, ab anno primo Nativitatis Christi, usque ad Excidium Hierosolymæ. (Ugol. vol. 24.)
Caltageronis, Urbis pulcherrimæ Siciliæ, Antiquitates, a M. Pace. (Græv. Thes. Ital.)
Calveto, Urbanus. Novæ Novi Orbis Historiæ Libri Tres, ex Ital. H. Benzonis. Item Insul. Canar. Descriptio; et de Gallorum Expeditione in Floridam. 8vo. Apud. E. Vignon. 1578.
Calvin, John. Institution of Christian Religion, tr. by T. Norton. fol. Lond. 1634.
———, ——. Institutes of the Christian Religion, tr. by J. Allen. 3 vols. 8vo. Lond. 1813.
———, ——. Institutio Christianæ Religionis. 8vo. Genevæ. 1569.

Calvin, John. Institutiones Christianæ Religionis, etc. fol. Amst. 1667.
———, ——. How Tumults may be avoided. 16mo. Lond. 1550.
———, ——. Contra Libellum Calvini, in quo ostendere conatur Hæreticos jure Gladii coercendos esse. 16mo. 1612.
———, ——. Harmonia Evangelica. fol. Genevæ. 1582.
———, ——. Commentarii in Isaiam Prophetam. fol. Apud E. Vignon. 1583.
———, ——. Prælectiones in Danielem. fol. Apud B. Vincentium. 1571.
———, ——. Opera Omnia, cum Vita ejus. 9 vol. fol. Amst. 1667—71.
Calvinus, J. W. Vide Kahl.
Calvisius, Sethus. Opus Chronologicum. 4to. Francof. 1629.
Camarra, Lucius. De Teate Antiquo. (Græv. Thes. Ital.)
Cambridge, (Eng.) Petition of the Fellows of Trinity College against Dr. Bentley. 8vo. 1709.
————, ——. Advice of an Old Tory to the Vice-Chancellor. 8vo. Lond. 1751.
————, ——. Narrative of the late Extraordinary Proceedings against the W——r Club. 3d ed. 8vo. Lond. 1751.
————, ——. Academic; or a Disputation on the State of the University. 8vo. Lond. 1751.
————, ——. Remarks on the Academic. 8vo. Lond. 1751.
————, ——. Cantabrigia Depicta. 12mo. Camb. 1763.
————, ——, Guide. 8vo. Camb. 1804.
————, ——. Costume of the University. See Harraden.
————, ——. Triposes from 1754 to 1807, inclusive. 12mo.
————, ——. Leges, sive Statuta Acad. Cantab. 4to. MS.
————, ——, Problems. 8vo. Camb. 1810.
Cambridge Coach Robbery, in verse. fol. Lond. 1728.
Cambridge, (N. E.) Platform of Church-Discipline. 4to. Lond. 1653.
————, ———. The Same. 4to. Camb. 1671.
————, ———. ————. 12mo. Bost. 1808.
————, ———. See Harvard University.
Cambridge Concordance. See Newman, S.
Cambridge, Owen. Poems. See Chalmers, A.
Camden, Wm. Remaines concerning Brittaine. 4to. Lond. 1629.
———, ——. Anglica, Normannica, Hibernica, Cambrica, a Veteribus scripta. fol. Francof. 1603.
———, ——. Rerum Anglicarum et Hibernicarum Annales, regnante Elisabetha. 8vo. Lug. Bat. 1639.
———, ——. Britannia. 4to. Lond. 1600.
———, ——. ———. fol. Lond. 1607.
———. ——. Britannia, or a Chorographical Description of Great Britain and Ireland; tr. from the Latin, with Additions, by Gibson. 2 vols. fol. Lond. 1722.
———, ——. The Same. 4th ed. 2 vols. fol. Lond. 1772.
———, ——. Camdeni et Illustrium Virorum ad eum Epistolæ; cum Vita ejus, et Annalium Regni Jacobi I Apparatu. 4to. Lond. 1691.

Camden, Wm. History of Queen Elizabeth. See Kennet, W.
———, ——. Annals of King James I. See Kennet, W.
———, ——. Institutio Græcæ Grammatices, a J. Ward. 12mo. Lond. 1763
Camerarius, Joach. De Comicis Versibus. (Gronov. vol. 8.)
———, ——. Historia Rei Nummariæ. (Id. 9.)
———, ——. Hippocomicus, seu de Curandis Equis, etc. (Id. 11.)
———, ——. Commentarius in Nov. Fœd. Vide Testamentum Novum.
Camerarius, Joh. De Obligatione Reproborum Credendi in Christum, etc. 4to. Tubingæ. 1753.
Camerino, Joseph. Novelas Amorosas. 4to. Madrid. 1736.
Cameron, Joannes. Opera. fol. Geneve. 1658.
———, ———. Examination of Popish Prejudices; from the French. 4to. Oxford. 1626.
Camoens, Luis de. Os Lusiadas; Nova Ediçao correcta, e dada á luz, por J. M. de Souza-Botelho. 4to. Paris. 1817.
Campanus, T. M. Enchiridion Oratorium. 12mo. Amst. 1564.
Campbell, Archibald. Discourse proving that the Apostles were no Enthusiasts. 8vo. Lond. 1730.
———, ———. Necessity of Revelation. 8vo. Lond. 1739.
———, ———. Authenticity of the Gospel History. 2 vols. 8vo. Edin. 1759.
———, ———. Enquiry into the Original of Moral Virtue. 8vo. Lond. 1734.
Campbell, Colen. Vitruvius Britannicus, or the British Architect. 3 vols. fol. Lond. 1731.
Campbell, Geo. Lectures on Ecclesiastical History; with an Essay on Christian Temperance and Self-Denial. 2 vols. 8vo. Lond. 1800.
———, ——. The Four Gospels, tr. from the Greek; with Dissertations and Notes. 2 vols. 4to. Lond. 1789.
———, ——. The Same. 4 vols. 8vo. Bost. 1811.
———, ——. Dissertation on Miracles. 8vo. Lond. 1762.
———, ——. ———. 12mo. Edin. 1766.
———, ——. ———. 12mo. Edin. 1796.
———, ——. The Same, with Sermons and Tracts, &c. 2 vols. 8vo. Edin. 1797.
———, ——. The Same. 8vo. Edin. 1823.
———, ——. Lectures on Systematic Theology and Pulpit Eloquence. 8vo. Bost. 1810.
———, ——. Philosophy of Rhetoric. 2 vols. 8vo. Lond. 1776.
———, ——. The Same. 8vo. Bost.
Campbell, John. History of the Spanish America. 8vo. Lond. 1741.
———, ——. Lives of the Admirals. 4 vols. 8vo. Lond. 1761.
———, ——. Political Survey of Britain. 2 vols. 4to. Lond. 1774.
———, ——. Considerations on the Nature of the Sugar Trade. 8vo. Lond. 1763.

Campbell, John. On the Constitution and Administration of Great Britain. Parts I. and II. 8vo. Lond. 1747.
———, ——. Hermippus Redivivus. See Cohausen.
Campbell, John. Reports at N. P. in B. R. and C. B. from 1807 to 1816 4 vols. 8vo. N. York. 1810—21.
Campbell, John. Travels in South Africa. 8vo. Andover. 1816.
Campbell, J. W. History of Virginia to 1781. 12mo. Phil. 1813.
Campbell, Tho. Essay on English Poetry. 18mo. Bost. 1819.
Campe, J. H. Allgemeine Revision des gesammten Schul-und Erziehungswesens, von einer Gesellschaft Praktischer Erzieher. 14 Theile. 12mo. Hamb. etc. 1785—90.
Camper, P. Œuvres. 3 vol. 8vo. et Atlas. fol. Paris. 1803.
———, —. Dissertation sur la Différence des Traits du Visage, trad. du Hollandois par D. B. Q. d'Isjonval. 4to. Utrecht. 1791.
———, —. Dissertation sur les Variétés Naturelles de la Physionomie des Hommes, trad. du Hollandois par H. J. Jansen. 4to. Paris. 1792.
———, —. Anatomie des Eléphans. fol. Paris. 1802.
Campillo y Cosio, J. del. Nuevo Sistema de Gobierno Económico para la América. 8vo. Madrid. 1789.
Camus, A. G. Sur la Distribution et le Classement des Livres d'une Bibliothèque. (Instit. Lit. vol. 1)
———, ——. Sur l'Histoire du Polytypage et de la Stéréotype. (Id. 3 et 5.)
———, ——. Sur l'Impression des Cartes Géographiques et d' autres Objects en Caractères Mobiles. (Id. 5.)
———, ——. Sur le Teurdanck. (Id. 3 et 5.)
———, ——. Notice d'un Livre imprimè à Bamberg en 1462. (Id. 2.)
———, ——. Sur l'Ecrit intitulé, "De Mirabilibus Auscultationibus," imprimé parmi les Ouvrages d'Aristote. (Id. 2.)
———, ——. Histoire des Animaux. Vide Aristoteles.
———, ——. Mémoire sur les Collections de Voyages des De Bry et De Thevenot. 4to. Paris. 1802.
Canada. Thoughts on the Canada Bill. 8vo. Lond. 1791.
———. Jugement rendu souverainement dans l'Affaire du Canada. 4to. Paris. 1763.
———. Vide Bigot. Vide Martel.
———. Letter to a Commander in Chief of His Majesty's Forces in Canada. 8vo. Lond. 1760.
———. Mémoires sur le Canada. 3 vol. 4to. Paris. 1763.
———. See Nova Scotia. See Quebeck.
Canadian Freeholder. 3 vols. 8vo. Lond. 1777—9.
Canals. Historical Account of the Canal Navigation in Pennsylvania. 4to. Phil. 1795.
———. Reports of the Directors of the Western Inland Lock-Navigation Company to the Legislature. 12mo. Albany. 1798.
———. Facts and Arguments respecting the Utility of an Extensive Plan of Inland Navigation in America. 8vo. Phil. 1805.
———. Report to the Legislature of New-York respecting the Route of an Inland Navigation from the Hudson to Lakes Ontario and Erie. 8vo. N. York. 1811.

Canals. Advantages of the Proposed Canal from Lake Erie to the Hudson, illustrated in a Correspondence between G. Morris and R. Fulton. 8vo. 1814.

———. Remarks on the Proposed Canal from Lake Erie to the Hudson, by Atticus. 8vo. N. York. 1816.

———. Appeal to the Legislature of New-York on the subject of a Canal Communication between the Lakes and Hudson. 8vo. 1816.

———. Reports of the Canal Commissioners of New-York, and Acts of the Legislature, &c. 8vo. N. York. 1817.

———. Considerations on the Great Western Canal. 8vo. Brooklyn. 1818.

———. See Pennsylvania,—New-York, &c.

Cancellieri, Fr. Osservazioni sulla Divina Commedia di Dante. 12mo. Roma. 1814.

Cancer y Velasco, Ger. Obras Varias. 16mo. Lisboa. 1675.

Candamo, Fr. Banzes. Poesias Comicas. 2 tom. 4to. Madrid. 1722.

Candidus, J. Commentariorum Aquilejensium Libri Octo. (Græv. Thes. Ital.)

Caner, Henry. Sermon on the Death of Charles Apthorp, Esq. 8vo. Bost. 1758.

———, ———. Sermon on the Death of King George II. 8vo. Bost. 1761.

———, ———. Sermon at the Funeral of the Rev. Timothy Cutler. 4to. Bost. 1765.

———, ———. Thanksgiving Sermon. 4to. Bost. 1763.

Cange, C. du Fresne, du. Glossarium ad Scriptores Mediæ et Infimæ Græcitatis. 2 vol. fol. Lugd. 1688.

———, ———————. Glossarium ad Scriptores Mediæ et Infimæ Latinitatis. 6 vol. fol. Paris. 1733—6.

———, ———————. Supplementum. Vide Carpentier.

———, ———————. Notæ in Script. Byz.

Canini, Giov. Ang. Iconografia. fol. Roma. 1669.

———, —————. Images des Héros et des Grands Hommes de l'Antiquité, trad. de l'Italien. 4to. Amst. 1731.

Cannell, Joseph. Case of the Pretender stated, &c., a Sermon. 8vo. Lond. 1708.

Canning, Elizabeth. Refutation of Sir C. Gascoyne's Address respecting her Case. fol. Lond. 1754.

Canning, Geo. Letter to the Earl of Hillsborough on the Connexion between Gr. Britain and her Colonies. 8vo. Lond. 1768.

Canoersin, Guil. De Oppugnatis a Turca Constantinopoli, Nigroponto, etc.—De Captione Hydruntinæ Urbis. (Clauser de Rebus Turcicis.)

Canones S S. Apostolorum, Conciliorum, S S. Patrum, etc. fol. Paris. 1561.

———. Pandectæ Canonum. Vide Beveridge.

——— et Decreta Concilii Tridentini. 12mo. Lovanii. 1564.

——— ——————— ———————, cum Constitutionibus speciatim innovatis. 12mo. Lugd. 1734.

Canovai, Stanislao. Viaggi d'Amerigo Vespucci, etc. 8vo. Firenze. 1817.
Cantacuzenus, Joannes. Contra Mahometicam Fidem Christiana et Orthodoxa Assertio, Græce; cum Interpretatione Latina, a R. Gualthero. fol. Basil. 1543.
——————, ————. Historiæ. (Script. Byz.)
Canti Carnascialeschi dal tempo del Magnifico Lorenzo de' Medici. 2 vol. 4to. Cosmopoli. 1750.
Canus, Melchior, (Episc.) Opera. 4to. Bassani. 1746.
Capacius, J. C. Neapolitana Historia. 4to. Neapoli. 1607.
————, ——. In Nuptiis F. Ubaldi et C. Mediceæ Panegyricus.—In Funere C. Emanuelis Oratio. 4to. Neapoli. 1609.
————, ——. Puteolana Historia; et de Balneis Libellus. 4to. Neapoli. 1604.
————, ——. Antiquitates et Historiæ Campaniæ Felicis.—Antiq. et Hist. Neapol.—De Balneis. (Græv. Thes. Ital.)
Capata, Luys. Carlo Famoso. 4to. Valencia. 1565.
Cape Breton. Genuine Letters and Memoirs relating to the History of the Islands of Cape Breton and St. John. 8vo. Lond. 1760.
—— ————. Lettres et Mémoires pour servir à l'Histoire du Cap Breton. 12mo. La Haye. 1760.
—— ————. Wichtigkeit und Vortheil des Kap-Breton, ins Deutsche übersetzt. 8vo. Leipz. 1747.
—— ————. Remarks upon the Failure of the Expedition against Cape Breton. 8vo. Lond. 1757.
Capella, Galeatius. De Bello Mediolanensi, ab anno MDXXI. usque ad MDXXX. (Græv. Thes. Ital.)
———— ———. De Bello Mussiano. (Id.)
Capella, Martianus. De Musica. Vide Musicæ Auctores.
Caper, Flavius. De Orthographia.—De Verbis Dubiis. Vide Grammatici Veteres Latini.
Capicius, Scip. De Vate Maximo. Vide Sannazarius.
Capitolinus, Julius. Vide Rom. Hist. Scriptores.
Cappe, Catharine. Life of Newcome Cappe. See Cappe, N.
———, ————. Memoirs of the Life of, written by herself. 8vo. Lond. 1822.
Cappe, Newcome. Discourses chiefly on Devotional Subjects; with his Life by C. Cappe. Also a Sermon at his Interment, by W. Wood, and a Sermon on his Death by C. Wellbeloved. 8vo. York. 1805.
———, ————. Works. 5 vols. 8vo. York. 1802–19.
———, ————. Critical Remarks on Important Parts of Scripture, with Dissertations, and his Life by C. Cappe. 2 vols. 8vo. York. 1802.
———, ————. Explication of Terms in Scripture, &c. 12mo. Bost. 1818.
———, ————. Discourses on Providence. 8vo. York. 1795.
———, ————. The Same. 3d. ed. 12mo. York. 1818.
Cappellus, Jacobus. Vide Cappellus, Ludov.
Cappellus, Ludov. Critica Sacra. fol. Paris. 1650.

Capellus, Ludov. Commentarii et Notæ Criticæ in Vet. Test. Accessere J. Cappelli Observationes in eosdem Libros, etc. fol. Amst. 1689.

———, ———. Arcanum Punctationis revelatum, etc. 4to. Lug. Bat. 1624.

———, ———. In Davidis Lyram. (Ugol. vol. 32.)

Capsius, M. B. De Revelationibus Brigittæ Suecicæ. 4to. Vitemb. 1715.

Carabajal y Saavedra, Mariana. Novelas. 4to. Madrid. 1728.

Caracci. Scuola Perfetta per Imparare a Disegnare tutto il Corpo Humano. fol.

Caraccioli, L. A. M. Life of Madam de Maintenon; from the French. 12mo. Lond. 1753.

Carafa, Greg. In Opusculum de novissima Vesuvii Conflagratione Epistola Isagogica. 16mo. Neap. 1632.

Card, Henry. Reign of Charlemagne. 8vo. Lond. 1807.

Cardenas, Bern. de. Vide Documentos.

Cardenas z Cano, G. de. Ensayo Cronologico para la Historia General de la Florida. fol. Madrid. 1723.

Care, H. Draconica; or Penal Law touching Matters of Religion. 4to. Lond. 1688.

——, —. Modest Enquiry whether St. Peter were ever at Rome and Bishop of that Church. 4to. Lond. 1687.

Careri, Gemelli. Voyage du Tour du Monde; trad. de l'Italien. 6 vol. 12mo. Paris. 1719.

Carew, Rich. Way to learn the Latin Tongue. See Phillips, J. T.

Carew, Tho. Poems. See Chalmers, A.

Carey, J. Latin Prosody. 8vo. Lond. 1808.

——, —. Key to Propria quæ Maribus, etc. 12mo. Lond. 1805.

Carey, Math. Account of the Fever in Philadelphia. 8vo. Phil. 1793.

———, ——. Observations on Dr. Rush's Enquiry into the Origin of the Fever. 8vo. Phil. 1793.

———, ——. On the Ruinous Consequences of a Non-Renewal of the Charter of the Bank of the U. States. 8vo. Phil. 1810.

———, ——. American Pocket Atlas. 12mo. Phil. 1814.

———, ——. On Congressional Caucusses for President and Vice President. 8vo. Phil. 1816.

———, ——. Vindiciæ Hibernicæ. 8vo. Phil. 1819.

———, ——. Calm Address to the People of the Eastern States on the Representation of Slaves, &c. 12mo. Bost. 1814.

———, ——. Olive Branch. 3d ed. 12mo. Bost. 1815.

———, ——. —————. 4th ed. 2 vols. 12mo. Phil. 1815.

———, ——. —————. 10th ed. 8vo. Phil. 1818.

———, ——. Address to Wm. Tudor respecting his Remarks on the Olive Branch. 12mo. Phil. 1821.

Carey, Walter. Present State of England, 1627. (Harl. Miscel. vol. 3.)

Carey, Wm. Grammar of the Bengalee Language. 8vo. Serampore. 1801.

Carey, Wm. Bengalee Dialogues. 8vo. Serampore. 1801.
———, —. New Testament in Bengalee. 8vo. Serampore. 1801.
Caribbeana, containing Letters and Dissertations, with Poetical Essays, chiefly wrote by several Hands in the West-Indies. 2 vols. 4to. Lond. 1741.
Carion, Jo. Chronicorum ab Orbe Condito Libri III. 24to. Basil. 1564.
Carkeet, Sam. Sermon at the Young Men's Lecture. 8vo. Lond. 1719.
———, ——. Essay on the Conversion of St. Paul. 8vo. Lond. 1741.
Carkesse, Charles. Book of Rates. fol. Lond. 1726.
Carleton, Geo. (Bp.) Examination of a late Appeal on the Doctrines of the Pelagians and Arminians. 4to. Lond. 1626.
————, ————. Consensus Ecclesiæ Catholicæ contra Tridentinos. 12mo. Lond. 1613.
Carli, G. R. Conte. Opere. 18 tom. 8vo. Milano. 1784—7.
——, ————. Della Spedizione degli Argonauti in Colco. 4to. Venez. 1745.
——, ————. Delle Lettere Americane. 2 vol. 4to. Cosmopoli. 1780.
——, ————. Briefe über Amerika, aus dem Ital. 3 theile. 12mo. Gera. 1785.
——, ————. Lettres Américaines. 2 vol. 8vo. Bost. 1788.
Carlos, C. B. El Lazarillo de Ciegos Caminantes desde Buenos Ayres, etc. 8vo. Gijon. 1773.
Carmen Arabicum, Arab. et Lat. 4to.
Carmichael, Fred. Sermons on Important Subjects. 8vo. Edin. 1753.
—————, ——. Sermon before the Society for propagating Christian Knowledge. 8vo. Edin. 1753.
Carmichael, Rich. On Scrofula. 8vo. Lond. 1810.
—————, ——. On the Venereal Diseases which have been confounded with Syphilis. 4to. Dublin. 1814.
—————, ——. On Venereal Diseases. 8vo. Lond. 1818.
Carnot, L. N. M. Géométrie de Position. 4to. Paris. 1803.
———, ————. Mémoire sur la Relation de Cinq Points, etc. 4to. Paris. 1806.
Caro, Annibal. Opere. 8 vol. 8vo. Milano. 1807—12.
——, ————. Rime. 4to. Venetia. 1572.
Carolina. Two Charters granted by King Charles II. to the Proprietors; with the First and Last Fundamental Constitutions. 4to. Lond.
————. Description of its Present State. 4to. Lond. 1682.
————, New Description of, by John Archdale. 4to. Lond. 1707.
————. See North Carolina. See South Carolina.
Caroline, Queen. Verses on her Death. fol. Lond. 1738.
Carpentarius, Jac. Platonis cum Aristotele, in Universa Philosophia, Comparatio. 4to. Paris. 1573.

Carpenter, Joseph. Sermon on the Death of the Rev. John Warren. 8vo. Lond. 1742.
Carpenter, Lant. Examination of Bishop Magee's Statements respecting Unitarians, &c. 8vo. Bristol. 1820.
——, ——. Systematic Education. See Shepherd, W.
Carpentier, P. Glossarium Novum ad Scriptores Medii Ævi; seu Supplementum ad Auctiorem Glossarii Cangiani Editionem. 4 vol. fol. Paris. 1766.
Carpovius, Jac. Theologia Revelata Dogmatica. 4 vol. 4to. Francof, etc. 1753—65.
Carpue, J. C. On Restoring the Nose. 4to. Lond. 1816.
Carpzovius, Ben. Dav. De Pontificum Hebræorum Vestitu Sacro. (Ugol. vol. 12.)
Carpzovius, Joh. Ben. De Crethi et Phlethi. (Ugol. vol. 27.)
——, ——. De Nummis Effigiem Moysis Cornutam exhibentibus. (Id. 28.)
——, ——. De Chappa Hebræorum. (Id. 30.)
——, ——. De Sepultura Josephi Patriarchæ. (Id. 33.)
——, ——. De Vacca Rufa ad Num. xix. 4to. Lips. 1692.
——, ——. Sacræ Exercitationes in Epist. ad Heb. 8vo. Helmst. 1701.
——, ——. Stricturæ Theol. et Crit. in Epistolam ad Romanos, ex Philone Alexandrino. 12mo. Helmst. 1758.
Carpzovius, Joh. Got. Discalceatio Religiosa in Loco Sacro. (Ugol. vol. 29.)
——, ——. Defence of the Hebrew Bible, tr. from the Latin, with Notes, by M. Marcus. 8vo. Lond. 1729.
Carr, John. Dialogues of Lucian, from the Greek. 5 vols. 8vo. Lond. 1774.
Carra. Sur l'Abolition de la Traite des Noirs. 8vo. Paris. 1790.
Carrafa, Placidus. Montucæ Descriptio.—Sicaniæ Descriptio. (Græv. Thes. Ital.)
Carranza, Bart. Summa Conciliorum et Pontificum a Petro usque ad Paulum III. 12mo. Paris. 1550.
——, ——. Idem, a Petrum usque ad Pium IV. 16mo. Lugd. 1570.
Carranza, D. G. Description of the Coasts, Harbours, and Seaports of the Spanish West-Indies, from the Spanish; with Capt. Parker's Account of his taking Porto Bello, &c. 8vo. Lond. 1740.
Carrera, Petrus. Descriptio Ætnæ.—Monumenta Historica Urbis Catanæ.—Disquisitio de Vero Significatu Numismatum quorundam Messanensium, etc. (Græv. Thes. Ital.)
Carribbee. See Caribbeana,—Charibbee,—Charibbs.
Cartari, Vicenzo. Imagini delli Dei de gl' Antichi. 4to. Venetia. 1674.
Carte, Tho. Life of James Duke of Ormonde; with Letters by Charles I and II, himself, and others. 3 vols. fol. Lond. 1736.
——, ——. Collection of Original Letters and Papers. 2 vols. 8vo. Lond. 1739.

Carteau, Félix. Le Songe de Colomb, en Vers. 8vo. Bordeaux. 1809.
Carter, Edm. History of the University of Cambridge to the Year 1753. 8vo. Lond. 1753.
Carter, Elizabeth. Poems. 12mo. Lond. 1766.
———, ———. Works of Epictetus, tr. from the Greek, with Notes and Introduction. 4to. Lond. 1759.
Carter, Wm. Detail of the Engagements, &c. of the Royal and American Armies during the years 1775 and 1776, &c. 4to. Lond. 1784.
Cartes, Réné des. Vide Descartes.
Carthagena, Authentic Papers relating to the Expedition against. 8vo. Lond. 1744.
———, Journal of the Expedition to, &c. 8vo. Lond. 1744.
———, Relation de l'Expedition de Carthagene, en 1697. Vide Pointis.
Cartwright, John. American Independence the Interest and Glory of Great Britain. 8vo. Lond. 1775.
———, ———. Trident; or the National Policy of Naval Celebration, &c. 4to. Lond. 1802.
———, ———. English Constitution Produced and Illustrated. 8vo. Lond. 1823.
Cartwright, Tho. (Bp.) Sermon before the Gentlemen of Yorkshire. 4to. Lond. 1684.
———, ———. Inauguration Sermon. 4to. Lond. 1686.
Cartwright, Wm. Poems. See Chalmers, A.
Cartwrightus, Chr. Electa Thargumico-Rabbinica; sive Annotationes in Genesin. 8vo. Lond. 1648.
———, ———. Idem, in Exodum. 8vo. Lond. 1658.
Cartwritus, Tho. Commentaria Practica in Totam Historiam Evangelicam, etc. 4to. 1630.
———, ———. Harmonia Evangelica. 4to. Amst. 1627.
———, ———. Commentarii in Proverbia Salomonis. 4to. Amst. 1638.
———, ———. Metaphrasis et Homiliæ in Ecclesiastem. 4to. Amst. 1647.
Carus, Fr. Aug. Historia Sententiarum Ecclesiæ Græcæ de Accommodatione Christo inprimis et Apostolis tributa. 4to. Lips. 1793.
———, ———. Pscychologie der Hebräer. 8vo. Leipz. 1809.
Carver, Jonathan. New Universal Traveller. fol. Lond. 1779.
———, –. Travels through the Interior Parts of North America in 1766—8. 3d ed. 8vo. Lond. 1781.
———, –. The Same. 12mo. Bost. 1797.
Carwithen, J. B. S. View of the Brahminical Religion, in a Series of Discourses at the Bampton Lecture. 8vo. Lond. 1810.
Cary, D. Remarks on a Pamphlet, entitled, The Innocents Vindicated, &c. 8vo. Exon. 1718.
Cary, Henry. See Falkland, Lord.
Cary, Hen. Fr. Dante's Vision of Hell, &c. tr. from the Italian, with the Life of Dante, and Notes. 2d ed. 3 vols. 8vo. Lond. 1819.

Cary, John. Essay on the Coyn and Credit of England, &c. 8vo. Bristol. 1796.
——, ——. Discourse concerning the East India Trade. 4to. Lond. 1696.
——, ——. Storia del Commercio della Gran Brettagna, trad. da P. Génovesi, con un Ragionamento sul Commercio in universale, etc. di A. Genovesi. 3 vol. 8vo. Napoli. 1757.
Cary, John. Atlas of England and Wales. 4to. Lond. 1794.
Cary, Mordecai, (Bp.) Sermon before the Society for promoting Protestant Schools in Ireland. 4to. Dublin. 1744.
Cary, Samuel. Ignorance of the True Meaning of the Scriptures, and the Causes of it; a Sermon. 8vo. Bost. 1814.
——, ———. Sermon on the Sabbath of his Ordination. 8vo. Bost. 1819.
——, ———. Fast Sermon. 8vo. Bost. 1813.
——, ———. Address to the Merrimack Humane Society. 8vo. Newburyport. 1806.
——, ———. Review of English's "Grounds of Christianity Examined," &c. 12mo. Bost. 1813.
——, ———. Tribute of Respect to his Memory. 12mo. 1816.
Cary, Tho. Sermon on the last Lords-Day of assembling in the Old Meeting-house in Newburyport. 8vo. Newburyport. 1801.
——, ——. Sermon on the Death of the Rev. Samuel Webster. 8vo. Newburyport. 1796.
Cary, Tho. Masonic Oration. 8vo. Newburyport. 1801.
Caryl, Joseph. Exposition upon the Book of Job. 2 vols. fol. Lond. 1676—77.
Caryophilus, Blasius. De Antiquis Auri, Argenti, Stanni, Æris, Ferri, Plumbique Fodinis. 4to. Viennæ, etc. 1757.
Casa, Giovanni della. Opere. 4 vol. 8vo. Milano. 1806.
Casalius, J. B. De Ritu Nuptiarum, ac de Jure Connubiali Veterum.—De Tragœdia et Comœdia. (Gronov. vol. 8.)
———, ——. De Tricliniis, Conviviis, Hospitalitate, et Tesseris Veterum.—De Thermis et Balneis Veterum.—De Insignibus, Anulis, etc. (Id. 9.)
Casas, Barth. de las. (Bp.) Tears of the Indians, written in Spanish by Casaus, and made English by J. P. 8vo. Lond. 1656.
——, ————————. Voyages des Espagnols dans les Indes; trad. de l'Espagnol. 12mo. Paris. 1697.
——, ————————. Idem. 12mo. Paris. 1698.
——, ————————. Indiarum Devastationis et Excidii Narratio. 4to. Heidelb. 1664.
Casaubonus, Isaacus. Animadversiones in Athenæi Dipnosophistas. fol. Lugd. 1600.
————, ———. Diatriba in Dionem. Vide Dio Chrysostom.
————, ———. De Rebus Sacris et Ecclesiasticis. fol. Lond. 1614.
————, ———. In Nov. Test. Libros Notæ. 24to.
————, ———. Casauboniana, sive Varia de Scriptoribus Librisque Judicia, a J. C. Wolfio. 12mo. Hamburgi. 1710.

Casaubonus, Isaacus. Ad Epistolam Cardinalis Perronii Responsio. 4to. Lond. 1612.
———, ———. De Satyrica Græcorum Poesi et Romanorum Satira Libri Duo. 8vo. Halæ. 1774.
———, ———. Life of I. Casaubon. (Class. Journ. vol. 12.)
Casaubonus, Mericus. De Quatuor Linguis Commentatio. 12mo. Lond. 1650.
———, ———. De Verborum Usu. 24to. Lond. 1647.
———, ———. Treatise on Enthusiasme. 2d. ed. 12mo. Lond. 1656.
———, ———. Of Credulity and Incredulity in Things Divine and Spiritual. 12mo. Lond. 1670.
———, ———. Notæ in Libros M. Antonini. (Gataker.)
Case, Charles. Objections against allowing any Human Authority in Matters of Religion. 8vo. Chelmsford. 1772.
Casella, P. L. De Primis Italiæ Colonis. (Græv. Thes. Ital.)
Cases in Parliament. fol. Lond. 1698.
———, from 1722 to 1740. 4 vols. fol.
———, Special and Select, from the Year Books. 4to. Lond. 1641.
——— in Equity in the Time of Lord Talbot, by Williams. 8vo. Dublin. 1793.
Casimir. Vide Sarbievius.
Cassani, Joseph. Historia del Nuevo Reyno de Granada. fol. Madrid. 1741.
Cassebohm, J. F. De Aure Humana. 4to. Halæ Magd. 1734.
Cassianus, Johannes. Opera, cura H. Cuyckii. 12mo. Antv. 1578.
Cassini, C. F. Voyage to Newfoundland and Sallee. See Chappe-d'Auteroche.
Cassini, J. Eléments d'Astronomie.—Tables Astronomiques.—Méridienne de Paris.—Géométrie de l'Infini. Vide Acad. Royale des Sciences.
Cassiodorus, M. Aur. Opera Omnia, a J. Garettio. 2 tom. in 1 vol. fol. Rotomagi. 1679.
———, ———. Chronicon. Vide Rom. Hist. Scriptores.
Castalio, Josephus. Adversus Feminarum Prænominum Assertores Disputatio.—De Antiquis Puerorum Prænominibus. (Grævius, vol. 2.)
———, ———. De Templo Pacis, etc.—Explicatio ad Inscriptionem Obelisci Augusti.—De Columna Triumphali Imp. Antonini. (Id. 4.)
Castalio, Sebastianus. Dialogi Sacri. 24to. Edin. 1700.
———, ———. Vide Biblia. Vide Testamentum.
Castellane, M. le Compte de. Opinion on the Declaration of Rights delivered in 1789 in the French National Assembly. 8vo.
Castellanus, Pet. De Festis Græcorum. (Gronov. vol. 7.)
———, ———. De Esu Carnium.—De Mensibus Atticis, etc. (Id. 9.)
———, ———. Vitæ Veterum et Illustrium Medicorum. (Id.)
Castellio. Vide Castalio.

Castellionæus, J. A. Mediolanenses Antiquitates. (Græv. Thes. Ital.)
Castellus, Barthol. Lexicon Medicum Græco-Latinum, a Brunone. 4to. Lips. 1713.
Castellus, Edm. Lexicon Heptaglotton. 2 vol. fol. Lond. 1669.
———, ——. Vide Michaelis, J. D.
Castellus, G. L. Siciliæ et Objacentium Insularum Vet. Inscriptionum Nova Collectio, Prolegomenis et Notis illustrata. fol. Panormi. 1769.
Castelnau, Michel de. Mémoires. (Mém. de France, vol. 42—46.)
Casti, Giambattista. Animali Parlanti. 4 tom. 12mo. Amst. 1804.
——, ————. Novelle. 6 tom. 16mo. Parigi. 1801.
Castiglione. Pope's Essay on Man, tr. into Italian Verse. 1746. MS.
Castiglione, Baldessare. Il Libro del Cortegiano. 2 vol. 8vo. Milano. 1803.
————, ————. El Cortesano, trad. por Boscan. 12mo. Salamanca. 1581.
————, ————. Sylvæ. Vide Poemata Italorum.
————, ————. Carmina. Vide Fracastorius.
Castiglioni, Luigi. Viaggio negli Stati Uniti dell' America Settentrionale, fatto negli anni 1785, 1786, e 1787. 2 tom. 8vo. Milano. 1790.
————, ——. Reise durch die vereinigten Staaten von Nord-Amerika in den Jahren 1785, 1786 und 1787; aus dem Italienischen von M. Petersen. Th. 1. 8vo. Memmingen. 1793.
Castillejo, Christóbal de. Obras. 2 tom. 8vo. Madrid. 1792.
Castillioneus, Bonaventura. De Gallorum Insubrum Antiquis Sedibus. (Græv. Thes. Ital.)
Castillo, Alonso. La Quinta de Laura. 12mo. Madrid. 1732.
Castillon, Bd. Campaign of the Grand Army. 2 vols. 12mo. Bordeaux. 1806.
Cat may look upon a King. 12mo. Amst. 1714.
Cat, C. N. le. Physical Essay on the Senses; from the French. 8vo. Lond. 1750.
Catalogue of the Harleian Manuscripts in the British Museum. 2 vols. fol. Lond. 1759.
———————— Libraries of Lord Colerane, Mr. Baron Clarke, and the Rev. S. Dunster. 2 vols. 8vo.
———————— Books of the Library Company of Philadelphia. 8vo. Phil. 1789 and 1807.
———————— Library of the American Academy of Arts and Sciences. 12mo. 1802.
———————— Loganian Library. 8vo. Phil. 1795.
———————— Books in the Boston Athenæum. 8vo. Bost. 1810 and 1827.
———————— Books of the Salem Athenæum. 8vo. Salem. 1811, 1818, and 1826.
———————— Books in the Boston Library. 8vo.
———————— Library of the Massachusetts Historical Society 8vo. Bost. 1811.

Catalogue of the Library of the New-York Historical Society. 8vo. N. York. 1813.

——— Library of Theophilus Parsons. 8vo. Bost. 1814.

——— Library of Congress. 8vo. Washington. 1802—3.

——— Library of the United States. 4to. Washington. 1815.

———. Supplement to the above. 4to. Washington. 1820.

——— American Philosophical Society. 8vo. Phil. 1824.

——— Social Friends' Library at Dartmouth College. 12mo. Concord. 1820 and 1824.

——— United Fraternity's Library at Dartmouth College. 12mo. Concord. 1824.

——— Library of Dartmouth College. 8vo. Concord. 1825.

——— Library of the Law School of Harvard University. 8vo. Camb. 1826.

——— Porcellian Library in Harvard University. 8vo. Camb. 1827.

——— Library of Brown University. 8vo. Prov. 1826.

——— of Yale College Library. 8vo. New-Haven. 1823.

———, Lackington's. 8vo. Lond. 1806—8.

———, ———. 8vo. Lond. 1819.

———, Longman's. 8vo. Lond. 1814.

———, ———. 8vo. Lond. 1822.

———, Priestley's. 8vo. Lond. 1819.

——— of Literary History. 8vo.

——— of Publications relating to the Toleration of Protestant-Dissenting-Ministers, and the Repeal of the Corporation and Test Acts, from 1772 to 1790, inclusive. 8vo. Lond. 1790.

——— des Livres de la Bibliothèque des ci-devant soi-disant Jésuites du College de Clermont. 8vo. Paris. 1764.

——— ——— de M. le Comte de MacCarthy Reagh. 2 vol. 8vo. Paris. 1815.

——— du Jardin des Plantes à Gorenki. 8vo. Moscou. 1812.

——— Raisonné d'une Collection de Médailles. 4to. 1774.

Catalogues, Sale, of Booksellers in England, France, Germany, &c.

———, Various, of Colleges and other Institutions and Societies.

——— ——— of Medals, &c. of Dingley, Fairfax, Folkes, Mead, Selbye, Wren, sold by Langford. 8vo. Lond.

Catalogus Bibliothecæ Bodleianæ, opera T. Hyde. fol. Oxon. 1674.

——— ——— Universitatis Lugduno-Batavæ. fol. Lug. Bat. 1716.

——— ——— Harleianæ. 4 vol. 8vo. Lond. 1743—4.

——— ——— Collegii Harvardini. 4to. Bost. 1723.

——— ——— ———. 2 vol. 4to. Bost. 1790.

——— ——— Musei Britannici. 2 vol. in 1. fol. Lond. 1787.

Catalogus Bibliothecæ Collegii Alleghaniensis. 8vo. Meadville. 1823.

——— ——— Societatis Physicalis Regalis Edinburgenæ. 8vo. Edin. 1813.

——— Editionum Horatii in Bibliotheca Jacobi Douglas. 4to. Lond. 1739.

——— Numismaticus Musei Lefroyani. 8vo. Liburni. 1763.

———. Vide Bibliotheca. Vide Bibliothèque.

Catechism, Larger Westminster. 8vo. Glasgow. 1762.

———, Shorter Westminster. 8vo. Glasgow. 1762.

———, Short. 12mo. Bost. 1766.

——— of a Rellyite. 8vo. Portsmouth. 1782.

———, Brief Evangelical. 24to. N. York. 1817.

———. Vide Confessio Fidei. V. Confession of Faith.

Catechisticall Doctrine, Pattern of. 12mo.

Catena, Girol. Vita del Gloriosissimo Papa Pio V. 12mo. Roma. 1587.

Catesby, Mark. Natural History of Carolina, Florida, and the Bahama Islands, Fr. and Eng. 2 vols. fol. Lond. 1754.

———, ———. Hortus Europæ Americanus. 4to. Lond. 1767.

———, ———. Beschreibung von Carolina, Florida, und den Bahamischen Inseln, in das Deutsche übers. von G. L. Huth. fol. Nürnberg. 1755.

Catharine II. Empress of Russia. Grand Instructions to the Commissioners, appointed to frame a New Code of Laws for the Russian Empire; tr. from the Russian Language by M. Tatischeff. 4to. Lond. 1768.

Catholic Faith and Practice relating to Phillips's Life of Cardinal Pole. 8vo. Lond. 1765.

Catholics. Dangers with which Great Britain and Ireland are menaced by the Demands of Irish Roman Catholics. 8vo. Lond. 1817.

———. Proceedings of the General Committee in 1792—3 compared with those in 1810—11. 8vo. Lond. 1812.

———. Strong Reasons for Rejecting their Claims. 8vo. Lond. 1813.

———. See Church. See Popery.

Cato, Dionysius. Disticha de Moribus, ab Arntzenio. 8vo. Amst. 1754.

Cato, M. Porcius. De Re Militari. Vide Script. de Re Militari.

———, ———. De Re Rustica. Vide Script. de Re Rustica.

Catrou, Fr. et J. Roüillé. Histoire Romaine. 21 vol. 4to. Paris. 1725—48.

———, ———. Roman History, done into English by R. Bundy. 6 vols. fol. Lond. 1728—37.

Cattenburgh, Adrianus à. Spicilegium Theologiæ Christianæ. fol. Amst. 1726.

Catullus, C. Val. Opera, ex recensione J. Vossii. 4to. Lug. Bat. 1691.

———, ———. Opera, cum Commentario J. A. Vulpii. 4to. Patavii. 1737.

Catullus, C. Val. Catulli, Tibulli, et Propertii Opera, cum Notis Variorum. fol. Lutetiæ. 1604.
———, ———. Catulli, Tibulli, et Propertii Opera. 4to. Cant. 1702.
———, ———. Epithalamium de Nuptiis Pelei et Thetidos, a F. G. Doeringio. 8vo. Numburgi. 1778.
———, ———. Phaselus, et ad eam Parodiæ. 16mo. Lugd. 1593.
———, ———. Poems in English Verse, with the Latin Text, and Notes. 2 vols. 8vo. Lond. 1795.
———, ———. Epitalamio nelle Nozze di Peleo, e Teti, trad. da L. Dolce. 4to. Siena. 1751.
———, ———. Vide Encyclopädie der Lateinischen Classiker,—Corpus Poet. Lat.,—Collectio Pisaurensis Poet. Lat.
Cauche, Fr. Voyage à Madagascar, Isles adjacentes, et Coste d'Afrique. 4to. Paris. 1651.
Caulin, Ant. Historia de la Nueva Andalucia. fol. 1779.
Causa Dei contra Novatores, in answer to Dr. Hughes and Mr. Wilson. 8vo Lond. 1747.
Causes Célèbres, de Toutes les Cours Souveraines du Royaume. 154 tomes. 12mo. Paris. 1775—87. (Tomes 9 and 10, 1775, wanting.)
Causeus, M. A. De Signis Militaribus. (Grævius, vol. 10.)
———, ———. De Vasis, Bullis, etc.—De Mutini Simulacris.—De Æneis Antiquorum Lucernis. (Id. 12.)
Caussinus, Nic. De Eloquentia Sacra et Humana. 4to. Lugd. 1651.
———, —. Idem. 4to. Lugd. 1657.
———, —. Holy Court, &c., from the French. fol. Lond. 1650.
Cavalcanti, Bart. Trattati sopra gli ottimi Reggimenti delle Repubbliche. 8vo. Milano. 1805.
Cavallero Determinado, trad. de Leng. Franc. por H. de Acuña. 8vo. Salamanca. 1573.
Cavallo, Tiberius. On Electricity. 3d ed. 3 vols. 8vo. Lond. 1786—95.
———, ———. The Same. 4th ed. 3 vols. 8vo. Lond. 1795.
———, ———. On Air. 4to. Lond. 1781.
Cave, Wm. Apostolici; or Lives of the Primitive Fathers. fol. Lond. 1687.
——, ——. The Same. 4th ed. fol. Lond. 1716.
——, ——. Ecclesiastici; or Lives of the Fathers of the 4th Century. fol. Lond. 1683.
——, ——. Scriptorum Ecclesiasticorum Historia Literaria. 2 vol. fol. Oxon. 1740—3.
——, ——. Primitive Christianity. 8vo. Lond. 1675.
——, ——. ————————. 8vo. Lond. 1702.
——, ——. ————————. 7th ed. 8vo. Lond. 1728.
——, ——. Discourse on the Unity of the Catholick Church. 4to. Lond. 1684.
Cavitellius, Ludov. Cremonenses Annales. (Græv. Thes. Ital.)
Cawdrey, Dan. Diatribe Triplex; or a Threefold Exercitation,

concerning Superstition, Will-Worship, and Christmas Festivals. 12mo. Lond. 1654.
Cawdwell, Tho. Power of Synods Discussed. 8vo. Lond. 1724.
———, ——. Origin of Churches. 8vo. Lond. 1723.
Cawthorn, James. Poems. See Chalmers, A.
Cay, John. Abridgment of the Public Statutes. fol. Lond. 1739.
Cayenne. Neue Reise nach Cayenne. 8vo. Leipz. 1799.
Cayet, P. V. P. Mémoires. (Mém. de France, vol. 55—60.)
Caylus, M. le Comte de. Sur les Pierres Gravées. (Acad. des Inscrip. vol. 19.)
———, ———. De l'Amour des Beaux Arts chez les Grecs. (Id. 21.)
———, ———. De l'Architecture Ancienne.—De la Perspective des Anciens. (Id. 23.)
———, ———. Sur le xxxve. Livre de Pline.—Sur le xxxive. Livre de Pline —De la Sculpture et des Sculpteurs Anciens, selon Pline. (Id. 25.)
———, ——— ———. Sur le Papyrus.—Sur le Tombeau de Mausole. (Id. 26.)
———, ———. Sur la Peinture à l'Encaustique. (Id. 28.)
———, ———. Sur la Vénus d'Apelles, etc.—Examen d'un Passage de Pline. (Id. 30.)
———, ———. De la Gravure des Anciens. (Id. 32.)
Caylus, M. de. Histoire du Rapprochement des Végétaux. 12mo. Paris. 1806.
Cebes. Tabula, cum Versione et Notis J. Caselii. 4to. Lug. Bat. 1618.
———. ———, Holstenii;—Id., Schweighaeuseri. Vide Epictetus.
———. Picture of Cebes, tr. by Collier. Vide Antoninus. See also S. Johnson's Works.
Cecil, Sir Robert. Secret Correspondence with James VI. of Scotland. 12mo. Edin. 1766.
Cecil, Wm. Ld. Burleigh. Collection of State Papers, from 1542 to 1570, by S. Haynes. fol. Lond. 1740.
———, ———. Collection of State Papers, from 1571 to 1596, by W. Murdin. fol. Lond. 1759.
———, ——— ———. Advice to Queen Elizabeth. (Harl. Miscel. vol. 7.)
Cedrenus, Geo. Compendium Historiarum ab Initio Mundi usque ad J. Comneni Tempora. (Script. Byz.)
Ceillier, Remy. Histoire Générale des Auteurs Sacrés et Ecclesiastiques. 23 vol. 4to. Paris. 1729—63.
———, ———. Table Générale des Matières contenues dans l'Hist. Gén, par Rondet. 2 vol. 4to. Paris. 1782.
Celeusma, seu Clamor ad Theologos Hierarchiæ Anglicanæ. 4to. Lond. 1679.
Celibacy. Answer to a Discourse concerning the Celibacy of the Clergy. 4to. Oxford. 1688.
Cellarius, Christoph. Notitia Orbis Antiqui. 3 tomi. 4to. Cant. 1703—6.

Cellarius, Christoph. Geographia Antiqua, cura S. Patrick. 6ta ed. 2 vol. 8vo. Lond. 1731.
———, ———. Dictionary, Latin, Russian, and German. 8vo. 1746.
———, ———. Vide Holterhof, F.
———, ———. De Barbarismis et Idiotismis Sermonis Latini. 16mo. Jenæ. 1745.
———, ———. De Latinitate Mediæ et Infimæ Ætatis. 16mo. Jenæ. 1733.
———, ———. Isagoge in Linguam Arabicam. 8vo. Cizæ. 1686.
———, ———. De Excidio Sodomæ.—De Amœnitatibus Geog. et Hist. ex Itineribus S. Pauli collectis. (Ugol. vol. 7.)
———, ———. Collectanea Historiæ Samaritanæ. (Id. 22.)
———, ———. De Cn. Pompeii M. Expeditione Judaica.—Vindiciæ Josephi adversus Harduinum. (Id. 26.)
———, ———. De Studiis Romanorum Litterariis in Urbe et Provinciis. (Sallengre, vol. 3.)
Cellini, Benv. Due Trattati; Uno dell' Oreficeria, l'Altro della Scultura. 8vo. Milano. 1811.
———, ———. Vita di Cellini, da lui medesimo scritta. 2 vol. 8vo. Milano. 1806—11.
———, ———, Life of, translated by Nugent. 2 vols. 8vo. Lond. 1771.
Celsus, Aur. Corn. De Medicina, a Pantino. fol. Basil. 1552.
———, ———. De Medicina, cum Notis Variorum, cura T. J. ab Ameloveen. 8vo. Rotterdami. 1750.
———, ———. De Medicina, cum Notis Variorum, cura C. C. Krause. 8vo. Lips. 1766.
———, ———. Vide Haller, Art. Med. Principes.
———, ———. Of Medicine, translated, with Notes, by J. Greive. 8vo. Lond. 1756.
———, ———. Sentences. See Sprengell.
Celsus, Minus. Vide Socinus, L.
Celtic Language. Collection of Letters and Papers concerning it; with a Specimen of a Dictionary. 8vo. Edin. 1739.
——— ———. See Cleland, J.
Cenalis, Rob. De Vera Mensurarum Ponderumque Ratione. (Grævius, vol. 11.)
Cène, Charles le. Essay for a New Translation of the Bible, tr. from the French by H. Ross. 2d ed. 8vo. Lond. 1727.
Censorinus. De Die Natali, ex recensione H. Lindenbrogii, cum ejusdem et Variorum Notis. 12mo. Cant. 1695.
Census. See United States.
Centinel, Columbian, for the years 1785—6, and 1791—1822.
Cepède, (Comte de la.) Histoire Naturelle des Poissons. 5 vol. 4to. Paris. 1798—1803.
Cepion, Coriol. De Rebus Petri Mocœnici contra Turcas gestis. (Clauser de Rebus Turcicis.)
Cerdá y Rico, Fr. Vide Alfonso.

Cerisier, M. Destin de l'Amérique, ou Dialogues Pittoresques. 12mo. Lond. 1780.
Cermenate, J. de. Historia de Situ, Origine, et Cultoribus Ambrosianæ Urbis, ac de Mediolanensium Gestis sub Imperio Henrici VII, etc. (Græv. Thes. Ital.)
Cérutti. L'Aigle et le Hibou, Fable. 8vo. Glascow. 1783.
Cervántes Saavedra, M. de. Vida y Hechos del Ingenioso Cavallero Don Quixote de la Mancha. 2 vol. 4to. Madrid. 1730.
——— ————. El Tngenioso Hidalgo Don Quixote de la Mancha; Nueva Edicion, corregıda por la Real Academia Española. 4 vol. 4to. Madrid. 1780.
——— ————. El Ingenioso Hidalgo Don Quixote, de la Mancha; por J. A. Pellicer. 5 vol. 8vo. Madrid. 1797.
——— ————. Novelas Exemplares. 2 vol. 12mo. Valencia. 1797.
——— ————. Galatea. 2 vol. 8vo. Madrid. 1784.
——— ————. Trabajos de Persiles y Sigismunda. 2 vol. 8vo. Madrid. 1802.
——— ————. Viage al Parnaso; La Numancia; y El Trato de Argel. 8vo. Madrid. 1784.
——— ————. Comedias y Entremeses; con una Dıssertacion sobre las Comedias de España. 2 vol. 4to. Madrid. 1749.
——— ————. History of the Renowned Don Quixote de la Mancha; from the Spanish. 7th ed. by Ozell. 4 vols. 12mo. Lond. 1743.
Cervantez de Salazar, Fr. Vide Salazar.
Cesarotti, Melchior. Dell' Epistolario. 6 vol. 12mo. Firenze e Pisa. 1811—13.
———, ———. Poesie Originale. 12mo. Firenze. 1810.
———, ———. Versioni, Poesie Latine, e Iscrizioni. 12mo. Firenze. 1810.
———, ———. L'Iliade di Omero. 4 vol. 12mo. Pisa. 1802.
———, ———. Versione Letterale dell' Iliade. 8 vol. Firenze. 1804—9.
———, ———. Le Opere di Demostene, tradotte ed illustrate. 6 vol. 12mo. Firenze. 1807—9.
———, ———. De Lingua et Eloquentia. 12mo. Flor. 1810.
———, ———. Corso di Letteratura Greca. 3 vol. 12mo. Firenze. 1805—6.
———, ———. Vite dei Primi Cento Pontefici. 12mo. Firenze. 1810.
———, ———. Poesie di Ossian. 4 tom. 12mo. Firenze. 1807.
———, ———. Saggi sulla Filosofia delle Lingue e del Gusto. 12mo. Pisa. 1814.
———, ———. Satire di Giuvenale, ridotte in Italiano. 12mo. Parigi. 1805.
———, ———. Relazione Accademiche. 2 vol. 12mo. Pisa. 1812—15.
———, ——— Prose di Vario Genere. 2 vol. 12mo. Firenze. 1808—9.

Cesarotti, Melchior. Il Bardo della Selva Nera. Parte Prima. 8vo. Firenze. 1806.
Cespedes, Pablo de. Rimas. Vide Rioja.
Cespedes y Meneses, Gonzalo de. Poema Tragico del Español Gerardo. 4to. Madrid. 1788.
Cevallos, Pedro. Exposition of the Practices which led to the Usurpation of the Crown of Spain by the Emperor of the French. 8vo. Boston.
Cevallos, Pedro Ordonnez de. Beschryvinghe van West-Indien. fol. Amst. 1621.
———, ——————. Descriptio Indiæ Occidentalis. fol. Amst. 1622.
———, ——————. Description de l'Inde Occidentale. fol. Amst. 1622.
Cevellerius, A. R. Rudimenta Hebraicæ Linguæ. fol. 1567.
Chabanon, M. de. Dissertation sur Homère. (Acad. des Inscrip. vol. 30.)
————, ——. Discours sur Pindare.—Odes de Pindare. (Id. 32 et 37.)
Chabert, M. de. Voyage dans l'Amérique Septentrionale en 1750 et 1751. 4to. Paris. 1753.
Chadlicot, Tho. Speech in the behalfe of the King and Parliament. 4to. Lond. 1642.
Chais, Charles. Lettres sur les Jubilés et les Indulgences. 3 vol. 12mo. La Haye. 1751.
Chaise, F. de la. Project for Extirpating Hereticks. 4to. Paris. 1688.
Chalcondylas, Laonicus. Historia Turcarum. (Clauser de Rebus Turcicis.)
—————, ————. Idem. (Script. Byz.)
Chalmers, Alex. History of the University of Oxford. 2 vols. 8vo. Oxford. 1810.
————, ——. Works of the English Poets from Chaucer to Cowper, with Prefaces, by Dr. S. Johnson, &c. 21 vols. 8vo. Lond. 1810.
Chalmers, Geo. Opinions on Interesting Subjects of Public Law and Commercial Policy arising from American Independence. 8vo. Lond. 1784.
————, ——. Political Annals of the United Colonies. 4to. Lond. 1780.
————, ——. Life of Mary, Queen of Scots. 2 vols. 8vo. Phil. 1822.
————, ——. Estimate of the Comparative Strength of Britain during the Present and four Preceding Reigns, &c. To which is added an Essay on Population, by Lord Chief Justice Hale. 4to. Lond. 1782.
————, ——. Opinions of Eminent Lawyers on Various Points of English Jurisprudence, &c. 2 vols. 8vo. Lond. 1814.
Chalmers, Lionel. Account of the Weather and Diseases of South-Carolina. 2 vols. 8vo. Lond. 1776.

Chalmers, Lionel. Essay on Fevers. 8vo. Lond. 1768.
Chalmers, Tho. Evidence and Authority of the Christian Revelation. 12mo. Edin. 1815.
Chaloner, Th. De Republica Anglorum Instauranda.—In Laudem Henrici Octavi.—De Illustrium quorundam Encomiis. 4to. Lond. 1579.
Chambaud, Lewis. Dictionary, French and English. 4to. Lond. 1778.
———, ———. Idioms of the French and English Languages. 12mo. Lond. 1793.
———, ———. Fables Choisies. 12mo. Phil. 1796.
Chamberlayne, John. State of Great Britain. 8vo. Lond. 1710.
———, ———. The Same. 8vo. Lond. 1726.
———, ———. Oratio Dominica in Diversas Omnium fere Gentium Linguas versa, cum Dissertationibus de Linguarum Origine, etc. 4to. Amst. 1715.
Chambers, Ephraim. Cyclopædia. 7th ed. 2 vols. fol. Lond. 1751—2.
———, ———. Supplement, by Scott. 2 vols. fol. Lond. 1753.
Chambers, J., & W. J. Duane. Settlement of Emigrants from Ireland. 8vo. Washington. 1818.
Chambers, Sir Wm. Treatise on Civil Architecture. fol. Lond. 1759.
———, ———. Designs of Chinese Buildings, &c. fol. Lond. 1757.
Chambon. Commerce de l'Amérique par Marseille. 2 vol. 4to. Avignon. 1764.
Champ-d'Asile, Tableau Topographique et Historique du Texas. 8vo. Paris. 1819.
Champigny, Chevalier de. Etat Présent de la Louisiane. 8vo. La Haye. 1776.
Champion, Joseph. Poems of Ferdosi translated, with an Essay on his Life and Writings, &c. 4to. Calcutta. 1785.
Champion, Rich. Considerations on the Situation of Great Britain and the United States with respect to Commercial Connections. 8vo. Lond. 1784.
Champlain, Le Sieur de. Voyages de la Nouvelle France Occidentale, dicte Canada; avec un Traitté de la Marine. 4to. Paris. 1632.
Champs, Jean des. Religion Chrétienne prouvée par le Raisonnement. 8vo. Lond. 1754.
Chandler, Edw. (Bp.) Defence of Christianity from the Prophecies of the Old Testament. 8vo. Lond. 1725.
———, ———. The Same. 2d ed. 8vo. Lond. 1725.
———, ———. Vindication of the 'Defence.' 2 vols. 8vo. Lond. 1728.
———, ———. Christmas-Day Sermon. 8vo. Lond. 1718.
———, ———. Thanksgiving Sermon. 8vo. Lond. 1716.
———, ———. Sermon, Nov. 5th. 8vo. Lond. 1715.
———, ———. Sermon, Jan. 30th. 8vo. Lond. 1718.

Chandler, Edw. (Bp.) Sermon on Reformation of Manners. 4to. Lond. 1724.
Chandler, Geo. On the Diseases of the Eye. 8vo. Lond. 1780.
Chandler, Henry. Effort against Bigotry. 2d ed. 4to. Lond. 1709.
Chandler, Rich. Travels in Asia Minor. 4to. Oxford. 1775.
———, ——. Travels in Asia Minor and Greece. 3d ed. 2 vols. 4to. Lond. 1817.
Chandler, Sam. Vindication of the Christian Religion. 8vo. Lond. 1725.
———, ——. The Same. 2d ed. 8vo. Lond. 1728.
———, ——. Reflections on the Conduct of the Modern Deists. 8vo. Lond. 1727.
———, ——. Vindication of Daniel's Prophecies. 8vo. Lond. 1728.
———, ——. Witnesses of the Resurrection of Christ re-examined. 8vo. Lond. 1744.
———, ——. History of Persecution. 8vo. Lond. 1736.
———, ——. Letter to a Friend occasioned by Mr. Chandler's History of Persecution. 8vo. Lond. 1733.
———, ——. Paraphrase and Commentary on Joel. 4to. Lond. 1735.
———, ——. Dissertation on the Third Chapter of Joel. 4to. Lond. 1735.
———, ——. Paraphrase and Notes on the Epistles to the Galatians and Ephesians, with a Commentary on the Epistles to the Thessalonians. 4to. Lond. 1777.
———, ——. History of the Inquisition. See Limborch.
———, ——. Answer to the Remarks of Dr. Berriman on the above. 8vo. Lond. 1733.
———, ——. Second Letter to Dr. Berriman. 8vo. Lond. 1733.
———, ——. Letter to the Rev. Mr. Guyse. 8vo. Lond. 1730.
———, ——. Account of a Conference between two Romish Priests and some Protestant Divines. 8vo. Lond. 1735.
———, ——. Case of Subscription Reviewed. 8vo. Lond. 1748.
———, ——. Letter to him on the above. 8vo. Lond. 1748.
———, ——. Day-Thoughts on Wisdom and Goodness. 4to. Lond. 1753.
———, ——. Defence of the Ministry and Character of Joseph. 8vo. Lond. 1743.
———, ——. Critical History of the Life of David. 2 vols. 8vo. Lond. 1766.
———, ——. Review of the History of the Man after God's own Heart. 8vo. Lond. 1762.
———, ——. Sermon on Reformation of Manners. 8vo. Lond. 1738.
———, ——. Fast Sermon. 8vo. Lond. 1759.
———, ——. Plain Reasons for being a Christian. 4th ed. 12mo. Lond. 1773.
———, ——. Great-Britain's Memorial against the Pretender and Popery. 8th ed. 8vo. Lond.

Chandler, Sam. Notes of the Church; a Sermon at Salters-Hall. 8vo. Lond. 1735.
———, ——. Supplement to the Notes of the Church. 8vo. Lond. 1735.
———, ——. Sermon to the Society for the Relief of Widows and Children of Dissenting Ministers. 4to. Lond. 1736.
———, ——. Sermon before the same Society. 4to. Lond. 1749.
———, ——. Incurableness of Superstition, in Two Discourses at Little St. Helen's. 8vo. Lond. 1749.
———, ——. Sermons; with his Life. 2d ed. 4 vols. 8vo. Lond. 1769.
———, ——. Sermon on the Death of the Rev. Tho. Hadfield. 8vo. Lond. 1741.
———, ——. Sermon on the Death of the Rev. Geo. Smyth. 8vo. Lond. 1746.
———, ——. Sermon on the Death of the Rev. Moses Lowman. 8vo. Lond. 1752.
Chandler, T. B. Appeal to the Public in behalf of the Church of England in America. 8vo. N. York. 1767.
———, ——. The Same. 2d ed. 8vo. Lond. 1769.
———, ——. The Appeal Defended. 8vo. N. York. 1769.
Changery: an Allegoric Memoir of the Boston Exchange Office. 12mo. Bost. 1805.
Chanler, Isaac. Sermon from Acts xi. 23. 12mo. Bost. 1740.
Channing, Edw. T. Inaugural Discourse. 8vo. Camb. 1819.
———, ———. Oration, July 4th. 8vo. Bost. 1817.
Channing, Wm. Ellery. Fast Sermon. 8vo. Bost. 1810.
———, ———. ———. 8vo. Bost. 1812.
———, ———. Two Sermons on Infidelity. 8vo. Bost. 1813.
———, ———. Sermon from Jeremiah vi. 8. 8vo. Bost. 1814.
———, ———. Discourse on the Delivery of the Christian World from Military Despotism. 8vo. Bost. 1814.
———, ———. Convention Sermon on War. 8vo. Bost. 1816.
———, ———. Sermon at the Ordination of the Rev. John Emery Abbot. 8vo. Bost. 1815.
———, ———. Letter to the Rev. S. C. Thacher, on the Aspersions in the Panoplist on the Ministers in Boston. &c. 3d. ed. 8vo. Bost. 1815
———, ———. Remarks on the Rev. Dr. Worcester's Letter to him. 8vo. Bost. 1815.
———, ———. Remarks on Dr. Worcester's Second Letter. 8vo. Bost. 1815.
———, ———. Letter to him, by a Layman. 8vo.
———, ———. Sermon at the Ordination of the Rev. Jared Sparks. 12mo. Bost. 1819.
———, ———. Dudleian Lecture. 8vo. Bost. 1821.
———, ———. Sermon at the Ordination of the Rev. E. S. Gannett. 8vo. Bost. 1824.

Channing, Wm. Ellery. Discourse at the Dedication of the Second Congregational Unitarian Church in New York. 2d ed. 12mo. N. York. 1827.
Chanter, Isaac. Sermon from Acts II. 23, at Mr. Whitfield's Lecture in Charleston, S. C. 12mo. Bost. 1740.
Chanut, M. l'Abbé. Le Saint Concile de Trente, nouvellement traduit. 2de ed. 12mo. Paris. 1680.
Chanvalon, Thibault de. Voyage à la Martinique. 4to. Paris. 1763.
Chaplin, Daniel. Convention Sermon. 8vo. Bost. 1808.
Chaplin, Eben. Result of an Ecclesiastical Council. 1793.
Chapman, Geo. The Iliads of Homer, donne according to the Greeke. See Homer.
Chapman, Geo. Treatise on Education. 12mo. Lond. 1774.
Chapman, John. Primitive Antiquity explained and vindicated.—Remarks on a Letter to Dr. Waterland in relation to the Natural Account of Languages.—Phlegon Examined, &c.—Phlegon Reexamined. 8vo. Lond. 1742.
———, ——. Eusebius; or Christian's Defence against "The Moral Philosopher." 2 vols. 8vo. Camb. 1739—41.
Chapman, Nathan. Select Speeches. 5 vols. 8vo. Phil. 1807—8.
Chapman, Tho. On the Roman Senate. 8vo. Camb. 1750.
Chappe d'Auteroche, Jean. Voyage en Siberie, en 1761. 2 vol. en 3. 4to. Paris. 1768.
————————, ——. Voyage en Californie, etc. 4to. Paris. 1772.
————————, ——. Voyage to California to observe the Transit of Venus; with Cassini's Voyage to Newfoundland and Sallee. 8vo. Lond. 1778.
Chappelow, Leon. Commentary on Job, with the Hebrew Text and English Translation; also Paraphrase on a part of Job. 2 vols. 4to. Camb. 1752.
—————, ——. Grammatica Arabica. 8vo. Lond. 1730.
Chaptal, J. A. Elements of Chemistry; tr. from the French by W. Nicholson. 3d ed. 3 vols. 8vo. Lond. 1800.
Characters. See Public Characters.
Chardin, Sir John. Travels into Persia and the East Indies. fol. Lond. 1686.
———, ———. Voyages en Perse et autres Lieux de l'Orient. 4 vol. 4to. Amst. 1735.
Chardon. Code des Prises, ou Recueil des Edits, etc. sur la Course et l'Administration des Prises, depuis 1400 jusqu' à présent. 2 vol. 4to. Paris. 1784.
Charibbs. See St. Vincent.
Charibee Leeward Islands. Acts of Assembly passed in them. fol. Lond. 1734.
Charitable Institutions. Account of the Charity-Schools in Great Britain and Ireland, &c. 4to. Lond. 1711.
——— ———. Plan for a Working-School for Poor Children. 4to. Lond. 1758.
——— ———. Charity-School Sermon. 4to.

Charitable Institutions. Plan and Present State of the Charity at Horton for Poor Children. 4to. Lond. 1766.

—— ——. Royal Charter for an Hospital for Exposed and Deserted Children. 8vo. Lond. 1739.

—— ——. Plan for executing the Purposes of the above "Royal Charter." 8vo. Lond. 1740.

—— ——. Rules of the Mount Sion Society, at Charleston, (S. C.) 4to. Charleston. 1784.

—— ——. Rules of the South-Carolina Society established at Charleston in 1736. 6th ed. 8vo. Charleston. 1795.

—— ——. Act to Incórporate the German Society for the Relief of Distressed Germans in Pennsylvania; in English and German. 8vo. Phil. 1793.

—— ——. Account of the Salem Female Charitable Society. 8vo. Salem.

—— ——. Fifteen Reports of the Society for Bettering the Condition of the Poor. 8vo. Lond. 1797—1805.

—— ——. Information for Overseers, by the above Society. 12mo. Lond. 1799.

—— ——. Accounts of the Literary Fund Society. 8vo. Lond. 1799—1810.

—— ——. Act of Incorporation of the Massachusetts Congregational Charitable Society, with a Sketch of its Origin, &c. 8vo. Bost. 1815.

—— ——. First and Third Reports of the Connecticut Asylum for Deaf and Dumb Persons. 8vo. Hartford. 1807—9.

—— ——. Act to Incorporate the New-York Institution for the Instruction of the Deaf and Dumb. 8vo. N. York. 1819.

—— ——. Explanations of the Views of the Society for Employing the Female Poor; with the Constitution and By-Laws, &c. 8vo. Camb. 1825.

—— ——. See Hospitals.

Chariton Aphrodisiensis. De Chærea et Callirrhoe, Gr. et Lat. a Reiskio, cum Animadversionibus d'Orville. 4to. Amst. 1750.

Charity in all its Branches. 8vo. Lond. 1732.

Charlemagne, P. Réfutation d'un Ecrit de Charrault, intitulé: "Coup-d'œil sur St. Domingue." 8vo. Cap-Henry.

Charlemont, Memoirs of the Earl of. See Hardy, F.

Charles I. Sylloge Variorum Tractatuum, quibus Caroli Innocentia illustratur, etc. 4to. 1648—9.

——. Oglio of Traytors, &c. 16mo. Lond.

——. Speeches and Prayers of some of his Judges, &c. 4to. 1660—2.

——. Journal of the High Court of Justice for his Trial. See Nalson, J.

——. Memorials and Letters relating to the History of Britain in his Reign. See Dalrymple, Sir David.

——; Letters concerning. See Hammond, R.

Charles I. Declaration concerning the Tumults in Scotland. fol. Lond. 1639.
———. Inquiry concerning the Transactions of the Earl of Glamorgan. See Birch, T.
———. Bibliotheca Regia. 8vo. Lond. 1659.
———. Presbyterians Not Guilty of his Murder. 12mo. Lond. 1713.
———. Icon Basilikè. 8vo. Lond. 1727.
———, Sermon on the Martyrdom of, preached at Court in the last Century. 2d ed. 8vo. Lond. 1708.
———. Works, with his Trial and Death. 12mo. Hague.
———. The Same. 2 vols. 12mo. Aberdeen. 1766.
———. Account of his Reign. (Harl. Miscel. vol. 2.)
———. Trial of his Judges. (Id. 6.)
———. His Case, by J. Cooke.—His Case and Character, by S. Butler. (Somers, Tr. vol. 4.)
———. See Husband, E.,—James I.,—Parliament,—Regicides.
Charles II. Act of General Pardon, Indemnity, &c. 4to. Edin. 1660.
———. Act for the Uniformity of Public Prayers, &c. 4to. Lond. 1662.
———. Directions concerning Preachers. 4to. 1685.
———. Declaratio de Rebus Ecclesiasticis. 4to. Amst. 1690.
———. Articuli Pacis. 4to. Lond. 1662.
———. Articles of Peace with the Bashaw of Tunis. 4to. Lond. 1677.
———. Account of his Escape from Worcester. (Harl. Miscel. vol. 4.)
———. Copies of Two Papers, written by him. fol. Lond.
———. Remarks on the Two Papers. 4to.
———. Defence of the Papers. 4to. Lond. 1686.
———. Reply to the Answer made upon the Three Royal Papers. 4to. Lond. 1686.
———. Royal Oak; or Account of his Travels, &c. (Somers, Tr. vol. 10.)
Charles de Valois, Duc d'Angoulême. (Mém. de France. vol. 62.)
Charles, Joseph. Dispersion at Babel. 2 vols. 8vo. Lond. 1769.
Charleston, (S. C.) Rules of the Charlestown Chamber of Commerce. 12mo. Charleston. 1774.
———, ———. Ordinances of the City Council. 4to. Charleston. 1802.
———, ———, Rules of the Fellowship Society in. 3d ed. 8vo. Charleston. 1774.
———, ———. See Charitable Institutions. See Church.
Charlestown, (Mass.) Review of the Case of the Free Bridge between Boston and Charlestown. 8vo. Bost. 1827.
Charleton, Walter. Character of Charles II. 4to. Lond. 1661.
Charlevoix, P. Fr. Xavier de. Histoire de Paraguay. 3 vol. 4to. Paris. 1756.
———, ———. Idem. 6 vol. 12mo. Paris. 1757.
———, ———. Histoire de S. Domingue. 2 vol. 4to. Paris. 1730—1.

Charlevoix, P. Fr. Xavier de. Idem. 4 vol. 12mo. Amst. 1733.
——, ——. Histoire de la Nouvelle France. 6 vol. 12mo. Paris. 1744.
——, ——. Idem. 3 vol. 4to. Paris. 1744.
——, ——. Histoire du Japon. 9 vol. 12mo. Paris. 1736.
Charmilly, Venault de. Lettre à M. Bryan Edwards, en Réfutation de son Ouvrage sur St. Domingue. 4to. Lond. 1797.
Charnock, John. Memoirs of Lord Nelson. 12mo. N. York. 1807.
Charnock, Stephen. Works. 2 vols. fol. Lond. 1684.
Charron, Pierre. De la Sagesse. 16mo. Leide. chez J. Elsevier.
——, ——. Of Wisdome, tr. from the French by S. Lennard. 4to. Lond. 1630.
——, ——. Of Wisdom, tr. by G. Stanhope. 2 vols. 8vo. Lond. 1707.
Charte-Livry. Vide Dialogues.
Charters of Virginia, Maryland, Connecticut, Rhode-Island, Pennsylvania, Massachusetts Bay, and Georgia; with a Narrative of the Proceedings of the North-American Colonies, in consequence of the Stamp-Act. 4to. Lond. 1766.
—— granted by Charles II. to the Proprietors of Carolina; with the First and Last Fundamental Constitutions of that Colony. 4to. Lond.
Chas, J., et Lebrun. Histoire de la Révolution de l'Amérique Septentrionale. 8vo. Paris. 1801.
Chase, Sam. Answer and Pleas to the Articles of Impeachment exhibited against him. 8vo. Salem and Newburyport. 1805.
——, ——. Report of his Trial. See Evans, C.
Chastellux, F. J. (M. le Marquis de.) Voyages dans l'Amérique Septentrionale dans les Anneés 1780, 1781, et 1782. 2 vol. 8vo. Paris. 1786.
——, ——. Travels in N. America in 1780—2; from the French, with Notes. 2 vols. 8vo. Lond. 1787.
——, ——. Remarks on his Travels. 8vo. Lond. 1787.
——, ——. Discours en Vers. Vide Humphreys, D.
Chastre. (M. de la.) Mémoires. (Mém. de France. vol. 40.)
Chateaubriand, F. A. de. Travels in Greece, Palestine, &c. tr. from the French by F. Shoberl. 8vo. N. York. 1814.
——, ——. Recollections of Italy, England, and America. 8vo. Phil. 1816.
Chatelain, Henri. Sermons. 6 vol. 8vo. Amst. 1759—60.
Chatham, Earl of. See Pitt, Wm.
Chatterton, Tho. Works. 3 vols. 8vo. Lond. 1803.
——, ——. Poems. See Chalmers, A.
Chaucer, Geoffrey. Works, by Urry, with a Glossary. fol. Lond. 1721.
——, ——. Poems. See Chalmers, A.
Chaufepié, J. H. Historia Febris Flavæ Americanæ. 8vo. Halæ. 1794.

Chaulmer, Charles. Le Nouveau-Monde, ou l'Amérique Chrestienne, etc.—Suite du Nouveau-Monde. 12mo. Paris. 1659.

Chaumont, J. le Ray de. Address to the Agricultural Society of Jefferson County. 8vo. N. York. 1818.

Chauncy, Charles. Seasonable Thoughts on the State of Religion in New England. 8vo. Bost. 1743.

———, ———. Dr. T. B. Chandler's Appeal answered, in behalf of Non-Episcopal Churches in America. 8vo. Bost. 1768.

———, ———. Reply to Dr. Chandler's Appeal Defended. 8vo. Bost. 1770.

———, ———. Letter to a Friend on the Bp. of Landaff's Sermon. 8vo. Bost. 1767.

———, ———. The Same; with a Supplement, in Answer to Dr. Chandler. 8vo. Lond. 1768. See Fleming, C.

———, ———. Compleat View of Episcopacy. 8vo. Bost. 1771.

———, ———. Sacramental "Breaking of Bread" a Christian Duty, in Five Sermons. 8vo. Bost. 1772.

———, ———. Salvation for All Men. 2d ed. 8vo. Bost. 1782.

———, ———. ——— ———. 8vo. Lond. 1784.

———, ———. Letter to Dr. Mather, occasioned by his Reflexions on the Above. 12mo. Bost. 1782.

———, ———. To the Author of a Letter to Dr. Mather, by one of the Readers. 12mo. Bost. 1783.

———, ———. Benevolence of the Deity considered. 8vo. Bost. 1784.

———, ———. Divine Glory brought to View in the Condemnation of the Ungodly, in Reply to "Salvation for All Men," by a Friend to Truth. 8vo. Bost. 1782.

———, ———. Five Dissertations on the Fall. 8vo. Lond. 1785.

———, ———. Dudleian Lecture. 8vo. Bost. 1762.

———, ———. Convention Sermon. 8vo. Bost. 1744.

———, ———. Election Sermon. 8vo. Bost. 1747.

———, ———. Thanksgiving Sermon for the Reduction of Cape Breton. 8vo. Bost. 1745.

———, ———. Thanksgiving Sermon on occasion of the Repeal of the Stamp-Act. 8vo. Bost. 1766.

———, ———. Sermon on the Death of Mrs. E. Price. 8vo. Bost. 1732.

———, ———. Sermon on the Death of the Hon. N. Byfield. 8vo. 1733.

———, ———. Sermon on the Death of Deacon J. Williams. 8vo. Bost. 1737.

———, ———. Discourse on the Death of Mrs. L. Waldo. 8vo. Bost. 1741.

———, ———. Sermon on the Death of Deacon C. Thayer. 8vo. Bost. 1745.

———, ———. Sermon on the Death of Mrs. Anna Foxcroft. 8vo. Bost. 1749.

Chauncy, Charles. Sermon on the Death of Mr. Edward Gray. 8vo. Bost. 1757.

———, ———. Discourse on the Death of the Rev. Jonathan Mayhew. 8vo. Bost. 1766.

———, ———. Sermon on the Death of the Rev. Thomas Foxcroft. 8vo. Bost. 1769.

———, ———. Sermon at the Ordination of the Rev. Joseph Bowman. 8vo. Bost. 1762.

———, ———. Sermon at the Ordination of the Rev. Penuel Bowen. 8vo. Bost. 1766.

———, ———. Sermon on the Gift of the Spirit to Ministers. 8vo. Bost. 1742.

———, ———. Sermon on the Present Rebellion. 8vo. Bost. 1746.

———, ———. Sermon against Enthusiasm. 8vo. Bost. 1742.

———, ———. Sermon at an Execution for Murder. 8vo. Bost. 1754.

———, ———. Sermon on account of the Earthquake, Nov. 18, 1755. 8vo. Bost. 1755.

———, ———. Sermon on account of the late Earthquakes. 8vo. Bost. 1756.

———, ———. Twelve Sermons on Important Subjects. 8vo. Bost. 1765.

———, ———. Trust in God in the Day of Trouble, a Sermon. 8vo. Bost. 1770.

———, ———. Sermon at the Installment of the Rev. Tho. Frink. 8vo. Bost. 1744.

———, ———. Sketch of Eminent Men in New-England. (Mass. Hist. Coll. vol. 10.)

Chauncey, Nathaniel. Connecticut Election Sermon. 16mo. N. Lond. 1734.

Chausse, M. A. C. de la. De Insignibus Pontificis Maximi, etc.—De Deorum Simulacris, Idolis, etc. (Grævius, vol. 5.)

Chauvin, Stephanus. Lexicon Rationale. fol. Rotterdami. 1692.

Checkley, John. Speech upon his Tryal for publishing "The Short and Easy Method with the Deists," &c. 2d ed. 8vo. Lond. 1738.

———, ——. Discourse on Episcopacy. See Leslie, C.

Checkley, Sam. Sermon on the Death of King George I. 8vo. Bost. 1727.

———, ——. Sermon on the Death of the Rev. Wm. Waldron. 8vo. Bost. 1727.

———, ——. Sermon on the Death of Madam Lydia Hutchinson. 8vo. Bost. 1748.

———, ——. Election Sermon. 8vo. Bost. 1755.

Cheetham, James. Life of Thomas Paine. 8vo. N. York. 1809.

———, ——. Reply to Aristides. 8vo. N. York. 1804.

Cheever, Abijah. Case of Incisted Dropsy, &c. 16mo. Bost. 1794.

Cheever, Samuel. Election Sermon. 12mo. Bost. 1712.

Chefs-d'œuvre d'Eloquence et de Poésie Française. 12mo. Paris. 1812.
Chelsum, James. Reply to Gibbon's Vindication of his History. 12mo. Winchester. 1785.
Chemistry, Conversations on. 8th ed. 2 vols. 12mo. Lond. 1822.
Chemnitius, Mart. Loci Theologici. 3 vol. 4to. Francof. ad Mœn. 1591—2.
———, ———. Idem. fol. Franc. et Witteb. 1653.
———, ———. Examen Concilii Tridentini. 4to. Francof. 1606.
———, ———. Idem. fol. Francof. 1609.
———, ———. Harmonia Evangelica, Gr. et Lat. 4to. Francof. ad Mœn. 1608.
Chenevix, Rich. New Method of Secret Writing. (Journal of Science, vol. 10).
Chenier, J. de. Tableau Historique de l'Etat et des Progrès de la Littérature Française. 8vo. Paris. 1818.
Chesapeake, Frigate. Thoughts upon the Conduct of our Administration, more especially in reference to the Attack on the Chesapeake. 8vo. Bost. 1808.
Cheselden, Wm. Anatomy of the Human Body. 9th ed. 8vo. Lond. 1768.
———, ———. The Same. 13th ed. 8vo. Lond. 1792.
———, ———. ———. 2d Amer. ed. 8vo. Bost. 1806.
———, ———. On the Bones. fol.
Chesterfield, P. D. Stanhope, Earl of. Miscellaneous Works; with his Life, by M. Maty. 3 vols. 8vo. Dublin. 1777.
Cheston, R. B. Pathological Inquiries and Observations on Surgery. 4to. Glocester. 1766.
Chevalier. Lettres sur les Maladies de St. Domingue; sur ses Plantes; et sur le Remora et les Halcyons. 12mo. Paris. 1752.
Chevalier, J. B. le. Voyage de la Propontide et du Pont-Euxin. 2 vol. 8vo. Paris. 1800.
———, ———. Description of the Plain of Troy, tr. from the French by A. Dalzel. 4to. Edin. 1791.
Chevalier, Tho. On Gun-Shot Wounds. 12mo. Lond. 1804.
———, ———. The Same. 3d ed. 12mo. Lond. 1806.
———, ———. Introduction to Lectures on Surgery. 8vo. Lond. 1801.
Chevallier, Paulus. Oratio de Fructibus, qui ex juste temperata Cogitandi Libertate in Theologum redundant. 4to. Groningæ. 1752.
———, ———. Oratio de Literis Humanioribus, Optimo Religionis Christianæ Præsidio. 4to. Lug. Bat. 1764.
Cheverny, P. Hurault, Comte de. Mémoires. (Mém. de France, vol. 50, 51, et 52.)
Cheyne, Geo. On Health and Long Life. 8vo. Lond. 1724.
———, ———. Natural Method of Curing Diseases. 8vo. Lond. 1742.

Cheyne, Geo. Philosophical Principles of Religion. 8vo. Lond. 1715.
Cheynell, Fr. Sickness, Heresy, Death, and Burial of Wm. Chillingworth. 8vo. Lond. 1725.
Chiabrera Gabriello. Rime. 3 tom. 8vo. Milano. 1807.
Chiaramonti, (Card.) Vide Pius VII.
Chiaranda, J. P. Plutia, sive Platia, Civitas Siciliæ. (Græv. Thes. Ital.)
Chicoyneau, Fran. Traité de la Peste. 4to. Paris. 1744.
Chiesa, Lodovico della. Dell' Historia di Piemonte. 4to. Torino. 1608.
Chiffletius, J. J. Geminiæ Titulus Sepulcralis Explicatus.—De Orthonibus Æreis. (Sallengre, vol. 1.)
———, ——. De Linteis Sepulchr. Christi. 4to. Antv. 1688.
———, ——. Idem. (Ugol. vol. 33.)
———, ——. Fons Aqua Virgo. (Grævius, vol. 4.)
Chiffletius, P. F. De Fide Catholica Quinque Opuscula. 4to. Divione. 1656.
Chija, (Rab.) De Die Expiationum. (Ugol. vol. 1.)
Child, Sir Josiah. New Discourse on Trade. 5th ed. 12mo. Glasgow. 1751.
Chile. Compendio della Storia del Regno del Chile. 8vo. Bologna. 1776.
Chillingworth, Wm. Works. 7th ed. fol. Lond. 1719.
——— ———, ——. ———. 10th ed. fol. Lond. 1742.
Chimentellius, Val. Marmor Pisanum de Honore Bisellii. 4to. Bononiæ. 1666.
———, ——. Idem. (Grævius, vol. 7.)
Chinese. Miscellaneous Pieces relating to them. 2 vols. 12mo. Lond. 1762.
———. Mémoires sur la Chinois. 15 vol. 4to. Paris. 1791—7.
———. Dissertation on the Chinese Language. 4to. Serampore. 1809.
——— Almanac for 1811.
——— Catechism, (by Mr. Morrison.)
——— Gospel of Luke, (by Mr. Morrison.)
——— First Chapter of Genesis.
——— Tracts, (by Mr. Morrison.)
Chinese Spy. 6 vols. 12mo. Lond. 1765.
Chioccus, And. Musæum Calceolarianum Veronense. fol. Veronæ. 1622.
Chion. Epistolæ. Vide Memnon.
Chipman, Daniel. Vermont Reports. 8vo. Middlebury. 1824.
———, ——. Essay on the Law of Contracts. 8vo. Middlebury. 1822.
Chipman, Nathaniel. Sketches of the Principles of Government. 12mo. Rutland. 1793.
Chirurgici Libri Græcorum, Sorani et Oribasii, Gr. et Lat. ab A. Cocchio. fol. Florentiæ. 1754.
Chishull, Edm. Inscriptio Sigea Antiquissima. fol. Lond. 1721.

Chishull, Edm. Antiquitates Asiaticæ Christianam Æram antecedentes. fol. Lond. 1728.
——, ——. Visitation Sermon. 8vo. Lond. 1711.
Chitty, Joseph. On Pleading, by T. Day. 3 vols. 8vo. N. York. 1812—18.
——, ——. On Criminal Law, by R. Peters. 3 vols. 8vo. Phil. 1819.
——, ——. On Bills of Exchange. 8vo. Georgetown. 1817.
Choate, John. Reasons of Dissent from the Judgment of a Council. 8vo. Portsmouth. 1760.
——, ——. Remarks on the Rev. W. Hall's Answer to the above. 8vo. Bost. 1761.
Choisnin, Jean. Mémoires. (Mém. de France, vol. 54.)
Choppin, R. Sermon on the Death of the Rev. Joseph Boyse. 8vo. Dublin. 1729.
Chrestien, Florent. Vide Pibrac.
Christ. Sermon on his Passion, by J. G. 4to. Lond. 1686.
——, or Anti-Christ. 8vo. Lond.
——, the Mediator. 8vo. Lond. 1732.
——. Discourse concerning his Priesthood. 8vo. Lond. 1747.
——. Second Thoughts concerning his Sufferings and Death. 8vo. Lond. 1748.
——. Essay on his Fear of Death. 8vo. Lond. 1737.
——. Essay to solve the Difficulties that attend the several Accounts of his Resurrection, by a Fellow of Harvard College. 4to. Bost.. 1734.
——. Summary View of the New Testament Evidence respecting his Person.
——. Arguments from Scripture proving him to be the Supreme God. 8vo. Lond. 1719.
——. Answer to the Above. 8vo. Lond. 1723.
——. Two Discourses, on the Creation of All Things by Jesus Christ, and on the Resurrection of the Dead. 8vo. Lond. 1787.
——. Language of Scripture respecting the Saviour, in relation to God, the Father; by a Layman. 8vo. Bost. 1815.
——. See Messiah. See Trinity.
Christ, M. Dictionnaire des Monogrammes, Chiffres, Logogryphes, Rébus, etc. 8vo. Paris. 1750.
Christian Disciple. 6 vols. 8vo. Bost. 1813—18.
—— ——. New Series. 5 vols. 8vo. Bost. 1819—23.
—— Examiner. 5 vols. 8vo. Bost. 1824, et seqq.
—— Monitor. 10 vols. 12mo. Bost. 1809—11.
—— Register. fol. 1821, et seqq.
—— Spectator. New Series. 8vo. New-Haven. 1827, et seqq.
—— Doctrine, Views of. 12mo. Camb. 1828.
Christianity, The Practice of, by R. R. 12mo. Lond. 1623.
—— Not Founded on Argument. See Dodwell.
——. Observations on the Above, by a Christian Freethinker. 8vo. Lond. 1765.
—— Not Introduced by Power and Force; a Sermon by Sir R——d C——ks. 8vo. Lond. 1722.

Christianity. Essay towards a Summary of Gospel Christianity, &c. 8vo. Lond. 1726.

———. Proposal for a Charter to incorporate a Society for promoting Christian Knowledge among the poor Natives in Ireland. 4to. Lond. 1740.

———. State of the Society in Scotland for propagating Christian Knowledge. 8vo. Edin. 1741.

———. Abridgment of the Statutes and Rules of the Society in Scotland for propagating Christian Knowledge. 12mo. Edin. 1732.

———. Account of some late Proceedings of the Society for promoting Christian Knowledge. 8vo. 1789.

———. Account of the Massachusetts Society for promoting Christian Knowledge. 12mo. Camb. 1806.

———. Another. 12mo. Andover. 1815.

———. Ninth Report of the Protestant Episcopal Society for the Advancement of Christianity, &c. 8vo. Charleston, (S. C.) 1819.

———. Nature and Design of Christianity, extracted from a late Author. 10th ed. 12mo. Camb. 1808.

———. Evidences of its Truth. 8vo. Bost. 1813.

———. Reply to Two Deistical Works, entitled, "The New Trial of the Witnesses," &c. and G. Smith's "Not Paul but Jesus." By Ben David. 8vo. Lond. 1824.

———, Evidences of, by Watson, Jenyns, West, and Lyttleton. 18mo. Lond. 1824.

———. Vide Church,—Gospel,—Popery,—Protestants,—Religion,—Trinity, &c.

Christie, Wm. Discourses on the Divine Unity. 2d ed. 12mo. Montrose. 1790.

———, ———. Speech at the Grave of the Rev. Joseph Priestley. 8vo. Northumberland. 1804.

Christmannus, M. J. De Kalendario Romano. (Grævius, vol. 8.)

Chronicle, Boston, for 1768. 4to.

———, ——— 1769. fol.

———, Independent, for 1777—85. 9 vols. fol. Bost.

———, ——— 1789. fol. Bost.

———, ——— 1800—12. 13 vols. fol. Bost.

———, ——— 1818—19. 2 vols. fol. Bost.

———, American and British, of War and Politics, from May 10, 1773 to July 16, 1783. 8vo. Lond.

Chronique Réligieuse. 3 vol. 8vo. Paris. 1819.

Chroniques des Empereurs. 12mo.

Chrysostomus, S. Joannes. Opera, Græce; cum Notis Latinis, cura H. Savillii. 8 vol. fol. Etonæ. 1612.

———, ———. Homiliæ IV, Gr. et Lat. cum Notis, a C. F. Matthæo. 2 vol. 8vo. Misenæ. 1792.

———, ———. Eclogæ LII, Græce, cum Notis, a C. F. Matthæo. 8vo. Lips. 1807.

———, ———. Vide Raphelius.

Chubb, Tho. Previous Question with regard to Religion. 4th ed. 8vo. Lond. 1728.

——, ——. Supplement to the Prev. Quest. 8vo. Lond. 1725.

——, ——. Prev. Quest. and Supplement. 4to. Lond. 1730.

——, ——. Vindication of God's Moral Character. 8vo. Lond. 1726.

——, ——. The Same. 4to. Lond. 1730.

——, ——. Supplement to the Vindication; with the Case of Abraham's Offering up Isaac re-examined. 8vo. Lond. 1727.

——, ——. Examination of Barclay's Apology. 4to. Lond. 1730.

——, ——. Enquiry into the Grounds and Foundation of Religion; with a Dissertation on Math. xix, 21, in Answer to Stebbing; and an Answer to a private Letter on the subject of God's Foreknowledge. 8vo. Lond. 1740.

——, ——. On Persecution. 4to. Lond. 1730.

——, ——. Discourse concerning Reason; with Reflections on the comparative Excellency of Moral and Positive Duties. 8vo. Lond. 1733.

——, ——. Scripture-Evidence considered. Also Two Tracts: viz. on Virtue and Happiness; and Things offered to the Consideration of Believers and Unbelievers. 12mo. Lond. 1728.

——, ——. True Gospel of Jesus Christ asserted; with a Short Dissertation on Providence. 8vo. Lond. 1738.

——, ——. Letter to him on the above, by R. P. 8vo. Lond. 1739.

——, ——. True Gospel of Christ vindicated; with a Vindication of the Dissertation on Providence. 8vo. Lond. 1739.

——, ——. Discourse on Miracles; with an Enquiry, whether a Future State was taught by Moses and the Prophets. 8vo. Lond. 1741.

——, ——. Discourse of Miracles answered, in a Letter to him. 8vo. 1742.

——, ——. Enquiry concerning Redemption; with a Preface, upon Christianity founded on Argument. 8vo. Lond. 1743.

——, ——. Enquiries:—viz. On Justification; on Forgiveness of Sins; on Christ's Satisfaction; on the Justice of God; on Infinite Justice and Infinite Satisfaction; on Faith and Mysteries; on the Use of Reason in Matters of Revelation; on Prayer; on the Unity of the Church, or Body of Christ; whether Christ is sole King in his own Kingdom. 4to. Lond. 1730.

——, ——. Remarks on Morgan's Tracts. 4to. Lond. 1730.

——, ——. Reflections on Natural Liberty. 4to. Lond. 1730.

——, ——. Eight Discourses:—viz. On Natural Liberty; on the Glory of Christ; Thanks to the Author of "A friendly Admonition"; Things offered to the Consideration of Believers and Unbelievers; on Virtue and Happiness; on Virtue and Vice; on the Grounds and Extent of Authority and Liberty, with respect to Civil Government; and on Natural Punishments. 4to. Lond. 1730.

Chubb, Tho. Supremacy of the Father asserted. 4to. Lond. 1730.

——, ——. Human Nature vindicated. 8vo. Lond. 1726.

——, ——. The Same. 8vo. Lond. 1730.

——, ——. Friendly Admonition to Mr. Chubb. 8vo. Lond. 1727.

——, ——. Four Tracts;—Enquiry concerning the New Testament; on Britannicus's Letters; Case of Abraham; Equity and Reasonableness of a Future Judgment. 8vo. Lond. 1734.

——, ——. Two Treatises;—concerning Property; concerning Sin. 4to. Lond. 1730.

——, ——. Two Letters;—to Dr. Stebbing on Church Discipline; to Dr. Waterland on Covenants: also Defence of Protestantism. 8vo. Lond. 1736.

——, ——. Equity and Reasonableness of the Divine Conduct in Pardoning Repentant Sinners; with Two Dissertations, viz. on Titus iii. 10, 11; and on the Time for keeping a Sabbath. Also the Case of Pecuniary Mulcts with regard to Dissenters. 8vo. Lond. 1737.

——, ——. Four Dissertations;—on the History of Melchizedek; on the Temper and Behaviour of Esau and Jacob; on the Conduct of Balaam; and on Dr. Sherlock's Assertion, "Thus far all is well." 8vo. Lond. 1746.

——, ——. On the Opposition to Dr. Rundle's Election to the See of Gloucester. Also Three Tracts, viz. Answer to Stone's Second Remarks on the Case of Abraham, &c.; Discourse on Sincerity; Supplement to "The Equity and Reasonableness of a Future Judgment." 8vo. Lond. 1735.

——, ——. Grounds and Reasons of Two Solemnities, viz. on the 30th of January and 5th of November; also Sufficiency of Reason in Matters of Religion farther considered. 8vo. Lond. 1732.

——, ——. Ground and Foundation of Morality; with the First Section of the Author's Farewell to his Readers. 8vo. Lond. 1745.

——, ——. Short and Faithful Account of his Life. 8vo. Lond. 1747.

——, ——. Two Letters from one of the People called Quakers concerning him. 8vo. Lond. 1747.

——, ——. Vindication of the Memory of Mr. Chubb. 8vo. Lond. 1747.

Church. First and Second Booke of Discipline, &c. of the Kirk. 4to. 1621.

——. Assertion of the Government of the Church of Scotland. 4to. 1641.

——. Dispute against the English-Popish Ceremonies obtruded upon the Church of Scotland. 4to. 1637.

——. Jus Divinum Regiminis Ecclesiastici; or Divine Right of Church Government, by sundry Ministers of Christ. 4to. Lond. 1646.

——. The Same. 2d ed. 4to. Lond. 1647.

Church. Constitutions and Canons Ecclesiasticall. 4to. Lond. 1633.

——. Constitutions and Canons Ecclesiasticall. 4to. Lond. 1640.

——. Disputation concerning Church-Members and their Children, by an Assembly of Divines at Boston, N. E. 1657. 4to. Lond. 1659.

——. Two Papers of Proposals concerning the Doctrines and Discipline of the Church of England. 4to. Lond. 1661.

——. Complaints concerning Corruptions and Grievances in Church-Government, &c. 4to. Lond. 1660 and 1675.

——. Animadversions upon the above. 2d ed. 4to. Lond. 1676.

——. Succession of the Church and Sacraments, from Christ and his Apostles to the End of the World. 4to. Lond. 1686.

——. Apologeticall Relation of the Sufferings of Ministers and Professors of the Church of Scotland. 12mo. 1665.

——. Endeavour to rectifie some prevailing Opinions contrary to the Doctrine of the Church of England. 12mo. Lond. 1671.

——. Collection of Articles, &c. See Sparrow, A.

——. Discourse concerning the Unity of the Catholic Church maintained in the Church of England. 4to. Lond. 1684.

——. Instance of the Church of England's Loyalty. 4to. Lond. 1687.

——. New Test of the Church of England's Loyalty. 4to. Lond. 1687.

——. New Test, &c. examined. 4to. Lond. 1687.

——. Reply to the New Test. 4to. Lond. 1687.

——. Answer to the New Test. 4to.

——. Reflections upon the New Test, &c. 4to. Lond. 1687.

——. Answer to the Question, "What Respect ought the True Sons of the Church of England to bear to the Religion of that Church, whereof the King is a Member?" 4to. Lond. 1687.

——. Layman's Opinion in a private Letter to a Divine of the Church of England. 4to. 1687.

——. Layman's Answer to the Layman's Opinion. 4to. Lond. 1687.

——. Testimonie of Antiquity, shewing the Ancient Faith in the Church of England touching Sacraments, &c. 4to. Lond. 1687.

——. Church Government, Part V. concerning the English Reformation. 4to. Oxford. 1687.

——. Reflections on the above. 4to. Oxford. 1687.

——. Animadversions on the same. 4to. Oxford. 1687.

——. Church of England's Complaint in Vindication of her Loyalty. 4to.

——. Copy of an Address to the King by the Bp. of Oxon; with the Reasons for and against subscribing it. 4to. Lond. 1687.

——. Reply to the Reasons against Addressing. 4to. Lond. 1687.

Church. Vindication of a Sheet, concerning the Orders of the Church of England against some Reasons, &c. printed at Oxford. 4to. Lond. 1688.

———. Address to the Abp. of Canterbury and the Bishops upon the account of their late Petition. 4to. Lond. 1688.

———. Answer to the Petition of the Abp. of Canterbury, &c. 4to. Lond. 1688.

———. Address to the Ministers of the Church of England. 4to. Lond. 1688.

———. Discourse concerning the Churches Authority in Matters of Faith. 4to. Lond. 1687.

———. Discourse concerning the Adoration of the Host. 8vo. Lond. 1685.

———. Discourse concerning Auricular Confession. 12mo. Edin. 1686.

———. Layman's Faith touching the Supream and Infallible Guide of the Church. 4to. Lond. 1688.

———. Continuation of the Present State of the Controversy between the Church of England and the Church of Rome. 4to. Lond. 1688.

———. Abby and other Church Lands, not yet assured to such Possessors as are Roman Catholics. 4to.

———. Doctrine of Instituted Churches explained and proved from the Word of God. 4to. Lond.

———. Ancient State of the Church. 16mo.

———. Heads of Agreement assented to by the United Ministers in and about London, formerly called Presbyterian and Congregational. 4to. Lond. 1691.

———. Answer to the Memorial of the Church of England. 8vo. Lond. 1705.

———. Letter from a Country Attorney, concerning the Rights of the Christian Church. 8vo. Lond. 1709.

———. Safety of the Church under the Present Administration considered. 8vo. Lond. 1715.

———. Layman's Vindication of the Church of England, against Howell and Bennett. 8vo. Lond. 1716.

———. Answer to the Non-Jurors Charge of Schism. 8vo. Lond. 1716.

———. External Peace of the Church only attainable by a Zeal for Scripture and by Mutual Charity. 8vo. Lond. 1716.

——— of England's Apology for the Principles of the Dissenters, particularly as to Jan. 30th. 8vo. Lond. 1718.

——— Anatomy; or Representation of the Present Constitution of the Church of England. 8vo. Lond. 1718.

———. Platform of Church Discipline. See Cambridge, (N. E.)

———. Vindication of the Divine Authority of Ruling Elders in the Church. 12mo.

———. Reasons for uniting the Church and Dissenters; with a a Liturgy. 8vo. Lond.

———. Authority of the Church in Matters of Religion. 8vo. Lond. 1718.

Church. Essay towards restoring Primitive Communion. 8vo. Lond. 1724.

———. Modest Proof of the Order and Government settled by Christ and his Apostles. 12mo. Bost. 1723.

———. Sober Remarks on the "Modest Proof." See Wigglesworth, E.

———. Vindication of the Appendix to "Sober Remarks." 12mo. Bost. 1725.

———. Results of Three Synods in Massachusetts. 12mo. Bost. 1725.

———. Address to the Church of Scotland on the Growth of Deism and Immorality, &c. 8vo. Lond. 1739.

———. Claims of Church Authority considered, and the Rights of Private Judgment defended, in Answer to Z. Mudge. 8vo. Lond. 1749.

———. Answers to the Reasons of Dissent from a Resolution of the General Assembly. 8vo. Edin. 1750.

———. Attempt to promote Love and Unity between the Church of England and the Dissenters. 8vo. Lond. 1751.

———. Form of Presbyterial Church Government. 8vo. Glasgow. 1762.

———. Serious and Free Thoughts on the Present State of the Church of England. 8vo. Lond. 1755.

———. The Same. 4th ed. 8vo. Lond. 1774.

———. Disquisitions relating to the Church of England. 4to. Lond. 1749.

———. Claims of the Church of England seriously examined. 8vo. Lond. 1764.

———. Address to the Rational Advocates of the Church of England. 8vo. Lond. 1769.

———. The Religion of the Church of England the surest Establishment of the Royal Throne. 4to.

———. Antiquity and Authority of the Church of Rome proved from the Scriptures. 8vo. Lond. 1768.

———. Canons of the Church of Scotland. 4to. 1769.

———. Observations upon the Congregational Plan of Church Government. 12mo. Bost. 1773.

———. Thoughts on the Present State of the Church and of Religion. 4th ed. 8vo. Lond. 1774.

———. Letter to a Layman on the subject of the Rev. Mr. Lindsey's Proposal for a Reformed English Church. 8vo. Lond. 1774.

———. Letter to the Abp. of Canterbury on the present Opposition to any further Reformation. 8vo. Lond. 1774.

———. Treatise on the Nature and Constitution of the Christian Church. 8vo. Lond. 1773.

———. Constitution of the Independent Congregational Church in Charleston, S. C. 8vo. Charleston. 1787.

———. Observations on the Homilies of the Church of England. 8vo. Lond. 1790.

———. Journal of the Proceedings of the Episcopal Convention at Philadelphia. 8vo. Phil. 1790.

Church. Journal of the Proceedings of the Episcopal Convention at New-York. 8vo. N. York. 1817.
———. Pastoral Letter of the Episcopal Convention. 8vo. N. York. 1817.
———. Acts and Proceedings of the General Synod of the Reformed Dutch Church at Albany. 8vo. Albany. 1817.
———. Inquiry into the Right to change the Ecclesiastical Constitution of the Congregational Churches of Massachusetts, (by J. Lowell.) 8vo. Bost. 1816.
———. Vide Canones,—Clergy,—Convocation,—Dissenters,—Episcopal Church,—Popery,—Protestants,—Religion, &c.
Church Music, Tractate on, being an Extract from Mr. Peirce's Vindication of the Dissenters. 8vo. Lond. 1786.
Church, R. S. Digest of New-York Reports. 2 vols. 8vo.
Church, T. Entertaining Passages relating to Philip's War, &c. 4to. Bost. 1716.
Church, Tho. Vindication of the Miraculous Powers of the Church in the Three First Centuries. 8vo. Lond. 1750.
Churchill, Awnsham and John. Collection of Voyages and Travels. 8 vols. fol. Lond. 1704—47.
———, ———. Histoire de la Navigation, trad. de l'Anglois. 2 vol. 12mo. Paris. 1722.
Churchill, Charles. Poems. 2 vols. 4to. Lond. 1765.
———, ———. ———. See Chalmers, A.
Churchill. See Marlborough.
Churchman, John. Magnetic Atlas. 4to. Lond. 1794.
Churton, Ralph. Eight Bampton Lecture Sermons on the Prophecies. 8vo. Oxford. 1785.
Chytræus, David. Historia Augustanæ Confessionis. 4to. Francof. ad Mœn. 1578.
———, ———. In Leviticum. 12mo. Vitebergæ. 1575.
———, ———. Tabula Philosophica. (Gronov. vol. 10.)
Ciacconius, Pet. Columna Rostrata. (Grævius, vol. 4.)
Cibber, Colley. Character and Conduct of Cicero, considered, from Dr. Middleton's History of his Life, &c. 4to. Lond. 1747.
———, ———. Lives of the Poets of Great Britain and Ireland. 5 vols. 12mo. Lond. 1753.
———, ———. His Life, &c. 4th ed. 2 vols. 12mo. Lond. 1756.
———, ———. Letter to Mr. Pope. 8vo. Lond. 1744.
Cicero, M. T. Opera, ex P. Victorii Codicibus, a R. Stephano. 4 tomi. fol. Paris. 1538—9.
———, ———. Opera, cum Notis Variorum, cura J. Verburgii. 2 vol. fol. Amst. 1724.
———, ———. Opera, a J. Oliveto. 9 vol. 4to. Paris. 1740—2.
———, ———. ———. ed. 3tia. 9 vol. 4to. Genevæ. 1758.
———, ———. ———, ex recensione noviss. J. A. Ernesti, cum ejusdem Notis et Clave. 20 vol. 12mo. Bost. 1815—16.
———, ———. De Officiis, etc. cum Comment. Marsi et Aliorum. 4to. Lugd. 1519.

Cicero, M. T. De Officiis, etc. ex recensione J. G. Grævii, cum Notis Variorum; item F. Eulogii in Somnium Scipionis Disputatio. 8vo. Amst. 1688.

——, ——. De Officiis, etc. 12mo.

——, ——. De Officiis. 24to. Lond. 1740.

——, ——. Orationes, ex recensione J. G. Grævii, cum Notis Variorum. 3 tomi in 6 vol. 8vo. Amst. 1698—9.

——, ——. Orationes Quædam Selectæ, Notis illustratæ, in usum Acad. Exon. ed 4ta. a C. Folsom. 12mo. Bost. 1828.

——, ——. Orationes IV, cum Notis, a F. A. Wolfio. 8vo. Berol. 1801.

——, ——. Orationes Philippicæ in Antonium, cum Notis Variorum, a G. G. Wernsdorf. 2 vol. 8vo. Lips. 1821—2.

——, ——. Select Orations, English and Latin, with Notes, by Wm. Duncan. 8vo. New-Haven. 1811.

——, ——. Sex Orationum Partes, ab A. Maio. 8vo. Mediol. 1817.

——, ——. Oratio pro Marcello. Vide Wormius, O.

——, ——. Epistolæ ad Atticum, ex recensione J. G. Grævii, cum Notis Variorum. 2 vol. 8vo. Amst. 1684.

——, ——. Epistolæ, a P. Manutio, Aldi Filio. 12mo.

——, ——. Epistolæ ad Familiares, ex recensione Grævii, cum Notis Variorum. 2 vol. 8vo. Amst. 1677.

——, ——. Epistolæ ad Familiares, cum Commentario Anglico, a J. Ross. 2 vol. 8vo. Cant. 1749.

——, ——. Epistolæ ad Quintum Fratrem et ad Brutum, cum Notis Variorum, etc. 8vo. Hagæ Com. 1725.

——, ——. De Natura Deorum, cum Notis Variorum, cura J. Davisii. 8vo. Cant. 1733.

——, ——. De Natura Deorum 12mo. Glasguæ. 1741.

——, ——. De Natura Deorum, ex recensione Ernesti, cum Notis C. V. Kindervater. 8vo. Lips. 1796.

——, ——. Tusculanæ Disputationes, ex recensione J. Davisii, cum ejusdem Commentario. 8vo. Cant. 1708.

——, ——. De Oratore, in usum Delphini. 8vo. Oxon. 1714.

——, ——. De Oratore, a Z. Pearce et G. C. Harless. 8vo. Lips. 1816.

——, ——. De Oratore, a C. G. Schütz. 8vo. Lips. 1805.

——, ——. Orator ad M. Brutum, et de Claris Oratoribus, a P. Manutio, Aldi Filio. 12mo. Venet. 1546.

——, ——. Historia Philosophiæ Antiquæ, ex illius Scriptis coll. a F. Gedike. 8vo. Berol. 1815.

——, ——. De Republica, ab A. Maio. 8vo. Bost. 1823.

——, ——. Vide Encyclopädie der Lateinischen Classiker.

——, ——. Offices, tr. by Cockman. 5th ed. 12mo. Lond. 1732.

——, ——. The Same. 10th ed. 12mo. Dublin. 1792.

——, ——. Essay on Old Age, tr. by Melmoth, with Remarks. 8vo. Lond. 1773.

——, ——. On Old Age, and Friendship, tr. by Melmoth, with Remarks. 2 vols. 8vo. Lond. 1777.

Cicero, M. T. Letters to his Friends, tr. by Melmoth, with Remarks. 3 vols. 8vo. Lond. 1753.
———, ——. The Same. 4th ed. 3 vols. 8vo. Lond. 1789.
———, ——. Epistles to Brutus, &c. See Middleton. See Tunstall. See Markland.
———, ——. Orations against Catiline. See Gordon, T.
———, ——. Dialogues de la Vieillesse et de l'Amitié, trad. du Latin. 18mo. Paris. 1640.
———, ——. Lettres à Atticus, avec des Remarques, et le Texte Latin de l'Edition de Grævius; par Mongault. 6 vol. 12mo. Paris. 1738.
———, ——. Thesaurus Ciceronis. Vide Stephanus, C.
———, ——. Comment. in Orationem pro Marcello, etc. Vide Weiske.
———, ——. Comment. in Epistolas. Vide Manutius, C.
———, ——. Clavis Ciceroniana. Vide Ernesti, J. A.
Cid, Romancero e Historia del, recopilado por J. de Escobar. 16mo. Cadiz. 1702.
——, Chronica del. Vide Cronica.
——. Chronicle of the Cid. See Southey.
Cieça de Leon, Pedro de. La Chronica del Peru. 8vo. Antv. 1554.
Cincinnati. Reply to a late Pamphlet, entitled, "Considerations on the Society or Order of the Cincinnati." 12mo. Annapolis. 1783.
————. See Burke, Æ.
————. Proceedings of the Pennsylvania Society. 8vo. Phil. 1785.
Cinnamus, J. Historiarum Libri VI. (Script. Byz.)
Cinonio. Vide Mambelli.
Cinq-Arbres, J. Vide Quinquaboreus.
Cirrno And. De Urbe Roma. (Sallengre, vol. 2.)
Citizen's Companion; or the Trades-man's Mirrour. 8vo. Lond. 1673.
Citri de la Guette. Histoire de la Conqueste de la Floride, par les Espagnols, trad. du Portugais. 12mo. Paris. 1685.
City Reformation, prescribed by the Holy Bible. 8vo. Bost. 1823.
Civil Power in Things Sacred, Essay on. 8vo. Lond. 1739.
Clagett, Nich. (Bp) Consecration Sermon. 8vo. Lond. 1718.
———, ——. Visitation Sermon. 4to. Lond. 1726.
Claggett, Wm. Answer to the Representer's Reflections. 4to. Lond. 1688.
———, ——. Difference of the Case, between the Separation of Protestants from the Church of Rome, and of Dissenters from the Church of England. 4to. Lond. 1683.
———, ——. The Same. 4to. Lond. 1686.
———, ——. Persuasive to an ingenuous Tryal of Opinions in Religion. 4to. Lond. 1685.
———, ——. Discourse concerning the Worship of the Blessed Virgin and the Saints. 4to. Lond. 1686.
———, ——. View of the Controversy between the Representer and the Answerer, &c. 4to. Lond. 1687.

Claggett, Wm. State of the Church of Rome when the Reformation began. 4to. Lond. 1688.

———, ——. Captious Queries concerning the English Reformation answered. 4to. Lond. 1688.

———, ——. Prerogatives of St. Ann, Mother of the Mother of God. 4to. Lond. 1688.

———, ——. Humanity and Charity of Christians, a Sermon. 4to. Lond. 1687.

———, ——. Paraphrase and Notes on Chapters i, ii, iii, iv, v, vii, and viii, of St. John. 3d ed. 8vo. Lond. 1704.

———, ——. Seventeen Sermons; with the Summ of a Conference with Father Gooden on Transubstantiation. 4th ed. 8vo. Lond. 1704.

———, ——. Eleven Sermons; with Notes on St. John, and a Discourse of Church-Unity. 3d ed. 8vo. Lond. 1704.

———, ——. Rule of Faith. See Hutchinson.

Clairac, (M. le Chevalier de.) Field Engineer; tr. from the French, with Remarks, by John Muller. 8vo. Lond. 1760.

Clamor ad Cœlum. Vide Molinæus.

Clap, Roger, Memoirs of, by himself. 8vo. Bost. 1807.

Clap, Tho. (Pres.) On the Nature and Foundation of Moral Virtue and Obligation. 8vo. New Haven. 1765.

——, ——. History of Yale College. 8vo. New-Haven. 1766.

——, ——. Letter on Dr. Whitefield's Design to replace the New-England Ministers with those of Great Britain and Ireland. 16mo. Bost. 1745.

——, ——. Letter to the Rev. Mr. Edwards. 4to. Bost. 1745.

Clapmarius, Arn. De Arcanis Rerumpublicarum Libri vi, illustrati a J. Corvino, etc.—Accessit C. Besoldi de eadem Materia Discursus. 16mo. Amst. 1641.

Clapperton, Hugh. Travels. See Denham, D.

Claramontius, Scip. Cæsenæ Urbis Historia. (Græv. Thes. Ital.)

Claramontius, Simeon. Contentio Apologetica de Cæsena Triumphante adversus F. Liceti Oppositiones. (Græv. Thes. Ital.)

Clare, John, Earl of. Speech in the House of Lords of Ireland. 8vo. Dublin. 1800.

Clare, John. Poems descriptive of Rural Life and Scenery. 12mo. Lond. 1820.

Clarendon, Edw. Hyde, Earl of. History of the Rebellion and Civil Wars in England, begun in 1641. 3 vols. fol. Oxford. 1702. (A large paper copy; with Bp. Atterbury's Vindication of the Editors attached.)

———, ————————. The Same. (Small paper.)

———, ————————. State Papers containing the Materials for the History of the Rebellion. fol. Oxford. 1767.

———, ————————. See Oldmixon, J.

———, ————————. Religion and Policy. 2 vols. 8vo. Oxford. 1811.

———, ————————. His Life, written by himself. fol. Oxford. 1759. (Large paper.)

———, ————————. The Same. (Small paper.)

Clark, Gilb. Oughtredus Explicatus. 12mo. Lond. 1682.

Clark, John. Penmanship.
Clark, John. On the Diseases in Long Voyages to Hot Countries. 8vo. Lond. 1778.
Clark, Jonas. Artillery Election Sermon. 8vo. Bost. 1768.
——, ——. Election Sermon. 8vo. Bost. 1781.
Clark, Peter. Sermon on the Necessity of Grace in Conversion. 16mo. Bost. 1735.
——, ——. Dudleian Lecture. 8vo. Bost. 1763.
——, ——. Election Sermon. 8vo. Bost. 1739.
——, ——. Artillery Election Sermon. 8vo. Bost. 1736.
——, ——. Convention Sermon. 4to. Bost. 1745.
——, ——. Sermon at the Ordination of the Rev. Wm. Jenison. 8vo. Bost. 1728.
——, ——. Two Fast Sermons. 8vo. Bost. 1741.
——, ——. Two Letters concerning Baptism. 8vo. 1732.
——, ——. Defence of Infant Baptism. 8vo. Bost. 1752.
——, ——. Scripture Doctrine of Original Sin defended. 8vo. Bost. 1758.
Clark, S. Sermon on the Earthquake at Lisbon. 8vo. Lond. 1756.
Clark, Sam. Life and Death of Nebuchadnezzar and Cyrus. (Somers, Tr. vol. 7.)
Clark, Sam. Old and New Testament, with Annotations, &c. See Bible.
——, ——. Brief Concordance of the Holy Scriptures. 12mo. Lond. 1696.
Clark, Stephen M. Report of the Trial of, for Arson. 8vo. Salem. 1821.
Clark, Tho. Naval History of the United States. 2 vols. 12mo. Phil. 1814.
Clarke, Adam. Bibliographical Dictionary. 8 vols. 12mo. Lond. 1802—6.
——, ——. History of the Ancient Israelites; from the French of Fleury, with Additions. 12mo. Balt. 1811.
Clarke, Alured. Sermon, January 31. 4to. Lond. 1731.
Clarke, Edw. Letters concerning the Spanish Nation. 4to. Lond. 1763.
Clarke, Edw. Dan. Travels in Europe, Asia, and Africa. 2 vols. 8vo. Phil. 1811—15.
——, ——. The Same. 4th ed. 11 vols. 8vo. Lond. 1816—24.
——, ——. Greek Marbles brought from the Euxine, &c. 8vo. Camb. 1809.
——, ——. Syllabus of Lectures on Mineralogy. 8vo. Camb. 1807.
Clarke, Geo. S. Hebrew Criticism and Poetry. 8vo. Lond. 1810.
Clarke, John, (Dean.) Enquiry into the Cause and Origin of Evil. (Boyle's Lecture Sermons.)
——, ——. Rohault's System of Natural Philosophy, done into English. 8vo. Lond. 1729.
Clarke, John, (School-Master.) Examination of what has been advanced relating to Moral Obligation. 8vo. Lond. 1730.

Clarke, John, (School-Master.) Defence of Dr. Clarke's Demonstration of the Being and Attributes of God. 8vo. Lond. 1734.
———, ———————. Foundation of Morality considered. 8vo. York.
———, ———————. Essay upon Study. 2d ed. 12mo. Lond. 1737.
———, ———————. History of Justin, Latin and English. 5th ed. 8vo. Lond. 1759.
———, ———————. Cornelius Nepos, Latin and English. 10th ed. 8vo. Lond. 1765.
———, ———————. Suetonius, Latin and English. 2d ed. 8vo. Lond. 1739.
———, ———————. Judgment on Latin Exercises. See Phillips, J. T.
Clarke, John. Sermons. 8vo. Bost. 1799.
———, ——. Discourse at the Interment of the Rev. Charles Chauncy. 4to. Bost. 1787.
———, ——. Discourses to Young Persons. 12mo. Bost. 1804.
———, ——. Discourse before the Humane Society of Massachusetts. 8vo. Bost. 1793.
———, ——. Occasional Discourses. 12mo. Bost. 1804.
———, ——. Sermon at the Interment of the Rev. Samuel Cooper. 8vo. Bost. 1784.
———, ——. Discourse on the Death of N. W. Appleton, M. D. 8vo. Bost. 1796.
———, ——. Answer to the Question, "Why are you a Christian?" 8vo. Bost. 1795.
———, ——. Letters to a Student. 12mo. Bost. 1796.
———, ——. His Life and Character, (by Dr. Belknap.) (Mass. Hist. Coll. vol. 6.)
Clarke, John. On the Diseases of Children. Part I. 8vo. Lond. 1815.
Clarke, Joseph. Dr. Clarke's Notions of Space examined. 8vo. Lond. 1733.
———, ————. Farther Examination. 8vo. Lond. 1734.
Clarke, Matthew. Sermon on the Death of the Rev. John Foxon. 8vo. Lond. 1723.
———, ————. Sermon on the Death of the Rev. Jer. Smith. 8vo. Lond. 1723.
———, ————. Sermon on Reformation of Manners. 12mo. Lond. 1711.
———, ————. Two Sermons;—on 2 Tim. ii, 15; and on 1 Cor. iii, 6. 8vo. Lond. 1725.
Clarke, Sam. Scripture-Doctrine of the Trinity. 8vo. Lond. 1712.
———, ——. The Same. 2d ed. 8vo. Lond. 1719.
———, ——. ————. 3d ed. 8vo. Lond. 1732.
———, ——. Reply to the Objections of R. Nelson, &c. against the Scripture-Doctrine. 8vo. Lond. 1714.
———, ——. Apology for Dr. Clarke. 8vo. Lond. 1714.
———, ——. Collection of Queries on the Trinity. 8vo. Lond. 1716.

Clarke, Sam. Demonstration of the Being and Attributes of God. 5th ed. 8vo. Lond. 1719.
———, ——. The Same. 10th ed. 8vo. Lond. 1766. See also Boyle's Lecture Sermons.
———, ——. Letters to him on the above, with his Answers. See Atkey.
———, ——. Evidences of Natural and Revealed Religion. 5th ed. 8vo. Lond. 1719.
———, ——. The Same. 10th ed. 8vo. Lond. 1766. See also Boyle's Lecture Sermons.
———, ——. Papers, which passed between Mr. Leibnitz and Dr. Clarke on Nat. Phil. and Religion. 8vo. Lond. 1717.
———, ——. Letters to him on Liberty and Necessity, with his Answers. 8vo. Lond. 1717.
———, ——. Letter to him on Prescience, &c. 8vo. 1725.
———, ——. Letter to Mr. Dodwell on the Immortality of the Soul;—Remarks on it;—Defence of an Argument to prove the Immateriality and Immortality of the Soul;—Reply to the Defence;—Second Defence of the Argument;—Reflections on the Second Defence;—Third Defence of the Argument;—Answer to the Third Defence;—Fourth Defence of the Argument;—Reflections on Amyntor. 8vo. Lond. 1731.
———, ——. See Clarke, J.,—Dodwell,—Jackson,—Stebbing.
———, ——. Discourse concerning the Prophecies. 8vo. Lond. 1725.
———, ——. Paraphrase on the Four Evangelists. 7th ed. 2 vols. 8vo. Lond. 1736.
———, ——. The Same. 11th ed. 2 vols. 8vo. Lond. 1771.
———, ——. ————. 2 vols. 8vo. Lond. 1795.
———, ——. Exposition of the Church Catechism. 6th ed. 8vo. Lond. 1756.
———, ——. See Common Prayer.
———, ——. Six Sermons on several Occasions. 8vo. Lond. 1718.
———, ——. Eighteen Sermons on several Occasions. 3d ed. 8vo. Lond. 1734.
———, ——. Charity Sermon. 8vo. Lond. 1725.
———, ——. Sermons; with his Life, by Bishop Hoadly. 2 vols. fol. Lond. 1738.
———, ——. The Same. 5th ed. 2 vols. fol. Lond. 1742.
———, ——. ————. 7th ed. 11 vols. 12mo. Lond. 1749.
———, ——. ————. 8th ed. 8 vols. 8vo. Lond. 1756.
———, ——. Works, with his Life. 4 vols. fol. Lond. 1738.
———, ——. Memoirs of his Life and Sentiments. 8vo. 1731.
———, ——. See Emlyn. See Whiston.
Clarke, Sam. Collection of Promises of Scripture. 12mo. Bost. 1803.
Clarke, T. B. Survey of the Strength and Opulence of Great Britain. 8vo. Lond. 1801.
Clarke, Wm. Observations on the Conduct of the French, with regard to their Encroachments upon the British Colonies in

North America, &c. To which are added Observations concerning the Increase of Mankind, &c. (by B. Franklin.) 8vo. Bost. 1755.
Clarke, Wm. See Lewis, M.
Clarke, Wm. Connexion of the Roman, Saxon, and English Coins. 4to. Lond. 1767.
Clarkson, David. Discourse on Liturgies. 8vo. Lond. 1689.
———, ———. Primitive Episcopacy. 8vo. Lond. 1688.
———, ———. Case of Protestants in England under a Popish Prince. 4to. Lond. 1681.
Clarkson, Tho. On the Impolicy of the African Slave Trade. 8vo. Lond. 1788.
———, ——. Essay on the Slavery and Commerce of the Human Species. 3d ed. 8vo. Phil. 1787.
———, ——. The Same. 8vo. Lond. 1788.
———, ——. Answer to the "Essay." See Francklyn, G.
———, ——. On the Comparative Efficiency of Regulation or Abolition, as applied to the Slave Trade. 8vo. Lond. 1789.
———, ——. Life of Wm. Penn. 2 vols. 12mo. Phil. 1814.
———, ——. History of the Abolition of the Slave Trade. 2 vols. 12mo. Phil. 1808.
Clasenius, Dan. Theologia Gentilis. (Gronov. vol. 7.)
Classical Journal. See Journal.
Claubergius, Joh. De Cognitione Dei et Nostri. 12mo. Franeq. 1685.
Claude, Jean. Plaintes des Protestans cruellement Opprimez en France. 12mo. Cologne. 1686.
———, ———. Historical Defence of the Reformation. 4to. Lond. 1683.
———, ———. Œuvres Posthumes. 5 tom. 8vo. Amst. 1688—9.
———, ———. Answer to M. de Meaux's Book. 4to. Lond. 1687.
———, ———. The Greeks Opinion of the Eucharist, mis-represented by M. Claude. 4to. 1686.
Claudianus, Claudius. Opera, a T. Pulmanno, cum M. Antonii Del-rio Notis. 12mo. Antv. 1571—2.
———, ———. Idem, cum Aviani Fabulis. 16mo. Antv. 1585.
———, ———. ———. Vide Corpus Poet. Lat. Vide Collectio Pisaurensis.
———, ———. Panegyrick on the Third Consulate of Honorius, from the Original;—Fragments Imitated. (Warburton, Tracts.)
Clauser, Conradus. De Rebus Turcarum Gestis, ex Variis Scriptoribus. fol. Basil. 1556.
Clausson, R. C. Undersogelse om Amerikas Opdagelse har mere skadet end gavnet det menneskelige Kion. 12mo. Kiobenhavn. 1785.
Claveringius, Robertus. De Maimonide. (Ugol. vol. 8.)
Clavière, E. Adresse de la Société des Amis des Noirs à l'Assemblée Nationale. 8vo. Paris. 1791.
———. ——. De la France et des Etats-Unis. Vide Brissot.
———, ——. Considerations, on the Relative Situation of France and the United States. See Brissot.

Clavigero, F. S. Storia Antica del Messico. 4 tom. 4to. Cesena. 1780.

———, ——. History of Mexico, translated from the Italian by C. Cullen. 2 vols. 4to. Lond. 1787.

Clavis Apocalyptica. 4to. Camb. 1632.

Clay, Joseph. Observations on the Figure of the Earth. (Amer. Phil. Trans. vol. 5.)

Clayton, Humfrey. Family Religion the best Preservative against Infidelity and Popery; a Sermon. 8vo. Lond. 1735.

———, ———. Doctrine of Christ respecting the Eucharist. 8vo. Lond. 1736.

———, ———. Sacrament of the Lord's Supper, necessary to Salvation. 8vo. Lond. 1737.

Clayton, J. Flora Virginica, a J. F. Gronovio. 8vo. Lug. Bat. 1743.

———, ——— ——. Idem. 4to. Lug. Bat. 1762.

Clayton, Rob. (Bp.) Chronology of the Hebrew Bible vindicated. 4to. Lond. 1747.

———, ———. Essay on Spirit. 8vo. Lond. 1751.

———, ———. ———. 2d ed. 8vo. Lond. 1752.

———, ———. Letter to him on the Essay. 8vo. Lond. 1752.

———, ———. Defence of the Essay. 8vo. Lond. 1753.

———, ———. See Deity.

———, ———. Thoughts on Self-Love, Innate-Ideas, Free-Will, Taste, Sentiment, Liberty, and Necessity, &c. 8vo. Lond. 1753.

———, ———. Letters between him and Wm. Penn, concerning Baptism. 8vo. Lond. 1756.

———, ———. Doctrine of the Trinity, as usually explained, Inconsistent with Scripture and Reason. 8vo. Lond. 1754.

———, ———. Speech in the Irish House of Lords on Subscription to Articles and Creeds. 8vo. 1756.

———, ———. The Same. 2d ed. 8vo. Lond. 1758.

———, ———. ———, with a Biographical Notice. (Sparks, Collection of Essays, &c.)

———, ———. Dissertation on Prophecy, &c. 8vo. Lond. 1749.

———, ———. Vindication of the Histories of the Old and New Testament, in Three Parts. 8vo. Lond. 1753—8.

Cleanthus. Hymnus ad Deum. Vide Epictetus.

Cleaveland, Parker. Treatise on Mineralogy and Geology, 8vo. Bost. 1816.

———, ———. The Same. 2d ed. 2 vols. 8vo. Bost. 1822.

———, ———. Account of Fossil Shells, &c. (Mem. A. A. S. vol. 3.)

Cleland, Arch. Appeal to the Publick. 8vo. 1743.

———, ——. Institutes of Health. 12mo. Lond. 1761.

Cleland, John. Plan for the Retrieval of the Ancient Celtic. 4to.

———, ——. Way to Things by Words, and to Words by Things. 8vo. Lond. 1766.

Cleland, John. Specimen of an Etymological Vocabulary. 8vo. Lond. 1768.
———, ——. Additional Articles to the Specimen, &c. 8vo. Lond. 1769.
Clemens Alexandrinus. Opera, Gr. et Lat. cum Annotationibus Heinsii et Sylburgii. fol. Lug. Bat. 1616.
——— ————. Idem. fol. Lut. Paris. 1641.
——— ————. ——, per J. Potterum. 2 vol. fol. Oxon. 1715.
Clemens, Claudius. Musei Extructio, Instructio, Cura, Usus, etc. 4to. Lugd. 1635.
Clemens, Herm. Gid. De Labro Æneo. (Ugol. vol. 19.)
Clemens Romanus. Opera, Gr. et Lat. Vide Cotelerius.
——— ————. Epistola Prior ad Corinthios, Gr. et Lat., cum Fragmento Epist. Secundæ; a P. Junio. 4to. Oxon. 1633.
——— ————. Duæ Epistolæ, Syriace et Latine, a J. J. Wetstenio. fol. Lug. Bat. 1752.
——— ————. Dissertation upon the Two Epistles ascribed to him. See Lardner.
Clement, David. Bibliothèque Curieuse, Historique et Critique. 4 vol. 4to. Göttingen. 1750—3.
Clementinus, Clem. Lucubrationes de Re Medica. fol. Basil. 1535.
Clenche, W. St. Peter's Supremacy discussed. 4to. Lond. 1686.
Cleonidas. Harmonicum Introductorium, Interprete G. Valla;—L. Vitruvii Pollionis de Architectura Libri Decem;—Sexti Julii Frontini de Aquæductibus Liber Unus;—Angeli Policiani Panepistemon, et Lamia. fol. Venet. 1497.
Clerc, Dan. le. Histoire de la Médecine. 4to. La Haye. 1729.
——, ———. History of Physick, made English by Drake and Baden. 8vo. Lond. 1699.
Clerc, Jean le. Bibliothèque Universelle. 26 tom. 12mo. Amst. 1687—1718.
——, ———. Bibliothèque Choisie. 28 tom. 12mo. Amst. 1703—18.
——, ———. Bibliothèque Ancienne and Moderne. 28 tom. 12mo. Amst. et La Haye. 1714—27.
——, ———. Parrhasiana; or Thoughts upon several Subjects; done into English. 8vo. Lond. 1700.
——, ———. Ars Critica. 3 vol. 12mo. Amst. 1712.
——, ———. De l'Incrédulité. 12mo. Amst. 1696.
——, ———. Treatise of the Causes of Incredulity; from the French. 8vo. Lond. 1697.
——, ———. On the Inspiration of the Scriptures; from the French. 12mo. 1690.
——, ———. The Same. See Locke, J.
——, ———. Vide Grotius.
——, ———. On the Choice of our Religious Opinions. (Sparks, Collection of Essays, &c.)
——, ———. Histoire des Provinces-Unies des Pays Bas. 2 vol. fol. Amst. 1723—8.
——, ———. In Eusebii Onomasticon.—In Indicem Geographicum Sansonis. (Ugol. vol. 5.)

Clerc, Jean le. De Poesi Hebræorum. (Id. 31.)
——, ———. Opera SS. Patrum Apostol. Vide Cotelerius.
——, ———. Opera Philosophica, cum Stanleii Philosophia Orientali. 4 vol. in 3. 12mo. Amst. 1698.
——, ———. Idem. 4 vol. 12mo. Amst. 1722.
——, ———. Logica, Ontologia, et Pneumatologia. 12mo. Lond. 1692.
——, ———. Idem. 12mo. Cant. 1704.
——. ———. Vita et Opera. Accedunt J. G. Grævii et E. Spanhemii ad eum Epistolæ. 12mo. Amst. 1711.
——, ———. On the "Rights of the Church Asserted." 8vo. Lond. 1708.
——, ———. Vetus Testamentum, cum Paraphrasi, Dissertationibus, etc. Vide Testamentum Vetus.
——, ———. Idem, sine Dissertationibus. Vide Testamentum Vetus.
——, ———. Nov. Test. Vide Testamentum Novum.
——, ———. Historia Ecclesiastica. 4to. Amst. 1716.
——, ———. Silvæ Philologicæ. 8vo. Amst. 1711.
——. ———. Harmonia Evangelica, Gr. et Lat. cum Historia Christi, et Tribus Dissertationibus. fol. Amst. 1699.
——, ———. Idem. fol. Amst. 1700.
Clerc, N. G. le. Yu le Grand et Confucius, Histoire Chinoise. 4to. Soissons. 1769.
——, ———. Histoire de la Russie Ancienne. 3 vol. 4to. Paris. 1783—4.
——, ———. Histoire de la Russie Moderne. 3 vol. 4to. Paris. 1783—94.
——, ———. Atlas de la Russie Anc. et Mod. avec Tableaux Statistiques. 4to.
Clercq, Chrestien le. Nouvelle Relation de Gaspesie. 12mo. Paris. 1691.
Clergy. Address to the Clergy of New-England on their Opposition to the Rulers of the U. States. 12mo. Concord, N. H. 1814.
———. Discourse concerning the Celibacy of the Clergy. 4to. Oxford. 1687.
Clerk's Manual. 8vo. Lond. 1678.
Cléry. Journal of Occurrences during the Confinement of Louis XVI, tr. by R. C. Dallas. 12mo. Bost. 1799.
Clicquot de Blervache. Mémoire sur l'Etat du Commerce de la France. 8vo. Paris. 1790.
Clifford, Jeronimy, Case and Replication of the Legal Representatives of. 8vo. Lond. 1763.
Clifford, M. Treatise of Humane Reason; with A. M's Examination of the Same. 16mo. Lond. 1675.
———, —. The Same. 3d ed. 8vo. Lond. 1736.
Clifford, Samuel. Fast Sermon. 8vo. Lond. 1721.
Clifton, Fr. Hippocrates on Air, Water, and Situation; on Epidemical Diseases; and on Prognosticks: with Thucydides's Account of the Plague of Athens; translated and illustrated with Notes. 8vo. Lond. 1734.

Climacus, Joannes. Opera Omnia, Gr. et Lat. a M. Radero. fol. Lut. Paris. 1633.
Clinton, De Witt. Discourse before the New-York Historical Society, Dec. 6, 1811. (N. York Hist. Coll. vol. 2.)
———, ————. Introductory Discourse before the Literary and Philosophical Society of New-York. 4to. N. York. 1815.
———, ————. Discourse before the American Academy of the Arts. 8vo. N. York. 1816.
———, ————. Remarks on the Fishes of the Western Waters of New-York. (N. York, Tr. of the Lit. and Phil. Soc. vol. 1.)
Clinton, Sir Henry. Letter to the Commissioners of Public Accounts. 8vo. Lond. 1784.
———, ————. Narrative of his Conduct during Part of his Command in America. 5th ed. 8vo. Lond. 1783.
———, ————. The Same. 6th ed. 8vo. Lond. 1783.
———, ————. Reply to the "Narrative." 8vo. Lond. 1783.
———, ————. Observations on Earl Cornwallis's Answer to the "Narrative." 8vo. Lond. 1783.
———, ————. Observations on Stedman's History of the American War. 4to. Lond. 1794.
Clipsham, Rob. Grand Expedient for Suppressing Popery examined. 8vo. Lond. 1685.
Clodius, Chr. Aug. Su er Quinctiliani Judicio de Sublimitate Homeri. 4to. Lips. p1764.
Clodius, Joh. De Magia Sagittarum. (Ugol. vol. 23.)
Clodius, J. C. Liturgiæ Syriacæ Septimanæ Passionis Jesu Christi Excerptum. 4to. Lips. 1720.
———, ——. Lexicon Hebraicum Selectum. 8vo. Lips. 1744.
Cloppenburg, Joh. Opuscula. 16mo. Franekeræ. 1652.
Clowes, J. Summary View of the Doctrines of the New Jerusalem Church. 8vo. Lond. 1785.
Club-Room. 8vo. Bost. 1820.
Clugius, C. G. De Usu Formulæ qua interrogamus Infantes ante Sacram Lotionem de Fide. 4to. Vittemb. 1734.
Cluny. American Traveller. 4to. Lond. 1769.
———. Voyageur Américain, trad. de l'Anglois; avec un Précis sur l'Amérique Septentrionale, etc. par J. Mandrillon. 8vo. Amst. 1782.
Clusius, Carolus. Exotica, a C. Clusio, Garcia ab Orta, C. Acosta, et N. Monardo. Accessere N. Monardi Magna Medicinæ Secreta; præterea, P. Bellonii Observationes, et Libellus ejus de Neglecta Stirpium Cultura. fol. 1605.
———, ———. Historia Plantarum Rariorum. fol. Antv. 1601.
Cluverius, Phil. Geographia tam Vetus quam Nova. 4to. Lond. 1711.
————, ——. Idem, cura La Martinière. 4to. Amst. 1729.
————, ——. Introduction to Geography, tr. from the Latin. 12mo. Lond. 1657.

Cluverius, Phil. Sicilia Antiqua.—Sardinia et Corsica Antiquæ. (Græv. Thes. Ital.)
Cluverus, Joh. Historiarum Totius Mundi Epitome. 4to. Lug. Bat. 1639.
Cneuffelius, Andr. Epistola de Podagra Curata. 18mo. Amst. 1643.
Coal. Compleat Collier; or Directions for discovering where Coal lies. 12mo. Newcastle.
Coale, E. J. Mnemonika; or Chronological Tablets. 16mo. Balt. 1812.
Coalition. See France.
Cobarruvias Orozco, S. de. Tesoro de la Lengua Castellana. fol. Madrid. 1611.
Cobb, John. Eight Bampton Lecture Sermons. 8vo. Oxford. 1783.
Cobbett, Wm. The Democratic Judge. 8vo. Phil. 1798.
——, ——. New Year's Gift to the Democrats. 8vo. Phil. 1796.
——, ——. Porcupine's Political Censor for Nov. 1796. 8vo. Phil. 1796.
——, ——. Works, by Peter Porcupine. 2 vols. 8vo. Phil. 1795—6.
——, ——. Bloody Buoy. 12mo. Lond.
——, ——. Report of an Action against him, for a Libel on Dr. Rush. 8vo. Phil. 1800.
——, ——. Porcupine's Gazette, No. 779. 12mo. N. York. 1800.
——, ——. Address to the Clergy of Massachusetts. 12mo. Bost. 1815.
——, ——. British Honour and Humanity, &c. as exemplified in the Modest Publications of Mr. Wm. Cobbett. 8vo. Phil. 1796.
——, ——. A Year's Residence in the United States. 8vo. Lond. 1819.
Cobden, Edw. Sermon on Reformation of Manners. 12mo. Lond. 1736.
——, ——. Letter to, by a Parishioner. 8vo. Lond. 1738.
Cocceius, Joh. Lexicon et Commentarius Sermonis Hebr. et Chald. Vet. Testamenti. fol. Amst. 1669.
——, ——. Justification de feu M. Cocceius. Vide Joncourt.
——, ——. Opera Omnia.
——, ——. Vide Maius, J. H.
Cocchi, Ant. Del Vitto Pitagorico per uso della Medicina Discorso.
Coccius, M. A. De Clade Sontiaca. (Clauser, de Reb. Turcicis.)
Cochin, Henri. Œuvres. 6 vol. 4to. Paris. 1771—5.
Cochorella, B. Tremitanæ, olim Diomedeæ, Insulæ Descriptio. (Græv. Thes. Ital.)
Cockburn, Catharine. Works, Theological, Moral, Dramatic, and Poetical; with her Life, by T. Birch. 2 vols. 8vo. Lond. 1751.
Cockburn, Gul. Œconomia Corporis Animalis. 12mo. Lond. 1695.
Cockburn, John. Sermon on Marriage. 8vo. London.
——, ——. Answer to Queries on some Points of Religion. 8vo. Lond. 1717.

Cockburn, John. Remarks &c. occasioned by Burnet's History of his Own Times. 8vo. Lond. 1724.

———, ——. Defence of Dr. Cockburn against a Libel entitled, "A Vindication of the late Bishop Burnet." 8vo. Lond.

———, ——. Letter to his Friend, concerning Bourignianism. 4to. Lond. 1698.

———, ——. Bourignianism Detected. 4to. Lond. 1698.

Cockburn, John. Reis-beschryving door de Spaanse West-Indien, in de Jaaren 1730 en 1731; uit het Engels vertaalt. 12mo. Amst. 1740.

Cockburn, Patrick. Enquiry into the Truth and Certainty of the Mosaic Deluge. 8vo. Lond. 1750.

Cocker, Edw. London Writing Master.

———, ——. England's Penman. Lond. 1678.

———, ——. Young Clerk's Tutor. 9th ed. 12mo. Lond. 1680.

Cockman, Tho. Tully's Offices in English. 5th ed. 12mo. Lond. 1732.

———, ——. The Same. 12mo. Lond. 1792.

———, ——. Salvation by Christ Alone, in Two Sermons. 4th ed. 8vo. Lond. 1722.

Code des Prises. Vide Chardon.

—— de Commerce. 2 vol. en 1. 12mo. Paris. 1807.

—— Frédéric. Vide Frédéric.

—— Noir. Vide Recueil de Réglemens.

Code, (Mr.) Letter to a Clergyman relating to his Sermon on the 30th of January. 12mo. Lond. 1746.

Codex Alexandrinus. Vide Woide.

—— Cantabrigiensis, vel Bezæ. Vide Kipling.

—— Theodosianus, cum Commentariis J. Gothofredi, etc. 6 vol. fol. Lugd. 1665.

Codinus, Geo. De Officiis Magnæ Ecclesiæ et Aulæ Constantinopolitanæ.—De Originibus Constantinop. (Script. Byz.)

Codman, John. Sermon before the Foreign Missionary Society. 8vo. Bost. 1818.

———, ——. Artillery Election Sermon. 8vo. Bost. 1820.

Codomannus, L. Chronographia. (Somers, Tr. vol. 5.)

Coetlogon, Dennis de. Universal History of Arts and Sciences. 2 vols. fol. Lond. 1745.

Coffin, John G. On Cold and Warm Bathing, &c. 12mo. Bost. 1818.

——, ———. On Medical Education. 8vo. Bost. 1822.

Coffin, Paul. Election Sermon. 8vo. Bost. 1799.

Cogan, Tho. Philosophical Treatise on the Passions. 2d ed. 8vo. Bath. 1802.

———, ——. Ethical Treatise on the Passions. 2 vols. 8vo. Bath. 1807—10.

———, ——. Theological Disquisitions. 2 vols. 8vo. Lond. 1812—13.

———, ——. Letters to Mr. Wilberforce on Hereditary Depravity. 12mo. Bost. 1799.

Cogan, Tho. The Same; with a Biographical Notice, and Remarks on his Writings. (Sparks, Collection of Essays, &c.)
Cognet, Sir Martyn. Politique Discourses upon Trueth and Lying. tr. out of French by Sir E. Hoby. 4to. Lond. 1586.
Cogolludo, D. L. Historia de Yucathan. fol. Madrid. 1688.
Cohausen, J. H. Hermippus Redivivus; or the Sage's Triumph over Old Age and the Grave, tr. from the Latin by J. Campbell. 2d ed. 8vo. Lond. 1749.
Coin, Considerations about the Raising of, in a Letter to Mr. Locke. 12mo. Lond. 1696.
——, Review of the Universal Remedy for all Diseases incident to. 12mo. Lond. 1696.
——. See Money.
Coke, Sir Edw. First Institute. 7th ed. fol. Lond. 1670.
——, ——. ——. 12th ed. fol. Lond. 1738.
——, ——. ——, by Hargrave and Butler. 3 vols. 8vo. Phil. 1812.
——, ——. Third Institute. fol. Lond. 1648.
——, ——. Book of Entries. 2d ed. fol. Lond. 1671.
——, ——. Reports in 13 parts, by Geo. Wilson. 7 vols. 8vo. Dublin. 1793.
——, ——. Reports Abridged, by Sir Thomas Ireland, 1st Amer. ed. by J. A. Dunlap. 8vo. N. York. 1813.
——, ——. Law Tracts, by W. Hawkins. 8vo. Lond. 1764.
Coke, Roger. Detection of the Court and State of England during the four last Reigns. 8vo. Lond. 1697.
Coker, Dan. Journal of a Voyage for Sherbro in Africa. 8vo. Baltimore. 1820.
Colbatch. Account of the Court of Portugal under Pedro II. 8vo. Lond. 1700.
Colbatch, John. Examination of Echard's Account of the Marriage-Treaty between King Charles II. and Catherine of Portugal. 4to. Camb. 1733.
Colbatch, Sir John. Scheme for proper Methods against the Plague. 8vo. Lond. 1721.
Colbert, J. B. See Torcy, Marquis of.
Colby, S. Sermon, Jan. 30th. 8vo. Lond. 1709.
Colden, Cadwallader. History of the Five Indian Nations of Canada. 8vo. Lond. 1747.
——, ——. The Same. 3d ed. 2 vols. 12mo. Lond. 1755.
——, ——. His Conduct, as Lieut. Governor of New-York. 8vo. 1767.
Colden, Cadwallader, D. Life of Robert Fulton. 8vo. N. York. 1817.
Cole, Abdiah. See Culpeper.
Cole, T. Plan to exclude the French from the New-foundland Fishery. See Williams, G.
Cole, Tho. Discourse of Regeneration, Faith, and Repentance. 8vo. Lond. 1689.
Cole, Wm. Conversations on Algebra.

Coleman, Edw. On Respiration. 8vo. Lond. 1802.
Coleman, Wm. Collection of the Facts and Documents relative to the Death of Alexander Hamilton; with Orations, Sermons, &c. on his Life and Character. 8vo. N. York. 1804.
Coleridge, S. T. Biographia Literaria; or Biographical Sketches of my Literary Life and Opinions. 2 vols. 8vo. N. York. 1817.
———, ——. Wallenstein; from the German of F. Schiller. 8vo. Lond. 1800.
Coleti, Giandomenico. Dizionario Storico-Geografico dell' America Meridionale. 4to. Venezia. 1771.
Coligny, Gaspard de. Vide Colinius.
Colin, A. Histoire des Drogues, Espiceries, etc. par Garcie du Jardin, C. de la Coste, et N. Monard, translatée en François, et augmentée de beaucoup d'Annotations, etc. 8vo. Lyon. 1619.
Colinius, Gaspar. Vita ejus. 16mo. Ultrajecti. 1644.
———, ———. La Vie de Gaspard de Coligny. 12mo. Cologne. 1686.
———, ———. Mémoires de Gaspard de Coligni. (Mém. de France, vol. 40.)
Collard, John. Essentials of Logic. 12mo. Lond. 1796.
Collectanea Græca Majora, a Dalzel. 2 vol. 8vo. Cant. Nov. Angl. 1811—20.
——— ——— Minora, a Dalzel. 8vo. Cant. Nov. Angl. 1819.
——— Juridica. 2 vol. 8vo. Lond. 1791.
——— Maritima. See Robinson, Charles.
Collectio Pisaurensis Poetarum Latinorum. 6 tomi. 4to. Pisauri. 1766.
Colliber, Sam. Inquiry into the Existence and Nature of God, &c. 8vo. Lond. 1718.
———, ——. The Christian Religion founded on Reason. 8vo. Lond. 1729.
Collier, Jeremy. Essays on Moral Subjects. 5th ed. 3 vols. 8vo. Lond. 1703.
———, ———. Meditations, &c. See Antoninus, M.
———, ———. Historical Dictionary. See Moreri.
Collier, Wm. Gospel Treasury, chiefly from the London Evangelical Magazine. 2d ed. 4 vols. 12mo. Charlestown, Mass. 1810—11.
———, ——. Sermon at the Ordination of Brother Geo. W. Appleton. 8vo. Bost. 1819.
Collin de Bar. Histoire de l'Inde Ancienne et Moderne. 2 vol. 8vo. Paris. 1814.
Collin, Nich. Essay on those Inquiries in Natural Philosophy, at present most beneficial to the United States. (Amer. Phil. Trans. vol. 3.)
——, ——. Description of a Machine for Saving Persons from the Upper Stories of a House on Fire.—Philological View of some very Ancient Words in several Languages.—Description of a Speedy Elevator. (Id. 4.)

Collin, Nich. On the Climate of the Country about the River Delaware. (Id. New Series, 1.)

Collinges, John. Intercourses of Divine Love betwixt Christ and his Church. 4to. Lond. 1683.

Collins, Anthony. Discourse of Free-Thinking. 8vo. Lond. 1713.

——, ——. The Same; with Remarks on the Discourse, by Phileleutherus Lipsiensis. 4to. Lond. 1713—15.

——, ——. Vindication of the Divine Attributes. 8vo. Lond. 1710.

——, ——. Discourse on the Grounds and Reasons of the Christian Religion. 8vo. Lond. 1724.

——, ——. The Same; with a Letter to the Author. 8vo. Lond. 1737.

——, ——. Examination of the Discourse on the Grounds and Reasons of the Christian Religion. 8vo. Lond. 1724.

——, ——. Christian Religion not founded on Allegory, in Answer to the Discourse on the Grounds, &c. 8vo. Lond. 1724.

——, ——. True Grounds and Reasons of the Christian Religion, in Answer to the Discourse on the Grounds, &c. 8vo. Lond. 1725.

——, ——. Letter to the Author of a Discourse on the Grounds, &c. 8vo. Lond. 1726.

——, ——. Answer to a Letter concerning the Grounds, &c. 8vo. Lond. 1725.

——, ——. Review of the Controversy between the Author of a Discourse on the Grounds, &c. and his Adversaries. 8vo. Lond. 1726.

——, ——. Scheme of Literal Prophecy considered. 8vo. Lond. 1727.

——, ——. Letter to Dr. Rogers on his Eight Sermons. 8vo. Lond. 1727.

——, ——. Essay on the XXXIX Articles. 8vo. Lond. 1724.

——, ——. Philosophical Inquiry concerning Human Liberty. 12mo. Lond. 1717. (2 copies.)

——, ——. On Liberty and Necessity. 8vo. Lond. 1729.

——, ——. See Soul. 8vo. Lond. 1729.

——, ——. Essay concerning the Use of Reason in Propositions the Evidence whereof depends on Human Testimony. 8vo. Lond. 1709.

——, ——. Catalogue of his Library. 8vo. Lond. 1731.

Collins, Arthur. Letters and Memorials of State in the Reigns of Mary, Elizabeth, James I, Charles I and II, and Oliver's Usurpation, &c. 2 vols. fol. 1646.

Collins, John. Sector on a Quadrant; with an Appendix touching Reflective Dialling. 4to. Lond. 1658—9.

——, ——. Commercium Epistolicum J. Collins et Aliorum, de Analysi promota.—Accedit Commercium Epistolicum de Varia Re Mathematica inter Celeberrimos Mathematicos. 4to. Lond. 1712—25.

Collins, Wm. Poems. See Chalmers, A.
Collinson, John. Key to the Writings of the Principal Fathers of the Church, in Eight Bampton-Lecture Sermons. 8vo. Oxford. 1813.
Collius, Fr. De Sanguine Christi. 4to. Mediolani. 1617.
Colloquia Scholastica, (Latin, Russian, Modern Greek, French, and German.) 8vo. Moscow. 1800.
Collyer, David. Sacred Interpreter; or Practical Introduction to the Scriptures. 2d ed. 2 vols. 8vo. Lond. 1732.
——, ——. The Same. 5th ed. 2 vols. 8vo. Lond. 1796.
Collyer, Wm. B. Lectures on Scripture Facts. 8vo. Bost. 1813.
Colman, Benj. Imprecation against the Enemies of God Lawful and a Duty; a Sermon. 16mo. Bost. 1707.
——, ——. Government and Improvement of Mirth, in Three Sermons. 16mo. Bost. 1707.
——, ——. Sermon before the General Court. 12mo. Bost. 1719.
——, ——. Sermon before a Society of Young Men. 12mo. Bost. 1720.
——, ——. Jacob's Vow, a Sermon to a Young Gentleman upon his Entering on Worldly Business. 12mo. Bost. 1722.
——, ——. Four Sermons on the late Earthquake. 8vo. Bost. 1727.
——, ——. Twenty Sacramental Discourses. 8vo. Lond. 1728.
——, ——. Government the Pillar of the Earth, a Sermon. 8vo. Bost. 1730.
——, ——. Grace given us in the Preached Gospel, a Sermon. 8vo. Bost. 1732.
——, ——. The Merchandize of a People Holiness to the Lord, a Sermon. 8vo. Bost. 1736.
——, ——. Discourses upon the Parable of the Ten Virgins. 8vo. Lond. 1707.
——, ——. The Same; with his Life. 8vo. Bost. 1747—9.
——, ——. Sermon at a Lecture before the General Court. 12mo. Bost. 1708.
——, ——. Sermon on the Union of England and Scotland. 12mo. Bost. 1708.
——, ——. Great Duty of Waiting on God in our Straits and Difficulties, a Sermon. 8vo. Bost. 1737.
——, ——. The Unspeakable Gift of God, a Sermon. 8vo. Bost. 1737.
——, ——. The Withered Hand Restored, a Sermon. 8vo. Bost. 1739.
——, ——. Souls flying to Christ pleasant and admirable to behold, a Sermon. 8vo. Bost. 1740.
——, ——. The Glory of God in the Firmament of his Power, a Sermon. 8vo. Bost. 1743.
——, ——. Sermon on Saving Faith. 16mo. 1742.
——, ——. Argument for Family Worship. 8vo. Bost. 1728.
——, ——. Sermon on the Death of Mrs. Abigail Foster. 16mo. Bost. 1711.

Colman, Benj. Sermon on the Death of the Rev. Thomas Bridge. 16mo. Bost. 1715.

———, ——. Sermon on the Death of the Hon. Joseph Dudley. 12mo. Bost. 1720.

———, ——. Sermon on the Death of Mr. David Stoddard. 12mo. Bost. 1723.

———, ——. Sermon on the Death of the Rev. John Leverett, President of Harvard College. 12mo. Bost. 1724.

———, ——. Sermon on the Death of the Rev. Cotton Mather. 12mo. and 8vo. Bost. 1728.

———, ——. Sermon on a Tragical Duel. 8vo. Bost. 1728.

———, ——. Sermon on the Death of Wm. Welsteed, Esq. 8vo. Bost. 1729.

———, ——. Sermon on the Death of the Rev. Solomon Stoddard. 8vo. Bost. 1729.

———, ——. Sermon on the Death of the Hon. Simeon Stoddard. 8vo. Bost. 1730.

———, ——. Sermon on the Death of Thomas Hollis, Esq. 8vo. Bost. 1731.

———, ——. Sermon on the Death of the Rev. Peter Thacher. 8vo. Bost. 1739.

———, ——. Sermon on the Death of Samuel Holden, Esq. of London. 4to. Bost. 1740.

———, ——. Sermon on the Death of the Rev. Wm. Cooper. 8vo. Bost. 1744.

———, ——. Sermon at the Ordination of the Rev. Ebenezer Pemberton. 8vo. Bost. 1727.

———, ——. Sermon at the Ordination of the Rev. Samuel Cooper. 8vo. Bost. 1746.

———, ——. Election Sermon. 16mo. Bost. 1718.

———, ——. Another. 16mo. Bost. 1723.

———, ——. Thanksgiving Sermon. 12mo. Bost. 1716.

———, ——. Duty of Parents to Pray for their Children, a Sermon. 12mo. Bost. 1723.

———, ——. Sermon Preparatory to a Fast. 8vo. Bost. 1734.

———, ——. Artillery Election Sermon. 8vo. Bost. 1738.

———, ——. Dissertation on the Three first Chapters of Genesis. 8vo. Bost. 1735.

———, ——. Letter to the Rev. Mr. Williams on the Rev. J. Davenport's Confession and Retractations. 16mo. Bost. 1744.

———, ——. Observations on receiving the Small-Pox by Ingrafting or Inoculating. 16mo. Bost. 1721.

———, ——. The Same; to which is prefixed an Historical Introduction by D. Neal. 8vo. Lond. 1722.

———, and Wm. Cooper. Two Sermons on a Day of Prayer. 12mo. Bost. 1723.

Colman, Geo. Comedies of Terence, translated into Familiar Blank Verse. 4to. Lond. 1765.

Colman, Henry. Discourse to the Plymouth and Norfolk Bible Society at their First Annual Meeting. 8vo. Bost. 1816.

———, ——. Sermons. 8vo. Bost. 1820.

Colman, Henry. Fast Sermon. 8vo. Bost. 1812.
———. ———. Artillery Election Sermon. 8vo. Bost. 1818.
———, ———. Sermon at the Ordination of the Rev. Daniel Kimball. 8vo. Bost. 1818.
———, ———. Discourse before the Humane Society of Massachusetts. 8vo. Bost. 1812.
———, ———. Discourse on Pastoral Duty. 8vo. Bost. 1822.
———, ———. Discourse on Religious Institutions. 8vo. Salem. 1825.
———, ———. Half-Century Sermon, July 4th. 8vo. Salem. 1826.
Colnett, Wm. Sermon on Reformation of Manners. 4to. Lond. 1711.
Colonial Journal. Nos. 1 and 2. (1 vol.) 8vo. Lond. 1816.
——— Policy of Great Britain. 8vo. Lond. 1816.
Colonies. State of the British and French Colonies in North America, &c. 8vo. Lond. 1755.
———. Serious Considerations on the Present State of Affairs in the Northern Colonies. 8vo. N. York. 1754.
———. Good Humour; or a Way with the Colonies. 8vo. Lond. 1766.
———. Free and Calm Consideration of the Misunderstanding between Great Britain and the American Colonies, (by Mr. Prescott of Danvers.) 12mo. Salem. 1774.
———. Authentic Papers from America. 8vo. Lond. 1775.
———. Histoire de la Fondation des Colonies des Anciennes Républiques, trad. de l'Anglois par Cérisier. 8vo. Utrecht. 1778.
———. Geschichte der Kolonisirung der Freien Staaten des Alterthums; aus dem Engl. 12mo. Leipz. 1778.
———. Historische und Politische Betrachtungen über die Colonien, etc. 12mo. Bern. 1779.
———. Historische, Statistische, Geographische Belustigungen. 8vo. Leipz. 1781—2.
———. See Antilles,—Britain,—British Colonies,—France,—Spain, &c.
Colonization Society. Fifth Annual Report of the American Society for Colonizing the Free People of Colour of the United States. 8vo. Washington. 1822.
Colquhoun, P. On the Commerce and Police of the Thames. 8vo. Lond. 1800.
———, —. On Indigence. 8vo. Lond. 1806.
Colson, Nathaniel. Mariners New Kalender. 4to. Lond. 1724.
Colton, Benj. Connecticut Election Sermon. 16mo. N. Lond. 1738.
Columbus, Christopher. Personal Narrative of his First Voyage to America; from the Spanish, (by Samuel Kettell.) 8vo. Bost. 1827.
———, ———. Elogi Storici di Cristoforo Colombo e di Andrea d'Oria. Vide Durazzo.
———, ———. Vide Novus Orbus.
Columella, L. J. M. De Re Rustica. Vide Script. Rei Rusticæ.
———, ———. De Cultu Hortorum. Vide Corpus Poet. Lat.

Columella, L. J. M. Of Husbandry, tr. into English. 4to. Lond. 1745.
Coluthus. Rape of Helen, tr. into English Verse by Fr. Fawkes. See Chalmers, A.
Comber, Tho. Companion to the Altar. 8vo. Lond. 1678.
———, ——. Companion to the Temple. 2 vols. 8vo. Lond. 1679.
———, ——. Occasional Offices of Matrimony, Burial, &c. explained. 8vo. Lond. 1679.
———, ——. Short Discourses upon the whole Common-Prayer. 8vo. Lond. 1688.
———, ——. Church History cleared from the Roman Forgeries. 4to. Lond. 1695.
———, ——. Discourse concerning the Second Council of Nice. 4to. Lond. 1688.
Combes, Fr. Historia de Mindanao, Iolo, y sus Adyacentes. fol. Madrid. 1667.
Comenius, J. A. Pansophiæ Prodromus. 16mo. Lond. 1639.
———, ——. Idem; cum Dissertatione de Sermonis Latini Studio. 16mo. Lug. Bat. 1644.
———, ——. Eruditionis Scholasticæ Atrium; cum Fortio Redivivo. 12mo. Noribergæ. 1659.
———, ——. Schola-Ludus, seu Encyclopædia Viva; h. e. Januæ Linguarum Praxis Comica. 16mo. Lond. 1664.
———, ——. Physicæ ad Lumen Divinum reformatæ Synopsis. 16mo. Amst. 1645.
———, ——. Janua Linguarum Reserata, Gr. Lat. et Gal. 8vo. Amst. 1643.
———, ——. Gate of Languages Unlocked. 8vo. Lond. 1650.
———, ——. The Same. 8vo. Lond. 1673.
———, ——. Ratio Disciplinæ in Unitate Fratrum Bohemorum, etc. 12mo. Amst. 1660
Comes, Natalis. Mythologia, sive Explicatio Fabularum; item M. A. Tritonii Mythologia. 4to. Patavii. 1616.
Comines, Phil. de. Mémoires, contenans l'Histoire des Roys Louys XI et Charles VIII. fol. Paris. 1649.
———, ———. Mémoires. (Mém. de France, vol. 10, 11, et 12.)
———, ———. Memoirs; from the French. 2 vols. 8vo. Lond. 1823.
Comings, Fowler. Sermons. 2 vols. 8vo. Birmingham. 1790.
Commelinus, Joh. Hortus Amstelodamensis. 2 vol. fol. Amst. 1697—1701.
Commencement, a Poem, recited before the Phi Beta Kappa Society, at Cambridge, Aug. 29, 1811, (by Wm. Biglow.) 8vo. Salem. 1811.
Commentaries and Essays, published by the Society for promoting the Knowledge of the Scriptures. vol. 1. 8vo. Lond.
Commentarii Societatis Philologicæ Lipsiensis, cura C. D. Beckii. 2 vol. 8vo. Lips. et Plaviæ. 1801—2.
Commerce. Observations on the Commerce of the American States with Europe and the West Indies. 8vo. Lond. 1783.

Commerce. Free and Candid Review of the above. 8vo. Lond. 1784.

————. Seventh Essay on Free Trade and Finance. 8vo. Phil. 1785.

————. Opinions respecting the Commercial Intercourse between the United States and the Dominions of Great Britain, &c. 8vo. Bost. 1797.

————. Remarques sur plusieurs Branches de Commerce et de Navigation. Vide Héguerty, d'.

————. Vide Compañia. Vide Trade.

Common Law. See Law.

Common-Place-Book to the Holy Bible. 4to. Lond. 1725.

Common-Prayer-Book. fol. 1629.

————————, for the use of the Church of Scotland. fol. Edin. 1637.

————————, Irish and English; with the Elements of the Irish Language. 8vo. Lond. 1712.

————————. 4to. Camb. 1758.

————————. 8vo. Oxford. 1770.

————————, reformed according to the Plan of Dr. S. Clarke. 12mo. Lond. 1774, and 8vo. 1775.

————————. 12mo. Phil. 1786, and 1791.

————————, with the Gospel of St. Mark, in the Mohawk Language. 8vo. Lond. 1787.

————————, Reformed, &c. 2d ed. 4to. Lond. 1802.

————————, No Divine Service. 4to. Lond.

————————, The Old Non-Conformist touching the Book of Common-Prayer, and Ceremonies. 4to. Lond. 1660.

————————, Anatomie of the. 4to. 1661.

————————, Queries relating to the. 8vo. Lond. 1774.

————————. See Liturgy.

Common Sense; or the Englishman's Journal. Vol. I. 12mo. Lond. 1738.

Commons, Proceedings and Debates of the House of, in 1620 and 1621. 2 vols. 8vo. Oxford. 1766.

————, Debates of the House of, from 1667 to 1694, collected by A. Grey. 10 vols. 8vo. Lond. 1763.

————, History and Proceedings of the House of, from the Reformation to the Present Time. 14 vols. 8vo. Lond. 1742—4.

————. See Parliament.

Comnenus, Joannes. Descriptio Montis Atho. (Montfaucon, Palæographia Græca.)

Compañia, Real, de Comercio para las Islas de Santo Domingo, Puerto-Rico, y la Margarita. 16mo. Madrid. 1755.

————, ——, Guipuzcoana de Caracas, etc. 4to. 1765.

Compendium, English, containing the Genealogies of all the Nobility of England, &c. 11th ed. 3 vols. 12mo. Lond. 1760.

————, Scots. 7th ed. 12mo. Lond. 1764.

————, Irish. 5th ed. 12mo. Lond. 1756.

———— of the Usuall Hands of England, Netherlands, France, Spaine and Italie, with the Hebrew, Samaritan, Caldæan, &c. by R. Daniel. fol. Lond. 1663.

Comperat, Car. De Certitudine quam quis habere possit et debeat de sua coram Deo Justificatione. 4to. Sedani. 1666.
Compiegne de Veil, Ludov. Præfatio in Opera Maimonidis. (Ugol. vol. 8.)
Comyn, Sam. On Contracts. 3d Amer. ed. 2 vols. 8vo. Brookfield. 1822.
Comyns, Sir John. Alphabetical Digest of the Laws of England. 5 vols. fol. Lond. 1762–7.
Conæus, Geo. De Duplici Statu Religionis apud Scotos. 4to. Romæ. 1628.
Conant, Silvanus. Letter on the Death of his Consort; with a Poem to her Memory (by Judge Oliver.) 4to. N. Lond. 1759.
Concilia Magnæ Britanniæ, etc. Vide Wilkins, D.
———. Synodicon in Gallia Reformata. Vide Quick.
———. Vide Canones, Carranza, Trente.
Conciliatory Hints, by Philodemus. 4to. Charleston. 1784.
Concilium Tridentinum, ex ultima recognitione Joannis Gallemart, etc. 8vo. Col. Agrip. 1727.
Conclavi de' Pontefici Romani. 4to. 1667.
Concord, Extracts from the Proceedings of the Convention at, and of the Town of Boston. 8vo. Bost. 1779.
Concordantiæ Majores Bibliorum. fol. Basil. 1506, et 1521.
————. Œconomia Methodica Concordantiarum Scripturæ Sacræ, a G. Bulloco. fol. Antv. 1572.
———— Bibliorum Vulgatæ Editionis. fol. Antv. 1642.
————. Vide Buxtorfius, Clark, Cruden, etc.
Concubine, The Fair; with the Lady's Last Shift. 8vo. Lond. 1732.
Condamine, C. M. de la. Voyage dans l'Intérieur de l'Amérique Méridionale. 8vo. Paris. 1745.
————, ————. Idem. 8vo. Francfort au Mein. 1779.
————, ————. Journal du Voyage à l'Equateur, etc, Vide Académie Royale des Sciences.
————, ————. Supplément au Journal. 4to. Paris. 1752.
————, ————, Barrère, und Bouguer. Reisen nach Guiana. Vide Barrère.
Conder, John. Sermon at the Ordination of the Rev. John Stafford. 8vo. Lond. 1758.
———, ———. Exhortation at the Ordination of the Rev. Richard Winter. 8vo. Lond. 1759.
Condillac, E. B. Œuvres. 23 vol. 8vo. Paris. 1798.
———, ———. On the Origin of Human Knowledge, tr. by Nugent. 8vo. Lond. 1756.
Condorcet, J. A. N. C. Marquis de. Esquisse d'un Tableau Historique des Progrès de l'Esprit Humain. 8vo. Paris. 1798.
Conen, Geo. Sermon at the Parish-Church of St. George the Martyr, in Southwark. 4to. Lond. 1745.
Conerus, C. F. De Ignoto Atticorum Deo ad Act. xvii, 23. 4to. Helmst. 1725.
Confederation. See Congress, Continental.

Conference between the Commissioners of Massachusetts-Bay and of New-York, at New-Haven, in 1767. 4to. Bost. 1768.

Confessio Fidei in Conventu Theologorum elaborata; cum Catechismo Duplice, Majori Minorique. 12mo. Cantab. 1659.

——— ——— in Comiciis Augustæ, Anno 1530.

Confession of Faith, owned and consented unto by the Elders and Messengers of the Churches assembled at Boston. 12mo. Bost. 1680.

———, Large Preface to the Assembly's. 8vo. Lond. 1720.

———, the Larger and Shorter Catechisms, with the Sum of Saving Knowledge contained in the Holy Scriptures, &c. of Publick Authority in the Church of Scotland. 8vo. Glasgow. 1762.

———. Auguspurgische Confession. fol. Franck. 1572.

———. See Articles of Faith, Creeds, &c.

Confucius Sinarum Philosophus, sive Scientia Sinensis Latine exposita, opera Patrum Societatis Jesu fol. Paris. 1687.

Congo. Beschrijvinge van't Koninckrijck Congo, etc. 4to. Amst. 1658.

Congregational Church. See Church.

Congress, Continental. Extracts from its Votes and Proceedings, Sept. 5th 1774. 8vo. Phil. and Bost.

———, ———. Address of the Twelve United Colonies of North America by their Representatives in Congress to the People of Ireland. 8vo. Phil. 1775.

———, ———. Speech in Support of its Petition to the King. 8vo. Lond. 1775.

———, ———. What think ye of the Congress Now? or an Enquiry how far the Americans are bound by the Decisions of the late Continental Congress. 8vo. N. York. 1775.

———, ———. Free Thoughts on its Proceedings in 1774. 8vo. N. York. 1775.

———, ———. Defence of its Resolutions and Address, in reply to "Taxation No Tyranny."

———, ———. Declaration of the Causes and Necessity of taking up Arms, &c. 8vo. Lond. 1775.

———, ———. Declaration of Independence, July 4th, 1776.

———, ———. Rights of Great Britain asserted; being an Answer to the General Congress. 10th ed. 8vo. Lond. 1776.

———, ———. Strictures upon its Declaration. 8vo. Lond. 1776.

———, ———. Lettres d'un Membre du Congrès Améri-quain à divers Membres du Parlement d'Angleterre. 8vo. Phil. 1779.

———, ———. Observations on the American Revolution. 8vo. Phil. 1779.

———, ———. Address and Recommendations to the States. 8vo. Phil. 1783.

———, ———. Report of the Board of Treasury relative to the Establishment of a Mint, April 8, 1786.

Congress, Continental, Journals of, from 1774 to 1788. 13 vols. 8vo.
———, ———. Secret Journals of the Proceedings of Congress, from its First Meeting to the Dissolution of the Confederation. 4 vols. 8vo. Bost. 1821.
———, ———. See American Revolution,—British Colonies,—Papinian, Letters of, &c.
Congress of the United States. Congressional Debates in 1810—11. No. I.
———. Address of Members of the House of Representatives to their Constituents on the War with Great Britain. 8vo. Bost. 1812.
———. See United States.
Congreve, Wm. Works. 2 vol. 12mo. Lond. 1774.
———, ———. Poems. See Chalmers, A.
Conimbricensis Collegii Societas Jesu. Vide Aristoteles.
Coningham, James. Sermon on Reformation of Manners. 12mo. Lond. 1714.
Connecticut. Charter granted by Charles II; with Acts and Laws to 1728. fol. New-London.
———. Acts and Laws, from 1784 to 1794. fol. New-London.
———. Acts and Laws. 8vo. Hartford. 1796.
———. System of the Laws, by Z. Swift. 2 vols. 8vo. Windham. 1795—6.
———. State of the Lands, said to be once within the bounds of its Charter, West of New-York, considered. 8vo. N. York. 1770.
———. Examination of its Claims to Lands in Pennsylvania. 8vo. Phil. 1774.
———. Articles of Agreement of the Connecticut Gore Land Company. 18mo. 1796.
———. Plea, &c. respecting Western Lands. 8vo.
———, General History of. 8vo. Lond. 1781.
——— Election Sermons. 3 vols. 12mo. 1710—69.
——— Reports. 8vo. Hartford. 1817.
———. See Charters. See Deaf and Dumb.
Conon et Parthenius. Narrationes, a Kanne. 12mo. Gŏttingæ. 1798.
———. Idem. Vide Hist. Poet. Scriptores.
Conradus, Petrus. De necessario, sed probe administrando, Rationis Usu in Religionis Revelatæ Negotio. 4to. Franeq. 1752.
Conringius, Herm. De Republica Hebræorum. (Ugol. vol. 24.)
———, ———. De Nummis Hebræorum. (Id. 28.)
———, ———. De Studiis Liberalibus Romæ et Constantinopolis. (Sallengre, vol. 3.)
Conscience, Plea for the Rights of. 8vo. Bost. 1753.
———, Discourse on Liberty of. 12mo. Lond. 1661.
Consett, Henry. Practice of the Spiritual or Ecclesiastical Courts, &c. 8vo. Lond. 1685.
Consett, Tho. State and Regulations of the Church of Russia, &c. 8vo. Lond. 1729.
Constable, John. On Accuracy of Style. 8vo. Lond. 1731.

Constantinus, Rob. **Lexicon Græco-Latinum.** **2 vol.** **fol.** **Paris.** **1592.**

Constantius the Apostate; being a short Account of his Life, &c., in answer to "Julian the Apostate, &c." 8vo. Lond. 1683.

Constitutional Information, Society for. See Society.

Constitutions of Government. See United States,—England,—France, &c.

Contarenus, Fr. Historia Hetruriæ, etc. (Græv. Thes. Ital.)

Contarenus, Vinc. De Frumentaria Romanorum Largitione. (Grævius, vol. 8.)

Contarini, Gasp. Della Republica et Magistrati di Venetia. 12mo. Venet. 1591.

———, ———. De Magistratibus et Republica Venetorum. (Græv. Thes. Ital.)

Conventicles, Letter concerning; with a Reply. 4to.

Convention between Great Britain and Spain. 4to. Lond. 1739.

———. See Treaty.

Conversations on Botany. 2d ed. 12mo. Lond. 1818.

——— on Chemistry, (by Margaret Bryan.) 8th ed. 2 vols. 8vo. Lond. 1822.

Conversations principally on the Aborigines of North America. 18mo. Salem. 1828.

Conveyancer, Modern. 3d ed. 3 vols. 8vo. Lond. 1725.

Convocation, Report of the Committee of the Lower House of, concerning Dangerous Positions and Doctrines contained in the Bishop of Bangor's Preservative. 8vo. Lond. 1717.

———. Report vindicated from Misreports. 8vo. Lond. 1717.

———. Prolocutors Answer to a Letter from a Member of Lower House. 8vo. Lond. 1718.

———. Prolocutor's Letter to Dr. Edward Tenison. 8vo. Lond. 1718.

———. Remarks upon the Lord Bishop of Bangor's Treatment of the Clergy and Convocation. 8vo Lond. 1817.

———. Clergy Vindicated. 8vo. Lond. 1817.

———. See Church.

Conwell, Henry, (Bp.) Pastoral Charge. 12mo. Phil. 1821.

Conybeare, John, (Bp.) The Mysteries of the Christian Religion credible, a Sermon. 8vo. Oxford. 1723.

———, ———. The Same. 2d ed. 8vo. Oxford. 1725.

———, ———. Truth of the Christian Religion proved from Miracles, a Sermon. 8vo. Oxford. 1725.

———, ———. Sermon before the Society for promoting Working-Schools in Ireland. 4to. Lond. 1752.

———, ———. Expediency of a Divine Revelation, a Sermon. 8vo. Lond. 1728.

———, ———. The Same. 3d ed. 8vo. Lond. 1733.

———, ———. Scripture Difficulties considered, a Sermon. 8vo. Oxford. 1733.

———, ———. Sermons. 2 vols. 8vo. Lond. 1757.

———, ———. Defence of Revealed Religion. 8vo. Lond. 1732.

Cook, Eben. The Sot-Weed Factor; or a Voyage to Maryland: a Satyr in Burlesque Verse. 4to. Lond. 1708.
Cook, James. Remarks on a Passage from the River Balise to Merida. 8vo. Lond. 1769.
——, ——. Voyage towards the South Pole and round the World in 1772—5. 3d ed. 2 vols. 4to. Lond. 1779.
——, ——. Voyage to the Pacific Ocean in 1776—9. 3 vols. (Third vol. by J. King.) 4to. Lond. 1784.
——, ——. Troisième Voyage de Cook, trad. de l'Anglois. 3me ed. 8vo. Paris. 1783.
——, ——. Vide Engel,—Forster,—Hawkesworth.
——, ——, Life of. See Kippis, A.
Cook, S. Penmanship.
Cook, Wm. Sermon at the Ordination of the Rev. Samuel Baldwin. 8vo. Bost. 1757.
——, ——. Sermon at the Ordination of the Rev. Elisha Marsh. 12mo. Bost. 1742.
Cooke, Edw. Voyage to the South Sea and round the World, in 1708—11. 8vo.
Cooke, Sam. Sermon for a Memorial of the Bloody Tragedy at Lexington. 8vo. Bost. 1777.
——, ——. Election Sermon. 8vo. Bost. 1770.
Cooke, Tho. Works of Hesiod, tr. from the Greek into English Verse. 4to. Lond. 1728.
——, ——. The Same. 12mo. Lond. 1740.
——, ——. ————. See Chalmers, A.
Cooke, Wm. Sermon at the Ordination of the Rev. Thomas Green. 8vo. Lond. 1710.
Cooke, Wm. Enquiry into the Patriarchal and Druidical Religion, Temples, &c. 4to. Lond. 1755.
Coollidge, Sam. Sermon on the Death of Queen Caroline. 8vo. Bost. 1738.
Coope, Rich. Letter to the Proprietors of the South-Sea Company. 8vo. Lond. 1739.
Cooper, Anthony Ashley. See Shaftesbury.
Cooper, Astley. Anatomy and Treatment of Inguinal and Congenital Hernia. fol. Lond. 1804.
——, ——. Anatomy and Treatment of Crural and Umbilical Hernia. fol. Lond. 1807.
Cooper, Edw. Sermon before the London Society for promoting Christianity among the Jews. 8vo. Lond. 1819.
Cooper, Geo. On Equity Pleading. 8vo. Lond. 1809.
Cooper, James. Spy. 2 vols. 12mo. New-York. 1822.
——, ——. Pioneers. 2 vols. 12mo. New-York. 1823.
Cooper, John Gilbert. Life of Socrates. 3d ed. 8vo. Lond. 1750.
——, ————. On Taste. 8vo. Lond. 1757.
——, ————. Poems. 12mo. Lond. 1764.
——, ————. ——. See Chalmers, A.
Cooper, J. T. Oration by him, and Poem by R. Hooper, at the Departure of the Senior Class from Harvard University. 8vo. Camb. 1811.

Cooper, (Rev. Mr.) History of S. America. 12mo. Lond. 1789.
———, ———. History of N. America. 12mo. Lond. 1789.
Cooper, Sam. Sermon in Boston before the Society for encouraging Industry, &c. 8vo. Bost. 1753.
———, ———. Sermon before the General Court on the Reduction of Quebec. 8vo. Bost. 1759.
———, ———. Dudleian Lecture. 2d ed. 8vo. Bost. 1774.
———, ———. Sermon on the Death of George II. 8vo. Bost. 1761.
———, ———. Sermon at the Ordination of the Rev. J. Jackson. 8vo. Bost. 1760.
———, ———. Artillery Election Sermon. 8vo. Bost. 1751.
———, ———. Election Sermon. 8vo. Bost. 1756.
———, ———. Sermon, Oct. 25th, 1780, the Day of the Commencement of the Constitution, &c. 8vo.
Cooper, Sam. First Lines of the Practice of Surgery. 8vo. Lond. 1807.
———, ———. On the Diseases of the Joints. 12mo. Lond. 1807.
———, ———. Dictionary of Practical Surgery. 8vo. Lond. 1818.
Cooper, Tho. Information respecting America. 8vo. Lond. 1794.
———, ———. Extract of a Letter on Emigration. 8vo.
Cooper, Wm. The Doctrine of Predestination unto Life explained and vindicated in Four Sermons. 12mo. Bost. 1765.
———, ———. Election Sermon. 8vo. Bost. 1740.
———, ———. Sermon at the Ordination of the Rev. Robert Breck. 8vo. Bost. 1736.
———, ———. Sermon on the Death of the Hon. William Tailer. 8vo. Bost. 1732.
———, ———. Sermon on the Death of the Rev. Peter Thacher. 8vo. Bost. 1739
———, ———. Sermon on the late awful Earthquake. 12mo. Bost. 1727.
———, ———. Remarks on his Objections to the Rev. Mr. Ashley's Sermon, by J. F. 3d ed. 4to. Bost. 1743.
———, ———. Letter to him, by J. F. 8vo. Bost. 1742.
Cooper, Wm. (Abp.) Two Occasional Discourses. 4to. Lond. 1763.
Cooper, Wm. Guide in the Wilderness. 8vo. Dublin. 1810.
Coote, Charles. History of England to the Peace of 1783. 9 vols. 8vo. Lond. 1802.
———, ———. History of Modern Europe from the Peace of 1763 to the Treaty of Amiens; being a Continuation of Russell's Modern Europe. 2 vols. 8vo. Phil. 1811—22.
Copeland, Tho. On the Diseases of the Rectum and Anus. 8vo. Lond. 1814.
———, ———. On the Diseased Spine. 8vo. Lond. 1815.
Copenhagen. Vide Acta Literaria Hafniensia.
———, ———. Tableau de l'Académie Royale de Peinture, Sculpture, et Architecture de Copenhague. 18mo.
Copernicus, Nicol. De Revolutionibus Orbium Cœlestium, etc. fol. Basil. 1566.

Coram, Tho. Petition to the Princess of Wales for the Establishment of a Foundling Hospital. 1737. MS.
Coray, A. Prodromus Bibliothecæ Græcæ. 8vo. Paris. 1805.
——, —. Bibliotheca Græca. vol. 1—7, et 14. 8vo. Paris. 1807–22.
——, —. Parerga Bibliothecæ Græcæ. vol. 1, 2. 8vo. Paris. 1809—10.
Corbet, John. Military Government of Gloucester during the Civill Warre. 4to. Lond. 1645.
——, ——. On the Decrees and Operations of God. 4to. Lond. 1683.
——, ——. Kingdom of God among Men. 12mo. Lond. 1679.
Corbet, Rich. (Bp.) Poems. See Chalmers, A.
Cordus, Val. Dispensatorium: item G. Rondeletii de Theriaca Tractatus, et Fr. Dissaldei Pharmaconetes, etc. 18mo. Lug. Bat. 1637.
Coreal, Fr. Voyages aux Indes Occidentales, trad. de l'Espagnol; avec une Relation de Raleigh et le Voyage de Narborough, trad. de l'Anglois. 3 vol. 12mo. Amst. 1722.
Corinna. Carmina. Vide Poetriæ Octo.
Cornarius, J. De Conviviis Veterum Græcorum. (Gronov. vol. 9.)
——, –. Eclogæ in Dialogos Platonis Omnes, cura J. F. Fischeri, etc. 8vo. Lips. 1771.
Cornaro, L. Discorsi della Vita Sobria. 8vo. Lond. 1768.
——, —. On a Sober and Temperate Life; from the Italian. 8vo. Lond. 1768.
——, —. The Same. 12mo. Lond. 1779.
Corneille, Pierre. Théatre, avec des Commentaires par Voltaire. 12 vol. 8vo. 1765.
——, ——. Idem. 8 vol. 4to. Genève. 1774.
——, ——. ——. 12 vol. 8vo. Paris. 1797.
Corneille, Thomas. Poëmes Dramatiques. 5 vol. 12mo. Paris. 1738.
Cornelius, Elias. Review of the Rev. Mr. Colman's Sermon. 8vo. Bost. 1825.
Cornewall, Fred. Assize Sermon. 8vo. Lond. 1710.
Cornutus, J. Canadensium Plantarum Historia, etc. 4to. Paris. 1635.
Cornwallis, Earl. Answer to that Part of Sir Henry Clinton's "Narrative," which relates to his Conduct. 8vo. Lond. 1783.
——, ——. See Clinton, Sir H.
Cornwallis, H. Visitation Sermon. 3d ed. 12mo. Lond. 1708.
Cornwallis, Sir Wm. Praise of Richard III. (Somers, Tr. vol. 5.)
Corporation and Test Acts shown to be of no Importance to the Church of England. 8vo. Lond. 1736.
————————. Letter to the Lord Mayor, &c. in which the Nature and Design of the Corporation Act is considered. 8vo. Lond. 1738.
————————. Letter to the Bishops on the Corporation and Test Acts, &c. 8vo. Lond. 1789.
————————. Address to the Bishops on a Letter from one of them to his Clergy. 8vo. Lond. 1790.

Corporation and Test Acts. See Catalogue,—Dissenters,—Test.
Corps Diplomatique. Vide Barbeyrac,—Dumont,—Négociations,—Rousset,—St-Prest.
Corpus Veterum Poetarum Latinorum, Profanorum et Ecclesiasticorum, a Maittaire. 2 vol. fol. Lond. 1713.
——— Juris Civilis, cum Notis Variorum, opera S. van Leeuwen. 2 vol. fol. Amst. et Lug. Bat. 1663.
——— ————. 2 vol. 8vo. Amst. 1700.
——— ————, a G. A. Spangenburg. 2 vol. 4to. Gottingæ. 1776—97.
——— ————. Vide Justinianus Imperator.
Correa de Serra, J. On the Soil of Kentucky. (Amer. Phil. Tr. N. S. vol. 1.)
Corry, John. Life of Washington. 8vo. Lond. 1800.
——, ——. Life of Joseph Priestley. 12mo. Birmingham. 1804.
Corry, Wm. Reflections upon Liberty and Necessity;—Remarks on the Reflections;—Replies, &c. 8vo. Lond. 1763.
Corsinus, Edvardus. Notæ Græcorum. fol. Florentiæ. 1749.
———, ————. Fasti Attici. 4 vol. 4to. Florentiæ. 1744—56.
Corte, Girolamo dalla. L'Istoria di Verona. 2 vol. 4to. Verona. 1594.
Corte Real, Hieron. Golfo de Lepanto. 4to. 1578.
Cortenovis, A. M. Sopra una Inscrizione Greca d' Aquileja Dissertazione. 8vo. Bassano. 1792.
Cortes, Hernan. Historia de Nueva-España, aumentada por Lorenzana. fol. Mexico. 1770.
———, ———. Briefe des Ferdinand Cortes, übers. von J. J. Stapfern. 2 Bände. 8vo. Heidelb. 1779.
———, ———. Vide Novus Orbis.
Cortusii, G. et A. Historia de Novitatibus Paduæ et Lombardiæ.—Supplementum ad Historiam. (Græv. Thes. Ital.)
Corvinus, A. J. F. Digesta per Aphorismos. 16mo. Amst. 1642.
Corvinus, Messalla. De Progenie Augusti Libellus. (Rom. Hist. Scriptores.)
Cosin, John, (Bp.) Scholastical History of the Canon of the Scripture. 8vo. Lond. 1672.
Cosmas Indopleustes. Topographia Christiana. (Montfaucon, Collectio Nova.)
Costa. Vide Acosta.
Costa, E. M. da. Natural History of Fossils. vol. 1. Part 1. 4to. Lond. 1757.
——, ———. Elements of Conchology. 8vo. Lond. 1776.
Costantini, Giuseppe Ant. Vide Pupieni.
Costanzo, Ang. di. Istoria di Napoli. 3 vol. 8vo. Milano. 1805.
Costard, Geo. Letter concerning the Rise and Progress of Astronomy among the Ancients. 8vo. Lond. 1746.
———, ——. History of Astronomy. 4to. Lond. 1767.
———, ——. Observations on Job. 8vo. Oxford. 1747.
———, ——. Dissertations on the Word *Kesitah*, mentioned in Job; and on the Word *Hermes*. 8vo. Oxford. 1750.
———, ——. Dissertationes II Critico-Sacræ. 8vo. Oxon. 1752.
Coste, Pierre. Hieron. Vide Xenophon.

Costeker, (Mr.) The Fine Gentleman; or Compleat Education of a Young Nobleman. 8vo. Lond. 1732.
Cota, Rodriguez. Calisto y Melibea, Tragicomedia. 16mo. Tarragona. 1595.
Cotelerius, J. B. SS. Patrum Apostolicorum Opera, Gr. et Lat. cum Notis. 2 vol. fol. Lut. Par. 1672.
———, ——. SS. Patrum Apostol. Opera, Gr. et Lat. cum Notis Variorum; item, G. Beveregii Codex Canonum Ecclesiæ Primitivæ vindicatus, J. Usserii Dissertationes Ignatianæ, et J. Pearsonii Vindiciæ Epistolarum S. Ignatii, etc. cura J. Clerici. 2 vol. fol. Amst. 1698.
———, ——. Idem. 2 vol. fol. Amst. 1724.
———, ——. Ecclesiæ Græcæ Monumenta. 4 vol. 4to. Lut. Par. 1677—92.
Cotes, Roger. Hydrostatical and Pneumatical Lectures; with Notes, by R. Smith. 8vo. Lond. 1738.
Cotta, Joh. Oda. Vide Poemata Italorum.
——, ——. Carmina. Vide Fracastorius.
Cotting, Uriah. Boston and Roxbury Mill Corporation. 8vo. Bost. 1818.
Cotton, Charles. Poems. See Chalmers, A.
Cotton, Clement. Complete Concordance to the Bible. fol. Lond. 1631.
Cotton, John. The Way of Life. 4to. Lond. 1641.
———, ——. Powring out of the Seven Vials. 4to. Lond. 1645.
———, ——. Churches Resurrection. 4to. Lond. 1642.
———, ——. Exposition upon the First Epistle of John. fol. Lond. 1656.
———, ——. Exposition of Ecclesiastes. 12mo. Lond. 1654.
———, ——. Way of the Churches in New England. 4to. Lond. 1645.
———, ——. Abstract of Laws and Government. 4to. Lond. 1655.
———, ——. Bloody Tenet washed and made white in the Blood of the Lambe. 4to. Lond. 1647.
———, ——. God's Mercie mixed with his Justice. 4to. Lond. 1641.
———, ——. Holinesse of Church-Members. 4to. Lond. 1650.
———, ——. Christ the Fountaine of Life. 4to. Lond. 1651.
———, ——. Covenant of Grace. 3d ed. 12mo. Lond. 1671.
Cotton, John. Sermon after repeated Shocks of the Earthquake. 12mo. Bost. 1728.
———, ——. Election Sermon. 12mo. Bost. 1753.
Cotton, John. Two Sermons on a Day of Humiliation for the Drought and War. 8vo. Bost. 1757.
———, ——. Practice of the Churches of New-England, relating to Baptism, vindicated. 8vo. Bost.
Cotton, Nathaniel. Poems. See Chalmers, A.
Cotton, Sir Rob. and Sir J. Hayward. Histories of the Lives and Raignes of Henry III. and Henry IV. of England. 12mo. Lond. 1642.

Cotton, Sir Rob. Cottoni Posthuma: Divers Choice Pieces on the Right and Power of Parliament. 8vo. Lond. 1679.

———, ———. Antiquity and Dignity of Parliaments. (Harl. Miscel. vol. 2.)

Cotton, Tho. Sermon on Reformation of Manners. 12mo. Lond. 1702.

Cotton, Ward. Sermon before the Female Society in Boylston for the Aid of Foreign Missions. 8vo. Worcester. 1817.

Coulomb, C. A. Théorie des Machines Simples. 4to. Paris. 1821.

Coulter, Tho. Method of Cultivating Peach Trees. (Amer. Phil. Tr. vol. 5.)

County and Town Officer. See Massachusetts.

Courayer, P. F. Declaration of my last Sentiments on the different Doctrines of Religion; from the French. 12mo. Lond. 1787.

Courier de Boston. 4to. 1789.

Cournand, (M. l'Abbé de.) Réponse aux Observations d'un Habitant des Colonies. 8vo.

Court, M. Histoire de la Guerre des Camisards, sous le Règne de Louis XIV. 3 vol. 12mo. Alais. 1819.

Court, John. Works of Flavius Josephus. See Josephus.

Courtalon, (l'Abbé.) Atlas de l'Allemagne. 4to. Paris. 1774.

Courtenay, James. On the Propriety of establishing a National Observatory. 8vo. Charleston. 1827.

Courts. See Ecclesiastical Courts.

Coutinho. Vide Cunha.

Couture, (M. l'Abbé.) De la Vie Privée des Romains. (Acad. des Inscrip. vol. 1.)

Covel, John. Some Account of the Present Greek Church. fol. Camb. 1722.

Covelli, N. Vide Monticelli, T.

Covenant. See Solemn League.

Coventry, Henry. Philemon to Hydaspes, on the Subject of False Religion, in 5 parts. 8vo. Lond. 1738—44.

Coverdale, Miles, (Bp.) Dedication to his Bible. (Somers, Tr. vol. 9.)

———, ———. Letters of Saintes and Martyrs. 4to. Lond. 1564.

Coward, Wm. Grand Essay; or a Vindication of Reason and Religion, against Impostures and Philosophy. 8vo. Lond. 1704.

———, ———. Second Thoughts concerning the Human Soul. 2d ed. 8vo. Lond. 1704.

———, ———. Just Scrutiny; or Serious Enquiry into the Modern Notions of the Soul. 12mo. Lond.

———, ———. Search after Souls. 2 vols. in 1. 4to. 1706.

———, ———. Observations on Dr. Charlton's "Immortality of the Soul demonstrated by the Light of Nature." 8vo. Lond. 1659.

———, ———. Observations on Mr. Wadsworth's Book of the Soul's Immortality. 8ve. Lond. 1670.

Cowell, Joh. Institutiones Juris Anglicani. 16mo. 1630.

Cowley, Abraham. Works. 10th ed. 3 vols. 8vo. Lond. 1707.
——, ———. Vision concerning Cromwell. (Harl. Miscel. vol. 5.)
——, ———. Poems. See Chalmers, A.
Cowper, Henry. Reports in B. R. from 14 Geo. III. to 18 Geo. III. 2 vols. 8vo. Bost. 1809.
Cowper, Spencer. Speech at the Enthronement of Richard, Lord Bishop of Durham. 4to. Durham. 1753.
Cowper, Wm. Anatomy of Humane Bodies. fol. Oxford. 1698.
Cowper, Wm. Poems. 2 vols. 12mo. Phil. 1803.
——, ——. ———. See Chalmers, A.
——, ——. Iliad and Odyssey of Homer, translated into English Blank Verse. 4 vols. 8vo. Bost. 1814.
——, ——. Life and Posthumous Writings. See Hayley.
Cow-Pox. Report on the Cow-Pock Inoculation, by the Physicians to the Vaccine-Pock Institution. 8vo. Lond. 1803.
———. Statement of Evidence from Trials by Inoculation of Variolous and Vaccine Matter, (by the Same.) 8vo. Lond. 1804.
Cox, Michael, (Bp.) Sermon before the Society for promoting Protestant Schools in Ireland. 4to. Dublin. 1748.
Cox, Rich. History of Ireland. 2 vols. fol. Lond. 1689—90.
Coxe, Dan. Description of the English Province of Carolana, &c. 8vo. Lond. 1722.
——, ——. The Same. 8vo. 1741.
Coxe, J. R. Emporium of Arts and Sciences. Nos. 1—10. 8vo. Phil. 1812—13.
Coxe, R. S. Cases in the Supreme Court of New-Jersey, from 1790 to 1795. 8vo. Burlington, N. J. 1816.
Coxe, Tench. Statement of the Arts and Manufactures of the United States, for 1810. 4to. Phil. 1814.
——, ———. Brief Examination of Lord Sheffield's Observations on the Commerce of the United States. 8vo. Lond. 1792.
——, ———. View of the United States of America. 8vo. Phil. 1794.
——, ———. The Same. 8vo. Lond. 1795.
Coxe, Wm. Travels into Poland, Russia, Sweden, and Denmark. 2 vols. 4to. Lond. 1788.
——, ——. The Same. 5 vols. 8vo. Lond. 1791.
——, ——. Voyage en Pologne, etc. trad. de l'Anglois par Mallet. 2 vol. 4to. Genève. 1786.
——, ——. Travels in Switzerland. 3 vols. 8vo. Lond. 1791.
——. ——. Account of the Russian Discoveries, &c. 4to. Lond. 1780.
——, ——. The Same. 8vo. Lond. 1787.
——, ——. Découvertes des Russes, etc. trad. de l'Anglois. 4to. Paris. 1781.
——, ——. Travels. (Pinkerton, vols. 5 and 6.)
——, ——. Memoirs of the Duke of Marlborough. 6 vols. 8vo. Lond. 1820.
——, ——. Memoirs of Horatio, Lord Walpole. 3d ed. 2 vols. 8vo. Lond. 1820.

Coxe, Wm. Memoirs of Sir Robert Walpole. 4 vols. 8vo. Lond. 1816.

——, ——. Memoirs of the Kings of Spain of the House of Bourbon. 2d ed. 5 vols. 8vo. Lond. 1815.

——, ——. History of the House of Austria. 2d ed. 5 vols. 8vo. Lond. 1820.

Coyer, H. A. Ueber die Riesen in Patagonien. 12mo. Danzig. 1769.

Crabb, Geo. Order and Method of Instructing Children, with Strictures on the Modern System of Education. 12mo. Lond. 1801.

——, ——. English Synonymes. 8vo. N. York. 1826.

Crabbe, Geo. Borough. 12mo. Phil. 1810.

——, ——. Tales of the Hall. 2 vols. 12mo. Bost. 1819.

——, ——. Poems. 8vo. Lond. 1808.

Cradock, Tho. Version of the Psalms. 8vo. Annapolis. 1756.

Cradock, Walter. Gospel-Holinesse, in Nine Sermons. 4to. Lond. 1651.

——, ——. Mount Sion, or the Privilege and Practice of the Saints, in Ten Sermons. 4to. Lond. 1649.

——, ——. Gospel-Libertie, in Nine Sermons. 4to. Lond. 1648.

——, ——. Glad Tydings from Heaven; a Sermon. 4to. Lond. 1648.

——, ——. Divine Drops from the Fountain of the Holy Scriptures. 4to. Lond. 1650.

——, ——. The Saints Fulnesse of Joy; a Thankesgiving Sermon. fol. Lond. 1646.

Crafts, Wm. Oration before the Phi Beta Kappa Society. 8vo. Camb. 1817.

Cragius, N. De Republica Lacedæmoniorum. (Gronov. vol. 5.)

Cragius, Tho. Jus Feudale. ed. 3tia. fol. Edin. 1732.

Crakelt, Wm. Entick's Dictionary. See Entick.

Cramer, J. U. de. Observationes Juris Universi. 6 vol. 4to. Darmstadii. 1789—92.

Cramerius, J. J. De Ara Exteriori Templi Secundi. (Ugol. vol. 10.)

Cramerus, M. Fr. De Corona Ammonitica. 4to. Vitemb. 1720.

Cramond, R. and H. Letter to the National Assembly of France. 4to. Lond. 1789.

Cranch, Wm. Reports of Cases in the Supreme Court of the United States. 9 vols. 8vo. Washington and N. York. 1812—17.

Cranmer, T. (Abp.) Translation of the Bible. See Bible.

——, ——. Answer unto a Crafty and Sophisticall Cavillation devised by S. Gardner concerning the Sacrament. fol. Lond. 1551.

Cranz, David. Historie von Grönland. 2 Theile. 8vo. 1770.

——, ——. Fortsetzung der Historie von Grönland. 8vo. Barby. 1770.

——, ——. History of Greenland; from the High-Dutch. 2 vols. 8vo. Lond. 1767.

——, ——. Kort Beskrivelse over Gronland. 8vo. Viborg. 1775.

Cranz, David. Anmærkninger over Crantzes Historie om Gronland. 8vo. Kiobenhavn.

——, ——. Alte und Neue Brüder-Historie. 8vo. Barby. 1772.

——, ——. Fortsetzung der Brüder-Historie. 3 Theile. 8vo. Barby, etc. 1791—1816.

——, ——. History of the United Brethren, translated from the German, with Notes, by La Trobe. 8vo. Lond. 1780.

Crashaw, Richard. Poems. See Chalmers, A.

Crasso, Lorenzo. Elogii d' Huomini Letterati. 2 vol. 4to. Venet. 1666.

Crassus, Nic. De Forma Reipublicæ Venetæ. (Græv. Thes. Ital.)

Crassus, Nic. Jun. Elogia Patritiorum Venetorum Belli Pacisque Artibus Illustrium. (Græv. Thes. Ital.)

Craufurd, Tho. History of the University of Edinburgh from 1580 to 1646. 8vo. Edin. 1808.

Crausius, Joh. De Succoth Benoth. (Ugol. vol. 23.)

Crawford, Adair. On Animal Heat. 8vo. Lond. 1788.

Crawford, Charles. Observations upon Negro-Slavery. 12mo. Phil. 1784.

Crawford, John. Masonic Address. 8vo. Baltimore. 1802.

Crawfurd, John. History of the Indian Archipelago. 3 vols. 8vo. Edin. 1820.

Crebillon, P. J. de. Œuvres. 2 vol. 12mo. Paris. 1743.

Creeds, Considerations on the Nature and Use of. 8vo.

——, Unreasonableness of. 4to. Lond. 1706.

——. Remarks on the Athanasian Creed, &c. by a Lady. 8vo. Lond.

——, Thoughts concerning. 8vo. Bost. 1813.

——. Things set in a Proper Light, by an Orthodox Clergyman of Massachusetts. 8vo. Bost. 1814.

——. See Articles of Religion,—Confession of Faith,—Subscription, &c.

Crellius, Joh. Opera. Vide Fratrum Polonorum.

——, ——. Two Books touching One God the Father; from the Latin. 4to. 1665.

Crellius, S. Initium Evangelii S. Joannis ex Antiquitate Ecclesiastica restitutum. 8vo. 1726.

Cremonensis, C. B. De Decretis Atheniensium. 4to. Romæ. 1785.

Crescenzi, Piero de. Trattato della Agricoltura. 3 vol. 8vo. Milano. 1805.

Crescimbeni, G. M. L'Istoria della Volgar Poesia. 6 vol. 4to. Venez. 1731.

Cresner, A. His Vindication from the Aspersions of A. Pulton. 4to. Lond. 1687.

Cresolius, Ludov. Theatrum Veterum Rhetorum, Oratorum, etc. (Gronov. vol. 10.)

Crespel, Emanuel. Voyages dans le Canada, etc. 12mo. Francf. sur le Meyn. 1752.

Crespel, Emanuel. Reisen nach Canada, aus dem Französischen. 12mo. Franckf. und Leipz. 1751.
———, ———. Voyage au Nouveau-Monde, etc. 12mo. Amst. 1757.
Creutzer, C. A. L. Leibnitii Doctrina de Mundo Optimo sub examen revocata denuo. 12mo. Lips. 1795.
Creuxius, Fr. Historia Canadensis. 4to. Paris. 1664.
Creuzer, Fr. Symbolik und Mythologie. 4 Bände. 8vo. Leipz. und Darmst. 1810—12.
———, —. Studien. Vide Daub.
Creuzer, G. F. Die Historische Kunst der Griechen. 8vo. Leipz. 1803.
Crèvecœur, (M. Saint-John de.) Lettres d'un Cultivateur Américain. 2 tom. 8vo. Paris. 1784.
———, ———. Idem. 3 tom. 8vo. Paris. 1787.
———, ———. Voyage dans la Haute Pensylvanie, et dans l'Etat de New-York. 3 tom. 8vo. Paris 1801.
———, ———. Letters from an American Farmer. 8vo. Lond. 1782.
———, ———. The Same. 8vo. Lond. 1783.
———, ———. Remarks on the Letters. 8vo. Lond. 1783.
Crevier, J. B. L. History of the Roman Emperors; tr. from the French by J. Mills. 10 vols. 8vo. Lond. 1755—61.
———, ———. See Rollin, C.
———, ———. Tractatus Varii. 8vo. Lond. 1788.
Crewe, N. Oratio in Memoriam Publicorum Benefactorum, etc. (Ugol. vol. 31.)
Crichton, Alex. On Mental Derangement. 2 vols. 8vo. Lond. 1798.
Criminal Law. See Law.
Crinesius, Christoph. Chaldaicum Lexicon. 4to. Norib. 1628.
Crinitus, Petrus, (Ricci.) Oda. Vide Poemata Italorum.
Crisis. 8vo. 1754.
———. Nos. 7 and 8. 8vo. New-Lond. 1775.
———. Extraordinary. 8vo. Phil. 1780.
———. See British Colonies. See Stamp Act.
Crisp, John. On Vision. 8vo. Lond. 1796.
Crispinus, Jo. Lexicon Græco-Latinum. fol. 1595.
———, —. Actiones et Monimenta Martyrum. fol. Genevæ. 1560.
Crispus, Joh. De Naxo a Turcis Occupata. (Clauser de Rebus Turcicis.)
Critica Sacra, sive Annotata Doctissimorum Virorum in Vetus et Novum Testamentum; quibus accedunt Tractatus Varii Theologico-Philologici. 8 tomi. in 9 vol. fol.
Crito, or Essays on Various Subjects. See Burgh.
Croce, G. C. Vita; con Varie Operette Poet. 4to. Verona. 1738.
Crockett, G. F. H. On the Abolition of Capital Punishments. 8vo. Georgetown, Ky. 1823.

Croes, John. Discourse on the Death of Washington. 8vo. Phil. 1800.
Croesius, Gerard. De Velando Capite Muliebri. (Ugol. vol. 29.)
Croft, Geo. Eight Bampton-Lecture Sermons. 8vo. Oxford. 1786.
Croft, Herbert, (Bp.) Naked Truth; or True State of the Primitive Church. 4to. 1675.
——, ————. Author of Naked Truth Stript Naked. 4to. Lond. 1676.
——, ————. See Turner, F.
——, ————. Short Discourse concerning the Reading his Majesties late Declaration in the Churches. 4to. Lond. 1688.
——, ————. Answer to a Paper importing a Petition of the Abp. of Canterbury, and Six other Bishops, to his Majesty. 4to. Lond. 1688.
Crofton, Zach. Vertue and Value of Baptism, &c. 4to. Lond. 1663.
——, ——. Hard Way to Heaven, a Sermon. 4to. Lond. 1662.
——, ——. Reformation not Separation; with an Appendix in Answer to it. 4to. 1662.
Croix, M. de la. Défence des Constitutions Américaines. Vide Adams, J.
——, ————. Verfassung der vornehmsten Europäischen und der Vereinigten Amerikanischen Staaten; aus dem Franz. 6 Bände. 8vo. Leipz. 1805.
Croix, S. F. la. Vide Lacroix.
Crombie, Alex. Essay on Philosophical Necessity. 8vo. Lond. 1793.
——, ——. Gymnasium, sive Symbola Critica. 2 vol. 8vo. Lond. 1812.
Crome, A. F. W. Ueber die Grösse, Volksmenge, Clima, und Fruchtbarkeit des Nordamerikanischen Freystaats. 12mo. Dessau und Leipz. 1783.
Crompton, Rich. L'Office et Auctoritie de Justices de Peace. 4to. Lond. 1617.
——, ——. L'Auctoritie et Jurisdiction des Courts. 4to. Lond. 1637.
Cromwell, Oliver. History and Policie reviewed. See Dawbeny.
——, ——. Short Critical Review of his Political Life. 12mo. Glasgow. 1763.
——, ——. Perfect Politician. 12mo. Lond. 1681.
——, ——, World's Mistake in. See Bethel.
——, ——, Treatment of the Body of. (Harl. Miscel. vol. 2.)
——, ——. Sermon in 1649. (Id. 4.)
——, ——. Complaint of Injustice: or Dispute with Pope Alexander VI, for Precedency in Hell. (Id. 7.)
——, ——, Vindication of, against Ludlow. (Somers, Tr. vol. 3.)
——, ——. Memoirs of Oliver Cromwell, and of his Sons, Richard and Henry. 3d ed. 2 vols. 8vo. Lond. 1822.
Cronica del Cid. fol. Burgos. 1593.

Cronica del Rey Don Rodrigo. fol. Toledo. 1549.
——— de España. fol. Zamora. 1541.
——— del Rey Don Juan II. fol. Logroño. 1517.
——— del Rey Don Jaume I. Vide Muntaner.
———. Coleccion de las Cronicas de los Reyes de Castilla, etc. Vide Ayala.
——— de Don Alvaro de Luna. Vide Luna.
———. Vide Alfonso.
Cronichette Antiche di Varj Scrittori. 4to. Firenze. 1733.
Cronstedt, Axel, Fred. Essay towards a System of Mineralogy; from the Swedish. 8vo. Lond. 1770.
Crophius, J. B. Antiquitates Macedonicæ. (Gronov. vol. 6.)
Crosby, Tho. History of the English Baptists. 4 vols. 8vo. Lond. 1738.
Crosse, Wm. Workes of C. C. Salustius; from the Latin. 12mo. 1629.
Croswell, Andrew. Part of an Exposition of Paul's Journey to Damascus; with an Appendix on Military Cruelties. 2d ed. 12mo. Bost. 1768.
———, ———. On Commencement Drollery. 4to. Bost. 1771.
———, ———. Letter to, on the above. 8vo. Bost. 1771.
———, ———. Observations on Warburton's Sermon before the Society for Propagating the Gospel. 8vo. Bost 1768.
Croswell, W. Description of the Mercator Map of the Starry Heavens. 8vo. Bost. 1810.
Crowley, Rob. Confutation of the Thirteen Articles N. Shaxton (Bp.) subscribed to, &c. 12mo. Lond. 1548.
Crown Circuit Companion. 8vo. N. York. 1816.
Crowther, Bryan. On the White-Swelling. 8vo. Lond. 1808.
Croxall, Sam. Consecration Sermon. 4to. Lond. 1724.
Croy, Charles de. Ampliation du Discours intitulé; "Histoire Veritable des Choses passées soubz le Gouvernement de Charles de Croy, Prince de Chimay." 12mo. 1589.
Cro⁻e, M. V. la. Histoire du Christianisme des Indes. 2 vol. 12mo. La Haye. 1758.
———, ———. Vindiciæ Veterum Scriptorum contra Harduinum. 12mo. Rotterdam. 1708.
Crozet, C. Descriptive Geometry. 8vo. N. York. 1821.
Crucius, Jac. Epistolæ. 12mo. Amst. 1650—51.
Cruden, Alex. Concordance to the Scriptures. 4to. Lond. 1761.
Cruikshank, Wm. Surgery. MS. 10 vols. 4to.
———, ———. Lectures on Surgery. MS. 20 vols. 4to.
———, ———. Anatomy of the Absorbing Vessels. 4to. Lond. 1790.
Cruise, Wm. Digest of the Laws of England respecting Real Property. 7 vols. 8vo. N. York. 1808.
Crusca, Accademici della. Vide Accademici.
Crusius, Chr. Aug. Opuscula Philosophico-Theologica. 12mo. Lips. 1750.
Crusius, J. A. De Nocte et Nocturnis Officiis apud Veteres. (Sallengre, vol. 2.)

Crusius, L. Lives of the Roman Poets. 2 vols. 12mo. Lond. 1733.
Cruso, Tim. Twenty-four Sermons at Pinners Hall. 12mo. Lond. 1699.
——, ——. Discourses upon the Rich Man and Lazarus. 12mo. Lond. 1697.
——, ——. Three Last Sermons; and Sermon on the 5th of Nov. 12mo. Lond. 1698.
Crutwell, C. Concordance of Parallels, from Bibles and Commentaries. 4to. 1790.
Cruylius, Liv. Descriptio Faciei Variorum Locorum Urbis Romæ. (Grævius, vol. 4.)
Cruys, Cornelius. Nieuw Pas-kaart Boek, behelsende de groote Rivier Don, etc. fol.
Cruz, San Juan de la. Vide Juan.
Cruz y Cano, Ramon de la. Teatro. 10 tom. 12mo. Madrid. 1786—91.
Cryselia de Lidaceli. 12mo. Paris. 1609.
Ctesias Cnidius. Vide Herodotus.
Cuba, Original Papers relating to the Expedition to. 8vo. Lond. 1744
Cubi i Soler, Mariano. New Spanish Grammar. 12mo. Baltimore. 1822.
——, ——. The Same. 2d ed. 12mo. Balt. 1825.
——, ——. ——. 3d ed. 12mo. N. York. 1826.
——, ——. ——. 4th ed. 12mo. Balt. 1828.
——, ——. New Pocket Dictionary of the English and Spanish Languages. 2 vols. 18mo. Balt. 1823.
——, ——. Gramática de la Lengua Castellana. 18mo. Balt. 1824.
——, ——. English and Spanish Conductor. 18mo. Balt.
——, ——. Traducteur François. 12mo. Balt. 1826.
——, ——. Idem. 2de edit. 12mo. Bost. 1828.
——, ——. Traductor Español. 12mo. Balt. 1826.
——, ——. Idem. ed. 2da. 12mo. Bost. 1828.
——, ——. Estractos de los mas Célebres Escritores Españoles. 12mo. Balt. 1827.
——, ——. Observations on a Practical System of Translation, &c. 8vo. Bost. 1828.
——, ——. English Translator. 12mo. Camb. 1828.
Cubières, M. de, (l'aîné.) Sur le Magnolier Auriculé. 8vo. Versailles.
——, ——. Sur le Genévrier Rouge de Virginie. 8vo. Versailles. 1805.
Cubillo, Alvaro. El Enano de las Musas, Comedias, y Obras Diversas. 4to. Madrid. 1654.
——, ——. Comedias. 4to.
Cudena. Beschrybung des Portugiesischen Amerika, herausgegeben von Lessing. 12mo. Braunschweig. 1780.
Cudworth, Ralph. Intellectual System of the Universe. fol. Lond. 1678.

Cudworth, Ralph. The Same; also his Discourse on the Lord's Supper, and Two Sermons; with his Life, by T. Birch. 2d ed. 2 vols. 4to. Lond. 1743.
———, ———. On Eternal and Immutable Morality. 8vo. Lond. 1731.
———, ———. Deus Justificatus. 12mo. Lond. 1688.
Cueva, Juan de la. Conquista de la Bética; Poema Heroyco. 2 tom. 12mo. Madrid. 1795.
Cuffe, Henrie. Differences of the Ages of Mans Life, &c. 16mo. Lond. 1607.
Cullen, Charles. History of Mexico. See Clavigero.
Cullen, Wm. First Lines of the Practice of Physic. 4 vols. 8vo. Edin. 1784.
———, ———. The Same. 4 vols. 8vo. Edin. 1788.
———, ———. ———, with Notes, by P. Reid. 2 vols. 8vo. Edin. 1802.
———, ———. Materia Medica. 2 vols. 8vo. Dublin. 1789.
———, ———. The Same. 2 vols. 4to. Edin. 1789.
———, ———. ———, by Barton. 3d Amer. ed. 8vo. Phil. 1808.
———, ———. Clinical Lectures. 8vo. Lond. 1797.
———, ———. Institutions of Medicine. Part I. Physiology. 8vo. Edin. 1785.
———, ———. Synopsis Nosologiæ Methodicæ. ed. 3tia. 2 vol. 8vo. Edin. 1780.
———, ———. Idem. ed. 6ta. 2 vol. 8vo. Edin. 1795.
———, ———. Essay on producing Cold by Evaporation.
Culloden, Account of the Battle of. 8vo. Lond. 1749.
Culpeper, Nich. New Method of Physick. 16mo. Lond. 1654.
———, ———. Practice of Physick, chiefly from L. Riverius; by N. Culpeper, A. Cole, and W. Rowland; with Select Medicinal Counsels, by J. Fernelius. fol. Lond. 1672.
Cultivateur Américain, La Science du, par Gel. Chast****-Destere. 8vo. 1800.
Cumberland, Rich. (Bp.) Sanchoniatho's Phœnician History, tr. from Eusebius. 8vo. Lond. 1720.
———, ———. Origines Gentium Antiquissimæ. 8vo. Lond. 1724.
———, ———. De Legibus Naturæ. 4to. Lond. 1672.
———, ———. Idem. 8vo. Dublini. 1720.
———, ———. Letter on the Character of Dr. Bentley. 8vo.
———, ———. Scripture Weights and Measures. 8vo. Lond. 1686.
Cumberland, Rich. The Observer. 5 vols. 12mo. Lond. 1787—90.
———, ———. ———. 4 vols. 8vo. Lond. 1786—8.
———, ———. Exodiad, a Poem, written in conjunction with Sir J. B. Burges. 4to. Lond. 1807.
———, ———. Retrospection. 4to. Bost. 1812.
Cuming, F. Sketches of a Tour to the Western Country, &c. 12mo. Pittsburgh. 1810.

Cuming, Patrick. Sermon before the Society in Scotland for propagating Christian Knowledge. 8vo. Edin. 1760.
Cumings, Henry. Occasional Sermons. 8vo. Bost. 1767—1802.
———, ———. Half Century Discourse at Billerica. 8vo. Camb. 1813.
———, ———. Election Sermon. 8vo Bost. 1783.
———, ———. Thanksgiving Sermon. 8vo. Bost. 1798.
Cumming, A. Sermon at his own Instalment as Colleague to Dr. J. Sewall. 8vo. Bost. 1761.
Cumming, John. Discourse to a Society of Young Men. 8vo. Lond. 1719.
———, ———. Sermon on the Death of the Rev. Benjamin Robinson. 8vo. Lond. 1724.
———, ———. Grounds of the present Differences among the London Ministers. 8vo. Lond. 1720.
———, ———, Apostles Creed better than the Assembly's Catechism, in a Letter to. 8vo. Lond. 1720.
Cummings, Archibald. Two Sermons on Christian Unity. 12mo. Phil. 1737.
Cummings, J. A. New Testament Questions. 12mo. Bost. 1817.
———, ———. See Testament.
———, ———. Geography, Ancient and Modern. 12mo. Bost. 1825.
Cunæus, Petrus. De Republica Hebræorum. 16mo. Lug. Bat. 1631.
———, ———. Idem. (Ugol. vol. 3.)
———, ———. Orationes, etc. 12mo. Lips. 1720.
Cunha de Azeredo Coutinho, J. J. da. Ensaio Economico sobre o Comercio de Portugal e suas Colonias. 4to. Lisboa. 1794.
———, ———. Politischer Versuch über den Handel Portugals und seiner Kolonien; aus dem Portugiesischen übers. von Murhard. 12mo. Hamb. 1801.
———, ———. Informaçâo dada ao Ministro de Estado dos Negocios da Fazenda D. Rodrigo de Sousa Coutinho. 4to. Lisboa. 1807.
———, ———. Repostas dadas, etc. 4to. Lisboa. 1808.
———, ———. Defeza de D. J. J. da Cunha. 4to. Lisboa. 1808.
Cunn, Sam. Euclid's Elements of Geometry; from the Latin Translation of Commandine, with Treatises by Dr. Keil. 3d ed. by John Ham. 8vo. Lond. 1733.
Cunningham, John. Poems. See Chalmers, A.
Cunningham, J. W. Velvet Cushion. 12mo. Lond. 1814.
———, ———. The Same. 16mo. Bost. 1815.
Cunningham, T. Law Dictionary. 3d ed. 2 vols. fol. Lond. 1783.
———, —. History of Taxes, &c. 3d ed. 8vo. Lond. 1778.
Cunningham, Wm. Correspondence with Adams. See Adams, J.
Cuperus, Gisbertus. Apotheosis Homeri. 4to. Amst. 1683.

Cuperus, Gisbertus. Harpocrates. 4to. Traj. ad Rhen. 1687.
———, ———. De Elephantis in Nummis Obviis. (Sallengre, vol. 3)
Curcellæus, Steph. Opera Theologica. fol. Amst. 1675.
———, ———. Dissertationes adversus S. Maresium. 12mo. Amst. 1659.
Curio, Hieronymus. Lexicon Græco-Latinum. fol. Basil. 1541.
Curiositez de la Nature et de l'Art, aportées dans deux Voyages des Indes, (par C. Biron.) 12mo. Paris. 1703.
Currie, Wm. Description of the Malignant Fever in Philadelphia. 8vo. Phil. 1793.
———, ———. Review of Dr. Rush's Account of the Yellow Fever. 8vo. Phil. 1794.
———, ———. Historical Account of the Climates and Diseases of the United States. 8vo. Phil. 1792.
———, ———. Causes of the Insalubrity of Flat and Marshy Situations, &c. (Amer. Phil. Tr. vol. 4.)
Curry, James. On Apparent Death from Drowning, Suffocation, &c. 8vo. Northampton. 1792.
Curtis, Wm. Botanical Magazine. 13½ vols. 8vo. Lond. 1793—1806.
Curtius, Q. R. De Rebus Gestis Alexandri Magni. 16mo. Amst. 1671.
———, ———. Idem, in usum Delphini. 4to. Paris. 1678.
———, ———. ———, ———. 8vo. Lond. 1705.
———, ———. ———, cum Notis Variorum. 8vo. Amst. 1684.
———, ———. ———, ———, cura Snakenburg. 4to. Delphis et Lug. Bat. 1724.
———, ———. History of the Wars of Alexander the Great, tr. by J. Digby. 2 vols. 12mo. Lond. 1747.
Cusanus, C. The Idiot. 16mo. Lond. 1650.
Cushing, Caleb. Address to the Senior Class. 8vo. Camb. 1821.
———, ———. Oration, July 4th. 8vo. Newburyport. 1821.
———, ———. Oration before the Washington Light Infantry Company. 8vo. Newburyport. 1822.
———, ———. Practical Principles of Political Economy. 8vo. Camb. 1826.
———, ———. Eulogy on Adams and Jefferson. 8vo. Camb. 1826.
———, ———. History and Present State of Newburyport. 12mo. Newburyport. 1826.
———, ———. See Pothier.
Cushing, Jacob. Sermon at the Ordination of the Rev. Samuel Williams. 8vo. Bost. 1766.
———, ———. Sermon at the Ordination of the Rev. Elijah Brown. 8vo. Bost. 1771.
———, ———. Sermon at the Ordination of the Rev. Jacob Biglow. 8vo. Bost. 1772.
———, ———. Sermon at the Ordination of the Rev. N. Underwood. 8vo. Bost. 1793.

Cushing, Jacob. Discourse at the Interment of the Rev. J. Jackson. 8vo. Bost. 1797.
Cushing, Tho. H. (Col.) Trial of, before a Court Martial at Baton-Rouge. 8vo. Phil. 1812.
Cutler, Manasseh. Century Discourse. 8vo. Salem. 1815.
———, ———. Account of American Plants. (Mem. A. A. S. vol. 1.)
Cutler, Timothy. Sermon on the Death of the Hon. Thomas Greaves. 8vo. Bost. 1747.
———, ———. Connecticut Election Sermon. 8vo. N. Lond. 1717.
Cuvier, G. Règne Animal. 4 vol. 8vo. Paris. 1817.
———, —. Anatomie Comparée. 5 vol. 8vo. Paris. 1805.
———, —. Lectures on Comparative Anatomy; from the French. 2 vols. 8vo. Lond. 1802.
———, —. Recherches sur les Ossemens Fossiles de Quadrupèdes. (Annales du Mus. d'Hist. Nat.)
———, —. Essay on the Theory of the Earth, translated from the French, with Notes, &c. by R. Jameson. 3d ed. 8vo. Edin. 1817.
———, —. The Same; with Observations on the Geology of North America, by S. L. Mitchell. 8vo. N. York. 1818.
Cyclopædia. Vide Rees, A.
Cypriano de Valera. Vide Biblia Española.
Cyprianus, Sanctus. Opera, cum Annotationibus J. Pamelii. 3 tomi in 1 vol. fol. 1593.
———, ———. Idem. 3 tomi in 1 vol. fol. Paris. 1633.
———, ———. ——, a S. Baluzio. fol. Paris. 1726.
———, ———. De Bono Patientiæ, cum Notis, a J. Stephano. 16mo. Oxon. 1633.
———, ———. De Idolorum Vanitate. Vide Minutius Felix.
Cyrillus, Alexandrinus. Opera, Gr. et Lat. cura J. Auberti. 6 tomi in 7 vol. fol. Lutetiæ. 1638.
———, ——— et Joannes Damascenus. Argumenta contra Nestorianos; accedunt M. Psellus de Trinitate et Charitonymus Christonymus pro Divinitate Christi; Gr. et Lat. cum Notis J. Wegelini. 12mo. Aug. Vind. 1611.
Cyrillus Hierosolymitanus. Opera, Gr. et Lat. cum Notis, a T. Milles. fol. Oxon. 1703.

D

DABNEY, J. P. Selection of Hymns and Psalms for Social and Private Worship. 18mo. Andover. 1821.
———, ——. The Same. 9th ed. 18mo. Camb. 1828.
———, ——. Prayers, adapted to Family and Private Use. 2d ed. 18mo. Camb. 1829.
———, ——. Annotations on the New Testament. 12mo. Camb. 1829.
Dacier, André. La Poétique d'Aristote, trad. en François, avec des Notes. 12mo. Amst. 1733.
Dafforne, Rich. Merchants Mirrour. See Malynes, G.
Daggett, Naphtali. Sermon on the Death of President Clap. 4to. New-Haven. 1767.
———, ———. Sermon at the Ordination of the Rev. J. Howe. 8vo. Bost. 1773.
Dahl, J. C. G. De Αὐθεντίᾳ Epistolarum Petrinæ Posterioris atque Judæ, etc. 4to. Rostochii. 1807.
——, ———. Chrestomathia Philoniana. 12mo. Hamb. 1800.
Dahlman, S. Beskrifning om S. Barthelemy. 12mo. Stockholm. 1786.
Dähnert, J. C. Platt-Deutsches Wörter-Buch. 4to. Stralsund. 1781.
Dairval, Baudelot de. De l'Utilité des Voyages. 2 vol. 12mo. Rouen. 1727.
Dalager, Lars. Grönlandske Relationer. 4to. Kiöbenhavn.
Dalboquerque, Alfonso. Commentarios. 2 vol. 8vo. Lisboa. 1774.
Dale, Ant. van. Dissertationes IX, Antiquitatibus, quin et Marmoribus, Rom. et Gr. illustrandis inservientes. 4to. Amst. 1702.
——, ———. Dissertationes de Origine ac Progressu Idololatriæ et Superstitionum ; de Vera ac Falsa Prophetia ; uti et de Divinationibus Idololatricis Judæorum. 4to. Amst. 1696.
——, ———. De Oraculis Veterum Ethnicorum, etc. 4to. Amst. 1700.
——, ———. Dissertatio super Aristea de LXX Interpretibus ; cui Aristeæ Textus subjungitur, Gr. et Lat. ; additur Historia Baptismorum ; item Dissertatio super Sanchoniathone. 4to. Amst. 1705.
Dale, Sam. Pharmacologia. 12mo. Lond. 1710.
Dalechamp, J. Histoire des Plantes. 2 vol. fol. Lyons. 1653.
Dalgleish, Wm. Sermon before the Society for propagating Christian Knowledge. 8vo. Edin. 1808.
Dalhusius, J. H. Salvation of Protestants asserted and defended. 4to. Lond. 1689.

Dallæus, J. De Pœnis et Satisfactionibus Humanis. 4to. Amst. 1649.

———, —. De Vero Usu Patrum Libri Duo; e Gallico redditi. 4to. Genevæ. 1686.

———, —. On the Right Use of the Fathers; from the French. 4to. Lond. 1675.

Dallas, A. J. Reports of Cases in the Courts of the United States and Pennsylvania. 4 vols. 8vo. Phil. 1806—7.

———, —. Exposition of the Causes and Character of the late War. 8vo. Washington. 1815.

Dallington, Sir Rob. Aphorismes Civil and Militarie, from Guicciardine. fol. Lond. 1629.

Dalmas. Recherches sur la Fièvre Jaune. 8vo. Paris. 1803.

Dalrymple, Alex. Account of the Discoveries made in the South Pacific Ocean previous to 1764. 8vo. Lond. 1767.

———, —. Historical Collection of Voyages and Discoveries in the South Pacific Ocean. 4to. Lond. 1770.

———, —. Spanish Pretensions fairly discussed. 8vo. Lond. 1790.

———, —. Journal of the Expeditions to the North of California, in 1768—70. 4to. Lond. 1790.

Dalrymple, Sir David, (Lord Hailes.) Historical Memorials concerning the Provincial Councils of the Scottish Clergy. 4to. Edin. 1769.

———, ———. Examination of some of the Arguments for the High Antiquity of Regiam Majestatem; and an Inquiry into the Authenticity of Leges Malcolmi. 4to. Edin. 1769.

———, ———. Memorials and Letters relating to the History of Britain in the Reigns of James I, and Charles I. 2 vols. 8vo. Glasgow. 1766.

Dalrymple, Gilbert. Letter from Edinburgh to Dr. Sherlock. 8vo. Lond. 1718.

Dalrymple, Sir John. On Feudal Property. 12mo. Lond 1759.

Dalrymple, John, (Earl of Stair.) State of the National Debt, Income, and Expenditure, with Reflections applicable to the Present Crisis. 12mo. Edin. 1776.

———, ———. The Same. 4th ed. fol. Lond. 1776.

Dalrymple, Wm. Travels through Spain and Portugal, &c. 4to. Lond. 1777.

Dalton, John. Sermon, Nov. 5th. 4to. Lond. 1747.

Dalton, Michael. Office and Authoritie of Sherifs. fol. Lond. 1623.

Dalzel, Andrew. Substance of Lectures on the Ancient Greeks, and on the Revival of Greek Learning in Europe. 2 vols. 8vo. Edin. 1821.

———, —. Vide Collectanea Græca.

Damascenus, Janus. De Arte Curandi. 4to. Basil. 1543.

Damascenus, Joannes. Opera, Gr. et Lat. cum Notis, a M. Lequien. 2 vol. fol. Paris. 1712.

———, ———. Vide Cyrillus Alexandrinus.

Damascenus, Nic. De Moribus Græcorum, etc. (Gronov. vol. 6.)
Damascius. Excerpta ex Libro ejus de Principiis. Vide Anecdota Græca a Wolfio.
Damm, C. T. Lexicon Homerico-Pindaricum, cura J. M. Duncan. 4to. Glasguæ. 1824.
Dampier, Wm. New Voyage round the World. 2 vols. 8vo. Lond. 1703—5.
———, ——. Voyages of Dampier and Others. 4 vols. 8vo. Lond. 1729.
Dana, Daniel. Discourse on the First Sabbath after his Ordination. 8vo. Newburyport. 1794.
——, ——. Two Fast Sermons. 8vo. Newburyport. 1799.
——, ——. Discourse on the Death of Washington. 8vo. Newburyport. 1800.
——, ——. Discourse on Music. 8vo. 1803.
——, ——. Connexion between Moral and Intellectual Improvement, an Address to the Phi Beta Kappa Society in Dartmouth College. 8vo. Exeter. 1817.
Dana, James. Century Discourse at Wallingford, April 9th, 1770. 12mo. New-Haven.
——, ——. Sermon on the Death of Charles Whittelsey, Esq. 8vo. Bost. 1764.
——, ——. Sermon on the Death of Mr. J. Hall. 8vo. New-Haven. 1765.
——, ——. African Slave Trade, a Discourse delivered before the Connecticut Society for the Promotion of Freedom. 8vo. New-Haven. 1791.
——, ——. Two Discourses;—on Faith, and on the Inscrutability of Providence. 8vo. Bost. 1767.
——, ——. Sermon on the Death of the Rev. Chauncey Whittelsey. 8vo. Bost. 1787.
——, —— Sermon at the Installation of the Rev. A. Holmes. 8vo. Bost. 1792.
Dana, J. F. On the "American Water Burner." 8vo.
——, ——. Report on a Disease afflicting Neat Cattle. 8vo. Concord, N. H. 1822.
——, ——, and S. L. Outlines of the Mineralogy and Geology of Boston and its Vicinity, with a Geological Map. 8vo. Bost. 1818.
Dana, Joseph. Two Discourses on Prov. xv, 8. 8vo. Newburyport. 1782.
——, ——. Fast Sermon. 8vo. Bost. 1799.
——, ——. Convention Sermon. 4to. Bost. 1801.
——, ——. Sermon at the Ordination of the Rev. D. Dana. 8vo. Newburyport. 1795.
——, ——. Sermon on the Death of the Rev. Joseph M'Kean. 8vo. Newburypost. 1818.
Dana, R. H. Oration before the Washington Benevolent Society of Cambridge. 8vo. Camb. 1814.
——, ——. Poems. 18mo. Bost. 1827.
——, ——. Idle Man. 8vo. N. York. 1821.
Dana, Sam. Masonic Address. 8vo. 1797.

Dana, Sam. Answer to the Report of the Committee of the House of Representatives. 8vo. Bost. 1808.
Dana, Sam. Discourse on the History of the First Church in Marblehead. 8vo. Bost. 1816.
Danæus, Lambertus. Orationis Dominicæ Explicatio. 8vo. Genevæ. 1582.
———, ———. De Vera Peccatorum Remissione adversus Purgatorium. 12mo.
———, ———. Opuscula Theologica. fol. 1583.
Dancer, Tho. History of the late Expedition against Fort San Juan; with Observations on Climate, Infection, and Contagion. 4to. Kingston. 1781.
———, ———. Catalogue of Plants in the Botanical Garden, Jamaica. 4to. St. Jago de la Vega. 1792.
Danchet. Le Sacre de Louis XV. fol.
Dane, Nathan. General Abridgment of American Law. 8 vols. 8vo. Bost. 1823.
Danegeld, Short Account of, &c. 4to. Lond. 1756.
Danet, P. Dictionnaire François et Latin. 4to. Lyon. 1738.
———, —. Dictionarium Latinum et Gallicum. 4to. Lugd. 1738.
———, —. Dictionary of the Greek and Roman Antiquities; from the French. 4to. Lond. 1700.
Danforth, Sam. Election Sermon. 16mo. Bost. 1714.
Danforth, Tho. Discourse before the Humane Society. 8vo. Bost. 1808.
Daniel, Græce, secundum Theodotionem, cura R. Holmes. fol.
———, secundum Septuaginta, ex Chisiano Codice; Gr. et Lat. 4to. Goettingæ. 1774.
———. See Bertholdt,—Blayney,—Wintle.
Daniel, Gabriel. History of France; from the French. 5 vols. 8vo. Lond. 1726.
Daniel, Richard. See Compendium.
Daniel, Sam. History of England from the Conquest to the End of Edward III. (Kennet, Hist. of Eng. vol. 1.)
———, ———. Poems. See Chalmers, A.
Daniell, J. On some Phenomena attending the Process of Solution. (Journal of Science, vol. 1.)
Dannhaverus, J. C. Politica Biblica. (Ugol. vol. 24.)
———, ———. De Sacrosancta Spiritus Sancti Poesi. (Id. 31.)
Danson, Tho. Friendly Debate between Satan and Sherlock. 16mo. 1676.
Dante Alighieri. Divina Commedia, con Illustrazioni, da Rosini. 4 vol. fol. Pisa. 1804.
———, ———. ———, da Portarelli. 3 vol. 8vo. Milano. 1804—5.
———, ———. ———, da Lombardi. 4 vol. 4to. Roma. 1815—17.
———, ———. ———, da Biagioli. 3 vol. 8vo. Parigi. 1818—19.
———, ———. Vision, translated by H. F. Cary. 2d ed. 3 vols. 8vo. Lond. 1819.

Danverian History of the Affairs of Europe for the Year 1731. 8vo. Lond. 1732.
D'Anvers. See Anvers.
Danz, Joh. Andr. Literator Ebræo-Chaldæus. ed. 3tia, 4ta, et 5ta. 8vo. Jenæ. 1715—45.
——, ————. Interpres Ebræo-Chaldæus. ed. 2da, 3tia, et 5ta. 8vo. Jenæ. 1694—1745.
——, ————. Interpretis Ebræo-Chaldæi Synopsis. ed. 4ta, et 7ma. 8vo. Jenæ. 1746.
——, ————. Compendium Grammaticæ Ebræo-Chaldaicæ. ed. 5ta, 6ta, et 8va. 8vo. Jenæ.
——, ————. Manuductio, Viam ostendens Compendiosam ad Ebrææ Linguæ Analysin facilius instituendam, etc. ed. 4ta. 8vo. Jenæ. 1732.
——, ————. Paradigmata Nominum Simplicium ac Verborum Integra. ed. 4ta, 5ta, 6ta, et 7ma. 8vo. Jenæ. 1716—51.
——, ————. Rabbinismus Enucleatus. ed. prima, 3tia, 6ta, 8va, et 9na. 8vo. Jenæ. 1699—1751.
——, ————. Aditus Syriæ Reclusus. ed. prima, 4ta, 6ta, et 7ma. 8vo. Jenæ. 1689—1752.
——, ————. Baptismus Proselytorum Judaicus. (Ugol. vol. 22.)
——, ————. De Re Militari Hebræorum. (Id. 27.)
Dapper, O. Beschreibung des Welt-teils Amerika, und des Sud-Landes. fol. Amst. 1673.
D'après de Mannevillette. Carte Reduite de l'Ocean Oriental Septentrional. Atlantic fol.
Darby, Wm. Geographical Description of the State of Louisiana. 8vo. Phil. 1816.
——, ——. The Same. 8vo. N. York. 1817.
——, ——. Emigrant's Guide. 8vo. N. York. 1818.
Darcie, Abr. True and Royall History of the famous Empresse Elizabeth, Queene of England. 4to. Lond. 1625.
Dares Phrygius. De Excidio Trojæ. Vide Dictys.
Darien, Defence of the Scots Settlement at, &c. 8vo. Edin. 1699.
———. Defence Answered. 8vo. Lond. 1699.
Dartmoor Prison, Massacre in. See Journal.
Dartmouth College. Sketches of the History of Dartmouth College and Moors' Charity School. 8vo. 1815.
———— ————. Review of the "Sketches." 8vo. 1815.
———— ————. Vindication of the Official Conduct of the Trustees of Dartmouth College. 8vo. Concord. 1815.
———— ————. See Freeman, P. R.
———— ————. Narrative of the Church Difficulties, which were the Origin of President Wheelock's Disaffection to the Trustees and Professors of the College, by B. Dewey and others, 8vo. Hanover. 1815.
———— ————, Case of, by T. Farrar. 8vo.
———— ————. Outline of the Arguments on the part of the Plaintiffs, in the Cause between the Trustees and William H. Woodward. 8vo.

Dartmouth College. See Catalogue.
Darwin, Erasmus. Temple of Nature. 8vo. New-York. 1804.
———, ———. Phytologia. 4to. Lond. 1800.
———, ———. Zoonomia. 3d ed. 4 vols. 8vo. Lond. 1801.
Daserus, L. H. De Augustiniana Decalogi Divisione. 4to. Stuttgardiæ. 1733.
Dassovius, Theod. Imagines Hebræarum Rerum. (Ugol. vol. 9.)
———, ———. De Ritibus Mesusæ. (Id. 21.)
———, ———. Vidua Hebræa. (Id. 30.)
Dathe, J. A. Disputatio in Canticum Mosis, Deut. xxxii. 4to. Lipsiæ. 1769.
———, ———. Opuscula ad Crisin et Interpretationem Vet. Testamenti spectantia. 8vo. Lips. 1796.
———, ———. Pentateuchus, Latine, cum Notis. 8vo. Halæ. 1781.
———, ———. Idem. 8vo. Halæ. 1791.
———, ———. Libri Historici Vet. Testamenti, Latine, cum Notis. 8vo. Halæ. 1784.
———, ———. Psalmi, Latine, cum Notis. 8vo. Halæ. 1787.
———, ———. Idem. 8vo. Halæ. 1784.
———, ———. Jobus, Proverbia Salomonis, Ecclesiastes, Canticum Canticorum, Latine, cum Notis. 8vo. Halæ. 1789.
———, ———. Prophetæ Majores et Minores, Latine, cum Notis. 8vo. Halæ. 1779.
———, ———. Prophetæ Majores, Latine, cum Notis. 8vo. Halæ. 1785.
———, ———. Prophetæ Minores, Latine, cum Notis. 8vo. Halæ. 1773.
———, ———. Idem. 8vo. Halæ. 1790.
Dati, C. R. Vite de' Pittori Antichi. 8vo. Milano. 1806.
Daub, Carl, und Fried. Creuzer. Studien. 6 Bände. 8vo. Frankf. und Heidelb. 1805—11.
Daubeney, Charles. Appendix to the "Guide to the Church." 2 vols. 8vo. Lond. 1799.
———, ———. Vindiciæ Ecclesiæ Anglicanæ. 8vo. Lond. 1803.
Daubuz, Charles. Perpetual Commentary on the Revelation of St. John. fol. Lond. 1720.
Daudin, F. M. Mémoires dans les Annales du Muséum d'Histoire Naturelle.
Daumius, C. Epistolæ. Vide Reinesius, T.
Davanzati, B. Scisma d'Inghilterra, con altre Operette. 8vo. Padova. 1727.
———, ———. Idem. 8vo. Milano. 1807.
Daveis, Charles, S. Address on Adams and Jefferson. 8vo. Portland. 1826.
———, ———. Address on the Commemoration at Fryeburg, May 19, 1825. 8vo. Portland. 1825.
Davenant, Joh. (Episc.) Expositio Epistolæ Pauli ad Colossenses. fol. Cant. 1639.
———, ———. Prælectiones Duæ Theologicæ. fol. Cant. 1631.

Davenant, Joh. (Episc.) Determinationes XLIX Quaestionum Theologicarum. fol. Cant. 1634.
Davenant, Sir Wm. Discourse upon Gondibert. 24to. Paris. 1650.
———, ———. First Days Entertainment at Rutland-House. 16mo. Lond. 1657.
———, ———. Poems. See Chalmers, A.
Davenport, James. Confessions and Retractations. 12mo. Bost. 1744.
———, ———. Examination of the Retractations. 12mo. Bost.
———, ———. Lines to him. 12mo. Bost.
Davenport, John. The Power of Congregational Churches asserted and vindicated. 12mo. Lond. 1672.
Davenport, W. Protestant Expostulator upon the Controversies between the Bishop of Bangor and Others. 8vo. Lond. 1718.
Daventer, Henry à. Art of Midwifery Improved; from the Latin. 8vo. Lond. 1723.
David, F. A. Antiquités Etrusques, Grecques, et Romaines. 5 vol. 4to. Paris. 1785—7.
———, ———. Muséum de Florence. 8 vol. 4to. Paris. 1787—1802.
———, ———. Antiquités d'Herculanum. 12 vol. 4to. Paris. 1780—1803.
———, ———. Histoire de France, représentée par Figures accompagnées de Discours. 5 vol. 4to. Paris. 1787—96.
———, ———. Histoire de Russie, représentée par Figures accompagnées de Discours. 2 vol. 4to. Paris. 1797—9.
———, ———. Histoire d'Angleterre, représentée par Figures accompagnées de Discours. 3 vol. 4to. Paris. 1784—1800.
Davidson, James. Short Introduction to Latin Grammar. 9th ed. 12mo. Phil. 1820.
Davidson, Wm. Arithmetic, &c. 12mo. Lond.
Davie, J. C. Letters from Paraguay. 8vo. Lond. 1805.
Davies, Benj. Account of Philadelphia. 12mo. Phil. 1794.
Davies, Edw. Celtic Researches. 8vo. Lond. 1804.
Davies, Jo. Antiquæ Linguæ Britannicæ et Linguæ Latinæ Dictionarium. fol. Lond. 1632.
Davies, Sir John. Poems. See Chalmers, A.
Davies, Myles. Athenæ Britannicæ. 2 vols. 8vo. Lond. 1716.
Davies, Sam. (Pres.) Sermons adapted to the Family and the Closet. 3 vols. 8vo. Lond. 1767.
———, ———. Sermon on the Death of King Geo. II; with the Life of the Author, by D. Bostwick. 8vo. Bost. 1761.
———, ———. State of Religion among the Protestant Dissenters in Virginia. 8vo. Bost. 1751.
———, ———. Sermon to Capt. Overton's Company of Volunteers. 8vo. Phil. 1756.
———, ———. Sermon before the Militia of Hanover County in Virginia. 16mo. Lond. 1758.
———, ———. Virginia's Danger and Remedy; Two Discourses. 12mo. Williamsburg. 1756.

Davies, Tho. Life of David Garrick. 2 vols. 12mo. Bost. 1818.
Davila, A. C. Dell' Istoria delle Guerre Civili di Francia. 6 vol. 8vo. Milano. 1807.
——, ——. History of the Civil Wars of France, tr. from the Italian by E. Farneworth. 2 vols. 4to. Lond. 1758.
Davis, Daniel. Oration, July 4th. 8vo. Portland. 1796.
Davis, Henry, (Pres.) Inaugural Oration. 8vo. Bost. 1810.
Davis, Hugh. De Jure Uniformitatis Ecclesiasticæ; or of the Rights belonging to an Uniformity in Churches. fol. Lond. 1659.
Davis, John. Discourse before the Massachusetts Historical Society, Dec. 22, 1813. 8vo. Bost. 1814. See also Mass. Hist. Coll. 2d Series, vol. 1.
——, ——. Eulogy on Washington. (Mem. A. A. S. vol. 2.)
——, ——. Attempt to explain the Inscription on Dighton Rock. (Id. 3.)
Davis, John. Oration, July 4th. 8vo. Worcester. 1816.
Davis, John. Travels in the United States. 8vo. Lond. 1803.
Davis, Sir John. Abridgment of the Eleaven Bookes of Reports of Sir Edward Cook; from the French. 12mo. Lond. 1651.
Davis, Nathanael. Reise nach den Spanisch-Americanischen Gold-Minen. Vide Wafer, L.
Davis, Rich. Sense of the United Nonconforming Ministers, in and about London, concerning his Errors, &c. 4to. Lond. 1693.
D'Avissonus, W. Oblatio Salis, sive Gallia Lege Salis Condita. 8vo. Paris. 1657.
Davy, Sir Humphry. Researches Chemical and Philosophical. 8vo. Lond. 1800.
——, ————. Elements of Agricultural Chemistry. 8vo. N. York. 1815.
——, ————. Elements of Chemical Philosophy, Part I. vol. 1. 8vo. Phil. 1812.
——, ————. On the Wire-Gauze Safe-Lamps, for preventing Explosions from Fire-damp, &c. (Brande, Journal, vol. 1.)
Dawbeny, H. Historie and Policie reviewed, in the Heroick Transactions of the late Lord Protector. 8vo. Lond. 1659.
Dawes, Ric. Miscellanea Critica. 8vo. Lipsiæ. 1800.
Dawes, Tho. Oration on the 5th of March. 4to. Bost. 1781.
——, ——. Oration July 4th. 8vo. Bost. 1787.
Dawes, Sir Wm. (Abp.) Sermon before the Society for Propagating the Gospel in Foreign Parts. 8vo. Lond. 1709.
Dawson, Benj. Examination of Dr. Rutherforth's Argument respecting Subscription. 8vo. Lond. 1766.
——, ——. Letter to Dr. Rutherforth respecting Subscription. 8vo. Lond. 1767.
——, ——. Examination of an Essay on Establishments in Religion. 8vo. Lond. 1767.
——, ——. Address to the Writer of a Second Letter to the Author of the Confessional. 8vo. Lond. 1768.
——, ——. Answer to Letters concerning Confessions of Faith. Parts 1, 2, and 3. 8vo. Lond. 1768—9.

Dawson, Benj. Short and Safe Expedient for Terminating the present Debates about Subscriptions. 8vo. Lond. 1769.
———, ——, Three Letters to, on the Reformation of the Church of England. 8vo. Lond. 1771.
———, ——. Dissertatio Inauguralis de Summo Bono. 4to. Glasguæ. 1750.
———, ——. On the Logos, in Eight Sermons. 8vo. Lond. 1765.
Dawson, Joan. Lexicon Novi Testamenti. 3tia ed. 8vo. Lond. 1766.
Day, Jeremiah. Introduction to Algebra. 8vo. New-Haven. 1814.
Day, Tho. Reports of Cases in the Sup. Court of Errors of Connecticut in 1802—4. 4 vols. 8vo. Hartford. 1806.
Daye, James. Sermon on the Death of the Rev. Caleb Rotherham. 8vo. Lond. 1752.
Dazille. Observations sur les Maladies des Nègres. 8vo. Paris. 1776.
Deaf and Dumb. Vox Oculis subjecta. Vide Green, F.
——————. First and Third Reports of the Connecticut Asylum for Deaf and Dumb Persons. 8vo. Hartford. 1817—19.
——————. Act to Incorporate the New-York Institution for the Deaf and Dumb, &c. 8vo. N. York. 1819.
Dean, Paul. Artillery Election Sermon. 8vo. Bost. 1816.
Dean, R. On the Future Life of Brute Creatures. 12mo. Lond. 1768.
Deane, Sam. Election Sermon. 8vo. Bost. 1794.
———, ——. Discourse on the Death of the Rev. T. Smith. 8vo. Portland. 1795.
Deane, Sam. Discourse on Christian Liberty. 8vo. Camb. 1825.
Deane, Silas. Address to the United States of North America; with a Letter to the Hon. Robert Morris. 8vo. Lond. 1784.
———, ——. See Lee, A.
Dearborn, Benj. Columbian Grammar. 12mo. Bost. 1795.
Dearborn, H. (Gen.) Account of the Battle of Bunker Hill. (Portfolio, vol. 5.)
————, ————. See Putnam, D.
Dearborn, H. A. S. Oration, July 4th. 8vo. Salem. 1806.
Dease, Wm. Theory and Practice of Surgery. vol. 1. 8vo. Lond. 1780.
———, ——. On the Methods for the Cure of the Hydrocele, and of Cutting for the Stone. 8vo. Dublin. 1782.
———, ——. On the Venereal Disease. 8vo. Dublin. 1779.
———, ——. On Midwifery and on the Disorders of Women and Children. 8vo. Dublin. 1783.
———, ——. On Wounds of the Head. 8vo. Lond. 1776.
Death-Bed-Repentance, Hazard of. 8vo. Lond. 1708.
Debates. See United States.
Debiel, Ludov. Utilitas Rei Numariæ Veteris. 8vo. Viennæ. 1733.
Debonnaire, Louis. Leçons de la Sagesse sur les Défauts des Hommes. 3 vol. 12mo. Paris. 1751.
—————, ——. L'Esprit des Loix Quintessencié. 2 vol. 12mo. 1751.

De Boze, Gros. Vide Boze.
Debt. See National Debt.
Decalves, Alonzo. Reisebeschreibung. 12mo. Phil. 1796.
Décandolle, A. P. Astragalogia. fol. Paris. 1802.
————, ——. Idem. 4to. Paris. 1802.
————, ——. Mémoires dans les Annales du Muséum d'Histoire Naturelle.
————, ——. On the Effect of Elevation above the Level of the Sea upon the Geography of Plants in France. (Brande, Journal, vol. 4.)
————, ——. Histoire Naturelle des Plantes Grasses. fol. Paris. 1799.
————, ——. Icones Selectæ Plantarum. 4to. Paris. 1820.
Decker, Sir Matthew. Essai sur les Causes du Déclin du Commerce Etranger de la Grande Bretagne; trad. de l'Anglois. 2 vol. 12mo. 1757.
Declaration of Independence, Biography of the Signers of the. See American Independence.
Dedham, Statement of the Proceedings in, respecting the Settlement of a Minister, &c. 8vo. Camb. 1819.
Deductio, sive Declaratio Ord. Hollandiæ, West-Frisiæque, etc. 24to. Lug. Bat. 1654.
Defection considered, and the Designs of those who divided the Friends of the Government, set in a True Light. 2d ed. 8vo. Lond. 1717.
Deffand, Madame du. Lettres. 4 vol. 12mo. Lond. 1810.
De Foe, Dan. More Reformation, a Satyr upon himself. 4to. Lond.
———, ——. Robinson Crusoe; with "The True-born Englishman," &c. 3 vols. 8vo. Lond. 1790.
———, ——. History of the Devil. 5th ed. 12mo. Lond. 1754.
———, ——. Original Power of the People of England, &c. 8vo. Lond. 1769.
———, ——. Religious Courtship; with an Appendix on Servants. 10th ed. 12mo. Lond. 1762.
Degen, J. F. Ueber die Philosophie des Anakreons. 12mo. Erlang.
Deist's Creed, with the Free-Thinker's annext. 8vo. Lond. 1731.
——— Religion, Summary Account of the. 8vo. Lond 1745.
Deity. Argument to prove the Unity and Perfections of God *a priori*. 8vo. Lond. 1735.
———. Wisdom the first Spring of Action in the Deity. See Grove, H.
———. Existence de Dieu montrée par les Merveilles de la Nature. 4to. Paris. 1725.
———. Discourse on the Service of God. 8vo. Lond. 1743.
———. Moral Discourse on the Attributes of God, occasioned by Clayton's "Essay on Spirit." 8vo. Lond. 1754.
Delambre, J. B. J. Méthodes Analytiques pour la Détermination d'un Arc du Méridien, etc. 4to. Paris. 1800.

Delambre, J. B. J. Vide Méchain.
Delamer, Henry, (Earl of Warrington.) Works. 8vo. Lond. 1694.
Delamétherie, J. C. Leçons de Minéralogie. 2 vol. 8vo. Paris. 1812.
———, —. Journal de Physique, de Chimie, et d'Histoire Naturelle. 13 vol. 4to. Paris. 1793—1802.
———, —. Vide Rozier, Fr.
Delany, Patrick. Sermon before the Society for promoting English Protestant Working-Schools in Ireland. 4to. Lond. 1744.
———, ———. Twenty Sermons on Social Duties, &c. 8vo. Lond. 1750.
———, ———. Sixteen Discourses on Doctrines and Duties, &c. 8vo. Lond. 1754.
———, ———. Abstinence from Blood defended. 8vo. Lond. 1734.
———, ———. Revelation examined with Candour. 4th ed. 3 vols. 8vo. Lond. 1745.
———, ———. Historical Account of the Life and Reign of David. 4th ed. 2 vols. 8vo. Lond. 1769.
———, ———. Observations upon Lord Orrery's Remarks on the Life and Writings of Swift. 8vo. Lond. 1754.
Delaplaine. Repository of the Lives and Portraits of Distinguished American Characters. vol. 1. part 1. 4to. Phil. 1816.
Delarbre, A. Flore d'Auvergne. 8vo. Clermont-Ferrand. 1795.
Delaune, Tho. Present State of London. 12mo. Lond. 1690.
———, —. Plea for Non-Conformists. 12mo. Lond. 1712.
———, —. The Same. 12mo. Bost. 1763.
Delbrück, J. F. F. Homeri Religionis quæ ad Bene Beateque Vivendum Heroicis Temporibus fuerit Vis. 12mo. Magdeburgi. 1797.
D'Elci, Angelo. Satire. 8vo. Firenze. 1817.
Deleuze. Mémoires dans les Annales du Muséum d'Histoire Naturelle.
Delille, Jacques. Poésies Fugitives. 12mo. Paris. 1802.
———, ———. La Pitié. 12mo. Paris. 1804.
———, ———. Dithyrambe sur l'Immortalité de l'Ame, suivi du Passage du St. Gothard, Poëme par Mme. la Duchesse de Devonshire, trad. de l'Anglais, avec l'Original. 12mo. Paris. 1802.
———, ———. L'Imagination. 2 vol. 12mo. Paris. 1806.
———, ———. Les Jardins. 12mo. Paris. 1803.
———, ———. L'Enéide. Vide Virgilius.
———, ———. Les Géorgiques. Vide Virgilius.
———, ———. Le Paradis Perdu. Vide Milton.
Delme, Philip. Letter to a Godly Christian under Affliction. 4to. Lond. 1703.
De Lolme, J. L. See Lolme, J. L. de.
Delpino, J. G. Dictionary, Spanish and English, &c. fol. Lond. 1763.
Del Rè, Ant. Antiquitates Tiburtinæ. (Græv. Thes. Ital.)
Demades. Vide Oratores Græci, a Reiskio.
———. Vide Demosthenes.

Demetrius Cydonius. De Contemnenda Morte. Vide Græci Auctores Minores.
Demetrius Phalerius. De Elocutione. 8vo. Glasg. 1743.
——— ———. Idem. Vide Rhetores Selecti.
Democrates. Aureæ Sententiæ. Vide Opuscula Mythologica.
Democratiad, a Poem. 8vo. Phil. 1796.
Democratic Society in Philadelphia. Articles and Regulations agreed upon by its Members. 8vo. Phil. 1793.
——— Songster. 12mo. Baltimore. 1801.
De Moivre, Abr. Doctrine of Chances. 3d ed. 4to. Lond. 1756.
Demontiosius, Ludov. De Sculptura, Cælatura, Gemmarum Scalptura, et Pictura Antiquorum. (Gronov. vol. 9.)
Demophilus. Similitudines. Vide Opuscula Mythologica.
Demos in Council, a Poem. 12mo. Bost. 1799.
Demosthenes. Opera Demosthenis et Æschinis, Gr. et Lat. a Wolfio. fol. Aurel. Allob. 1607.
———. Opera Demosthenis, Æschinis, Dinarchi, et Demadis, Gr. et Lat. cum Notis, a J. Taylor. tomi 2 et 3. [All that was published.] 4to. Cant. 1747.
———. Opera. Vide Oratores Græci, a Reiskio.
———, Æschines, Dinarchus, et Demades. Orationes de Legatione, et de Corona, Gr. et Lat. cum Notis, a J. Taylor. 2 vol. 8vo. Cant. 1769.
———. Selectæ Orationes, Gr. et Lat. cum Notis, a R. Mounteney. ed. 4ta. 8vo. Lond. 1764.
———. Oratio in Midiam, cum Notis, a G. L. Spalding. 8vo. Berol. 1794.
———. Orations; with the Oration of Dinarchus against him, and the Orations of Æschines on the Crown, tr., with Notes, by T. Leland. 3 vols. 8vo. Lond. 1757—70.
———. The Same. 3d ed. 3 vols. 8vo. Lond. 1777.
———. Orations of Demosthenes and Æschines, tr. with Notes, by P. Francis. 2 vols. 4to. Lond. 1757—8.
———. Opere, tradotte ed illustrate da M. Cesarotti. 6 vol. 12mo. Firenze. 1807—9.
Dempsterus, Tho. De Etruria Regali. 2 vol. fol. Flor. 1723—4.
———. Kalendarium Romanum. (Grævius, vol. 8.)
Denham, Sir John. Poems; with the Sophy. 4th ed. 8vo. Lond. 1703.
———, ———. Poetical Works. 16mo. Lond. 1793.
———, ———. ———. See Chalmers, A.
———, ———. Version of the Psalms of David. 8vo. Lond. 1714.
Denham, D. and H. Clapperton. Travels in Africa. 8vo. Bost. 1826.
Denham, Joseph. Charity Sermon. 8vo. Lond. 1737.
———, ———. Sermon before the Society for the Relief of Widows and Orphans of Dissenting Ministers. 8vo. Lond. 1741.
Denholm, James. History of Glasgow, &c. 3d ed. 8vo. Glasg. 1804.
Denina, Carlo. Delle Rivoluzioni d' Italia. 6 vol. 8vo. Venez. 1816.
———, ———. Essay on the Revolutions of Literature, tr. from the Italian by J. Murdock. 12mo. Lond.

Denisart. Collection de Décisions Nouvelles et de Notions relatives à la Jurisprudence. 9 vol. 4to. Paris. 1783—90.
Denison, Dan. Irenicon, or a Salve for New-England's Sore. 16mo. 1684.
Denman, Tho. On Midwifery. 2d ed. 2 vols. 8vo. Lond. 1801.
———, ——. Aphorisms on the Use of the Forceps and Vectis. 4th ed. 12mo. Lond. 1793.
Denmark. De Regno Daniæ et Norwegiæ, etc. Tractatus Varii. 16mo. Lug. Bat. 1629.
———. The Danish Laws; or the Code of Christian V, tr. into English. 8vo. Lond. 1756.
———. See Copenhagen.
Donne, John. Consecration Sermon. 4to. Lond. 1737.
Denny, Austin. Oration, July 4th. 8vo. Worcester. 1818.
Denon, Vivant. Travels in Egypt, tr. from the French by A. Aikin. 2 vols. 8vo. N. York. 1803.
Dent, Arthur. Plain Man's Path-Way to Heaven. 27th ed. 12mo. Lond. 1648.
Dent, Giles. Character of a Good Prince, &c. a Sermon. 8vo. Lond. 1712.
——, ——. Sermon, Nov. 5th. 8vo. Lond. 1713.
——, ——. Sermon, Nov. 5th. 8vo. 1715.
Denys, J. Description des Costes de l'Amérique Septentrionale. 2 vol. 12mo. Paris. 1672.
———, –. Beschrijving der Kusten van Noord-America.—Natuurlyke Historie van Noord-America. 4to. Amst. 1688.
D'Eon de Beaumont. Vide Eon de Beaumont, le Chevalier d'.
Depons, F. Voyage à la Partie Orientale de la Terre-Ferme dans l'Amérique Méridionale. 3 vol. 8vo. Paris. 1806.
———, —. Voyage to the Spanish Main in South-America; from the French. 3 vols. 8vo. N. York. 1806.
Depravity, Remarks on the Calvinistic Doctrine of. 8vo. Stockbridge. 1822.
Derham, Rob. Manuell, or Briefe Treatise of some Rights of Parliament, &c. 16mo. Lond. 1647.
Derham, Wm. Astro-Theology. 8vo. Lond. 1715.
———, ——. The Same. 3d ed. 8vo. Lond. 1719.
———, ——. ————. 8vo. Lond. 1721.
———, ——. Physico-Theology. 3d ed. 8vo. Lond. 1714.
———, ——. The Same. 4th ed. 8vo. Lond. 1716.
———, ——. ————. See Boyle's Lecture Sermons.
De Rossi. Vide Rossi.
Desaguliers, J. T. Course of Experimental Philosophy. 3d ed. 2 vols. 4to. Lond. 1763.
Desaussure, H. W. Reports in Chancery in South Carolina. 3 vols. 8vo. Columbia. 1817.
Desbois, A. de la Chesnaye. Système Naturel du Règne Animal. 2 vol. 8vo. Paris. 1754.
Des-Cartes, R. Discourse of a Method for the well guiding of Reason and the Discovery of Truth in the Sciences. 16mo. Lond. 1649.

Des-Cartes, R. Geometria, Latine, cum Notis, opera F. à Schooten. 4to. Amst. 1659—61.
————, —. Idem. 4to. Amst. 1683.
————, —. Musicæ Compendium. 4to. Amst. 1683.
————, —. Opera Philosophica. 4to. Amst. 1656.
————, —. ————. 4to. Amst. 1672.
————, —. ————. 4to. Amst. 1685.
————, —. Epistolæ. 4to. Amst. 1682.
————, —. ————. 4to. Amst. 1683.
————, —. Opuscula Posthuma, Physica et Mathematica. 4to. Amst. 1701.
Description, Topographical and Historical, of Boston. 8vo. Bost. 1794.
————, ————. (Mass. Hist. Coll. vol. 3.)
Desfontaines. Mémoires dans les Annales du Muséum d'Histoire Naturelle.
————. Tableau de l'Ecole de Botanique du Jardin du Roi. 8vo. Paris. 1815.
Desgodetz, Ant. Edifices Antiques de Rome. fol. Paris. 1682.
Deslandes, A. F. B. Essai sur les Intérêts du Commerce Maritime. 16mo. La Haye. 1754.
————, ————. Histoire Critique de la Philosophie. 3 vol. 12mo. Lond. 1742.
————, ————. Recueil de différens Traités de Physique et d'Histoire Naturelle. 3me ed. 3 vol. 12mo. Paris. 1750—3.
Despagne, John. Eating of the Body of Christ considered; from the French. 16mo. Lond.
————, ————. Shibboleth; from the French. 16mo. Lond. 1655.
Despauterius, Joh. Commentarii Grammatici. fol. Paris. 1537.
Desportes, J. B. R. P. Histoire des Maladies de S. Domingue. 3 vol. 12mo. Paris. 1770.
Desvoeux, A. V. Philosophical and Critical Essay on Ecclesiastes. 4to. Lond. 1760.
Deuber. Geschichte der Schiffahrt im Atlantischen Ozean. 12mo. Bamberg. 1814.
Devarius, Mat. De Græcæ Linguæ Particulis. 12mo. Norib. 1718.
Devèze, J. Sur la Fièvre Jaune. 8vo. Paris. 1804.
————, —. Mémoire au Roi, etc. 4to. Paris. 1821.
Devil let Loose, a Discourse on the National Fast. 8vo. Bost. 1799.
Devonshire, Georgiana, Duchess of. Passage of St. Gothard. See Delille.
Devotion, Eben. Sermon at the Ordination of the Rev. N. Huntington. 4to. N. Lond. 1750.
————, ————. Connecticut Election Sermon. 8vo. N. Lond. 1753.
D'Ewes, Sir Simonds. See Ewes, Sir Simonds d'.
Dewey, L. D. Documents relative to his Dismission from the Theological Seminary in New-York. 8vo. N. York. 1816.
De Witt, Benj. Account of Minerals in New-York. (Mem. A. A. S. vol. 2.)
Dexter, Franklin. Oration, July 4th. 8vo. Bost. 1819.

Dexter, Sam. Address to the Electors of Massachusetts. To which is added a Temperate Examination of it, (by J. Lowell.) 8vo. Bost. 1814.
Deylingius, S. De Origine Circumcisionis Judaicæ. (Ugol. vol. 22.)
——————, –. De Fletu super Thammuz. (Id. 23.)
——————, –. De Israele Jehovæ Dominio. (Id. 24.)
——————, –. De Sceptro Judæ, etc.—De Judæorum Jure Gladii, etc.—De Familia et Genealogia Herodiadum. (Id. 26.)
——————, –. De Re Nummaria Veterum Hebræorum. (Id. 28.)
Deyron. Antiquités de Nismes. 4to. Nismes. 1663.
Dialetto Napoletano. 16mo. Napoli. 1789.
Dialling performed instrumentally by our Hemisphere in Plane. 4to. Lond. 1652.
Dialogue between John Faustus a Conjurer, and Jack Tory his Friend. 16mo. Bost. 1720.
———— between a Gentleman of London and an honest Alderman on the Grievances of the Nation. 8vo. Lond. 1747.
———— between a Clergyman of the Church of England and a Lay-Gentleman. 8vo. Lond. 1792.
Dialogues in a Library. 12mo. Lond. 1797.
Dialogues Critiques et Philosophiques, par M. l'Abbé de Charte-Livry, (J. F. Bernard.) 12mo. Amst. 1730.
Diamante, J. B. Comedias. 2 vol. 4to. Madrid. 1674.
Diaper, Wm., and J. Jones. Oppian's Halieuticks, translated from the Greek. 8vo. Oxford. 1722.
Diario de los Literatos de España. 7 tom. 12mo. Madrid. 1737—42.
Diaz del Castillo, Bernal. Historia Verdadera de la Conquista de la Nueva-España. fol. Madrid. 1632.
————————, ————. True History of the Conquest of Mexico, tr. from the Spanish by M. Keatinge. 4to. Lond. 1800.
————————. ————. The Same. 2 vols. 8vo. Lond. 1803.
Dibdin, Tho. F. Introduction to Rare and Valuable Editions of the Classics, &c. 8vo. Lond. 1804.
————, ————. The Same. 2 vols. 12mo. Lond. 1808.
————, ————. Bibliotheca Spenceriana. 4 vols. 8vo. Lond. 1814—15.
Dicæarchus. Geographica Quædam. (Gronov. vol. 11.)
Dick, Rob. Sermon before the Society in Scotland for propagating Christian Knowledge. 8vo. Edin. 1762.
Dickinson, John. Letters from a Farmer. 8vo. Lond. 1768.
————, ———. The Same. 8vo. Bost. 1768.
————, ———. ————. 8vo. Phil. 1774.
————, ———. Lettres d'un Fermier de Pensylvanie, trad. de l'Anglois. 8vo. Amst. 1769.
————, ———. New Essay on the Constitutional Power of Great Britain over the Colonies; with the Resolves of the Committee for the Province of Pennsylvania, &c. 8vo. Phil. 1774.
————, ———. Remarks on the "New Essay." 8vo. Lond. 1775.
————, ———. Speech in the House of Assembly of Pennsylvania, May 24th, 1764; with a Preface by Dr. Smith. 8vo. Lond. 1764.

Dickinson, John. Reply to a Piece called the Speech of Joseph Galloway, Esq. 8vo. Lond. 1765.
————, ——. Late Regulations respecting the British Colonies considered. 8vo. Phil. 1765.
————, ——. Letters of Fabius on the Federal Constitution, &c. 8vo. Wilmington. 1797.
Dickinson, John. Sermon on the Death of the Queen. 8vo. Lond. 1737.
Dickinson, Jonathan. Defence of Presbyterian Ordination. 12mo. Bost. 1724.
————, ————. Familiar Letters on Religious Subjects. 8vo. Bost. 1745.
————, ————. On Baptismal Regeneration. 8vo. Bost. 1744.
————, ————. Vindication of God's Sovereign Free Grace. 8vo. Bost. 1746.
————, ————. Second Vindication. 8vo. Bost. 1748.
Dickinson, Jonathan. Geschichte von dem Schiffbruche in dem Meerbusem von Florida, etc. 12mo. Frankf. und Leipz. 1774.
Dickinson, Moses. Connecticut Election Sermon. 16mo. Lond. 1755.
Dickinson, Nodes. On Burns and Scalds. 8vo. Lond. 1818.
Dickinson, Rodolphus. Geography. 8vo. Bost. 1813.
————, ————. View of Massachusetts Proper. 8vo. Greenfield. 1813.
————, ————. Digest of the Powers and Duties of Sheriffs, &c. 8vo. Greenfield. 1810.
Dickson, David. Vide Dicsonus.
Dickson, Wm. Letters on Slavery. 8vo. Lond. 1789.
Dicsonus, David. Expositio Analytica Omnium Apostolicarum Epistolicarum. 4to. Glasguæ. 1645.
————, ————. Therapeutica Sacra. 4to. Lond. 1656.
Dictionarium Historicum ac Poeticum. 4to. Lugd. 1579.
Dictionary, English-German, &c. vol. 1. 8vo. Lancaster. 1812.
————, English and Portuguese, and vice versa, by J. A. fol. Lond. 1701.
———— of Arts and Sciences. See Gregory, G. See Owen, W.
Dictionnaire François, Italien, Allemand, Latin, et Russe. 2 vol. 4to. Moscow. 1784—7.
———— des Synonymes de la Langue Française, par Girard, Beauzée, Roubaud, etc. 3 vol. 12mo. Paris. 1801.
————, Nouveau, d'Histoire Naturelle, appliquée aux Arts, à l'Agriculture, à l'Economie Rurale et Domestique, à la Médecine, etc. par une Société de Naturalistes, et d'Agriculteurs. 36 vol. 8vo. Paris. 1816—19.
Dictys et Dares. De Bello et Excidio Trojæ, in usum Delphini; cum Interpretatione A. Daceriæ, et Notis Variorum. Item J. Iscani Poema, cum Notis S. Dresemii. 4to. Amst. 1702.
————————. Della Guerra Troiana, trad. per T. Porcacchi. 4to. Verona. 1734.
Diderot, D. Encyclopédie des Sciences, etc. par une Societé de

Gens de Lettres; mis en ordre par M. Diderot, et quant à la Partie Mathématique, par M. D'Alembert. 28 vol. (dont 11 de Planches.) fol. Paris. 1751—72.

Diderot, D. Supplément à l'Encyclopédie. 5 vol. (dont un de Planches.) fol. Paris. 1776—7.

———, —. Table Analytique et Raisonnée. 2 vol. fol. Paris. 1780.

Didier, Constantius. De Febre Flava Americana. 4to. Gottingæ. 1800.

Diemerbroeck, Isbrandus de. Anatome Corporis Humani. 4to. Genevæ. 1680.

Dièreville. Relation du Voyage du Port-Royal de l'Acadie. 12mo. Amst. 1710.

————. Reise nach Portroyal in Acadien; aus dem Franz. 8vo. Göttingen. 1751.

Dies Dominica. De illius Observatione. 4to. 1639.

Diessbach, A. G. N. de. Il Zelo Meditativo. 8vo. Torino. 1774.

Diest, Henricus à. De Ratione Studii Theologici. 24to. Hardervici. 1634.

Dietericus, J. C. Sparsio Florum. (Ugol. vol. 30.)

Dietzschius, Dan. De Cultu Molochi. (Ugol. vol. 23.)

Dieu, Ludov. de. Grammatica Linguarum Hebr. Chald. et Syr. inter se collatarum. 4to. Lug. Bat. 1628.

——, ————. In Acta Apostolorum. 4to. Lug. Bat. 1634.

——, ————. In Pauli Epistolam ad Romanos, etc. 4to. Lug. Bat. 1646.

Digby, George, (Lord.) Speeches concerning Grievances, and the Trienniall Parliament, in 1640.—Speech concerning Bishops and the City Petition, in 1640.—Speech upon the Attainder of the Earle of Strafforde, in 1641, &c. (Parliament, Speeches and Passages.)

Digby, John. Philosophical Account of Nature in General, &c.; from the French. 8vo. Lond. 1722.

———, ——. History of the Wars of Alexander the Great, tr. from Quintus Curtius, &c. 3d ed. 2 vols. 12mo. Lond. 1747.

Digby, Sir Kenelme. Two Treatises;—viz. on the Nature of Bodies, and of Mans Soule. fol. Paris. 1644.

———, ——————. The Same. 4to. Lond. 1658.

———, ——————. On the Cure of Wounds by the Powder of Sympathy; from the French. 4th ed. 12mo. Lond. 1664.

Dike, Jer. See Dyke.

Dilherrus, J. M. Grammatica Syriaca. 18mo. Hal. Sax. 1646.

————, ——. Eclogæ Sacræ. 18mo. Jenæ. 1638.

————, ——. Atrium Linguæ Sanctæ Hebraicæ. 12mo. Norib. 1659.

Dillenius, J. J. Hortus Elthamensis. 2 vol. fol. Lond. 1732.

Dillon, J. T. Travels through Spain. 2d ed. 4to. Lond. 1782.

Dillon, Wentworth. See Roscommon, Earl of.

Diluvium. De Diluvii Universalitate Dissertatio Prolusoria. 16mo. Genevæ. 1667.

Dimsdale, Tho. Present Method of Inoculating for the Small-Pox. 5th ed. 8vo. Lond. 1769.

Dinarchus. Orationes. Vide Oratores Græci, a Reiskio.

———. ———. Vide Demosthenes.

Dinocourt. Mozanino. 4 vol. 12mo. Paris. 1825.

Dinouart, A. J. T. L'Eloquence du Corps, ou l'Action du Prédicateur. 12mo. Paris. 1761.

Dio Chrysostomus. Orationes, ex recensione J. J. Reiske. Accesserunt J. Casauboni in Dionem Diatriba, et F. Morelli Scholia et Collectanea in Dionem. 2 vol. 8vo. Lips. 1798.

———. Notæ et Emendationes in Dionem. (Anecdota Gr. a Wolfio.)

Diodati, Dominicus. De Christo Græce loquente. 8vo. Neapoli. 1766.

Diodati, J. La Biblia. Vide Biblia Italiana.

———, –. Il Nuovo Testamento. Vide Testamento.

———, –. Annotations upon the Bible. 3d ed. fol. Lond. 1651.

Diodorus Siculus. Bibliothecæ Historicæ Libri qui supersunt, Gr. et Lat. cum Notis Variorum, a P. Wesselingio. 2 vol. fol. Amst. 1746.

——— ———. Historical Library, made English by G. Booth. fol. Lond. 1700.

Diogenes Laertius. De Vitis Clarorum Philosophorum, Gr. et Lat. cum Notis Variorum, a M. Meibomio. 2 vol. 4to. Amst. 1692.

——— ———. Idem, Latine, ex Versione Ambrosii. 24to. Lugd. 1593.

Diomedes. De Arte Grammatica. Vide Grammatici Veteres Latini.

Dion, Cassius. Historiæ Romanæ, Gr. et Lat. cum Notis Variorum, cura H. S. Reimari. 2 vol. fol. Hamb. 1750—2.

———, ———. Hist. Rom. Fragmenta, a J. Morellio. 12mo. Bassani. 1798.

———, ———. Delle Guerre de' Romani, trad. da N. Leoniceno. 12mo. Venet. 1548.

———, ———. The Emperor Augustus his Two Speeches, translated out of Dion Cassius. 4to. Lond. 1675.

Dionis du Séjour, A. P. Traité Analytique des Mouvemens Apparens des Corps Célestes. 2 vol. 4to. Paris. 1786—9.

Dionysius Areopagita. Opera, Gr. et Lat. cum Notis, cura P. Lansselii et B. Corderii, etc. 2 vol. fol. Paris. 1644.

——— ———. Idem. 2 vol. fol. Venet. 1755—6.

Dionysius Halicarnassensis. Opera Omnia, Gr. et Lat. cum Notis, per J. Hudsonum. 2 vol. fol. Oxoniæ. 1704.

——— ———. Opera Omnia, Gr. et Lat. cum Notis Variorum, cura J. J. Reiske. 6 vol. 8vo. Lips. 1774—7.

——— ———. De Structura Orationis, Gr. et Lat. a J. Upton. 8vo. Lond 1702.

——— ———. De Compositione Verborum, a Fr. Goeller; accesserunt variæ Lectiones in Themistii Orationibus quibusdam, a Fr. Jacobs. 8vo. Jenæ. 1815.

——— ———. De Compositione Verborum, Gr. et Lat. cum Notis Variorum, a G. H. Schæfer. 8vo. Lips. 1808.

Dionysius Halicarnassensis. Delle Cose Antiche della Città di Roma, trad. per F. Venturi. 2 vol. 4to. Verona. 1738.
Dionysius Periegetes. Orbis Descriptio, Gr. et Lat. cum Commentariis Eustathii. 8vo. Oxon. 1710.
———, ————. Geographia, Gr. et Lat. cum Notis, ab Edv. Wells. ed. 4ta. 8vo. Lond. 1726.
———, ————. Vide Eustathius.
Dionysius, P. L. Sacrarum Vaticanæ Basilicæ Cryptarum Monumenta Æreis Tabulis incisa, et a P. L. Dionysio Commentariis illustrata. fol. Romæ. 1773.
Dionysius Thrax. Grammatica, cum Scholiis. (Anecdota Græca, a Bekkero.)
Diophantus Alexandrinus. Arithmetica, Gr. et Lat. cum Commentariis C. G. Bacheti, etc. fol. Tolosæ. 1670.
Dioscorides, Pedacius. Opera Omnia, Gr. et Lat. a J. A. Saraceno. fol. 1598.
Diplomatick Policy of Mr. Madison unveiled, (by J. Lowell.) 8vo.
Director, El Pequeño, de los Niños. 16mo. Phil. 1811.
Discourse on the Wickedness and Danger of fomenting Divisions in a State. 8vo. Lond. 1733.
Discourses, Practical, concerning Hearing the Word, by several Ministers. 12mo. Lond. 1713.
————. See Sermons.
Diseases. See West-India Diseases.
Disney, John. Sermon before the Mayor against Popery. 8vo. Lond. 1721.
———, ——. Sermon before the Mayor on the Justice and Religion of Magistrates. 8vo. Lond. 1724.
———, ——. Assize Sermon. 8vo. Lond. 1724.
———, ——. ————. 8vo. Lond. 1727.
———, ——. Reflections of a Devout Solitude. 8vo. Lond. 1703.
———, ——. Second Essay upon the Execution of the Laws against Immorality and Profaneness. 8vo. Lond. 1710.
Disney, John. Sermons. 2 vols. 8vo. Lond. 1793.
———, ——. Sermon on Industry. 12mo. Newark. 1781.
———, ——. Fast Sermon. 8vo. Lond. 1782.
———, ——. Visitation Sermon. 4to. Lond. 1777.
———, ——. Reasons for Resigning the Rectory of Panton, &c. 8vo. Lond. 1783.
———, ——. Memoirs of the Life and Writings of A. A. Sykes. 8vo. Lond. 1785.
———, ——. Memoirs of the Life and Writings of John Jortin. 8vo. Lond. 1792.
———, ——. Remarks on the Bishop of Lincoln's Charge to the Clergy of his Diocese. 8vo. Bath. 1812.
———, ——. Friendly Dialogue between a Unitarian and an Athanasian; with a Second Dialogue between Eugenius and Theophilus. (Unitarian Tracts, vol. 2.)
Disney, John. Laws of Gaming, &c. 8vo. Lond. 1806.
———, ——. Collection of Acts of Parliament relative to County and Borough Elections. 8vo. Lond. 1811.

Dispensations of God to Mankind, Essay on the Several. 8vo. Lond. 1728.

————. Remarks on the above. Part I. 8vo. Lond. 1737.

Dispensatory, New. 3d ed. 8vo. Lond. 1770.

D'Israeli. Vide Israeli, J. d'.

Dissaldeus, Fr. Pharmaconetes. Vide Cordus.

Dissen, L. G. De Temporibus et Modis Verbi Græci. 4to. Gottingæ. 1808.

——, ——. Disquisitionum Philologicarum Specimen Primum. 4to. Gottingæ. 1813.

Dissen, Ludov. De Philosophia Morali in Xenophontis de Socrate Commentariis tradita. 4to. Gottingæ. 1812.

Dissenters. Perswasive to Moderation to Church Dissenters, submitted to the King and Councel. 4to. Lond. 1685.

————. Collection of Cases and other Discourses written to recover Dissenters to the Communion of the Church of England. fol. Lond. 1694.

————. The Same. 3d ed. 3 vols. 8vo. Lond. 1718.

————. Their Case, as affected by the late Bill proposed in Parliament for Preventing Occasional Conformity. 4to. Lond. 1703.

————. Rights of Protestant Dissenters. 4to. Lond. 1705.

————. Enquiry into the Present State of Dissenters in England and Presbyterians in Scotland. 8vo. Lond. 1712.

————. Interest of England respecting them. 4to. Lond. 1703.

————. Case of the Protestant Dissenters respecting the Sacramental Test. 8vo.

————. Vindication of the Principles and Practice of the Protestant Dissenters. 8vo. Lond.

————. Apology of the Church of England for the Principles of Dissenters in Church and State. 8vo. Lond. 1718.

————. Observations on the Present State of the Dissenting Interest, &c. 8vo. Lond. 1731.

————. Vindication of the Religious and Political Principles and Worship of the Dissenters. 8vo. Lond. 1737.

————. On the Conduct of the Tories, the Whigs, and the Dissenters. 8vo. Lond. 1739.

————. Humble Address to the Protestant Dissenters relating to the Election of Persons to Represent them in Parliament. 12mo. Lond. 1741.

————. Answer to the Enquiry, Why are you a Dissenter from the Church of England? 8vo. Lond. 1772.

————. The Same. 8vo. Bost. 1773.

————. Two Letters to the Rt. Rev. Prelates, who a Second Time rejected the Dissenters' Bill. 8vo. Lond. 1773.

————. Cause of the Petitioners examined; with a Defence of the Doctrine of the Trinity. 8vo. Lond. 1773.

————. Opposition Opposed. 8vo. Bedford. 1773.

————. Address to Protestant Dissenters relating to the approaching Election of Members of Parliament. 8vo. Lond. and Bost. 1774.

Dissenters. Dissenting Gentleman's Letters to White. See Towgood, M.
———. Appeal to Government in favour of them. 8vo. Lond. 1787.
———. Right of Protestant Dissenters to a Complete Toleration. 8vo. Lond. 1789.
———. See Catalogue,—Church,—Non-Conformists, &c.
Dissertationum Ludicrarum et Amœnitatum Scriptores Varii. 12mo. Lug. Bat. 1644.
Distributive Justice, Treatise on; confined chiefly to Will-Making. 8vo. Lond. 1751.
Dithmarsus, C. M. Systema Ethicum. 12mo. Marpurgi. 1626.
Ditton, Humphry. Discourse concerning the Resurrection of Jesus Christ. 8vo. Lond. 1714.
———, ———. The Same. 3d ed. 8vo. Lond. 1722.
———, ———. ———. 4th ed. 8vo. Lond. 1727.
———, ———. Treatise of Perspective. 8vo. Lond. 1712.
———, ———. General Laws of Nature and Motion. 8vo. Lond. 1709.
Diurnall of Sea Designes of Foreign Princes. 4to. Lond. 1642.
———. See Journal.
Divine Glory brought into View, in the Condemnation of the Ungodly. 8vo. Bost. 1782.
Dixon, Geo. Remarks on the Voyages of John Mears, Esq. 4to. Lond. 1790.
———, ——. Further Remarks, &c. 4to. Lond. 1791.
———, ——. Voyage round the World by Captains Portlock and Dixon. 4to. Lond. 1789.
———, ——. Voyage autour du Monde, par les Capitaines Portlock et Dixon, trad. de l'Anglois par M. Lebas. 2 vol. 8vo. Paris. 1789.
———, ——. See Portlock.
Doane. See M'Clary Owners.
Dobbs, Arthur. Account of the Countries about Hudson's Bay. 4to. Lond. 1744.
———, ———. Remarks upon Capt. Middleton's Defence of his Conduct in a Voyage for Discovering the North West Passage. 8vo. Lond. 1744.
———, ———. See Letter from a Russian Sea-Officer.
Dobrizhoffer, M. Geschichte der Abiponer, aus dem Lateinischen übersetzt von A. Kreil. 3 Theile. 8vo. Wien. 1783—4.
Dobson, Susan. History of the Troubadours, collected and abridged from the French of M. de St. Palaye. 12mo. Lond. 1807.
Doctor and Student. See St. German.
Doctrines. See Church,—Scripture,—Treatises, &c.
Documents, Public. See United States, &c.
Documentos de la Compañia en el Paraguay. 4 tom. 4to. Madrid. 1768—70.
Dodd, A. C. The Contrast; or Strictures on Dr. Price's "Additional Observations on Civil Liberty," &c. 8vo. Lond. 1777.

Dodd, Charles. List of All the eminent Writers of Controversy, since the Reformation, &c. (Somers, Tracts. vol. 3.)
Dodd, Wm. Hymns of Callimachus, translated from the Greek into English Verse, with Notes, &c. 4to. Lond. 1755.
——, ——. Sermons to Young Men. 3 vols. 12mo. Lond. 1771.
Doddridge, Sir John. Opinions of Antiquaries touching the Power &c. of Parliament. 16mo. Lond. 1658.
——, ——. Treatise of Estates. See Noy, Sir Wm.
Doddridge, Philip. Works. 5 vols. 8vo. Leeds. 1802—4.
——, ——. Sermon on the Death of the Rev. John Norris. 8vo. Northampton. 1738.
——, ——. Sermon on the Death of a Child. 2d ed. 8vo. Lond. 1740.
——, ——. Family Expositor. 6 vols. 4to. Lond. 1760.
——, ——. The Same. 4th ed. 6 vols. 4to. Lond. 1763.
——, ——. ——. 6 vols. 8vo. Charlestown. 1807.
——, ——. New Translation of the New Testament, extracted from the above. 2 vols. 12mo. Lond. 1765.
——, ——. On Family Religion. 12mo. Northampton. 1804.
——, ——. Peace Sermon. 8vo. Lond. 1749.
——, ——. Life of Col. James Gardiner. 4th ed. 12mo. Lond. 1763.
——, ——. Rise and Progress of Religion in the Soul. 12mo. Edin. 1762.
——, ——. The Same. 10th ed. 12mo. Lond. 1771.
——, ——. Lectures on Pneumatology, Ethics, and Divinity. 4to. Lond. 1763.
——, ——. The Same. 2d ed. 4to. Lond. 1776.
——, ——. ——. 4th ed. 2 vols. 8vo. Lond. 1799.
——, ——. Letters between him and Others, with Notes, by Tho. Stedman. 8vo. Shrewsbury. 1790.
——, ——. Perspecuity and Solidity of the Evidences of Christianity, in a Letter to the Author of a Pamphlet, entitled "Christianity not founded on Argument." 8vo. Lond. 1742.
——, ——. Second Letter to the Same. 8vo. Lond. 1743.
——, ——. Hymns. 3d ed. 12mo. Lond. 1766.
——, ——. Principles of the Christian Religion in Verse. 12mo. Lond. 1767.
——, ——. Poem to his Memory. 4to. Lond. 1752.
——, ——. Practical Discourses on Regeneration. 8vo. Lond. 1742.
——, ——. The Same. 4th ed. 12mo. Lond. 1766.
——, ——. ——, with Two Sermons on Salvation by Grace. 12mo. Bost. 1823.
——, ——. Substance of Two Sermons on the Flight of the Rebels from Sterling. 8vo. Lond. 1746.
——, ——. Christian Candour and Unanimity stated, &c. in a Sermon. 8vo. Lond. 1750.

Doddridge, Philip. Sermons to Young Persons. 4th ed. 12mo. Lond. 1760.
———, ———. Ten Sermons on the Power and Grace of Christ. 4th ed. 12mo. Lond. 1760.
———, ———. Sermons and Religious Tracts. 3 vols. 12mo. Lond. 1761.
———, ———. Sermon at a Meeting of Ministers. 8vo. Lond. 1742.
Dodington, Geo. Bubb, (Lord Melcombe.) Diary, by H. P. Wyndham. 8vo. Salisbury. 1784.
Dodsley, Rob. Preceptor. 2d ed. 2 vols. 8vo. Lond. 1754.
———, ———. Collection of Poems by Several Hands. 6 vols. 12mo. Lond. 1763.
———, ———. Economy of Human Life. 18mo. Camb. 1827.
———, ———. Poems. See Chalmers, A.
———, ———. See Register, Annual.
Dodson, Joseph. Twelve Discourses. 8vo. Lond. 1728.
Dodson, Michael. New Translation of Isaiah, with Notes. 8vo. Lond. 1790.
———, ———. Life of Sir Michael Forster. 8vo. Lond. 1811.
Dodwell, Henry. Separation from Episcopal Government proved Schismatical. 4to. Lond. 1679.
———, ———. Two Discourses against the Romanists. 4to. 1688.
———, ———. Dissertationes in Irenæum. 8vo. Oxon. 1689.
———, ———. De Ætate Phalaridis, et de Ætate Pythagoræ. 8vo. Lond. 1704.
———, ———. De Parma Equestri Woodwardiana, a Hearne. 8vo. Oxon. 1713.
———, ———. Dissertatio Singularis de Pontificum Romanorum Primæva Successione, usque ad Annales Cl. Cestriensis Cyprianicos. Vide Pearson, J.
———, ———. Epistolary Discourse, proving the Soul naturally Mortal, &c. 8vo. Lond. 1706.
———, ———. Reply to Mr. Clark's Defence of his Letter to him, &c. 8vo. Lond. 1709.
———, ———. Reflections on Mr. Clark's Second Defence. 8vo. Lond. 1711.
———, ———. Answer to Mr. Clark's Third Defence. 8vo. Lond. 1711.
———, ———. Letter to him on Mr. Clark's Answer to his Epistolary Discourse. 8vo. Lond. 1709.
———, ———. Invitation to Gentlemen to acquaint themselves with History. (Preface to Wheare's Method.)
Dodwell, Henry. Christianity not founded on Argument. 3d ed. 8vo. Lond. 1743.
Dodwell, Wm. Reply to Toll's Defence of Middleton's Free Enquiry, &c. 8vo. Lond. 1751.
Doederlein, J. C. Institutio Theologi Christiani. 2 vol. 8vo. Norimb. et Altorfii. 1797.

Doederlein, J. C. Esaias, Latine, cum Notis. ed. 3tia. 8vo. Norimb. et Altorfii. 1789.

———, ——. Curarum Exeget. et Crit. in Quædam Vet. Testamenti Oracula Specimen. 12mo. Alt. et Norimb. 1770.

———, et J. H. Meisner. Vide Biblia Hebraica.

Doederlinus, J. A. De Nummis Germaniæ Mediæ, etc. 4to. Norimb. 1729.

———, ——. De Patellis Iridis. 4to. Suobaci. 1739.

Doederlinus, G. M. De Candelabris Judæorum. (Ugol. vol. 11.)

Dolce, L. Historia degl' Imperatorí Greci, etc. 4to. Vinet. 1569.

——, —. Vide Catullus.

Doletus, Steph. De Re Navali. (Gronov. vol. 11.)

Dolomieu, Déodat de. Sur les Iles Ponces. 8vo. Paris. 1788.

———, ———. On the Earthquakes in Calabria in 1783. (Pinkerton, vol. 5.)

Dolscius, Paulus. Psalterium Davidis, Versibus Elegiacis (Græce) redditum. 12mo. Basil. 1555.

Domat, J. Civil Law in its Natural Order; together with the Public Law, tr. from the French, with Remarks, by William Strahan. 2 vols. fol. Lond. 1722.

———, –. The Same. 2d ed. 2 vols. fol. Lond. 1737.

Domenichi, L. Nobiltà delle Donne. 12mo. Vinet. 1551.

———, —. Polibio tradotto. Vide Polybius.

Domes-Day Book, Particulars concerning. 4to. Lond. 1756.

Dominis, M. A. de. (Abp.) De Republica Ecclesiastica. fol. Heidelb. 1618.

———. ———. Reasons for Abandoning Popery, &c.; —Treatment of his Body after Death. (Somers, Tracts. vol. 4.)

Donatus, Ælius. De Grammatica. Vide Grammatici Vet. Lat.

Donatus, Alex. Roma Vetus ac Recens, etc. (Grævius, vol. 3.)

Doni, A. F. I Marmi. 4to. Vinegia. 1552.

Donius, J. B. De Utraque Pænula. (Grævius, vol. 6.)

———, —. De Restituenda Salubritate Agri Romani. 4to. Florentiæ. 1667.

———, —. Idem. (Sallengre, vol. 1.)

Donne, John. Poems. See Chalmers, A.

Donovan, C. Instructions for Collecting and Preserving various Subjects of Natural History; with a Treatise on the Management of Insects. 8vo. Lond. 1794.

———, —. British Shells. 8vo.

Doolittle. Narrative of Mischief done by the French and Indian Enemy, on the Western Frontiers of Massachusetts-Bay, in 1743—8.

Doolittle, Tho. Complete Body of Practical Divinity. fol. Lond. 1723.

Dorchester, Memorial of the Proprietors of the New South Meeting-House in, to the Ministers of the Boston Association. 8vo. Bost. 1813.

Dorffer, Balthassar. De Sepulcro Christi. (Ugol. vol. 33.)

Doria, A. Vide Durazzo.

Dorien, J. H. A. De Cherubinis Sanctisanctorum. (Ugol. vol. 8.)

Dorigny, E. N. Pinacotheca Hamptoniana.
Döring, F. W. Anleitung zum Uebersetzen aus dem Deutschen ins Lateinische. 2 Theile. 8vo. Jena und Leipz. 1814—15.
Dorophagus, the great Patriot of the North, Essay on the Memory and Character of. 4to.
Dorotheus. Lives of the Prophets, Apostles, and 70 Disciples. See Hanmer, M.
Dorr, Edw. Connecticut Election Sermon. 8vo. Hartford. 1765.
Dorset, C. Sackville, Earl of. Poems. See Chalmers, A.
Dorvo-Soulastre. Voyage par terre de Santo-Domingo au Cap-Français. 8vo. Paris. 1809.
Dosius, Jo. Ant. Urbis Romanæ Ædificiorum Reliquiæ. fol. 1569.
Dossie, Rob. Institutes of Experimental Chemistry. 2 vols. 8vo. Lond. 1759.
——, ——. Observations on the Pot-Ash brought from America 8vo. Lond. 1767.
——, ——. Memoirs of Agriculture, &c. vol. 1. 8vo. Lond. 1768.
Douespe, Samuel de la. Sermons. 8vo. La Haye. 1752.
Doughty, Edw. On the Yellow Fever. 8vo. Lond. 1816.
Doughty, Tho. Coronation Sermons, &c. 8vo. Lond. 1728.
Douglas, James. Comparative Description of all the Muscles in a Man and in a Quadruped; with an Account of the Blood-Vessels and Nerves. 8vo. Edin. 1775.
——, ——. Vide Catalogus.
Douglas, John, (Bp.) Vindication of Milton from the Charge of Plagiarism, brought against him by Lauder. 8vo. Lond. 1751.
——, ——. Criterion; or Miracles Examined. 8vo. Lond. 1754.
——, ——. The Same. 8vo. Lond. 1807.
Douglas, Rob. Peerage of Scotland. fol. Edin. 1764.
Douglas, Sylvester. Reports in B. R. from 19 to 21 Geo. III. 2 vols. 8vo. Lond. 1790.
Douglas, Walter. Eleven Sacramental Sermons. 8vo. Edin. 1725.
Douglass, Wm. Inoculation of the Small Pox, as practised in Boston, considered. 12mo. Bost. 1722.
——, ——. Practical History of a New Epidemical Eruptive Miliary Fever. 8vo. Bost. 1736.
——, ——. Summary, Historical and Political, of the British Settlements in North America. 2 vols. 8vo. Bost. 1749.
——, ——. The Same. 2 vols. 8vo. Lond. 1755.
——, ——. ——. 2 vols. 8vo. Lond. 1760.
Dousa, G. De Itinere suo Constantinopolitano Epistola. (Gronov. vol. 6.)
Dove, John. Strictures on Agriculture. 12mo. Lond. 1770.
D'Overbeke. Vide Overbeke.
Dow, Alex. History of Indostan; from the Persian. 3 vols. 4to. Lond. 1770—2.
Dow, Moses. Fast Sermon. 8vo. Salem. 1813.
Dowglasse, Rob. Sermon at the Down-Sitting of this last Parliament of Scotland. 4to. Lond. 1661.

Dowglassius, Guil. Academiarum Vindiciæ. 4to. Aberdoniæ. 1659.
Downame, Geo. (Bp.) Treatise concerning Antichrist. 4to. Lond. 1603.
———, ———. Treatise of Justification. fol. Lond. 1633.
Downame, John. Christian Warfare against the Devil, &c. fol. Lond. 1634.
Doyle and Valine. Genuine Copies of all the Letters between the Lord Chancellor and the Sheriffs of London, &c. relative to their Execution. 8vo. Lond. 1770.
Draco Stratonicensis. De Metris Poeticis;—J. Tzetzæ Exegesis in Homeri Iliadem;—a G. Hermanno. 8vo. Lips. 1812.
——— ———. Appendix ad Draconem Stratonicensem, complectens Trichæ, Eliæ Monachi, et Herodiani Tractatus de Metris, a F. de Furia. 8vo. Lips. 1814.
Drake, Daniel. Picture of Cincinnati and the Miami Country, &c. 12mo. Cincinnati. 1815.
———, ———. Account of the Valley of the Ohio. (Amer. Phil. Tr. N. S. vol. 2.)
Drake, Nathan. Essays illustrative of the Tatler, Spectator, and Guardian. 3 vols. 12mo. Lond. 1805.
———, ———. Essays illustrative of the Rambler, Adventurer, and Idler, &c. 2 vols. 12mo. Lond. 1809.
Drama. See British Drama.
Dran, H. F. le. Observations in Surgery; from the French. 3d ed. 8vo. Lond. 1758.
———, ———. Consultations in Surgery; from the French. 8vo. Lond. 1766.
———, ———. Operations in Surgery; from the French. 5th ed. 8vo. Lond. 1781.
Dräseke, J. H. B. Predigten für Denkende Verehrer Jesus. 5 Theile. 8vo. Lüneburg. 1812—14.
———, ———. Predigten über die Letzten Schiksale unsers Herrn. 8vo. Lüneburg. 1816.
———, ———. Ueber Ideale und ihre Beziehung auf Lebensgenusz und Lebensfrieden. 12mo. Bremen. 1816.
Draxe, Tho. Bibliotheca Scholastica; or Treasurie of Ancient Adagies, &c. 8vo. Lond. 1633.
———, ———. Calliepeia. 8vo. Lond. 1643.
Drayton, John. View of South-Carolina. 8vo. Charleston. 1802.
———, ———. Memoirs of the American Revolution, as relating to South-Carolina, &c. 2 vols. 8vo. Charleston. 1821.
Drayton, Michael. Poems. See Chalmers, A.
Dreams and Visions, Treatise on; with a Discourse on Madness. 12mo.
Drechsler, Wolfgangus. De Turcorum Origine, etc. (Clauser de Rebus Turcicis.)
Drelincourt, Charles. Les Visites Charitables. 3 vol. 8vo. Amst. 1731.
———, ———. Sonnets Chrétiens. 12mo. Amst. 1731.
Dreschlerus, J. G. De Cithara Davidica. (Ugol. vol. 32.)

Dreux, Pet. **Oratio de Latina in Republica Litteraria Communi Lingua Servanda. 4to. Zutph. 1775.**
Drew, Rob. Sermon on occasion of the Act for the Relief of Insolvent Debtors. 8vo. Lond. 1725.
——, ——. Sermon on Reformation of Manners. 8vo. Lond. 1735.
Drexelius, Hieremias. Nicetas, seu Triumphata Incontinentia. 16mo. Col. Agrip. 1631.
Drummond, Rob. (Abp.) Sermons on Public Occasions, &c. 8vo. Edin. 1803.
Drummond, Wm. Poems. See Chalmers, A.
Drummond, Sir Wm. Satires of Persius tr. into English Verse, with Notes. 8vo. Lond. 1799.
————, ——. Review of the Governments of Sparta and Athens. 8vo. Lond. 1794.
————, ——. Academical Questions. vol. 1. 4to. Lond. 1805.
Drummond, W. A. (Bp.) Lawfulness of Breaking Faith with Heretics proved to be a Doctrine of the Church of Rome, in Two Letters. 12mo. Edin. 1778—9.
Drummond, W. H. First Book of Lucretius on the Nature of Things, tr. into English Verse. 12mo. Edin. 1808.
Drury, D. Illustrations of Natural History, Fr. and Eng. 3 vols. 4to. Lond. 1770–82.
Drusius, Joh. (Drieche.) De Voce Elohim. 12mo. Francof. 1603.
——, ————. Responsio ad Quæstiones Anonymi Theologici. 12mo. Francof. 1606.
——, ————. Commentarius in Pentateuchum. 4to. Franek. Fris. 1617.
——, ————. Ad Loca Difficiliora Josuæ et Judicum Commentarius. 4to. Franek. Fris. 1618.
——, ————. Historia Ruth, Latine, cum Commentario. etc 4to. Amst. 1632.
——, ————. Grammatica Linguæ Sanctæ. 4to. Franek. 1612.
——, ————. Commentarius in Prophetas Minores. 4to. Amst. 1627.
——, ————. De Hasidæis. (Ugol. vol. 22.)
Dryden, John. Works of Virgil, tr. into English Verse. 3d ed. 3 vols. 12mo. Lond. 1709.
——, ——. Ovid's Metamorphoses, tr. See Garth.
——, ——. Poetical Miscellanies; by the most Eminent Hands. 6 vols. 12mo. Lond. 1702—9.
——, ——. Miscellaneous Works; with his Life. 4 vols. 8vo. Lond. 1760.
——, ——. Poems.—Translations of Virgil and Juvenal. See Chalmers, A.
——, ——. Plutarch's Lives, tr. from the Greek, with a Preface and Life of Plutarch. 6 vols. 8vo. Lond. 1758.
——, ——. Essay on Natural Religion as opposed to Divine Revelation. 8vo. 1746.
——, ——. See Fresnoy, C. A. du.

Dryfhoud, A. De Prædestinatione et Creatione. 4to. Traj. ad Rhen. 1768.

Duane, Wm. Hand-Book for Infantry. 5th ed. 8vo. Phil. 1813.

———, ———. Mississippi Question fairly stated, &c. 8vo. Phil. 1803.

Duane, Wm. J. Law of Nations, investigated in a Popular Manner. 8vo. Phil. 1809.

———, ———. See Chambers, J.

Dublin. Abstract of the Proceedings of the Incorporated Society in Dublin, for promoting English Protestant Schools in Ireland. 4to. Lond. 1737.

———. Brief Review of the Rise and Progress of the above Society. 8vo. Dublin. 1744.

———. Hospital Reports in Medicine and Surgery. 2 vols. 8vo. d. 1817—18.

———. Chartæ et Statuta Collegii Trinitatis juxta Dublin. 4to. 1768.

———. Comparative View of the Schools of Physic of Dublin and Edinburgh. 8vo. Dublin. 1818.

Dubois, J. A. Description of the People of India; translated from the French MS. 2 vols. 8vo. Phil. 1818.

Du Bos, J. B. Réflexions Critiques sur la Poësie et sur la Peinture. 6me ed. 3 vol. 12mo. Paris. 1755.

———, ———. Les Intérêts de l'Angleterre malentendus dans la Guerre Presente. 12mo. Amst. 1714.

Dubreuil, (le P.) La Perspective Pratique. 2de ed. 3 vol. 4to. Paris. 1663.

Dubroca. Leben des J. J. Dessalines, aus dem Franz. 12mo. Leipz. 1805.

Dubuisson, M. Lettres Critiques et Politiques sur les Colonies et le Commerce des Villes Maritimes de France. 8vo. Paris. 1785.

Ducange, C. du Fresne. Vide Cange.

Ducas, Michaelis. Historia Byzantina, Gr. et Lat. (Script. Byz.)

Duchal, James. Presumptive Arguments for the Truth and Authority of the Christian Religion. 8vo. Lond. 1753.

———, ———. Sermons. 3 vols. 8vo. Lond. 1765.

Duche, J. Caspipina's Letters, with the Life of William Penn. 2 vols. 12mo. Bath. 1777.

Duchesne de Versailles. Mémoires dans les Annales du Muséum d'Histoire Naturelle.

Duck, Stephen. Poems. 4th ed. 12mo. Lond. 1764.

Duclos. Sur l'Origine et les Révolutions des Langues Celtique et Françoise. (Acad. des Inscrip. vol. 15.)

Duclos, (l'Abbé.) Dictionnaire Bibliographique. Vide Cailleau.

Ducœurjoly, S. J. Manuel des Habitans de St. Domingue. 2 vol. 8vo. Paris. 1803.

Dudley, Paul. Essay on the Merchandise of Slaves and Souls of Men. 4to. Bost. 1731.

Dudley, Sir Rob. Dell' Arcano del Mare. fol. Firenze. 1646.

Dudley, Tho. Massachusetts, or the First Planters of New-England. 12mo. Bost. 1696.

Duer, Wm. Alex. Letter to C. D. Colden, Esq. in Answer to Strictures, in his "Life of Robert Fulton," upon a Report to the Legislature of New-York respecting Steam Navigation, &c. 8vo. Albany. 1817.
Duez, N. Dittionario Italiano et Francese. 8vo. Leide. 1660.
Duff, Wm. Essay on Original Genius. 8vo. Lond. 1767.
Duffield, Geo. Peace Sermon. 8vo. Bost. 1784.
Dufief, N. G. Nature Displayed in her Mode of Teaching Language to Man. Adapted to the French. 2d ed. 2 vols. 8vo. Phil. 1806.
Dufresne. Mémoires dans les Annales du Muséum d'Histoire Naturelle.
——, ——. Vide Fresne. Vide Cange.
Dugdale, Richard. See Surey Demoniack.
Dugdale, Sir Wm. Monasticon Anglicanum; from the Latin. fol. Lond. 1718.
———, ———. See Stevens, J.
———, ———. Antiquities of Warwickshire, by Wm. Thomas. 2d ed. 2 vols. fol. Lond. 1730.
———, ———. Chronica Juridicialia. 8vo. Lond. 1739.
Du Halde. Vide Halde.
Du Hamel du Monceau, H. L. Traité des Arbres Fruitiers. 2 vol. 4to. Paris. 1768.
———————, ———. Physique des Arbres. 2 vol. 4to. Paris. 1758.
———————, ———. Insecte de l'Angoumois. 12mo. Paris. 1762.
———————, ———. Traité des Arbres et Arbustes qui se cultivent en France. 2 vol. 4to. Paris. 1755.
———————, ———. Elements of Agriculture, tr. from the French by P. Miller. 2 vols. 8vo. Lond. 1764.
Du Hamel, J. B. Regiæ Scientiarum Academiæ Historia. 4to. Paris. 1698.
Dujardin et Peyrilhe. Histoire de la Chirurgie. 2 vol. 4to. Paris. 1774—80.
Duke, Richard. Poems. See Roscommon.
——, ———. ———. See Chalmers, A.
Duke, Richard. Fifteen Sermons. 8vo. Oxford. 1714.
——, ———. Assize Sermon. 4to. Lond. 1704.
Dukerus, Alex. Comi Urbis Historia, etc. (Græv. Thes. Ital.)
Dulaney. Considerations on the Propriety of Taxing the British Colonies for the purpose of a Revenue. 8vo. Lond. 1766.
Dulcinus, Barth. De Bononia. (Græv. Thes. Ital.)
Du Marsais. Vide Marsais.
Dumesnil, J. B. Gardin. Latin Synonyms; tr. from the French, &c. by J. M. Gosset. 8vo. Lond. 1809.
Dummer, Jeremiah. Discourse on the Holiness of the Sabbath. 8vo. Bost. 1763.
———, —. De Christi ad Inferos Descensu. 4to. Lug. Bat. 1702.

Dummer, Jeremiah. Defence of the New-England Charters. 8vo. Lond.
———, —. The Same. 8vo. Lond. 1766.
———, —. Letter on the Late Expedition to Canada. 8vo. Bost.
Dummer, Wm. (Lt. Gov.) Conferences with the Eastern Indians in 1726 and 1727. 4to. Bost. 1754.
Dumont. See Mont, J. du.
Dumont, G. M. B. Vide Mascrier, (l'Abbé le.)
Dumont, Jean. Corps Universel Diplomatique du Droit des Gens. 8 vol. fol. Amst. et La Haye. 1726—31.
———, —. Supplément au Corps Universel, par J. Barbeyrac et J. Rousset. 5 vol. fol. Amst. et La Haye. 1739.
Du Moulin. Vide Molinæus.
Dumouriez. Vie du Général Dumouriez. 3 vol. 12mo. Hamb. 1795.
Dunbar, Sam. Sermon on Brotherly Love. 8vo. Bost. 1749.
———, —. Artillery Election Sermon. 8vo. Bost. 1748.
———, —. Righteousness by the Law Subversive of Christianity, a Sermon. 8vo. Bost. 1751.
———, —. Sermon at the Ordination of the Rev. E. Grosvenor. 8vo. Bost. 1763.
———, —. Election Sermon. 8vo. Bost. 1760.
Dunbar, Wm. Account of the Language of Signs among certain North American Indians. (Amer. Phil. Tr. vol. 6.)
———, —. Meteorological Observations in 1799 and 1800. (Id.)
———, —. On Fossil Bones in Louisiana, and on Lunar Rainbows. (Id.)
———, —. Description of the Mississippi;—Appendix to the Same. (Id.)
Duncan, Andrew. Elements of Therapeutics. 2 vols. 12mo. Lond. 1773.
———, —. The Same. 2 vols. 12mo. Edin. 1773.
———, —. Medical Cases, from the Records of the Edinburgh Dispensatory. 3d ed. 8vo. Edin. 1784.
———, —. Medical and Philosophical Commentaries. 20 vols. 8vo. Edin. 1774—95.
———, —. Heads of Lectures on the Institutions of Medicine. 5th ed. 8vo. Edin. 1801.
———, —. On Pulmonary Consumptions. 8vo. Edin. 1816.
———, —. See Simson, T.
Duncan, Andrew, (Jun.) Edinburgh New Dispensatory. 8vo. Edin. 1803.
———, ————. Edinburgh Clinical Reports. 8vo. Edin. 1818.
Duncan, Andrew, (Sen. and Jun.) Annals of Medicine. 8 vols. 8vo. Edin. 1796—1804.
Duncan, Rob. Exposition of the Epistle to the Hebrews. 8vo. Edin. 1731.
Duncan, Wm. Elements of Logic. 5th ed. 12mo. Lond. 1764.

Duncan, Wm. New York-Directory and Register for 1793 and 1794. 2 vols. 12mo.
Dunciad, New, with Notes. 4to. Lond. 1742.
Duncombe, Giles. Trials per Pais. 5th ed. 8vo. Lond. 1718.
Duncombe, John. Letters by several Eminent Persons, including the Correspondence of John Hughes, Esq., with Notes. 2d ed. 3 vols. 8vo. Lond. 1773.
Dundas, Henry. Tracts relative to the Conduct of the War in the West Indies, collected from his Speech, &c. 4to. Lond. 1796.
Dunham, Josiah. Oration, July 4th. 8vo. Hanover. 1798.
———, ———. Funeral Oration on Washington. 8vo. 1800.
Duni, Emmanuele. Origine e Progressi del Cittadino, e del Governo Civile di Roma. 2 vol. 8vo. Roma. 1763—4.
Dunlap, Andrew. Oration, July 4th. 8vo. Salem. 1810.
Dunlap, Wm. Archers; with an Account of Switzerland. 8vo. N. York. 1796.
———, ———. Tell the Truth and Shame the Devil; a Comedy, in Two Acts. 8vo. N. York. 1797.
Dunlop, John. History of Roman Literature. 2 vols. 8vo. Lond. 1823.
Dunlop, Wm. Preface to the Westminster Confession, &c. 8vo. Lond. 1720.
———, ———. The Same. 2d ed. 8vo. Lond. 1724.
———, ———. Sermons and Lectures. 2 vols. 12mo. Glasgow. 1747.
Dunster, Isaiah. Sermon at the Instalment of the Rev. J. Green, jr. 8vo. Bost. 1763.
Dunton, John. Hazard of a Death-Bed Repentance; to which is added Conjugal Perjury. 12mo. Lond. 1708.
———, ———, Life of, and Journal. (Mass. Hist. Coll. N. S. vol. 2.)
Dupaty. Lettres sur l'Italie en 1785. 8vo. Paris. 1792.
Dupin, L. E. Bibliothèque des Auteurs Ecclesiastiques. 19 vol. 4to. Paris. 1693—1715.
———, ———. Compendious History of the Church; from the French. 4 vols. 12mo. Lond. 1713.
———, ———. Ecclesiastical History; from the French. 8 vols. fol. Lond. 1692—1725.
———, ———. Evangelical History; from the French. 2 vols. 8vo. Lond. 1750.
———, ———. Library of Historians; from the French. 4th ed. 2 vols. 8vo. Lond. 1709.
———, ———. History of the Canon and Writers of the Books of the Old and New Testament; from the French. fol. Lond. 1699.
Dupleix, Mémoire pour le Sieur. 4to. Paris. 1759.
Dupleix, Scipion. Histoire de Louis le Juste, XIII du Nom, Roy de France. fol. Paris. 1635.
Du Ponceau, P. S. English Phonology. (Amer. Phil. Tr. N. S. vol. 1.)
—————, ———. Discourse on the Early History of Pennsylvania. 8vo. Phil. 1821.

Du Ponceau, P. S. On the Jurisdiction of the Courts of the United States. 8vo. Phil. 1824.
———, ——. See Bynkershoek.
———, ——. Grammar of the Language of the Lenni Lenape or Delaware Indians, tr. from the German MS. of the late Rev. D. Zeisberger, for the Amer. Phil. Transactions. 4to. Phil. 1827.
———, ——. See Eliot, J.
Dupont de Nemours. Sur les Végétaux, les Polypes, et les Insectes. (Amer. Phil. Tr. vol. 5.)
———, ——. Sur la Théorie des Vents. (Id. vol. 6.)
———, ——. Notice sur la Vie et les Ecrits de M. Joël Barlow. 4to. 1813.
———, ——. Sur l'Education Nationale dans les Etats-Unis d'Amérique. 2de éd. 8vo. Paris. 1812.
Duportail. Love and Patriotism! or the Extraordinary Adventures of M. Duportail, late Major-General in the Armies of the United States. 12mo. Phil. 1797.
Duportus, Jac. Gnomologia Homerica. 4to. Cant. 1660.
———, ——. Metaphrasis Libri Psalmorum Græcis Versibus contexta. 4to. Cant. 1666.
Dupuis. Sur les Pélasges. (Instit. Lit. vol. 2 et 3.)
———. De l'Influence des Habitans du Golfe Persique et des Côtes Méridionales de la Perse, etc. sur l'Europe et sur l'Asie Mineure. (Id. vol. 5.)
———. Origine de Tous les Cultes. 3 vol. 4to. Paris. 1795.
Dupuy. Sur la Manière dont les Anciens rallumoient le Feu Sacré. (Acad. des Inscrip. vol. 35.)
———. Sur les Voyelles de la Langue Hébraïque, et des Langues Orientales. (Id. 36.)
Dupuy, P. Vide Satyre Ménippée.
Dupuy, (le Baron de.) Deuxième Lettre à M. H. Henry, sur les Habitans d'Hayti. 8vo. Cap-Henry.
Durand, F. J. Sermons pour les principales Solemnités, Chrétiennes, etc. 3 vol. 8vo. Lausanne. 1773.
Durand, Laur. Cantiques de l'Ame Dévote. 12mo. Lyon.
Durandus a Sancto Porciano. In Sententias Theologicas P. Lombardi Commentariorum Libri Quatuor. fol. Lugd. 1595.
Durazzo, Ippolito. Elogj Storici di Christoforo Colombo e di Andrea d'Oria. 4to. Parma. 1781.
Dureau de la Malle. Mémoires dans les Annales du Muséum d'Histoire Naturelle.
Duree, John. Severall Formes of Government, received in the Reformed Churches beyond the Seas. 4to. Oxford. 1641.
Durell, D. Critical Remarks on the Books of Job, Proverbs, Psalms, Ecclesiastes, and Canticles. 4to. Oxford. 1772.
———, ——. Parallel Prophecies of Jacob and Moses examined, &c. 4to. Oxford. 1763.
Durellus, J. Patronus Bonæ Fidei in Causa Puritanorum contra Hierarchicos Anglos. 8vo. 1672.

Duresme, Tho. Ezekiel's Wheels; a Treatise concerning Divine Providence. 8vo. Lond. 1653.
Durette. Treatise concerning the Abuse of Confessions of Faith, &c.; from the French. 8vo. Lond. 1718.
Durham, James. Dying Man's Testament to the Church of Scotland. 8vo. Edin. 1659.
———, ———. Exposition of the X Commandments; with a Resolution of Cases of Conscience. 4to. Lond. 1675.
Durie, John. Reformed Librarie Keeper. 16mo. Lond. 1650.
Durnford, C. See Willes, Ld. C. J.
———, and E. H. East. Term Reports in B. R. from 26 to 34 Geo. III. 5 vols. 8vo. Lond. 1794—1800.
Durnford, Tho. Assize Sermon. 8vo. Lond. 1715.
Durret. Voyage de Marseille à Lima, etc. 12mo. Paris. 1720.
Dutch Design Anatomized; or a Discovery of the Wickedness of the Intended Invasion. 4to. Lond. 1688.
——— Reasoner, on the Earl of Chesterfield's Embassy and the Emperor's Death; done from the French. 8vo. Lond. 1745.
———. Sentiments of a Dutch Patriot; from the Dutch. 8vo. Lond. 1746.
———. Voyages of the Dutch to the North of Europe. (Pinkerton, vol. 1.)
———. See Holland.
Dutens, L. Recherches sur l'Origine des Découvertes attribuées aux Modernes. 2 vol. in 1. 8vo. Paris. 1766.
Duties. Considerations on the High Duties which the Nation labors under. 4th ed. 8vo. Lond. 1744.
——— on Importations into the United States, in 1794—5. 8vo.
———. See United States.
Dutrône, J. F. Précis sur la Canne. 8vo. Paris. 1791.
———, ———. Histoire de la Canne, etc. 8vo. Paris. 1801.
Dutton, T. Warnings of the Spirit to Edinburgh and Glasgow. 12mo. Lond. 1710—11.
Duty. See Whole Duty of Man.
Duvallon, B. Vue de la Colonie Espagnole du Mississipi, en l'Année 1802. 8vo. Paris. 1803.
Du Verney. Diseases of the Bones, tr. by S. Ingham. 8vo. Lond. 1762.
Dwight, Henry. Farewell Sermon. 8vo. Utica. 1817.
Dwight, Nathaniel. Geography. 12mo. Bost. 1796.
Dwight, Theodore. Oration before the Connecticut Society for the Promotion of Freedom, &c. 8vo. Hartford. 1794.
———, ———. Oration, July 4th. 8vo. Hartford. 1792.
Dwight, Timothy. On the History, Eloquence, and Poetry of the Bible. 8vo. New-Haven. 1772.
———, ———. Sermon at the Opening of the Theological Institution in Andover, and Ordination of the Rev. E. Pearson. 8vo. Bost. 1808.
———, ———. Conquest of Canaan. 12mo. Hartford. 1785.
———, ———. Sermon at the Ordination of the Rev. N. W. Taylor. 8vo. N. York. 1812.

Dwight, Timothy. Greenfield Hill, a Poem. 8vo. N. York. 1794.
———, —. Remarks on the Review of Inchiquin's Letters in the Quarterly Review. 8vo. Bost. 1815.
———, —. Travels in New-England and New-York. 4 vols. 8vo. New-Haven. 1821—2.
Dyer, G. History of the University and Colleges of Cambridge. 2 vols. 8vo. Lond. 1814.
Dyer, Sir James. Reports in the time of Henry VIII., Edward VI., Mary, and Elizabeth. fol. Lond 1688.
—. ———. The Same, translated by John Vaillant. 3 vols. 8vo. Dublin. 1794.
Dyer, John. Poems. See Chalmers, A.
Dyer, Mary. Brief Statement of her Sufferings occasioned by the Shakers. 12mo. Bost. 1818.
Dyer, Wm. Collection of Psalms and Hymns. 12mo. Lond. 1767.
—, —. Believer's Golden Chain, &c. 12mo. Lond. 1763.
Dying Legacy of an Aged Minister of the Gospel to the United States. 8vo. Bost. 1783.
Dyke, Daniel. Workes. 2 vols. 4to. Lond. 1633—35.
—, ———. Treatises of Repentance and of Christs Temptations, &c. 4to. Lond. 1635.
Dyke, Jeremy. Discourses;—on Quenching the Spirit; Sinners Suite for Pardon; Right Eating and Digesting the Word; and the Purchase and Possession of Truth. 12mo. Lond. 1640.
Dynus, Fr. Antiquitates Etruriæ.—De Antiquitatibus Umbrorum, etc. (Græv. Thes Ital.)

E

Eachard, John. Works. 11th ed. 8vo. Lond. 1705.
Earbery, Matthias. Deism Examined and Confuted. 8vo. Lond. 1697.
Earle, Jabez. Hearing without Doing not sufficient to Salvation, a Sermon. 4to. Lond. 1706.
——, ——. Sinful Anger contrary to Charity, a Sermon. 8vo. Lond. 1721.
——, ——. Sermon on the Birth-Day of King William. 8vo. Lond. 1725.
——, ——. Sermon against Purgatory. 8vo. Lond. 1735.
——, ——. Sermon at the Ordination of Mr. William Hunt. 8vo. Lond. 1725.
——, ——. Fast Sermon. 8vo. Lond. 1727.
——, ——. Sermon on Reformation of Manners. 12mo. Lond. 1704.
Earle, Sir James. On the Operation for the Stone. 8vo. Lond. 1803.
——, ————. New Operation for the Cataract. 8vo. Lond. 1801.
——, ————. On the Cure of the Curved Spine. 8vo. Lond. 1799.
——, ————. On the Means of Lessening the Effect of Fire on the Human Body. 8vo. Lond. 1799.
Earthquakes. Account of the Earthquake at Lima, Oct. 28, 1746; with a Description of Peru;—also an Account of the Earthquake at Jamaica, June 7, 1692. 8vo. Lond. 1748.
————. Boanerges; an Essay concerning Earthquakes. 12mo. Bost. 1727.
————. Account of the Earthquake and Fire at Lisbon. 12mo. Bost. 1756.
————. Letter of Consolation and Counsel to the People of England, occasioned by the late Earthquakes. 8vo. Lond. 1750.
————, Sacred Philosophy of. 8vo. Lond. 1750.
————. Address to the Cities of London and Westminster, occasioned by the late Earthquake. 3d ed. 8vo. Lond. 1750.
————. Nouveaux Détails Historiques et Météorologiques du Tremblement de Terre de Messine, etc. 4to. Paris. 1783.
————. Description de l'Etna et du Vésuve, pour servir de Supplément aux "Nouveaux Détails," etc. 4to. Paris. 1783.
East, Edw. H. Reports in B. R. from 41 George III. by T. Day. 16 vols. 8vo. Phil. 1817.
——, ———. Pleas of the Crown. 2 vols. 8vo. Phil. 1806.

East, Edw. H. See Durnford.

Eastburn, Benj. Doctrine of Absolute Reprobation refuted. 16mo Bost. 1732.

Eastburn, James, & Co. Plan of the Literary Rooms. 8vo. N. York. 1817.

Easterbrooks, Joseph. Election Sermon. 4to. Bost. 1705.

East-India Company. Letters to and from the Company's Servants, at Bengal, &c. relative to Treaties and Grants from the Country Powers, from 1756 to 1766, inclusive; also a Letter from the Nabob of Arcot to the Company, &c. 4to. Lond. 1772.

East Indies. See India.

Eaton, Amos. Manual of Botany for the Northern and Middle States. 2d ed. 12mo. Albany. 1818.

——, ——. The Same. 12mo. Albany. 1822.

——, ——. Index to the Geology of the Northern States, &c. 8vo. Leicester. 1818.

Eaton, S. and T. Taylor. Congregational-Way Justified. 4to. Lond. 1646.

Eaton, Wm. (Gen.) Life of. 8vo. Brookfield. 1813.

Ebel, J. Tergeminum Specimen Disputationis a Magistro qui est ipsa Veritas habitæ ex Matth. c. xxii. demonstratum. 4to. Jenæ. 1699.

Ebeling, C. D. Amerikanische Bibliothek. 2 Stücke. 8vo. Leipz. 1777.

——, ——. Erdbeschreibung und Geschichte von Amerika. 7 Bände. 8vo. Hamburg. 1795—1816.

——, ——. Idem. (The author's interleaved copy, with his manuscript additions.)

——, ——, und Prof. Hegewisch. Amerikanisches Magazin. 8vo. Hamb. 1797.

Ebenaverus. B. F. De Dignitate ad Vitam Æternam Dissertatio. 4to. Vitemb. 1734.

Ebertus, Jac. Tetrasticha Hebræa in Textus Evangelicos, etc. (Ugol. vol. 31.)

Ebertus, Theodorus. Poetica Hebraica, Harmonica, Metrica, etc. (Ugol. vol. 31.)

Eburne, Rich. On the Maintenance of the Ministerie. 4to.

Ecclesiastes, New Translation of, by B. Hodgson. 4to. Oxford. 1790.

——————. Vide Rossi, G. B. de. Vide Palm, J. H. van der.

Ecclesiastical Benefice. Justice of the present Law which gives the Successor in any Ecclesiastical Benefice all the Profits from the Day of Avoidance, justified, &c. 4to. Lond. 1703.

—————— Council. Remarks on the Doings and Results of one, holden in Brimfield in March 1801, &c. 8vo. Bost. 1801.

—————— Courts, State of, delineated, &c. 4to. Lond. 1733.

—————— ——————. Letter to the Author of the Vindication of the Ecclesiastical Commissioners, concerning the Legality of that Court. 4to.

—————— Estates Invalidated. Lond. 1745.

—————— Governors, Obedience to, and Tryal of Doctrines. 4to. 1687.

Ecclesiastical History. See Magdeburg.
——— Jurisdiction, Brief View of, as practised in England. 8vo. Lond. 1733.
——— Revenues, History of. See Simon, R.
——— Small Dues, Letter concerning the late Act of Parliament relating to. 8vo. 1750.
———. See Church.
Ecclesiasticus. Vide Bretschneider.
Echard, Laurence. History of England. 3d ed. fol. Lond. 1720.
———, ———. Remarks on the History. 8vo. Lond. 1724.
———, ———. Ecclesiastical History. 4th ed. 2 vols. 8vo. Lond. 1718.
———, ———. The Same. 6th ed. 2 vols. 8vo. Lond. 1722.
Echevelar, Manuel de. Instruccion de las Derrotas y Navegaciones en la America Septentrional. 4to. Cadiz. 1753.
Eckermann, J. C. R. Ecklärung aller Dunkeln Stellen des Neuen Testaments. 3 Bände. 8vo. Kiel. 1806—8.
Eckhardus, Henricus. De Ordine Ecclesiastico et Politico. 12mo. Lips. 1612.
Eckhel, J. Doctrina Nummorum Veterum. 8 vol. 4to. Vindobonæ. 1792—8.
Eckley, Joseph. Dudleian Lecture in 1806. 8vo. Bost. 1810.
———, ———. Sermon at the Installation of the Rev. H. Holley. 8vo. Bost. 1809.
———, ———. Thanksgiving Sermon. 8vo. Bost. 1798.
———, ———. Discourse before the Boston Female Assylum. 8vo. Bost. 1802.
———, ———. Artillery Election Sermon. 8vo. Bost. 1792.
———, ———. Divine Glory brought to View in the Condemnation of the Ungodly, &c. 8vo. Bost. 1782.
Ecoles Normales, Seances des. 14 vol. (vol. 14ème, planches.) 8vo. Paris. 1800—1.
Edda. Vide Grimm. Vide Rühs.
Eddis, Wm. Letters from America. 8vo. Lond. 1792.
Eddius, Steph. Vita S. Wilfridi. (Gale, Scriptores xv.)
Eddowes, Ralph. Sermons. 12mo. Phil. 1817.
———, ———. Sermon on the Unity of God. 8vo. Phil. 1813.
Eddy, Tho. Hints for an Improved Mode of Treating the Insane in the Asylum. 12mo. N. York. 1815.
Eden, Robert. Visitation Sermon. 4to. Lond. 1754.
Eden, R., and R. Willes. History of the Travayles in the East and West Indies. 4to. Lond. 1577.
Eden, Robert. Jurisprudentia Philologica. 4to. Oxonii. 1744.
Eden, Wm. (Lord Auckland.) Principles of Penal Law. 2d ed. 8vo. Lond. 1771.
Edgeworth, Maria. Parent's Assistant. 3 vols. 18mo. Bost.
———, ———. Moral Tales. 3 vols. 12mo. Phil. 1810.
———, ———. Tales of Fashionable Life. 3 vols. 12mo. Bost. 1812.
———, ———. Popular Tales. 2 vols. 12mo. Poughkeepsie. 1813.

Edgeworth, Maria. Harrington and Ormond. 3 vols. in 2. 12mo.
———, ———. Patronage. 3 vols. 12mo. Phil. 1814.
———, ———. Cottage Dialogues. 12mo. Phil. 1811.
———, ———, and R. L. Practical Education. 3 vols. 8vo. Lond. 1801.
———, ———. Readings on Poetry. 18mo. Bost. 1816.
Edinburgh. Medical Essays and Observations published by a Society in Edinburgh. 5 vols. in 6. 8vo. Edin. 1733—44.
———. Essays and Observations, Physical and Literary, published by a Society in Edinburgh. 3 vols. 8vo. Edin. 1754—71.
———. Medical and Philosophical Commentaries, by a Society in Edinburg, &c. 2d ed. 8 vols. 8vo. Lond. 1774—83.
———. Medical and Surgical Journal. 14 vols. 8vo. 1805—18.
———. Medical and Physical Dictionary, by R. Morris and others. 2 vols. 4to. Edin. 1807.
———. New Dispensatory. See Duncan, A.
———. System of Anatomy. 2 vols. 8vo. Edin. 1784.
———. Memorial concerning the Surgeons Hospital at Edinburgh. 12mo. 1737.
———, Proposals for certain Public Works in. 8vo. 1752.
———, Medical School of. 8vo. Edin. 1819.
———. See Dublin,—Oxford,—Pharmacopœia,—Review.
Edmonds, (Dr.) Compleat Collection of All the Articles and Clauses which relate to the Marine, in the Several Treaties now subsisting between Great Britain and other States, &c. 8vo. Lond. 1760.
Edmundson, H. Lingua Linguarum. 12mo. Lond. 1655.
Education. The great Benefit of the Christian Education of Children, a Sermon. 4to. Lond. 1662.
———, A Thought relating to. 8vo. Lond. 1732.
———. The Expence of University Education Reduced. 2d. ed. 8vo. Lond. 1733.
———. Of Education. 8vo. Lond. 1734.
———, Thoughts on, by the Author of Britain's Remembrancer, (James Burgh.) 8vo. Lond. 1747.
———, Essay on Modern. 8vo. Lond. 1747.
———. Third Report of the Directors of the American Society for Educating Pious Youth for the Gospel-Ministry. 8vo. Andover. 1813.
———. See Schools.
Edward II, History of the Life and Reign of. See Falkland, Lord.
Edwards, Bryan. Thoughts on the Proceedings of Government respecting the Trade of the West India Islands with the United States. 2d ed. 8vo. Lond. 1784.
———, ———. Proceedings of the Governor and Assembly of Jamaica in regard to the Maroon Negroes; with an Introductory Discourse respecting the Maroons. 8vo. Lond. 1796.
———, ———. Speech on the Slave Trade. 8vo. Lond. 1790.
———, ———. Historical Survey of St. Domingo. 4to. Lond. 1797.

Edwards, Bryan. Vide Charmilly.
———, ———. History of the British West Indies. 3 vols. 4to. Lond. 1793—1801.
———, ———. The Same. 2 vols. 4to. Lond. 1794.
———, ———. ————. 4 vols. 8vo. Phil. 1806.
———, ———. Continuation of the History, (by another hand.) 2 vols. 8vo. Lond. 1819.
———, ———. History of the West Indies abridged. 8vo. Lond. 1798.
———, ———. Atlas for the History of the West Indies. 4to. Charleston. 1810.
———, ———. Histoire de l'Ile St. Domingue, extraite de l'Histoire des Antilles de M. Edwards, trad. de l'Anglois par J. B. J. Breton. 12mo. Paris. 1802.
———, ———. Histoire des Indes Occidentales, trad. de l'Anglois. 8vo. Paris. 1801.
Edwards, Geo. Gleanings of Natural History, English and French, with Coloured Figures. 4to. Lond. 1758.
Edwards, John. On the Authority, Style, and Perfection of the Old and New Testament. 3 vols. 8vo. Lond. 1693—5.
———, ——. Exercitations on Important Places in the Old and New Testament. 8vo. Lond. 1702.
———, ——. Thoughts on the Causes of Atheism, &c. 8vo. Lond. 1695.
———, ——. Demonstration of the Existence and Providence of God. 8vo. Lond. 1696.
———, ——. Accession Sermon. 8vo. Lond. 1714.
———, ——. Enquiry into Four Remarkable Texts of the New Testament. 8vo. Camb. 1692.
———, ——. Further Enquiry into several Remarkable Texts. 2d ed. 8vo. Lond. 1694.
———, ——. The Preacher, a Discourse, shewing his Office and Employment; also the Hearer. 3 vols. 8vo. Lond. 1705—9.
———, ——. Sermons on Special Occasions. 8vo. Lond. 1698.
———, ——. History or Survey of All the Dispensations and Methods of Religion. 2 vols, 8vo. Lond. 1699.
———, ——. Veritas Redux; or Evangelical Truths Restored. 8vo. Lond. 1707.
———, ——. Doctrine of Faith and Justification set in a True Light. 8vo. Lond. 1708.
———, ——. New Discoveries of the Uncertainty, &c. of Knowledge. 8vo. Lond. 1714.
———, ——. Theologia Reformata; or the Body and Substance of the Christain Religion. 3 vols. fol. Lond. 1713—26.
———, ——. Treatise of Repentance. 8vo. Lond. 1718.
Edwards, Jonathan. Preservative against Socinianism. 3d ed. 4to. Oxon. 1698.
Edwards, Jona. (Pres.) Life of D. Brainerd. 8vo. Bost. 1749.
———, ——— ———. Works, with his Life. 8 vols. 8vo. Worcester. 1808.
———, ————. Enquiry concerning the Freedom of the Will. 8vo. Lond. 1790.

Edwards, Jona. (Pres.) Observations on the Language of the Muhhekaneew Indians. 8vo. New-Haven. 1788.

———, ———. The Same, with Notes by J. Pickering. 8vo. Bost. 1823.

———, ———. Farewell-Sermon at Northampton. 8vo. Bost. 1751.

———, ———. Answer to his Sermon on the Spirit of God. 12mo. Bost. 1743.

———, ———. Treatise concerning Religious Affections. 12mo. Edin. 1789.

———, ———. The Same. 12mo. Bost. 1794.

———, ———. Two Letters cited by the Rev. Tho. Clap. 16mo. Bost. 1745.

———, ———. Sermon at the Boston Public Lecture. 16mo. Bost. 1731.

———, ———. Sermon on the Death of the Rev. D. Brainerd. 8vo. Bost. 1747.

———, ———. Sermon on the Death of the Hon. J. Stoddard. 16mo. Bost. 1748.

———, ———. Humble Inquiry concerning the Qualifications requisite to a Complete Standing in the Visible Church; with an Appendix by Mr. Foxcroft. 4to. Bost. 1749.

———, ———. Narrative of the Work of God in the Conversion of many hundred Souls in Northampton, of New-England. 12mo. 1738. See also Williams, W.

———, ———. Doctrine of Original Sin defended. 12mo. Dublin. 1768.

Edwards, Jonathan. The Injustice and Impolicy of the Slave Trade, a Sermon. 8vo. 1791.

Edwards, Peter. Candid Reasons for Renouncing the Principles of Antipædobaptism. 12mo. Windsor. 1802.

Edwards, Tho. Antapologia; or Answer to the Apologeticall Narration of certain Members of the Assembly of Divines. 4to. Lond. 1644.

Edwards, Tho. Duæ Dissertationes: I. De Variantibus Lectionibus et Mendis quæ in Sacram Scripturam irrepserunt. II. De Prædestinatione Paulina. 8vo. Cant. 1768.

———, ———. New English Translation of the Psalms from the Hebrew, reduced to Metre by Bishop Hare, with Notes, &c. 8vo. Camb. 1755.

———, ———. In Libros Veteris Testamenti Poeticos. 8vo. Cant. 1762.

———, ———. Two Dissertations;—on Religious Bigotry; and on the Qualifications and Canons, necessary for the right Interpretation of the New Testament. 8vo. Camb. 1766.

———, ———. The Doctrine of Irresistible Grace not in the New Testament. 8vo. Camb. 1759.

Edwards, Tho. Reports of Cases in the High Court of Admiralty. vol. 1. 8vo. Lond. 1810—12.

Edwards, Timothy. Connecticut Election Sermon. 16mo. N. Lond. 1732.

Eells, Edw. Connecticut Election Sermon. 16mo. Hartford. 1767.
Eells, Nathaniel. Election Sermon. 8vo. Bost. 1743.
——, ————. Reasons for inviting Mr. Whitefield to preach.
Egan, A. Romanists Designs detected and Jesuits Practices discovered. 4to. Lond. 1674.
*Egede, Hans. Det gamle Gronlands Nye Perlustration, etc. 4to. Kiobenhaven. 1741.
———, ——. Des Alten Grönlandes neue Perlustration; aus den Dänischen. 4to. Copenhagen. 1792.
Egede, Hans. Nachricht vom Anfange und Fortgange der Gronländischen Mission. 4to. Hamb. 1740.
———, ——. Beschreibung und Natur-Geschichte von Grönland, übers. von J. G. Krünitz. 12mo. Berlin. 1763.
Egede, Paul. Continuation af Relationerne betreffende den Grönlandske Missions Tilstand og Beskaffenhed. 4to. Kiobenhavn.
———, ——. Efterretninger om Gronland uddrag'ne af en Journal holden fra 1721 til 1788. 8vo. Kiobenhavn.
Egen, J. F. W. Ueber die Homerischen Gleichnisse. 12mo. Magdeburg. 1790.
Egesippus. De Excidio Urbis Hierosolymitanæ. Vide Orosius.
Eggelingius, J. H. Mysteria Cereris et Bacchi in Vasculo ex uno Onyche. 4to. Bremae. 1682.
—————, ——. Idem. (Gronovius, vol. 7.)
Eggers, H. P. von. Ueber die Wahre Lage des Alten Ostgrönlands. 12mo. Kiel. 1794.
Eginhartus. Vita et Gesta Caroli Magni. Vide Witichindus.
Egmont, J. Perceval, Earl of. Second Series of Facts and Arguments to prove that the Abilities of the Two B——rs are not more extraordinary than their Virtues. 8vo. Lond. 1749.
———, ————————. Letter from a Person of Distinction, in Answer to the above, &c. 8vo. Lond.
———, ————————. Letter to the Author of an Examination of the Principles, &c. of the Two B——rs. 8vo. Lond. 1749.
———, ————————. Conduct of the Two B——rs Vindicated. 8vo. Lond. 1749.
Egnatius, J. B. De Romanis Principibus. Vide Rom. Hist. Scriptores. vol. 3.
———, ——. De Origine Turcarum. (Clauser, de Reb. Turcicis.)
Egypt, Reflections on the Natural Foundation of the High Antiquity of Government, Arts, and Sciences in. 8vo. Oxford. 1743.
———. Trois Relations d'Ægypte, par C. Lambert, J. Albert, et S. Seguezzi. 4to. Paris. 1651.
———. Relation de l'Egypte par Abd-Allatif. Vide Sacy.
———. Description de l'Egypte, ou Recueil des Observations et des Recherches qui ont été faites en Egypte pendant l'Expédition de l'Armée Française, publié par les Ordres de sa Majesté l'Empereur Napoléon le Grand. Planches et Texte. Paris. 1808—25.
Ehrenmalm, Arwid. Travels into Western Nordland, &c. (Pinkerton, vol. 1.)

Eichhorn, J. G. Repertorium für Biblische und Morgenländische Litteratur. 18 Theile. 8vo. Leipz. 1777—86.

———, ——. Commentarius in Apocalypsin. 2 vol. Gottingæ. 1791.

———, ——. Einleitung in das Alte Testament. 4 Bände. 8vo. Leipz. 1803.

———, ——. Idem. 5 Bände. 8vo. Göttingen. 1823.

———, ——. Einleitung in das Neue Testament. 3 Bände. 8vo. Leipz. 1804.

———, ——. Litterärgeschichte. 2 Bände. 8vo. Göttingen. 1812—14.

———, ——. Geschichte der Litteratur. 6 Bände. 8vo. Göttingen. 1805—11.

———, ——. Antiqua Historia ex ipsis Veterum Scriptorum Græcorum Narrationibus contexta, Græce. 4 vol. 8vo. Lips. 1811—12.

Einari, Halfdanus. Historia Literariæ Icelandiæ. 8vo. Haun. et Lips. 1786.

Eisenmenger, J. A. Entdecktes Judenthum. 2 Theile. 4to. 1700.

Eisenschmidius, J. C. De Ponderibus et Mensuris Romanorum, Græcorum, Hebræorum; nec non de Valore Pecuniæ Veteris, etc. 12mo. Argent. 1737.

———, ——. Idem. (Ugol. vol. 28.)

Eldik, E. H. van. Suspicionum Specimen. (Thesaurus Crit. Nov.)

Election. See Predestination.

Electioneering Tracts. "Look before You Leap." 8vo. Newburyport. 1805.

——— ———. Who shall be Governor, Strong or Sullivan? 8vo. 1806.

——— ———. Touchstone to the People of the United States, on the Choice of a President. 8vo. N. York. 1812.

——— ———. Hamilton to the Federalists, on the Choice of a President. 8vo. N. York. 1812.

——— ———. See Address,—Appeal, &c.

Elegant Extracts. See Knox, V.

Elegantiæ Latinæ. See Valpy, E.

Elegiaca Græca. 8vo. Oxon. 1759.

Elegy on the Times, first printed at Boston in 1774. 8vo. New-Haven. 1775.

Eliot, Andrew. Sermon against an Inordinate Love of the World. 8vo. Bost. 1744.

——, ———. Sermon before the Execution of Levi Ames for Burglary. 8vo. Bost. 1773.

——, ———. Twenty Sermons. 8vo. Bost. 1774.

——, ———. Sermon on the Death of the Rev. John Webb. 8vo. Bost. 1750.

——, ———. Thanksgiving Sermon for the Reduction of Quebec, 8vo. Bost. 1759.

——, ———. Sermon at the Ordination of the Rev. Joseph Roberts. 8vo. Bost. 1754.

Eliot, Andrew. Sermon at the Ordination of the Rev. Ebenezer Thayer. 8vo. Bost. 1766.
——, ———. Sermon at the Ordination of his Son. 8vo. Bost. 1774.
——, ———. Fast Sermon. 8vo. Bost. 1753.
——, ———. Dudleian Lecture. 8vo. Bost. 1771.
——, ———. Election Sermon. 8vo. Bost. 1765.
Eliot, Jared. Connecticut Election Sermon. 8vo. N. Lond. 1738.
——, ——. On Field-Husbandry. 12mo. N. Lond. 1751.
Eliot, John. Mamusse Wunneetupanatamwe Up-Biblum God naneeswe Nukkone Testament kah wonk Wusku Testament. (Bible in the Massachusetts Indian Language.) 4to. Camb. 1663.
——, ——. Idem. 4to. Camb. 1685.
——, ——. Manitowompæ Pomantamoonk Sampwshanau Christianoh Uttoh woh an Pomantog Wussikkitteahonat God. 12mo. Camb. 1685.
——, ——. New Testament translated into the Indian Language. 4to. Camb. 1661.
——, ——. Grammar of the Massachusetts Indian Language; with Notes, &c. by P. S. Du Ponceau, and an Introduction, &c. by John Pickering. 8vo. Bost. 1822.
——, ——. Account of Indian Churches in New England. (Mass. Hist. Coll. vol. 10.)
Eliot, John. Sermon before the New-North Religious Society, upon the Completion of their House of Worship. 8vo. Bost. 1804.
——, ——. Thanksgiving Sermon. 8vo. Bost. 1794.
——, ——. Sermon from Prov. viii. 31. 8vo. Bost. 1800.
——, ——. Sermon at the Ordination of the Rev. J. McKean. 8vo. Bost. 1797.
——, ——. Biographical Dictionary of New-England. 8vo. Bost. 1809.
——, ——. Ecclesiastical History of Massachusetts. (Mass. Hist. Coll. 2d Series, vol. 1.)
——, ——, Characters of. See McKean, J. See Mass. Hist. Coll. 2d Series, vol. 1.)
——. See Elliot.
Elis, Clement. Folly of Atheism demonstrated. 12mo. Lond. 1692.
Elizabeth, (Queen.) Instance of her Power of Dispensing with Acts of Parliament. fol. Lond. 1687.
————, ————. Injunctions as well to the Clergie, as to the Laitie.—Visitation Articles. 4to. Lond. 1600.
————, ————. Golden Speech to her last Parliament. (Harl. Miscel. vol. 1.)
Ellend, G. C. Exercitatio Exegetica de illis, qui Prophetæ vocantur in Novo Fœdere. 4to. Helmst. 1732.
Ellery, Christopher. Defence against Calumny; or Haman in the shape of Christopher Ellery, Esq. hung upon his own Gallows; being the Substance of certain Publications respecting the Accusation against John Rutledge, &c. 8vo. 1803. See Rutledge, J.

Ellesmere, T. (Ld. Chancellor.) Speech on the Post-Nati. 4to. Lond. 1609.
Ellicott, Andrew. Journal from 1796 to 1800. 8vo. Phil. 1803.
———, ———. Astronomical and other Papers in the Transactions of the American Philosophical Society.
Elliot, Rob. Specimen of Bishop Burnet's Posthumous History; with Lesley's Character of an Enthusiast. 3d ed. 8vo. Lond.
Elliott, J. On Vision and Hearing; on Harmonic Sounds; on Combustion; and on Animal Heat. 8vo. Lond. 1780.
Elliott, Stephen. Botany of South Carolina and Georgia. vol. 1. Nos. 4, 5, and 6. 8vo. Charleston, S. C. 1817—21.
———. See Eliot.
Ellis. Letter to a Friend reflecting on some Passages in a Letter to the D. of P. 4to. Lond. 1687.
——. Defence of the preceding. 4to. Lond. 1688.
——. Protestant Resolved. 4to. Lond. 1688.
Ellis. Summary of the Roman Law. See Taylor, J.
Ellis, Asa. Country Dyer's Assistant. 12mo. Brookfield, (Mass.) 1798.
Ellis, Geo. Specimens of Early English Metrical Romances. 3 vols. 8vo. Lond. 1805.
Ellis, Henry. Reise nach Hudsons Meerbusen; aus dem Englischen. 8vo. Göttingen. 1750.
——, ———. Voyage de la Baye de Hudson, trad. de l'Anglois. 2 vol. en 1. 12mo. Paris. 1749.
Ellis, Henry. Journal of the Proceedings of the late Embassy to China. 8vo. Phil. 1818.
Ellis, James. Narrative of the late Law-Suits relative to Property devoted to Pious Uses in Rehoboth. 12mo. Warren. 1795.
Ellis, John. Knowledge of Divine Things from Revelation. 8vo. Lond. 1743.
——, ——. The Same. 2d ed. 8vo. Lond. 1747.
Ellis, John. Method of Preventing the Premature Decay of Peach Trees. (Amer. Phil. Tr. vol. 5.)
Ellis, Ph. Five Sermons before the King and Queen. 4to. Lond. 1686.
Ellis, Wm. English Exercises. 7th ed. 12mo. Lond. 1816.
Ellis, Wm. Tour round Hawaii. 12mo. Bost. 1825.
Ellys, Anthony, (Bp.) Spiritual and Temporal Liberty of Subjects in England. 4to. Lond. 1765.
Ellys, Sir Richard. Fortuita Sacra; cum Commentario de Cymbalis. 8vo. Rotterodami. 1727.
——, ————. Idem. 8vo. Traj. ad Rhen. 1744.
Eloquence of the United States. See Williston, E. B.
Eloy, N. F. J. Dictionnaire Historique de la Médicine. 4 vol. 4to. Mons. 1778.
Elsasser, der Patriotische, eine Wochenschrift. 12mo. Strassb. und Colmar. 1777.
Else, Joseph. Works, containing a Treatise on the Hydrocele, &c. 8vo. Lond. 1782.
Elsley, (Rev. Mr.) Annotations on the Four Gospels and the Acts of the Apostles. 3 vols. 8vo. Lond. 1812.

Elsner, Jacobus. Observationes Sacræ in Novi Fœderis Libros. 2 vol. 8vo. Traj. ad Rhen. 1720—8.
Elsner, Jo. De Terra Gosen. 4to. Francof. ad Viadrum. 1735.
Elstob, Elizabeth. Rudiments of Grammar for the English-Saxon Tongue, &c. 4to. Lond. 1715.
Elsynge, Henry. Manner of holding Parliaments in England. 8vo. Lond. 1768.
Elton, C. A. Specimens of the Classic Poets, tr. into English Verse, with Notes. 3 vols. 8vo. Lond. 1814.
Elwall, (Mr.) Account of his Trial for Publishing a Book in Defence of the Unity of God. 8vo. Birmingham. 1788.
Ely, Ezra Stiles. Contrast between Calvinism and Hopkinsianism. 8vo. N. York. 1811.
—, ———. Theological Review. vols. 1, 2. 8vo. Phil. 1818—19.
Embargo Laws. Examination of their Constitutionality, by Fr. Blake. 8vo. Worcester. 1808.
——— ——. See Massachusetts.
Emerson. Exhortation respecting a Variety of Ministers. 16mo. Bost. 1742.
Emerson, Brown. Sermon on the Death of the Rev. Daniel Hopkins. 8vo. Salem. 1815.
———, ———. Discourse before the Salem Female Charitable Society. 8vo. Salem. 1811.
Emerson, Wm. Doctrine of Fluxions. 8vo. Lond. 1757.
———, ——. Cyclomathesis. 8vo. Lond. 1763.
———, ——. Treatise of Algebra. 8vo. Lond. 1764.
———, ——. Arithmetic of Infinites; Conic Sections; Curve Lines. 8vo. Lond. 1767.
———, ——. System of Astronomy. 8vo. Lond. 1769.
———, ——. Mathematical Tracts, viz. Combinations, &c.; Chronology; Calculation, &c.; Gauging; Surveying. 8vo. Lond. 1770.
———, ——. Principles of Mechanics. 2d ed. 4to. Lond. 1758.
———, ——. Mechanics; Projection of the Sphere, &c. 8vo. Lond. 1769.
———, ——. Elements of Optics. 8vo. Lond. 1768.
———, ——. Elements of Geometry. 8vo. Lond. 1763.
———, ——. Elements of Trigonometry. 2d ed. 8vo. Lond. 1764.
———, ——. Mathematical Principles of Geography; Navigation; Dialling. 8vo. Lond. 1770.
Emerson, Wm. Historical Sketch of the First Church in Boston; with Two Sermons, on leaving the Old, and entering the New House of Worship. 8vo. Bost. 1812.
———, ——. Sermon on the Decease of the Rev. Peter Thacher. 8vo. Bost. 1803.
———, ——. Sermon on the Death of Mr. Charles Austin. 8vo. Bost. 1806.
———, ——. Discourse before the Massachusetts Humane Society. 8vo. Bost. 1807.

Emerson, Wm. Artillery Election Sermon. 8vo. Bost. 1799.
———, ———, Oration, July 4th. 8vo. Bost. 1802.
Emigrant's Guide; or Picture of America. 8vo. Lond. 1816.
Emigration. Look before you Leap. 3d ed. 8vo. Lond. 1796.
———. See Cooper, T.
Emlyn, S. See Hale, Sir Matthew.
Emlyn, Tho. Memoirs of the Life and Sentiments of Dr. Samuel Clarke. 8vo. Lond. 1731.
———, ———. Sermons. 8vo. Lond. 1742.
———, ———. Answer to Mr. Martin's Critical Dissertation on 1 John v, 7. 8vo. Lond 1719.
———, ———. Reply to Martin's Examination of the "Answer." 8vo. Lond. 1720.
———, ———. Dr. Bennet's New Theory of the Trinity examined. 8vo. Lond. 1718.
———, ———. On a Book, entitled, the Doctrine of the Blessed Trinity stated and defended, &c. 8vo. Lond. 1719.
———, ———. Collection of Tracts relating to the Deity, &c. of Christ. 8vo. Lond. 1719.
———, ———. Memoirs of his Life and Writings. 8vo. Lond. 1746.
———, ———. Humble Inquiry into the Scripture-Account of Jesus Christ. 5th ed. 8vo. Bost. 1756.
———, ———. The Same.—Danger of Rashness in Censuring others as Heretics.—Biographical Notice of him. (Sparks, Collection, vol. 4.)
Emmius, Ubbo. De Græcia Veteri.—De Carthagine. (Gronov. vol. 4.)
Emmons, Nathaniel. Sermons. 8vo. Bost. 1813.
———, ———. Fast Sermon. 8vo. Salem. 1802.
———, ———. Election Sermon. 8vo. Bost. 1798.
———, ———. Sermon before the Massachusetts Missionary Society. 8vo. Charlestown. 1800.
———, ———. Convention Sermon. 4to. Bost. 1804.
———, ———. Sermon at the Ordination of the Rev. J. Emerson. 8vo. Salem. 1803.
———, ———. Sermon at the Installation of the Rev. H. Weeks. 8vo. Bost. 1815.
Emms, Robert. Excellency and Advantage of the Gospel Dispensations. 8vo. Lond. 1732.
Emott, James. Speech in the House of Representatives of the United States, Jan. 1813. 8vo. Alexandria.
Empedocles Agrigentinus. Carminum Reliquiæ, cum Annotationibus; item, de Vita et Philosophia ejus, etc. a F. G. Sturz 2 tomi in 1 vol. 8vo. Lips. 1805.
Empereur, Constantinus l'. Oratio Inauguralis, de Linguæ Hebrææ Dignitate ac Utilitate. 4to. Lug. Bat. 1627.
———, ———. De Legibus Ebræorum Forensibus. 4to. Lug. Bat. 1637.
Enciso, Ambrosio Alvarez de. Discurso sobre las Ventajas de las Sociedades Economicas. 8vo. Zaragoza. 1784.
Encyclopädie der Lateinischen Classiker. 20 Bände. 12mo. Braunschweig. 1790—6.

Encyclopædia Britannica. 2d ed. 10 vols. 4to. Edin. 1778—83.
————. Dobson's Edition; with a Supplement. 21 vols. 4to. Phil. 1798—1803.
———— Perthensis. See Aitchison, A.
————, Edinburgh. See Brewster.
————. Vide Alstedius, J. H. Vide Cyclopædia.
Encyclopédie. Vide Diderot.
Encyclopédie Méthodique par Lamarcke et Poiret.
Enfant, J. l'. Vide Lenfant.
Enfield, Wm. Sermons for Families. 2 vols. 12mo. Lond. 1769—72.
———, ——. History of Philosophy. 2 vols. 4to. Lond. 1791.
———, ——. The Same. 2 vols. 8vo. Dublin. 1792.
Engel, (le Bailly d'.) Essai sur cette Question; Quand et Comment l'Amérique a-t-elle été peuplée? 4to. Amst. 1767.
———, ————. Mémoires et Observations Géographiques et Critiques sur la Situation des Pays Septentrionaux de l'Asie et de l'Amérique. 4to. Lausanne. 1765.
———, ————. Geographische Nachrichten und Anmerkungen über die Lage der Nördlichen Gegenden von Asien und Amerika, etc.; aus dem Franz. 4to. Mietau, etc. 1772.
———, ————. Neuer Versuch über die Lage der Nördlichen Gegenden von Asia und Amerika, etc. 4to. Basel. 1777.
———, ————. Anmerkungen über Cooks Reise-Relation, etc. 12mo. 1780.
Engelstoft, L. Commentatio de Pretio Literarum Romanarum. 4to. Hauniæ. 1803.
England, Discourse on the Nationall Excellencies of, by R. H. 8vo. Lond. 1658.
———. England's Present Interest. 4to. 1675.
———. England's Miseries, (under the Stuarts.) 12mo. Lond. 1692.
———, State of, in 1588. 8vo. Lond. 1746.
———, Ancient Customs of. 4to.
———. Plan of the English Commerce. 8vo. Lond. 1728.
———. Enquiry into the Conduct of our Domestick Affairs from the Year 1721. 8vo. Lond. 1734.
———, Second Letter to the People of, on Foreign Subsidies, &c. 2d ed. 8vo. Lond. 1755.
———, Parliamentary, or Constitutional History of, to the Restoration of Charles II, by several Hands. 2d ed. 24 vols. 8vo. Lond. 1761—2.
———, Letter from the Elephant to the People of. 4to. Lond. 1764.
———, Essay on the Constitution of. 2d ed. 8vo. Lond. 1766.
———. Select Collection of Letters on its Government, Liberty, and Constitution. 2d ed. 3 vols. 12mo. Lond. 1763.
———. Conduct of the late Administration examined. 8vo. Lond. 1767.
———, Letters on the Present State of. 8vo. Lond. 1772.
———. Examination into the Conduct of the Present Adminis-

tration, from the Year 1774, and a Plan of Accommodation with America. 8vo. Lond. 1778.

———. See Affairs,—Anglia,—Angleterre,—Britain,—Great Britain,—Church,—New-England,—Parliament,—Scriptores, etc.

England, Geo. Enquiry into the Morals of the Ancients. 4to. Lond. 1735.

Englefield, Sir Henry. Determination of the Orbits of Comets. 4to. Lond. 1793.

English Fortune-Teller, or a New Almanacke. 4to. 1642.

English, Geo. B. Grounds of Christianity examined. 12mo. Bost. 1813.

———, ——. Letter to the Rev. Mr. Cary on his Review of the above. 12mo. Bost. 1813.

———, ——. Letter to the Rev. Mr. Channing on his Two Sermons on Infidelity. 12mo. Bost. 1813.

———, ——. See Cary, S. See Everett, E.

———, ——. Expedition to Dongola and Sennaar. 8vo. Bost. 1823.

English Language. Reflections on it, in the Nature of Vaugelas's Reflections on the French, &c. 12mo. Lond. 1770.

English Pilot; Part 5. 2d ed. fol. Lond. 1720.

Eniedinus, Geo. Explicationes Locorum Veteris et Novi Testamenti, ex quibus Trinitatis Dogma stabiliri solet. 4to.

Ennius, Quintus. Fragmenta, cum Notis, a F. Hesselio. 4to. Amst. 1707.

———, ———. Vide Epigrammata et Poematia Vetera.

———, ———. Vide Corpus Poetarum Latinorum.

Enquiry into the Principles and Tendency of certain Public Measures. 8vo. Phil. 1794.

Ensor, Geo. Principles of Morality. 8vo. Lond. 1801.

——, ——. Independent Man. 2 vols. 8vo. Lond. 1806.

Enthusiasm, Nature and Consequences of. See Trinity.

————, Fine Picture of, chiefly drawn by Dr. John Scott. 8vo. Lond. 1744.

Entick, John. New Latin and English Dictionary; by William Crakelt. 2 vols. 12mo. Lond. 1787—9.

Entretiens de Guillaume de Nassau et du Général Montgommery. 12mo. Lond. 1776.

Entries. See Brown, W.,—Registrum,—Small,—Thesaurus.

Enty, John. Defence of the Proceedings of the late Assembly at Exon, in Reply to Mr. Peirce. 8vo. Lond. 1719.

——, ——. Further Defence. 8vo. Lond. 1720.

——, ——. Reply to the above. 8vo. Lond. 1721.

——, ——. See Peirce, J.

Enzina, Sebastian de la. Vide Testamento.

Eon de Beaumont, (le Chevalier d'.) Loisirs. 13 vol. 8vo. Amst. 1774.

Ephemeriden, neue Allgemeine Geographische. Band 1, und Bd. 2, Stücke, 2, 3, 4. 8vo. Weimar. 1817.

Ephemerides Motuum Cœlestium. Vide Manfredius.

Ephémérides des Mouvemens Célestes, pour les Années 1715, jusqu'en 1800, par Desplaces, La Caille, et La Lande. 9 vol. 4to. Paris. 1716—92.
Ephemeris, Gr. MS.
Ephemeris Parliamentaria. Vide Fuller, W.
Ephraem Syrus, Sanctus. Opera Omnia, Græce, Syriace, Latine, cum Interpretatione, Notis, etc. 6 vol. fol. Romæ. 1732—43.
Epictetus. Enchiridion, cum Cebetis Tabula; accessere Arriani Commentarii de Epicteti Disputationibus; Gr. et Lat. ab H. Wolfio. Item, Porphyrius, de Abstinentia, de Vita Pythagoræ, etc., Gr. et Lat. cura L. Holstenii. 12mo. Cant. 1655.
———. Dissertationes ab Arriano collectæ; nec non Enchiridion et Fragmenta, Gr. et Lat. cum Notis, a J. Uptono. 2 vol. 4to. Lond. 1741.
———. Idem, a J. Schweighæusero. 5 tomi in 6 vol. 8vo. Lips. 1799—1800.
———. Enchiridion, Cebetis Tabula, Prodici Hercules, et Cleanthis Hymnus; Omnia Gr. et Lat. 12mo. Glasg. 1744.
———. Manuale, et Cebetis Tabula, Gr. et Lat. a J. Schweighæusero. 8vo. Lips. 1798.
———. Epictetus his Morals, with Simplicius his Comments, made English from the Greek by G. Stanhope, &c. 4th ed. 8vo. Lond. 1721.
———. Works, translated from the Greek by Elizabeth Carter, with Notes, &c. 2d ed. 4to. Lond. 1759.
Epicurus. Fragmenta. (Herculanensium Voluminum quæ, etc.)
Epigrammata Antiquæ Urbis. 4to. Romæ. 1521.
——— et Poematia Vetera. 12mo. Paris. 1590.
Epiphanius, Sanctus. Opera. fol. Basil. 1544.
———, ———. Opera, Gr. et Lat. 2 tomi in 1 vol. fol. Paris. 1622.
——— ———, ———. De Ponderibus et Mensuris. (Ugol. vol. 28.)
Episcopal Church. Certain Briefe Treatises, by divers Learned Men, concerning Episcopacie. 4to. Oxford. 1641.
——— ———. Episcopal and Priestly Claims freely examined. 8vo. Lond. 1737.
——— ———. Address to the Protestant Episcopal Church of Maryland. To which is added a Sermon to the Convention, by William Smith. 8vo. Balt. 1784.
——— ———. Journal of the Proceedings of the Convention in Philadelphia. 8vo. Phil. 1790.
——— ———. Lessons and Hymns. 8vo.
——— ———. Journal of the Proceedings of the Convention in Maryland. 8vo. Balt. 1791.
——— ———. Journal of the Proceedings of the Convention in New-York. 8vo. N. York. 1792.
——— ———. Circular to the Clergy, &c. of the Eastern Diocese of the United States. 12mo. Bost. 1816.
——— ———. Trial of Episcopacy, by R. C. C. 18mo. Bost. 1817.

Episcopal Church. Pastoral Letter from the Bishops in the United States. 8vo. Phil. 1820.
——— ———. Address by A. Eaton, J. Morss, and T. Carlile. 8vo. 1820.
——— ———. Reply to the Review of Dr. Wyatt's Sermon and Mr. Sparks's Letters on the Episcopal Church, &c. 8vo. Bost. 1821.
——— ———. See Church.
Episcopius, Simon. Opera Theologica. Necnon Horæ Hebraicæ et Talmudicæ in Acta Apostolorum, etc.; auctore Johanne Lightfoot. fol. Hagæ-Com. 1678.
Epistle, Panegyrical, to Mr. Tho. Snow. 2d ed. fol. Lond. 1721.
Epistle, Poetical, to his Excellency George Washington. 4to. Lond. 1780.
———, ———, on the Fall of Man, (by J. Byron.) fol. Lond. 1749.
Epistles, Apostolical. See Macknight, J.
———, Elegant, from the Best Writers. See Knox, V.
———. See Letters. See Washington.
Epistola Pauli ad Galatas, etc. Arabice et Latine. Vide Spcy.
——— S. Judæ, Arabice et Latine. Vide Kirstenius.
——— D. Johannis, Syriace et Latine, ab A. Sennerto. 4to. Wittenberg. 1652.
Epistolæ Virorum Eruditorum. Vide Limborch, P. à.
Ἐπιτάφιοι τῶν Παλαιῶν. Funeral Eulogies upon Military Men. See Bentham, E.
Equinox, Autumnal. Compendious Way of finding it by Arithmetic. 8vo.
Erasmus, Desiderius. Opera Omnia, cum Notis Variorum, a J. Clerico. 10 vol. fol. Lug. Bat. 1703—6.
———, ———. Annotationes in Novum Testamentum. fol. Basil. 1522.
———, ———. Paraphrasis in Novum Testamentum. 4to. Hannov. 1668.
———, ———. Vide Testamentum Novum.
———, ———. Enchiridion Militis Christiani. 12mo. Lug. Bat. 1641.
———, ———. Moriæ Encomium, cum G. Listrii Commentariis. 12mo. Lug. Bat. 1648.
———, ———. Stultitiæ Laudatio. 12mo. Lond. 1765.
———, ———. Colloquia. 24to. Amst. 1650.
———, ———. ———. 12mo. Basil. 1656.
———, ———. ———, cum Notis Variorum, a C. Schrevelio. 8vo. Amst. 1693.
———, ———. ———, cum Scholiis. 8vo. Lond. 1717.
———, ———. Epistolarum D. Erasmi Libri xxxi; et P. Melancthonis Libri iv; quibus adjiciuntur T. Mori et L. Vivis Epistolæ. fol. Lond. 1642.
———, ———. Complaint of Peace; from the Latin. 8vo. Lond. 1802.

Erasmus, Desiderius. De Civilitate Morum Puerilium. 12mo. 1631. Rostochii.

———, ———. Idem. 12mo. 1733.

———, ———. Lingua. 16mo. Lug. Bat. 1641.

———, ———. Adagiorum Omnium, Gr. et Lat. Aureum Flumen, per T. Cortehoevium. 8vo. Antv. 1530. Vide etiam Adagia.

———, ———. Catalogus Lucubrationum, etc. 12mo. Basil. 1523.

———, ———. De Copia Verborum et Rerum. 16mo. Amst. 1645.

———, ———. Ecclesiastes. 8vo. Lond. 1730.

———, ———, Life of. See Jortin, J.

Erastus, Tho. De Excommunicatione. 4to. Pesclavii. 1589.

Eratosthenes. Geographicorum Fragmenta, a G. C. F. Seidel. 12mo. Goettingæ. 1789.

———. Catasterismi, Gr. et Lat. cum Commentario, cura J. C. Schaubach. 8vo. Gottingæ. 1795.

———. ———. Vide Opuscula Mythologica.

———. Cribrum. Vide Horsley, S. (Bp.)

Erberg, Mattia d'. Vide Biblia Italiana.

Ercilla, Alonso de. La Araucana. 2 vol. 8vo. Madrid. 1776.

Erdmann, Charles. Das Gelbe Fieber in Philadelphia. 8vo. Phil. 1799.

Ericus, Joh. Observationum ad Antiquitates Septentrionales pertinentium Specimen. 18mo. Hafniæ. 1769.

Erinna. Carmina. Vide Poetriæ Octo.

Erizzo, Sebastiano. Discorso sopra le Medaglie de gli Antichi. 4to. Vinegia. 1568.

———, ———. Le Sei Giornate. 8vo. Lond. 1794.

———, ———. ———. 8vo. Milano. 1805.

Ἑρμῆς ὁ Λόγιος. (Modern Greek Journal. 1813 and 1816. 2 vols. 8vo. Vienna.)

Ernesti, J. A. Clavis Ciceroniana. 8vo. Lips. 1738.

———, ———. Observationes Philologico-Criticæ in Aristophanis Nubes et Flav. Josephi Antiq. Jud. Accesserunt G. Olearii Notæ ad Suidam. 8vo. Lips. 1795.

———, ———. Neue Theologische Bibliothek. Vide Kraft, F. W.

———, ———. Prælectiones Theologico-Exegeticæ super Pauli Epistola ad Romanos. MS. Lips. 1766.

———, ———. Opuscula Philologica. ed. 2da. 8vo. Lug. Bat. 1776.

———, ———. Opuscula Theologica. ed. 2da. 8vo. Lips. 1792.

———, ———. Opuscula Varii Argumenti. 8vo. Lips. 1794.

———, ———. Opuscula Oratoria. 8vo. Lug. Bat. 1767.

Ernesti, J. C. G. Commentatio de Usu Vitæ Communis ad Interpretationem Novi Testamenti. (Muntinghe, Syl. Opusc.)

Ernesti, J. C. T. Lexicon Technologiæ Græcorum Rhetoricæ. 8vo. Lips. 1795.

Eroberung von Mexico und Peru; aus dem Französischen. 8vo. Frankf. und Leipz. 1770.

Erpenius, Tho. Rudimenta Linguæ Arabicæ.—Catalogus Librorum Arabicorum. 12mo. Leidæ. 1620.

———, ——. Rudimenta Linguæ Arabicæ. Florilegium Sententiarum Arabicarum, et Clavim Dialectorum adjecit A. Schultens. 4to. Lug. Bat. 1733.

———, ——. Grammatica Arabica, cum Fabulis Locmani, Arab. et Lat. etc. 4to. Lug. Bat. 1656.

———, ——. Idem, ab A. Schultens. 4to. Lug. Bat. 1748, et 1767.

———, ——. Orationes Tres de Linguarum Hebrææ atque Arabicæ Dignitate. 16mo. Leidæ. 1621.

Error, Innocency of, asserted and vindicated. 3d ed. 8vo. Lond. 1729.

Erskine. Reflections on Gaming, Annuities, and Usurious Contracts. 8vo. Lond. 1776.

Erskine, Eben. and Ralph. Sermons on Several Subjects. 8vo. Bost. 1744.

Erskine, John. Sketches of Church History and Theological Controversy. 2 vols. 12mo. Edin. 1790—97.

———, ——. Discourses. 8vo. Edin. 1798.

———, ——. Theological Dissertations. 12mo. Lond. 1765.

Erskine, Ralph. Sermons and Practical Works. 2 vols. fol. Glasgow. 1764—5.

———, ——. Gospel Sonnets. 12mo. Worcester. 1798.

———, ——. See Erskine, E.

Erskine, Tho. (Lord.) Speeches, collected by J. Ridgway. 2 vols. 8vo. N. York. 1813.

Erythræus, Janus Nicius. Vide Roscius, J. V.

Escalona, G. de. Gazophilacium Regium Perubicum. fol. Matriti. 1775.

Escandon, J. de. und B. Nusdorfer. Geschichte von Paraguay; aus Spanischen Handschriften übersetzt, etc. 12mo. Frankf. und Leipz. 1769.

Eschenawer, J. M. De Necessitate Bonorum Operum. 4to. Argent. 1706.

Eschenburg, J. J. Handbuch der Klassischen Literatur. 8vo. Berlin und Stettin. 1816.

———, ——. Vide Lessing.

Escobar, J. de. Vide Cid.

Escoiquiz, Juan de. Mexico Conquistada. 3 vol. 8vo. Madrid. 1798.

Esmangart, Charles. Des Colonies Françaises, et en particulier de Saint-Domingue. 8vo. Paris. 1802.

Espagne, J. d'. Eating of the Body of Christ, tr. out of French by J. Rivers. 12mo. Lond. 1655.

———, ——. Shibboleth, or Reformation of several Places in the Translations of Bibles. 12mo. Lond. 1655.

Espen, Z. B. van. Opera Omnia. 6 tomi in 3 vol. fol. Col. Agrip. 1729.

———, ———. Opera Omnia Canonica. 3 vol. fol. Lovanii. 1732.

Espine, J. de l'. Discourse touching the Tranquilitie and Contentation of the Minde; from the French. 4to. Camb. 1592.
Espriella's Letters. See Southey, R.
Esquilache, Fr. de Borja, Principe de. Obras en Verso. 4to. Amberes. 1663.
———, ———. Napoles Recuperada. 4to. Zaragoza. 1651.
Esquimaux Gospels. See Gospels.
Esquisse Intéressant du Tableau des Causes des Révolutions de l'Amérique Septentrionale. 8vo. Phil. 1783.
Ess, Leander van. Auszüge über das Nothwendige und Nützliche Bibellesen aus den Kirchenvätern, etc. 8vo. Sulzbach. 1816.
—, ———. Die Heiligen Schriften des Neuen Testaments übersetzt. 8vo. Sulzbach. 1820.
—, ———. Idem. 12mo. Sulzbach. 1821.
—, ———. ——. 8vo. Sulzbach. 1823.
Essayists, British. See Addison,—Cumberland,—Johnson,—World, Looker-on, &c.
Essays by the Students of the College of Fort William in Bengal, with Theses in the Oriental Languages. 8vo. Calcutta. 1802.
——— Commercial and Political. 8vo. Newcastle. 1777.
——— and Observations Physical and Literary. See Edinburgh.
Essex, Declaration of the County of, in Massachusetts, by its Delegates at Ipswich, July 21, 1812. 8vo. Salem. 1812.
Essex, A. Capel, Earl of. Letters, while Lord Lieutenant of Ireland, in 1675; with his Life. 4to. Lond. 1770.
Estaing, (M. le Comte d'.) Extrait du Journal d'un Officier de la Marine de son Escadre. 8vo. 1782.
Esteius, D. Oratio de Certitudine Salutis. 16mo. Amst. 1658.
Esther, Book of. See Barnes, J. See Yeates, T.
Estiene, Henri. Apologie pour Hérodote. 3 vol. 12mo. La Haye. 1735.
Estrades, Godfrey, Count d'. Letters and Negotiations; from the French. 3 vols. 8vo. Lond. 1711.
Estwick, Sam. Considerations on the Negro Cause, commonly so called. 2d ed. 8vo. Lond. 1773.
Etiro, Partenio. Vide Aretino, P.
Etlinger, Henricus. Pseudocatechista Racoviensis Explosus. 4to. Altd. 1705.
Etna. Vide Earthquakes.
Eton, W. Survey of the Turkish Empire. 8vo. Lond. 1799.
——. The Same. 3d ed. 8vo. Lond. 1801.
Etrobius, Jo. De Tuniceæ Urbis et Gouletæ Expugnatione. (Clauser, de Rebus Turcicis.)
Ettmüller, Mich. Opera Omnia. 2 vol. fol. Francof. ad Mœn. 1688, et 1708.
———, ——. Medicus Theoria et Praxi Generali Instructus. 4to. Francof. ac Lips. 1685.
Etymologicon Magnum, opera F. Sylburgii. 4to. Lips. 1816.
Euboicus, Nic. De Origine et Rebus Gestis Turcarum. (Clauser, de Rebus Turcicis.)

Eucharist. Two Discourses concerning the Adoration of our Saviour in the Eucharist. 4to. Oxford. 1687.
———. See Lord's Supper.
Eucherius Episcopus. Epistola ad Faustum Presbyterum. (Ugol. vol. 7.)
Eucherius de Quintiis, Camillus. Vide Quintiis.
Euclides. Opera Omnia, Gr. et Lat. ex recensione D. Gregorii. fol. Oxon. 1703.
———. Sex Libri Priores de Geometricis Principiis, Gr. et Lat. etc. a J. Scheubelio. fol. Basil. 1550.
———. Elementorum Libri Sex Priores, Lat. a C. Malapertio. 16mo. Duaci. 1620.
———. Elementorum Libri xv. Gr. et Lat. 12mo. Lutetiæ. 1557.
———. Elementorum Libri xv. Gr. et Lat.; item Data, Lat. opera I. Barrow. 12mo. Lond. 1659.
———. Datorum Liber. Vide Horsley, S. (Bp.)
———. Elements of Geometry, by J. Leeke and G. Serle. fol. Lond. 1661.
———. Elements; with Archimedes's Theorems of the Sphere and Cylinder, &c. by I. Barrow and T. Haselden. 8vo. Lond. 1732.
———. Elements, from the French of M. de Chales. 4th ed. 12mo. Lond. 1704.
———. Elements from the Latin Translation of Commandine. See Cunn, S.
———. Elements and Data, by R. Simson. 6th ed. 8vo. Edin. 1781.
———. Grondbeginsels der Meetkunst, door P. Steenstra. 8vo. Leyden. 1779.
———. Introductio Harmonica, Gr. et Lat. Vide Musicæ Auctores Antiquæ.
Eugenio, or Virtuous and Happy Life. (By T. Beach.) fol. Lond. 1737.
Euler, Leonhardus. Institutiones Calculi Differentialis. 4to. Berol. 1755.
———, ———. Introductio in Analysin Infinitorum. 2 vol. 4to. Lugd. 1797.
———, ———. Methodus Inveniendi Lineas Curvas. 4to. Lausan. et Genev. 1744.
———, ———. Scientia Navalis. 2 vol. 4to. Petropoli. 1749.
———, ———. Letters on Physics and Philosophy, tr. from the French, by H. Hunter. 2d ed. 2 vols. 8vo. Lond. 1802.
Eunapius. De Vitis Philosophorum et Sophistarum. 12mo. Col. Allob. 1616.
Euphormionis Lusinini, sive J. Barclaii Satyricon; accessit Conspiratio Anglicana. 18mo. Lug. Bat. 1655.
——————— ———. Vide Barclaius, J.
Euphrasén, B. A. Reise nach St. Barthelemi, St. Eustache und St. Christoph; aus dem Schwedischen. 12mo. Göttin. 1798.
Euripides. Tragœdiæ, Fragmenta, Epistolæ, Gr. et Lat. ex editione J. Barnesii, cum Scholiis, et Notis Variorum, cura C. D. Beckii. 3 vol. 4to. Lipsiæ. 1778—88.

Euripides. Tragœdiæ et Fragmenta, cum Scholiis Gr. et Notis, cura A. Matthiæ. 8 vol. 8vo. Lips. 1813—24.

———. Tragœdiæ, Gr. et Lat. ex recensione S. Musgrave. Item Epistolæ et Fragmenta. 10 vol. 8vo. Glasguæ. 1797.

———. Medea et Phœnissæ, Gr. et Lat. cum Scholiis Gr. etc.; opera W. Piers. 8vo. Cant. 1703.

———. Medea, cum Annotationibus, a P. Elmsley. 8vo. Oxon. 1818.

———. Hecuba, cum G. Hermanni Animadversionibus. 8vo. Lips. 1800.

———. Hecuba, Orestes, Phœnissæ, et Medea, cum Notis, a R. Porson. 8vo. Lips. 1807.

———. Alcestis, cum Diatriba, et Annotatione perpetua, a G. A. Wagner. 8vo. Lips. 1800.

———. Ion, cum Notis et Commentario perpetuo, etc. studio F. Hülsemann. 8vo. Lips. 1801.

———. Iphigenia in Aulide, cum Commentario, a J. G. C. Höpfner. 8vo. Halæ. 1795.

———. Hercules Furens, a G. Hermanno. 12mo. Lips. 1810.

———. Supplices Mulieres, Gr. et Lat. cum Notis. Accedit Quæstio Grammatica de Græcorum Quinta Declinatione Imparisyllabica, etc. 4to. Lond. 1763.

———. Troades, Electra, et Iphigenia in Tauris, cum Notis, ab A. Seidler. 12mo. Lips. 1812—13.

———. Hippolytus, cum Annotationibus, cura J. H. Monk. 8vo. Cant. 1811.

———. Tragedies, translated by R. Potter. 2 vols. 4to. Lond. 1781—3.

———. Medea, Treurspel, naar het Grieksch van Euripides in Jambische Verzen gevolgd door N. G. van Kampen. 8vo. Haarlem. 1811.

———. Vide Heath, B.,—Jacobs, F.,—Wagner, G.

Europe, Secret History of. 4th ed. 8vo. Lond. 1724.

———, Present State of. 6th ed. 8vo. Lond. 1761.

———, General Table of. 4to. 1669.

———, Political State of, for the year 1792. 8vo.

———. See Danverian History,—Everett,—Lessons,—Wise, &c.

Eusebius Pamphilus, (Episc.) Præparatio Evangelica, Gr. et Lat. cum Notis, a Fr. Vigero. fol. Paris. 1628.

———, ———. Chronicon, ab Hieronymo Latine versum. 4to. Paris. 1518.

———, ———. Thesaurus Temporum Eusebii, Gr. et Lat. cum Notis, etc. a J. Scaligero. fol. Amst. 1658.

———, ———. Historia Ecclesiastica, et de Vita Imp. Constantini; quibus subjicitur Oratio Constantini ad Sanctos, et Panegyricus Eusebii; Gr. et Lat. cum Adnotationibus, ab H. Valesio. fol. Moguntiæ. 1672.

———, ———. Eusebii Pamphili, Socratis Scholastici, Hermiæ Sozomeni, Theodoriti et Evagrii, item Philostorgii et Theodori Lectoris, Historiæ Ecclesiasticæ, Gr. et Lat. cum Annotationibus, a G. Reading. 3 vol. fol. Cant. 1720.

Eusebius Pamphilus, (Episc.) Ecclesiastical Historie. See Hanmer, M.

——— ———————. Liber contra Hieroclem. Vide Philostratus.

——— ———————. Commentarii in Psalmos et in Hesaiam. Vide Montfaucon.

——— ———————. Onomasticon, Latina Interpretatione S. Hieronymi, etc. (Ugol. vol. 5.)

Eustace, J. C. Classical Tour through Italy. 2 vols. 8vo. Phil. 1816.

Eustace, J. S. Lettres sur les Crimes du Roi George III. 8vo. Paris.

———, —. Official and Private Correspondence. 8vo. Paris. 1796.

Eustachius, Bart. Tabulæ Anatomicæ, cum Notis, etc. J. M. Lancisii. fol. Romæ. 1728.

Eustachius, Fr. Summa Philosophiæ Quadripartita; de Rebus Dialecticis, Ethicis, Physicis, et Metaphysicis. 8vo. Cant. 1648.

————, —. Ethica. 16mo. Cant. 1654.

Eustathius. De Ismeniæ et Ismenes Amoribus, Gr. et Lat. a L. H. Teuchero. 12mo. Lips. 1792.

Eustathius. Commentarii in Dionysium Periegetam, ab A. Polito. 8vo. Col. Allob. 1741.

————. Commentarii in Homeri Iliadem, Gr. et Lat. cum Notis, ab A. Polito. 3 vol. fol. Florentiæ. 1730—5.

Eutropius. Historiæ Romanæ Breviarium, in Usum Delphini. 4to. Paris. 1683.

Evagrius Scholasticus. Vide Eusebius,—Theodoretus,—et Hanmer, H.

Evangelia, Arabice et Latine. fol. Romæ. 1591.

————. Evangeliorum Fragmenta, Græce, MS.

————, Gothice et Anglo-Saxonice, cum Notis T. Mareschalli. Accessit Glossarium Gothicum, etc. F. Junii. 4to. Dordrechti. 1665.

————, Gothice, cum Interpretatione Latina et Annotationibus E. Benzelii. Edidit, Observationes suas adjecit, et Grammaticam Gothicam præmisit E. Lye. 4to. Oxon. 1750.

————, Persice et Latine, per A. Whelocum. fol. Lond. 1657.

————. See Gospel.

Evangeliarium Quadruplex. Vide Blanchinus.

Evangelical Guardian and Review. vol. 1. Nos. 1—4. 8vo. N. York. 1817.

———— Treasury. Proposal for one, humbly tendered to the Churches. 4to.

Evangelistarium, Gr. MS.

Evangelistarum iv Collatio. Vide Anecdota Græca, a Wolfio.

Evangelium secundum Matthæum. Vide Barrett, J.

Evans, Caleb. Discourses on the Atonement. 12mo. Bristol. 1789.

Evans, Charles. Report of Judge Chase's Trial. 8vo. Balt. 1805.

Evans, Estwick. Pedestrious Tour of Four Thousand Miles through the Western States, &c. in 1818. 12mo. Concord, N. H. 1819.
Evans, Israel. Thanksgiving Sermon for the Peace. 8vo. N. York. 1783.
Evans, J. Fast Sermon. 4to. Charles-Town, S. C. 1745.
Evans, John. Letter to Mr. Cumming concerning Scripture-Consequences. 8vo. Lond. 1719.
———, ——. Second Letter. 8vo. Lond. 1722.
———, ——. Thanksgiving Sermon. 4to. and 8vo. Lond. 1706.
———, ——. Sermon, Nov. 5th. 8vo. Lond. 1720.
———, ——. Sermon on the Death of the Rev. Daniel Williams. 8vo. Lond. 1716.
———, ——. Sermon on the Death of Mrs. A. King. 8vo. Lond. 1726.
———, ——. Fast Sermon. 8vo. Lond. 1727.
———, ——. Coronation Sermon. 8vo. Lond. 1722.
———, ——. ——————. 8vo. Lond. 1727.
———, ——. Sermon upon 2 Kings iv, 26. 8vo. Lond. 1727.
———, ——. Sermon on Reformation of Manners. 12mo. Lond. 1707.
———, ——. Sermon to Young People. 8vo. Lond. 1717.
———, ——. ——————. 8vo. Lond. 1728.
———, ——. Practical Discourses on the Christian Temper. 2 vols. 8vo. Lond. 1723.
———, ——. The Same. 2d ed. 2 vols. 8vo. Lond. 1725.
———, ——. ————. 6th ed. 2 vols. 8vo. Lond. 1770.
———, ——. Charity Sermon. 8vo. Lond. 1729.
———, ——. Sermon from 2 Chron. xv, 2. 8vo. Lond. 1720.
———, ——, and James Read. Three Sermons on Opening a New Meeting-Place. 8vo. Lond. 1730.
Evans, John. Sketch of the Denominations of the Christian World. 12mo. Bost. 1807.
———, ——. Sequel to the Sketch of the Denominations of the Christian World. 12mo. Bost. 1811.
Evans, Lewis. Geographical, Historical, Political, Philosophical, and Mechanical Essays. 4to. Phil. 1755.
———, ——. The Same, MS. fol.
Evanson, Edw. Dissonance of the Evangelists. 2d ed. 8vo. Gloucester. 1805.
———, ——. Letter to Dr. Priestley's Young Man, &c. respecting the above. 8vo. Ipswich. 1794.
———, ——. Arguments against and for the Sabbatical Observance of Sunday. 8vo. Ipswich. 1792.
Evanthius et Donatus. De Tragœdia et Comœdia. (Gronov. vol. 8.)
Evarts, Jeremiah. Oration, July 4th. 8vo. Charlestown. 1812.
Eveleigh, John. Bampton Lecture Sermons, &c. 8vo. Oxford. 1794.
Evelyn, John. Discourse of Medals. fol. Lond. 1697.
———, ——. Sylva; or a Discourse of Forest-Trees, with Notes by A. Hunter. 4to. York. 1776.
———, ——. Sculptura, or the History and Art of Chalcography. 2d ed. 12mo. Lond. 1755.

Evelyn, John. Fumifugium. 4to. Lond. 1661.
——, ——. Memoirs of his Life and Writings; with the Private Correspondence between Charles I, and Sir E. Nicholas, &c. 2d ed. 2 vols. 4to. Lond. 1819.
Everett, Alex. H. Eighteen Hundred and Twenty; a Poem. Part 1. 8vo. Lond. 1821.
——, ——. Europe. 8vo. Bost. 1822.
——, ——. A Few Notes on certain Passages in the North American Review respecting "Europe." 8vo. Bost. 1823.
——, ——. New Ideas on Population. 8vo. Bost. 1823.
——, ——. America. 8vo. Phil. 1827.
Everett, Edw. Defence of Christianity against G. B. English. 12mo. Bost. 1814.
——, ——. Sermon at the Interment of the Rev. J. L. Abbot. 8vo. Bost. 1814.
——, ——. Sermon at the Dedication of the First Congregational Church in New York. 8vo. Bost. 1821.
——, ——. On an Inscription from the Columbarium of the Freedmen and Slaves of Livia Augusta. (Mem. A. A. S. vol. 4.)
——, ——. Account of Greek Manuscripts procured at Constantinople, now in Harvard College Library. (Id.)
——, ——. Letter to John Lowell, Esq. in Reply to his "Remarks on a Pamphlet printed by the Professors and Tutors of Harvard University." 8vo. Bost. 1824.
——, ——. Synopsis of a Course of Lectures on the History of Greek Literature. 8vo.
——, ——. Oration before the Phi Beta Kappa Society. 8vo. Bost. 1824.
——, ——. Oration at Plymouth, Dec. 22, 1824. 8vo. Bost. 1825.
——, ——. Oration at Concord, April 19, 1825. 8vo. Bost. 1825.
——, ——. Claims of Citizens of the United States on Naples, Holland, and France. 8vo. Camb. 1826.
——, ——. Speech in Congress on the Subject of Retrenchment. 8vo. Washington. 1828.
——, ——. Address at the Erection of a Monument to John Harvard, Sept. 26, 1828. 8vo. Bost. 1828.
Everett, John. Oration before the Senior Class of Harvard University. 8vo. Bost. 1818.
Everett, Moses. Sermon at the Ordination of the Rev. Oliver Everett. 8vo. Bost. 1782.
Everett, Oliver. Eulogy on Washington. 8vo. Charlestown. 1800.
Evia, Xacinto de. Ramillete de Varias Flores Poeticas. 4to. Madrid. 1676.
Ewer, John, (Bp.) Sermon before the Society for the Propagation of the Gospel in Foreign Parts. 4to. Lond. 1767.
——, ————. Remarks on the above Sermon. See Chauncy, C.
——, ————. Letter to him from a Petitioner. 8vo. Marlb. 1774.

Ewes, Sir Simonds d'. Journals of all the Parliaments during the Reign of Queen Elizabeth; by P. Bowes. fol. Lond. 1682.
Ewing, Alex. Synopsis of Practical Mathematics. 8vo. Edin. 1779.
Ewing, John. Account of the Transit of Venus and Mercury over the Sun.—Improvement in the Construction of Godfrey's (commonly called Hadley's) Quadrant. (Amer. Phil. Tr. vol. 1.)
Excerpta Varia Græcorum Sophistarum ac Rhetorum, Gr. et Lat. cum Notis, a L. Allatio. 8vo. Romæ. 1641.
——— ex Historicis Græcis. 12mo. Lips. 1778.
——— e Scriptoribus Latinis, cum Notis. 8vo. Bost. 1810.
——— ex Auctoribus Classicis, in usum Collegii Stæ. Mariæ Baltimorensis. 2 vol. 12mo. Balt. 1820.
Excise Laws, Short History of the Nature and Consequences of, &c. 8vo. Phil. 1795.
Executors, Office and Duty of. 12mo. Lond. 1641.
Exegetisches Handbuch des Neuen Testamentes. 5 vol. 8vo. Leipz. 1794—1800.
Exeter College, Defence of the Rector and Fellows of, against the Accusations of Dr. Huddesford. 8vo. Lond. 1754.
Exhortation addressed to the People of London, occasioned by a Proclamation for a Fast. 8vo. Lond. 1756.
Exmoor Scolding, &c. 6th ed. 8vo. Exon. 1668.
Exon, Account of what was transacted in the Assembly of Ministers at. 8vo. Lond. 1719.
——. See Enty, J.—Hallett, J.—Peirce, J.
Expatriation, Review of Hay's Treatise on, (by J. Lowell.) 8vo. Bost. 1814.
Experience preferable to Theory; an Answer to Dr. Price's Observations on Civil Liberty, &c. 8vo. Lond. 1776.
Experiens, P. Callimachus. De Uladislao Rege, sive Clade Varnensi. (Clauser de Rebus Turcicis.)
Exter, Joachimus ab. De Podagra, etc. 8vo. Franeq. 1789.
Extracts. See Elegant Extracts.
Eybenius. De Ordine Equestri Veterum Romanorum. (Sallengre, vol. 1.)
Eyre, Robert. Assize Sermon. 4to. Lond. 1700.
——, ——. Sermon, Jan. 30th. 8vo. Lond. 1708.

F

FABER, BASIL. Thesaurus Eruditionis Scholasticæ. fol. Lips. 1726.
——, ——. Idem. 2 vol. fol. Francof. et Lips. 1749.
Faber, Geo. Stanley. Dissertation on the Prophecies. 2 vols. 8vo. Lond. 1806.
——, ——. A Practical Treatise on the Ordinary Operations of the Holy Spirit. 8vo. Lond. 1813.
——, ——. Horæ Mosaicæ, the Substance of Eight Sermons at the Bampton Lecture. 2 vols. 8vo. Oxford. 1801.
——, ——. Remarks on the Pyramid of Cephrenes. (Classical Journal. vol. 21.)
Faber, J. Psalterium Quincuplex. Vide Psalterium.
Faber, John. Kit-Cat Club, done from the Original Paintings of Sir Godfrey Kneller. fol. 1735.
Faber, P. De Re Athletica, Ludisque Veterum Gymnicis, Musicis, etc. (Gronov. vol. 8.)
——, —. De Magistratibus Romanorum. (Sallengre, vol. 3.)
Faber, Tanaquil. Method of Teaching the Learned Languages. See Phillips, J. T.
——, ——. Vitæ Poetarum Græcorum. (Gronov. vol. 10.)
Fabre, J. C. Vide Fleury, Claude.
Fabregou, M. Description des Plantes qui naissent ou se renouvellent aux Environs de Paris. 6 vol. 12mo. Paris. 1740.
Fabretti, Raph. De Aquis et Aquæductibus Veteris Romæ. 4to. Romæ. 1680.
——, ——. Idem. (Grævius, vol. 4.)
——, ——. Inscriptionum Antiquarum quæ in Ædibus Paternis asservantur Explicatio, etc. fol. Romæ. 1702.
Fabricias, or Letters to the People of Great Britain on the American War. 8vo. Lond. 1782.
Fabricius, Geo. Antiquitatis Monumenta ex Marmoribus, etc. veteribus collecta. 12mo. Basil. 1549.
——, ——. Descriptio Urbis Romæ. (Grævius, vol. 3.)
Fabricius, Guido. Vide Boderianus, G. F.
Fabricius, Hieron. Opera Chirurgica. ed. 25ta. fol. Patavii. 1666.
——, ——. Opera Omnia Anatomica et Physiologica. fol. Lips. 1687.
Fabricius Hildanus, Guil. Opera Omnia. Additus M. A. Severini Liber de Efficaci Medicina. fol. Francof. ad Mœn. 1646.
——, ——. Idem. fol. Francof. ad Mœn. 1682.
Fabricius, J. L. De Ludis Scenicis. (Gronov. vol. 8.)

Fabricius, Jo. Historia Bibliothecæ Fabricianæ. 6 vol. in 3. 4to. Wolffenb. 1717—23.
Fabricius, Jo. Alb. Bibliotheca Græca. 14 vol. 4to. Hamb. 1708—28.
———, ———. Idem. 14 vol. 4to. Hamb. 1718—28.
———, ———. Bibliotheca Latina. 2 vol. 4to. Venet. 1728.
———, ———. Idem, ab Ernesti. 3 vol. 4to. Lips. 1773—4.
———, ———. Bibliotheca Ecclesiastica. fol. Hamb. 1718.
———, ———. Bibliographia Antiquaria. 4to. Hamb. et Lips. 1716.
———, ———. Salutaris Lux Evangelii Toti Orbi per Divinam Gratiam exoriens. 4to. Hamb. 1731.
———, ———. Codex Pseudepigraphus Veteris Testamenti. 2 vol. 12mo. Hamb. 1722—3.
———, ———. Vide Josephus, Vet. Christ. Scriptor.
———, ———. Codex Apochryphus Novi Testamenti. 3 vol. 12mo. Hamb. 1719.
———, ———. Delectus Argumentorum, et Syllabus Scriptorum qui Veritatem Religionis Christianæ asseruerunt. 4to. Hamb. 1725.
Fabricius, Joh. Christ. Entomologia. 8 vol. 8vo. Hafniæ, etc. 1775—94.
———, ———. Mantissa Insectorum. 2 vol. 8vo. Hafniæ. 1787.
———, ———. Voyage en Norwège, etc. trad. de l'Allemand. 8vo. Paris. 1802.
Fabricius, Otho. Fauna Groenlandica. 8vo. Hafn. et Lips. 1780.
Fabritius, K. M. E. Ueber den Herrschenden Unfug auf teutschen Universitäten, Gymnasien und Lycäen. 8vo. Mainz. 1822.
Fabronius, Ang. Vitæ Italorum. 20 vol. 8vo. Pisis. 1778—1805.
Facciolatus, J. See Forcellinus.
Facilides, S. G. De Auctoritate Canonica Apocalypseos Johannis. 4to. Lips. 1751.
Facius, Barthol. De Bello Veneto Clodiano. (Græv. Thes. Ital.)
———, ———. De Rebus Gestis ab Alphonso Primo, Neapolitanorum Rege. (Id.)
Fac Simile des Aeltesten bisher bekannten Teutschen Druckes. 4to. München. 1808.
Facts and Documents relating to the Controversy between Great Britain and America. 8vo. Bost. 1813.
Faerno, Gabr. Centum Fabulæ ex Antiquis Auctoribus delectæ. 12mo. Lond. 1672.
Fæschius, Sebast. De Nummo Pylæmenis Evergetæ, Regis Paphlagoniæ. (Gonov. vol. 9.)
Fagel, G. (Baron de.) Letter concerning the Repeal of the Test and the Penal Laws. 4to.
———, ——— ———, Animadversions on the above. 4to. Lond. 1688.
Fairbanks, Jason. Report of his Trial for the Murder of Elizabeth Fales. 1st, 2d, and 3d editions. 8vo. Bost. 1801.

Faireclough, John. Vide Featley, D.

Fairfax, Edw. Recovery of Jerusalem, done into English Heroical Verse from the Italian of Tasso, &c. 5th ed. 2 vols. 12mo. Windsor. 1817.

Faith, Account of, in Answer to a Roman Catholick. 4to. Lond. 1661.

—— Necessary to Salvation, &c. 4to. Oxford. 1688.

——, Inquiry concerning. 8vo. Lond. 1744.

——. Discourse on the Nature and Excellency of Saving Faith, &c. 12mo. Bost. 1742.

——, Law, and Church of Christ. Fundamental Positions, &c. concerning them. fol.

—— and Practice represented in Fifty-four Sermons, by Six Ministers. 2 vols. 8vo. Lond. 1735, and 1739.

——. See Articles of Religion,—Creeds,—Religion, &c.

Falcandus, Hugo. De Rebus Gestis in Siciliæ Regno Historia. (Græv. Thes. Ital.)

Falco, Bened. de. Antiquitates Neapolis, etc. (Græv. Thes. Ital.)

Falconbridge, Alex. Account of the Slave Trade on the Coast of Africa. 2d ed. 16mo. Lond. 1788.

Falconer, Tho. Bampton Lecture Sermons. 8vo. Oxford. 1811.

Falconer, Wm. The Shipwreck. 3d ed. 8vo. Lond. 1769.

————, ——. Poems. See Chalmers, A.

————, ——. Universal Dictionary of the Marine. 4to. Lond. 1769.

Falconer, Wm. Remarks on the Influence of Climate, &c. on the Disposition, Manners, &c. of Mankind. 8vo. Lond. 1781.

————, ——. On the Poison of Copper. 12mo. Lond. 1774.

Falconerius, Octavius. De Pyramide C. Cestii Epulonis.—De Latere ex Ædificii Vet. Ruderibus eruto, etc. (Grævius, vol. 4.)

—————, ————. Inscriptiones Athleticæ Notis illustratæ. (Gronov. vol. 8.)

—————, ————. De Nummo Apamensi, Deucalionei Diluvii Typum exhibente. (Id. vol. 10.)

Falconet, Camille. Sur les Principes de l'Etymologie.—Sur le Mot *Dunum*.—Sur les Anciennes Horloges. (Acad. des Inscrip. vol. 20.)

Falda, G. B. Le Fontane di Roma, disegnate et intagliate da G. B. Falda, date in luce da G. G. de Rossi. fol.

Faldo, John. Twenty one Divines defended against William Penn's "Just Rebuke." 8vo. Lond. 1675.

Falkland, H. Cary, Lord. Of the Infallibilitie of the Church of Rome; with a View of the Exceptions to it by a Romanist. 8vo. Oxford. 1646.

————, ——————. History of Edward II, King of England; with the Rise and Fall of his Favorites, Gaveston and the Spencers. fol. Lond. 1680.

Falkland's Island. Papers relating to the late Negociation with Spain, and the Taking of Falkland's Island from the British. 4to. Lond. 1777.

Falkner, Tho. Description of Patagonia, &c. 4to. Hereford. 1774.

Falkner, Wm. Vindication of Liturgies. 8vo. Lond. 1680.
——, ——. Two Treatises;—1. on Reproaching and Censure; 2. an Answer to Mr. Serjeant's Sure-Footing: with Three Sermons. 4to. Lond. 1684.
Fallopius, Gabr. Opera Omnia. 2 tomi in 1 vol. fol. Francof. 1600.
Falsterus, Christ. Amœnitates Philologicæ. 8vo. Amst. 1729.
Familiæ Romanæ Nobiliores, e Fulvii Ursini Commentariis. (Grævius, vol. 7.)
Family Prayers and Moral Essays in Prose and Verse. 8vo. Lond. 1769.
—— Tablet, containing a Selection of Original Poetry. 12mo. Bost. 1796.
—— Worship, Letter to the Protestant Dissenters relating to the Neglect of. 8vo. Lond. 1720.
Fancourt, Sam. Sermon at the Ordination of the Rev. H. Lane. 8vo. Sarum. 1734.
——, ——. Essay concerning Certainty and Infallibility. 8vo. Lond. 1720.
——, ——. Enthusiasm Retorted. 8vo. Lond. 1722.
——, ——. Greatness of Divine Love vindicated. 8vo. Lond. 1727.
——, ——. What Will be, Must be; or Future Contingencies No Contingencies. 8vo. Sarum. 1730.
——, ——. Appendix to the above. 8vo. Lond. 1732.
——, ——. Certain Futurity of Free Actions No Contradiction, in Answer to his Pamphlet on Free Agency. 8vo. Lond. 1733.
——, ——. Narrative. 4to. Lond. 1747.
Fara, J. F. De Rebus Sardois Historia. (Græv. Thes. Ital.)
Farbaky, Joh. De Justitia Christi nobis per Fidem imputata. 4to Altorfii. 1736.
Faringdon, Anthony. Sermons. 3 vols. in 2. fol. Lond. 1672—4.
Farmer, Hugh. Inquiry into the Nature and Design of Christ's Temptations in the Wilderness. 2d ed. 8vo. Lond. 1765.
——, ——. The Same. 3d ed. 8vo. Lond.
——, ——. ——. 4th ed. 12mo. Lond. 1805.
——, ——. Essay on the Demoniacs of the New Testament. 8vo. Lond. 1775.
——, ——. The Same. 2d ed. 12mo. Lond. 1805.
——, ——. Letter to Dr. Worthington in Answer to his "Impartial Enquiry into the Case of the Gospel Demoniacks." 8vo. Lond. 1778.
——, ——. Dissertation on Miracles. 8vo. Lond. 1771.
——, ——. The Same. 8vo. Edin. 1798.
——, ——. ——. 12mo. Lond. 1804.
——, ——. Examination of Mr. Le Moine's Treatise on Miracles. 8vo. Lond. 1772.
——, ——. Prevalence of the Worship of Human Spirits in the Ancient Heathen Nations. 8vo. Lond. 1783.

Farmer, John. Historical Memoir of Billerica, Mass. 8vo. Amherst, N. H. 1816.
———, ———. Historical Sketch of Amherst, N. H. 8vo. Amherst. 1820.
———, ———, and J. B. Moore. Gazetteer of New-Hampshire. 12mo. Concord. 1823.
Farmers, Address to, on interesting Subjects. 12mo. Salem. 1796.
Farquhar, John. Sermons. 3d ed. 2 vols. 12mo. Lond. 1778.
Farr, Sam. On Animal Motion. 8vo. Lond. 1771.
———, ———. Elements of Medical Jurisprudence. 12mo. Lond. 1815.
Farrar, John. Elementary Treatise on Arithmetic, taken principally from the Arithmetic of Lacroix, and tr. into English, with Alterations and Additions. 2d ed. 8vo. Camb. N. E. 1821.
———, ———. Introduction to the Elements of Algebra, selected from the Algebra of Euler. 2d ed. 8vo. Camb. N. E. 1821.
———, ———. Elements of Algebra, tr. from the French of S. F. Lacroix. 8vo. Camb. N. E. 1818.
———, ———. The Same. 2d ed. 8vo. Camb. N. E. 1825.
———, ———. Elements of Geometry, tr. from the French of A. M. Legendre. 8vo. Camb. N. E. 1819.
———, ———. The Same. 2d ed. 8vo. Camb. N. E. 1825.
———, ———. Elementary Treatise of Plane and Spherical Trigonometry, tr. from the French of Lacroix and Bézout. 8vo. Camb. N. E. 1820.
———, ———. The Same. 2d ed. 8vo. Camb. N. E. 1826.
———, ———. Elementary Treatise on the Application of Trigonometry. 8vo. Camb. 1822.
———, ———. First Principles of the Differential and Integral Calculus, taken chiefly from the Mathematics of Bézout, and tr. from the French. 8vo. Camb. N. E. 1824.
———, ———. Elementary Treatise of Mechanics. 8vo. Camb. N. E. 1825.
———, ———. Elements of Electricity, Magnetism, and Electro-Magnetism. 8vo. Camb. N. E. 1826.
———, ———. Experimental Treatise of Optics. 8vo. Camb. N. E. 1826.
———, ———. Elementary Treatise of Astronomy. 8vo. Camb. N. E. 1827.
———, ———. Elements of Natural Philosophy, by E. S. Fischer, tr. from the French of Biot. 8vo. Bost. 1827.
———, ———. Account of the Storm of the 23d of September, 1815. (Mem. A. A. S. vol. 4.)
Farrar, Timothy. Report of the Case of the Trustees of Dartmouth College against William H. Woodward. 8vo. Portsmouth, N. H. 1819.
Farre, J. R. On Malformations of the Human Heart. 8vo. Lond. 1814.
Farrer, John. Sermons at the Bampton Lecture. 8vo. Oxford. 1804.

Farresley, Tho. Reports in B. R. in the time of Sir John Holt. fol. Lond. 1716.
Farrol, Geo. Thanksgiving Sermon. 8vo. Lond. 1716.
Fascitellus, Honoratus. Carmina. 4to. Patavii. 1731.
——, ——. In Obitum Arsilli Medici et Poetæ. (Poem. Ital.)
Fasoldus, Joh. De Festis Græcorum. (Gronov. vol. 7.)
Fast Sermon on Isaiah lix. 1, 2. 12mo. Lond. 1718.
———— on Psalm lxviii, 30. 2d ed. 8vo. Lond. 1712.
————. See Devil Let Loose.
—— Sermons, from 1770 to 1801. 8vo.
Fasti Consulares Anonymi, cum Dissertatione H. Noris. (Grævius. vol. 11.)
——. Anonymus de Præfectis Urbi ex temporibus Gallieni; ut et Fragmentum Fastorum ab Anno Christi 205 ad 354. (Id.)
Fathers. Vide Monumenta S. Patrum Orthodoxographa.
Fauchet, J. Coup d'Œil sur l'Etat Actuel de nos Rapports Politiques avec les Etats-Unis. 8vo. Paris. 1797.
Faucon, N. Grammaire Française. 12mo. Bost. 1810.
Faujas de Saint Fond. Mémoires dans les Annales du Muséum d'Histoire Naturelle.
Fauno, Lucio. Delle Antichità della Citta di Roma. 12mo. Venet. 1548.
——, ——. De Antiquitatibus Romæ. (Sallengre, vol. 1.)
Faustinus Presbyter. Opera. 12mo. Oxon. 1678.
Fawcett, Benj. Sermon on the encouraging Prospect that Religious Liberty will be enlarged. 8vo. Shrewsbury. 1773.
———, ——. See Baxter, R.
Fawcett, J. Sermons. 8vo. Lond. 1749.
Fawcett, Joseph. Sermons at the Old Jewry. 2 vols. 8vo. Lond. 1801.
Fawkes, Fr. Idylliums of Theocritus, tr. from the Greek into English Verse, with Notes. 8vo. Lond. 1767.
———, —. The Same. See Chalmers, A.
———, —. Argonautics of Apollonius Rhodius.—Rape of Helen by Coluthus.—Works of Anacreon.—Works of Sappho.—Idylliums of Bion and Moschus.—Loves of Hero and Leander by Musæus. All tr. into English Verse. See Chalmers, A.
———, —. Poems. See Chalmers, A.
Faxardo, Diego de Saavedra. Republica Literaria. 8vo. Madrid. 1788.
Faye, Geo. de la. Principes de Chirurgie. 12mo. Paris. 1761.
Fayette, Marquis de la. See Washington.
Fayus, Jac. Defensio Religionis, necnon Mosis et Gentis Judaicæ. 12mo. Ultrajecti. 1709.
Fazellus, Tho. De Rebus Siculis. fol. Panormi. 1558.
———, ———. ————————. 2 vol. fol. Catanæ. 1749—51.
———, ———. ————————. (Græv. Thes. Ital.)
Fearne, Charles. On Contingent Remainders and Executory Devises. 2 vols. 8vo. Dublin. 1794—6.
Fearon, H. B. Sketches of America. 8vo. Lond. 1818.
Featley, Dan. (Faireclough.) League Illegal. 4to. Lond. 1660.

Featley, Dan. (Fairclough.) Clavis Mystica. fol. Lond. 1636.
———, —————. Sermon at the Funeral of Mr. Bennet. 8vo. Lond. 1708.
Febronius, Justinus. De Statu Ecclesiæ. 4to. Col. et Franc. 1777.
Feder, C. A. L. Observationum Criticarum in Auctores Vet. Gr. et Lat. Specimen Quadruplex. 8vo. Heidelb., etc. 1818.
Federal Government, Essay on the Seat of the, &c. 8vo. Phil. 1789.
Federalist, on the New Constitution, written in 1788 by Mr. Hamilton, Mr. Madison, and Mr. Jay. 8vo. Hallowell, (Me.) 1826.
————. Le Fédéraliste, trad. de l'Anglois. 2 vol. 8vo. Paris. 1792.
Federalist, containing Strictures on Phocion's Pamphlet against Thomas Jefferson's Pretensions to the Presidency; in Two Parts. 8vo. Phil. 1796.
Fees, Table of. 12mo. Lond. 1694.
Fehmelius, A. G. De Criteriis Errorum circa Religionem Communibus. 4to. Lips. 1713.
Fein, Chr. Fr. De Signis Temporum dijudicandis ad Matth. xvi, 3. 4to. Helmst. 1725.
Feithius, Everardus. Antiquitates Homericæ. (Gronov. vol. 6.)
Felde, Joh. à. Elementa Juris Universi et, in specie, Publici Justinianæi. 4to. Franc. et Lips. 1664.
Felini, P. M. Trattato Nuovo delle Cose Maravigliose di Roma. 12mo. Roma. 1610.
Felinus, Aretius. Vide Bucer.
Felix, M. Minucius. Octavius; C. Cyprianus de Idolorum Vanitate, cum Observationibus N. Rigaltii; et Julius Firmicus de Profana ac Vera Religione. 16mo. Oxon. 1662.
———, —————. Octavius, cum Notis Variorum, ex recensione J. Gronovii. Accedunt C. Cyprianus de Idolorum Vanitate, et J. Firmicus de Errore Profanarum Religionum. 8vo. Lug. Bat. 1709.
———, —————. Octavius, and Tertullian's Apology for the Primitive Christians, rendered into English. 8vo. Lond. 1708.
———, —————. See Reeves, W.
Fell, John, (Bp.) Gentleman's Calling. 8vo. Lond. 1677.
———, —————. Ladies Calling. 8vo. Oxford. 1677.
———, —————. Whole Duty of Man.—Gentleman's Calling.—Ladies Calling.—Government of the Tongue.—Art of Contentment.—Christian's Birth-Right. fol. Lond. 1703.
———, —————. Art of Contentment. 8vo. Oxford. 1705.
———, —————. Government of the Thoughts. 8vo. Lond. 1700.
———, —————. Government of the Tongue. 4th ed. 8vo. Oxford. 1675.
———, —————. Officium Hominis; trad. ex Lingua Anglicana. 12mo. Lond. 1680.
———, —————. Paraphrase and Annotations upon all St. Paul's Epistles, by him and others. 3d ed. 8vo. Lond. 1702.

Fell, John, (Bp.) The Established Religion in Opposition to Popery. 4to. Lond. 1688.

——, ————. Vide Testamentum Novum. Vide Whole Duty of Man.

Fellowes, Rob. Body of Theology. 2 vols. 8vo. Lond. 1807.

————, ——. Guide to Immortality. 3 vols. 8vo. Lond. 1804.

————, ——. Christian Philosophy. 3d ed. 8vo. Lond. 1800.

————, ——. Religion without Cant. 8vo. Lond. 1801.

————, ——. Brief Treatise on Death. 12mo. Lond. 1805.

Feltham, Owen. Lusoria; with a Taste of some Letters. fol. Lond. 1661 and 1667.

————, ————. Resolves, Divine, Moral, Political. 8th ed. fol. Lond. 1661.

————, ————. The Same. 10th ed. fol. Lond. 1677.

————, ————. ————; with a Short Account of his Life and Writings, by J. Cumming. 8vo. Lond. 1806.

Felton, Henry. Dissertation on Reading the Classics, &c. 5th ed. 12mo. Lond. 1753.

————, ————. Sermons on the Creation, Fall, and Redemption of Man. 8vo. Lond. 1748.

Female Scripture Characters, exemplifying Female Virtues. 12mo. Bost. 1816.

Fendt, Tobias. Monumenta Sepulcrorum. fol. Vratisl. 1574.

Fénel. Plan Systématique de la Religion, etc. des Anciens Gaulois. (Acad. des Inscrip. vol. 24.)

Fénélon, Fr. de Salignac de la Motte. Œuvres; avec sa Vie. 9 vol. 4to. Paris. 1787—92.

————, ————————————. Examen de Conscience pour un Roi; avec la Vie de l'Auteur. 12mo. Lond.

————, ————————————. Œuvres Spirituelles. 4 vol. 12mo. 1752.

————, ————————————. Sermons Choisis sur Divers Sujects. 12mo. Paris. 1744.

————, ————————————. Œuvres Philosophiques. 12mo. Paris. 1739.

————, ————————————. Les Aventures de Télémaque. 2 vol. 12mo. Paris. 1763.

————, ————————————. Idem. 12mo. Lond. 1796.

————, ————————————. The Adventures of Telemachus, &c. done from the French by Mr. Ozell. 2 vols. 12mo. Lond. 1715.

————, ————————————. Le Avventure di Telemaco, trad. dal Francese. 2 vol. 12mo. Avignone, etc. 1804.

————, ————————————, Réflexions sur la Rhétorique et sur la Poétique. 12mo. Amst. 1717.

————, ————————————. Dialogues sur l'Eloquence, etc. 12mo. Paris. 1764.

————, ————————————. Dialogues concerning Eloquence, tr. from the French, with Notes, by William Stevenson. 8vo. Lond. 1722.

Fénélon, Fr. de Salignac de la Motte, Life of. 12mo. Lond. 1723.
———, ———. Dialogues des Morts, avec quelques Fables. 2 vol. 12mo. Paris. 1752.
———, ———. On the Ballance of Europe. (Somers, Tr. vol. 16.)
Fenin, Pierre de. Mémoires. (Mém. de France, vol. 5.)
Fenn, Joseph. Algebra. 4to. Dublin.
———, ———. History of Mathematics, &c. 4to. Dublin.
Fennell, James, Apology for his Life. 8vo. Phil. 1814.
Fenning, Dan. On Algebra. 3d ed. 12mo. Lond. 1759.
Fenton, Elijah. Poems. See Chalmers, A.
Fenwick, Athanasius. Essay on Volition and Pleasure. 8vo. Phil. 1818.
Fenwick, Sir John. Contemplations on Life and Death. (Harl. Miscel. vol. 1.)
Ferber, J. J. On the Oryctography of Derby; from the German. (Pinkerton, vol. 2.)
Ferdosi, Poems of. See Champion, J.
Ferf, H. N. Specimen Critico-Theologicum de Fide et Auctoritate Matthæi. 8vo. Traj. Bat. 1790.
Ferguson, Adam. History of the Roman Republic. 3 vols. 4to. Lond. 1783.
———, ———. The Same. 3 vols. 8vo. Dublin. 1783.
———, ———. ———. 3 vols. 8vo. Phil. 1805.
———, ———. ———. 3 vols. 8vo. Phil. 1811.
———, ———. Essay on the History of Civil Society. 5th ed. 8vo. Lond. 1782.
———, ———. Principles of Moral and Political Science. 2 vols. 4to. Edin. 1792.
———, ———. The Same. 2 vols. 4to. Lond. 1795.
Ferguson, James. Select Mechanical Exercises. 8vo. Lond. 1778.
———, ———. Lectures on Select Subjects in Mechanics, Hydrostatics, &c. 9th ed. 8vo. Lond. 1799.
———, ———. The Same, with Notes, &c. by D. Brewster, revised by R. Patterson. 2 vols. 8vo., and 1 vol. of Plates, 4to. Phil. 1806.
———, ———. Introduction to Astronomy. 8vo. Lond. 1769.
———, ———. Astronomy. 4to. Lond. 1773.
———, ———. The Same, with Notes, &c. by D. Brewster. 2 vols. 8vo., and 1 vol. of Plates, 4to. Phil. 1817.
Fergusson, Alex. Religious Establishment in Scotland examined; a Tract occasioned by the late Persecution against the late Rev. A. Fergusson. 8vo. Lond. 1771.
Fermin, Phil. Histoire Naturelle de la Hollande Equinoxiale. 8vo. Amst. 1765.
———, ———. Développement parfait du Crapaud de Surinam. 8vo. Maestricht. 1765.
———, ———. Abhandlungen von der Surinamischen Kröte oder Pipa, etc.; aus dem Franz. 8vo. Braunschweig. 1776.
———, ———. Description de Surinam. 2 vol. 8vo. Amst. 1769.
———, ———. Tableau de Surinam. 8vo. Maestricht. 1778.

Fermin, Phil. History of Surinam; from the French. 8vo. Lond. 1781.

——, ——. Uebersicht des gegenwärtigen und ehemaligen Zustandes der Kolonie Surinam; aus dem Engl. 16mo. Göttingen. 1788.

Fern, Robert. Sermon on the Death of the Rev. Edward Prime. 8vo. Lond. 1710.

Fernandez, Alonso. Historia Ecclesiastica de Nuestros Tiempos. fol. Toledo. 1611.

Fernandez, Diego. Historia del Peru. 4to. Sevilla. 1571.

Ferne, H. Church of England-Man's Reasons for not making the Decisions of Ecclesiastical Synods the Rule of his Faith. 8vo. Lond. 1717.

Fernelius, Jo. Monalosphærium, Partibus constans Quatuor. fol. Paris. 1526.

———, —. Cosmotheoria. fol. Paris. 1528.

———, —. Medicina. fol. Lut. Paris. 1554.

———, —. De Febribus. 8vo. Amst. 1664.

———, —. De Morbis Universalibus et Particularibus. 8vo. Lug. Bat. 1645.

———, —. De Abditis Rerum Causis. 8vo. Lug. Bat. 1644.

———, —. Consiliorum Medicinalium Liber, selectus a J. Palmario. 8vo. Lug. Bat. 1644.

Ferrario, Giulio. Poesie Pastorali e Rusticali, raccolte ed illustrate con Note. 8vo. Milano. 1808.

Ferrarius, Fr. Bern. De Veterum Acclamationibus et Plausu. (Grævius, vol. 6.)

Ferrarius, Octavianus. De Origine Romanorum. (Græv. vol. 1.)

Ferrarius, Octavius. Opera Varia. 2 vol. 12mo. Wolffenb. 1711.

———, ———. De Re Vestiaria.—Analecta de Re Vestiaria. (Grævius, vol. 6.)

———, ———. De Veterum Lucernis Sepulchralibus. (Id. 12.)

———, ———. Oratio de Laudibus Urbis Patavii. (Græv. Thes. Ital.)

———, ———. De Pantomimis et Mimis. (Sallengre, vol. 2.)

Ferrebee, Mich. Sermon on St. Matthew's Day. 4to. Lond. 1732.

Ferreira Sylva, Silvestre. Relaçao do Sitio da Nova Colonia do Sacramento. 4to. Lisboa. 1748.

Ferretius, Jo. Bapt. Musæ Lapidariæ Antiquorum in Marmoribus Carmina sculpta. fol. Veronæ. 1672.

Ferriar, John. Medical Histories and Reflections. 4 vols. 8vo. Lond. 1792—1813.

——, ——. On Digitalis Purpurea. 8vo. Manchester. 1799.

Ferrus, Ant. Apparatus Statuarum novissime in Destructis Cumis inventarum, etc. (Græv. Thes. Ital.)

Férussac, (M. le Baron.) Bulletin Universel des Sciences et de l'Industrie. 8vo. Paris. 1824 et seqq.

Fessenden, Tho. G. Democracy Unveiled. 12mo. Bost. 1805.

———, ———. Original Poems. 12mo. Phil. 1806.

Fessenden, Tho. G. Modern Philosopher, or Terrible Tractoration. 8vo. Phil. 1806.
Festus, Sex. Pompeius. Vide Flaccus, M. Verrius.
Feuillée, Louis. Journal des Observations Phys. Math. et Botan. faites sur les Côtes Orientales de l'Amérique Méridionale, et dans les Indes Occidentales. 3 vol. 4to. Paris. 1714.
Fever, Enquiry into a late Essay on the Bilious. 2d ed. 8vo. Kingston (Jamaica.) 1750.
——. Essay on Fevers, &c. 8vo. Lond. 1768.
——. Extrait des Délibérations de l'Assemblée des Professeurs de la Faculté de Médecine de Paris sur la Fièvre Jaune. 4to. 1817.
——. See Yellow Fever.
Fevre de la Boderie. Vide Boderianus, G. F.
Feyjoo, Miguel. Relacion descriptiva de Truxillo del Peru. fol. Madrid. 1763.
Feyjóo y Montenegro, B. G. Teatro Critico Universal. 8 vol. 4to. Madrid. 1778—9.
——————, ——. Cartas Eruditas, y Curiosas. 5 vol. 4to. Madrid. 1777.
——————, ——. Idem. 5 vol. 4to. Madrid. 1781.
——————, ——. Ilustracion Apologetica al Primero y Segundo Tomo del Teatro Critico. 4to. Madrid. 1777.
——————, ——. Indice General, etc. 4to. Madrid. 1774.
Ficinus, Marsilius. De Vita, Moribus, et Scriptis ejus.—Apologia pro M. Ficino. (Schelhorn, vol. 1.)
Ficoroni, Fr. de'. Le Vestigia e Rarità di Roma Antica.—Singolarità di Roma Moderna. 4to. Roma. 1744.
Fiddes, Rich. Thanksgiving Sermon. 4to. York. 1703.
——, ——. Body of Divinity. 2 vol. fol. Lond. 1718—20.
——, ——. Treatise of Morality formed upon the Principles of Natural Reason only. 8vo. Lond. 1724.
——, ——. Life of Cardinal Woolsey. fol. Lond. 1726.
Fidell, Tho. Perfect Guide for a Studious Young Lawyer. 8vo.
Field of Mars; being an Alphabetical Digestion of the principal Naval and Military Engagements from the 9th Century to the Peace of 1801. 2 vols. 4to. Lond. 1801.
Fielding, Henry. Works, with his Life. 8 vols. 8vo. Lond. 1771.
———, ———. The Same, with Murphy's Essay on his Life and Genius. 14 vols. 8vo. N. York. 1813—16.
———, ———. Enquiry into the Causes of the late Increase of Robbers, &c. 8vo. Lond. 1751.
Fielding, John. British Peerage. 18mo. Lond. 1783.
Fielding, Sir John. Receipts and Disbursements relating to his Plan for the Apprenticing of Distressed Boys to the Sea-Service, &c. 8vo.
Fielding, S. Lives of Cleopatra and Octavia. 4to. Lond. 1757.
Fights of Faith, in Two Parts; (a Poem.) 8vo. Bost. 1821.
Filangieri, Gaetano. La Scienza della Legislazione. 5 vol. 8vo. Filadelfia. 1799.

Filangieri, Gaetano. Idem. 5 vol. 8vo. Fil. 1807.
Filmer, Sir Robert. Patriarcha, or the Natural Power of Kings. 8vo. Lond. 1680.
———, ———. The Same. 12mo. Lond. 1685.
———, ———. See Tyrrell, Sir James.
———, ———. Freeholders Grand Inquest, &c. To which are added Observations upon Forms of Government. 8vo. Lond. 1680.
———, ———. Difference between an English and Hebrew Witch. 8vo. Lond. 1680.
Filson, John. Discovery, Settlement, and Present State of Kentucky. 8vo. Wilmington. 1784.
——, ——. The Same. 12mo. N. York. 1793.
——, ——. Histoire de Kentucke, trad. de l'Anglois par M. Carraud. 8vo. Paris. 1785.
Finæus Orontius. De Rebus Mathematicis. fol. Lut. Par. 1556.
Finances, le Commerce, la Marine, et les Colonies. 2 vol. 8vo. Paris. 1802.
———. See Commerce.
Finch, Sir Henry. Law. fol. Lond. 1613.
Finch, Leopold Wm. Restoration Sermon. 4to. Lond. 1701.
Finch, Robert P. Fast Sermon. 4to. Lond. 1747.
——, ———. Thanksgiving Sermon. 4to. Lond. 1749.
Finch, Tho. Precedents in Chancery, from 1689 to 1722. fol. Lond. 1733.
Finch, Wm. Bampton Lecture Sermons. 8vo. Oxford. 1797.
Findlay, Robert. Vindication of the Sacred Books and of Josephus. 8vo. Glasgow. 1770.
Findley, Wm. History of the Insurrection in Pennsylvania. 8vo. Phil. 1796.
Finley, Anthony. New American Atlas. fol. Phil. 1826.
Finley, Samuel. Christ Triumphing, and Satan Raging; a Sermon. 12mo. Bost. 1742.
Fino, Alemanio. Historia di Crema. 4to. Venet. 1566.
Fioravanti, Leon. Il Tesoro della Vita Humana. 4to. Vinet. 1570.
Firenze. Costituzioni della Imperiale e Reale Accademia Economico-Agraria dei Georgofili di Firenze. 4to. Firenze. 1817.
———. Costituzioni e Regolamenti dell' Instituto Fiorentino. 4to. Firenze. 1819.
Firenzuola, Agnolo. Opere. 5 vol. 8vo. Milano. 1802.
Firmicus, Julius Maternus. De Errore Profanarum Religionum. 12mo. Argent. 1562. Vide etiam Felix, M. M.
———, ————. Astronomicorum Libri Octo. (Astronomici Veteres Latini.)
Firmin, Giles. Real Christian. 4to. Lond. 1670.
——, ——. The Same. 8vo. Bost. 1742.
Fischer, C. A. Beyträge zur genauern Kenntniss der Spanischen Besitzungen in Amerika. 12mo. Dresden. 1802.
Fischer, J. C. Vita J. V. Roscii, vulgo Jani Nicii Erythræi dicti. 12mo. Col. Ubiorum. 1739.

Fischer, J. F. Prolusiones de Variis Locis in Utroque Testamento. Accessit Commentatio super Loco quodam Epistolæ ad Hebræos. 8vo. Lips. 1779.

———, ——. Animadversiones ad Velleri Grammaticam Græcam. 4 vol. 8vo. Lips. 1798—1801.

Fischer, E. S. See Farrar, J.

Fish, Elisha. Japhet dwelling in the Tents of Shem. 2d ed. 8vo. Bost. 1773.

Fish, Joseph. Sermon at the Ordination of the Rev. William Vinal. 8vo. Newport. 1747.

——, ———. Connecticut Election Sermon. 16mo. New-London. 1760.

Fisher, Edw. Marrow of Modern Divinity. 9th ed. 12mo. Lond. 1699.

Fisher, John, (Bp.) Mornynge Remembrance of the Prynces Margarete, Moder unto Kinge Henry VII. 8vo. Lond. 1708.

Fisher, Nathaniel. Sermon at Salem at the Execution of Henry Blackburne for Murder. 8vo. Bost. 1796.

Fisher, Payne. See Piscator.

Fisher, Samuel. Rusticus ad Academicos; The Rustick's Alarm to the Rabbies. 8vo. Lond. 1660.

Fisher, Wm. Thanksgiving Sermon. 8vo. Lond. 1716.

Fishery, Ancient Right of the English Nation to the American, &c. See Bollan.

Fisk, Samuel. Election Sermon. 8vo. Bost. 1731.

Fiske, Nathan. Twenty-two Sermons, chiefly Practical. 8vo. Worcester. 1794.

——, ———. Oration at Brookfield on the Capture of Lord Cornwallis. 4to. Bost. 1781.

——, ———. Dudleian Lecture. 8vo. Bost. 1796.

Fitch, James. Connecticut Election Sermon. 4to. Camb. 1674.

Fitz-Gerald, Gerald. Essay on the Originality and Permanency of the Biblical Hebrew. 8vo. Dublin. 1796.

Fitz-Herbert, Sir Anthony. Natura Brevium. 8vo. Lond. 1598.

————, ————. ————. 8vo. Lond. 1652.

————, ————. ————. 6th ed. 8vo. Lond. 1718.

————, ————. On Husbandry. (Husbandry, Tracts on.)

Flaccus, C. Valerius. Argonauticon Libri Octo, cum Notis Variorum, cura P. Burmanni. Accedunt Orphei Argonautica, Lat. 4to. Leidæ. 1724.

———, ————. Idem, a T. C. Harles. 8vo. Altenb. 1781.

———, ————. ——. 8vo. Biponti. 1786.

———, ————. ——. Vide Corpus Poet. Lat., et Collectio Pisaurensis.

Flaccus, M. Verrius, et Sex. Pompeius Festus. De Verborum Significatione, cum Notis, ab A. Augustino. 12mo. Venet. 1560.

———, ——————. Idem, cum Notis A. Dacerii et aliorum, in Usum Delphini. 4to. Amst. 1699.

Flacius Illyricus, M. Francowitz. Catalogus Testium Veritatis qui ante nostram Ætatem Pontificum Romanorum Primatui, etc. reclamarunt. fol. 1608.
Flacour, le Sieur de. Histoire de l'Isle Madagascar.—Rélation de l'Isle Madagascar. 4to. Paris. 1661.
Flagg, James. See Gardiner, Silvester.
Flaminius, M. Anton. Carmina. Vide Fracastorius. Vide Poemata Italorum.
Flamsteed, John. Historia Cœlestis Britannica. 3 vol. fol. Lond. 1725.
Flatt, J. F. Magazin für christliche Dogmatik und Moral. 3 Bände. 8vo. Tübingen. 1797—1802.
——, ——. Vide Süskind.
Flavel, Jo. Tractatus de Demonstratione. 12mo. Oxon. 1624.
Flavel, John. Works; with his Life. 2d ed. 2 vols. fol. 1716.
——, ——. The Same. 3d ed. 2 vols. in 1. fol. Edin. 1731.
——, ——. On Mental Errors;—Answer to P. Cary;—Synopsis of Antinomian Errors;—Sermon on Gospel Unity. 8vo. Lond. 1691.
Fléchier, Esprit. Œuvres Complettes. 10 vol. 8vo. Nismes. 1782.
Fleet, John. Anniversary Discourse before the Massachusetts Humane Society. 8vo. Bost. 1797.
——, ——. Dissertatio Inauguralis Medica. 4to. Bost. 1795.
Fleet, T. and J. Pocket Almanack and Massachusetts Register, for 1779—99. 18mo. Bost.
——, ——. See Massachusetts.
Fleetwood, Wm. (Bp.) Life and Death of the B. Virgin. 4to. Lond. 1688.
——, ——. Life and Miracles of St. Wenefride, with her Litanies. 8vo. Lond. 1713.
——, ——. Chronicon Preciosum; or an Account of English Gold and Silver Money, &c. 8vo. Lond. 1745.
——, ——. Sermon before the Queen. 4to. Lond. 1693.
——, ——. Sermon against Clipping. 4to. Lond. 1694.
——, ——. Four Sermons. 2d ed. 8vo. Lond. 1712.
——, ——. Two Sermons on the Justice of Paying Debts. 8vo. Lond. 1718.
——, ——. Sermon upon Swearing. 8vo. Lond. 1721.
——, ——. Charge to his Clergy. 8vo. Lond. 1723.
——, ——. Sermon, November 5th. 4to. Lond. 1704.
——, ——. Thanksgiving Sermon. 4to. Lond. 1704.
——, ——. ——. 8vo. Lond. 1708.
——, ——. ——. 8vo. Lond. 1716.
——, ——. Complete Collection of Sermons, Tracts, &c. fol. Lond. 1737.
——, ——. Essay upon Miracles. 8vo. Lond. 1702.
——, ——. Sermon on the Death of the Duke of Gloucester. 8vo. Lond. 1708.
——, ——. Sermon, January 30th. 8vo. Lond. 1710.

Fleming, Caleb. Remarks on Chubb's Dissertation on Providence. 8vo. Lond. 1738.

———, ———. Remarks on Chubb's Vindication of his True Gospel. 8vo. Lond. 1739.

———, ———. Animadversions upon Chubb's Discourse on Miracles. 8vo. Lond. 1741.

———, ———. Truth and Modern Deism at Variance; with Remarks on Dr. Watts's "Glory of Christ." 8vo. Lond. 1746.

———, ———. True Deism the Basis of Christianity. 8vo. Lond. 1749.

———, ———. Immorality of Profane Swearing. 8vo. Lond.

———, ———. A Future State to be expected on the Principles of Reason. 8vo. Lond. 1739.

———, ———. Theophilus to Gaius, on the Inexpediency of Forms of Prayer. 8vo. Lond. 1753.

———, ———. Three Letters on Systematic Taste. 8vo. Lond. 1755.

———, ———. Apology for a Protestant Dissent from a National Church. 8vo. Lond. 1755.

———, ———. No Protestant Popery, a Letter to Mr. Pike. 8vo. Lond.

———, ———. Three Questions resolved concerning Popery. 8vo. Lond. 1757.

———, ———. Natural and Revealed Religion at Variance. 8vo. Lond. 1758.

———, ———. Survey of the Search after Souls. 8vo. Lond. 1758.

———, ———. Defence of the "Survey." 8vo. Lond. 1759.

———, ———. Tyburn Saints Doubtful Characters. 8vo. Lond. 1760.

———, ———. Discourse on the Sufferings of Christ. 8vo. Lond.

———, ———. Doctrine of the Eucharist considered. 8vo. Lond. 1763.

———, ———. Root of Protestant Errors examined. 4to. Lond. 1767.

———, ———. Civil Establishments in Religion, the Ground of Infidelity. 8vo. Lond. 1767.

———, ———. Supplement to a Letter to a Friend, on American Bishops. 8vo. Lond. 1768. See Chauncy, C.

———, ———. Œconomy of the Sexes. 8vo. Lond. 1751.

———, ———. Devout Laugh. 8vo. Lond. 1750.

———, ———. St. Paul's Heretic. 8vo. Lond. 1735.

———, ———. Appeal to the People of England in Defence of the Clergy. 8vo. Lond.

———, ———. Plain and Rational Account of the Law of the Sabbath. 8vo. Lond. 1736.

———, ———. Jesuit Unmasked. 8vo. Lond. 1738.

———, ———. Plunging a Subject of Bigotry, when made essential to Baptism. 8vo. Lond. 1741.

Fleming, Caleb. Pædo-Baptist's Sense of Positive Institutions defended. 8vo. Lond.
———, ———. A Plea for Infants. 8vo. Lond. 1742.
———, ———. Defence of Infant-Baptism. 8vo. Lond. 1744.
———, ———. Farther Defence of Infant-Baptism. 8vo.
———, ———. Challenge, occasioned by an Answer to a late Treatise on the Subjects and Mode of Baptism. 8vo. Lond. 1743.
———, ———. Plain Reasons for Infant-Baptism. 8vo. Lond. 1750.
———, ———. Essay on the Scripture-Account of Man's Redemption. 8vo. Lond. 1745.
———, ———. On Warburton's Alliance. 8vo. Lond. 1748.
———, ———. Catholic-Epistle. 8vo. Lond.
———, ———. St. Paul's Orthodoxy, a Sermon. 8vo. Lond. 1759.
———, ———. Equality of Christians in the Province of Religion; a Discourse. 8vo. Lond. 1760.
———, ———. Sermon on the Death of the Rev. J. Foster. 8vo. Lond. 1753.
———, ———. Scale of First Principles, Religious and Moral, calculated for Youth. 12mo. Lond. 1755.
———, ———. Fund raising for the Italian Gentleman. 8vo. Lond. 1750.
———, ———. Necessity not the Origin of Evil. 8vo. Lond. 1757.
———, ———. Modern Plan upon which the Minds and Manners of Youth may be formed. 8vo. Lond. 1748.
Fleming, John. Catalogue of Indian Medicinal Plants and Drugs. (Asiatic Researches, vol. 11.)
Fleming, Malcolm. Introduction to Physiology, in Lectures on the Animal Œconomy. 8vo. Lond. 1759.
Fleming, Rob. Fulfilling of the Scripture. 3d ed. 8vo. 1681.
———, ———. Discourse to the Societies for Reformation of Manners. 2d ed. 12mo. Lond. 1700.
Fleta, seu Comment. Juris Anglicani, Seldeni. 2d ed. 4to. Lond. 1685.
Fletcher, Fr. The World Encompassed by Sir Francis Drake. 4to. Lond. 1628.
Fletcher, Giles. Poems. See Chalmers, A.
Fletcher, Phineas. Purple Island, Piscatorie Eclogs, and other Poetical Miscellanies. 4to. Camb. 1633.
———, ———. Poems. See Chalmers, A.
Fletcher, Robert. Copy of the Record, in the Case of R. Fletcher vs. John Peck. 8vo. Bost. 1808.
Fletcher, Tho. (Bp.) Sermon before the Society for promoting Protestant Schools in Ireland. 4to. Dublin. 1746.
Fletcher, Wm. State of the Action brought by him against William Vassall for Defaming him. 4to. Bost. 1753.
Fleury, (Cardinal.) Memoirs of his Life and Administration. 8vo. Lond. 1743.
Fleury, Claude. Histoire Ecclésiastique; avec la Continuation, par J. C. Fabre; et la Table Générale des Matières, par Rondet. 37 vol. 4to. Paris. 1728—58.

Fleury, Claude. Ecclesiastical History to A. D. 870, tr. from the French by H. Herbert. 5 vols. 4to. Lond. 1727.
———, ———. Mœurs des Israelites. 12mo. Paris. 1712.
———, ———. In Poesim Universam, et Hebræorum potissimum. (Ugol. vol. 31.)
Flexman, R. Charity Sermon. 8vo. Lond. 1752.
Flicke, Rob. Voyage to the Azores. (Pinkerton, vol. 1.)
Flint, James. Election Sermon. 8vo. Bost. 1815.
———, ———. Sermon at the Ordination of the Rev. N. Whitman. 8vo. Camb. 1814.
Flint, Timothy. Recollections of the last Ten Years passed in the Valley of the Mississippi. 8vo. Bost. 1826.
Floræ Lusitanicæ et Brasiliensis Specimen; et Epistolæ a Carolo à Linné, etc. 8vo. Conimb. 1788.
Florence. Vide Firenze.
Florent d'Illiers. Mémoires. (Mém. de France, vol. 7.)
Flores, Joseph. Especifico nuevamente descubierto para la Curacion del Cancro. 4to. Madrid. 1782.
Florian, J. P. C. de. Numa Pompilius. 16mo. Paris. 1812.
———, ———. Gonzalve de Cordoue. 2 vol. 18mo. Paris. 1820.
Florida, Gulf of. See Windward Passage.
Florus, L. Annæus. Rerum Romanarum Libri IV; cui subjungitur L. Ampelii Liber Memorialis; a M. Maittaire. 12mo. Lond. 1715.
———, ———. Epitome Rerum Romanarum, cum Versione Anglica, a J. Clarke. 8vo. Lond. 1739.
———, ———. Epitome of Roman History, made English. 12mo. Lond. 1714.
———, ———. Vide Rom. Hist. Scriptores.
Flosculi Historici delibati, nunc delibatiores redditi. Vide Bussières.
Floyer, John. Treatise of the Asthma. 8vo. Lond. 1717.
Fludd, Robert. De Naturæ Simia. fol. Oppenh. 1618.
Flynt, Henry. Twenty Sermons. 8vo. Bost. 1739.
———, ———. Sermon at the Thursday-Lecture in Boston. 8vo. Bost. 1729.
———, ———. Sermon to the Scholars in the College Hall. 8vo. Bost. 1736.
———, ———. Oratio Funebris in Obitum Rev. Benjaminis Wadsworth. 8vo. Bost. 1737.
Fobes, Perez. Election Sermon. 8vo. Bost. 1795.
Foe, Daniel de. See De Foe.
Folieta, Ubertus. Opuscula Varia de Linguæ Latinæ Usu et Præstantia, etc. 4to. Romæ. 1579.
———, ———. Historiæ Genuensium Libri XII.—Clarorum Ligurum Elogia.—Conjuratio Joan. Ludov. Flisci.—Tumultus Neapolitani.—Cædes P. L. Farnesii, Placentiæ Ducis.—De Sacro Fœdere in Selimum.—Variæ Expeditiones in Africam, cum Obsidione Melitæ.—De Ratione Scribendæ Historiæ.—Tiburtinum Hippolyti Cardinalis Ferrariensis.—Brumanus, sive de Laudibus Urbis Neapolis, etc. (Græv. Thes. Ital.)

Folkes, Martin. Tables of English Silver and Gold Coins, reprinted, with Plates &c.; by the Society of Antiquaries. 2 vols. 4to. Lond. 1763.
———, ———. Catalogue of his Collection of Mathematical Instruments, Gems, Pictures, &c. 8vo. 1755.
———, ———. Catalogue of his Library. 8vo. 1755.
Follen, Charles. Deutsches Lesebuch für Anfänger. 12mo. Camb. 1826.
———, ———. Practical Grammar of the German Language. 12mo. Bost. 1828.
Folsom, Peter. Eulogy on Washington. 8vo. Gilmanton. 1800.
Fonblanque, John. Treatise of Equity. 3d ed. 2 vols. 8vo. Phil. 1807.
Foncemagne, M. de. Sur la Succession au Royaume quant aux Filles. (Acad. des Inscrip. vol. 8.)
Fonseca, Manoel da. Vida do Padre Belchior de Pontes. 4to. Lisboa. 1752.
Fontaine, J. de la. Fables. 2 vol. 12mo. Paris. 1811.
———, ———. Œuvres Diverses. 3 vol. 12mo. Paris. 1729.
———, ———. Loves of Cupid and Psyche, tr. from the French by Mr. Lockman. 8vo. Lond. 1744.
Fontana, Carlo. Discorso sopra l'Antico Monte Citatorio. fol. Roma. 1708.
———, ———. Templum Vaticanum et ipsius Origo, etc. 2 vol. fol. Romæ. 1694.
Fontana, Dominicus. Contignationes ac Pontes Nicolai Zabaglia, etc. fol. Romæ. 1743.
Fontana, Nicolas. On the Nicobar Isles and the Fruit of the Mellori. (Asiatic Researches, vol. 3.)
Fontanini, Giusto. Della Eloquenza Italiana. 4to. Venez. 1737.
———, ———. Biblioteca dell' Eloquenza Italiana. 2 vol. 4to. Parma. 1803—4.
———, ———. De Corona Ferrea Longobardorum. (Græv. Thes. Ital.)
———, ———. De Antiquitatibus Hortæ Coloniæ Etruscorum. (Id.)
Fontanus, Jac. De Bello Rhodio. (Clauser de Rebus Turcicis.)
Fontenelle, B. le Bovier de. Œuvres. 3 vol. fol. La Haye. 1728—9.
———, ———. Elogium of Sir Isaac Newton. 4to. Lond. 1727.
———, ———. Histoire des Oracles. 12mo. La Haye. 1728.
———, ———. Answer to the History of Oracles. See Baltus.
———, ———. Entretiens sur la Pluralité des Mondes, avec les Dialogues des Morts. 12mo. Paris. 1762.
Fonticulanus, Aug. Belli Bracciani, Aquilæ gesti, Narratio. (Græv. Thes. Ital.)
Foot, Wm. Essay on Education. 8vo. Bristol. 1747.
Forbes, Duncan. Letter concerning important Discoveries in Philosophy and Theology. 4to. Lond. 1732.

Forbes, Duncan. Works on Religion, Natural and Revealed. 2 vols. 12mo. Edin.
———, ———. The Same. 12mo. Glasgow. 1788.
———, ———. ———. 8vo. Lond. 1809.
———, ———. Thoughts concerning Religion. 5th ed. 12mo. Dundee. 1799.
———, ———. Reflexions on the Sources of Incredulity. 12mo. Edin. 1750.
Forbes, Eli. Artillery Election Sermon. 8vo. Bost. 1771.
———, —. Sermon on the Conquest of Canada. 8vo. Bost. 1761.
———. —. Sermon at the Funeral of John Low, Esq. 8vo. Newburyport. 1797.
———, —. Election Sermon. 8vo. Bost. 1795.
———, —. Convention Sermon. 4to. Charlestown. 1799.
———, —. Sermon at Salem, and Result of an Ecclesiastical Council respecting Dr. Whitaker. 8vo. Salem. 1784.
———, —. Sermon at the Dedication of a Grammar School House in Gloucester. 8vo. Newburyport. 1795.
Forbes, Murray. On Gravel and Gout, &c. 8vo. Lond. 1793.
Forbes, Patrick. View of Public Transactions in the Reign of Queen Elizabeth. 2 vols. fol. Lond. 1740—1.
Forbes, Sir Wm. Account of the Life and Writings of James Beattie. 8vo. N. York. 1806.
Forbesius à Corse, Joh. Opera Omnia. 2 vol. fol. Amst. 1703.
———————, —. Arnoldi Montani Forbesius Contractus. 12mo. Amst. 1668.
Forcatulus, Steph. De Origine Valesiorum.—De Fœminis Illustribus, etc. 8vo. Paris. 1579.
Forcellinus, Ægidius. Totius Latinitatis Lexicon, consilio et cura Jacobi Facciolati, opera et studio Ægidii Forcellini. 4 vol. fol. Patav. 1771.
Ford, Edward. On the Disease of the Hip Joint, &c. 8vo. Lond. 1794.
Ford, John. Dramatic Works, with Notes, &c. by H. Weber. 2 vols. 8vo. Edin. 1811.
Ford, Stephen. Epistle to the Church in Chippin-Norton. 4to. Oxford. 1657.
Ford, Timothy. Eulogy on John Adams. 8vo. Charleston, S. C. 1826.
Fordun, John. Scotichronicon. Vide Gale, Scriptores xv,—et Hearne, T.
Fordyce, David. Elements of Moral Philosophy. 12mo. Lond. 1758.
———, ———. Dialogue on the Art of Preaching. 3d ed. To which is added, a Sermon on the Eloquence, and an Essay on the Action, of the Pulpit, by J. Fordyce. 12mo. Lond. 1755.
Fordyce, Geo. Elements of the Practice of Physic. 5th ed. 8vo. Lond. 1784.
———, ———. The Same. 6th ed. 8vo. Lond. 1791.
———, ———. On Digestion. 2d ed. 8vo. Lond. 1791.
———, ———. On Simple Fever. 2 vols. 8vo. Lond. 1794—8.

Fordyce, James. Sermon on the Death of the Rev. S. Lawrence. 8vo. Lond. 1760.
———, ——. Ordination Sermon. 12mo. Glasgow. 1755.
———, ——. Eloquence of the Pulpit, an Ordination Sermon. 12mo. Glasgow. 1755.
———, ——. See Fordyce, D.
———, ——. Sermons to Young Women. 2 vols. 12mo. Lond. 1766.
Fordyce, Wm. On Putrid and Inflammatory Fevers, &c. 8vo. Lond. 1773.
———, ——. Review of the Venereal Disease and its Remedies. 8vo. Lond. 1777.
Foreigners, Argument against Employing and Ennobling. 8vo. Lond. 1717.
Forman, Charles. Letter concerning the Imperial Company of Commerce in the Netherlands. 8vo. Lond. 1725.
Formey, J. H. S. History of Philosophy and Philosophers. 12mo. Lond. 1766.
Formosa, Das Verwarloste. 12mo. Nürnberg. 1677.
Forner, J. P. Oracion Apologética por la España y su Mérito Literario. 8vo. Madrid. 1786.
Foronda, Valentin de. Miscelanea. 12mo. Madrid. 1787.
Forrest, Alex. Eucharistical Psalmody. 12mo. Lond. 1754.
Forrester, Tho. Hierarchical Bishops Claim to a Divine Right tried at the Scripture-Bar. 4to. Edin. 1699.
Forskäll, Peter. Flora et Fauna Ægyptiaca. 4to.
Forster, Edward. Arabian Nights, translated; with Engravings, from Pictures by Robert Smirke. 5 vols. 8vo. Lond. 1802.
Forster, Geo. Voyage round the World with Capt. Cook. 2 vols. 4to. Lond. 1777.
———, ——. Letter to the Earl of Sandwich. 4to. Lond. 1778.
———, ——. Journey from Bengal to England. 2 vols. in 1. 4to. Lond. 1798.
———, ——. Geschichte der Reisen an der Nordwest und Nordost Küste von Amerika, etc. aus dem Englischen. 3 Bände. 4to. Berlin. 1791.
Forster, Jo. Dictionarium Hebraicum. fol. Basil. 1557.
Forster, J. R. Flora Americæ Septentrionalis. 8vo. Lond. 1771.
———, ——. Catalogue of the Animals of North America. 8vo. Lond. 1771.
———, ——. Novæ Species Insectorum. 8vo. Lond. 1771.
———, ——. Catalogue of North American Plants. 8vo. Lond. 1771.
———, ——. Observations made during a Voyage round the World. 4to. Lond. 1778.
———, ——. Liber Singularis de Bysso Antiquorum. 8vo. Lond. 1776.
———, ——. Introduction to Mineralogy. 8vo. Lond. 1768.
———, ——. Genera Plantarum Australasiæ. 4to. Lond. 1776.
———, ——. Travels in Sicily, &c. See Riedesel.

Forster, Nathaniel. Dissertation upon the Account supposed to have been given of Christ by Josephus. 8vo. Oxford. 1749.
———, —. Vide Biblia Hebraica.
Forster, Tho. Two Letters from a late Dissenting Teacher; with an Answer to the former, and Animadversions on the latter. 8vo. Lond. 1764.
———, ———. Brief Defence of the Divine Institution of the Episcopal Order. 8vo. Lond. 1768.
Forster, Tho. Researches about Atmospheric Phænomena. 2d ed. 8vo. Lond. 1815.
Forsyth, Joseph. Remarks on Antiquities, Arts, and Letters, during an Excursion in Italy in 1802—3. 8vo. Bost. 1818.
Fortescue, Sir John. Commendation of the Lawes of England, tr. by R. Mulcaster; with the original Latin. 12mo. Lond. 1616.
———, ———. De Laudibus Legum Angliæ. fol. Lond. 1737.
———, ———. The Same, tr. into English, with the Notes of Selden, &c. 2d ed. fol. Lond. 1741.
Fortia, M. Travels in Sweden. (Pinkerton, vol. 6.)
Fortia d'Urban, (M. de.) Œuvres Diverses. 11 vol. 12mo. Paris. 1807—9.
Fortiguerra, Niccolò. Ricciardetto. 3 vol. 8vo. Milano. 1813.
Foscarini, Marco. Della Letteratura Veneziana. fol. Padova. 1752.
Foschi, N. Trattenimento Mensile. Genn. Febbr. e Mar. 1816. 12mo. Napoli.
Foster, Daniel. Election Sermon. 8vo. Bost. 1790.
Foster, Edmund. Sermon at the Ordination of the Rev. J. Osgood. 8vo. Worcester. 1792.
Foster, Isaac. Holiness of Infants explained and improved. 8vo. Bost. 1766.
———, ———. Defence of Religious Liberty. 8vo. Worcester. 1780.
Foster, James. Account of the Behaviour of the Earl of Kilmarnock after his Sentence, &c. 8vo. Lond. 1746.
———, ———. Vindication of the above. 8vo. Lond. 1746.
———, ———. Natural and Social Virtue.
———, ———. Answer to Dr. Stebbing's Letter on Heresy. 8vo. Lond. 1735.
———, ———. Answer to Dr. Stebbing's Second Letter on Heresy. 8vo. Lond. 1736.
———, ———. Essay on Fundamentals. 8vo. Bost. 1809.
———, ———. Answer to Dr. Stebbing's "True State of the Controversy." 8vo. Lond. 1737.
———, ———. Usefulness, Truth, &c. of the Christian Revelation. 8vo. Lond. 1731.
———, ———. Sermons. 4 vols. 8vo. Lond. 1744—55.
———, ———. Sermon on the Death of the Rev. Thomas Emlyn. 8vo. Lond. 1741.
———, ———. Sermon on the Death of the Rev. John Ashworth. 8vo. Lond. 1742.

Foster, James. Discourses on all the Principal Branches of Natural Religion and Social Virtue. 2 vols. 4to. Lond. 1749—52.

——, ——. Biographical Notice of him.—Essay on Fundamentals in Religion.—Image of God in Man.—On Mysteries.—Rules for Reading the Scriptures.—On Heresy.—On a Uniformity of Belief in Religion.—The Death of Christ considered as Sacrifice.—On the Nature of a Heavenly Conversation.—Enthusiasm in Religion.—The Glory of God promoted by the Moral Rectitude of his Creatures.—Expediency and Benefits of a Revelation. (Sparks, Collection of Essays, &c. in Theology.)

Foster, John. Essay on Accent and Quantity, &c. 8vo. Eton. 1763.

Foster, John. Fast Sermon. 8vo Camb. 1805.

——, ——. Sermon on Infidelity. 8vo. Camb. 1802.

——, ——. Sermon before the Society for propagating the Gospel among the Indians and Others in North America. 8vo. Camb. 1817.

——, ——. Artillery Election Sermon. 8vo. Bost. 1809.

Foster, John. Essays. 2d Amer. ed. 2 vols. in 1. 12mo. Bost. 1811.

Foster, Sir Michael. Examination of the Scheme of Church-Power, laid down in the Codex Juris Ecclesiastici Anglicani, &c. 8vo. Lond. 1735.

——, ————. The Same. 3d ed. 8vo. Lond. 1736.

——, ————. Answer to the above. See Andrew, Dr.

——, ————. Report of some Proceedings on the Commission for the Trial of the Rebels in 1746, &c. fol. Oxford. 1762.

Foster, Samuel. Miscellanies; or Mathematical Lucubrations, in Latin and English, by J. Twysden. fol. Lond. 1659.

Fothergill, A. On the Formation of Ice Islands, and the Means of avoiding them. (Mem. A. A. S. vol. 3.)

Fothergill, Anthony. Wicked Christians Practical Atheists. 8vo. Lond. 1755.

Fothergill, Geo. Sermons. 2 vols. 8vo. Oxford. 1765.

Fothergill, John. Works; by J. C. Lettsom. 3 vols. 8vo. Lond. 1783—4.

————, ——. The Same. 4to. Lond. 1784.

————, ——. Account of Peter Collinson. 4to. Lond. 1770.

Fothergill, S. On Tic Douloureux. 12mo. Lond. 1804.

————, ——. See London Medical and Physical Journal.

Foucher. Sur la Religion des Perses et les Ecrits de Zoroastre. (Acad. des Inscrip. vol. 25, 27, 29, 31, et 39.)

————. Systèmes de Pythagore, de Platon, etc. (Id. 29.)

————. Sur la Religion de la Grèce. (Id. 34, 35, 36, 38.)

Foundling, First Twenty Years of the Life of a. 12mo. Bost. 1812.

Fountaine, Andr. Numismata Anglo-Saxonica et Anglo-Danica. Vide Antiquæ Literaturæ Septentrionalis.

Fourcroy, A. F. Lectures on Chemistry and Natural History, tr. from the French by T. Elliot. 2 vols. 8vo. Edin. 1785.

Fourcroy, A. F. Synoptic Tables of Chemistry, tr. from the French by William Nicholson. fol. Lond. 1801.

———, ——. Mémoires dans les Annales du Muséum d'Histoire Naturelle.

———, ——. Vide Journal de l'Ecole Polytechnique.

Foureau de Beauregard. Vide Beauregard.

Fourmont, Steph. Réflexions sur l'Origine des Anciens Peuples. 2 vol. 4to. Paris. 1747.

Fowler, Edw. (Bp.) Sermon on Reformation of Manners. 12mo. Lond. 1699.

———, ———. Propositions by which the Doctrine of the Trinity may be explained according to the Ancient Fathers. 8vo. Lond. 1719.

Fowler, Geo. Wandering Philanthropist. 12mo. Phil. 1810.

Fowler, John. Summary Account of Tobago. 8vo. Lond. 1774.

Fowler, Tho. Medical Reports on the Effects of Blood-Letting, &c. in the Acute and Chronic Rheumatism. 8vo. Lond. 1795.

———, ——. Medical Reports on the Effects of Tobacco. 8vo. Lond. 1785.

Fowles, Susanna. Second Part of the Boy of Bilson; or a True Relation of the Impostor, S. Fowles. 4to. Lond. 1698.

Fownes, Joseph. Enquiry into the Principles of Toleration. 8vo. Shrewsbury. 1773.

Fox, C. J. History of the Early Part of the Reign of James II. 8vo. Phil. 1808.

——, ——, Characters of. See Parr, S.

——, ——, Memoirs of. See Trotter, J. B.

Fox, Edw. Formulæ Medicamentorum Selectæ. 8vo. Lond. 1777.

Fox, George. Battle-Door for Teachers to learn Plural and Singular. fol.

——, ———. Journal of his Life and Labours in the Ministry. 3d ed. fol. Lond. 1765.

——, ———. Last Will. (Harl. Miscel. vol 7.)

Fox, John. Booke of Martyrs. 3 vols. fol. Lond. 1631—2.

——, ——. The Same. 3 vols. fol. Lond. 1641.

——, ——. ———, with his Life in Latin and English. 9th ed. 3 vols. fol. Lond. 1684.

——, ——. Ad Angliæ Proceres pro Afflictis Fratribus Supplicatio. 16mo. Basil. 1557.

Fox, Joseph. Natural History of the Human Teeth. 4to. Lond. 1803.

——, ———. History and Treatment of the Diseases of the Teeth, &c. 4to. Lond. 1806.

Foxcroft, Francis. Catalogue of the Graduates of Harvard College, MS. 1764.

Foxcroft, Tho. Discourse on Kindness. 16mo. Bost. 1720.

———, ——. Sermon on the State of the Dead. 16mo. Bost. 1722.

———, ——. Sermon on Death. 16mo. Bost. 1726.

———, ——. Sermon on the Conquest of Canada. 8vo. Bost. 1760.

Foxcroft, Tho. Occasional Sermons. 12mo. Bost. 1722.
———, ——. God's Face set against an Incorrigible People, a Sermon. 16mo. Bost. 1724.
———, ——. Discourse Preparatory to the Choice of a Minister. 8vo. Bost. 1727.
———, ——. Thursday-Lecture Sermon after the Earthquake. 8vo. Bost. 1727.
———, ——. Sermon on the Day of Prayer occasioned by the late Earthquakes. 8vo. Bost. 1756.
———, ——. Pleas of Gospel-Impenitents refuted, in Two Sermons. 12mo. Bost. 1730.
———, ——. Lesson of Caution to Young Sinners, a Sermon. 12mo. Bost. 1733.
———, ——. Sermon at the Old-Church Lecture. 8vo. Bost. 1740.
———, ——. Sermon at a Family-Meeting in private. 8vo. Bost. 1742.
———, ——. Sermon, January 1st. 8vo. Bost. 1747.
———, ——. Saints united Confession, in Disparagement of their own Righteousness. 8vo. Bost. 1750.
———, ——. Observations on the Rise and Primitive State of New England, a Sermon. 8vo. Bost. 1730.
———, ——. Sermon at the Old-Church-Lecture. 8vo. Bost. 1756.
———, ——. Sermon at his Ordination. 16mo. Bost. 1718.
———, ——. Sermon at the Ordination of the Rev. John Lowell. 16mo. Bost. 1726.
———, ——. Sermon at the Ordination of the Rev. John Taylor. 16mo. Bost. 1728.
———, ——. Sermon at the Ordination of Mr. Z. Thayer, to the Office of Deacon. 8vo. Bost. 1731.
———, ——. Sermon on the Death of his Mother. 16mo. Bost. 1721.
———, ——. Sermon on the Decease of Mr. John Coney and others. 16mo. Bost. 1722.
———, ——. Sermon on the Death of Dame Bridget Usher. 16mo. Bost. 1723.
———, ——. Sermon on the Death of George I, and the Accession of Geo. II. 8vo. Bost. 1727.
———, ——. Sermon on the Death of the Hon. Penn Townsend. 8vo. Bost. 1727.
———, ——. Sermon on the Death of the Rev. William Waldron. 8vo. Bost. 1727.
———, ——. Sermon on the Death of the Rev. John Williams and Rev. Thomas Blowers. 8vo. Bost. 1729.
———, ——. Sermon on the Death of the Rev. Benjamin Wadsworth. 8vo. Bost. 1737.
———, ——. Ruling and Ordaining Power of Congregational Bishops or Presbyters defended. 12mo. Bost. 1724.
———, ——. See Edwards, Jona.
———, ——. Letter to him, by J. F. 4to. Bost. 1745.

Foxe, Luke. North-West Fox, or Fox from the North-West Passage. 4to. Lond. 1635.
Fracastorius, Hieron. Carmina. Item M. A. Flaminii et aliorum Carmina. 12mo. Venet. 1759.
———, ——. Vide Poemata Italorum.
———, ——. Della Sifilide, Libri Tre, volgarizzati da Benini. 8vo. Milano. 1813.
Fragment, concerning Mun and Tom. 8vo. Lond.
———, Another, concerning Mun, Tom, and Dun. 8vo. Lond.
Fragmenta Vestigii Veteris Romæ, ex Lapidibus Farnesianis, nunc primum in lucem edita, cum Notis J. P. Bellorii. (Grævius, vol. 4.)
Fraguerius, Cl. Fr. Carmina. Vide Poetæ Recentiores.
Fraguier. Sur la Manière dont Virgil a imité Homère. (Acad. des Inscrip. vol. 2.)
Frambesarius, N. Abr. Examen Practicum de recta Curandarum Febrium Ratione. 12mo. Lug. Bat. 1640.
———, ——. Scholæ Medicæ. Quibus accessit Ambrosiopœa. 12mo. Lug. Bat. 1647.
France. Le Tocsain contre les Massacreurs et Auteurs des Confusions en France. 8vo. Reims. 1579.
———. Discours sur l'Etat de France. 12mo. 1588.
———. Historical Collection of Tragicall Massacres, &c. in France, from the Reign of Henry II. to that of Henry IV; tr. from the French. fol. Lond. 1598.
———. Résponse à la Lettre touchant les Droicts du Roy sur le Temporel de MM. du Clergé, etc. 4to. 1663.
———. Conformité de la Discipline Ecclésiastique des Protestans de France avec celle des Anciens Chrêtiens. 4to. Quevilly. 1678.
———. Enquiry into the Revenue, Credit, and Commerce of France. 8vo. Lond. 1742.
———. Present State of the Revenues and Forces of France and Spain compared with those of Great Britain. 8vo. Lond. 1740.
———. Letters concerning the Present State of the French Nation, &c. 8vo. Lond. 1769.
———. Impartial History of the late Revolution in France. 2 vols. 8vo. Lond. 1794.
———. Frankreichs Verfahren gegen Amerika. 12mo. Hamb. 1798.
———. What is our Situation? and What our Prospects? or a Demonstration of the Insidious Views of Republican France. 8vo. Lond. 1799.
———. La Coalition et la France. 8vo. Lond. et Phil. 1817.
———. Peace-Republicans' Manual; or the French Constitution of 1793, in French and English, &c. 8vo. N. York. 1817.
———. Lettres sur la Situation de la France. 8vo. Paris. 1820.
———. See Académie,—Britain,—French,—Mémoires,—Paris,—Recueil,—Treaties, &c.
Francheville, M. de. Siècle de Louis XIV. 2 vol. 4to. Lond. 1752.

Francis, Convers. Errors in Education, a Discourse. 8vo. Hingham. 1828.

——, ——. Address, July 4th. 8vo. Camb. 1828.

——, ——. Discourse before the Middlesex Bible Society. 12mo. Bost. 1828.

Francis, Henry. Sermon on the Death of the Rev. John Foxon. 8vo. Lond. 1723.

Francis, John. Reflections on the Character of David. 8vo. Lond. 1764.

Francis, J. W. See Hosack, D.

Francis, Lydia Maria. Hobomok, a Tale of Early Times. 12mo. Bost. 1824.

——, ——. The Rebels. 12mo. Bost. 1825.

——, ——. Moral Lessons in Verse. 18mo. Camb. 1828.

Francis, Philip. Poetical Translation of the Works of Horace, with the Original Text and Notes. 3d ed. 2 vols. 4to. Lond. 1749.

——, ——. The Same. 4 vols. 12mo. Lond. 1747—56.

——, ——. ——. See Chalmers, A.

——, ——. Orations of Demosthenes, translated into English, with Notes. 2 vols. 4to. Lond. 1757—8.

Francis, Richard. Maxims of Equity; with the Case of the Earl of Coventry. fol. Lond. 1728.

——, ——. Grounds and Rudiments of Law and Equity. 2d ed. fol. Lond. 1751.

Franciscus, Erasmus. Guineischer und Americanischer Blumen-Pusch. 8vo. Nürnberg. 1669.

Franck, J. F. De Usu Accentuum S. Codicis Ebræi. 4to. Wittebergæ. 1717.

——, ——. De Induitione Novi Hominis. 4to. Argent. 1701.

Francke, Wilhelmus. De Christi Crucifixi Derelictione. 4to. Wittenb. 1695.

Franckel, D. H. (Arch-Rabbi.) Thanksgiving Sermon, for the King of Prussia's Victory, Dec. 5, 1757, preached at the Synagogue of the Jews in Berlin; from the German Original. 9th ed. 12mo. Bost. 1758.

Franckius, A. H. Manuductio ad Lectionem Scripturæ Sacræ. 8vo. Lond. 1706.

——, ——. Programmata in Academia Hallensi proposita. 12mo. Halæ Magd. 1714.

——, ——. Prælectiones Hermeneuticæ. 12mo. Halæ Magd. 1723.

——, ——. Nov. Test. Gr., et Hodier. Gr. Vide Test. Nov.

——, ——. Vita ejus; et Narratio Rerum in Ecclesiis Germaniæ. Vide Mather, S.

——, ——. De Gratia et Veritate. 12mo. Halæ Magd. 1733.

——, ——. Idea Studiosi Theologiæ et Monita Pastoralia Theologica. 12mo. Halæ Magd. 1723.

——, ——. Christus S. Scripturæ Nucleus, etc. 12mo. Halæ Magd. 1724.

Franckius, A. H. Prælectiones de Methodo Studii Theologici;—

Uberior Explicatio Prælectionum Hermeneuticarum suarum;—Prælectionum Hermeneuticarum suarum Succinctior Explicatio; —Introductio Exegetica in Libros Omnes Vet. Testamenti Historicos;—Introductio Generalis in Lectionem Prophetarum;—Collegium Pastorale ad Ductum Epistolæ ad Titum; MSS.

——, ——. Vide Franckius, G. A.

Franckius, G. A. Programmata in Academia Fridericiana proposita. Adjectæ sunt A. H. Franckii Reliquiæ Programmatum et Aliorum Opusculorum. 12mo. Hal. Magd. 1735.

Franckius, Jo. Val. Callinus; sive De Origine Carminis Elegiaci Tractatio. Accedunt Tyrtæi Reliquiæ, cum Proœmio et Critica Annotatione. 8vo. Alt. et Lips. 1816.

Francklin, R. 'Ορθοτονία; seu Tractatus de Tonis in Lingua Græcanica. 16mo. Lond. 1630.

Francklin, Tho. Works of Lucian; from the Greek. 4 vols. 8vo. Lond. 1781.

——, ——. Tragedies of Sophocles, tr. from the Greek into English Blank Verse. 4to. Lond. 1759.

——, ——. Dissertation on Antient Tragedy. 4to.

——, ——. Epistles of Phalaris, tr. from the Greek; with Select Epistles of eminent Greek Writers. 8vo. Lond. 1749.

——, ——. Sermons. 4th ed. 3 vols. 8vo. Lond. 1790.

Francklyn, G. Observations occasioned by the Attempts to effect the Abolition of the Slave Trade. 8vo. Lond. 1789.

——, —. Answer to the Rev. Mr. Clarkson's Essay on Slavery. 8vo. Lond. 1789.

——. See Franklin.

Franco, Agoustine, dit Medina, (Espion Français,) Procès Verbal d' Interrogatoires de. 4to. Cap-Henry. 1814.

Francœur, L. B. Traité Elémentaire de Mécanique. 3me. ed. 8vo. Paris. 1804.

François, (M. le.) Réflexions Critiques sur la Médecine. 2 vol. 12mo. 1723.

Francus, G. G. Lexicon Sanctum. 12mo. Hanoviæ. 1634.

Frank, John. Sermon on the Death of the Rev. Bennet Stevenson. 8vo. Lond. 1756.

Franklin, Benj. Works consisting of his Life and Essays. 2 vols. 12mo. N. York. 1794.

——, ——. Interest of Great Britain considered with regard to her Colonies. 8vo. Bost. 1760.

——, ——. The Same. 8vo. Lond. 1760.

——, ——. ——. 2d ed. 8vo. Lond. 1761.

——, ——. Two Tracts;—Information to those who would remove to America; and Remarks concerning the Savages of North America. 8vo. Lond. 1784.

——, ——. Memoirs of his Life and Writings, written by himself to a late Period, and continued by his Grandson, W. T. Franklin. 4to. Lond. 1818.

——, ——. Private Correspondence. 4to. Lond. 1817.

——, ——. The Same. 2d ed. 2 vols. 8vo. Lond. 1817.

——, ——. Observations concerning the Increase of Mankind, Peopling of Countries, &c. 4to.

Franklin, Benj. Political, Miscellaneous, and Philosophical Pieces. 8vo. Lond. 1779.

———, ——, Examination of, relative to the Repeal of the Stamp Act. 8vo. Lond. 1767.

———, ——. Auszug der Anmerkungen, etc. 8vo.

———, ——. Œuvres, trad. de l'Anglois par B. Dubourg. 2 vol. en 1. 4to. Paris. 1773.

———, ——. Account of the New Invented Pennsylvania Fire-Places. 8vo. Phil. 1744.

———, ——. Experiments and observations on Electricity; in Letters to Mr. P. Collinson. 4to. Lond. 1751.

———, ——. The Same; with Letters and Papers on Philosophical Subjects. 4to. Lond. 1756.

———, ——. Works. 5 vols. 8vo. Phil. 1809.

———, ——. On the Causes and Cure of Smokey Chimnies. (Amer. Phil. Tr. vol. 2.)

———, ——. Letter proposing a slow sensible Hygrometer for certain Purposes. (Id.)

———, ——, Description of a New Stove for burning Pit-coal, and consuming all its Smoke. (Id.)

———, ——. Conjectures concerning the Formation of the Earth. (Id. 3.)

———, ——. New and Curious Theory of Light and Heat. (Id.)

———, ——. On making large Sheets of Paper in the Chinese Manner. (Id.)

———, ——. Queries and Conjectures relating to Magnetism and the Theory of the Earth. (Id.)

———, ——. 'Η 'Επιστήμη τοῦ Καλοῦ 'Ριχάρδου. (Poor Richard's maxims in Modern Greek.) 16mo. Paris. 1823.

Franklin, John. Narrative of a Journey to the Shores of thePolar Sea, in the Years 1819, 20, 21, and 22. 4to. Lond. 1823.

Franklin, W. T. Life of Dr. Franklin. See Franklin, B.

———. See Francklin.

Franks, John. On Animal Life, and Apparent Death, &c. 8vo. Lond. 1790.

Franz, F. C. Ueber die Kultur der Amerikaner. 12mo. Stuttgart. 1788.

Franzius, Wolfgangus. Historia Animalium Sacra. 12mo. Witteb. 1624.

Fraser, James. History of Nadir Shah, Emperor of Persia; and a Catalogue of Oriental MSS. 8vo. Lond. 1742.

Fraseus, Petrus. De Regio Patronatu Indiarum. 2 tomi. fol. Matriti. 1775.

Fratrum Polonorum, qui Unitarii appellantur, Bibliotheca, continens Opera Omnia J. Crellii Francii, L. Wolsogenii, F. Socini Senensis, et Exegetica J. Schlichtingii a Bucowiec. 8 vol. fol. Irenopoli. 1656.

——— ———. Idem. 9 vol. fol. Irenopoli et Eleutheropoli. 1656—92.

Frédéric II, (King of Prussia.) Code Frédéric, trad. de l'Allemand. 2 vol. en 3. 12mo. 1751—5.

Frédéric II, (King of Prussia.) The Frederician Code; from the French. 2 vols. 8vo. Lond. 1761.

———, ———. Memoirs of the House of Brandenburgh, &c. 12mo. Lond. 1751.

———, ———. The Same. 12mo. Lond. 1758.

———, ———. Epitre à M. Voltaire, Fr. et Angl. 4to. Lond. 1758.

———, ———. Œuvres Posthumes. 15 vol. 8vo. Berlin. 1789.

———, ———. Posthumous Works, tr. by Thomas Holcroft. 13 vols. 8vo. Lond. 1789.

Free Bridge. See Charlestown.

Free, John. Petition to the King, and Letter to the Earl of Bute, concerning the hard Case of an eminent Divine. 8vo. Lond. 1762.

——, ——. Speech on the English Constitution. 2d ed. 8vo. Lond. 1753.

——, ——. Seasonable Reflections upon the Importance of the Name of England. 8vo. Lond. 1755.

——, ——. Monthly Reviewers reviewed, by an Antigallican. 8vo. Lond. 1755.

——, ——. Poems. 8vo. Lond. 1751.

——, ——. The Same. 12mo. Lond. 1757.

——, ——. Stigand, or the Anti-Gallican; a Poem. 4to. Lond. 1750.

——, ——. Three Essays on the Employment of Time. 8vo. Lond. 1750.

——, ——. Essay towards a History of the English Tongue. 8vo. Lond. 1749.

——, ——. Matrimony made Easy. 2d ed. 8vo. Lond. 1764.

——, ——. Sermon before the University of Oxford. 8vo. Lond. 1743.

——, ——. A Volume of Sermons before the University of Oxford, with a Latin Oration on Transubstantiation. 8vo. Lond. 1750.

——, ——. Sermon before the Anti-Gallicans. 8vo. Lond. 1753.

——, ——. Sermon before the Same. 4to. Lond. 1756.

——, ——. Sermon before a Society of Florists. 2d ed. 8vo. Lond. 1764.

——, ——. Sermon before the University of Oxford. 2d ed. 8vo. Lond. 1764.

——, ——. Sermon upon 1 Peter iii, 8. 4to. Lond. 1756.

——, ——. Voluntary Exile; or the English Poets Sermon in Verse. 4to. Lond. 1765.

——, ——. Short View of the Brunswick-Genealogy. 4to.

——, ——. Speech to the Clergy of London at Sion College, May 8th. 8vo. Lond. 1759.

——, ——. Sermon on the Death of William Allen. 2d ed. 8vo. Lond. 1768.

——, ——. The Same. 3d ed. 8vo. Lond. 1768.

Free, John. Anniversary Sermon on the same occasion. 8vo. Lond. 1769.
——, ——. Sermon, Nov. 5th, 1745. 8vo. Lond. 1746.
——, ——. Sermon, January 30th. 8vo. Lond. 1753.
——, ——. Articles proposed to the Consideration of the Company of Salters in London, &c. 8vo. Lond. 1758.
——, ——. Rules for the Discovery of False Prophets; a Sermon at Oxford against the Methodists. 4to. and 8vo. Lond. 1758.
——, ——. The Same. 3d ed. 8vo. Lond. 1759.
——, ——. Edition of the Rev. J. Wesley's Letters, with Notes. 8vo. Lond. 1759.
——, ——. Display of the Bad Principles of the Methodists. 8vo. Lond. 1759.
——, ——. Remarks upon Mr. Jones Letter from the Mansions Above. 8vo. Lond. 1759.
——, ——. Plan for a Free University; with a Sketch of an Universal Liturgy for Foreign Students. 8vo. Lond. 1766.
——, ——. Petition to the House of Commons relative to the Conduct of the Abps. of Canterbury and York. 8vo. Lond. 1763.
——, ——. Two Stages in Physiology. 8vo. Lond. 1762.
Freedom, the First of Blessings. 4to.
———— of Speech and Writing upon Public Affairs considered. 4to. Lond. 1766.
Freeman, James. Collection of Psalms and Hymns. 12mo. Bost. 1799.
————, ——. Sermons on Particular Occasions. 8vo. Bost. 1812.
————, ——. See Allen, S.
————, ——. Liturgy. 8vo. Bost. 1785.
————, ——. Remarks on the American Universal Geography. 8vo. Bost. 1793.
————, ——. Description of Cape Cod. 8vo. Bost. 1802.
————, ——. Thanksgiving Sermon. 8vo. Bost. 1796.
————, ——, and Samuel Cary. Funeral Sermons. 8vo. Bost. 1820.
Freeman, P. R. Refutation of Aspersions in the "Vindication" of the Present Trustees of Dartmouth College on the Memory of their Predecessors. 4to. Portsmouth. 1816.
Freeman, Richard. Reports of Cases in Law and Equity. fol. Lond. 1742.
Freeman, Samuel. Discourse concerning Invocation of Saints. 4to. Lond. 1684.
————, ——. Dialogue concerning the Catholick Church. 4to. Lond. 1687.
Freeman, Samuel. Town Officer. 12mo. Bost. 1793.
Free-Thinker. 3 vols. 8vo. Lond. 1722—3.
Freherus, Marquardus. Sapphirus Constantii Imp. Aug. exposita a M. Frehero. 4to. Heidelb. 1681.
————, ——. Cecropistromachia. (Grævius, vol. 9.)

Freherus, Marquardus. De Re Monetaria veterum Romanorum et hodierni apud Germanos Imperii. (Id. 11.)

———, ———. Decisiones Areopagiticæ. (Gronov. vol. 5.)

Freigius, J. T. De Martini Forbisseri Angli Navigatione in Regiones Occidentis et Septentrionis, Narratio Historica, ex Gallico Sermone in Latinum translata. 12mo. Norib. 1580.

———, ———. Prædagogus. 12mo. Basil. 1582.

Freind, Joh. Opera Omnia Medica. fol. Lond. 1733.

———, —. Emmenologia. 8vo. Oxon. 1703.

———, —. Idem. 12mo. Rotterod. et Lug. Bat. 1711.

———, —. ——, tr. from the Latin by T. Dale. 8vo. Lond. 1752.

———, —. On Fevers, and on the Small Pox, tr. from the Latin by T. Dale. 8vo. Lond. 1730.

———, —. History of Physick, from the Time of Galen to the beginning of the 16th Century; with the Author's Life, &c. 4th ed. 2 vols. 8vo. Lond. 1750.

———, —. De Febribus. Vide Hippocrates.

Freind, Rob. Sermon, January 30th. 8vo. Lond. 1710.

Freinshemius, Jo. De Calidæ Potu. (Gronov. vol. 9.).

Freke, Tho. Sin and Danger of Rebelling against the Light. 8vo. Lond. 1716.

——, ——. Heroick Christian, a Sermon. 8vo. Lond. 1714.

——, ——. Sermon on Reformation of Manners. 12mo. Lond. 1704.

French Colonies. Relation de ce qui s'est passé en la Nouvelle France en l'année 1637, etc. 8vo. Rouen. 1638.

——— ———. Geschichte und Handlung der Französischen Pflanzstädte in Nordamerika. 12mo. Stutgart. 1756.

——— ———. La Ligne de Démarcation, ou Plan pour l'Approvisionnement des Isles Françoises. 4to.

——— ———. Recueil de Réglemens, Edits, etc. concernant les Colonies Françaises; avec le Code Noir. 12mo. Paris. 1765.

——— ———. Mémoires des Commissaires du Roi et de ceux de sa Majesté Britannique, sur les Possessions et les Droits respectifs des deux Couronnes en Amérique. 6 vol. 12mo. Paris. 1756.

——— ———. Observations des Négocians de Bordeaux sur l'Arrest du Conseil du 30 Août 1784. 8vo. Paris. 1784.

——— ———. Considérations sur l'Admission des Navires Neutres aux Colonies Françoises de l'Amérique en Tems de Guerre. 12mo. 1779.

——— ———. Mémoire sur le Commerce Etranger avec les Colonies Françaises de l'Amérique. 8vo. Paris. 1785.

——— ———. Essai sur l'Administration des Colonies Françoises. 8vo. Paris. 1788.

——— ———. Extraits des Régistres de l'Agence du Directoire Exécutif aux Isles du Vent. 4to. Port de la Liberté. 1798.

——— ———. Conversation d'un Officier d'Artillerie, sur les Colonies. 8vo.

——— ———. See Canada,—Colonies,—Recueil, etc.

French Constitution of 1793, in French and English, with Debates on it in the National Convention, &c. 8vo. N. York. 1817.
rench Invasions, Complete History of. from the Revolution. 8vo. F Lond. 1744.
French Prisoners of War. Proceedings of the Committee for Clothing them. fol. Lond. 1760.
——— ——————. See France.
French, Ebenezer. Oration, July 4th. 8vo. Bost. 1805.
French, Jacob. New American Melody. Bost. 1789.
French, Jona. Election Sermon. 8vo. Bost. 1796.
———, ——. Thanksgiving Sermon. 8vo. Newburyport. 1804.
———, ——. Sermon at the Ordination of the Rev. Jonathan French, jr. 8vo. Portsmouth. 1802.
———, ——. Sermon at the Ordination of the Rev. Daniel Oliver. 8vo. Newburyport. 1787.
French, Jonathan. Sketch of North Hampton, N. H. (Mass. Hist. Coll. N. S. vol. 4.)
Frenckel, G. N. Controversiæ inter Limborchium et Vitringam de Sensu Scripturæ Mystico jam nuper agitatæ Discussio. 4to. Kiliæ. 1716.
Frend, Wm. Thoughts on Subscription. 8vo. St. Ives. 1788.
———, ——. Appendix to the above. 8vo. St. Ives. 1789.
———, ——. Address to the Members of the Church of England and Protestant Trinitarians in general, against the Worship of the Trinity. 2d ed. 8vo. Lond. 1788.
———, ——. Second Address. 2d ed. 8vo. Lond. 1789.
———, ——. Mr. Coulthurst's Blunders exposed. 8vo. Lond. 1789.
———, ——. Account of some late Proceedings of the "Society for Promoting Christian Knowledge." 8vo. 1789.
Freneau, Philip. Poems. 3d ed. 2 vols. 12mo. Phil. 1809.
Freret, Nicolas. Sur l'Etude des Anciennes Histoires.—Sur les Principes de l'Art d'Ecrire, et en particulier sur les Fondemens de l'Ecriture Chinoise. (Acad. des Inscrip. vol. 6.)
———, ——. Sur le Nom de *Mérovingiens*. (Id. 20.)
———, ——. Sur la Religion des Gaulois, et sur celle des Germains. (Id. 24.)
Fresne, Carolus du. De Portu Iccio. Vide Gibson, E.
———, —————. Vide Cange, C.
Fresne, R. T. du. De Charondæ Effigie in Catanensi Nummo expressa. (Gronov. vol. 10.)
Fresnoy, C. A. du. Art of Painting, Latin and English, with Remarks, by J. Dryden; with an Account of Eminent Painters, by R. Graham. 2d ed. 8vo. Lond. 1716.
———, —————. The Same. 8vo. Lond. 1750.
Fréville, A. F. L. de. Histoire des Nouvelles Découvertes faites dans la Mer du Sud en 1767—70. 2 vol. 8vo. Paris. 1774.
Frey, Andrew. True Account of himself and the Moravians. 8vo. Lond. 1753.
Frey, J. S. C. F. Hebrew, Latin, and English Dictionary. 2 vols. 8vo. Lond. 1815.
——, —————. Hebrew Grammar. 8vo. Lond. 1813.

Frey, J. S. C. F. Biblia Hebraica.—Lexicon Hebraico-Chaldaico-Latino-Biblicum. 2 vol. 8vo. Lond. 1812—14.

Freyre, Fr. de Brito. Nova Lusitania, Historia da Guerra Brasilica. fol. Lisboa. 1675.

———, ———. Viage da Armada e Frotas do Brasil. fol. 1655.

———, ———. Relação da Viagem do Brazil. 24to. Lisboa. 1657.

Frézier, Amadeus Francis. Relation du Voyage de la Mer du Sud. 2 vol. 12mo. Amst. 1717.

———, ———. Idem. 4to. Paris. 1716.

———, ———. ———. 4to. Paris. 1732.

Friedemannus, F. T. De Media Syllaba Pentametri Græcorum Elegiaci. Vide Spitzner, F.

Friederich, A. Geschichte der Heidelberger Bibliothek. 8vo. Karls. 1816.

Friedlibius, P. H. Theologia Exegetica. fol. Francof. ad Mœn. 1660.

Friendship, True, distinguished from that which is False, in a Short Narrative of the Life of Jack Saunders. 12mo. Bost. 1812.

Frink, Tho. Election Sermon. 8vo. Bost. 1758.

———, ———. Sermon at the Ordination of Mr. John Willard. 8vo. Bost. 1757.

Frisbie, Levi. Inaugural Address. 8vo. Camb. 1817.

———, ———. See Norton, A.

———, ———. Miscellaneous Writings; with Notices of his Life and Character, by A. Norton. 8vo. Bost. 1823.

Frisby, Levi. Oration at the Interment of the Rev. Moses Parsons. 8vo.

Frisius, Jo. Dictionarium Latino-Germanicum. fol.

Fritsch, J. G. Disputatio; utrum Veteres Americam noverint, nec ne. 8vo. Curiæ Regnitianæ. 1796.

Fritzsche, C. F. A. Evangelium Matthæi. 8vo. Lips. 1826.

Frobisher, Sir Martin. Passage by the Northwest. (Eden and Willes, Travayles.)

———, ———. Trois Navigations pour chercher un Passage à la Chine, etc. par la Mer Glaciale, en 1576—8, trad. de l'Anglois. 12mo. Amst. 1720.

———, ———. Vide Freigius, J. T. Vide Recueil.

Frœlich, Erasmus. Annales Regum et Rerum Syriæ Numis Veteribus illustrati. fol. Viennæ. 1754.

Froger, T. Voyage of M. de Gennes to the Streights of Magellan, &c. 8vo. Lond. 1698.

Froissart, Sir John. Vide Frossardus.

Frölich, Wenceslaus. Vide Mader, A.

Fromentin, E. Observations on a Bill before Congress respecting the Titles to Land within the Territory of Orleans, &c. 8vo.

Frontinus, Sextus Julius. Opera. 8vo. Biponti. 1788.

———, ———. De Aquæductibus Romæ Commentarius, opera J. Poleni. 4to. Patavii. 1722.

———, ———. Idem. (Grævius, vol. 4.)

———, ———. ———. Vide Cleonidas.

Frontinus, Sextus Julius. Libri Quatuor Strategematicon, cum Notis Variorum, cura N. Schwebelii. 8vo. Lips. 1772.
———, ————. Vide Scriptores de Re Militari.
Fronto, M. C. De Differentiis Vocabulorum. Vide Grammatici Veteres Latini.
———, ————. Opera Inedita, etc., ab A. Maio. 2 vol. 8vo. Francof. ad Mœn. 1816.
Frossard, M. La Cause des Esclaves Nègres et des Habitans de la Guinée. 2 vol. 8vo. Lyon. 1789.
Frossardus, Jo. Historiarum Epitome, a J. Sleidano collecta et Latinitate donata. Vide Rerum Britannicarum Scriptores Vetustiores.
Frothingham, N. L. Sermon on the Death of the Rev. J. McKean. 8vo. Bost. 1818.
————, ——. Artillery Election Sermon. 8vo. Bost. 1825.
Fry, Edmund. Pantographia, containing all known Alphabets. 8vo. Lond. 1799.
Fuel, Plan for supplying the City of New-York with. 8vo. N. York. 1814.
——, Experiments to determine the Comparative Value of the principal Varieties of, &c. by Marcus Bull. (Amer. Phil. Tr. vol. 3. N. S.)
——. Defence of the "Experiments," by M. Bull. 8vo. Phil. 1828.
——. Short Reply to the "Defence," (by J. Bigelow.) 8vo. Bost. 1828.
——. Answer to the "Short Reply," by M. Bull. 8vo. Phil. 1828.
Fuero Juzgo. Vide Academia Real Española.
Fuessly, J. G. Inseckten. 4to. Winterthour. 1794.
Fugitive Pieces on various Subjects, by several Authors. 2 vols. 12mo. Lond. 1765.
Fuhrmann, W. D. Handbuch der Classischen Literatur. 4 Bände. 8vo. Halle. 1807—10.
————, ——. Handbuch der Theologischen Literatur. 2 Bände. 8vo. Leipz. 1818—19.
Fulbecke, Wm. Pandectes of the Law of Nations. 4to. Lond. 1602.
———, ——. Parellel. 16mo. Lond. 1602.
Fulgentius, F. P. Mythologicon;—Virgiliana Continentia;—Expositio Sermonum Antiquorum. (Mythographi Latini.)
Fulgentius, Sanctus. Opera. Item, Opera J. Maxentii. 4to. Hagenau. 1519.
Fulke, Wm. See Testament, New.
Fuller, Andrew. The Gospel its own Witness. 8vo. Clipstone. 1799.
Fuller, Sam. Canonica Successio Ministerii Ecclesiæ Anglicanæ Reformatæ vindicata. 4to. Cant. 1690.
Fuller, Stephen. Act of the Assembly of Jamaica respecting Slaves. 4to. Lond. 1788.
——, ———. Two Reports from a Committee of the Assembly of Jamaica respecting the Slave-Trade, &c. 4to. Lond. 1789.
Fuller, Tho. Historie of the Holy Warre. fol. Camb. 1640.

Fuller, Tho. Holy State;—Profane State. fol. Lond. 1642.
——, ——. Church-History of Britain. fol. Lond. 1656.
——, ——. History of the University of Cambridge. fol. Lond. 1655.
——, ——. History of Waltham Abbey. fol. Lond. 1655.
——, ——. Pisgah-Sight of Palestine, &c. fol. Lond. 1662.
——, ——. History of the Worthies of England. fol. Lond. 1662.
Fuller, Tho. Pharmacopœia Extemporanea. 4th ed. 8vo. Lond. 1730.
——, ——. Idem. 5th ed. 8vo. Lond. 1740.
Fuller, Timothy. Oration, July 4th. 8vo. Bost. 1809.
——, ——. Address to the Massachusetts Peace Society. 8vo. Bost. 1827.
Fuller, Wm. Ephemeris Parliamentaria. fol. Lond. 1654.
Fulmannus, Gul. Rerum Anglicarum Scriptorum Veterum. Tom. 1. fol. Oxoniæ. 1684.
Fulton, Robert. Treatise on the Improvement of Canal Navigation. 4to. Lond. 1796.
——, ——. Torpedo War. 4to. N. York. 1810.
——, ——. See Canals.
Fulvius, Andr. Antiquitates Urbis. fol. Romæ. 1527.
Fumanus, Adam. Carmina. Vide Fracastorius.
Fumus, Barth. Summa sive Aurea Armilla. 8vo. Antv. 1576.
Funccius, Joh. Nic. De Adolescentia Latinæ Linguæ. 4to. Marburgi Cattorum. 1723.
——, ——. De Virili Ætate Latinæ Linguæ. 2 vol. 4to. Marb. Cat. 1727—30.
——, ——. De Imminenti Latinæ Linguæ Senectute. 4to. Marb. Cat. 1736.
Funcius, J. Chronologia. Vide Witichindus.
Fundanus, M. Phrases Poeticæ. 16mo. Rothomagi. 1621.
Funera et Ritus Veterum Christianorum. (Anecdota Gr. a Wolfio.)
Funeral Discourses. 8vo. 1761—1803.
—— Sermons. See Sermons.
—— Sermons, Orations, and Odes, Essay on the Original of. 8vo. Lond. 1729.
—— Solemnities, Brief Dissertation on. 8vo. Lond. 1745.
Funke, C. P. Real-Schullexicon. 5 Theile. 8vo. Brauns. 1800—5.
——, ——. Atlas der Alten Welt. Weimar. 1800.
Furius, Frid. Bononia. 8vo. Lug. Bat. 1819.
Furlong, Laurence. American Coast Pilot. 8vo. Newburyport. 1800.
Furneaux, Philip. Sermon on the Death of the Rev. H. Miles. 8vo. Lond. 1758.
——, ——. Fast Sermon. 8vo. Lond. 1758.
——, ——. Charity Sermon. 8vo. Lond. 1755.
——, ——. Letters to Mr. Justice Blackstone on his Exposition of the Act of Toleration, &c. 8vo. Lond. 1770.
——, ——. The Same. 2d ed. 8vo. Lond. 1771.
Fuscus, Palladius. De Situ Oræ Illyrici. (Græv. Thes. Ital.)

Fusi, F. Bibliografia delle Opere contenute nella Collezione de' Classici Italiani. 8vo. Milano. 1814.
Future State, or a Discourse attempting some Display of the Souls Happiness in Heaven. 12mo. Lond. 1683.
——— ——. Necessity of believing it, in order to being truly Religious. 8vo. Lond. 1718.
Fyfe, Andrew. Compendium of Anatomy. 3 vols. 4to. Edin. 1800.
——, ————. The Same. 2 vols. 12mo. Edin. 1800.
——, ————. Outlines of Comparative Anatomy. 8vo. Edin. 1818.
Fysh, Henry. Sermon on Prov. x, 27. 8vo. Lond. 1738.

G

GAAB, L. Beiträge zur Erklärung des Hohenlied, und der Klaglieder. 12mo. Tübingen. 1795.

Gäbler, J. P. Journal für auserlesene Theologische Literatur. 5 Bände (1—5) und Bd. vi, St. 1. 8vo. Nürnberg. 1805—11.

Gadsden, C. E. Discourse on the Death of Bishop Dehon. 8vo. Charleston. 1817.

Gaetano, Enea. La Peste di Messina. 12mo. Venez. 1747.

Gaffarel, J. Curiositez inouyes sur la Sculpture Talismanique des Persans, Horoscope des Patriarches, et Lecture des Estoilles. 8vo. 1637.

Gage, Tho. New Survey of the West Indies. 4th ed. 8vo. Lond. 1699.

——, ——. Nouvelle Relation des Indes Occidentales, trad. de l'Anglois par B. H. O'Neil. 2 vol. 12mo. Paris. 1676.

——, ——. Idem. 4me ed. 2 vol. 12mo. Amst. 1720.

Gage, Tho. (Gen.) Letters. See Bernard, Sir F.—See Massachusetts.

Gagliardi, Paolo. Antico Statu de' Cenomani, etc. 8vo. Padova. 1724.

Gagnier, J. Vie de Mahomet. 2 vol. 12mo. Amst. 1732.

————, –. De Nummis Samaritanis. (Ugol. vol. 28.)

Gahn, J. T. De Causis cur Homo Christianus in hac Vita ad Perfectam Sanctitatem pervenire non possit. 4to. Altorfii. 1738.

Gail, J. B. Nouvelle Grammaire Grecque. 8vo. Paris. 1805.

——, ——. Le Jardin des Racines Grecques. 12mo. Paris. 1813.

——, ——. Anthologie Poétique Grecque. 8vo. Paris. 1801.

——, ——. Cour de Langue Grecque. 8vo. Paris. 1808.

Gailhard, J. Right of the Church asserted. 4to. Lond. 1660.

Gaillard, G. H. Sur les Lombards. (Acad. des Inscrip. vol. 32 et 35.)

Galard-Terraube, (M. le Vicomte de.) Tableau de Cayenne. 8vo. Paris. 1799.

Galateus, Ant. De Situ Japygiæ. (Græv. Thes. Ital.)

Gale, John. Reflections on Mr. Wall's History of Infant-Baptism. 8vo. Lond. 1711.

——, ——. Sermons, with his Life. 4 vols. 8vo. Lond. 1724—6.

Gale, Theophilus. Court of the Gentiles; or a Discourse touching the Original of Human Literature, from the Scriptures and Jewish Church. 2d ed. 3 vols. 4to. Oxon. 1672—8.

Gale, Tho. Historiæ Anglicanæ Scriptores Quinque. fol. Oxon. 1687.

Gale, Tho. Historiæ Britannicæ, Saxonicæ, Anglo-Danicæ, Scriptores xv. fol. Oxon. 1691.
Galenus, Claudius. Opera Omnia, Latine, per G. Gesnerum. 4 vol. fol. Lugduni. 1550.
———, ———. Idem, cum A. M. Brasavoli Indice. 5 vol. fol. Venet. 1609.
———, ———. Septima Classis, cum Oribasio de Laqueis et de Machinamentis, Latine. fol. Basil. 1561.
Galerie. 8vo. Paris. Avril. 1820.
Gales, J. C. Sulle Fumigazioni dello Zolfo. 8vo.
Galfredus Monumetensis. De Origine et Gestis Regum Britanniæ. Vide Rerum Britannicarum Scriptores Vet.
Galignani. Twenty-four Lectures on the Italian Language. 8vo. Lond. 1796.
Galilei, Galileo. Opere. 13 vol. 8vo. Milano. 1808—11.
———, ———. Systeme of the World. (Salusbury, T. Mathematical Collections.)
———, ———. Sidereus Nuncius. Vide Gassendus, P.
———, ———. Dialogues on Mechanicks and Local Motion, with an Appendix on the Center of Gravity; done into English from the Italian by T. & J. Weston. 4to. Lond. 1730.
Gallais, M. Histoire du Dix-Huit Brumaire et de Buonaparte, etc. 3 vol. 8vo. Paris. 1814—18.
Galland, Ant. De Tubæ Origine et Usu apud Veteres. (Ugol. vol. 32.)
Gallatin, Albert. Speech in Congress on the Foreign Intercourse Bill. 2d ed. 8vo. Phil. 1798.
———, ———. Sketch of the Finances of the United States. 8vo. N. York. 1796.
———, ———. Views of the Public Debt, Receipts, and Expenditures of the United States. 8vo. N. York. 1800.
Gallaudet, Tho. H. Discourses on Christian Faith and Practice. 8vo. N. York. 1818.
Gallesio, Georges. Traité du Citrus. 8vo. Paris. 1811.
Gallicanus, Vulcatius. Avidius Cassius. Vide Historiæ Augustæ Scriptores, et Rom. Hist. Scriptores.
Gallichon. Vide Roche Gallichon, J. C. de la.
Gallison, John. Address before the Massachusetts Peace Society. 8vo. Camb. 1820.
———, ———. Explanation of the Views of the Society for Employing the Female Poor, &c. 8vo. Camb. 1825.
Gallois, (M. le.) Experiments on the Principle of Life, tr. by N. C. and J. G. Nancrede. 8vo. Phil. 1813.
Galloway, Joseph. Speech in Answer to the Speech of John Dickinson, May 24, 1764. 8vo. Phil. 1765.
———, ———, Examination of, before the House of Commons. 8vo. Lond. 1789.
———, ———, Interrogatorien van. 8vo. 1781.
———, ———. Letter to Ld. H——e, on his Naval Conduct in the American War. 8vo. Lond. 1779.
———, ———. Letters to a Nobleman on the Conduct of the War in the Middle Colonies. 2d e 8vo. Lond. 1779.

Galloway, Joseph. Reply to the Observations of Gen. Howe on "Letters to a Nobleman," &c. 2d ed. 8vo. Lond. 1781.
———, ——. Cool Thoughts on the Consequences to Great Britain of American Independence, &c. 8vo. Lond. 1780.
———, ——. Candid Examination of the Mutual Claims of Great Britain and her Colonies. 8vo. N. York. 1780.
———, ——. Historical and Political Reflections on the Rise and Progress of the American Rebellion. 8vo. Lond. 1780.
Galloway, Samuel. Plan for a proposed Union between Great Britain and her Colonies. 8vo. N. York. 1775.
Galpine, John. Sermon on Reformation of Manners. 12mo. Lond. 1703.
Galt, John. Voyages and Travels in 1809, 1810 and 1811. 4to. Lond. 1812.
Galtruchius, P. Mathematicæ Totius Institutio. 16mo. Lond. 1683.
Gama, Ant. de. Felicidad de Mexico en el Principio, etc. 4to. Sevilla. 1685.
Gamba, Bartolommeo. Serie dell' Edizioni de' Testi di Lingua Italiana. 16mo. Milano. 1812.
Gamboa, Fr. Xavier de. Comentarios à las Ordenanzas de Minas. fol. Madrid. 1761.
Gambóa, P. S. de. Viage al Estrecho de Magallanes. 4to. Madrid. 1768.
Gamon, Achille. Mémoires. (Mém. de France, vol. 46.)
Gamucci, Bernardo. Antichità della Città di Roma. 8vo. Vineg. 1580.
Gand, Ludov. de. Parallelum Olivæ, nec non Olivarii Protectoris, etc. fol. Lond. 1656.
Gandini, M. A. Le Opere di Senofonte Ateniese, trad. dal Greco. 3 vol. 4to. Verona. 1736—7.
Ganilh, Charles. Inquiry into the Various Systems of Political Economy, tr. from the French by Boileau. 8vo. N. York. 1812.
Gaon, R. Chai. Carmen Ethicum, cum Versione Latina J. Eberti. (Ugol. vol. 31.)
Garcæus, Joh. Meteorologia. 8vo. Witeb. 1568.
Garces, G. Fundamento del Vigor y Elegancia de la Lengua Castellana. 2 vol. 8vo. Madrid. 1791.
Garcia, Fr. G. Origen de los Indios de el Nuevo Mundo. fol. Madrid. 1729.
Garcia, Vicent. Poesias Varias. 4to. Barcelona. 1700.
Garçias ab Orto. Aromatum et Simplicium aliquot Medicamentorum apud Indos nascentium Historia, a C. Clusio. 8vo. Antv. 1593.
——— ———. Vide Clusius, C.
Garci'aso de la Vega. Obras. 16mo. Madrid. 1796.
——— ———. Vide Boscan.
Garcilaso de la Vega, (el Inca.) Historia General del Peru, ó Comentarios Reales de los Incas. 2 vol. fol. Madrid. 1722—3.
——— ———. Idem. 13 vol. 16mo. Madrid. 1800—1.

Garcilaso de la Vega, (el Inca.) Royal Commentaries of Peru, rendered into English by Sir Paul Ricaut. fol. Lond. 1688.
——— ———————. Historia de la Florida. fol. Madrid. 1723.
——— ———————. Idem. 4 vol. 16mo. Madrid. 1803.
——— ———————. Histoire de la Conquête de la Floride, trad. de l'Espagnol par R. Richelet. 12mo. Paris. 1719.
Garden, Alex. Six Letters to the Rev. Geo. Whitefield; with Whitefields Answer to the First. 2d ed. 12mo. Bost. 1740.
———, ———. Doctrine of Justification, according to the Scriptures, and the Articles and Homilies of the Church of England vindicated, in a Letter to A. Croswell. 8vo. S. Carolina. 1742.
Gardener, Henry. New-Englands Vindication. 4to. Lond. 1660.
Gardenier, Barent. Examiner. vol. 1. 8vo. N. York. 1814.
Gardiner, James, (Bp.) Fast Sermon. 4to. Lond. 1695.
Gardiner, John. Speech on the Theatre.—Dissertation on the Ancient Poetry of the Romans. 8vo. Bost. 1792.
Gardiner, J. S. J. Convention Sermon at the Ordination of the Rev. James Bowers. 4to. Bost. 1802.
———, ———. Sermon before the Massachusetts Humane Society. 8vo. Bost. 1803.
———, ———. Address before the Massachusetts Charitable Fire Society. 8vo. Bost. 1803.
———, ———. Preservative against Unitarianism, a Sermon. 8vo. Bost. 1811.
———, ———. Sermon before the Society of Donations, &c. 8vo. Bost. 1813.
Gardiner, R. Vide Instructor Clericalis.
Gardiner, Richard. Account of the Expedition to the West Indies. 3d ed. 4to. Birmingham. 1762.
———, ———. Relation de l'Expédition aux Indes Occidentales. 3me ed. 4to. Birmingham. 1762.
Gardiner, Silvester. Tracts relating to the Case between him and James Flagg. 12mo. Bost. 1767.
Gardiner, W. Tables de Logarithmes. 4to. Avignon. 1770.
Gardiner, W. H. See Pickering, O.
Garidel, Joseph. Histoire des Plantes des Environs d'Aix. fol. Aix. 1715.
Garmannus, J. T. De Pane Lugentium. (Ugol. vol. 33.)
Garmston, John. Sermon to Prisoners for Debt. 8vo. Lond. 1715.
Garmston, Sh. Thanksgiving Sermon. 8vo. Lond. 1716.
———, ——. Sermon, November 5th. 8vo. Lond. 1716.
Garner, John. Le Nouveau Dictionnaire Universel, François-Anglois, et Anglois-François. 2 vol. 4to. Rouen. 1802.
Garnet, Tho. Account of the Drosacks. (Pinkerton, vol. 3.)
———, ———. Outlines of a Course of Lectures on Chemistry. 8vo. Lond. 1801.
Garnham, Rob. Edw. Letter to the Bishop of Chester on the subject of Two Sermons addressed by him to the Clergy of his Diocese. 8vo. Lond. 1790.

Garnier. Collection des Fruits de l'Asie, de l'Afrique, et de l'Amérique. 8vo. 1812.
Garnier, J. J. Sur Platon. (Acad. des Inscrip. vol. 32.)
———, —. Sur les Paradoxes Philosophiques. (Id. 35.)
Garth, Sir Samuel. Dispensary. 9th ed. 12mo. Lond. 1726.
———, ———. ———. 10th ed. 12mo. Lond. 1741.
———, ———. Poems. See Chalmers, A.
———, ———. Ovid's Metamorphoses, translated by Dryden, Addison, Garth, and others, and published by Sir S. Garth. 5th ed. 2 vols. 12mo. Lond. 1751.
Garuffius, J. M. Lucerna Lapidaria, quæ Titulos, Monimenta, Sepulchra, etc. tum Gentilium, tum Christianorum, Via Flaminia, et Arimini scrutatur. (Græv. Thes. Ital.)
Gascoigne, George. Poems. See Chalmers, A.
Gaspar da Madre de Deos, Fr. Memorias para a Historia da Capitania de S. Vicente. Vide Academia Real das Sciencias.
Gaspard de Saulx, Seigneur de Tavannes. Mémoires. (Mém. de France, vol. 27 et 28.)
Gass, P. Journal of the Voyages and Travels of a Corps of Discovery under Capts. Lewis and Clarke. 12mo. Pittsburgh. 1807.
———, —. The Same. 2d ed. 12mo. Phil. 1810.
Gassendus, Petrus. Vita N. Claudii Fabricii de Peiresc. 24to. Hagæ Com. 1651.
———, ———. Institutio Astronomica. Cui accesserunt Galilei Nuncius Siderius, et J. Kepleri Dioptrice. 8vo. Lond. 1653.
———, ———. Idem. 3tia ed. 8vo. Lond. 1683.
———, ———. Opera Omnia, curante N. Averanio. 6 vol. fol. Florentiæ. 1727.
———, ———. Kalendarium Romanum. (Grævius, vol. 8.)
Gastrell, Fr. (Bp.) Eight Sermons at Boyle's Lecture. 8vo. Lond. 1697.
———, ———. The Same. 2d ed. 8vo. Lond. 1703.
———, ———. Charity Sermon. 8vo. Lond. 1707.
———, ———. Certainty of the Christian Revelation. 8vo. Lond. 1699.
———, ———. Fast Sermon. 4to. Lond. 1704.
———, ———. Christian Institutes. 8vo. Lond. 1707.
———, ———. The Same. 9th ed. 12mo. Lond. 1762.
Gataker, Tho. De Nomine Tetragrammato Dissertatio. 12mo. Lond. 1645.
———, ———. Opera Critica;—Marci Antonini Imperatoris de Rebus suis Libri xii, Gr. et Lat., cum Commentario;—Opuscula Varia. fol. Traj. ad Rhen. 1698.
———, ———. Sermons. fol. Lond. 1637.
———, ———. De Diphthongis. 12mo. Lond. 1646.
Gatchel, Sam. Signs of the Times. 8vo. Danvers. 1781.
Gates, Hezekiah. King George's Right to the Crown of Great Britain. 8vo. Bost. 1769.

Gattus, Ant. Historia Gymnasii Ticinensis, etc. (Græv. Thes. Ital.)
Gaubius, H. D. Institutiones Pathologiæ Medicinalis. 3tia ed. 8vo. Leid. Bat. 1781.
———, ———. Institutions of Medical Pathology, tr. from the Latin by C. Erskine. 8vo. Edin. 1778.
Gaudentius Philosophus. Harmonica Introductio, Gr. et Lat. Vide Musicæ Auctores.
Gaufredus. Vide Malaterra.
Gauricus, Pomp, De Sculptura. (Gronov. vol. 9.)
Gavantus, Barth. Thesaurus Sacrorum Rituum. 3 vol. fol. Aug. Vind. 1763.
Gavin, Ant. Master-Key to Popery. 3d ed. 8vo. Lond. 1773.
Gay, Bunker. Sermon at Keene before the Inferior Court. 8vo. Portsmouth, N. H. 1773.
Gay, Eben. Sermon at the Funeral of the Rev. John Hancock. 8vo. Bost. 1744.
——, ——. Two Sermons on the Death of the Rev. Jonathan Mayhew. 8vo. Bost. 1766.
——, ——. Old Man's Calender, a Discourse. 12mo. Bost. 1781.
——, ——. Sermon at the Ordination of the Rev. Jonathan Dorby. 8vo. Bost. 1752.
——, ——. Sermon at the Ordination of the Rev. Caleb Gannet. 8vo. Bost. 1768.
——, ——. Sermon at the Installment of the Rev. G. Rawson. 8vo. Bost. 1756.
——, ——. Dudleian Lecture. 8vo. Bost. 1759.
——, ——. Election Sermon. 8vo. Bost. 1745.
——, ——. Thanksgiving Sermon. 8vo. Bost. 1771.
——, ——. Artillery Election Sermon. 8vo. Bost. 1728.
——, ——. Convention Sermon. 8vo. Bost. 1746.
Gay, John. Poems. 4to. Lond. 1720.
——, ——. ———. See Chalmers, A.
Gayll, Andr. Practicarum Observationum Libri Duo.—De Pace Publica.—De Pignationibus. fol. Col. Agrip. 1578.
Gaza, Theodorus. De Mensibus Atticis. (Gronov. vol. 9.)
——, —————. Introductionis Grammaticæ Libri Quatuor, Gr et Lat. 8vo. Basil. 1538.
——, —————. De Origine Turcarum. (Clauser, de Reb. Turc.)
Gazaignes, (l'Abbé Philibert.) Annales de la Société des soidisans Jésuites. 5 vol. 4to. Paris. 1764—71.
Gazeta de Literatura. 4to. Mexico. 1788—9.
Gazette, American, being a Collection of Addresses, &c. relating to the Dispute between Great Britain and her Colonies, &c. 6 Nos. (1—6.) 8vo. Lond. 1768—70.
———, Boston, and Country Journal, by Edes and Gill, &c. 16 vols. fol. Bost. 1769—84.
———, National, by P. Freneau. 2 vols. fol. Phil. 1791—2.
———, ———, by R. Walsh. 1820—2. fol. Phil.
———, Philadelphia. 1794—9. fol. Phil.

Gazette, Pennsylvania. 1761—8. fol. Phil.
———, Salem. 1792—1805. fol. Salem.
———, United States. 1789—93, 1795—7, 1801—8, 1818. fol. Phil.
———. See Centinel,—Chronicle,—Journal,—Palladium,—Repertory, &c.
Gazetteer, American. 3 vols. 12mo. Lond. 1762.
————, North American and West Indian. 2d ed. 12mo. Lond. 1778.
———— of the Towns in Massachusetts. 8vo. Bost.
———— of Upper Canada, &c. 8vo. N. York. 1812.
Gebelin, Court de. Monde Primitif analysé et comparé avec le Monde Moderne. 7 vol. 4to. Paris. 1773—81.
———, ————. Histoire Naturelle de la Parole. 8vo. Paris. 1776.
Geber Arabs. De Alchemia. 12mo. Argent. 1598.
Gedæus, H. B. De Instrumento Circumcisionis a Zippora et Josua adhibito. (Ugol. vol. 22.)
Geddes, Alex. Prospectus of a New Translation of the Bible, with Letters, &c. concerning it. 4to. Lond. 1786—94.
———, ——. Critical Remarks on the Hebrew Scriptures. vol. 1. 4to. Lond. 1800.
———, ——. Holy Bible, tr. from corrected Texts of the Originals, with Notes, &c. 2 vols. 4to. Lond. 1792—7. (Unfinished.)
———, ——. New Translation of the Psalms. 8vo. Lond. 1807.
———, ——. Vide Vater, J. S.
Geddes, James. Essay on the Composition of the Ancients, particularly Plato. 8vo. Glasgow. 1748.
Geddes, Mich. History of the Church of Malabar, done out of Portugueze into English. 8vo. Lond. 1694.
———, ——. Church-History of Ethiopia. 8vo. Lond. 1696.
———, ——. Miscellaneous Tracts relating to Spain, Portugal, and the Pope. 3 vols. 8vo. Lond. 1702—6.
———, ——. Tracts against Popery; with the Life of Don Alvaro de Luna. 8vo. Lond. 1715.
Gedoyn, N. Histoire de Dedale.—Histoire de Phidias. (Acad. des Inscrip. vol. 9.)
Gee, Edw. Veteres Vindicati, in an Expostulatory Letter to Mr. Sclater. 2d ed. 4to. Lond. 1687.
——, ——. Answer to the Nubes Testium. 4to. Lond. 1688.
——, ——. Vindication of the Author of the above "Answer." 4to. Lond. 1688.
——, ——. Letter to Father L. Sabran Jesuite. 4to. Lond. 1688.
——, ——. Second Letter to Sabran. 4to. Lond. 1688.
——, ——. Third Letter to Sabran. 4to. Lond. 1688.
——, ——. Primitive Fathers no Papists. 4to. Lond. 1688.
——, ——. Letter to the Licensers of Books concerning Sabran. 4to. Lond. 1688.
Gee, Joshua. Letter to the Rev. N. Eells, Moderator of the late Convention of Pastors in Boston. 4to. Bost. 1743.

Gee, Joshua. Sermon on the Death of Cotton Mather. 8vo. Bost. 1728.
Gee, Joshua. Trade and Navigation of Great Britain considered. 8vo. Lond. 1729.
——, ——. The Same. 3d ed. 8vo. Lond. 1731.
——, ——. ————. 12mo. Lond. 1767.
——, ——. Considérations sur le Commerce et la Navigation de la Grande Bretagne, trad. de l'Anglois. 12mo. Amst. 1750.
——, ——, and Others. Two Papers on the subject of Taxing the British Colonies in America. 8vo. Lond. 1767.
Geierus, Mart. Opera Omnia quæ Latine edita sunt. 2 vol. fol. Amst. 1695—6.
———, ——. Commentarius in Psalmos. fol. Dresdæ, etc. 1681.
Geigerus, G. E. De Hillele et Sammai. (Ugol. vol. 21.)
Gejerus, Mart. De Hebræorum Luctu. (Ugol. vol. 33.)
Gelli, Gio. Battista. Opere. 3 vol. 8vo. Milano. 1804—7.
——, ————. La Circe. 12mo. Venet. 1600.
Gellius, Aulus. Noctes Atticæ; ad usum Delphini. 4to. Paris. 1681.
———, ———. Idem, cum Notis J. Gronovii, etc. 4to. Lug. Bat. 1706.
Gelone, F. D. Manuel-Guide des Voyageurs aux Etats-Unis. 12mo. Paris. 1818.
Gemistus, Geo. Pletho. De iis quæ post Pugnam Mantinensem apud Græcos gesta sunt; cum Notis, ab H.G. Reichardo. 12mo. Lips. 1770. Vide etiam Herodotus.
————, ————. Dell' Istorie de' Greci, trad. in Ital. da G. A. dalla Bona. 4to. Verona. 1736.
Gendre, A. M. le. Essai sur la Théorie des Nombres. 4to. Paris. 1798.
———, ————. See Farrar, J.
Genebrardus, Gilb. Chronographiæ Libri iv, cum Appendice P. Victoris. fol. Paris. 1600.
Genèse, Conjectures sur la. 12mo. Bruxelles. 1753.
Genesee. Description of the Genesee Country. 4to. Albany. 1798.
———. Berichte über den Genesee-Distrikt. 8vo. 1791.
Genesius, Josephus. De Rebus Constantinopolitanis. (Byz. Scrip.)
Genest, E. J. Etat Politique Actuel de l'Angleterre. 10 vol. 12mo. 1757—9.
Genius der Zeit. Zehntes Stück. 8vo. 1798.
Genlis, (Madame de.) Manual of Expressions, French and English. 12mo. Bost. 1817.
———, ————. Jane of France; from the French. 2 vols. 12mo. Bost. 1817.
Genoa, History of the Revolutions of. 3 vols. 12mo. Lond. 1751.
———. Journal de ce qui s'est passé à Gènes et aux Environs, depuis le 11 d'Avril, 1747. 4to. Gènes. 1749.
———. Vide Gravier, J.
———. Journal of what happened at Genoa from the Irruption of the Austrian and Piedmontese Armies; tr. from the French. 8vo. Lond. 1747.

Genoa. Reflections on the late Convention between the Courts of Vienna and Turin for partitioning Genoa. 8vo. Lond. 1747.
Genovesi, Ant. Della Diceosina, o sia della Filosofia del Giusto, e dell' Onesto. 3 vol. 12mo. Napoli.
———, —. Lezioni di Commercio o sia d' Economia Civile. 2 vol. 12mo. Bassano. 1788.
———, —. Vide Cary, John.
———, —. Elementi di Fisica Sperimentale. 2 vol. 12mo. Napoli. 1791.
———, —. Meditazioni Filosofiche sulla Religione, e sulla Morale. 12mo. Bassano. 1783.
———, —. Lettere Filosofiche. 3za ediz. 12mo. Napoli. 1785.
———, —. Logica. 4ta ediz. 12mo. Napoli. 1790.
———, —. Delle Scienze Metafisiche. 12mo. Napoli. 1791.
Gentilis, Albericus. De Actoribus et Spectatoribus Fabularum non notandis Disputatio. (Gronov. vol. 8.)
Gentilis, Scipio. Commentarius in Pauli Epistolam ad Philemonem. 4to. Traj. ad Rhen. 1744.
Gentleman's Calling. See Fell, J. See Whole Duty of Man.
Gentleman's Recreation in Four Parts, viz. Hunting, Hawking, Fowling, and Fishing. 6th ed. 8vo. Lond. 1721.
——— Pocket Remembrancer for 1805, and 1813. 18mo. Phil.
Genty, (l'Abbé.) L'Influence de la Découverte de l'Amérique sur le Bonheur du Genre-Humain. 8vo. Paris. 1788.
Gentz, Fred. Fragments upon the Balance of Power in Europe; from the German. 8vo. Lond. 1806.
Geoffroy. Entomologia. 2 vol. 4to. Paris. 1800.
———. Mémoires dans les Annales du Muséum d'Histoire Naturelle.
Geographia Classica. 4to. Lond. 1712.
Geographische Belustigungen zur Erläuterung der neuesten Weltgeschichte. Stücke, 1, 2. 4to. Leipz. 1776.
Geological and Agricultural Survey, &c. See Rensselaer.
Geoponicorum, sive de Re Rustica, Libri xx, Cassiano Basso Collectore; Gr. et Lat.; a Jo. Nicolao Niclas. 4 vol. 8vo. Lips. 1781.
George II. Letters and Messages on occasion of the Birth of the Princess. 8vo. 1737.
——— —. Review of his Reign. 2d ed. 8vo. Lond. 1762.
George III, History of the Reign of, to May 1770. 8vo. Lond. 1770.
——— —. Sketch of his Reign, from 1780 to the close of 1790. 8vo. Lond. 1791.
Georgia, Impartial Enquiry into the State and Utility of the Province of. 8vo. Lond. 1741.
———. Grant to the Georgia Mississippi Company, the Constitution thereof, &c. 8vo. Augusta. 1795.
———. Case of the Georgia Sales on the Mississippi considered. 8vo. Lond. 1797.

Georgia. Memorial of the Agents of the New England Mississippi Land Company to Congress, &c. 8vo.
———. Remarks on the above "Memorial." 8vo. Washington City. 1805.
———. Case of the Georgia Sales considered. 8vo. Phil. 1797.
———. Grant to the Mississippi Land Company, &c. 8vo. Augusta. 1795.
———. See Bishop, A.
Georgical Essays. 12mo. Lond. 1769.
Georgius, C. S. De Chaldæo-Syrismis, Rabbinismis, et Persismis Dictioni Novi Fœderis immerito afflictis. 4to. Witteb. 1726.
Gerard, Alex. Dissertations on Subjects relating to the Genius and Evidences of Christianity. 8vo. Edin. 1766.
———, ——. Sermon on the Influence of the Pastoral Office on the Character. 8vo. Aberdeen. 1760.
———, ——. The Same. 2d ed. 8vo. Lond. 1762.
———, ——. Pastoral Care. 8vo. Lond. 1799.
———, ——. Essay on Taste; with Three Dissertations on Taste, by Voltaire, Montesquieu, and D'Alembert. 8vo. Lond. 1759.
Gerard, Gilbert. Institutes of Biblical Criticism. 2d ed. 8vo. Edin. 1808.
———, ———. The Same. 8vo. Bost. and Camb. 1823.
Gerardin, N. V. A. Mémoires sur la Fièvre Jaune. 8vo. Paris. 1820.
Gerardus, Joh. Theatrum Plantarum. fol. Lond. 1633.
Gerbelius, Nicolaus. In Græciæ Sophiani Descriptionem Explicatio. (Gronov. vol. 4.)
Gerbier, Sir Balthasar. The None-Such Charles his Character. 16mo. Lond. 1651.
Gerdesius, Dan. Historia Evangelii Renovati. 4 vol. 4to. Groningæ. 1744—52.
Gerhardius, Edv. Lectiones Apollonianæ. 8vo. Lips. 1816.
Gerhardus, Joh. Commentatio de Tribus Testibus in Cœlo. 4to. Jenæ. 1747.
————, ——. Meditationes Sacræ. 24to. Oxon. 1633.
Germaine, Lord George. Rights of Great Britain asserted against the Claims of America. 8vo. Lond. 1776.
German Society in New-York. Rules and Orders. 8vo. N. York. 1799.
Germanus, Dominicus. Fabrica Linguæ Arabicæ. fol. Romæ. 1639.
Germany, History of the Present Warres of, a Sixth Part. 4to. Lond. 1634.
Gerry, Elbridge. Speech to the Legislature of Massachusetts, June, 1811. 8vo.
——, ————. Speech to the Legislature, Jan. 1812. 8vo.
——, ————. Message, February, 1812. 8vo.
——, ————, Life of, by James T. Austin. 8vo. Bost. 1828.
Gervasius Dorobornensis. Chronica, etc. (Twysden, Scrip. x.)

Gery, Robert. Sermon on Opening the Church at Isleworth. 8vo. Lond. 1706.

Geschichte und Handlung der französischen Pflanzstädte in Nordamerika. 8vo. Stutgart. 1756.

———— der Kolonisirung der freien Staaten des Alterthums; aus dem Engl. 12mo. Leipz. 1778.

———— des Krieges zwischen Grossbritannien und den Vereinigten Bourbonischen Mächten und Nordamerikanischen Kolonien. Erster Band. 8vo. Leipz. 1780.

———— des Englisch-Französisch-Spanischen Krieges, aus Veranlassung des Aufstandes der Englischen Kolonien in Nordamerika. 8vo. Salzburg. 1780.

Geschichten derer Chiquitos, etc. 8vo. Wienn. 1729.

Gesellschaften, Ueber Gelehrte. Vide Jacobs, F.

Gesenius, Wilhelm. Geschichte der Hebräischen Sprache und Schrift. 8vo. Leipz. 1815.

———, ————. Hebräisch-Deutsches Handwörterbuch. 2 Theile. 8vo. Leipz. 1810—12.

———, ————. Lehrgebäude der Hebräischen Sprache. 8vo. Leipz. 1817.

———, ————. Versuch über die Maltesische Sprache. 8vo. Leipz. 1810.

———, ————. De Pentateuchi Samaritani Origine, Indole, et Auctoritate. 4to. Halæ. 1815.

Gesner, Conrad. Historia Animalium. 4 vol. fol. Tiguri. 1551—60.

Gesnerus, Jo. Matth. Novus Linguæ et Eruditionis Romanæ Thesaurus. 4 vol. fol. Lips. 1749.

————, ————. De Phœnicum Navigationibus. Vide Orpheus.

————, ————. Socrates Sanctus Pæderasta. Accedit Corollarium, de Antiqua Asinorum Honestate. 8vo. Traj. ad Rhen. 1769.

————, ————. Chrestomathia Græca. ed. 7ma. 8vo. Lips. 1780.

Gessner, S. Schriften. 3 Bände. 24to. Zürich. 1801.

————, –. New Idyls. 16mo. Phil. 1802.

————, –. Works, tr. from the German, with Notes, &c. 2 vols. 12mo. Lond. 1805.

Geuns, Matth. van. Orationes II de Civium Valetudine. 4to. Hardervici Gelrorum. 1791.

————, ————. Oratio de Providentia Politica, uno maximo Adversæ Civium Valetudinis Præsidio. 4to. Traj. ad Rhen. 1791.

Gewächse Amerikanische. 4 Bände. 8vo. Nürnberg. 1785—7.

Ghemara Hierosolymitana, cum Versione Latina, etc. (Ugol. vol. 17, 18, 20, 25, et 30.)

———— Babylonica, cum Versione Latina. (Id. 19 et 25.)

Ghilinus, Camillus. Telinæ Vallis ac Larii Lacus Descriptio. (Græv. Thes. Ital.)

Giannone, Pietro. Dell' Istoria Civile del Regno di Napoli. 4 vol. 4to. Napoli. 1723.

————, ————. Idem. 4 vol. 4to. Venez. 1766.

Giannone, Pietro. Opere Postume. 2 vol. 4to. Venez. 1768.
———, ———. Professione di Fede. 8vo.
———, ———. Vide Vernet, J. J.
Gibbon, Edw. History of the Decline and Fall of the Roman Empire. 3 vols. 4to. Lond. 1781—2.
———, ——. The Same. 6 vols. 4to. Lond. 1776—88.
———, ——. ————. 6 vols. 8vo. Lond. 1783.
———, ——. ————, with Memoirs of his Life and Writings. 8 vols. 8vo. Phil. 1804—5.
———, ——. Miscellaneous Works; and Memoirs of his Life and Writings, with Notes, &c. by Lord Sheffield. 5 vols. 8vo. Lond. 1814.
———, ——. Critical Observations on the Sixth Book of the Æneid. 8vo. Lond. 1770.
Gibbons, Tho. Two Discourses on the cruel Oppressions of Protestants in France, &c. 8vo. Lond. 1755.
———, ——. Sermon on the Earthquake at Lisbon. 8vo. Lond. 1755.
———, ——. Sermon on the Declaration of War against the French King. 8vo. Lond. 1756.
———, ——. Sermon to the Society for Promoting the Gospel among the Poor. 8vo. Lond. 1752.
———, ——. Hidden Life of a Christian. 2d ed. 12mo. Lond. 1756.
———, ——. Objections against the Application to the Legislature in behalf of Dissenters considered. 8vo. Lond. 1773.
Gibbs, Henry. Artillery Election Sermon. 16mo. Bost. 1704.
Gibbs, Philip. Letter to the Protestant Dissenters at Hackney. 8vo. Lond. 1737.
Gibelin, E. A. Sur le Gladiateur de Borghèse. (Inst. Lit. vol. 4.)
Gibert. Sur le Nom de *Mérovingiens.* (Acad. des Inscrip. vol. 20.)
———. Sur les Premiers Habitans de la Grèce. (Id. 25.)
———. Sur l'Année Grecque.—Sur l'Obélisque interprété par Hermapion. (Id. 35.)
Gibert, Balthasar. Jugemens des Savans, sur les Auteurs qui ont traité de la Rhétorique, etc. 4to. Amst. 1725.
Gibert, Carron de. Satyres de Perse, Lat. et Fr., avec des Notes, et des Poésies du même Traducteur. 12mo. Amst. 1771.
Gibraltar, a Bulwark to Great Britain. 8vo. Lond. 1725.
Gibson, Edmund, (Bp.) Codex Juris Ecclesiastici Anglicani. 2d ed. 2 vols. fol. Oxford. 1761.
———, ————. See Andrew, Dr.—See Foster, Sir M.
———, ————. Letter to Masters and Mistresses of Families in the Plantations. 4to. Lond. 1727.
———, ————. Letter to him, occasioned by his Pastoral Letter on Lukewarmness and Enthusiasm, and Mr. Whitfield's Answer. 8vo. Lond. 1739.
———, ————. Pastoral Letter against Infidels. 2d and 3d ed. 8vo. Lond. 1728.

Gibson, Edmund, (Bp.) Second Pastoral Letter against Infidels. 8vo. Lond. 1730.

———, —————. Third Pastoral Letter against Infidels. 1st and 2d ed. 8vo. Lond. 1731.

———, —————. Five Pastoral Letters. 12mo. Lond. 1760.

———, —————. Plea for Humane Reason, in a Letter to him. 8vo. Lond. 1730.

———, —————. Defence of the "Plea," in a Letter to him. 8vo. Lond. 1731.

———, —————. See Infidelity.

———, —————. Serious Advice to Persons who have been sick; from the 51st Lond. ed. 12mo. Bost. 1813.

———, —————. Assize Sermon. 8vo. Lond. 1706.

———, —————. Thanksgiving Sermon. 8vo. Lond. 1716.

———, —————. Sermon on Reformation of Manners. 4to. Lond. 1723.

———, —————. Chronicon Saxonicum. 4to. Oxon. 1692.

—————, ———. Portus Iccius Julii Cæsaris illustratus;—sive 1. G. Somneri ad Chiffletii Librum de Portu Iccio Responsio;—2. Caroli du Fresne Dissertatio de Portu Iccio. Tractatum utrumque Latine vertit, et Nova Dissertatione auxit E. Gibson. 12mo. Oxon. 1694.

Gibson, John B. Observations on Trap Rocks in Pennsylvania. (Amer. Phil. Tr. N. S. vol. 2.)

ibson, Wm. Treatise on the Diseases of Horses. 4to. Lond. G 1751.

Giffard, Wm. Cases in Midwifery. 4to. Lond. 1734.

Gifford, James. Elucidation of the Unity of God. 4th ed. To which is subjoined a Letter to the Abp. of Canterbury. 2d ed. 8vo. Lond. 1786.

Gifford, Wm. Satires of Juvenal, tr. into English Verse, with Notes. 4to. Lond. 1802.

———, ——. Baviad. 12mo. Lond. 1793.

Giggeius, Antonius. Thesaurus Linguæ Arabicæ. 4 vol. fol. Mediolani. 1632.

Gil, Alex. Logonomia Anglica. 4to. Lond. 1621.

Gil, Fr. Anweisung zu einer sichern Methode, die Völker vor den Blattern zu bewahren, etc.; aus dom Ital. 8vo. Leipz. 1795.

Gilbert, Benj. Narrative of the Captivity of him and his Family, by the Indians. 8vo. Phil. 1784.

Gilbert, Sir Jeffrey, (Ld. C. B.) Treatise on the Court of Exchequer. 8vo. Lond. 1758.

———, ——————. Law of Evidence. 8vo. Lond. 1760.

———, ——————. Abstract of Locke's Essay on Human Understanding. 8vo. Dublin. 1752.

———, ——————. Law of Tenures, by C. Watkins. 4th ed. 8vo. Lond. 1796.

Gilbert, John. Answer to the Bishop of Condom (now of Meaux) his Exposition of the Catholick Faith, &c. 4to. Lond. 1686.

Gilbert, John, (Abp.) Consecration Sermon. 4to. Lond. 1725.

Gilchrist, John. Strangers East Indian Guide to the Hindoostanee 12mo. Calcutta. 1802.

Gildas Sapiens. De Excidio et Conquestu Britanniæ. Vide Rerum Britannicarum Scriptores Vetustiores.

Gildon, Charles. Deist's Manual. 8vo. Lond. 1705.

Giles, Wm. Defence of Dr. Sherlock's Preservative against Popery. 2d ed. 4to. Lond. 1688.

Giles, Wm. B. Speech in the Senate of the United States on the Embargo Laws. 8vo. 1808.

——, ——. Speech on the Organization of the Courts of the United States. 8vo. Bost. 1802.

Gilij, F. S. Saggio di Storia Americana. 4 vol. 8vo. Roma. 1780—4.

——, ——. Nachrichten vom Lande Guiana; aus dem Italienischen. 8vo. Hamb. 1785.

Gill, John. Quiet and Easy Passage through Death to Glory, a Discourse. 8vo. Lond. 1760.

——, ——. Sermons on Justification. 8vo. Bost. 1744.

——, ——. Body of Divinity. 3 vols. 8vo. Lond. 1796.

——, ——. Exposition of the Old Testament. 6 vols. 4to. Lond. 1809—10.

——, ——. Exposition of the New Testament. 3 vols. 4to. Lond. 1809.

Gill, Obadiah, and Others. See Calef, R.

Gillespie, Geo. An Useful Case of Conscience discussed, concerning Idolaters. 4to. Edin. 1649.

Gillies, John. Aristotle's Ethics and Politics, from the Greek; with his Life, Notes, &c. 2 vols. 4to. Lond. 1797.

——, ——. Orations of Lycias and Isocrates, from the Greek; with their Lives, &c. 4to. Lond. 1778.

——, ——. History of Ancient Greece. 3 vols. 8vo. Dublin. 1786.

——, ——. The Same. 2 vols. 4to. Lond. 1786.

——, ——. ————. 4th ed. 4 vols. 8vo. Lond. 1801.

——, ——. ————. 4 vols. 8vo. Phil. 1814.

——, ——. History of the World from the Reign of Alexander to that of Augustus, &c. 2 vols. 4to. Lond. 1807.

——, ——. The Same. 3 vols. 8vo. Phil. 1809.

——, ——. View of the Reign of Frederick II of Prussia. 8vo. Lond. 1789.

Gilling, Isaac. Six Occasional Sermons. 8vo. Exon. 1702—11.

——, ——. Sermon at the Young-Men's Lecture. 8vo. Lond. 1719.

Gillissen, Ægidius. Oratio de Deistis. 4to. Franequeræ. 1762.

Gillius, Petrus. Lexicon Græco-Latinum. fol. Basil. 1577.

Gilman, Samuel. Funeral Address on E. P. Simons. 8vo. Charleston. 1823.

Gilmer, Fr. Wm. On the Geological Formation of the Natural Bridge of Virginia. (Amer. Phil. Tr. vol. 1. N. S.)

Gilpin, Bernard. Coronation Sermon. 8vo. Lond. 1717.

Gilpin, Wm. Life of Bernard Gilpin. 2d ed. 8vo. Lond. 1753.

——, ——. Life of Hugh Latimer. 8vo. Lond. 1755.

Gilpin, Wm. Lives of John Wicliff, Lord Cobham, John Huss, Jerome of Prague, and Zisca. 2d ed. 8vo. Lond. 1766.
——, ——. Lives of Reformers. 2 vols. 8vo. Lond. 1809.
——, ——. Exposition of the New Testament. 4to. Lond. 1790.
——, ——. The Same. 3d ed. 2 vols. 8vo. Lond. 1798.
Gimbernat, Ant. de. New Method of Operating for the Femoral Hernia; from the Spanish. 8vo. Lond. 1795.
Giovanni Fiorentino. Il Pecorone. 2 vol. 8vo. Lond. 1793.
———, ———. ———. 2 vol. 8vo. Milano. 1804.
Giovio, Paolo. Vide Jovius, Paulus.
Giraldus Cambrensis, Silvester. Topographia Hiberniæ;—Hibernia Expugnata;—Itinerarium Cambriæ. (Cambden, Anglica, etc.)
————, ———. Irish Historie, tr. from the Latin by John Hooker. (Hooker, Chronicles.)
Girard, G. Synonymes François. 2 vol. 12mo. Paris. 1796.
Giraud, P. F. F. J. Campagne de Paris en 1814, etc. 6me ed. 8vo. Paris. 1814.
Giraudeau, Bonav. Praxis Linguæ Sacræ. 4to. Rupellæ. 1757.
Girod-Chantrans. Sur les Conferves. 4to.
————. Voyage d'un Suisse dans l'Amérique pendant la dernière Guerre. 8vo. Neuchatel. 1785.
Gisbert, B. L'Eloquence Chrétienne. 12mo. Amst. 1728.
Gisborne, Tho. Enquiry into the Duties of Men in the Higher and Middle Classes of Society in Great Britain. 4to. Lond. 1794.
———, ——. The Same. 5th ed. 2 vols. 8vo. Lond. 1800.
———, ——. Enquiry into the Duties of the Female Sex. 8vo. Lond. 1797.
———, ——. The Same. 8vo. Lond. 1801.
———, ——. Principles of Moral Philosophy. 2d ed. 8vo. Lond. 1790.
———, ——. Testimony of Natural Theology to Christianity. 12mo. Phil. 1818.
———, ——. Familiar Survey of the Christian Religion. 2d ed. 8vo. Lond. 1799.
———, ——. The Same. 6th ed. 8vo. Lond. 1816.
———, ——. Sermons. 2 vols. 8vo. Lond. 1802—4.
———, ——. Familiar Exposition and Application of Paul's Epistle to the Colossians, in Eight Sermons; with Two Sermons on Parts of the Example of St. Paul. 12mo. Lond. 1816.
Giuseppe di S. Teresa, Gio. Istoria delle Guerre del Regno del Brazil. fol. Roma. 1698.
Gladwin, Fr. Vocabulary, English and Persian. 4to. Malda in Bengal. 1758.
———, ——. Ayeen Akberry. Vide Akber.
Glæser, J. A. De Instrumentis Hebræorum Musicis. (Ugol. vol. 32.)
Glanvill, Joseph. Considerations about Witchcraft; with Reflections on Drollery and Atheism. 4th ed. 8vo. Lond. 1668.
———, ———. Plus Ultra; or the Progress and Advancement of Knowledge since the Days of Aristotle. 8vo. Lond. 1668.

Glanvill, Joseph. Sadducismus Triumphatus; or a full and plain Evidence concerning Witches and Apparitions. 4th ed. 8vo. Lond. 1726.
———, ———. Essays on Important Subjects in Philosophy and Religion. 4to. Lond. 1676.
Glanvilla, Ranulphus de. De Legibus et Consuetudinibus Regni Angliæ. 16mo. 1604.
Glas, Geo. History of the Discovery and Conquest of the Canary Islands, tr. from a Spanish MS. To which is added a Description of the Islands. 4to. Lond. 1764.
Glas, John. Works. 4 vols. 8vo. Edin. 1761.
Glasewald, C. E. Observationes in Quintum Smyrnæum. 8vo. Viteb. 1817.
Glass, Tho. Twelve Commentaries on Fevers, tr. by N. Peters. 8vo. Lond. 1752.
———, ———. Commentarii Duodecim de Febribus. 8vo. Jenæ et Lips. 1771.
Glassius, Salomon. Philologia Sacra. 4to. Lips. 1705.
———, ———. Philologia Sacra, his Temporibus accommodata a J. A. Dathio et G. L. Bauero. 4 vol. 8vo. Lips. 1776—97.
Gleason, Benj. Oration, July 4th. 8vo. Bost. 1802.
Glen, (Gov.) Description of South-Carolina. 8vo. Lond. 1761.
Glennie, James. Doctrine of Universal Comparison, or General Proportion. 4to. Lond. 1789.
———, ———. Antecedental Calculus. 4to. Lond. 1793.
Glimpse of the State of the Nation, Feb. 22, 1814. 2d ed. 8vo. Phil. 1814.
Glisson, Fr. Tractatus de Ventriculo et Intestinis. 12mo. Amst. 1677.
Glover, Philip. Discourse concerning Virtue and Religion. 8vo. Lond. 1732.
———, ———. Argument *a priori* concerning the Existence and Perfections of God considered. 8vo. Lond. 1737.
———, ———. Inquiry concerning Virtue and Happiness. 8vo. Lond. 1751.
Glover, Richard. Leonidas, a Poem. 4to. Lond. 1737.
———, ———. The Same. 3d ed. 12mo. Lond. 1738.
———, ———. Poems. See Chalmers, A.
———, ———. Account of the late Application to Parliament by the Merchants of London, upon the Neglect of their Trade. 2d ed. 8vo. Lond. 1742.
———, ———. Substance of the Evidence on the Petition of the West-India Planters and Merchants to the House of Commons. 8vo. Lond.
———, ———. Remarks on the Above, by a West-India Planter. 8vo. Lond. 1777.
Glycas, Michael. Annales, Gr. et Lat. (Script. Byz.)
———, ———. ———, Gr. MS.
Gmelin, J. F. Apparatus Medicaminum. Vide Murray, A.
Gmelin, P. J. De Obligatione Reproborum Credendi in Christum. 4to. Tubingæ. 1730.

Gmelin, S. G. Historia Fucorum. 4to. Petropoli. 1768.
Gnomici Poetæ Græci, Gr. et Lat., a R. F. P. Brunck. 12mo. Argentorati. 1784.
———, ———. 12mo. Lips. 1817.
———, ———, a C. G. Heyne. 2 vol. 12mo. Lips. 1776.
Gobellinus, Jo. Pii II, Pontificis Maximi, Commentarii. 4to. Romæ. 1584.
Goclenius, Rodolphus. De Vita Proroganda. 12mo. Moguntiæ. 1608.
God. See Deity.
Goddard, James. State of the Case between him and the Managers of the Royal Family Privateers. 8vo. Lond. 1756.
Goddard, Jona. Unhappy Condition of the Practice of Physic in London. 4to. Lond. 1670.
Goddard, Wm. The Partnership; or the History of the Rise and Progress of the Pennsylvania Chronicle, &c. No. 1. 8vo. Phil. 1770.
Godden, Tho. Sermon before the Queen Dowager. 4to. Lond. 1686.
———, ———. Sermon before the Queen Dowager. 4to. Lond. 1688.
Godefroy, F. Recueil d'Estampes représentant les différents Evénemens de la Guerre de l'Indépendance des Etats-Unis. 4to. Paris.
Godfrey, Sir Edmondberry. Narrative of his Murder. 4to. 1678.
———, ———. See Quakers.
Godfrey, Tho. Jun. Juvenile Poems; with the Prince of Parthia, a Tragedy. 4to. Phil. 1765.
Godis, Antonius de. Chronica quæ exstant, ab Anno MCXCIV, usque ad MCCLX. (Græv. Thes. Ital.)
Godon, S. Observations to serve for a Mineralogical Map of Maryland. (Amer. Phil. Tr. vol. 6.)
———, —. Mineralogical Observations near Boston in 1807—8. (Mem. A. A. S. vol. 3.)
———, —. Mémoires dans les Annales du Muséum d'Histoire Naturelle.
Godwin, Edw. Accession Sermon. 8vo. Lond. 1727.
———, ———. Accession Sermon. 8vo. Lond. 1743.
———, ———. Accession Sermon. 8vo. Lond. 1744.
Godwin, Fr. (Bp.) Life of Queen Mary, tr. from the Latin, with Notes, by J. S. (Kennet, Hist. of England, vol. 2.)
———, ———. De Præsulibus Angliæ Commentarius, a G. Richardson. fol. Cant. 1743.
Godwin, Wm. Life of Geoffrey Chaucer, &c. 2 vols. 4to. Lond. 1803.
———, ———. Enquiry concerning Political Justice. 2 vols. 12mo. Phil. 1796.
———, ———. History of the Commonwealth of England. 2 vols. 8vo. Lond. 1824—6.

Godwyn, Tho. Roman Antiquities. 4to. Oxford. 1642.
———, ——. ——————. 14th ed. 4to. Lond. 1685.
———, ——. ——————. 15th ed. 4to. Lond. 1689.
———, ——. Rites of the Ancient Hebrews. 6th ed. 4to. Lond. 1641.
———, ——. The Same. 12th ed. 4to. Lond. 1685.
Goedart, Jean. Métamorphoses Naturelles, ou Histoire des Insectes. 3 vol. 12mo. La Haye. 1700.
Gœde, C. A. G. A Foreigner's Opinion of England, &c., tr. from the German by T. Horne. 8vo. Bost. 1822.
Goens, R. M. van. Oratio de Incrementis Literarum. 4to. Traj. ad Rhen. 1766.
——, ————. Diatriba de Cepotaphiis. 8vo. Traj. ad Rhen. 1763.
Goës, Damianus à. De Æthiopum Moribus;—Deploratio Lappianæ Gentis. 18mo. Lug. Bat. 1582.
——, ————. De Rebus Æthiopicis, etc. Vide Martyr, P.
Goes, G. F. D. De Variis, quibus usi sunt Græci et Romani, Philosophiæ Definitionibus, Commentatio. 4to. Ulmæ. 1811.
Goesgenius, J. A. De Usu Accentuum S. Codicis Ebræi. 4to. Vitembergæ. 1716.
Goethe, W. J. von. Werke. 20 Bände. 8vo. Stuttgard und Tübingen. 1815—19.
———, ————. Propyläen. 3 Bände. 8vo. Tübingen. 1798—1800.
———, ————. Kunst und Alterthum am Rhein und Mayn. 4 Hefte. 12mo. Stuttgard. 1816—18.
———, ————. Philipp Hackert. 8vo. Tübingen. 1811.
———, ————. Aus meinem Leben. 2 Theile. 12mo. Stuttgard und Tubingen. 1816.
———, ————, Memoirs of, written by himself; from the German. 8vo. N. York. 1824.
———, ————. Zur Farbenlehre. 2 Bände, 8vo., und Tafeln, 4to. Tübingen. 1810.
———, ————. Festgedischte. 8vo. Weimar. 1818.
———, ————. Zur Morphologie. Bd. 1. Heft 1. 8vo. Stuttgard und Tübingen. 1817.
———, ————. Ἰφιγένεια ἡ ἐν Ταυροῖς, μεταφρασθεῖσα ἐκ τοῦ Γερμανικοῦ ὑπὸ Ἰ. Παπαδοπούλου. 12mo. Jena. 1818.
Goetzius, F. L. De Molis et Pistrinis veterum. (Ugol. vol. 29.)
Goezius, Geo. Philologema de Osculo. (Ugol. vol. 30.)
Goguet, A. Y. Origin of Laws, Arts, and Sciences; and their Progress among the most Ancient Nations; from the French. 3 vols. 8vo. Edin. 1761.
Gold Coins, Considerations on Lowering the Value of, in Massachusetts-Bay; with a Projection of Gov. Hutchinson prefixed. 8vo. Bost. 1762.
Goldesborough, J. Reports. See Brownlow and Goldsborough.
Golding, C. Defence of the Warden of Winchester College. 8vo. Lond. 1758.

Goldingham, J. Account of the Seven Pagodas. (Asiatic Researches, vol. 5.)
Goldmann, G. A. F. De Linguis Vasconum Belgarum et Celtarum. 4to. Gottingæ. 1807.
Goldoni, Carlo. Commedie. 26 vol. 16mo. Lucca. 1809—12.
Goldsmith, Lewis. Exposition of the Conduct of France towards America. 2d ed. 8vo. N. York. 1810.
Goldsmith, Oliver. Grecian History. 2 vols. 8vo. Lond. 1800.
——, ——. Roman History. 2 vols. 8vo. Lond. 1770.
——, ——. ——. 2 vols. 8vo. Lond. 1786.
——, ——. ——. 2 vols. 8vo. Lond. 1805.
——, ——. History of England. 4 vols. 8vo. Lond. 1771.
——, ——. The Same; with Continuations, by M. Wood, and J. McKean. 2 vols. 8vo. Bost. 1814.
——, ——. Traveller. 4th ed. 4to. Lond. 1765.
——, ——. Poems. See Chalmers, A.
——, ——. Essays. 12mo. Lond. 1766.
——, ——. Miscellaneous Works. 4 vols. 8vo. Lond. 1821.
——, ——. History of the Earth and Animated Nature. 8 vols. 8vo. Lond. 1779.
——, ——. The Same. 4 vols. 8vo. Phil. 1795.
——, ——. Survey of Experimental Philosophy. 2 vols. 8vo. Lond. 1776.
Golitz, C. G. Ἀποσπασμάτια τῶν Ἱερῶν Γραμμάτων. 4to. Regiomonti. 1710.
Golius, Jac. Lexicon Arabico-Latinum. fol. Lug. Bat. 1653.
——, —. Vide Ahmed.
Golius, Theoph. Epitome Doctrinæ Moralis, ex Decem Libris Ethicorum Aristotelis. 12mo. Argent. 1631.
Gölnitzius, Abr. Itinerarium Belgico-Gallicum. 24to. Lug. Bat. 1631.
Goltzius, Hubertus. De Re Nummaria Antiqua Opera. 5 vol. fol. Antv. 1708.
Gomara, F. L. de. Historia de Mexico. 16mo. Anvers. 1554.
——, ——. Historia de las Indias;—Cronica de la Nueva-España. (Barcia, Historiadores Primitivos.)
——, ——. Account of Mexico. (Purchas, vol. 3.)
——, ——. Stryfe betweene the Spanyardes and Portugales, for the Division of the Indies, &c. (Eden and Willes.)
Gomarus, Fr. Opera Theologica Omnia. fol. Amst. 1664.
——, —. Syntagma Disputationum Theologicarum. 12mo. Roterodami. 1615.
——, —. Davidis Lyra. (Ugol. vol. 31.)
Gomez, Cosme. Leon Prodigioso. 2 vol. 4to. Sevilla. 1732.
Gomez de Cibdareal, F. Centon Epistolario. 4to. Madrid. 1775.
Góngora y Argote, Luis de. Obras. 4to. Brusselas. 1659.
——. Poesias. 8vo. Madrid. 1789.
Gonzales, Manoel. Voyage to England and Scotland. (Pinkerton, vol. 2.)

Gonzales de Salas, J. A. Nueva Idea de la Tragedia Antigua. 4to. Madrid. 1633.
Gooch, Benj. Chirurgical Works. 3 vols. 8vo. Lond. 1792.
Good, John Mason. Memoirs of Alexander Geddes. 8vo. Lond. 1803.
——, ————. Physiological System of Nosology. 8vo. Lond. 1817.
——, ————. Book of Nature. 2 vols. 8vo. Bost. 1826.
Goodale, Ebenezer, (Gen.,) Proceedings of the Court Martial for the Trial of. 8vo. Camb. 1812.
Goodman, John. Winter-Evening Conference between Neighbours. 7th ed. 8vo. Lond. 1698.
————, ——. Discourse on the Parable of the Prodigal Son. 5th ed. 8vo. Lond. 1700.
————, ——. Discourse concerning Auricular Confession. 4to. Lond. 1648.
Goodrich, C. A. Address before the Female Reading and Charitable Society. 8vo. Worcester. 1817.
Goodridge, Elijah P. (Major,) Report of the Trial of L. & L. Kenniston for the Robbery of. 8vo. Salem. 1817.
Goodwin, John. Defence of the Sentence passed upon the late King. 4to. Lond. 1649.
Goodwin, Philip. Evangelicall Communicant. 2d ed. 8vo. Lond. 1657.
Goodwin, Tho. State of Glory for Spirits of Just Men upon Dissolution demonstrated, a Sermon. 4to. Lond. 1657.
————, ——. Sermon on the Death of the Rev. S. Lobb. 2d ed. 12mo. Lond. 1699.
————, ——, On the Punishment of Sin in Hell; with a Sermon on a Future State of Glory. 8vo. Lond. 1680.
————, ——. Transubstantiation a peculiar Article of the Roman Catholic Faith. 4to. Lond. 1688.
————, ——. Moses et Aaron, cum Notis Hottingeri. (Ugol. vol. 3.)
————, ——. De Theocratia Israelitarum. (Id. 24.)
Gookin, Daniel. Historical Collections of the Indians in New-England.—Account of him. (Mass. Hist. Coll. vol. 1.)
Gordon. Essay on Government. 8vo. Lond. 1747.
————. Four Fundamental Points of Religion. 8vo. Lond. 1756.
Gordon, Alexander. Lives of Pope Alexander VI, and his Son, Cæsar Borgia. fol. Lond. 1729.
————, ————. Itinerarium Septentrionale; or a Journey over Part of Scotland. fol. Lond. 1726.
Gordon, Alexander. On the Epidemic Puerperal Fever of Aberdeen. 8vo. Lond. 1795.
Gordon, Cosmo, (Col.,) Trial of. 8vo. Lond. 1783.
Gordon, Jo. Specimen Animadversionum Criticarum in Priscam Evangeliorum Versionem Gothicam, etc. (Ihre, J.)
Gordon, John. Memoirs of his Life. 12mo. Lond. 1734.
Gordon, John. Outlines of Lectures on Human Physiology. 8vo. Edin. 1817.

Gordon, John. On the Structure of the Brain. 8vo. Edin. 1817.
Gordon, Patrick. Geographical Grammar. 6th ed. 8vo. Lond. 1711.
———, ———. The Same. 19th ed. 8vo. Lond. 1749.
———, ———. ———. 20th ed. 8vo. Lond. 1754.
Gordon, Tho. Cordial for Low Spirits. 3 vols. 12mo. Lond. 1763.
———, ——. Dissertation upon Bull-Baiting and Evening Lectures; with Occasional Meditations on the 30th of January. 8vo. Lond. 1718.
———, ——. Works of Sallust, tr. into English; with a Translation of Cicero's Four Orations against Catiline, &c. 4to. Lond. 1744.
———, ——. Works of Tacitus, tr. into English. 2 vols. fol. Lond. 1728—31.
———, ——. The Same. 2d ed. 4 vols. 8vo. Lond. 1737.
———, ——. Independent Whig. 2d ed. 8vo. Lond. 1722.
———, ——. The Same. 8th ed. 4 vols. 12mo. Lond. 1752—3.
———, ——. Pillars of Priestcraft and Orthodoxy shaken. 2 vols. 12mo. Lond. 1752.
———, ——. The Same. 4 vols. 12mo. Lond. 1768. (See Baron, R.)
———, ——. Cato's Letters, and Tracts. See Trenchard, J.
Gordon, Wm. Popery against Christianity. 8vo. Lond. 1719.
Gordon, Wm. History of the American Revolution. 4 vols. 8vo. Lond. 1788.
———, ——. Plan of a Society for the Support of Widows, &c. 8vo. Bost. 1772.
———, ——. Election Sermon. 8vo. Watertown. 1775.
———, ——. Sermon before the General Court, July 4th. 8vo. Bost. 1777.
Gore, Christopher. Masonic Oration. 4to. Bost. 1783.
Gorges, Ferdinando. America painted to the Life. 4to. Lond. 1659.
Gorgias Leontinus. Reliquiæ. Vide Oratores Græci, a Reiskio.
Gorham, John. Inaugural Address at Cambridge. 8vo. Bost. 1817.
———, ——. Elements of Chemical Science. 2 vols. 8vo. Bost. 1819.
Gorius, Ant. Fr. Gemmæ Antiquæ A. M. Zanettii, cum A. F. Gorii Notis Latinis, et eisdem Italice redditis ab H. F. Zanettio. fol. Venet. 1750.
———, ———. Museum Etruscum, exhibens Insignia Veterum Etruscorum Monumenta, etc. 2 vol. fol. Florentiæ. 1737.
Gorlæus, Abrahamus. De Anulis. Vide Kirchmannus, J.
Gorter, David de. Flora Belgica. 8vo. Harlemi. 1781.
Gorter, Joh. de. Chirurgia Repurgata. 4to. Lug. Bat. 1742.
Gosnold, Barth. Relation des Voyages de Gosnol, Prince, et Gilbert à la Virginie en 1602—3, trad. de l'Anglois. 12mo. Amst. 1720.
Gospel. Veritas Evangelica; or Gospel-Truth asserted in Sixteen useful Questions. 4to. Lond. 1687.

Gospel. Essay to prove its Credibility from the Doctrine of the Efficacy of Christ's Death. 8vo. Lond. 1761.
———. Its Truth and Divine Authority asserted. 8vo. Lond. 1707.
———. The Same. 2d ed.; with other Tracts by the same Author. 8vo. Lond. 1709.
———. See Christianity,—Evangelia,—John,—Luke,—Mark,—Matthew.
Gospel-Ministry, Divine Right of the. 4to. Lond. 1654.
———————. See Education,—Ministers,—Schools.
Gospels and the Acts in the Malayan Tongue. See Marshall, T.
——— in the Language of the Esquimaux Indians in Labrador, by Missionaries of the Unitas Fratrum. 12mo. Lond. 1813.
———. See Campbell,—Macknight,—Newcome,—Priestley,—Testament, New, &c.
Gostwyke, Wm. Thanksgiving Sermon. 4to. Camb. 1685.
Gottfriedt, J. L. Newe Welt und Americanische Historien. fol. Franck. 1655.
Göttingen. Göttingische Gelehrte Anzeigen. 8vo. 1815—21.
————. Commentarii Societatis Regiæ Scientiarum Gottingensis. 4 vol. 4to. Gottingæ. 1752—4.
————. Commentationes Societati Reg. Scient. Goett. per Annos 1758—62, oblatæ a J. D. Michaelis. 4to. Bremæ. 1763.
————. Novi Commentarii Societatis Regiæ Scientiarum Gottingensis. (vol. 1—3.) 3 vol. 4to. 1771—3.
Gottleber, J. C. Animadversiones ad Platonis Phædonem et Alcibiadem Secundum, etc. 8vo. Lips. 1771.
Gottus, F. L. Theologia Scholastico-Dogmatica, juxta Mentem D. Thomæ Aquinatis. 3 vol. fol. Venet. 1750.
Gouanus, Ant. Historia Piscium. 4to. Argent. 1770.
———, ——. Flora Monspeliensis. 8vo. Lugd. 1765.
———, ——. Hortus Monspeliensis. 8vo. Lugd. 1762.
Goudoever, A. van. Disputatio Philologica de Historicis Polybii Laudibus. 8vo. Traj. ad Rhen. 1808.
Gouge, Tho. Directions how to walk with God. 4to. Lond. 1661.
———, ——. Elegiac Essay on his Death. 12mo. Lond. 1700.
Gouge, Wm. Commentary on the Hebrewes. 4to. Lond. 1655.
Gough, Rich. Anecdotes of British Topography. 4to. Lond. 1768.
Gough, Strickland. Accession Sermon. 8vo. Lond. 1714.
———, ————. Sermon on the Rumour of an Invasion in Scotland. 8vo. Lond. 1745.
———, ————. Sermon at the Ordination of Joseph Denham. 8vo. Lond. 1714.
Gouldman, Fr. Dictionary, English and Latin. fol. Camb. 1678.
Gourdon. Request to Roman Catholicks to answer certain Queries. 4th ed. 4to. Lond. 1687.
Gourgaud, (Gen.) Vide Napoleon.
Governing, Art of. 2d ed. 8vo. Lond. 1722.
Government, Essay on, (by Gordon.) 8vo. Lond. 1747.
—————, Treatise on. 8vo. Lond. 1750.
—————, Thoughts on the Origin and Nature of. 8vo. Lond. 1769.

Government, Fragment on; with a Critique on Blackstone's Commentaries. 8vo. Lond. 1776.
——————. Vindication of the Patriarchal Form of. 8vo. Lond. 1711.
——————. See Law. See Politics.
Gowen, J. R. On the Glazing of Hot-houses,—Method of Constructing Flues for Hot-houses. (Horticultural Tr. vol. 3.)
Gower, John. Confessio Amantis. See Chalmers, A.
Goynæus, J. B. De Situ Istriæ. (Græv. Thes. Ital.)
Gozzi, Gasparo. Opere. 22 vol. 12mo. Venez. 1812.
Graaf, Regnerus de. Opera Omnia. 8vo. Lug. Bat. 1677.
Graberg, J. N. De Unctura Christi in Bethania facta. (Ugol. vol. 30.)
Grabius, J. E. Spicilegium SS. Patrum, ut et Hæreticorum, Seculi I, II, et III, Gr. et Lat. 2 vol. 8vo. Oxon. 1700.
————, ———. Idem. 2 vol. 8vo. Oxon. 1714.
————, ———. Vet. Test. ex Codice Alexandrino. Vide Testamentum Vetus.
————, ———. Liturgia, Gr. Vide Irenæus.
Gracian, Lorenzo. Obras. 2 vol. 4to. Amberes. 1669.
Gradonicus, J. H. De Siclo Argenteo Brixiæ anno 1744 reperto. (Ugol. vol. 28.)
Gradus ad Parnassum. 8vo. Lond. 1802.
Græca Majora, et Græca Minora. Vide Collectanea.
——— ————. ed. 4ta Americana. 2 vol. 8vo. Cant. 1824.
Græcæ Grammaticæ Compendium. 8vo. Lond. 1785.
Grævius, Jo. Geo. Thesaurus Antiquitatum Romanarum. 12 tomi. fol. Traj. ad Rhen., et Lug. Bat. 1694—9.
————, —————. Thesaurus Antiquitatum et Historiarum Italiæ, Neapolis, Siciliæ, Sardiniæ, Corsicæ, Melitæ, atque Adjacentium Terrarum Insularumque; cum Præfationibus P. Burmanni. 45 vol. in 24 tom. fol. Lug. Bat. 1704—25.
————, —————. Syntagma Variarum Dissertationum Rariorum. 4to. Ultrajecti. 1702.
————, —————. Epistolæ. Vide Clerc, J. le.
Graham. Letter to the Bishop of Bangor on his Sermon preached January 30. 12mo. Lond. 1750.
Graham, Maria. Letters on India. 8vo. Lond. 1814.
Graham, Richard. Short Account of the most Eminent Painters. See Fresnoy, C. A. du.
Grahame, James. Birds of Scotland, with other Poems. 12mo. Bost. 1807.
Grainger, James. Sugar-Cane a Poem. 4to. Lond. 1774.
—————, ————. Poems. See Chalmers, A.
Gramann, J. V. Vide Wakius, J. C.
Gramática de la Lengua Castellana compuesta por la Real Academia Española. 12mo. Madrid. 1796.
Grammar, English, with Critical Notes. 12mo. Lond. 1797.
—————, Essay towards an Universal and Rational. See Phillips, J. T.
—————. Les Nouveaux Rudimens de la Langue Latine. 12mo.
—————. See Latin Grammar.

Grammatical Essays;—I. On a Barbarism in the English Language;—II. On the Necessity of Grammatical Knowledge in order to a right Interpretation of the Scriptures. 8vo. Lond. 1768.

Grammatici Veteres Latini. fol. Paris. 1516.

————— —————, opera H. Putschii. 4to. Hanoviæ. 1605.

Grammaticus Leidensis, Grammaticus Meermannianus, et Grammaticus Augustanus. De Dialectis. Vide Gregorius Corinthius.

Granada. See Grenada.

Granada, Luis de. Guia de Pecadores. 4to. Madrid. 1777.

Grand Accuser the Greatest of all Criminals. 8vo. Lond. 1735.

Grand-Pierre, Dralsé de. Relation de Divers Voyages faits dans l'Afrique, dans l'Amérique, et aux Indes Occidentales. 12mo. Paris. 1718.

Granger. Reise durch Egypten in dem Jahre 1730, aus dem Franz. 8vo.

Granger, James. Biographical History of England. 2 vols. 4to. Lond. 1769.

Grant, Charles. English Prize Poem on the Restoration of Learning in the East. (Classical Journal, vol. 5.)

Grant, John. Institutes of Latin Grammar. 8vo. Lond. 1808.

Grant, Robert. Sketch of the History of the East-India Company. 8vo. Lond. 1813.

Grant, Wm. On the Nature and Cure of Fevers. 2d ed. 2 vols. 8vo. Lond. 1772.

——, ——. Essay on the Pestilential Fever of Sydenham. 8vo. Lond. 1775.

——, ——. Observations on the Origin and Progress of the Atrabilious Constitution and Gout. 8vo. Lond. 1781.

——, ——. Account of the Present Epidemic Cough and Fever. 8vo. Lond. 1776.

Grapheus, C. Carmina ad Damianum de Goes. Vide Legatio.

Grapius, Z. De Percussione Sepulchrali. (Ugol. vol. 33.)

Graserus, Conradus. Commentarius in Apocalypsin; cum Explicatione Visionis F. Nicolai. 4to. Tiguri. 1610.

Grasserus, Jac. Antiquitates Nemausenses. (Sallengre, vol. 1.)

Grassi, Giov. Notizie Varie sullo Stato Presente della Repubblica degli Stati Uniti dell' America Settentrionale. ed. 2da. 8vo. Milano. 1819.

Gratianus, Steph. Disceptationes Forensium Judiciorum. 2 vol. fol. Col. Allob. 1615.

Gratius Faliscus. Cynegeticon. Vide Corpus Poet. Lat.

Grattan, Henry. Speeches. vol. 1. 8vo. N. York. 1813.

Gratz. Kritisch-Historischer Kommentar über das Evangelium des Matthäus. 2 vol. 8vo. Tübingen. 1821—3.

Graunt, John. Natural and Political Observations upon the Bills of Mortality. 2d ed. 4to. Lond. 1662.

Grave, C. L. De Pythagoreorum et Essenorum Disciplina et Sodalitiis. 4to. Gottingæ. 1808.

Grave, La. Dissertation Critique sur 2 Sam. xxiii, 3, 4, 5. 4to. Stetin. 1721.
Grave, Poncet de la. Précis Historique de la Marine Royale de France. 2 vol. 12mo. Paris. 1780.
Gravenor. See Grosvenor.
Graverius, Jo. Theses Theologicæ de Bonorum Operum Relatione ad Vitam Æternam. 4to. Sedani. 1664.
Graves, Richard. Essay on the Character of the Apostles and Evangelists. 8vo. Lond. 1798.
——, ——. Lectures on the Four last Books of the Pentateuch. 2 vols. 8vo. Lond. 1815.
Gravesande, W. J. 's. Mathematical Elements of Natural Philosophy, tr. from the Latin by J. F. Desaguliers. 3d ed. 2 vols. 8vo. Lond. 1726.
Gravier, Jean. Recueil de toutes les Uniformes qui se sont signalé durant la Siège de la Ville de Gènes. 4to. Gènes. 1752.
Gray, Andrew. Spiritual Warfare. 12mo. Edin. 1672.
Gray, Ellis. Sermon at the Ordination of the Rev. Thaddeus Maccarty. 8vo. Bost. 1742.
Gray, Hugh. Letters from Canada. 8vo. Lond. 1809.
Gray, John C. Oration, July 4th. 8vo. Bost. 1822.
Gray, John. See Guthrie, Wm.
Gray, Rob. Key to the Old Testament. 3d ed. 8vo. Lond. 1797.
——, ——. Bampton Lecture Sermons. 8vo. 1796.
Gray, Tho. Poems; with Memoirs of his Life and Writings, by W. Mason. 4 vols. 12mo. York. 1778.
——, ——. Elegy, and Blair's Grave. 8vo. Lond. 1790.
——, ——. Poems; with his Life by Dr. Johnson. See Chalmers, A.
Gray, Tho. Discourse before the Massachusetts Humane Society. 8vo. Bost. 1805.
——, ——. Artillery Election Sermon. 8vo. Bost. 1819.
——, ——. Sermon on the Death of Governor Eustis. 8vo. Bost. 1825.
Graydon, Wm. Digest of the Laws of the United States. 2 vols. 8vo. Harrisburgh. 1803.
Grazzini, A. F. Novelle. 2 vol. 8vo. Lond. 1793.
Great Britain, Enquiry into the Reasons of the Conduct of, with relation to the Present State of Affairs in Europe. 8vo. Lond. 1727.
—— ——, New Survey of; or Magna Britannia et Hibernia, Antiqua et Nova. 6 vols. 4to. Lond. 1720—31.
—— ——, Political State of, for 1734—5, &c. 8vo.
—— ——. Great-Britain's Memorial against the Pretender and Popery. 12mo. Lond. 1745.
—— ——. Liberty and Right; or an Essay on the Constitution and Administration of Great Britain. 8vo. Lond. 1747.
—— ——, Right Method of maintaining Security in Person and Property to all the Subjects of. 8vo. Lond. 1751.
—— ——. Le Système Politique de la Grande-Bretagne dans la Conjoncture présente, mis dans tout son jour. 12mo. La Haye. 1755.

Great Britain, Military History of, for 1756, 1757. 8vo. Lond. 1757.

—— ——, View of the Internal Policy of. 12mo. Lond. 1764.

—— ——. Four Dissertations on the Reciprocal Advantages of a Perpetual Union between Great-Britain and her American Colonies, written for Mr. Sargent's Prize-Medal, by J. Morgan, S. Watts, F. Hopkinson, and a person unknown; with an Eulogium on the Delivery of the Medal, by Wm. Smith. 8vo. Phil. 1766.

—— ——. Letter to the Earl of Hillsborough on the Connexion between Great Britain and her Colonies. 8vo. Lond. 1768.

—— ——. Present State of the British Empire in Europe, America, Africa, and Asia. 8vo. Lond. 1768.

—— ——. Present State of the Nation. 8vo. Lond. 1768.

—— ——. Appendix to the Present State of the Nation. 8vo. Lond. 1769.

—— ——, Remarks on the "Appendix." 8vo. Lond. 1769.

—— ——. Political Essays concerning the Present State of the British Empire. 4to. Lond. 1772.

—— ——. Examination into the Conduct of the Present Administration, from 1774 to 1778, and a Plan of Accommodation with America. 8vo. Lond. 1778.

—— ——. View of the relative Situation of Great Britain and the United States, by a Merchant. 8vo. Lond. 1794.

—— ——, Prospectus, Charter, Ordinances, and Bye-Laws of the Royal Institution of, &c. 4to. Lond. 1800.

—— ——. Facts and Documents relating to the State of the Controversy between America and Great Britain, &c. 8vo. Bost. 1813.

—— —— and North America, Present State of, with regard to Agriculture, Population, Trade, and Manufactures. 8vo. Lond. 1767.

—— ——. See Britain,—Convention,—France,—Letter,—Minister,—Minority,—Motuum Britannicorum Verax Cushi,—Rerum Britannicarum Scriptores,—Standing Armies,—Treaties,—United States, &c.

Greaves, John. Miscellaneous Works. 2 vols. 8vo. Lond. 1737.

Grece, C. F. Facts and Observations respecting Canada and the United States. 8vo. Lond. 1819.

Green, Ashbel. Thanksgiving Sermon. 8vo. Phil. 1795.

——, ——. Letter to the Preacher of Liberal Sentiments. 12mo. 1792.

——, ——. Discourse on Doing Good. 8vo. Phil. 1822.

Green, Fr. "Vox Oculis Subjecta;" a Dissertation on the Art of imparting Speech to the Deaf and Dumb, &c. 8vo. Lond. 1783.

Green, George. Essay on the Application of Mathematical Analysis to the Theories of Electricity and Magnetism. 4to. Nottingham. 1828.

Green, J. Remarks in Support of the New Chart of North and South America. 4to. Lond. 1753.

Green, Joseph. Sermon at the Ordination of his Son. 8vo. Bost. 1753.
Green, Matthew. The Spleen, a Poem. 3d ed. 8vo. Lond. 1738.
——, ————. Poems. 12mo. Bost. 1804.
——, ————. ———. See Chalmers, A.
Green, Richard. Accession Sermon. Lond. 4to. 1756.
——, ————. Assize Sermon. 4to. Lond. 1745.
Green, Rob. Principles of Natural Philosophy. 8vo. Camb. 1712.
Green, Wm. Song of Deborah reduced to Metre; with a New Translation, &c. 4to. Camb. 1753.
——, ——. New Translation of the Prayer of Habakkuk, the Prayer of Moses, and the cxxxix Psalm. 4to. Camb. 1755.
Greene, Th. (Bp.) Four Discourses on the Four Last Things; viz. Death, Judgment, Heaven, and Hell. 12mo. Lond. 1765.
Greenhill, Tho. Art of Embalming. 4to. Lond. 1705.
Greenhill, Wm. Exposition upon the Nineteen First Chapters of Ezekiel. 2 vols. 4to. Lond. 1649—51.
Greenland. Rélation du Groenland à M. de la Mothe le Vayer. 12mo. Paris. 1647.
————. Nauwkeurige Beschrijvingh van Groenland aen Heer de la Mothe le Vayer. 4to. Amst. 1678.
Greenleaf, J. Abridgement of Burn's Justice of the Peace. 4to. Bost. 1773.
Greenleaf, Moses. Statistical View of Maine. 8vo. Bost. 1816.
Greenleaf, Simon. Report of Cases in the Supreme Court of Maine. 2 vols. 8vo. Hallowell. 1822—5.
Greenway, James. Beneficial Effects of the Cassia Chamæcrista in recruiting worn-out Lands. (Amer. Phil. Tr. vol. 3.)
Greenwood, Isaac. Philosophical Discourse on the Death of Thomas Hollis, Esq. 8vo. Bost. 1731.
Greenwood, Nich. Astronomia Anglicana. fol. Lond. 1689.
Grégoire. Mémoire en faveur des Gens de Couleur de St. Domingue, etc. adressé à l'Assemblée Nationale. 8vo. Paris. 1789.
————. Inquiry into the Intellectual and Moral Faculties of the Negroes, tr. by D. B. Warden. 8vo. Brooklyn. 1810.
————. Observations Critiques sur le Poëme de M. Joel Barlow, "The Colombiad." 8vo. Paris. 1809.
————. Critical Observations on Barlow's Columbiad. 8vo. Washington. 1809.
————. Seconde Lettre aux Electeurs du Département de l'Isère. 8vo. Paris. 1820.
Gregorius Corinthius, et Alii Grammatici. De Dialectis Linguæ Græcæ, cum Notis Variorum, a G. H. Schæfero. 8vo. Lips. 1811.
Gregorius de Valentia. De Rebus Fidei hoc tempore Controversis, etc. fol. Lugd. 1591.
Gregorius Francus, Gr. Lexicon Sanctum. 12mo. Hanov. 1634.
Gregorius, Joh. West-Indianische Reisse. 4to. Aldenb. 1627.
Gregorius Magnus, (Papa.) Opera; cum Vita ejus, a J. Diacono, etc. 6 tomi in 2 vol. fol. Paris. 1605.
———— ————————. Idem. 4 vol. fol. Paris. 1705.

Gregorius Nazianzenus. Opera, Gr. et Lat. 2 vol. fol. Paris. 1630.
——— ————. Orationes xvi, Gr. MS.
Gregorius Neocæsariensis, Macarius Ægyptius, et Basilius Seleuciensis. Opera Omnia, Gr. et Lat. fol. Paris. 1622.
Gregorius Nyssenus. De Resurrectione, Gr. et Lat. a F. Morello. 12mo. Lutetiæ. 1600. Vide etiam Anecdota Gr. a Wolfio.
——— ————. Opera, Latine. fol. Basil. 1562.
——— ————. Opera Gr. et Lat. cum Notis. 3 vol. fol. Paris. 1638.
Gregorius Turonensis. Opera; necnon Fredegarii Chronicum, cum aliis Antiquis Monumentis, etc. opera T. Ruinart. fol. Lut. Par. 1699.
Gregory, David. Astronomiæ Physicæ et Geometricæ Elementa. fol. Oxon. 1702.
———, ———. Elements of Astronomy, from the Latin; with E. Halley's Synopsis of the Comets. 2 vols. 8vo. Lond. 1715.
———, ———. Treatise of Practical Geometry; from the Latin. 9th ed. 8vo. Edin. 1780.
Gregory, (Dr.) Lectures on the Practice of Physic, as delivered at Edinburgh, 1770. 4 vols. 4to. MS.
Gregory, Geo. Letters on Literature, Taste, and Composition. 12mo. Phil. 1809.
———, ——. Dictionary of Arts and Sciences. 2 vols. 4to. Lond. 1806—7.
———, ——. Economy of Nature. 2d ed. 3 vols. 8vo. Lond. 1798.
———, ——. Essays Historical and Moral. 2d ed. 8vo. Lond. 1788.
———, ——. History of the Christian Church. 2 vols. 8vo. Lond. 1795.
Gregory, Jac. Conspectus Medicinæ Theoreticæ. 2 vol. 8vo. Edin. 1790.
Gregory, John. Observations on the Duties and Offices of a Physician, and on the Method of prosecuting Enquiries in Philosophy. 8vo. Lond. 1770.
———, ——. Lectures on the Duties and Qualifications of a Physician. 8vo. Lond. 1772.
———, ——. Comparative View of the State and Faculties of Man with those of the Animal World. 3d ed. 12mo. Lond. 1766.
———, ——. Elements of the Practice of Physic. 2d ed. 8vo. Lond. 1774.
Gregory, Olinthus. Treatise of Mechanics. 2d ed. 3 vols. (3d vol. plates.) 8vo. Lond. 1807.
Grellotus, Anth. Prodromus in Apocalypsin. 4to. Lug. Bat. 1675.
Grenada Planter. 8vo. Lond. 1768.
———. Observations upon the Report of the Board of Trade against the Grenada Laws. 8vo. Lond. 1770.
———. See Mansfield, Ld.
———. Letter to the Earl of H—b—h on Gr—n—da Affairs. 8vo. Lond. 1769.

Grenada. Audi Alteram Partem; or a Counter-Letter to the E—l of H—ll—gh on G—n—a Affairs. 8vo. Lond. 1770.
———. Narrative of the Proceedings upon the Complaint against Gov. Melvill. 8vo. Lond. 1770.
———, Brief Enquiry concerning the Insurrection in. 8vo. Lond. 1796.
———, Observations upon a Resolution of the Assembly of, passed May 11, 1795; and upon a Pamphlet in Vindication of the Government of that Colony. 8vo. Lond. 1796.
Grenius, Geo. De Rusticatione Romanorum.—De Villarum Antiquarum apud eosdem Structura. (Sallengre, vol. 1.)
Grenville, Geo. Regulations concerning the Colonies, and the Taxes imposed upon them, considered. 3d ed. 8vo. Lond. 1775.
Gresham-College in London, Account of; with the Life of the Founder, &c. 4to. Lond. 1707.
Greswell, W. Parr. Memoirs of Politianus, Sannazarius, Bembus, Fracastorius, Flaminius, and the Amalthei. 8vo. Manchester. 1801.
Greville, Fulke. See Brooke, Fulke Greville, Lord.
Grew, Nehemiah. Anatomy of Plants. fol. Lond. 1682.
——, ———. Anatomie des Plantes. fol. Lond. 1682.
——, ———. Cosmologia Sacra. fol. Lond. 1701.
Grey, A. Debates of the House of Commons. See Commons.
Grey, Richard. Method of Learning Hebrew without Points. To which is annexed the Book of Proverbs divided according to the Metre, &c. 8vo. Lond. 1738.
——, ——. Last Words of David, divided according to the Metre, with Notes. 4to. Lond. 1749.
——, ——. Vide Job.
Grey, Zachary. Examination of Neal's History of the Puritans. 3 vols. 8vo. Lond. 1736—9.
——, ——. Answer to "The Spirit of Ecclesiasticks," &c. 2d ed. 8vo. Lond. 1735.
Grice, C. le, Case of, 8vo.
Gridley, Selah. On the Importance and Associability of the Human Stomach. 8vo. Montpelier, Vt. 1816.
Griesbach, Jo. Jac. Symbolæ Criticæ. 2 vol. 8vo. Halæ. 1785—93.
———, ———. Commentarius Criticus in Textum Græcum Novi Testamenti. Particulæ I et II. 8vo. Jenæ. 1798—1811.
———, ———. Synopsis Evangeliorum. 8vo. Halæ. 1776.
———, ———. Idem. ed. 3tia. 8vo. Halæ, Sax. 1809.
———, ———. Vide Testamentum Novum.
———, ———, Biographical Memoir of, by A. F. Kothe. (Classical Journal, vol. 10.)
Grieve, James. Translation of Celsus. Vide Celsus.
——, ——. History of Kamtschatka and the Kurile Islands, &c. tr. from the Russian by J. Grieve. 4to. Gloucester. 1764.
Griffin, Edw. D. Sermon at the Funeral of the Rev. Alexander Macwhorter. 8vo. N. York. 1807.
———, ———. Inaugural Oration at Andover. 8vo. Bost. 1809.

Griffith, Elizabeth. Platonic Wife, a Comedy. 8vo. Lond. 1765.
Griffith, John. Journal in the Work of the Ministry. 8vo. Lond. 1779.
Griffith, Moses. On Hectic and Slow Fevers, and Pulmonary Consumption, &c. 8vo. Lond. 1799.
Griffith, Wm. Law Register of the United States. vols. 3 and 4. 8vo. Burlington, N. J. 1822.
Grillet, J., et F. Bechamel. Journal du Voyage dans la Goyane en 1674. 12mo.
———, ————. Journal of their Travels into Guiana; from the French. 8vo. Lond. 1698.
Grimké, Tho. S. Address on the Character and Objects of Science, before the Literary and Philosophical Society of South-Carolina. 8vo. Charleston. 1827.
Grimm, J. M. Exercitatio Philologica circa genuinum Verborum, ἐπιβαλὼν ἔκλαιε, Sensum, Marc. xiv, 72. 4to. Rintelii. 1729.
Grimm, J. W. und K. Lieder der alten Edda. 8vo. Berlin. 1815.
———, ————. Das Lied von Hildebrand und Hadubrand, und das Weissenbrunner Gebet. 4to. Cassel. 1812.
Grinæus, Simon. Novus Orbis. fol. Basil. 1555.
Grinsted Ballad. fol. Lond. 1750.
Griswold, A. V. (Bp.) Episcopal Convention Sermon. 8vo. Bost. 1811.
———, ————. Another. 8vo. N. York. 1817.
———, ————. Charge to the Clergy and Pastoral Letter. 12mo. Bost. 1816.
———, ————. Pastoral Letter. 8vo. Bost. 1821.
Griswold, J. New Periodical Publications proposed. 12mo. N. York. 1816.
Groddeckius, Gabr. De Ceremonia Palmarum in Festo Tabernaculorum. (Ugol. vol. 18.)
————, ——. De Judæis Præputium attrahentibus. (Id. 22.)
————, ——. De Antiquorum Hebræorum Purgationibus Castitatis. (Id. 30.)
Gronovius, Jacobus. Thesaurus Græcarum Antiquitatum. 12 vol. fol. Venet. 1732—7.
————, ——. Effigies Virorum ac Fœminarum Illustrium. (Thes. vol. 1, 2, 3.)
————, ——. Regia Auspicia.—Memoria Natalis Wilhelmi, Britanniarum Regis. fol. Lug. Bat. 1689.
Gronovius, J. F. Flora Virginica. Vide Clayton, J.
Gronovius, Joh. Fr. Observationum Libri Tres. 12mo. Lug. Bat. 1662.
————, ———. Observationum Liber Novus. 12mo. Davent. 1652.
————, ———. De Museo Alexandrino. (Gronov. Thes. vol. 8.)
————, ———. Notæ in Terentium. 8vo. Oxon. 1750.
Gronovius, L. T. Marmorea Basis Colossi Tiberio Cæsari erecti post horrendos Terræ Tremores. (Gronov. Thes. vol. 7.)

Gronovius, L. T. Bibliotheca Regni Animalis atque Lapidei. 4to. Lug. Bat. 1760.

Grose, Fr. The Olio. 2d ed. 8vo. Lond. 1796.

——, —. Classical Dictionary of the Vulgar Tongue; by Pierce Egan. 8vo. Lond. 1823.

Grosse, C. F. De Cultura Ingenii. 4to. Halæ Magd. 1699.

Grossis, J. B. de. Catanense Decachordum, sive Novissima Sacræ Ecclesiæ Catanensis Notitia. (Græv. Thes. Ital.)

Grossius, J. G. Theatrum Biblicum; sive Vindicatio Scripturæ a Corruptelis seu Falsis Interpretationibus. 4to. Basil. 1615.

Grosvenor, Benj. Sermon on Reformation of Manners. 2d ed. 12mo. Lond. 1705.

——, —. Coronation Sermon. 8vo. Lond. 1720.

——, —. Sermon, November 7th. 8vo. Lond. 1710.

——, —. Sermon on the Death of J. Deacle, Esq. 8vo. Lond. 1723.

——, —. Two Discourses on the Name and Temper of Jesus. 8vo. Lond. 1724.

——, —. Sermon against Popery. 8vo. Lond. 1735.

——, —. Cruelty in Religion no Service of God. 8vo. Lond. 1725.

——, —. Essay on the Christian Name. 8vo. Lond. 1728.

——, —. Mourner. 16mo. Bridgeport. 1810.

——, —. Sermon to a Society of Young Persons. 8vo. Lond. 1714.

Grotius, Hugo. De Veritate Religionis Christianæ, cum Dissertationibus et Notis Variorum, cura J. C. Koecheri. 3 vol. 12mo. Jenæ. 1726—39.

——, —. De Veritate Religionis Christianæ, cum Libris J. Clerici de Eligenda inter Dissentientes Christianos Sententia, et contra Indifferentiam Religionum, etc. 12mo. Hagæ-Com. 1734.

——, —. Idem. 12mo. Bost. 1809.

——, —. Truth of the Christian Religion, &c. done into English by J. Clarke. 6th ed. 8vo. Lond. 1761.

——, —. The Same. 11th ed. 8vo. Lond. 1800.

——, —. Opera Omnia Theologica. 3 tomi in 4 vol. fol. Amst. 1679.

——, — Idem. 4 vol. fol. Basil. 1732.

——, —. Commentatio ad Loca quædam Novi Testamenti, quæ de Antichristo agere putantur. 16mo. Amst. 1640.

——, —. Vide Maresius, S. Vide Tilenus, D.

——, —. Annotationes in Novum Testamentum. Cui subjuncti sunt Libri pro Veritate Religionis Christianæ. 3 vol. fol. Amst. et Paris. 1641—50.

——, —. Annotationes in Acta Apostolorum et Epistolas Apostolicas. fol. 1646.

——, —. Annotata ad Vetus Testamentum. 3 vol. fol. Lut. Par. 1644.

——, —. Annotationes in Vet. et Nov. Testamentum. 2 vol. 4to. Lond. 1727.

Grotius, Hugo. Historia Gotthorum, Vandalorum, et Langobardorum. 8vo. Amst. 1655.
———, ———. Annales et Historiæ de Rebus Belgicis. 16mo. Amst. 1658.
———, ———. Idem. 8vo. Amst. 1658.
———, ———. Excerpta ex Tragœdiis et Comœdiis Græcis, Gr. et Lat., cum Notis. 4to. Paris. 1626.
———, ———. De Jure Belli ac Pacis;—Commentatio in Epistolam ad Philemonem. 8vo. Amst. 1651.
———, ———. De Jure Belli ac Pacis;—Comment. in Epist. ad Philemonem;—Mare Liberum. 8vo. Amst. 1670.
———, ———. De Jure Belli ac Pacis; Mare Liberum; ac Libellum de Æquitate, etc., cum Notis, cura J. Barbeyrac. 8vo. Amst. 1720.
———, ———. Idem, cum Commentariis H. L. B. de Cocceii, etc. 4 vol. 4to. Lausannæ. 1751.
———, ———. Rights of War and Peace, tr. from the Latin, with Notes by J. Barbeyrac. fol. Lond. 1738.
———, ———. Le Droit de la Guerre et de la Paix, trad. par J. Barbeyrac, avec des Notes. 2 vol. 4to. Leide. 1759.
———, ———. Defensio Fidei Catholicæ de Satisfactione Christi adversus F. Socinum. 12mo. Oxon. 1636.
———, ———. De Antichristo. 12mo. Amst. 1640.
———, ———. Two Tracts on the Sacrament. 8vo.
———, ———. Epistolæ. fol. Amst. 1687.
———, ———. Vide Laet, J. de.
Grove, Henry. Works. 10 vols. 8vo. Lond. 1747.
———, ———. Posthumous Works. 6 vols. 8vo. Lond. 1741.
———, ———. New Year's Sermon. 8vo. Lond. 1719.
———, ———. Sermon, November 5th. 8vo. Lond. 1717.
———, ———. Sermon on the Death of Mrs. P. Welman. 8vo. Lond. 1730.
———, ———. Sermon on the Death of the Rev. R. Darch. 8vo. Lond. 1737.
———, ———. Sermon at the Ordination of the Rev. Thomas Amory and William Cornish. 8vo. Lond. 1731.
———, ———. System of Moral Philosophy. 2d ed. 2 vols. 8vo. Lond. 1749.
———, ———. The Same. 3d ed. 2 vols. 8vo. Lond. 1755.
———, ———. Evidence for our Saviour's Resurrection considered. 8vo. Lond. 1730.
———, ———. Friendly Monitor. 8vo. Lond. 1728.
———, ———. Discourse concerning the Nature of Christ's Kingdom. 8vo. Lond. 1735.
———, ———. Letter to the Rev. J. Ball, on a "New Way of Preaching." 8vo. Lond. 1737.
———, ———. On the Nature and Design of the Lord's Supper. 2d ed. 12mo. Lond. 1738.
———, ———. The Same. 9th ed. 12mo. Lond. 1784.
———, ———. Essay towards a Demonstration of the Soul's Immateriality. 8vo. Lond. 1718.

Grove, Henry. Wisdom the first Spring of Action in the Deity. 8vo. Lond. 1734.
Grove, Joseph. History of Cardinal Wolsey. 4 vols. 8vo. Lond. 1742—4.
Grove, Robert, (Bp.) Protestant and Popish Way of Interpreting Scripture compared. 4to. Lond. 1689.
Grsepsius, Stanislaus. De Multiplici Siclo et Talento Hebraico; item de Mensuris Hebraicis. (Ugol. vol. 28.)
Gruchius, Nic. De Comitiis Romanorum.—Responsio ad Binas C. Sigonii Reprehensiones.—Ad Posteriorem C. Sigonii Disputationem Refutatio. (Græv. vol. 1.)
Grundmann, Fr. Mordechæus Notis Philologicis illustratus. 4to. Wittemb. 1729.
Gruner, J. F. Introductio in Antiquitates Romanas. 8vo. Jenæ. 1746.
Gruner, J. R. De Oblatione et Consecratione Primitiarum. (Ugol. vol. 17.)
Gruterus, Janus. Inscriptiones Antiquæ Totius Orbis Romani, ex Recensione et cum Annotationibus J. G. Grævii. 2 vol. fol. Amst. 1707.
———, ———. Lampas, sive Fax Artium Liberalium, hoc est, Thesaurus Criticus. 7 tomi. 8vo. Francof. 1602—34.
Grynæus, Simon. Novus Orbis Regionum ac Insularum Veteribus Incognitarum, a Variis descriptus. fol. Basil. 1537.
Guadagnolus, Philippus. Breves Arabicæ Linguæ Institutiones. fol. Romæ. 1642.
Guadaloupe. Rapport fait par la Commission pour examiner la Situation du Volcan de la Guadeloupe. 4to. Guad. 1798.
Gualterus, Nicolas. Index Testarum. fol. Florentiæ. 1742.
Gualtherus, Rodolphus. In Pauli Epistolam ad Romanos Homiliæ. fol. Tiguri. 1572.
Guarin, Petrus. Grammatica Hebraica et Chaldaica. 2 vol. 4to. Lut. Par. 1724—6.
Guarini Gio. Batt. Il Pastor Fido. 8vo. Milano. 1807.
Guarnerius, J. B. Dissertationes Historicæ Catanenses, etc. (Græv. Thes. Ital.)
Guay-Trouin, M. du. Mémoires. 8vo. Amst. 1740.
Guazzo, S. Dialoghi Piacevoli. 12mo. Piacenza. 1587.
Gudius, G. F. De Hebraica Obstetricum Origine. 4to. Lips. 1724.
———, ———. Idem. (Ugol. vol. 30.)
Gudius, Marquardus. Epistolæ ejus, et Doctorum Virorum ad eum: item Claudii Sarravii Epistolæ; curante P. Burmanno. 4to. Hagæ-Com. 1714.
———, ———. Antiquæ Inscriptiones, Gr. et Lat. fol. Leovardiæ. 1731.
Guénée, Antoine. Lettres de Quelques Juifs Portugais et Allemands à M. de Voltaire. 12mo. Paris. 1769.
Guesclin, Bertrand du. Mémoires. (Mém. de France, vol. 3 et 4.)
Guiana, Pertinente Beschrijvinge van. 4to. Amst. 1676.
Guicciardini, Fr. Historia d' Italia. 4to. Venet. 1623.

Guicciardini, Fr. Idem. 10 vol. 8vo. Milano. 1803.
——————, —. Historie of Guicciardin, tr. from the Italian by G. Fenton. fol. Lond. 1578.
——————, —. History of Italy, tr. by A. P. Goddard; with the Author's Life. 10 vols. 8vo. Lond. 1753—6.
——————, —. Aphorismes. See Dallington, R.
——————, —. Paralipomena. Vide Thuanus.
Guicciardini, Lodov. Descrittione di Tutti i Paesi Bassi, etc. fol. Anversa. 1581.
Guide, Sure, to Heaven, with Advices for promoting Practical Religion. 12mo. Lond. 1704—5.
Guiffartus, Petrus. De Cordis Officio;—item de Proxima Lactis Materia. 4to. Rothomagi. 1652.
Guignes, J, de. Sur les Rois Grecs de la Bactriane. (Acad. des Inscrip. vol. 25.)
———, ———. Sur les Philosophes appelés *Samanéens*. (Id. 26.)
———, ———. Sur les Navigations des Chinois du Côté de l'Amérique, etc. (Id. 28.)
———, ———. Sur l'Origine des Lettres Phéniciennes, Hébraïques, etc. (Id. 29.)
———, ———. Mémoires relatifs à l'Histoire des Romains. (Id. 28 et 32.)
———, ———. Mémoires sur l'Histoire, la Littérature, la Philosophie, et la Religion des Chinois. (Id. 32, 36, 38, et 40.
———, ———. Sur les Hiéroglyphes Egyptiens. (Id. 34.)
———, ———. Sur la Religion des Egyptiens. (Id. 40.)
———, ———. Sur les Langues Orientales. (Id. 36.)
———, ———. Sur le Commerce des François dans le Levant avant les Croisades. (Id. 37.)
———, ———. Sur la Religion Indienne. (Id. 40.)
Guignes, (M. de.) Dictionnaire Chinois, Français, et Latin. fol. Paris. 1813.
Guillatière, (M. de la.) Account of a late Voyage to Athens, now Englished. 8vo. Lond. 1676.
Guillaume de Saulx, Seigneur de Tavannes. Mémoires. (Mém. de France. vol. 49.)
Guillebert, Joh. Theses Theol. de Certitudine quam quis habere possit et debeat de sua Justificatione. 4to. Sedani. 1665.
Guillermin, Gilbert. Précis Historique des Derniers Evénemens de la Partie de l'Est de Saint-Domingue. 8vo. Paris. 1811.
Guillié. Essai sur l'Instruction des Aveugles. 3me ed. 8vo. Paris. 1820.
Guillim, John. Display of Heraldry. 6th ed. fol. Lond. 1724.
Guillimannus, Fr. Helvetia, sive de Rebus Helvetiorum. 4to. Amiterni. 1623.
Guillotina, or a Democratic Dirge. 8vo. Phil. 1796.
Guiranus, Gaillardus. De Antiquitatibus Nemausensibus. (Sallengre, vol. 1.)
Guiscardi, Rob. Vide Ptolemæi Lucensis, etc.
Güldenapfel, G. T. Dissertatio Historico-Exegetica Josephi Archæologi de Sadducæorum Canone Sententiam exhibens. 4to. Jenæ. 1804.

Gulielmus, Janus. De Magistratibus Reipublicæ Romanæ. (Sallengre, vol. 3.)
Gulielmus Neubrigensis. Historia Rerum Anglicarum. Vide Hearne, T.
Gumble, Tho. Life of General Monck. 8vo. Lond. 1671.
Gumilla, J. El Orinoco Ilustrado. 2 vol. 4to. Madrid. 1745.
———, -. Histoire Naturelle, Civile, et Géographique de l'Orenoque, trad. de l'Espagnol, par M. Eidous. 3 vol. 12mo. Aignon. 1758.
Gummere, John. Elementary Treatise of Astronomy. 8vo. Phil. 1822.
Günther, G. F. C. Anleitung zum Uebersetzen aus dem Deutschen in das Griechische. 12mo. Halle. 1816.
———, ———. Deutsch-Griechisches Wörterbuch. 12mo. Halle. 1816.
Güntherus, G. G. De Servo Dei Electo ad Jes. xlii, 1. 4to. Marb. Cat. 1717.
Gurdon, Brampton. Christian Religion supported by the Prophecies. 8vo. Lond. 1728.
———, ———. Consecration Sermon. 4to. Lond. 1723.
Gurdon, Thornhagh. History of the High Court of Parliament; also of Court Baron and Court Leet. 2 vols. 8vo. Lond. 1731.
Gurnall, Wm. Christian in Compleat Armour. 5th ed. fol. Lond. 1669.
Gurney, Joseph. Report of the Trial of Dr. Dodd, &c. 4to. Lond. 1777.
Gurney, T. Trial of T. Murphy for Felony and Forgery. fol. Lond. 1753.
Gussetius, Jac. Commentarii Linguæ Hebrææ. fol. Amst. 1702.
———, —. Lexicon Linguæ Hebraicæ. ed. 2da. 4to. Lips. 1743.
Gutbirius, Ægidius. Lexicon Syriacum. 8vo. Hamb. 1667.
Gutherius, Jac. De Veteri Jure Pontificio Urbis Romæ Libri iv. (Grævius, vol. 5.)
———, —. De Jure Manium.—De Orbitate Toleranda. (Id. 12.)
———, —. De Officiis Domus Augustæ Publicæ et Privatæ. (Sallengre, vol. 3.)
Guthrie, G. J. On Gun-Shot Wounds of the Extremities. 8vo. Lond. 1815.
Guthrie, Wm. Christian's Great Interest. 12mo. Lond. 1705.
———, —. The Same. 12mo. Edin. 1763.
Guthrie, Wm. Quinctilianus his Institutes of Eloquence, tr. from the Latin, with Notes. 2 vols. 8vo. Lond. 1756.
———, —. New System of Modern Geography. 2 vols. 4to. Phil. 1794—5.
———, —. The Same, with an Atlas. 6th ed. 4to. Lond. 1795.
———, —. History of England. 3 vols. fol. Lond. 1744—51.
———, —, and John Gray. General History of the World. 12 vols. 8vo. Lond. 1764—7.
Gutierrez de Rubalcava. Vide Rubalcava.

Guy, Thomas. Act for Incorporating the Executors of his Last Will. 12mo. Lond. 1725.
Guyking, N. Disputatio ad Tit. i, 12, et Math. xii, 36. 4to. Traj. ad. Rhen. 1741.
Guyse, John. Sermon to the Society for the Relief of Widows and Children of Dissenting Ministers. 8vo. Lond. 1742.
———, ——. Standing Use of the Scripture to all the Purposes of a Divine Revelation, in Eleven Sermons. 12mo. Lond. 1790.
———, ——. Practical Exposition of the New Testament. 3 vols. 4to. Lond. 1739—42.
———, ——. Scripture Notion of Preaching Christ further vindicated, in a Letter to S. Chandler. 8vo. Lond. 1730.
Guyton-Morveau, L. B. Treatise on the Means of Purifying Infected Air, &c. tr. from the French by R. Hall. 8vo. Lond. 1802.
Guyton, Vincent, Taunay, et Berthollet. Sur la Restauration du Tableau de Raphaël, connu sous le Nom de *la Vierge de Foligno*. (Instit. Lit. vol. 5.)
Guzman, F. P. de. Generaciones y Semblanzas. 4to. Madrid. 1775.
———, ———. Triumphos Morales. 12mo. Sevilla. 1581.
Gylius, Petrus. De Bosporo Thracio.—De Topographia Constantinopoleos et de illius Antiquitatibus. (Gronov. vol. 6.)
Gyllenborg, Gortz, Sparre, and Others. Letters relating to a Design of raising a Rebellion in his Majesty's Dominions, tr. into English. 8vo. Lond. 1717.
Gyraldus, C. J. B. De Ferraria et Atestinis Principibus. (Græv. Thes. Ital.)
Gyraldus, L. G. De Comœdia. (Gronov. vol. 8.)

H

Haab, P. H. Hebräisch-Griechische Grammatik; nebst einer Vorrede von F. G. von Süskind. 8vo. Tübingen. 1815.
Haak, Theod. Dutch Annotations upon the Whole Bible, translated by T. Haak. 2 vols. fol. Lond. 1657.
Haan, L. F. Beschryving van de Straat Davids. 4to. Amst. 1719.
Habert, Ludov. Theologia Dogmatica et Moralis. 8 vol. 12mo. Venet. 1741.
Habington, John. Reign of Edward IV. (Kennet, Hist. of England, vol. 1.)
Habington, Wm. Poems. See Chalmers, A.
Hachette, M. Supplément de la Géométrie Descriptive. 4to. Paris. 1812.
Hacket, John. Life of Abp. Williams. fol. Lond. 1693.
Hackmannus, Dith. De Cemoscho Moabitarum Idolo. (Oelrichs, Opusc.)
Haeberlin, Fr. Dom. De Familia Augusta Wilhelmi Conquestoris Regis Angliæ. 4to. Gottingæ. 1745.
Hæduus, Quint. Descriptio Insulæ Melitæ. (Græv. Thes. Ital.)
Haenlein, H. K. A. Handbuch der Einleitung in die Schriften des Neuen Testamentes. 3 Theile. 8vo. Erlangen. 1801—9.
———, ———. Epistola Judæ. Vide Judas.
Haes, Gerhardus, de. De Paulino Velandæ Mulieris Præcepto ad 1 Corinth. xi, 10. 4to. Traj. ad Rhen. 1761.
Hafenrefferus, Sam. De Cutis Affectibus. 8vo. Ulmæ. 1660.
Haferung, Joh. C. Oratio Inauguralis. 4to.
Hagen, F. H. von der. Der Nibelungen Lied. 8vo. Breslau. 1816.
Hagerus, Jo. Consilium de Supplemento Lexici Arabico-Latini Goliani. 4to. Vitemb. 1719.
Hagiographa in the Orissa Language. 8vo.
Haguelonus, Petrus. Calendarium Trilingue. (Gronov. vol. 9.)
Hailes, Lord. See Dalrymple, Sir David.
Haithone. Historia delle Parti dell' Oriente. Vide Horologgi.
Hakewill, Geo. Apologie of the Power and Providence of God in the Government of the World. fol. Lond. 1635.
Hakewil, Wm. Libertie of the Subject, against the pretended Power of Impositions. 4to. Lond. 1641.
Hakluyt, Richard. Collection of the Early Voyages, Travels, and Discoveries of the English Nation. A new edition, with additions. 5 vols. 4to. Lond. 1809.

Halbkart, C. W. Psychologia Homerica. 12mo. Zullichaviæ. 1796.
Halde, J. B. du. Description of China, and Chinese-Tartary, together with the Kingdoms of Korea and Tibet; from the French, with Notes. 2 vols. fol. Lond. 1738—41.
Hale, Enoch. Experiments on the Production of Animal Heat by Respiration. 8vo. Camb. 1813.
——, ——. Boylston Medical Prize Dissertations. 8vo. Bost. 1821.
Hale, John. Modest Enquiry into the Nature of Witchcraft. 12mo. Bost. 1702.
Hale, Sir Matthew. History of the Pleas of the Crown, by S. Emlyn. 2 vols. fol. Lond. 1736.
——, ——————. Summary of the Law relating to the Pleas of the Crown. 6th ed. 8vo. Lond. 1759.
——, ——————. History of the Common Law of England. 8vo. Lond. 1713.
——, ——————. The Same. 3d ed. 8vo. Lond. 1739.
——, ——————. Letter of Advice to his Grandchildren. 12mo. Bost. 1817.
——, ——————. Metaphysical and Divine Contemplations on the Loadstone. 8vo. Lond. 1695.
Hale, Moses. Sermon at the Ordination of the Rev. J. Woodman. 8vo. Salem. 1772.
Hales, Guil. Analysis Æquationum. 4to. Dublini. 1784.
——, ——. New Analysis of Chronology. 3 vols. in 4. 4to. Lond. 1809—12.
Hales, John. Tracts concerning the Lord's Supper, Auricular Confession, and Schism. 8vo. See also Hoadly, B.
——, ——. Golden Remains. 4to. Lond. 1673.
——, ——. Letter to Abp. Laud, upon occasion of his Tract on Schism. 8vo. Lond. 1716.
——, ——, Life of.—Tract concerning Schism and Schismatics;—Letter to Abp. Laud;—On Private Judgment in Religion;—The Moral Christian;—Original Sin;—Sin against the Holy Ghost;—On Parables;—Abuses of Scripture;—On the Aid of the Spirit in Private Judgment;—The Literal Sense of Scripture to be preferred;—Whether the Church may err in Fundamentals;—On Ecclesiastical Jurisdiction. (Sparks, Collection of Essays, &c.)
Hales, Stephen. Statical Essays. 2d ed. 2 vols. 8vo. Lond. 1731—3.
——, ——. Account of a Useful Discovery to distill Sea-Water; also an Account of the great Benefit of Ventilators, &c. 2d ed. 8vo. Lond. 1756.
Haley, Rich. Request to Protestants to produce Scripture for their Tenets. 4to. Lond. 1686.
——, ——. Queries to the Protestants concerning the English Reformation. 4to. Lond. 1687.
——, ——. Answer to a Discourse against Transubstantiation. 4to. Lond. 1687.

Haley, Rich. Transubstantiation Defended. 4to. Lond. 1687.
Halfpenny, Wm. and John. Country Gentleman's Pocket Companion and Builder's Assistant. 2d ed. 8vo. Lond. 1756.
Halhed, N. B. Code of Gentoo Laws, from a Persian Translation made from the Shanscrit. 8vo. Lond. 1781.
Haliday, Samuel. Sermon on the Death of the Rev. Michael Bruce. 8vo. Belfast. 1735.
——, ——. Reasons against the Imposition of Subscription. 8vo. Lond. 1724.
——, ——. Letter to the Rev. G. Kennedy on his Answer to the above. 8vo. Belfast. 1726.
——, ——. Letter to the Rev. F. Tredel on his Remarks on the above. 8vo. Belfast. 1726.
Halifax, C. Montague, Earl of. Works; with his Life and Times. 8vo. Lond. 1715.
——, ——————. Poems. See Chalmers, A.
Halifax, Sir Geo. Savile, Marquis of. Miscellanies. 8vo. Lond. 1704.
Hall, Basil. Account of a Voyage of Discovery to the West Coast of Corea and the Great Loo-Choo Island. 8vo. Phil. 1818.
Hall, (Capt.) History of the Civil War in America. 2d ed. vol. 1. 8vo. Lond. 1780.
Hall, C. H. Bampton Lecture Sermons. 8vo. Oxford. 1799.
Hall, Fr. Travels in Canada and the United States in 1816 and 1817. 8vo. Bost. 1818.
——, —. The Same. 2d ed. 8vo. Lond. 1819.
Hall, Gordon, and Samuel Newell. The Conversion of the World; or the Claims of Six Hundred Millions, &c. 2d ed. 12mo. Andover. 1818.
Hall, John E. American Law Journal. 6 vols. 8vo. Phil. 1808—17.
Hall, Joseph, (Bp.) Works. fol. Lond. 1628.
——, ————. Satires in Six Books. 12mo. Oxford. 1753.
——, ————. Poems. See Chalmers, A.
Hall, Prince. Masonic Charge. 8vo. Bost. 1792.
——, ———. Masonic Charge. 8vo. Bost. 1797.
Hall, Robert. Modern Infidelity considered with respect to its Influence on Society, in a Sermon. 8vo. Charlestown. 1801.
——, ———. Sermons; with a Treatise on the Holy Spirit. 8vo. N. York. 1814.
——, ———. Sermon on the Death of the Princess Charlotte. 12mo. Bost. 1818.
Hall, Samuel. Connecticut Election Sermon. 16mo. N. Lond. 1746.
Hall, Tomaso. Orazione Funebre in occasione della Morte della Baronessa Giacomina Elisa de Schubart, trad. dall' originale Inglese da E. Capuzzi. 4to. Lond. 1814.
Hall, Willard. Answer to Col. Choate. 8vo. Bost. 1761.
Hall, Wm. Sermon before the Queen Dowager. 4to. Lond. 1686.

Hallam, Henry. View of the State of Europe during the Middle Ages. 4 vols. 8vo. Phil. 1821.
———, ———, Letters to, from the North of Italy. 2 vols. 8vo. Lond. 1819.
Hallaran, Wm. S. On Insanity. 2d ed. 8vo. Cork. 1818.
Halleck, F. G. Fanny, (a Poem.) 8vo. N. York. 1819.
Haller, Albertus de. Bibliotheca Anatomica. 2 vol. 4to. Tiguri. 1774—7.
———, ———. Disputationes Chirurgicæ Selectæ. 5 vol. 4to. Lausannæ. 1755—6.
———, ———. Disputationes Anatomicæ Selectæ. 8 vol. 4to. Gottingæ. 1746—52.
———, ———. Opuscula Anatomica. 8vo. Gottingæ. 1751.
———, ———. Medical, Chirurgical, and Anatomical Cases and Experiments, by him and others; from the Swedish. 8vo. Lond. 1758.
———, ———. Pathological Observations. 8vo. Lond. 1756.
———, ———. Vide Uratislavia.
———, ———. Elementa Physiologiæ Corporis Humani. 5 vol. 4to. Lausannæ. 1757—63.
———, ———. Idem. 8 vol. 4to. Lausannæ et Bernæ. 1757—66.
———, ———. Primæ Lineæ Physiologiæ. 12mo. Gottingæ. 1751'
———, ———. Idem. 8vo. Edin. 1767.
———, ———. First Lines of Physiology; from the Latin. 8vo. Edin. 1786.
———, ———. The Same, by Wm. Cullen. 8vo. Edin. 1801.
———, ———. Artis Medicæ Principes; Hippocrates, Aretæus, Alexander, Aurelianus, Celsus, Rhazes; Latine, etc. 11 vol. 8vo. Lausannæ. 1769—74.
———, ———. Bibliotheca Botanica. 2 vol. 4to. Lond. 1771.
———, ———. Historia Plantarum Helveticarum. 2 vol. fol. Bernæ. 1768.
———, ———. Icones Plantarum Helvetiæ. fol. Bernæ. 1795.
———, ———. Letters to his Daughter on the Truths of the Christian Religion; from the German. 12mo. Lond. 1807.
———, ———. Sammlung kleiner Hallerischer Schriften. 3 Theile. 8vo. Bern. 1772.
Haller, G. E. von. Schweizerisches Münz- und Medaillen-Kabinet. 2 Theile. 8vo. Bern. 1780—1.
Hallet, Joseph. Notes on Texts of Scripture and Discourses. 3 vols. 8vo. Lond. 1729—36.
———, ———. The Belief of the Subordination of the Son of God to his Father, No Characteristic of an Arian. 8vo. Exon. 1719.
———, ———. Reflections on the Defence of the Account of the Reasons for Withdrawing from the Preaching of J. Hallet and J. Peirce. 8vo. Lond. 1720.
———, ———. Reflections on some Passages in Mr. Peirce's Answer to Enty. 8vo. Lond. 1721.

Hallet, Joseph. Immorality of the Moral Philosopher. 8vo. Lond. 1737.

——, ——. The Same. 2d ed. 8vo. Lond. 1740.

——, ——. Vindication of the Above. 8vo. Lond. 1737.

——, ——. Rebuke to the Moral Philosopher. 8vo. Lond. 1740.

——, ——. See Morgan, T.

——, ——. Consistent Christian; a Confutation of Chubb's "True Gospel of Jesus Christ, asserted." 8vo. Lond. 1738.

——, ——. Defence of a Discourse on the Impossibility of proving a Future State by the Light of Nature. 8vo. Lond. 1731.

Halley, Edmund. Atlas Maritimus et Commercialis. fol. Lond. 1728.

——, ——. Astronomical Tables, &c. 4to. Lond. 1752.

——, ——. Tables Astronomiques pour les Planètes et les Comètes, etc. par M. Delalande. 8vo. Paris. 1759.

——, ——. Papers in the Philosophical Transactions of the Royal Society.

——, ——. Vide Apollonius Pergæus,—Menelaus,—Serenus.

Hallier, Fr. De Sacris Electionibus et Ordinationibus. ed. 3tia. 3 vol. fol. Romæ. 1749.

Hallifax, Sam. (Bp.) Three Sermons on Subscription to the xxxix Articles. 3d ed. 8vo. Camb. 1772.

——, ——. Twelve Sermons on the Prophecies concerning the Christian Church. 8vo. Lond. 1776.

Halling, Sol. The Messiah, attempted in English Blank Verse; from the German of Klopstock. 8vo. Georgetown, (S. C.) 1810.

Halloran, Sylvester O'. See O'Halloran.

Halyburton, Tho. Natural Religion insufficient, and Revealed necessary, to Man's Happiness in his Present State. 4to. Edin. 1714.

——, ——. Ten Sermons before and after the celebration of the Lord's Supper. 8vo. Edin. 1721—3.

Hamel. Vide Du Hamel.

Hamelsveld, Isbrandus van. Oratio, de Statu Rei Christianæ Hodierno, etc. 4to. Traj. ad Rhen. 1784.

Hamilton to the Federalists of the United States on the Choice of a President. 8vo. N. York. 1812.

Hamilton. Philosophical Essays. 12mo. Edin. 1768.

Hamilton, Alex. Account of the East Indies. 2 vols. 8vo. Lond. 1744.

Hamilton, Alex. Outlines of the Theory and Practice of Midwifery. 5th ed. 8vo. Edin. 1803.

——, ——. On the Management of Female Complaints, and of Infants. 5th ed. 8vo. Edin. 1804.

Hamilton, Alex. Letter from Phocion to the Considerate Citizens of New-York. 8vo. Phil. 1784.

Hamilton, Alex. Mentor's Reply to Phocion. 8vo. Phil. 1784.
———, ——. Second Letter from Phocion. 8vo. Phil. 1784.
———, ——. Defence of the British Treaty. 8vo. N. York. 1794.
———, ——. Observations on Certain Documents contained in Nos. V, and VI of "The History of the United States for the year 1796," refuting the charge of Speculation. 8vo. Phil. 1797.
———, ——. Letter concerning President Adams. 2d and 3d ed. 8vo. N. York. 1800.
———, ——. The Same, new Edition, with a Preface. 8vo. Bost. 1809.
———, ——. Answer to his Letter concerning President Adams, by a citizen of New-York. 8vo. N. York. 1800.
———, ——. Letter to him, occasioned by his Letter to President Adams, by a Federalist. 8vo.
———, ——. Speeches of him and others on the Trial of H. Croswell. 8vo. N. York. 1804.
———, ——. Reports, as Secretary of the Treasury. (United States, Reports.)
———, ——. Works. 3 vols. 8vo. N. York. 1810.
———, ——. See Federalist.
Hamilton, C. A. Mémoires de Grammont. 2 vol. 12mo. 1760.
———, ——. Idem. 2 vol. 18mo. Paris. 1816.
Hamilton, David. De Praxeos Regulis.—De Febre Miliari. 12mo. Lond. 1710.
Hamilton, Elizabeth. Translation of the Letters of a Hindoo Rajah. 2 vols. 16mo. Bost. 1819.
———, ————. Letters addressed to the Daughter of a Nobleman. 2 vols. 12mo. Salem. 1821.
Hamilton, Hugh. Attempt to prove the Existence and Absolute Perfection of the Supreme Unoriginated Being in a Demonstrative Manner. 8vo. Lond. 1785.
———, ——. Geometrical Treatise of the Conic Sections; from the Latin. 4to. Lond. 1773.
Hamilton, James. On Purgative Medicines. 8vo. Edin. 1805.
Hamilton, James. Engravings to facilitate the Study of Midwifery. 8vo. Lond. 1796
Hamilton, John. Tables of Observations, &c. made on the Atlantic Ocean. (Amer. Phil. Tr. N. S. vol. 2.)
Hamilton, Robert. On the Marsh Remittent Fever. Also on the Water Canker, &c. 8vo. Lond. 1801.
Hamilton, Wm. Life of James Bonnell, Esq. 4th ed. 8vo. Lond. 1718.
Hamilton, Wm. Letters on the Basaltes of the Northern Coast of the County of Antrim. (Pinkerton, vol. 4.)
Hamilton, Wm. Sermon before the Society in Scotland for Propagating Christian Knowledge. 8vo. Edin. 1732.
Hamilton, Sir Wm. Campi Phlegræi; ou Observations sur les Volcans des Deux Siciles, Angl. et Fr. fol. Paris. 1799.

Hammius, J. S. Scrutatio Principii Primi Theologici. 4to. Ratisbonæ. 1706.

Hammond, Henry. Practicall Catechisme.—Large Additions to the Catechisme.—Of Conscience, Scandal, Will-Worship, and Superstition.—Of Sinnes of Weaknesse, Wilfulnesse, &c.—Of Resisting the Lawful Magistrate under Colour of Religion.—Of Idolatry.—View of the New Directory and Vindication of the Ancient Liturgy of the Church of England.—View of Some Exceptions made by a Romanist to Lord Falkland's Discourse of the Infallibilitie of the Church of Rome.—Of a Late or Death-Bed Repentance. 4to. Oxford. 1645—6.

———, ———. Practical Catechism. 7th ed. Whereunto is added the Reasonableness of Christian Religion. 8vo. Lond. 1662.

———, ———. The Same. 14th ed. 8vo. Lond. 1700.

———, ———. Reasonableness of Christian Religion. 2d ed. 16mo. Lond. 1650.

———, ———. Vide Testamentum Novum.

———, ———. Paraphrase and Annotations upon the Psalms. fol. Lond. 1659.

———, ———. Paraphrase and Annotations upon all the Books of the New Testament. 7th ed. fol. Lond. 1702.

———, ———. Exhortatory to all true Sons of the Church of England. 12mo. Lond. 1656.

———, ———. Sermons. fol. Lond. 1675.

———, ———. Works. 4 vols. fol. Lond. 1684—1702.

Hammond, James. Poems. See Chalmers, A.

Hammond, John. Practical Surveyor. 4th ed. 8vo. Lond. 1765.

Hammond, N. Elements of Algebra. 8vo. Lond. 1742.

———, —. The Same. 4th ed. 8vo. Lond. 1772.

Hammond, Robert, (Col.) Letters between him and the Committee of Lords and Commons at Derby House, relating to Charles I. 8vo. Lond. 1764.

Hampden, John, Trial of, in the Case of Ship-Money, &c. fol. Lond. 1719.

———, ——. Speech on the King's Accusation of High Treason, against himself and others. (Somers, Tr. vol. 6.)

Hampton, Geo. Remarks upon the Rev. Mr. Taylor's "Scripture Doctrine of Atonement Examined." 8vo. Lond.

———, ——. Jesus Christ the Mediator between God and Man. 8vo. Lond. 1733.

———, ——. The Same. 2d ed. 8vo. Lond. 1761.

Hampton, James. General History of Polybius, in Five Books; from the Greek. 4to. Lond. 1756.

———, ———. Two Extracts from the Sixth Book of the General History of Polybius; from the Greek. 4to. Lond. 1764.

———, ———. Extracts from Books 6—17 of Polybius; from the Greek. 2 vols. 8vo. Lond. 1773.

Hanapus, N. Virtutum et Vitiorum Exempla. fol. Basil. 1555.

Hanau, Treaty of. Occasional Letter from a Gentleman in the

Country to his Friend in Town, concerning the Treaty negociated at Hanau in 1743. 8vo. Lond. 1749.
Hanau, Treaty of. Modest and Impartial Reply to a Pamphlet entitled, *A Second Series of Facts and Arguments*, &c. with some Remarks on the *Occasional Letter*. 8vo. Lond. 1749.
———, ———. See Egmont, Earl of.
Hancock, John. Sermons at Boyle's Lecture. 8vo. Lond. 1707.
———, ——. The Same. See Boyle's Lecture Sermons.
———, ——. Febrifugum Magnum; or Common Water the best Cure for Fevers, and probably for the Plague. 8vo. Lond. 1722.
Hancock, John. Election Sermon. 12mo. Bost. 1722.
———, ——. Sermon at the Ordination of his Son. 12mo. Bost. 1726.
———, ——. Sermon at the Instalment of the Rev. T. Harrington. 8vo. Bost. 1748.
Hancock, John. Discourse on the Death of the Hon. Edmund Quincy. 8vo. Bost. 1738.
———, ——. Discourse on the Works of Grace. 8vo. Bost. 1742.
———, ——. Examiner, or Gilbert against Tennent. 12mo. Bost. 1748.
———, ——. Letter in Reply to the Rev. Mr. Gee. 4to. Bost.
Hancock, John, (Gov.) Oration, March 5th, 1774. 2d ed. 8vo. Bost. 1774.
———, ————. Biographical Sketch of his Life and Character (by J. Sullivan.) 12mo. Bost.
Handbuch. Vide Exegetisches Handbuch.
Handel, Geo. Fr. Memoirs of his Life. 8vo. Lond. 1760.
———, ———. Messiah. fol. Lond.
Handsome Jack, or an Example for Sailors. 12mo. Bost. 1813.
Hankius, Martinus. De Byzantinarum Rerum Scriptoribus. 4to. Lips. 1677.
Hanmer, Jonathan. Exercitation upon Confirmation. 8vo. Lond. 1657.
Hanmer, Meredith. Auncient Ecclesiastical Histories of the first Six Hundred Yeares after Christ, from the Greeke of Eusebius, Socrates, and Evagrius. Whereunto is annexed Dorotheus, of the Lives of the Prophets, Apostles, and 70 Disciples; with a Chronographie. fol. Lond. 1585.
———, ——. The Same. 3d ed. fol. Lond. 1607.
Hannekenius, P. L. De Cura Domestica Romanorum. (Sallengre, vol. 1.)
Hanover, Popular Prejudice concerning Partiality to the Interests of. 8vo. Lond. 1743.
Hanover Street Church. See Religious Freedom.
Hansen, F. A. Numophylacium Ehrencronianum, etc. 4to.
Hansenius, J. B. De Jurejurando Veterum. (Græevius, vol. 5.)
Hanway, Jonas. Historical Account of the British Trade over the Caspian; with a Journal of Travels through Russia, Persia, Germany, and Holland, &c. 3d ed. 2 vols. 4to. Lond. 1762.

Hanway, Jonas. Letter to the Marine Society, on the Piety and Policy of that Institution. 4th ed. 4to. Lond. 1758.
———, ——. Appeal for Mercy to the Children of the Poor. 4to. Lond. 1766.
Harcourt, Robert. Voyage to Guiana. (Harl. Miscel. vol. 6, and Purchas, vol. 4.)
Harder, Jac. Clericus Percussor. 4to. Rostochii. 1708.
Hardie, James. Account of the Malignant Fever at New-York. 8vo. N. York. 1799.
——, ——. American Remembrancer. 12mo. Phil. 1795.
——, ——. Philadelphia Directory and Register. 8vo. Phil. 1793.
——, ——. The Same. 2d ed. 8vo. Phil. 1794.
Hardion, J. Sur l'Oracle de Delphes. (Acad. des Inscrip. vol. 3.)
———, –. Sur le Sault de Leucade. (Id. 7.)
———, –. Sur l'Origine et les Progrès de la Rhétorique dans la Grece. (Id. 13, 15, 16, 19, et 21.)
Hardouin, John. Vide Harduinus, J.
Hardres, Sir Thomas. Reports of Cases in the Court of Exchequer from 1655 to 21 Car. II. 2d ed. 8vo. Dublin. 1792.
Hardt, A. J. von der. Commentatio ad R. Isaaci Aramæ Dissertationem Rabbinicam de Usu Linguæ in Proverbium Judæorum de Camelis. 4to. Helmst. 1729.
——, —————. Vide Arama.
——, —————. Dissertatio Philologica in Pirke Avot. 4to. Helmst. 1728.
Hardt, Herm. von der. Via in Caldæam Brevis et Expedita, in Fundamentis Linguæ, etc. ed. 4ta. 12mo. Helmst. 1732.
Harduinus, Jo. Ad Censuram Scriptorum Veterum Prolegomena. 8vo. Lond. 1766.
————, —. Vide Croze, M. V. la.
————, —. Nummi Antiqui Populorum et Urbium Illustrati. 4to. Paris. 1684.
————, —. Opera Selecta. fol. Amst. 1709.
————, —. De Baptismo Quæstio Triplex. 4to. Paris. 1687.
————, —. De Nummis Herodiadum. (Ugol. vol. 24.)
————, —. De Nummis Samaritanis. (Id. 28.)
————, —. Comment. in Nov. Test. fol. Amst. 1741.
Hardwicke, P. Yorke, Earl of. Speech upon giving Judgment against the Earl of Kilmarnock, &c. fol. Lond. 1746.
————, ——————, Cases in B. R. in the time of. 8vo. Dublin. 1794.
Hardwicke, Tho. Journey to Sirinagur. (Asiatic Researches, vol. 6.)
Hardy, Fr. Memoirs of the Earl of Charlemont. 2d ed. 2 vols. 8vo. Lond. 1812.
Hardy, Samuel. Vindication of the Church of England in requiring Subscription. 8vo. Lond. 1773.
Hardy, Wm., Trial of, for the Murder of an Infant. 8vo. Bost. 1807.

Hare, Francis, (Bp.) Concio ad Clerum. 4to. Lond. 1722.
——, ———. The Above examined, &c. by a Gentleman. 4to. Lond. 1722.
——, ———. Two Sermons on Rom. xiii, 1, 2. 4to. Lond. 1723.
——, ———. Psalmorum Liber in Versiculos metrice divisus; cum Dissertatione de Antiqua Hebræorum Poesi, etc. 8vo. Lond. 1736.
——, ———. Idem. (Ugol. vol. 31.)
——, ———. Sermon on Reformation of Manners. 8vo. Lond. 1731.
——, ———, Letter to, concerning the above Sermon. 8vo. Lond. 1731.
——, ———. Victory Sermon. 3d ed. 8vo. Lond. 1709.
——, ———. Accession Sermon. 8vo. Lond. 1716.
——, ———. Sermon, January 30th. 8vo. Lond. 1710.
——, ———. Visitation Sermon. 8vo. Lond. 1719.
——, ———. Vide Neal, D.
——, ———. Letter of Thanks to him for the above. 8vo. Lond. 1719.
——, ———. Scripture vindicated from the Misinterpretations of the Bishop of Bangor. 8vo. Lond. 1721.
——, ———. D——n of W——r still the Same, by an Impartial Hand. 8vo. Lond. 1720.
——, ———. Examination of the Facts and Reasonings in his Sermon preached on the 31st of January last. 8vo. Lond. 1732.
——, ———. Difficulties and Discouragements which attend the Study of the Scriptures, &c. 7th ed. 8vo. Lond. 1716.
——, ———. The Same. 9th ed. 8vo. Lond. 1729.
——, ———. ————. 12mo. Bost. 1749.
——, ———. ————. 8vo. Lond. 1766.
——, ———. ————. 8vo. Bost. 1809.
——, ———. ————; with a Biographical Notice of him. (Sparks, Collection of Essays, &c.)
——, ———. Censure of the Lower House of Convocation upon the above "Difficulties and Discouragements," &c.
——, ———. Works. 2d ed. 4 vols. 8vo. Lond. 1755.
Hare, Jo. England's proper and only Way to an Establishment in Honour, Freedom, Peace, and Happiness. (Harl. Miscel. vol. 6.)
Hareborne, Wm. Voyage to Constantinople. (Hakluyt, vol. 2.)
Harembergius, J. C. Oculus Moysis et Christi e Monte editissimo Palæstinam spectantium. (Ugol. vol. 7.)
————, ——. De Vocibus Hebraicis, Ex. xxv, 4. xxvi, 1. xxviii, 5, 6, 33, etc. (Ugol. vol. 13.)
————, ——. De Vocibus Hebraicis, 1 Paral. xxix, 7. Esdr. ii, 69. Nehem. vii, 70, 71, 72. (Id. 28.)
————, ——. De Domo inducta Minio. (Id. 29.)
Hargrove, E. Anecdotes of Archery. 12mo. York. 1792.
Harington, J. H. Description of a Cave near Gya. (Asiatic Researches, vol. 1.)

Harington, J. H. On the Burmha Game of Chess. (Id. 7.)
———, ——. On the Authorities of Mosulman Law. (Id. 10.)
Haririus. Tres Priores Consessus, Arab. et Lat., cum Notis, ab A. Schultens. 4to. Franeq. 1731.
———. Consessus Quartus, Quintus et Sextus, Arab. et Lat., cum Notis; accedunt Monumenta Vetustiora Arabiæ; cura A. Schultens. 4to. Lug. Bat. 1740.
Harkenrothius, J. E. De Monte Sublimi in quo Christus a Diabolo tentatus perhibetur.—In quædam Loca Hesychii.—De Rachele.—De Ænon prope Salem. (Ugol. vol. 7.)
Hariot, Tho. Admiranda Narratio de Commodis et Incolarum Ritibus Virginiæ. (De Bry, vol. 1.)
———, ——. Voyage to Virginia, &c. (Hakluyt, vol. 3.)
Harlan, R. On the Poison of the Rattlesnake. (Amer. Phil. Tr. N. S. vol. 3.)
Harle, Jonathan. Two Discourses; on the Frailty of Man, and on Conformity to Christ.—Psalms and Hymns. 8vo. Lond. 1730.
———, ————, Life of. See Horsley, J.
Harleian Miscellany. 8 vols. 4to. Lond 1744.
——— ————. 2d ed. 8 vols. 4to. Lond. 1753.
Harles, T. C. Introductio in Historiam Linguæ Græcæ. 2 tomi in 3 vol. 8vo. Altenb. 1792—5.
———, ——. Supplementa ad Introductionem Hist. Ling. Gr. 2 vol. 8vo. Jenæ. 1804—6.
———, ——. Introductio in Notitiam Litteraturæ Romanæ. 2 vol. 8vo. Lips. 1794.
Harley, Richard. Faults on Both Sides. (Somers, Tr. vol. 15.)
Harley, Robert, (Earl of Oxford.) Essay on Public Credit.—Essay on Loans. (Somers, Tr. vol. 2.)
———, ——————————. Vindication of Rights of the Commons. (Id. 8.)
———, ——————————. Reasons for Im—— the L——d H—— T——r, and Some Others of the P—— M——. 12mo. Lond.
———, ——————————. See Harleian Miscellany.
Harman, Paul. Materia Medica, done from the Latin, with Observations, &c. by E. Strother. 2 vols. 8vo. Lond. 1727.
Harmer, Tho. Observations on Various Passages of Scripture. 3d ed. 4 vols. 8vo. Lond. 1797.
———, ——. The Same, with Additions, &c. by A. Clarke. 4th ed. 4 vols. 8vo. Lond. 1808.
———, ——. The Same. 5th ed. 4 vols. 8vo. Lond. 1816.
———, ——. Outlines of a New Commentary on Solomon's Song. 8vo. Lond. 1768.
Harmoniæ Evang. Chemnitio-Lyserianæ, ed. Gerhard. 2 vol. 4to. Jenæ. 1626—7.
Harmony without Uniformity, being a Philosophical Defence of Liberty and Charity. 8vo. Lond. 1740.
Haroldus, Fr. Lima Limata Consiliis, etc. fol. Romæ. 1673.
Harpe, Jean Fr. de la. Du Fanatisme dans la Langue Révolutionnaire. 8vo. Paris. 1797.

Harpe, Jean Fr. de la. Correspondence Littéraire. 2de ed. 4 vol. 8vo. Paris. 1804.
——, ————. Œuvres. 6 vol. 8vo. Paris. 1778.
——, ————. Lycée, ou Cours de Littérature Ancienne et Moderne. 16 tom. en 19 vol. 8vo. Paris. 1799—1805.
Harper, Robert G. Address to his Constituents on the British Treaty; with a Letter from Gov. Jay. 8vo. Phil. 1796.
——, ————. Speech on the Foreign Intercourse Bill in 1798. 8vo.
——, ————. Observations on the Dispute between the United States and France. 4th Amer. ed. 8vo. Bost. 1798.
——, ————. Letter to one of his Constituents on the Proceedings of Congress. 8vo. Phil. 1798.
——, ————. Speech in 1797, relative to the Conduct of France. 8vo. Phil. 1798.
——, ————. Speech on the Reduction of the Army. 12mo. Phil. 1800.
——, ————. Letter to his Constituents. 8vo. Portsmouth. N. H. 1801.
——, ————. Speech at the Celebration of the Recent Triumphs of the Causepof Mankind in Germany. 8vo. Bost. 1814.
——, ————. Correspondence with Robert Walsh, jun. respecting Russia. 8vo. Phil. 1813.
Harpocration, Valerius. De Vocibus Liber, cum Notis J. Gronovii. Accedit H. Stephani in Isocratem Diatribe. 4to. Lug. Bat. 1696.
——, ————. Vide Valesius.
Harraden, R. Costume of the University of Cambridge. 4to. Camb. 1803.
——, ————, and Son. Cantabrigia Depicta. 4to. Camb. 1809.
Harrington, James. Common-Wealth of Oceana. fol. Lond. 1656.
——, ————. Oceana and Other Works; with his Life, by J. Toland. fol. Lond. 1700.
——, ————. The Same, with Additions. 3d ed. fol. Lond. 1747.
Harrington, Sir John. Nugæ Antiquæ, or Original Papers in Prose and Verse, with Notes, by T. Park. 2 vols. 8vo. Lond. 1804.
Harrington, Timothy. Ill-boding Symptoms on a Stupid People, a Discourse. 8vo. Bost. 1756.
Harris, James. Hermes. 8vo. Lond. 1751.
——, ————. ————. 2d ed. 8vo. Lond. 1765.
——, ————. Philological Enquiries. 8vo. Lond. 1781.
——, ————. Three Treatises, on Art; Music, Painting, and Poetry; and Happiness. 8vo. Lond. 1744.
——, ————. The Same. 8vo. Lond. 1765.
Harris, John, (Bp.) Eight Sermons at Boyle's Lecture. 4to. Lond. 1698.
——, ————. The Same. See Boyle's Lecture Sermons.

Harris, John, (Bp.) Sermon before the Lord Mayor. 4to. Lond. 1705.
———, ———. Use and Lawfulness of Publick Feasting, a Sermon. 8vo. Lond. 1706.
———, ———. Evil of Universal Applause, a Sermon. 8vo. Lond. 1718.
———, ———. Sermon, January 30th. 4to. Lond. 1735.
Harris, John. Complete Collection of Voyages and Travels. 2 vols. fol. Lond. 1705.
———, ———. The Same, with Additions. 2 vols. fol. Lond. 1764.
———, ———. Lexicon Technicum. 2d ed. 2 vols. fol. Lond. 1708—10.
———, ———. Remarks on some late Papers relating to the Universal Deluge. 8vo. Lond. 1697.
Harris, Joseph. Treatise of Opticks. 4to. Lond. 1775.
Harris, S. Commentary on Isaiah LIII, with Dissertations and Queries. 2d ed. 4to. Lond. 1739.
Harris, Thaddeus M. Natural History of the Bible. 12mo. Bost. 1793.
———, ———. The Same. 8vo. Bost. 1820.
———, ———. Journal of a Tour into the Territory Northwest of the Alleghany Mountains, &c. 8vo. Bost. 1805.
———, ———. Sermon at the Ordination of the Rev. John Pierce. 8vo. Bost. 1797.
———, ———. Sermon at the Installation of the Rev. Abiel Abbot. 8vo. Salem. 1804.
———, ———. Sermon at the Ordination of the Rev. C. H. Shearman. 8vo. Dover, N. H. 1807.
———, ———. Sermon at the Ordination of the Rev. E. Pratt. 8vo. Bost. 1807.
———, ———. Sermon at the Ordination of the Rev. S. Osgood. 8vo. Springfield, Mass. 1809.
———, ———. Sermon at the Ordination of the Rev. E. Randall. 8vo. New-Bedford. 1814.
———, ———. Sermon at the Ordination of the Rev. L. Capen. 8vo. Bost. 1815.
———, ———. Discourse on the Death of Washington. 8vo. Charlestown. 1800.
———, ———. Discourse on the Death of his Mother. 8vo. Charlestown. 1801.
———, ———. Discourse at the Funeral of Deacon A. White. 8vo. Bost. 1804.
———, ———. Sermon on the Death of the Hon. James Bowdoin. 4to. Bost. 1811.
———, ———. Discourse at the Funeral of Ebenezer Wales, Esq. 8vo. Bost. 1813.
———, ———. Discourse at the Funeral of Moses Everett, Esq. 8vo. Bost. 1813.
———, ———. Sermon on New Year's Day. 8vo. Bost. 1796.

Harris, Thaddeus M. Sermon on the Execution of Jason Fair banks. 8vo. Dedham. 1801.

——, ————. Fast Sermon. 8vo. Bost. 1798.

——, ————. Century Discourse to the Religious Society of Young Men in Dorchester. 8vo. Charlestown. 1799.

——, ————. Artillery Election Sermon. 8vo. Bost. 1805.

——, ————. Discourse on Covenant Engagements; with an Address to Baptized Children. 8vo. Bost. 1802.

——, ————. Address at the Interment of Three Persons who were drowned. 8vo. Bost. 1804.

——, ————. Discourse before the Humane Society of Massachusetts; with the Life Boat, a Poem, by a Member of the Society. 8vo. Bost. 1806.

——, ————. Masonic Discourses. 8vo. Charlestown. A. L. 5801.

——, ————. Sermon before the Union Lodge in Dorchester. 8vo. Bost. 1807.

——, ————. Constitutions of the Fraternity of Free and Accepted Masons, &c. 4to. Worcester. 1792.

——, ————. Dedication Sermon. 8vo. Bost. 1806.

——, ————. Sermon from 1 Corinthians x, 17. 8vo. Bost. 1806.

——, ————. Sermon from Ephesians ii, 17, 18. 8vo. Bost. 1806.

——, ————. Thanksgiving Sermon. 8vo. Bost. 1807.

——, ————. Discourse at Plymouth on the Landing of our Ancestors. 8vo. Bost. 1808.

——, ————. Address before the Washington Benevolent Society. 8vo. Bost. 1813.

——, ————. Good Wishes for Youth, expressed in a Discourse. 8vo. Bost. 1804.

——, ————. On Christian Sensibility, a Sermon preached in the Family of Dr. Disney. 8vo. Lond. 1811.

——, ————. Discourse before the Boston Female Asylum; with Hymns, composed at several times for the Asylum. 8vo. Bost. 1813.

——, ————. Caution against Suicide. 8vo. Bost. 1812.

——, ————. Textuary. 8vo. Bost. 1818.

——, ————. See Sewall, Stephen.

Harris, Tho. Popery and Slavery Displayed. 3d ed. 8vo. Lond. 1745.

Harris, Tho., and John M'Henry. Maryland Reports, from 1700 to 1799. 4 vols. 8vo. N. York and Annapolis. 1809—18.

——, ——, and Reverdy Johnson. Reports in Maryland, from 1800 to 1805. 8vo. Annapolis. 1821.

Harris, Walter. De Morbis Acutis Infantium, et de Morbis Gra vioribus. 8vo. Lond. 1705.

——, ——. On the Acute Diseases of Infants, &c. tr. by J. Martyn. 8vo. Lond. 1742.

Harris, Walter. History of the Life and Reign of William III, King of England, &c. fol. Dublin. 1749.
Harris, Wm. Sermon to Young People. 8vo. Lond. 1707.
———, ——. Sermon to Young Men. 8vo. Lond. 1716.
———, ——. Practical Discourses on the Messiah. 8vo. Lond. 1724.
———, ——. Two Sermons on the Reasonableness of Believing in Christ, &c. 8vo. Lond. 1729.
———, ——. Discourse on Transubstantiation. 8vo. Lond. 1735.
———, ——. Self-Dedication. 12mo. Lond. 1717.
———, ——. Sermon, Nov. 5th. 8vo. Lond. 1713.
———, ——. Sermon at the Ordination of Mr. John Treen and Mr. B. Owen. 8vo. Lond. 1725.
———, ——. Sermon at the Ordination of Mr. Thomas Payne. 8vo. Lond. 1729.
———, ——. Sermon at the Ordination of the Rev. Wiliam Ford and S. Parks. 8vo. Lond. 1731.
———, ——. Sermon on the Death of Mrs. B. Barker. 8vo. Lond. 1719.
———, ——. Sermon on the Death of the Rev. John Billingsly. 8vo. Lond. 1722.
———, ——. Sermon on the Death of Mr. John Mercer. 8vo. Lond. 1725.
———, ——. Sermon on the Death of the Rev. Samuel Harvey. 8vo. Lond. 1729.
———, ——. Sermon on the Death of the Rev. Joshua Oldfield. 8vo. Lond. 1730.
———, ——. Sermon on the Death of the Rev. John Evans. 8vo. Lond. 1730.
———, ——. Sermon on the Death of the Rev. Daniel Mayo. 8vo. Lond. 1733.
———, ——. Funeral Discourses. 8vo. Lond. 1736.
———, ——. Two Fast Sermons. 8vo. Lond. 1740.
———, ——. Two Sermons on Lukewarmness in Religion; with a Discourse concerning False Zeal. 8vo. Lond. 1732.
Harris, Wm.. Account of the Life and Writings of James I, King of Great Britain. 8vo. Lond. 1753.
———, ——. Life and Writings of Charles I. 8vo. Lond. 1758.
———, ——. Life and Writings of Charles II. 2 vols. 8vo. Lond. 1758—66.
———, ——. Account of Hugh Peters. 8vo. Lond. 1751.
———, ——. Life of Oliver Cromwell. 8vo. Lond. 1762.
———, ——. Observations on National Establishments of Religion. 8vo. Lond. 1767.
Harris, Wm. Sermon at the Funeral of Mrs. Martha Roads. 12mo. Bost 1795.
Harrison, Amos. Sermon on the Death of Mr. Job Harrison. 2d ed. 8vo. Lond. 1724.
———, ——. Sermon on the Duties and Dignities of Gospel Ministers. 8vo. Lond. 1742.

Harrison, Amos. New Year's Gift to the Thirtieth of January Preachers. 2d ed. 8vo. Lond. 1742.
———, ——. "New Year's Gift" Defended. 8vo. Lond. 1743.
———, ——. Remarks on the Vicar's Complaint against some of his Parishioners for not paying Tythes, &c. 8vo. Lond. 1742.
Harrison, David. Melancholy Narrative of his Distressful Voyage and Miraculous Deliverance. 8vo. Lond. 1766.
Harrison, J. B. Discourse on the Prospects of Letters and Taste in Virginia. 8vo. Camb. 1828.
Harrison, Joseph. Practice of the Court of Chancery. 2 vols. 8vo. Phil. 1807.
Harrison, Tho. Sermon on Phil. i, 20. 8vo. Lond. 1729.
———, ——. Sermon on the Death of Mrs. I. Ewer. 8vo. Lond. 1724.
Harrison, Wm. Chronicles. See Holinshed, R.
Harryson (Bale), Johan. Yet a Course at the Romyshe Foxe. 12mo. Zurich. 1543.
Harte, Walter. Essay on Reason. 3d ed. fol. Lond. 1736.
——, ———. Essays on Husbandry. 8vo. Lond. 1764.
——, ———. The Same. 2d ed. 8vo. Lond. 1770.
——, ———. Poems. See Chalmers, A.
Hartford, Proceedings of the Convention of New-England Delegates at. 3d ed. 8vo. Bost. 1815.
Hartley, David. Observations on Man. 2 vols. 8vo. Lond. 1749.
———, ——. Theory of the Mind, on the Principle of the Association of Ideas, &c. by J. Priestley. 8vo. Lond. 1775.
———, ——. Review of the "Observations" and "Theory." 8vo 1791.
———, ——. De Lithontriptico a J. Stevens nuper invento. Accedunt Conjecturæ de Sensu, Motu, et Idearum Generatione. 8vo. Bath. 1746.
———, ——. Prayers and Religious Meditations. 8vo. Camb. 1821.
———, ——. See Priestley, J.
Hartley, David. Substance of a Speech in Parliament upon the State of the Nation and the present Civil War with America. 2d ed. 4to. Lond. 1776.
———, ——. Letters on the American War. 3d ed. 4to. Lond. 1778.
Hartley, Tho. Nine Queries concerning the Trinity, &c. proposed to E. Swedenborg; with his Answers. 8vo. Lond. 1786.
Hartmann, A. Th. Die Hebräerin am Putztische und als Braut. 3 Theile. 12mo. Amst. 1809—10.
Hartmann et Millard. Le Texas, ou Notice Historique sur le Champ d'Asile. 8vo. Paris. 1819.
Hartmannus, H. L. Chronologia Symposii Platonis. 4to. Lips. 1798.
Hartsinck, J. J. Beschryving van Guiana. 2 vol. 4to. Amst. 1770.
Harvard Register. 8vo. Cambridge. 1828.

Harvard University. Pietas et Gratulatio Collegii Cantabrigiensis apud Novanglos. 4to. Bost. 1761.

——— ———. Foundation of the Massachusetts Professorship of Natural History at Harvard College. 12mo. Bost. 1805.

——— ———. Statement of Facts, (relating to the Disturbance in 1807,) by Students. 12mo.

——— ———. Statutes relating to the Degree of Doctor in Medicine. 8vo. Bost. 1811.

——— ———, Constitution of, with an Appendix. 8vo. Camb. 1812.

——— ———. Observations on the Proposition for Increasing the Means of Theological Education at the University in Cambridge. 8vo. Camb. 1815.

——— ———. Report of the Committee of the Society for the Promotion of Theological Education in Cambridge University. 8vo. Bost. 1824.

——— ———, Constitution of the Society for the Promotion of Theological Education in. 8vo. Bost. 1825.

——— ———. Report of the Committee of the Association of the Members of the Federal Street Society for Benevolent Purposes, on the Application of the Directors of the Theological School in Cambridge. 8vo. Camb. 1825.

——— ———. Circular of the Directors of the Theological School. 8vo. Bost. 1825.

——— ———. Report of a Committee of the Board of Overseers respecting the State of the University, and the Changes it would be expedient to recommend to the Corporation for its adoption, May 4, 1824. 8vo.

——— ———. Remarks on the above "Report," by one, lately a Member of the Immediate Government of the College, (Prof. Norton.) 8vo. Camb. 1824.

——— ———. Memorial of Professors and Tutors, to the Corporation, relative to the Mode, in which the Corporation ought of Right to be constituted. 8vo. Camb. 1824.

——— ———. Another Memorial from the Same. 8vo. 1824.

——— ———. Remarks on the "Memorial," by an Alumnus of Harvard College, (John Lowell.) 8vo. Bost. 1824.

——— ———. Letter to John Lowell, Esq. in Reply to the "Remarks," by Edward Everett. 8vo. Bost. 1824.

——— ———. Further Remarks on the "Memorial," by an Alumnus of Harvard College, (John Lowell.) 8vo. Bost. 1824.

——— ———. Report of a Committee of the Overseers of Harvard College, January 6, 1825. 8vo. Camb. 1825.

——— ———. Report of a Committee of the Overseers on the Memorial of the Resident Instructers. 8vo. 1825.

——— ———. See Norton, A.,—Ticknor, G.,—United States Literary Gazette, vols. 2 and 3.

——— ———. Mathematical Exercises by Undergraduates, for the Exhibitions in the Chapel. MSS.

——— ———. Laws, Catalogues, Theses, Prize Dissertations MSS., &c.

Harvrad University. See Cambridge,—Catalogue,—Catalogus,—Massachusetts,—Whitefield, &c.
Harveianæ Orationes Anniversariæ. Vide Harveius, G.
Harveius, Guil. Opera Omnia, a Collegio Medicorum Londinensium edita; cum Vita ejus. 4to. Lond. 1766.
———, ——. Exercitationes Anatomicæ de Motu Cordis et Sanguinis Circulatione.—J. Walæus, de Motu Chyli et Sanguinis.—J. de Back, de Corde. 12mo. Lond. 1660.
———, ——. De Generatione Animalium. 12mo. Amst. 1651.
———, ——. Orationes Anniversariæ in Theatro Collegii Regalis Medicorum Londinensium ex Harvæi Instituto. 4to. Lond. 1746—64.
Harvey, James. Justice of Peace. 2d ed. 12mo. Lond. 1734.
Harvey, Joseph. Reply to Parker's "Proscription Delineated." 8vo. Hartford. 1819.
Harvey, Wm. See Harveius, Guil.
Harwood, Sir Busick. Synopsis of a Course of Lectures on Anatomy and Physiology. 8vo. Camb. 1787.
———, ————. System of Comparative Anatomy and Physiology. 4to. Lond. 1796.
Harwood, Edward. Introduction to the Study and Knowledge of the New Testament. 2 vols. 8vo. Lond. 1767—71.
———, ———. Life and Character of Christ. 8vo. Lond. 1772.
———, ———. Five Dissertations on Religious Subjects. 8vo. Lond. 1772.
———, ———. Liberal Translation of the New Testament, with Notes. 2 vols. 8vo. Lond. 1768.
———, ———. Account of the Conversion of a Deist. 8vo. Lond. 1762.
———, ———. View of the Editions of the Greek and Roman Classics. 3d ed. 12mo. Lond. 1782.
———, ———. Biographia Classica. 2d ed. 2 vols. 12mo. Lond. 1750.
Harwood, Tho. Grecian Antiquities. 8vo. Lond. 1801.
Hasæus, Jac. Dissertatio de Tuckiim. (Ugol. vol. 7.)
———, ——. Dissertatio ad Illustrationem Jobi xl, 31, (vel 26,) et Jesaiæ xviii, 1. (Id. 29.)
———, ——. Vide Hasæus, T.
———, ——. De Inquinatis Sardiensium Vestimentis ad Illustrationem Apoc. iii, 4. (Id.)
———, ——. De Inscriptione Psalmi 22. (Id. 32.)
Hasæus, Theodorus. De Monte Sublimi.—De Sabulonis præ Sidone Præstantia.—De Naphthalitide Apostolorum Patria.—De Gente Kau, Kau. (Ugol. vol. 7.)
———, ————. De Vera Origine, et Significatione Vocis *Astartes*. (Id. 23.)
———, ————. De Ligno Sittim.—De Rubo Mosis.—De Lapide Fundamenti. (Id. 8.)
———, ————. Ad Dissertationem J. Hasæi de Esai xviii, 1, Supplementum. (Id. 29.)

Hasæus, Theodorus. De Decreto Tiberii Imperatoris, quo Christum referre voluit in Numerum Deorum. (Oelrichs, Coll. Opusculorum.)
———, ———, et C. Ikenius. Thesaurus Novus Theologico-Philologicus. 2 vol. fol. Lug. Bat. et Amst. 1732.
Haselbauer, Fr. Fundamenta Grammatica Ling. Hebr. et Chald. 8vo. Pragæ. 1742.
Haselden, Tho. Euclide's Elements, and Data. 8vo. Lond. 1732.
Hasenclever. Lebensgeschichte des Kaufmanns Hasenclever in Landshut. 8vo. Hamburg. 1796.
Haskard, (Dr.) Discourse about the Charge of Novelty made by the Papists upon the Church of England. 4to. Lond. 1685.
Haslewood, Fr. Sermon, January 30th. 8vo. Lond. 1721.
———, —. Sermon, November 5th. 4to. Lond. 1721.
Hassel, J. Tour of the Isle of Wight. (Pinkerton, vol. 2.)
Hasselquist, Fred. Voyages and Travels in the Levant; from the Swedish. 8vo. Lond. 1766.
Hassenfratz, J. H. Cours de Physique Céleste. 8vo. Paris. 1803.
Hassler, F. R. Papers on the Survey of the Coast of the United States. (Amer. Phil. Tr. N. S. vol. 2.)
Hastings, Warren. See Impey, Sir Elijah.
Hauboldus, C. G. Institutiones Juris Romani Litterariæ. 8vo. Lips. 1809.
Haug, J. F. De Theologia Mystica. 4to. Argent. 1701.
Hauksbee, Fr. Physico-Mechanical Experiments on Various Subjects. 2d ed. 8vo. Lond. 1719.
———, —. Experiments, Mechanical, Optical, &c. 4to.
Hautchamp, B. M. du. Histoire Générale et Particulière du Visa. 4 vol. 12mo. La Haye. 1743.
Hauxley, Edw. Navigation Unvailed. 2 vols. 8vo. Lond. 1743.
Haüy, Réné Just. Traité de Minéralogie. 4 vol. 8vo. Paris. 1801.
———, ———. Mémoires dans les Annales, du Muséum d'Histoire Naturelle.
———, ———. Elementary Treatise of Natural Philosophy, tr. from the French, with Notes, by O. Gregory. 2 vols. 8vo. Lond. 1807.
Havana, Journal of the Siege of, by an Officer. 8vo. Lond. 1762.
———. Memorias de la Real Sociedad Económica de la Habana. 4to. Habana. 1817; y Números 13—15, 19—30, 1818—19.
———, Letters from the, in 1820, containing an Account of the Present State of Cuba, and Observations on the Slave Trade. 8vo. Lond. 1821.
Haven, Jason. Artillery Election Sermon. 8vo. Bost. 1761.
———, ———. Election Sermon. 8vo. Bost. 1769.
Haven, N. A. Remains; with a Memoir of his Life, by Geo. Ticknor. 8vo. Camb. 1827.
———, ———. The Same. 2d ed. 12mo. Bost. 1828.
Haven, Samuel. Convention Sermon. 8vo. Portsmouth. 1760.
———, ———. Peace Sermon. 8vo. Portsmouth. 1763.
———, ———, Dudleian Lecture. 8vo. Bost. 1798.

Havercampus, Sigebertus. Thesaurus Morellianus Numismaticus. 2 vol. fol. Amst. 1734.
————, ————. Nummophylacium Reginæ Christinæ, Latine et Gallice. fol. Hagæ. Com. 1742.
Havestadt, Bernardus. Res Chilenses. 3 tomi in 2 vol. 8vo. Monasterii Westphaliæ. 1777.
Havre de Grace Company, Articles of Association of the. 8vo. Phil. 1797.
Hawes, Noyes P. United States' Spelling Book. 12mo. Portland. 1824.
Hawes, W. Transactions of the Royal Humane Society, 1774—94. vol. 1. 8vo. Lond.
Hawker, Robert. Sermons on the Divinity and Operations of the Holy Ghost. 8vo. Bath. 1794.
————, ————. The Same. 2d ed. 12mo. Bath. 1796.
Hawkesworth, John. Account of Voyages of Discovery in the Southern Hemisphere, performed by Byron, Wallis, Carteret, and Cook. 3 vols. 4to. Lond. 1773.
————, ——. Adventurer. 4th ed. 4 vols. 12mo. Lond. 1762.
————, ——. ————. 4 vols. 12mo. Lond. 1770.
————, ——. ————. 4 vols. 12mo. Phil. 1803.
Hawkins, Abraham. On the Agave Americana. (Horticultural Tr. vol. 4.)
Hawkins, James. Answer to the Rev. Thomas Reynolds. 8vo. Lond. 1723.
Hawkins, Sir John. Voyages to the West Indies. (Hakluyt, vol. 3.)
Hawkins, Sir John. Life of Dr. Samuel Johnson. See Johnson, S.
Hawkins, Sir Richard. Voyage to the South Sea. (Purchas, vol. 4, and Callander, vol. 2.
Hawkins, Tho. Origin of the English Drama. 3 vols. 12mo. Oxford. 1773.
Hawkins, Wm. Relations of Occurents in the Country of the Great Mogoll. (Purchas, vol. 1.)
Hawkins, Wm. Pleas of the Crown. 2 vols. fol. Lond. 1716.
Hawkins, Wm. Pretences of Enthusiasts Confuted, a Sermon. 8vo. Oxford. 1769.
————, ——. Discourses on Scripture Mysteries, preached at the Bampton Lecture. 8vo. Oxford. 1787.
Hawkwood, Sir John, Memoirs of. 4to. Lond. 1782.
Hawley, Jacobus. Oratio Harveiana. 4to. Lond. 1747.
Hawley, Wm. Letter to Bishop Kemp on the Choice of a Chaplain to Congress. 8vo. Washington. 1822.
Hawney, Wm. Compleat Measurer. 4th ed. 12mo. Lond.
————, ——. ————————. 13th ed. 12mo. Lond. 1769.
Haworth, A. H. On the Cultivation of Crocuses. (Horticultural Tr. vol. 1.)
Hay, Wm. Religio Philosophi. 2d ed. 8vo. Lond. 1754.
——, ——. Essay on Deformity. 3d ed. 8vo. Lond. 1755.
Hayden, H. H. Geological Essays. 8vo. Baltimore. 1820.

Hayes, Charles. Treatise of Fluxions. fol. Lond. 1704.
Hayes, Thomas. On Coughs and Colds. 12mo. Walpole, N. H. 1808.
Haygarth, John. Inquiry how to prevent the Small-Pox, &c. 8vo. Bath. 1801.
———, ——. Medical Transactions. 4 vols. 8vo. Lond. 1801.
———, ——. On the Prevention of Infectious Fevers. 8vo. Lond. 1801.
Hayley, Thomas. Sermon before the King on Religious Impositions. 8vo. Lond. 1716.
———, ———. Sermon before the King on Charity. 8vo. Lond. 1718.
Hayley, Wm. Sermon on Reformation of Manners. 12mo. Lond. 1699.
Hayley, Wm. Poems and Plays. 6 vols. 8vo. Lond. 1785.
———, ——. Life and Posthumous Writings of William Cowper. 2 vols. 12mo. Bost. 1803.
———, ——. The Same. 2d ed. 3 vols. 4to. Chichester. 1803—4.
Haym, Nic. Fr. Biblioteca Italiana. 4to. Venez. 1741.
———, ———. Idem. 4 vol. 8vo. Milano. 1803.
Hayne, Tho. Linguarum Cognatio. 8vo. Lond. 1648.
Haynes, Hopton. Scripture Account of the Attributes and Worship of God; and of the Character and Offices of Christ. 2d ed. 8vo. Lond. 1790.
Hayter, John. Account of Herculaneum. (Class. Journ. vol. 7.)
Hayter, Tho. (Bp.) Charge to his Clergy. 8vo. Lond. 1732.
———, ——. Sermon before the King. 2d ed. 4to. Lond. 1752.
———, ——. Sermon before the Governors of the London Hospital, &c. 4to. Lond. 1759.
———, ——. Sermon before the Society for promoting English Protestant Working-Schools in Ireland. 4to. Lond. 1754.
Hayus, Joh. De Rebus Japonicis, Indicis, et Peruanis Epistolæ Recentiores. 12mo. Antv. 1605.
Hayward, Sir John. Life of King Edward VI. (Kennet, vol. 2.)
———, ———. Lives of Henry III, and IV. See Cotton, Sir R.
Hazard, Ebenezer. Historical Collections of State Papers, &c. intended as Materials for a History of the United States of America. 2 vols. 4to. Phil. 1792—4.
———, ———. Remarks on Schermerhorn's Report concerning the Western Indians. (Mass. Hist. Coll. N. S. vol. 4.)
Hazlitt, Wm. Eloquence of the British Senate; with Notes. 2 vols. 8vo. N. York. 1810.
Head, Joseph. Enthusiasm, a Poem delivered before the Phi Beta Kappa Society. 8vo. Bost. 1809.
Heads of Milton, Marvell, Sidney, Ludlow, Locke, and Newton, &c. fol.

Heads of Illustrious Persons. See Birch, T.
Hearne, Tho. Johannis de Fordun Scotichronicon. 5 vol. 8vo. Oxon. 1722.
———, ———. Johannis Glastoniensis Chronica de Rebus Glastoniensibus. 2 vol. 8vo. Oxon. 1726.
———, ———. Peter Langtoft's Chronicle. 2 vols. 8vo. Oxford. 1725.
———, ———. Leland's Itinerary. 2d ed. 9 vols. in 5. 8vo. Oxford. 1745.
———, ———. Robert of Gloucester's Chronicle. 2 vols. 8vo. Oxford. 1724.
———, ———. Joannis Rossi, Antiquarii Warwicensis, Historia Regum Angliæ. ed. 2da. 8vo. Oxon. 1745.
———, ———. Thomæ Sprotti Chronica. 8vo. Oxon. 1719.
———, ———. Liber Niger Scaccarii. 2 vol. 8vo. Oxon. 1728.
———, ———. Thomæ de Elmham Vita et Gesta Henrici Quinti, Anglorum Regis. 8vo. Oxon. 1727.
———, ———. Walteri Hemingford Historia de Rebus Gestis Edvardi I, II, et III. 2 vol. 8vo. Oxon. 1731.
———, ———. T. Caii Vindiciæ Antiquitatis Academiæ Oxoniensis contra J. Caium. 2 vol. 8vo. Oxon. 1730.
———, ———. Collection of Discourses by Eminent Antiquaries on English Antiquities. 8vo. Oxford. 1720.
———, ———. Acta Apostolorum Græco-Latine, Litteris Majusculis, e Codice Laudiano. 8vo. Oxon. 1715.
———, ———. Chronicon Prioratus de Dunstaple. 2 vol. 8vo. Oxon. 1733.
———, ———. History and Antiquities of Glastonbury. 8vo. Oxford. 1722.
———, ———. Historia Vitæ et Regni Ricardi II, a Monacho quodam de Evesham, etc. 8vo. Oxon. 1729.
———, ———. Adami de Domerham Historia de Rebus Gestis Glastoniensibus. 2 vol. 8vo. Oxon. 1727.
———, ———. Benedictus Abbas de Vita et Gestis Henrici II. et Ricardi I. 2 vol. 8vo. Oxon. 1735.
———, ———. Guilielmi Neubrigensis Historia Rerum Anglicarum. 3 vol. 8vo. Oxon. 1719.
———, ———. Hemingi Chartularium Ecclesiæ Wigorniensis. 2 vol. 8vo. Oxon. 1723.
———, ———, Life of, See Huddesford, W.
———, ———. Vide Dodwell, H. Vide Nelus, T.
Heart, Jonathan. Observations on the Ancient Works of Art, Native Inhabitants, &c. of the Western Country. (Amer. Phil. Tr. vol. 3.)
Heath, Benj. Notæ sive Lectiones ad Tragicos Græcos. 4to. Oxon. 1762.
Heath, Rob. Royal Astronomer and Navigator. 4to. Lond. 1760.
———, ———. Account of the Islands of Scilly. (Pinkerton, vol. 2.)
Heath, Thomas. Essay towards a New English Version of Job; with a Commentary, &c. 4to. Lond. 1756.

Heath, Wm. (Gen.) Memoirs. 8vo. Bost. 1798.

Heathcote, Ralph. Two Sermons at Boyle's Lecture. 2d ed. 8vo. Lond. 1763.

Hebediesu. Catalogus Librorum Chaldæorum, Syriace et Latine, cum Notis, ab A. Ecchellensi. 8vo. Romæ. 1653.

Heberden, Wm. Commentaries on the History and Cure of Diseases. 2d ed. 8vo. Lond. 1803.

Hebrew Language. Its Majesty and Copiousness illustrated. 8vo. Lond. 1744.

Heckewelder, John. On the Bird Nine-Killer.—On the Big Naked Bear. (Amer. Phil. Tr. vol. 4.)

———, ——. On the Beaver. (Id. 6.)

———, ——. Account of the History, Manners, and Customs of the Indian Nations of Pennsylvania, &c. (Transactions of the Hist. and Lit. Committee of the Amer. Phil. Society, vol. 1.)

Heckhing, J. C. Responsiones ad G. Bulli contra Doctrinam de Justificatione Fidei Objectiones. 4to. Tubingæ. 1733.

Hedenus, J. Q. Scissio Vestium Hebræis et Gentilibus usitata. (Ugol. vol. 29.)

Hedericus, Benj. Lexicon Manuale Græcum. 4to. Lond. 1727.

———, ——. Idem. 3tia ed. 4to. Lond. 1755.

———, ——. ——. 4to. Lond. 1803.

———, ——. ——. 4to. Lond. 1821.

———, ——. Mythologisches Lexicon. 8vo. Leipz. 1770.

Hedge, Levi. Elements of Logic. 12mo. Camb. 1816.

———, ——. The Same. 3d ed. 12mo. Bost. 1821.

———, ——. Eulogy on the Rev. Joseph McKean. 8vo. Camb. 1818.

———, ——. Brown's Philosophy abridged. See Brown, T.

Hedges, Wm. On the Hydrangea Hortensis. (Horticult. Tr. vol. 3.)

Hédouville, le Sieur de. Vide Sallo.

Heereboord, Adrianus. Logica. 12mo. Cant. 1633.

———, ———. ———. 12mo. Cant. 1680.

———, ———. Meletemata Philosophica. 4to. Amst. 1680.

Heeren, A. H. L. Geschichte des Studiums der Classischen Litteratur. 2 Bände. 8vo. Göttingen. 1797—1801.

———, ———. Vide Menander Rhetor.

———, ———. Ueber die Statue des Schleifers. 8vo.

———, ———. Ideen über die Politik, den Verkehr, und den Handel der Vornehmsten Völker der Alten Welt. 2 Theile. 8vo. Göttingen. 1815.

———, ———. Handbuch der Geschichte der Staaten des Alterthums. 8vo. Göttingen. 1817.

———, ———. History of the States of Antiquity, tr. from the German, by George Bancroft. 8vo. Northampton, Mass. 1828.

———, ———. Essai sur l'Influence des Croisades, trad. de l'Allemand par C. Villers. 8vo. Paris. 1808.

Hegelmaier, T. G. De Θεοπνευστίᾳ. 4to. Tubingæ. 1784.

Hegendorphinus, C. Vide Macropedius, G.

Hegenitius, Gotfr. Itinerarium Frisio-Hollandicum, et A. Ortelii Itinerarium Gallo-Brabanticum. Accedit G. Loysii Pervigilium Mercurii. 18mo. Lug. Bat. 1667.
Hegesippus. Vide Egesippus.
Hegewisch, Professor. Vide Ebeling.
Héguerty, (d'.) Essai sur les Intérets du Commerce Maritime. 12mo. La Haye. 1754.
———, —. Remarques sur plusieurs Branches de Commerce et de Navigation. 2 parties. 12mo. 1757.
Heidegger, J. H. Exercitationes Biblicæ contra Capellum, Simonem, Spinosam, et Alios; cum Vita ejus, etc. 4to. Tiguri. 1700.
———, —. Dissertationes Selectæ. 4 vol. 4to. Tiguri. 1674—97.
———, —. De Historia Sacra Patriarcharum. 4to. Amst. 1667.
———, —. Enchiridion Biblicum. ed. 5ta. 8vo. Jenæ. 1723.
Heilandus, S. Aristotelis Ethica, Latine. Vide Aristoteles.
Heilmannus, J. D. Opuscula, maximam partem Theologici Argumenti, cura E. J. Danovii. 2 vol. 12mo. Jenæ. 1774—8.
Heineccius, J. G. Opera ad Universam Jurisprudentiam, Philosophiam, et Litteras Humaniores pertinentia. 8 vol. 4to. Genevæ. 1744—9.
———, —. Elementa Juris Germanici. 2 vol. 8vo. Halæ. 1736—7.
———, —. Elementa Juris Naturæ et Gentium. ed. 2da. 8vo. Halæ. 1742.
———, —. Elementa Juris Civilis secundum Ordinem Institutionum. 8vo. Lips. 1740.
———, —. Elementa Juris Civilis secundum Ordinem Pandectarum. 12mo. Francof. 1747.
———, —. Antiquitatum Romanarum Jurisprudentiam illustrantium Syntagma. 8vo. Argent. 1755.
———, —. Dictata ad Elementa Juris Civilis. 8vo. 1744.
Heineken, (le Baron de.) Idée Générale d'une Collection Complette d'Estampes. 8vo. Leips. et Vien. 1771.
Heinricus, Dan. De Judiciis Hebræorum. (Ugol. vol. 26.)
Heinsius, Dan. Exercitationes Sacræ ad Novum Testamentum. 4to. Cant. 1640.
———, —. Herodes Infanticida, Tragœdia. 12mo. Lug. Bat. 1632.
Heinsius, Theod. Volksthümliches Wörterbuch der Deutschen Sprache. 4 Bände. 8vo. Hannov. 1818—22.
Heinzius, A. F. De Terra Gosen. 4to. Francof. ad Viad. 1735.
Heisen, Henr. De Voce ὁ ἀγαπητός, Matth. iii, 17. (Oelrichs, Coll. Opusculorum.)
Heister, Laurence. System of Surgery; from the Latin. 4th ed. 4to. Lond. 1750.
———, ———. The Same. 8th ed. 4to. Lond. 1768.

Heister, Laurence. Compendium Anatomicum. 2 vol. 8vo. Norimb. et Altorfi. 1732.
———, ———. Idem. 2 tomi in 1 vol. 8vo. Amst. 1748.
———, ———. ——. 12mo. Edin. 1777.
———, ———. Compendium of Anatomy; from the Latin. 8vo. Lond. 1752.
———, ———. Institutiones Chirurgicæ. 2 vol. 4to. Amst. 1739.
Held, Joh. De Deo Abscondito, ex Esa. xlv, 15. 4to. Wittenbergæ. 1690.
Heliodorus. Æthiopicorum Libri x, Gr. et Lat., cum Animadversionibus J. Bourdelotii. 8vo. Lut. Par. 1619.
———. Idem, a C. G. Mitscherlich. 2 vol. 8vo. Argent. 1798.
———. ——, Gr. cum Notis, a Coray. 2 vol. 8vo. Paris. 1804.
Hell Torments. See Torments.
Hellanicus Lesbius. Fragmenta, a F. G. Sturzio. Vide Græci Auctores Minores.
Hellenbroek, Abr. Sermon from Canticles ii, 15, tr. from the Dutch. 8vo. Bost. 1742.
Hellenica. Vide Siebelis, C. G.
Hellenius, Fr. English and Low-Dutch Instructer. 3d ed. 18mo. Rotterdam. 1677.
Hellerus, J. J. De Deo Ignoto Atheniensium. (Gronov. vol. 7.)
Helmont, J. B. van. Opera. ed. 4tia. fol. Lugd. 1667.
Helms, A. Z. Tagebuch einer Reise durch Peru. 8vo. Dresden. 1798.
Heloisa. Vide Abelardus.
Helsham, Richard. Lectures in Natural Philosophy. 5th ed. 8vo. Lond. 1777.
Helvetiæ Descriptio. 16mo. Lug. Bat. 1627.
Helvicus, Chistophorus. Theatrum Historicum et Chronologicum. ed. 5ta. fol. Oxon. 1651.
Helyot, (le Père.) Histoire des Ordres Religieux, et Militaires. 8 vol. 4to. Paris. 1792.
Hemans, Felicia. Poems. 2 vols. 8vo. Bost. 1826—7.
———, ———. Hymns on the Works of Nature. 12mo. Bost. 1827.
Hemingford, Walter. De Rebus Gestis Edvardi I, II, et III. Vide Hearne, T.
———, ———. Chronica. (Gale, Script. XV.)
Hemingus. Chartularium Ecclesiæ Wigorniensis. Vide Hearne, T.
Heminway, Jacob. Connecticut Election Sermon. 16mo. N. Lond. 1740.
Hémisphère, (l'.) Journal Littéraire et Politique, May, 1810. Phil.
Hemmenway, Moses. Seven Sermons on the Obligation &c. of the Unregenerate to strive for Eternal Life. 8vo. Bost. 1767.
———, ———. Discourse concerning the Church. 8vo. Bost. 1792.
———, ———. Election Sermon. 8vo Bost. 1784.

Hemmenway, Moses. Sermon at the Ordination of the Rev. M. Calef. 8vo. Hallowell. 1795.
Hemmersam, Michael. Guineische Reiss-Beschreibung. 12mo. Nürnberg. 1663.
Hemmingius, Nic. De Pastore Christiano. 12mo. · 1590.
Henault, C. J. F. Chronological Abridgment of the History of France, tr. from the French by Mr. Nugent. 5th ed. 2 vols. 8vo. Lond. 1762.
Henchman, Nathaniel. Sermon on the Death of the Hon. John Burrill. 16mo. Bost. 1721.
———, ——. Reasons for Declining to admit Mr. Whitfield into his Pulpit. 12mo. Bost. 1745.
———, ——. Letter to the Rev. Mr. Hobby respecting Mr. Whitfield. 4to. Bost. 1745.
Hencke, G. J. De Usu LXX Interpretum in N. Testamento. 4to. Halæ Magd. 1721.
———, ——. De Textu N. Testamenti Græco. ed. 3tia. 4to. Halæ Magd. 1721.
Henderson, Alex. Review and Consideration of two late Pamphlets, relating to Episcopacy, &c. 4to. Edin. 1706.
Henderson, Geo. Account of the British Settlement of Honduras. 12mo. Lond. 1811.
———, ——. Short View of the Administrations in the Government of America. 8vo. Lond. 1802.
Hendreich, Petrus. Massilia, ejus Situs, etc. (Gronovius, vol. 6.)
Hendy, A. D. Oxford Prize Essay, on the Utility of Classical Learning in subserviency to Theological Studies. (Class. Journ. vols. 6 and 18.)
Hendy, James, und John Rollo. Ueber die Drüsenkrankheit in Barbados; aus dem Engl. 8vo. Frank. am Main. 1788.
Hengham, Radulphus de. Summæ. 18mo. Lond. 1616.
Hening, Wm. W. Statutes at Large; being a Collection of All the Laws of Virginia, from the First Session of the Legislature, in 1619. 13 vols. 8vo. Phil. 1823.
———, ———. New Virginia Justice. 3d ed. 8vo. Richmond. 1820.
———, ———, and Wm. Munford. Reports in the Supreme Court of Appeals of Virginia. 4 vols. 8vo. Flatbush and N. York. 1809—11.
Henley, David, (Col.), Proceedings of a Court-Martial held at Cambridge for the Trial of. 8vo. Bost. 1778.
Henley, John. History and Advantages of Divine Revelation, &c. a Sermon. 4to. Lond. 1725.
———, ——. Samuel Sleeping in the Tabernacle; or the Model of Christian Preaching Asserted. 8vo. Lond.
Hennepin, L. Nouveau Voyage dans l'Amérique Septentrionale. 12mo. Amst. 1711 et 1720.
———, —. Beschryving van Louisiana. 4to. Amst. 1688.
———, —. New Discovery of a vast Country in America, with a Continuation, giving an Account of De la Salle's Attempts upon the Mines of St. Barbe, &c. 8vo. Lond. 1698.

Hennert, Joh. Fred. Oratio de Ingenio Mathematici. 4to. Traj. ad Rhen. 1764.

——, ——. De Matheseos Studio, etc. 4to. Traj. ad Rhen. 1765.

Henninius, H. C. Notæ ad Bergierium. (Grævius, vol. 10.)

——, ——. Græcam Linguam non esse pronunciandam secundum Accentus. Addita est J. Vossii de Accentibus Græcanicis Sententia. 8vo. Traj. ad Rhen. 1684.

Henry VIII. Love-Letters to Ann Boleyn, and Two Letters from her to Wolsey, with her Last to Henry VIII. (Harl. Miscel. vol. 3.)

Henry, Alex. Travels in Canada and the Indian Territories, between the Years 1760 and 1776. 8vo. N. York. 1809.

Henry, Matthew. Works; Sermons and Tracts, with his Life, &c. fol. Lond. 1726.

——, ——. Sermon, Nov. 5th. 8vo. Lond. 1712.

——, ——. Directions for Daily Communion with God. 4th ed. 12mo. Lond. 1720.

——, ——. Life of Lieut. Illidge. 2d ed. 12mo. Lond. 1722.

——, ——. Exposition of the Old and New Testaments. 5th ed. 6 vols. fol. Edin. 1760.

——, ——. The Same. 6 vols. 4to. Edin. 1797—1800.

——, ——. Sermon at the Ordination of Mr. Atkinson. 8vo. Lond. 1713.

——, ——. Sermon on Reformation of Manners. 8vo. Lond. 1712.

Henry, Robert. History of Great Britain. 4th ed. 12 vols. 8vo. Lond. 1805.

——, ——. Sermon before the Society for propagating Christian Knowledge. 8vo. Edin. 1773.

Henry, Wm. Epitome of Experimental Chemistry, with Notes, &c. by B. Silliman. 2d Amer. ed. 8vo. Bost. 1810.

Hensler, P. G. Geschichte der Lustseuche. 2 Bände. 12mo. Altona und Hamb. 1783—9.

Hentz, N. M. On the Alligator of North America. (Amer. Phil. Tr. N. S. vol. 2.)

——, ——. Description of Eleven New Species of North American Insects. (Id. vol. 3.)

Hephæstion Alexandrinus. Enchiridion de Metris et Poemate, cum Scholiis, et Animadversionibus J. C. de Pauw. 4to. Traj. ad Rhen. 1726.

—— ——. Idem, cum Notis Variorum, curante T. Gaisford. Accedit Procli Chrestomathia Grammatica. 8vo. Oxon. 1810.

Heraclides Ponticus. Fragmenta de Rebus Publicis, cum Commentario, a G. D. Koeler. 8vo. Halæ Sax. 1804.

—— ——. Fragmenta. Vide Coray

—— ——. Allegoriæ Homeri. Vide Opuscula Mythol.

—— ——. Vide Memnon.

Heraclitus. De Incredibilibus. Vide Opuscula Mythologica.

Herald, American, and General Advertiser, by Powars and Willis. fol. Bost. 1784.
——— of Freedom, and Federal Advertiser. fol. Bost. 1790.
Heraldry. See Compendium.
Herbelot, Barth. d'. Bibliothèque Orientale. fol. Paris. 1697.
———, ———. Idem. 4 vol. 4to. La Haye. 1777—9.
Herbert, Edw. Lord, of Cherbury. Life and Reign of Henry VIII. fol. Lond. 1649.
———, ———. The Same. fol. Lond. 1682.
———, ———. ———. (Kennet, Hist. of England, vol. 2.)
———, ———. His Life, written by himself. 3d ed. 4to. Lond. 1778.
———, ———. De Religione Gentilium. 4to. Amst. 1663.
———, ———. Idem. 4to. Amst. 1700.
———, ———. De Veritate. 4to. Lut. Par. 1633.
———, ———. Dialogue between a Tutor and his Pupil. 4to. Lond. 1768.
Herbert, Geo. The Temple; Sacred Poems and Private Ejaculations; with his Life. 13th ed. 12mo. Lond. 1709.
Herbert, Sir Tho. Some Yeares Travels into Africa, and Asia the Great. fol. Lond. 1677.
———, ———. Relation du Voyage de Perse et des Indes Orientales, trad. de l'Anglois. 4to. Paris. 1673.
Herbert, Wm. On the Amaryllis Longifolia. (Horticult. Tr. vol. 3.)
———, ———. On the Culture of Hyacinths.—On the Culture of the Amaryllis. (Id. 4.)
Herborn, Nicolaus. De Indis Convertendis. (Novus Orbis.)
Herculanensium Voluminum Quæ Supersunt. Tomi 1, 2. fol. Neapoli. 1793—1809.
——— ———, Dissertationes Isagogicæ ad Explanationem. Pars I. fol. Neapoli. 1797.
Herculaneum. Catalogo degli Antichi Monumenti di Ercolano. Tomo 1. fol. Napoli. 1755.
———. De' Bronzi di Ercolano. 2 tom. fol. Napoli. 1767—71.
———. Le Pitture Antiche d' Ercolano. 5 tom. fol. Napoli. 1757—79.
Herder, J. G. Von der Gabe der Sprachen. 12mo. Riga. 1794.
———, ———. Von der Auferstehung. 12mo. Riga. 1794.
———, ———. Vom Erlöser der Menschen. 12mo. Riga. 1796.
———, ———. Von Gottes Sohn. 12mo. Riga. 1797.
———, ———. Vom Geist des Christenthums. 12mo. Riga. 1798.
———, ———. Von Religion. 12mo. Leipz. 1798.
———, ———. Briefe, das Studium der Theologie betreffend. 4te Ausg. 2 Theile. 12mo. Weimar. 1816.
———, ———. Maran-atha. 8vo. Riga. 1779.
———, ———. Outlines of a Philosophy of the History of Man, tr. from the German by T. Churchill. 4to. Lond. 1800.

Herder, J. G. Oriental Dialogues on the Spirit and Beauties of the Sacred Poetry of the Hebrews. 8vo. Lond. 1801.
Heresbachius, Conr. Historia de Factione Monasteriensi sub J. Bocaldo Leydensi Anabaptistarum quondam Rege, etc. 8vo. Amst. 1650.
———, ——. Foure Bookes of Husbandrie, collected by him, Englished and increased by B. Googe. 4to. Lond. 1586.
Heresy, Dissertation on the Nature of. 8vo. Lond. 1731.
——. St. Paul's Heretic. 8vo. Lond. 1735.
——. See Church,—Religion, &c.
Herfer, D. A. Denckwürdige Schiff-Reise nach dem Gross-Hertzogthum Moscovien oder Russland. 4to. Jahr. 1678.
Héricart de Thury, (M. le Vicomte.) Rapport fait à la Société d'Encouragement pour l'Industrie Nationale, sur les Lames Damassées de M. Degrand-Gurgey, de Marseille. 4to. Paris. 1820.
Hering, J. H. Beschryving van het Eiland Curaçao. 8vo. Amst. 1779.
Heringa, J. Oratio de Theologiæ in Scholis Institutione, etc. 4to. Traj. ad Rhen. 1794.
Heriot, Geo. Travels through the Canadas. 4to. Lond. 1807.
Héritier de Brutelle, C. L. l'. Stirpes Novæ. 2 vol. fol. Paris. 1784—5.
———, ——. Sertum Anglicum. fol. Paris. 1788.
———, ——, Catalogue des Livres de la Bibliothèque de feu. 8vo. Paris. 1805.
Herkern, Forms of. See Balfour, F.
Herle, Charles. Wisdom's Tripos. 12mo. Lond. 1670.
Hermann, Mart. Gottf. Handbuch der Mythologie, etc. 3 Theile. 8vo. Berlin und Stettin. 1787—95.
Hermann. Vide Herrmann.
Hermannus Comes Nuenarius. Brevis Narratio de Origine et Sedibus Priscorum Francorum. Vide Witichindus.
Hermannus, Godofredus. De Metris Poetarum Græcorum et Romanorum. 8vo. Lips. 1796.
———, ———. Elementa Doctrinæ Metricæ. 8vo. Lips. 1816.
———, ———. De Emendanda Ratione Græcæ Grammaticæ. Accedunt Herodiani Aliorumque Libelli nunc primum editi. 8vo. Lips. 1801.
———, ———. De Usu Antistrophicorum in Græcorum Tragœdiis. 4to. 1810.
———, ———. Observationes Criticæ in quosdam Locos Æschyli et Euripidis. 8vo. Lips. 1798.
———, ———. De Versibus Spuriis apud Æschylum. 4to. Lips. 1814.
———, ———. De Æschyli Glaucis. 4to. Lips. 1812.
———, ———. De Antiquitate Orphei Argonauticorum. 4to. Lips. 1811.
———, ———. De Legibus quibusdam subtilioribus Sermonis Homerici. 4to. 1812.
———, ———. De Mythologia Græcorum Antiquissima Dissertatio. 4to. Lips. 1817.

Hermas, Sanctus. Pastor. Vide Barnabas. Vide Cotelerius.
Hermias. Irrisio Gentilium Philosophorum. Vide Tatianus.
Hermogenes. Ars Oratoria, Gr. et Lat., cum Commentariis G. Laurentii. 8vo. Col. Allob. 1614.
Hernandez, Fr. Nova Plantarum, Animalium, et Mineralium Mexicanorum Historia. fol. Romæ. 1651.
Herne, Tho. Account of Pamphlets published in the Bangorian Controversy to the End of the Year 1718. 8vo. Lond. 1719.
——, ——. Continuation of the Account to the End of the Year 1719. 8vo. Lond. 1720.
——, ——. Account of Books and Pamphlets written in the Controversy concerning the Trinity since the Year 1712, &c. 8vo. Lond. 1720.
Herodes Atticus. Quæ supersunt, cum Adnotationibus, a R. Fiorillo. Præfixa est Epistola C. H. Heynii. 8vo. Lips. 1801.
——, ——. Vide Oratores Græci, a Reiskio.
Herodianus. Vide Draco Stratonicensis. Vide Hermannus, G.
Herodianus. Historiæ sui Temporis Libri viii, cum A. Politiani Interpretatione Latina, et Notis, cura D. Parei. 8vo. Lond. 1639.
——. Historiarum Libri viii, Gr. et Lat. cum Notis. 8vo. Oxon. 1704.
——. Idem, Græce, ex Recensione F. A. Wolfii. 12mo. Halis. 1792.
——. ——, cum Versione Bergleri et Notis Variorum, curante T. G. Irmisch. 5 vol. 8vo. Lips. 1789—1805.
Herodianus, Ælius. Philetærus. Vide Mœris.
Herodotus. Libri Novem, Latine, Interprete Laurentio Valla. fol. 1537.
——. Historiarum Libri Novem; cum G. Gemisti, de iis quæ post Pugnam ad Mantineam gesta sunt, Libris ii; a J. Camerario. fol. Basil. 1541.
——. Historiarum Libri ix, cum Notis G. H. Schaefer. 3 vol. 8vo. Lips. 1800—3.
——. Herodoti et Ctesiæ quæ extant Opera et Fragmenta, Gr., ab A. C. Borheck. 3 vol. 8vo. Lemgoviæ. 1808.
——. Apparatus ad Herodotum intelligendum et interpretandum Augusti C. Borheck. 5 vol. 8vo. Lemgoviæ. 1795—8.
——. Historiarum Libri ix, cum Vita Homeri, etc. Gr. et Lat., cum Notis, a G. Jungermano. fol. Francof. 1608.
——. Historiarum Libri ix, cum Vita Homeri, etc., Gr. et Lat., cum Notis, a P. Wesselingio. fol. Amst. 1763.
——. Historiarum Libri ix, Gr. et Lat. cum Adnotationibus Variorum, a J. Schweighæusero. 6 vol. 8vo. Argentorati et Paris. 1816.
——. Lexicon Herodoteum. Vide Schweighæuser.
——. Libri qui Enarrationem Pugnarum inter Græcos et Persas complectuntur, a D. Schulz. 8vo. Halis. 1809.
——. Περὶ Ὁμήρου. Vide Reineldius, J.; et Opuscula Mythologica, a Gale.
——. Greca Istoria, con la Vita d' Omero, trad. da G. C. Becelli. 2 vol. 4to. Verona. 1733.

Herodotus. Histoire d' Hérodote, trad. du Grec, avec des Remarques, etc. par M. Larcher. 7 vol. 8vo. Paris. 1786.
——————. History of Herodotus, translated from the Greek, with Notes, by William Beloe. 4 vols. 8vo. Lond. 1791.
——————. The Same. 4 vols. 8vo. Phil. 1814.
——————. Vide Bredow,—Estiene,—Wesseling.
Heron, Robert. Letters of Literature. See Pinkerton, J.
Herport, (Rev. Mr.) Essay on Truths of Importance to the Happiness of Mankind; from the German. 8vo. Lond. 1768.
Herr, Michael. Die New Welt. fol. Strassburg. 1534.
Herrera, Ant. de. Historia de las Indias Occidentales. 4 vol. fol. Amberes. 1728.
————, —————. Idem. 4 vol. fol. Madrid. 1730.
————, —————. Description des Indes Occidentales, trad. de l'Espagnol; avec la Navigation de J. le Maire. fol. Amst. 1622.
————, —————. Novus Orbis, Metaphraste C. Barlæo.—Navigationis Australis Jacobi le Maire Descriptio, etc. fol. Amst. 1622.
————, —————. Beschrijvinghe van West-Indien. fol. Amst. 1622.
————, —————. Histoire des Indes Occidentales, trad. de l'Espagnol par N. de la Coste. 3 vol. 4to. Paris. 1660—71.
————, —————. History of America, tr. into English by J. Stevens. 2d ed. 6 vols. 8vo. Lond. 1740.
————, —————. Account of the First Discovery of America. (Churchill, Coll. vol. 5.)
Herrera, Fernando, de. Rimas. 2 vol. 8vo. Madrid. 1786.
————, —————. Egloga Venatoria. Vide Rioja.
Herring, Tho. (Abp.) Fast Sermon. 4to. Lond. 1747.
Herrmann, Fr. Die Deutschen in Nordamerika. 12mo. Lübden. 1806.
Herty, Tho. Digest of the Laws of the United States to March 1799. 8vo. Baltimore. 1800.
———, ———. Digest of the Laws of Maryland to Nov. 1797. 8vo. Baltimore. 1799.
Hervey, James. Two Sermons on Rom. v, 19. 12mo. Lond. 1769.
————, —————. Aspasio vindicated and Imputed Righteousness defended; with Mr. J. Wesley's Letter to him. 12mo. Edin. 1765.
————, —————. Meditations and Contemplations. 10th ed. 2 vols. 12mo. Lond. 1753.
————, —————. The Same. 16th ed. 2 vols. 12mo. Lond. 1761.
————, —————. Substance of Three Fast Sermons. 8vo. Lond. 1757.
Hervey, Tho. Letter to Sir Thomas Hanmer. 8vo. Lond. 1741.
Heshusius, D. T. Comment. in Psalmos. fol. Helmst. 1586.
Hesiodus. Quæ extant, Gr. et Lat., cum Notis Variorum, opera C. Schrevelii. 8vo. Amst. 1657.
——————. Idem. 8vo. Cant. 1672.
——————. ———, ex recensione J. G. Grævii, cum Notis. 8vo. Amst. 1667.

Hesiodus. Idem, cum Notis Variorum, a T. Robinson. 4to. Oxon. 1737.
———. Scutum Herculis, cum Scholiis et Commentario, etc., a C. F. Heinrich. 8vo. Vratislaviæ. 1802.
———. Theogonia, cum Observationibus, a F. A. Wolfio. 8vo. Halæ Sax. 1783.
———. Works, translated from the Greek, with Notes, by Thomas Cooke. 4to. Lond. 1728.
———. The Same. 2d ed. 12mo. Lond. 1740.
———. Vide Bavermeister. Vide Poetæ Gr. Minores.
Hess, J. G. Life of Ulrich Zwingle, tr. from the French by Lucy Aikin. 8vo. Lond. 1812.
Hess, J. J. Geschichte der drey letsten Lebensjahre Jesu, samt dessen Jugendgeschichte. 2 Bände. 12mo. Tübingen. 1779.
——, ——. Lebensgeschichte Jesu. 2 Bände. 12mo. Tübingen. 1784—7.
——, ——. Ueber die Lehren, Thaten und Schicksale unsers Herrn; ein Anhang zu der Lebensgeschichte. 12mo. Tübingen. 1793.
Hesse, J. G. G. Commentatio de Religione Christiana Philosophiæ Stoicæ nec Æmula nec Patrona. (Muntinghe, Syll. Opusc.)
Hesychius. Lexicon, cum Notis Variorum, a J. Alberti. 2 vol. fol. Lug. Bat. 1746.
———. Lexicon, sive Supplementa ad Editionem Hesychii Albertinam, cum Notis, a N. Schow. 8vo. Lips. 1792.
———. Glossæ Sacræ, cum Notis, a J. C. G. Ernesti. 8vo. Lips. 1785.
———. Vide Pricæus.
———. Notæ et Emendatt. in Hesych. Lexic. (Anecdota Gr., a Wolfio.)
Heubnerus, J. L. De Academiis Hebræorum. (Ugol. vol. 21.)
Heumannus, C. A. De Selah. (Ugol. vol. 32.)
Heustis, Jabez W. On the Topography and Diseases of Louisiana. 8vo. N. York. 1817.
Hevelius, Joh. Cometographia. fol. Gedani. 1668.
Hewit, Alex. Account of the Rise and Progress of the Colonies of S. Carolina and Georgia. 2 vols. 8vo. Lond. 1779.
Hewson, Wm. Experimental Inquiries into the Properties of the Blood, &c. 3 vols. 8vo. Lond. 1772—7.
———, ——. The Same. 3d ed. 8vo. Lond. 1780.
Hexerey, Nord-Schwedische. Vide Sincerus.
Hey, John. Lectures in Divinity. 4 vols. 8vo. Camb. 1796—8.
Hey, Wm. Observations in Surgery. 8vo. Lond. 1803.
Heylyn, John. Sermon on Reformation of Manners. 8vo. Lond. 1721.
———, ——. Another. 4to. Lond. 1729.
———, ——. Theological Lectures; with an Interpretation of the New Testament, &c. 2 vols. 4to. Lond. 1749—61.
———, ——. Consecration Sermon. 8vo. Lond. 1738.
Heylyn, Peter. Historical and Miscellaneous Tracts; with an Account of the Author. fol. Lond. 1681.

Heylyn, Peter. Summe of Christian Theologie contained in the Apostles Creed. fol. Lond. 1673.
——, ——. Help to English History. 12mo. Lond. 1709.
——, ——. Cosmographie. 2d ed. fol. Lond. 1657.
——, ——. The Same. 5th ed. fol. Lond. 1677.
——, ——. Plus Ultra; being an Examination of Dr. Heylin's History of the Church of England, in a Letter to him. 4to. Lond. 1661.
Heym, J. Nouveau Dictionnaire Russe-François et Allemand. 3 vol. 4to. Moscow. 1799—1802.
Heyne, Chr. G. Sammlung Antiquarischer Aufsatze. 8vo. Lips. 1779.
——, ——. Opuscula Academica. 5 vol. 8vo. Göttingæ. 1785—1801.
——, ——. Vide Homerus. Vide Virgilius.
——, ——, Life of. (Classical Journal, vols. 19 and 20.)
Heywood, Henry. Defence of Dr. Whitby's Treatise on Original Sin. 8vo. Lond. 1740.
Heywood, James. Sermon on his Majesty's late Indisposition. 8vo. Lond. 1756.
Heywood, Thomas. Apology for Actors. (Somers, Tr. vol. 5.)
Hibbert, Henry. Body of Divinity. fol. Lond. 1662.
Hickeringill, Edmonde. Jamaica Viewed. 3d ed.—Test of Spiritual Courts. 3d ed.—Priest-Craft, its Character and Consequences. 3d ed.—Vindication of the Character of Priest-Craft. 2d ed.—Survey of the Earth in its general Vileness and Debauch. 2d ed.—The Parliament-Tacks inquired into.—Essays. 4to. Lond. 1705.
——, ——. Works. 3 vols. 8vo. Lond. 1716.
Hickes, George. Speculum B. Virginis; a Discourse from Luke, i, 28. 4to. Lond. 1686.
——, ——. Spirit of Enthusiasm Exorcised. 3d ed. 4to. Lond. 1683.
——, ——. Sermon on 1 Cor. x, 13. 2d ed. 4to. Lond. 1683.
——, ——. Sermon, January 30th. 4to. Lond. 1683.
——, ——. Vindication of the Church of England. 4to. Lond. 1687.
——, ——. Answer to his "Christian Priesthood Asserted," &c. 8vo. Lond. 1709.
——, ——. Grammatica Anglo-Saxonica et Mœso-Gothica. —Grammatica Islandica R. Jonæ.—Edv. Bernardi Etymologicon Britannicum. 4to. Oxon. 1689.
——, ——. Linguarum Vett. Septentrionalium Thesaurus Grammatico-Criticus et Archæologicus. Vide Antiquæ Literaturæ Septentrionalis Libri Duo.
——, ——. See Baptism.
Hickman, Charles. Sermon before the Queen. 4to. Lond. 1690.
——, ——. Sermon before the Queen. 4to. Lond. 1692.
——, ——. Thanksgiving Sermon. 2d ed. 4to. Lond. 1690.

Hickman, Henry. Laudensium Apostasia. 4to. Lond. 1660.
Hierarchy. The Powers claimed by it examined. 8vo. Lond. 1735.
———. See Andrew, Dr.—See Foster, Sir M.
Hierocles. Commentarius in Aurea Pythagoreorum Carmina, Gr. et Lat., a J. Curterio. 16mo. Lond. 1654.
———. Aurea Pythagoreorum Carmina, Gr. et Lat., cum Adnotationibus, a T. Marcilio. 16mo. Lond. 1654.
———. De Providentia et Fato, Gr. et Lat., a F. Morello. 8vo. Lutetiæ. 1597.
———. Facetiæ, Gr. et Lat. 8vo. Lond. 1654.
———. Facéties, Gr. et Fr. 8vo. Paris. 1812.
Hieronymo Corte Real. Vide Corte Real.
Hieronymus a S. Helena, Paulus. Moralis Theologiæ Medulla. fol. Bononiæ. 1753.
Hieronymus, Sanctus. Opera, per Erasmum. 9 tomi in 4 vol. fol. Basil. 1565.
———, ———. ———, a J. Martianay. 5 vol. fol. Paris. 1693—1706.
———, ———. Epistolæ Selectæ, opera P. Canisii. 8vo. Coloniæ. 1625.
———, ———. Vitaspatrum. 4to. Lugd. 1502.
———, ———. Vide Biblia Latina. Vide Eusebius.
Higden, Wm Sermon, January 30th. 8vo. Lond. 1711.
Higdenus, Ranulphus. Polychronicon. (Gale, Scriptores xv.)
Higgins, Fr. Sermon on Ash-Wednesday. 8vo. Lond. 1707.
———, —. Thanksgiving Sermon. 8vo. Lond. 1707.
Higginson, Fr. New-Englands Plantation; or a Short and True Description of the Commodities and Discommodities of that Countrey. 8vo. Lond. 1630.
———, —. The Same. (Mass. Hist. Coll.)
Higginson, John. Election Sermon. 4to. Bost. 1663.
Hilarius Pictaviensis. Lucubrationes, per Erasmum. fol. Basil. 1570.
——— ———. Opera, a Benedictinis. fol. Paris. 1693.
Hildersam, Arthur. CLII Lectures upon Psalme LI. fol. Lond. 1635.
———, ———. Lectures on the Fourth of John. fol. Lond. 1629.
Hill, Geo. Sermon before the Society for propagating Christian Knowledge. 8vo. Edin. 1787.
Hill, James. Cases in Surgery. 8vo. Edin. 1772.
Hill, John. Sermons on Several Occasions. 8vo. Lond. 1748.
Hill, Sir John. General Natural History. 3 vols. fol. Lond. 1748—52.
—, ———. Vegetable System. 6 vols. 4to. Lond. 1759—63.
Hill, Richard. Pietas Oxoniensis; or an Account of the Expulsion of Six Students from Oxford. 2d ed. 8vo. Lond. 1768.
—, ———. Goliath Slain. 8vo. Lond. 1768.

Hill, Richard. Letter to the Rev. Dr. Nowell concerning his Answer to "Pietas Oxoniensis." 8vo. Lond. 1769.
Hill, Sir Richard. Apology for Brotherly Love, and for the Doctrines of the Church of England, &c. 8vo. Lond. 1798.
Hill, Samuel. Catholic Balance. 4to. Lond. 1687.
——, ———. Debate on the Justice and Piety of the Present Constitution, under K. William. 8vo. Lond. 1696.
Hill (or Hyll), Tho. Profitable Arte of Gardening; with the Arte of Graffing and Planting of Trees.—Right Ordering of Bees. 4to. Lond. 1593.
Hill, Tho. Trade of Truth; a Fast Sermon. 4to. Lond. 1642.
Hillary, Wm. Inquiry into the Means of Improving Medical Knowledge, &c. 8vo. Lond. 1761.
———, ——. Beobachtungen über die Veränderungen der Luft, etc., aus dem Engl. 8vo. Leipz. 1776.
Hillenius, Fr. English and Low-Dutch Instructer. 3d ed. 12mo. Rotterdam. 1677.
Hiller, Matth. Hieropyticon, sive Commentarius in Plantas S. Scripturæ. 4to. Traj. ad Rhen. 1725.
——, ———. De Vestibus Fimbriatis Hebræorum. (Ugol. vol. 21.)
Hillhouse, Augustus L. Description of the European Olive Tree. 4to. Paris. 1818.
Hillhouse, James A. The Judgment, a Vision. 12mo. N. York. 1821.
Hilliard, Timothy. Two Fast Sermons. 8vo. Bost. 1774.
———, ————. Sermon at the Ordination of the Rev. Henry Ware. 8vo. Salem. 1788.
———, ————. The Same. 2d ed. 12mo. Camb. 1828.
———, ————. Sermon at the Ordination of the Rev. J. Andrews. 8vo. Newburyport. 1789.
———, ————. Dudleian Lecture. 12mo. Bost. 1788.
Hilliard, William. Address before the Massachusetts Charitable Mechanic Association. 8vo. Camb. 1827.
Hilliard d'Auberteuil. Essais Historiques et Politiques sur les Anglo-Américains. 3 vol. 8vo. Bruxelles. 1781—2.
——— ————. Idem. 2 vol. 4to. Bruxelles. 1782.
——— ————. Histoire de l'Administration de Lord North. 2 vol. 8vo. Lond. 1784.
——— ————. Considérations sur l'Etat présent de St. Domingue. 2 vol. 8vo. Paris. 1776—7.
——— ————. Nouvelles Considérations sur St. Domingue, en Réponse à celles de M. H. D. Vide Buisson.
Himerius Sophista. Eclogæ et Declamationes, Gr. et Lat., cum Commentario, etc., a G. Wernsdorfio. 8vo. Gottingæ. 1790.
——— ———. Oratio, qua Laudes Urbis Constantinopoleos etc. celebrantur, Gr. et Lat., cum Commentario, a T. C. Harles. 12mo. Erlangæ. 1785.
Hincks, Edw. On Secret Writing. (Brande, Journal, vol. 12.)
Hincmarus, (Archiepiscopus Remensis.) Opera, cura J. Sirmondi. 2 vol. fol. Lut. Par. 1645.

Hinde, Robert. Modern Practice of the Court of Chancery. 8vo. Dublin. 1786.

Hindmarsh, Robert. Letters to Dr. Priestley, containing Proofs of the Divinity of Christ, and of the Divine Mission of Swedenborg. 8vo. Lond. 1792.

Hindoostanee Intelligencer, and Oriental Anthology. Nos. 1—13. 4to. Calcutta. 1801—2.

——————, Strangers East Indian Guide to the. See Gilchrist, J.

Hingham, Narrative of the Proceedings of the North-Parish of, with an Appendix. 8vo. Salem. 1807.

Hint; or a Free Thought or Two, offered to the consideration of those British-Heroes who have overcome the Fear of an Oath or a Curse. 8vo. Lond.

Hints, Conciliatory, by Philodemus. 4to. Charleston. 1784.

——, Ten, addressed to Wise Men, concerning the Dispute which ended Nov. 8, 1809, in the Dismission of Mr. Jackson. 8vo.

Hinton, Edward. Visitation Sermon. 4to. Lond. 1720.

Hippesley. Essays on the Populousness of Africa, on the Trade of the Gold Coast, &c. 8vo. Lond. 1765.

Hippocrates. Opera Omnia, Gr. et Lat., cum Annotationibus, ab A. Fœsio. 2 vol. fol. Genevæ. 1657—62.

——————. Opera Omnia, Gr. et Lat., a J. A. Vander Linden. 2 vol. 8vo. Lug. Bat. 1665.

——————. De Morbis Popularibus Lib. 1 et 3, Gr. et Lat His accomodavit Novem de Febribus Commentarios J. Freind. 8vo. Lond. 1717.

——————. Sententiæ Definitivæ, Gr., Lat., Hebr., studio M. A. Gaiotii. 8vo. Romæ. 1647.

——————. De Visu Libellus, Gr. et Lat., cum Notis Variorum, a J. H. Jugler. 8vo. Helmst. 1792.

——————. Aphorismi, Gr. et Lat., cum Comment., a M. Lister. 12mo. Tubingæ. 1730.

——————. Aphorisms of Hippocrates and the Sentences of Celsus, with Explanations, &c., by Sir C. Sprengell. 2d ed. 8vo. Lond. 1735.

——————. On Air, Water, and Situation, on Epidemical Discases, and on Prognosticks. See Clifton, F.

——————. Erotiani, Galeni, et Herodoti Glossaria in Hippocratem, Gr. et Lat., cum Animadversionibus, a J. G. F. Franzio. 8vo. Lips. 1780.

——————. 'Ορκὸς, 'Αφορίσμοι, καὶ Νόμος. MS. 1733. (Most beautifully executed by John Thomasine, for Doctor Mead, and presented to Harvard College, through Ward Nicholas Boylston, Esq., by John Nichols, Esq. LL. D. of Kensington, near London.)

Hippolytus, Sanctus. Opera, Gr. et Lat., cum Notis Variorum, etc., curante J. A. Fabricio. 2 vol. fol. Hamburgi. 1716—18.

Hipponax et Ananius. Fragmenta, a F. T. Welckero. 4to. Gottingæ. 1817.

Hirsch, J. C. Bibliotheca Numismatica. fol. Norimb. 1760.

Hirschius, J. G. De Discrepantia et Consensu Psalmi xviii, et 2 Sam. xxii. 4to. Lips. 1736.

Hirt, J. F. Orientalische und Exegetische Bibliothek. 8 Theile. 12mo. Jena. 1772—6.

——, ——. Neue Orientalische und Exegetische Bibliothek. 4 Theile. 12mo. Jena. 1776—9.

Hirtius, A. De Bellis Alexandrino et Africano. Vide Cæsar, C. J.

Hirtius, J. F. Biblia Ebræa Analytica. 8vo. Jenæ. 1753.

Hispanorum Clarorum Opuscula Selecta et Rariora, tum Latina, tum Hispana, magna ex parte nunc primum in lucem edita. vol. 1. 4to. Matriti. 1781.

Histoire Naturelle de l'Ephémère. 8vo.

——— ————. Vide Annales du Muséum d'Histoire Naturelle.

Histoire Philosophique de l'Homme. 8vo. Lond. 1766.

Historia Belgicorum Tumultuum. 12mo. Amst. 1641.

———. Vide Bussières, J. de.

Historia delle Cose passate tra'l Sommo Pontefice Paolo V, e la Republica di Venetia, gl' Anni 1605, 1606, 1607. 4to. Mirandola. 1624.

Historiæ Augustæ Scriptores VI, cum Notis Variorum, accurante C. Schrevelio. 8vo. Lug. Bat. 1661.

——— Byzantinæ Scriptores. Vide Byzantinæ.

——— Poeticæ Scriptores Antiqui, Gr. et Lat., cum Notis, etc. 8vo. Paris. 1675.

——— Romanæ Scriptores Latini Veteres, cum Notis, a B. C. Haurisio. 3 vol. fol. Heidelb. 1743—8.

Historical Applications and Occasional Meditations upon several Subjects, by a Person of Honour. 12mo. Lond. 1670.

——— Collections out of Protestant Historians concerning the Changes of Religion from Henry VIII to Queen Elizabeth. 8vo. 1674.

——— Collections, concerning District-Successions, and Deprivations, during the Three First Centuries of the Church. 8vo. Lond. 1713.

——— Collections. See Massachusetts, New-York, &c.

——— Register, with a Chronological Diary. 25 vols. 8vo. Lond. 1714—38.

History of Baptism; or One Faith, One Baptism. 12mo. Lond. 1678.

———, Pleasant and Compendious, of the First Inventers and Instituters of the most famous Arts, Misteries, Laws, &c. in the World. 12mo. Lond. 1685.

———, Compleat, of the Late Rebellion. 2d ed. 8vo. Lond. 1716.

———, Universal. 7 vols. fol. Lond. 1736—44.

———, ———. Additions. fol. Lond. 1750.

———, ———. 60 vols. 8vo. Lond. 1747—63.

———, ———. Geographische Belustigungen zur Erläuterung der neuesten Weltgeschichte. Stücke, 1, 2. 4to. Leipz. 1776.

——— of the British Dominions in North America. 4to. Lond. 1773.

——— of the British Empire from 1765 to the End of 1783, by a Society of Gentlemen. 2 vols. 8vo. Phil. 1798.

History, Compendious, of the late War. 8vo. Bost. 1815.
Hitchcock, Edward. Sketch of the Geology, Mineralogy, and Topography of the Connecticut. 8vo. New-Haven. 1823.
Hitchcock, Enos. Discourse on the Death of Washington. 4to. Providence. 1800.
———, ——. Sermon on the Death of Mrs. S. Bowen. 8vo. Providence. 1800.
———, ——. Memoirs of the Bloomsgrove Family. 2 vols. 12mo. Bost. 1790.
———, ——. Sermon at the Ordination of the Rev. E. Fiske. 8vo. Providence. 1799.
Hitchcock, Gad. Election Sermon. 8vo. Bost. 1774.
———, ——. Sermon to a Military Company. 8vo. Bost. 1757.
———, ——. Dudleian Lecture. 8vo. Bost. 1779.
———, ——. Sermon at the Ordination of the Rev. E. Hitchcock. 8vo. Salem. 1771.
Hoadly, Benj. (Bp.) Measures of Submission to the Civil Magistrate considered. 8vo. Lond. 1706.
———, ——. The Same. 4th ed. 8vo. Lond. 1710.
———, ——. Original of Civil Government; with an Answer to Dr. F. Atterbury's Charge of Rebellion. 8vo. Lond. 1710.
———, ——. Nature of the Kingdom or Church of Christ, a Sermon before the King. 15th ed. 8vo. Lond. 1717.
———, ——. Answer to a Calumny cast upon him by Dr. Sherlock. 8vo. Lond. 1718.
———, ——. Preservative against the Principles and Practices of the Non-Jurors. 4th ed. 8vo. Lond. 1717.
———, ——. Reasonableness of Conformity to the Church of England. 3d ed. 8vo. Lond. 1712.
———, ——. The Same. 4th ed. 8vo. Lond. 1720.
———, ——. Remarks upon Dr. Sherlock's Considerations offered to the Bishop of Bangor. 8vo. Lond. 1718.
———, ——. Answer to the Five Important Queries, &c. by a Divine of the Church of England. 8vo. Lond. 1718.
———, ——. Answer to the Representation of the Convocation. 8vo. Lond. 1718.
———, ——. Defence of the First Head of the Charge of the Committee of the Lower House of Convocation against him. 8vo. Lond. 1818.
———, ——. Letter to him from a Gentlewoman. 8vo. Lond.
———, ——, Answer to Dr. Sherlock's "Condition and Example of our Saviour Vindicated." 8vo. Lond. 1718.
———, ——. Common Rights of Subjects defended, &c. in Answer to the Dean of Chichester. 8vo. Lond. 1719.
———, ——. Tracts relating to the Bangorian Controversy. 3 vols. 8vo. Lond. 1717—19.
———, ——. Account of Pamphlets published in the Bangorian Controversy. 8vo. Lond. 1719.
———, ——. The D——n of W——r still the same; or, his New Defence of the Bishop of Bangor's Sermon, &c. considered. 8vo. Lond. 1720.

Hoadly, Benj. (Bp.) See Baker,—Convocation,—Davenport,—Hare,—Herne,—Law,—Norris,—Pyle,—Sherlock,—Snape,—Sykes,—Whitby, &c.

——, ———. Brief Defence of Episcopal Ordination. 8vo. Lond. 1707.

——, ———. Choose which you Please; or Dr. Sacheverell and Mr. Hoadly drawn to the Life. 8vo. Lond. 1710.

——, ———. Discourses concerning the Terms of Acceptance with God. 8vo. Lond. 1711.

——, ———. The Same. 7th ed. 8vo. Lond. 1766.

——, ———. Several Tracts formerly published, now collected into one volume; viz. a Letter to Fleetwood, concerning Miracles; a Letter about the Bishop's Votes upon the Occasional Bill; a Letter to Atterbury, concerning Virtue and Vice; a Second Letter, in Answer to his Large Vindication; a Vindication of the Ancient Prophets, in Answer to Sir R. Bulkeley; Some Considerations offered to the Bishop of Exeter; Humble Reply to the Bishop of Exeter; Queries to the Authors of the late Discourse of Free-Thinking. To which are added Six Sermons; viz. concerning the Evils, of which Christianity hath been made the Occasion; and concerning the Extremes of Implicit Subjection, and Infidelity. 8vo. Lond. 1715.

——, ———, Biographical Notice of; Dedication to the Pope;—On the Nature of the Kingdom of Christ;—On Divisions among Christians. (Sparks, Collection of Essays, &c.)

——, ———. Plain Account of the Nature and End of the Lord's Supper, &c. 6th ed. 12mo. Lond. 1761.

——, ———. Defence of the "Plain Account"; with a Tract concerning the Lord's-Supper, by J. Hales. 8vo. Lond. 1735.

——, ———. Second Letter to the Author of the "Plain Account." 8vo. Lond. 1735.

——, ———. Proper Answer to "the Winchester Converts." 8vo. Oxford. 1735.

——, ———. Farther Defence of the "Plain Account." 8vo. Lond. 1735.

——, ———. "Plain Account," vindicated against the Misrepresentations, &c. of Dr. R. Warren. 8vo. Lond. 1737.

——, ———. See Lord's Supper. See Warren, R.

——, ———. Sermon on Submission to the Civil Magistrate. 8vo. Lond. 1706.

——, ———. The Same. 4th ed. 8vo. Lond. 1710.

——, ———. Sermon before the Society of Ancient Britons. 8vo. Lond. 1717.

——, ———. Twenty Sermons. 8vo. Lond. 1755.

——, ———. Sixteen Sermons, with Six upon Public Occasions. 2d ed. 8vo. Lond. 1758.

——, ———. Assize Sermon. 12mo. and 8vo. Lond. 1708.

——, ———. Another. 8vo. Lond. 1708.

——, ———. Sermon, Nov. 5th. 2d ed. 8vo. Lond. 1715.

——, ———. Sermon, Jan. 30th. 4to. Lond. 1720.

——, ———. Works. 3 vols. fol. Lond. 1773.

Hoadly, Benjamin. Oratio Anniversaria Harveiana. 4to. Lond. 1742.

Hoadly, Benj., and B. Wilson. Observations on a Series of Electrical Experiments. 8vo. Lond. 1756.

Hoadly, John, (Abp.) Assize Sermon. 3d ed. 8vo. Lond. 1707.

———, —————. Another. 12mo. Lond. 1708.

———, —————. Sermon, Jan. 30th. 8vo. Lond. 1718.

———, —————. Consecration Sermon. 8vo. Lond. 1716.

Hobart, John Henry, (Bp.) Charge to the Clergy of the Protestant Episcopal Church in the State of New-York. 8vo. N. York. 1815.

———, —————. Address before the Auxiliary New-York Bible and Common Prayer Book Society. 8vo. N. York. 1816.

———, —————. Address before the New-York Protestant Episcopal Missionary Society of Young Men and Others. 8vo. N. York. 1817.

———. —————. Thanksgiving Sermon. 8vo. N. York. 1815.

Hobart, Sir Henry. Reports. fol. Lond. 1658.

Hobart, Noah. Serious Address to the Episcopal Separation in New-England. 12mo. Bost. 1748.

———, ———. Second Address; with Mr. Dickinson's Answer to Mr. Wetmore. 8vo. Bost. 1751.

———, ———. Sermon at the Ordination of the Rev. Noah Welles. 8vo. Bost. 1747.

———, ———. Connecticut Election Sermon. 16mo. N. Lond. 1751.

Hobbes, Tho. Philosophicall Rudiments concerning Government and Society. 12mo. Lond. 1651.

———, ———. Leviathan; or the Matter, Forme, and Power of a Commonwealth. fol. Lond. 1651.

———, ———. Leviathan; sive de Materia, Forma, et Potestate Civitatis. 4to. Lond. 1678.

———, ———. Answer to Dr. Bramhall's Book called "the Catching of the Leviathan," &c. 8vo. Lond. 1682.

———, ———. Moral and Political Works. fol. Lond. 1750.

———, ———. Treatise of Libertie and Necessity. 16mo. Lond. 1654.

———, ———. Dialogue on the Common Law. 8vo. Lond. 1681.

———, ———. Considerations upon his Reputation, Religion, &c. 8vo. Lond. 1681.

———, ———. Vita ejus. 8vo. Carolopoli. 1681.

———, ———. Behemoth; or History of the Civil-Wars of England. 8vo. Lond. 1682.

———, ———. Answer to Sir William D'Avenant's "Discourse upon Gondebert." 16mo. Paris. 1650.

———, ———. Art of Rhetoric. 12mo. Lond. 1681.

———, ———. Seven Philosophical Problems, and Two Propositions of Geometry. 8vo. Lond. 1682.

———, ———. Ten Dialogues of Natural Philosophy. 8vo. Lond. 1678.

Hobbes, Tho. Lux Mathematica. Vide Wallis, J.
———, ——. Historical Narration of Heresie, and the Punishment thereof. 8vo. Lond. 1682.
———, ——. Dying Legacy. (Somers, Tr. vol. 1.)
———, ——. See Homer. See Thucydides.
Hobby, Wm. Artillery Election Sermon. 8vo. Bost. 1747.
———, ——. Vindication of the Itinerancy and Conduct of Whitefield. 4to. Bost. 1745.
———, ——. Vindication of the Protest against Mr. Edwards Dismission. 8vo. Bost. 1751.
———, ——. Twig of Birch for Billy's Breech, &c. against Mr. Hobby. 4to. 1744.
Hodder, James. Arithmetick. 28th ed. 12mo. Lond. 1719.
Hodge, John. Accession Sermon. 8vo. Lond. 1751.
Hodge, Michael. Oration before St. Peter's Lodge. 8vo. Newburyport. A. L. 5802.
Hodges, Nath. Account of the Plague in London in 1665; with an Essay on Pestilential Diseases, by J. Quincy. 8vo. Lond. 1720.
———, ——. The Same. 3d ed. 8vo. Lond. 1721.
———, ——. Sermon on the Death of the Rev. J. Stennett. 8vo. Lond. 1713.
Hodges, Walter. Elihu, or an Enquiry into the Principal Scope and Design of the Book of Job. 4to. Lond. 1750.
———, ———. Letter to the Bishop of Oxford on Dr. Hodges's Interpretation of Elohim; with a Letter to the Rev. J. Jortin in vindication of Dr. Middleton. 8vo. Lond. 1752.
Hodgson, Bernard. Solomon's Song, the Proverbs of Solomon, and Ecclesiastes; from the Hebrew, with Notes. 4to. Oxford. 1786—90.
Hodgson, James. System of the Mathematics. 2 vols. 4to. Lond. 1723.
Hodgson, Robert. Life of Bishop Porteus. 8vo. Lond. 1811.
————, ———. The Same. 12mo. New York. 1811.
Hodson, J. L. Plain Reasons for being a Protestant. 12mo. Lond.
Hody, Humphrey. Resurrection of the (same) Body Asserted. 8vo. Lond. 1694.
——, ————. De Græcis Illustribus Linguæ Græcæ Instauratoribus. 8vo. Lond. 1742.
——, ————. Contra Historiam Aristeæ de LXX Interpretibus Dissertatio. 8vo. Oxon. 1684.
——, ————. De Bibliorum Textibus Originalibus, Versionibus Græcis, et Latina Vulgata. fol. Oxon. 1705.
Hoeke, P. van. Lucubrationes in Catechismum Palatinum. 4to. Lug. Bat. 1711.
Höen, M. W. Beschreibung von der unglücklichen Reise nach Carolina und Pensylvanien, etc. 12mo. Franckf. und Leipz. 1711.
Hofer, Fr. J. Abhandlung vom Kaffee. 12mo. Frankf. und Leipz. 1781.

Hoffman, David. Course of Legal Study. 8vo. Baltimore. 1817.
———, ———. Introductory Lecture, &c. 8vo. Balt. 1823.
Hoffman, Jo. Maur. Syntagma Pathologico-Therapeuticum. 4to. Lips. 1728.
Hoffman, L. W. Alter und Neuer Münz-Schlüssel. 4to. Nürnberg. 1692.
Hoffmann, Friderich. Fabrikernes Flor, som et Middel til Dannemarks Opkomst. 4to. Kiobenhavn. 1772.
Hoffmann, Imman. Rabulismi Exegetici Partis Socinianæ, a L. Melliero, Specimina. 4to. Tubingæ. 1731.
Hoffmannus, Fr. Opera Omnia Physico-Medica. 6 vol. fol. Genevæ. 1748—53.
————, —. System of the Practice of Medicine, tr. from the Latin, by William Lewis, &c. 2 vols. 8vo. Lond. 1783.
Hoffmannus, Maur. Monographia Salicum. fol. Lips. 1785.
Hofmannus, J. G. Grammatica Hebræa. 12mo. Giessæ. 1765.
Hofmannus, Jo. Jac. Lexicon Universale. 4 vol. fol. Lug. Bat. 1698.
Hogæus, Gul. Paraphrasis in Jobum Poetica. 12mo. Lond. 1682.
Hogan, Edmund. Pennsylvania State Trials. 8vo. Phil. 1794.
———, ———. Prospect of Philadelphia, and Check on the Next Directory. Part I. 2d ed. 8vo. Phil. 1796.
Hogarth, Wm. Analysis of Beauty. 8vo. Lond. 1753.
Hogg, James. Winter Evening Tales. 2 vols. 12mo. N. York. 1820.
Hoheisel, C. L. De Molis Manualibus Veterum. (Ugol. vol. 29.)
Hohmannus, H. A. Thomæ Woolstoni de Miraculis Christi Paralogismi examinati. 4to. Lips. 1730.
Holbach, P. T. Baron d'. Le Christianisme Dévoilé. 12mo. Lond. 1767.
Holberg, L., Baron de. Introduction to Universal History, tr. from the Latin, with Notes, by G. Sharpe. 2d ed. 8vo. Lond. 1758.
Holbrook, Abiah. Specimens of Penmanship. fol.
Holbrook, Anthony. Pastoral and Magisterial Duties of the Gospel Ministry asserted. 8vo. Lond. 1718.
Holden, Lawrence. Paraphrase on the Books of Psalms, Job, Proverbs, and Ecclesiastes, with Notes. 4 vols. 8vo. Lond. 1763.
Holder, H. E. Essay on Negro Slavery in Barbadoes. 8vo. Lond. 1788.
Holder, Wm. Elements of Speech. 8vo. Lond. 1669.
Holditch, Robert. Emigrant's Guide to the United States. 8vo. Lond. 1818.
Holdsworth, Edward. Remarks and Dissertations on Virgil; and some other Classical Observations; with Notes, &c. by Mr. Spence. Item, Muscipula. 4to. Lond 1768.
Holdsworth, Wm., and Wm. Aldridge. Natural Short-Hand. 8vo. Lond.
Hole, Richard. Remarks on the Arabian Nights' Entertainments. 8vo. Lond. 1797.
Holford, Miss. Margaret of Anjou, a Poem. 12mo. Phil. 1816.

Holinshed, Raphaell. Chronicles of England, Scotland, and Ireland, by R. Holinshed, W. Harrison, J. Hooker, and Others. fol. Lond. 1586.
Holland. History of the Republic of Holland. 2 vols. 8vo. Lond. 1705.
———. Vaderlandsche Historie. 2 vol. 8vo. Amst. 1759.
———. Guide des Voyageurs en Hollande. 12mo. La Haye. 1781.
———. Gegenwärtiger Zustand der Besizungen der Holländer in Ostindien; aus dem Franz. 8vo. Nürnberg. 1781.
———. Vide American Independence,—Berbice,—Deductio,—Dutch,—Surinam, &c.
Holland, H. Heroologia Anglica. fol. 1620.
Holland, H. R. Fox, Lord. Some Account of the Life and Writings of Lope de Vega. 8vo. Lond. 1806.
Holland, John. Two Sermons on the Folly and Guilt of Intemperance. 8vo. Lond. 1750.
Holland, Joseph. Som sober Inspections made into the Cariage and Consults of the late Long Parliament. 3d ed. 12mo. Lond. 1658.
Holland, Philip. Importance of Learning, a Sermon. 8vo. Warrington. 1760.
Hollebeek, Ewaldus. Dissertatio Theologica de Optimo Concionum Genere. 8vo. Lug. Bat. 1770.
————, ————. Vide Sibellius. Vide Verboom.
Hollerius, Jac. De Morbis Internis.—Institutiones Chirurgicæ, etc. 8vo. Lugd. 1588.
Holles, Denzil, Lord. Memoirs. 8vo. Lond. 1699.
Hollinworth, Richard. Catechist Catechized. 4to. Lond. 1653.
Hollingsworth, S. Dissertation on the Manners, Governments, and Spirit of Africa; with Observations on the Applications to Parliament for Abolishing Slavery. 4to. Edin. 1788.
Hollis, Thomas, Memoirs of. 2 vols. 4to; with an Index in 1 vol. 4to. Lond. 1780.
Hollis, Thomas Brand, Memoirs of. 4to. Lond. 1808.
Holm, T. C. Kort Beskrifning om Provincien Nya Swerige uti America. 4to. Stockholm. 1702.
———, ———. Extract of a Translation of the History of New Sweed Land. (New-York Hist. Coll. vol. 2.)
Holmes, Abiel. Life of President Stiles. 8vo. Bost. 1798.
———, ———. History of Cambridge. 8vo. Bost. 1801.
———, ———. Memoir of Stephen Parmenius of Buda; with a Latin Poem, composed by him, and translated into English. (Mass. Hist. Coll. vol. 9.)
———, ———. Memoir of the Moheagan Indians. (Id.)
———, ———. American Annals. 2 vols. 8vo. Camb. 1805.
———, ———. Annals of America, from the Discovery by Columbus in the year 1492, to the year 1826. 2d (American) ed. 2 vols. 8vo. Camb. 1829.
———, ———. Address to the American Antiquarian Society. 8vo. Bost. 1814.

Holmes, Abiel. Memoir of the French Protestants, who settled at Oxford in Massachusetts, in 1686, &c. 8vo. Camb. 1826.

———, ——. Historical Sketch of the English Translations of the Bible. 8vo. Camb. 1815.

———, ——. Address before the Washington Benevolent Society. 8vo. Camb. 1813.

———, ——. Sermon on the Death of Governor Sumner. 8vo. Camb. 1799.

———, ——. Sermon at the Funeral of Dr. Tappan. See Tappan, D.

———, ——. Sermon on the Death of President Willard. 8vo. Camb. 1804.

———, ——. Sermon at the Funeral of the Rev. David Osgood. 8vo. Camb. 1822.

———, ——. Thanksgiving Sermon. 8vo. Bost. 1795.

———, ——. Fast Sermon. 8vo. Camb. 1809.

———, ——. Christmas Sermon. 8vo. Camb. 1810.

———, ——. Discourse before the Society for Propagating the Gospel among the Indians and Others in North America. 8vo. Bost. 1808.

———, ——. Discourse before the Society for Foreign Missions. 8vo. Camb. 1813.

———, ——. Discourse at Plymouth, at the Anniversary Commemoration of the First Landing of the Fathers. 8vo. Camb. 1806.

———, ——. Two Discourses on the Completion of the Second Century from the Landing of the Forefathers of New England at Plymouth. 8vo. Camb. 1821.

———, ——. Discourse at the Opening of the new Alms-house in Cambridge. 8vo. Camb. 1818.

———, ——. Convention Sermon. 8vo. Camb. 1819.

———, ——. Dudleian Lecture. 8vo. Camb. 1810.

———, ——. Sermon at the Ordination of the Rev. D. Kendal. 8vo. Worcester. 1803.

———, ——. Sermon at the Ordination of the Rev. William Bascom. 8vo. Camb. 1805.

———, ——. Sermon at the Ordination of the Rev. John Bartlett. 8vo. Camb. 1811.

———, ——. Sermon at the Inauguration of the Rev. Ebenezer Porter, Professor of Sacred Rhetoric in the Theological Institution at Andover. 8vo. Bost. 1812.

———, ——. Sermon at the Ordination of the Rev. Thomas B. Gannett. 8vo. Camb. 1814.

———, ——. Sermon at the Ordination of the Rev. Hosea Hildreth. 8vo. Camb. 1825.

Holmes, David. Letter to the Church of Christ in Amherst, N. H. 8vo. Bost. 1823.

Holmes, Robert. Four Religious Tracts; with a Discourse on Humility. 8vo. Oxford. 1788.

———, ———. Eight Sermons at the Bampton Lecture, on the Prophecies and Testimony of John the Baptist, &c. 8vo. Oxford. 1782.

Holmes, Robert. Vide Daniel. Vide Testamentum Vetus.
Holstenius, L. Notæ et Castigationes in Stephanum Byzantium de Urbibus. fol. Lug. Bat. 1684.
———, —. In Veterem Picturam Nymphæum referentem. (Grævius, vol. 4.)
———, —. De Fulcris, seu Verubus Dianæ Ephesiæ Simulacro appositis. (Gronovius, vol. 7.)
Holt, Sir John, Reports in B. R. in the time of. fol. Lond. 1737.
Hölterhof, Fr. Der Russische Cellarius, oder Etymologisches Russisches Wörterbuch, etc. 8vo. 1771.
Holtzberger, G. V. De Dei Gratia Universali. 4to. Argent. 1723.
Holtzhausen, Fr. De Informatione Catechetica ex Ebr. v, 12. 4to. Argent. 1700.
Holwell, J. Z. India Tracts, by Mr. Holwell and his Friends. 2d ed. 4to. Lond. 1764.
———, ———. Historical Events relative to Bengal and Indostan, &c. 2d ed. 2 vols. 8vo. Lond. 1766—7.
Holwell, Wm. Mythological, Etymological, and Historical Dictionary. 8vo. Lond. 1793.
Holyday, Barten. Sermon on Faith. 4to. Lond. 1654.
Holyoke, Edward. Doctrine of Life, or of Mans Redemption. 4to. Lond. 1658.
Holyoke, Edw. (Pres.) Convention Sermon. 8vo. Bost. 1741.
———, ———. Sermon at the Ordination of the Rev. J. Diman. 8vo. Bost. 1737.
———, ———. Election Sermon. 8vo. Bost. 1736.
———, ———. Answer to Mr. Whitefield. 4to. Camb. 1744.
Holyoke, Samuel. Columbian Repository of Sacred Harmony. 4to. Exeter, N. H.
———, ———. Occasional Musick. 4to. Exeter. 1802.
———, ———. Hark! from the Tombs, &c. 8vo. Exeter.
———, ———. Exeter. 8vo. Exeter. 1798.
Holyoke, Tho. Dictionary, English and Latin. fol. Lond. 1677.
Holy Scriptures. Sufficiency and Perfection of them as a Rule of Faith and Manners. 8vo. Lond. 1719.
——— ———. See Bible,—Scriptures,—Testament, &c.
Holywood, John. See Sacrobosco.
Homannus, J. B. Atlas Methodicus. fol. Norimb. 1719.
———, ———. Atlas Germaniæ Specialis; Opus inceptum a J. B. Homanno, et ab Homannianis Heredibus continuatum. fol. Norimb. 1753.
Home, Sir Everard. On the Properties of Pus. 4to. Lond. 1788.
———, ———. On Strictures in the Urethra and in the Œsophagus. 2d ed. 2 vols. 8vo. Lond. 1797—1803.
———, ———. On the Treatment of Ulcers on the Legs, &c. 2d ed. 8vo. Lond. 1801.
———, ———. On Cancer. 8vo. Lond. 1805.
———, ———. On the Treatment of the Diseases of the Prostate Gland; with a Letter from Professor Brande on Calculi. 2 vols. 8vo. Lond. 1811—18.

Home, Sir Everard. Papers in the Philosophical Transactions and in Nicholson's Journal.

Home, Fr. Medical Facts and Experiments. 8vo. Lond. 1759.

———, —. Principia Medicinæ. ed. 3tia. 8vo. Edin. 1770.

———, —. Clinical Experiments, Histories, and Dissections. 2d ed. 8vo. Lond. 1782.

———, —. The Same. 3d ed. 8vo. Lond. 1783.

———, —. Principles of Agriculture and Vegetation. 3d ed. 8vo. Lond. 1762.

Home, Henry. See Kames, Lord.

Home, John. History of the Rebellion in 1745. 4to. Lond. 1802.

Home, Robert. Efficacy and Innocency of Solvents examined. 8vo. Lond. 1783.

Homer, Jonathan. Sermon on the Death of his only Child. 8vo. Bost. 1804.

———, ————. Century Sermon. 8vo. Bost. 1792.

———, ————. Artillery Election Sermon. 8vo. Bost. 1790.

Homerus. Ilias et Ulyssea, cum Interpretatione. fol. Basil. 1535.

————. Ilias et Odyssea, cum Commentariis Eustathii. 4 vol. fol. Romæ. 1542—50.

————. Opera, Gr. et Lat. Accessit Plutarchi Homeri Vita. fol. Basil. 1551.

————. ———, Gr. et Lat., cum Scholiis et Notis, cura J. Barnes. 3 vol. 4to. Cant. 1711.

————. ———, cum Scholiis Didymi. 4 vol. 4to. Oxon. 1792—7.

————. ———. Vide Poetæ Græci Heroici.

————. Homeri et Homeridarum Opera et Reliquiæ, ex recensione F. H. Wolfii. 4 vol. 8vo. Lips. 1804—7.

————. Ilias, cum Scholiis Didymi. 8vo. Oxon. 1695.

————. ———. 8vo. Oxon. 1714.

————. ———, Gr. et Lat. 8vo. Lond. 1736.

————. ———. 8vo. Oxon. 1743.

————. ———, cum Scholiis, a Villoison. fol. Venet. 1788.

————. ———. 2 vol. (a Maittaire.) 12mo. Lond. 1816.

————. ———, cum brevi Annotatione, curante C. G. Heyne. 2 vol. 8vo. Lips. 1804.

————. ———, Gr. et Lat., cum Annotationibus, a S. Clarke. 2 vol. 4to. Lond. 1729—32.

————. ———, Gr. et Lat., cum brevi Annotatione. Accedunt Variæ Lectiones et Observationes Veterum Grammaticorum, cum Nostræ Ætatis Critica, curante C. G. Heyne. 8 vol. 8vo. Lips. 1802.

————. Ἰλιὰς μετὰ Παλαιᾶς Παραφράσεως ἐξ Ἰδιοχείρου τοῦ Θεοδώρου Γαζῆ. 4 vol. 8vo. Florentiæ. 1811.

————. Iliados Libri i, v, ix; cum Scholiis Brevibus, etc. in Usum Scholarum. 8vo. Lond. 1760.

————. Iliadis Liber xxii, cum Scholiis Porphyrii et aliorum, a L. C. Valckenaer. Accessit ejusdem Dissertatio, de Præstantissimo Codice Leidensi, et de Scholiis in Homerum ineditis. 8vo. Leovardiæ. 1747.

Homerus. Homeri et Homeridarum Opera et Reliquiæ, ex recensione F. A. Wolfii. vol. 1. (Iliad, Lib. i—xii.) fol. Lips. 1806.

———. Epitome Iliados. Vide Poetæ Lat. Minores.

———. Odyssea, Gr. et Lat. cum Notis, a S. Clarke. 2da ed, 2 vol. 8vo. Lond. 1758.

———. ———, cum Batrachomyomachia, Hymnis, ceterisque Poematiis, a F. A. Wolfio. 8vo. Halæ Sax. 1784.

———. ———, etc. ex recensione F. A. Wolfii. 2 vol. 8vo. Lips. 1807.

———. Hymnus in Cererem, Gr. et Lat., cum Notis, a D. Ruhnkenio. Accedunt Duæ Epistolæ Criticæ ejusdem in Homeridarum Hymnos et Hesiodum. 8vo. Lug. Bat. 1782.

———. Hymni Homerici, cum Reliquis Carminibus Minoribus. Addita est D. Zeni Versio Batrachomyomachiæ Dialecto Vulgari, et T. Prodromi Galeomyomachia, cum Animadversionibus, a C. D. Ilgen. 8vo. Halis Sax. 1796.

———. Hymni et Batrachomyomachia, Gr. et Lat., cum Animadversionibus, ab A. Matthiæ. 8vo. Lips. 1805.

———. Hymni et Epigrammata, cum Notis, a G. Hermanno. 8vo. Lips. 1806.

———. Index Vocabulorum. Vide Seberus.

———. Die Batrachomyomachie und Galeomyomachie, Griechisch, mit Anmerkungen, etc. von A. C. Borheck. 8vo. Lemgo. 1789.

———. Ilias und Odyssee, von J. H. Voss. 4te Auflage. 4 Bände. 8vo. Stuttg. und Tübingen. 1814.

———. L' Iliade di Omero, da M. Cesarotti. 4 vol. 12mo. Pisa. 1802.

———. Versione Letterale dell' Iliade, da M. Cesarotti. 8 vol. 12mo. Firenze. 1804—9.

———. The Iliads of Homer donne according to the Greeke, by George Chapman. fol. Lond. 1610.

———. The Iliads and Odysses of Homer, tr. out of Greek into English, by Thomas Hobbes. 2d ed. 12mo. Lond. 1677.

———. The Iliad and Odyssey, translated from the Greek by A. Pope. 2 vols. 12mo. Edin. 1763.

———. The Same, with Notes. 11 vols. 12mo. Lond. 1750—2.

———. The Same. 11 vols. 8vo. Lond. 1760.

———. The Same, with Additional Notes, by G. Wakefield. 11 vols. 8vo. Lond. 1796.

———. Iliad and Odyssey, tr. into English Blank Verse by William Cowper. 4 vols. 8vo. Bost. 1814.

———. Vita ejus. Vide Opuscula Mythologica.

———. Vide Besseldt,—Bongiovanni,—Delbrück,—Duportus,—Egen.—Eustathius,—Halbkart,—Hermannus,—Klotzius,—Knight,—Koes,—Köppen,—Marées,—Nast,—Patrick,—Quintus,—Riccius,—Schott,—Seberus,—Spitzner,—Spohn,—Tzetz,—Ursinus.—Wetstenius,—Wolfius,—Wood.

Homes, Wm. Proposals of some Things to be done in our Administering Ecclesiastical Government. 8vo. Bost. 1732.

Homiliæ. Vide Mosanus, G.
Homilies, Observations on the. See Church.
Honcamp, Mathias. Justificatio Apologiæ Sanctarum Scripturarum et SS. Patrum adversum Censuram J. Clerici, etc. 12mo. Moguntiæ. 1710.
Honduras. Full Answer to the King of Spain's last Manifesto, respecting the Bay of Honduras, and the Mosquito Shore. 8vo. Lond. 1779.
Honesty 's best Policy, or Penitence the Sum of Prudence. 4to.
Hontan, le Baron de la. Voyages dans l'Amérique Septentrionale. 2 vol. 12mo. Amst. 1705.
———, ————. Idem. 2 vol. 12mo. La Haye. 1709.
———, ————. ——. 3 vol. 12mo. Amst. 1728.
———, ————. New Voyages to North America; with New Voyages to Portugal and Denmark; from the French. 2 vols. 8vo. Lond. 1703.
Hood, (Commodore.) Letters. See Bernard, Sir Fr. See Massachusetts.
Hoogeveen, Henricus. Doctrina Particularum Linguæ Græcæ. 2 vol. 4to. 1769.
————, ————. Idem. Recensuit, breviavit, et auxit C. G. Schütz. 8vo. Dessaviæ et Lips. 1782.
————, ————. Idem. 8vo. Lips. 1806.
————, ————. ——. 8vo. Glasguæ. 1813.
Hooght, Everardus van der. Vide Biblia Hebraica.
Hooke, Andrew. On the National Debt and Capital. 8vo. Lond. 1750.
Hooke, N. Roman History. 3d ed. 4 vols. 4to. Lond. 1757—71.
———, —. Observations on the Roman Senate, as treated by Vertot, a Gentleman, Middleton, and Chapman. 4to. Lond. 1758.
Hooke, Rob. Lectures and Collections relating to Comets and the Microscope. 4to. Lond. 1678.
———, ——. On Helioscopes, &c. 4to. Lond. 1676.
———, ——. Philosophical Collections. 4to. Lond. 1681.
———, ——. On Lamps, Waterpoises, &c. 4to. Lond. 1677.
———, ——. On the Power of Springing Bodies. 4to. Lond. 1678.
———, ——. Philosophical Experiments and Observations. 8vo. Lond. 1726.
———, ——. Micrographia. fol. Lond. 1665.
———, ——. ————. fol. Lond. 1745.
———, ——. Posthumous Works. fol. Lond. 1705.
Hooke, Wm. New Englands Teares for Old Englands Feares; a Fast Sermon. 8vo. Lond. 1641.
Hooker, John, alias Vowell. Chronicles. See Holinshed, R.
Hooker, John. Sermon at the Funeral of the Rev. Joseph Hunt. 8vo. Bost. 1776.
Hooker, Richard. Lawes of Ecclesiastical Politie. fol. Lond. 1617.
———, ————. Works, with his Life by I. Walton. fol. Lond. 1705.

Hooker, Richard. The Same. fol. Lond. 1723.
———, ———. Ecclesiasticall Politie. Books vi and viii. 4to.
———, ———. Causes of the Continuance of these Contentions concerning Church Government. 4to. Lond. 1641.
Hooker, Thomas. The Poor Doubting Christian drawn to Christ. 12mo. Bost. 1743.
Hooker, Wm. J. Journal of a Tour in Iceland in 1809. 2d ed. 2 vols. 8vo. Lond. 1813.
Hoole, Charles. Rudiments of Latine Grammar. 12mo. Lond. 1657.
Hoole, John. Jerusalem Delivered, translated from the Italian of Tasso. 2d ed. 2 vols. 12mo. Lond. 1764.
——, ——. The Same. 1st American from the 8th London edition, with Notes. 2 vols. 8vo. Newburyport. 1810.
——, ——. The Same. See Chalmers, A.
——, ——. Orlando Furioso, translated from the Italian of Aristo, with Notes. 6 vols. 12mo. Lond. 1807.
——, ——. The Same. See Chalmers, A.
——, ——. Dramas and Other Poems, translated from the Italian of Metastasio. 3 vols. 8vo. Lond. 1800.
Hooper, Geo. (Bp.) Works. fol. Oxford. 1757.
———, ———. Sermon, January 31st. 4to. Lond. 1704.
———, ———. Inquiry into the State of the Ancient Measures, the Attick, the Roman, and especially the Jewish, &c. 8vo. Lond. 1721.
Hooper, Robert. Medical Dictionary. 12mo. Lond. 1799.
———, ———. Anatomist's Vade-Mecum. 2d ed. 12mo. Lond. 1800.
———, ———. The Same. 2d American edition. 12mo. Windsor. 1809.
———, ———. Physician's Vade-Mecum. 12mo. Albany. 1809.
Hooper, Wm. Sermon at the Funeral of Thomas Greene, Esq. 4to. Bost. 1763.
———, ——. Apostles neither Impostors nor Enthusiasts, a Sermon. 8vo. Bost. 1742.
Hoornbeeck, Joh. Apologia pro Ecclesia Christiana Hodierna, non Apostatica. 12mo. Amst. 1647.
—————, ——. Commentarius de Paradoxis et Heterodoxis Weigelianis. 16mo. Ultrajecti. 1646.
—————, ——. Socinianismi Confutatio. 2 vol. 4to. Ultrajecti. 1650.
Hopkins, David. Vocabulary, Persian, Arabic, and English, abridged from Wilkins's quarto edition of Richardson's Dictionary. 8vo. Lond. 1810.
Hopkins, Ezekiel, (Bp.) Works. 3d ed. fol. Lond. 1710.
Hopkins, John. See Psalms.
Hopkins, Samuel. Two Discourses, on the Knowledge of Sin, and on being born of God. 8vo. Bost. 1768.
———, ———. Sin, thro' Divine Interposition, an Advantage to the Universe, in Three Sermons. 8vo. Bost. 1773.

Hopkins, Samuel. System of Doctrines contained in Divine Revelation explained and defended. 2 vols. 8vo. Bost. 1793.
Hopkins, Samuel. Historical Memoirs relating to the Housatunnuk Indians; with a Character of the Rev. John Sergeant, &c. 4to. Bost. 1753.
Hopkins, Wm. Appeal to the Common Sense of all Christian People on Church Authority in Matters of Faith. 2d ed. 12mo. Lond. 1754.
——, ——. Trinitarian Controversy Reviewed; or a Defence of the Appeal. 8vo. Lond. 1760.
Hopkinson, Fr. Machine for Measuring a Ship's Way through the Sea. (Amer. Phil. Tr. vol. 2.)
——, —. Dissertation on the reciprocal Advantages of a Perpetual Union between Great Britain and her Colonies. See Great Britain.
Hopkinsonius, Joh. Descriptio Paradisi. (Ugol. vol. 7.)
Horapollo, (Orus Apollo.) Hieroglyphica, Gr. et Lat., cum Notis, curante J. C. de Pauw. 4to. Traj. ad Rhen. 1727.
Horatius, Q. Flaccus. Opera, cum A. Mureti Scholiis et Aldi Manutii Annotationibus. 8vo. Venet. 1561.
——, ——. Opera, a T. Pulmanno. 16mo. Antv. 1566.
——, ——. Opera, cum Comment. Variorum, et Scholiis J. Bond, accurante C. Schrevelio. 8vo. Lug. Bat. 1663.
——, ——. Poemata, cum Commentariis J. Min-ellii. 12mo. Rotterodami. 1677.
——, ——. Opera. 4to. Cant. 1699.
——, ——. ——, cum Scholiis, a J. Bond. 12mo. Amst. 1712.
——, ——. ——, ex Recensione et cum Notis R. Bentleii. ed. 3tia. 4to. Amst. 1728.
——, ——. Horatii, A. Persii, et J. Juvenalis Opera, a Valentino Curio. 8vo. Basil. 1531.
——, ——. Opera, cum Notis Variorum, a C. Combe. 2 vol. 4to. Lond. 1792.
——, ——. Opera, illustravit C. G. Mitscherlich. 2 vol. 8vo. Reutlingæ. 1815—16.
——, ——. ——, cum Scholiis Vet. et Notis, a J C. Zeunio. 8vo. Lond. 1809.
——, ——. ——, a J. H. Jaeck. 12mo. Vinariæ. 1821.
——, ——. ——. Vide Corpus Poetarum Lat.
——, ——. Carmina atque Epodon Liber, cum Comment. B. P. Spilimbergii. 4to. Venet. 1524.
——, ——. Sermonum Libri Quatuor. 4to. Venet. 1584.
——, ——. Carmina Selecta, in Usum Scholarum Belgicæ. 12mo. Bruxelles. 1779.
——, ——. Carmina Expurgata, cum Notis J. Juventii et Aliorum. 8vo. Cant. 1806.

Horatius, Q. Flaccus. Eclogæ, sive Satiræ et Epistolæ Selectæ, cum Scholiis, a J. C. Müller. 8vo. Magontiaci. 1790.

———, ———. Eclogæ, cum Scholiis Veteribus, Notis, etc., a J. C. Zeunio. 8vo. Lips. 1802.

———, ———. Ausgewählte Oden und Lieder von Horaz. Vide Encyclopädie der Lat. Class.

———, ———. Satyren, erklärt von L. F. Heindorf. 8vo. Breslau. 1815.

———, ———. Epistolæ ad Pisones et Augustum; with an English Commentary, Notes, and Critical Dissertations, by Mr. Hurd. 2d ed. 2 vols. 12mo. Lond. 1753.

———, ———. The Same. 4th ed. 3 vols. 12mo. Lond. 1766.

———, ———. Poetical Translation of the Works of Horace, with the Original Text, and Notes, by Philip Francis. 3d ed. 2 vols. 4to. Lond. 1749.

———, ———. The Same. 4th ed. 4 vols. 12mo. Lond. 1750.

———, ———. ———. 6th ed. 4 vols. 12mo. Lond. 1756.

———, ———. Odes, Epodes, and Carmen Seculare, translated into English Prose, with the Original, and Notes, by D. Watson. 8vo. Lond. 1741.

———, ———. Satires, Epistles, and Art of Poetry, translated into English Prose, with the Original, and Notes. 5th ed. 8vo. Lond. 1760.

———, ———. Works, translated into English Prose, with the Original, and Notes, by D. Watson and S. Patrick. 4th ed. 2 vols. 8vo. Lond. 1760.

Horchius, Henricus. De Igne Sacro, et Musica.—Canones Hermeneutici S. Scripturæ. (Ugol. vol. 32.)

Horn, George. Treatises on Leeches. 8vo. Lond. 1798.

Horn, Jo. Commentatio de Sententiis eorum Patrum quorum Auctoritas ante Augustinum plurimum valuit de Peccato Originali. 4to. Gottingæ. 1801.

Horne, Andrew. Myrror of Justice. 12mo. Lond. 1642.

Horne, Geo. (Bp.) Commentary on the Psalms. 3d ed. 3 vols. 12mo. Perth. 1794.

———, ———. The Same. 6th ed. 2 vols. 8vo. Oxford. 1798.

———, ———. ———. 8th ed. 2 vols. 8vo. Lond. 1806.

———, ———. Discourses. 3d ed. 4 vols. 8vo. Lond. 1799.

———, ———. Sixteen Sermons. 3d ed. 8vo. Lond. 1800.

———, ———. Visitation Sermon. 16mo. Lond. 1788.

———, ———. Letter to Dr. Priestley by an Undergraduate. 2d ed. 16mo. Oxford. 1787.

———, ———. His Life. See Jones, W.

Horne, Jo. van. Microcosmus. 18mo. Lug. Bat. 1662.

Horne, John. On Infant Baptism. 4to. Lond. 1654.

Horne, John. See Tooke.

Horne, Thomas. Manuductio in Ædem Palladis. 12mo. Lond. 1641.

Horne, Tho. H. Introduction to the Study of Bibliography. 2 vols. 8vo. Lond. 1814.

———, ———. Introduction to the Study and Knowledge of the Scriptures. 3 vols. 8vo. Lond. 1818.

———, ———. The Same. 4 vols. 8vo. Phil. 1825.

Horneck, Anthony. Consecration Sermon. 4to. Lond. 1689.

———, ———. Sermon before the King and Queen. 4to. Lond. 1689.

———, ———. Account of Edmund Slater's Return to the Communion of the Church of England. 4to. Lond. 1689.

———, ———. Great Law of Consideration. 7th ed. 8vo. Lond. 1698.

Horneman, C. F. De Canone Veteris Testamenti.—De Versione LXX Interpretum. 8vo. Hauniæ. 1776.

Horneman, C. Frees. Clavis Dialectorum Orientalium. (Acta Literaria Hafniensia.)

Horniceus, D. De Novo Legislatore Christo contra Socinianos et Arminianos. 4to. Wittenbergæ. 1691.

Hornius, Geo. Historia Ecclesiastica, et Historia Politica. Accedit L. Capelli Hist. Jud. Compendium, et Continuatio. 12mo. Lug. Bat. 1687.

———, ——. Arca Mosis. 12mo. Lug. Bat. 1669.

———, ——. De Originibus Americanis. 8vo. Hagæ Com. 1652.

———. ——. Orbis Antiqui Delineatio. fol. Amst. 1653.

Horologgi, Ioseppe. Historia degli Imperatori Greci, descritta da Niceta; a questi sono aggiunti gli Annali de gli Imperatori di Constantinopoli, con l'Historia delle Parti dell' Oriente scritta da Haithone, trad. in Ling. Ital. 4to. Venet. 1562.

Horrebows, P. Nouvelle Description de l'Islande, avec des Observations Critiques sur l'Hist. Nat. de cette Isle par M. Anderson; trad. de l'Allemand. 2 vol. 12mo. Paris. 1764.

Horsey, Jerome. Voyage from Mosco to England. (Hakluyt, vol. 1.)

Horsley, (Mr.) Considerations on the High Duties examined. 8vo. Lond. 1744.

Horsley, John. Enquiry into the Objection against the Resurrection of Christ from his not appearing to the Jews. 4to. Lond. 1704.

———, ——. The Same. 8vo. Lond. 1730.

———, ——. Sermon on the Death of the Rev. Jonathan Harle; with an Account of his Life. 8vo. Lond. 1730.

Horsley, John. Britannia Romana; or the Roman Antiquities of Britain. fol. Lond. 1732.

Horsley, Samuel, (Bp.) Tracts in Controversy with Dr. Priestley on the Belief of the First Ages in our Lord's Divinity, with Notes, &c. 8vo. Gloucester. 1789.

———, ————. See Priestley, J.

———, ————. Critical Disquisitions on the Eighteenth Chapter of Isaiah. 4to. Lond. 1799.

———, ————. Hosea, translated from the Hebrew, with Notes, 2d ed., and a Sermon on Christ's Descent into Hell. 4to. Lond. 1804.

Horsley, Samuel, (Bp.) Sermons. 3 vols. 8vo. Dundee. 1810.
———, ————. Nine Sermons on our Lord's Resurrection, &c. with a Dissertation on the Prophecies of the Messiah dispersed among the Heathen. 8vo. Lond. 1815.
———, ————. Euclidis Data.—Additamentum Datorum.—Problematum Delectus.—Archimedis Circuli Dimensio.—Cribrum Eratosthenis.—De Numeris Primis et Compositis.—Sphericorum Liber Singularis.—J. Keilii de Natura et Arithmetica Logarithmorum Tractatus. 8vo. Oxon. 1803.
Horsmanden, Daniel. New-York Conspiracy, or a History of the Negro Plot in 1741. 4to.
————, ——. The Same. 8vo. N. York. 1810.
Horstius, J. M. Paradisus Animæ Christianæ, cum Manuali Pietatis. 12mo. Coloniæ. 1644.
Hortensius, Lambertus. De Annabaptistis. 12mo. Amst. 1636.
Horticultural Society of London. Transactions. 4to. Lond. 1807 et seqq.
———— ————. Charter and Bye-Laws. 8vo. Lond. 1822.
Horto, Garcias ab. Vide Garcias ab Orto.
Horton, Tho. Expositions on Psalms, iv, xlii, li, and lxiii. fol. Lond. 1675.
Hosack, David. Observations on the Establishment of the College of Physicians and Surgeons in New-York, &c. 8vo. N. York. 1811.
———, ———. Case of Aneurism of the Femoral Artery. 8vo. N. York. 1812.
———, ———. Observations on Vision. 8vo. N. York. 1813.
———, ———. Introductory Discourse to Lectures on the Theory and Practice of Physic; with a Tribute to the Memory of Dr. Benjamin Rush. 8vo. N. York. 1813.
———, ———. Treatment of the Typhoid State of Fever. 8vo. N. York. 1815.
———, ———. System of Practical Nosology, &c. 8vo. N. York. 1818.
———, ———. Observations on the Peripneumonia Typhodes, now prevailing in several Districts of the United States. 8vo. N. York. 1813.
———, ———. Observations on the Surgery of the Ancients. 8vo. N. York. 1813.
———, ———. Syllabus of Lectures on Botany. 8vo. N. York. 1795.
———, ———. The Same. 8vo. N. York. 1814, and 1815.
———, ———. Course of Studies for the Private Medical School in New-York. 8vo. N. York. 1816.
———, ———. Syllabus of Lectures on the Theory and Practice of Physic, &c. 8vo. N. York. 1816.
———, ———. Biographical Memoir of Hugh Williamson, M. D. LL. D. 8vo. N. York. 1820. See also New-York Historical Collections, vol. 3.
———, ———. Inaugural Discourse before the New-York Historical Society. (New-York Hist. Coll. vol. 3.)

Hosack, David. Catalogue of Plants in the Elgin Botanic Garden. 18mo. N. York. 1806.

——, ——. The Same. 2d ed. 8vo. N. York. 1811.

——, ——. Statement of Facts relating to the Elgin Botanic Garden. 8vo. N. York. 1811.

——, ——. Medical Essays. 2 vols. 8vo. N. York. 1824.

——, ——. Inaugural Discourse before the New-York Horticultural Society. 8vo. N. York. 1824.

——, ——. Observations on the Medical Character. 8vo. N. York. 1826.

——, ——, and J. W. Francis. American Medical and Philosophical Register. 2d ed. 4 vols. 8vo. N. York. 1814.

Hosea. See Horsley, S.

Hosmer, Stephen. Connecticut Election Sermon. 16mo. N. Lond. 1720.

Hospinianus, Rodolphus. De Festis Diebus Judæorum, Græcorum, Romanorum, et Turcarum. fol. Tiguri. 1592.

——, ——. Idem. fol. Tiguri. 1593.

Hospital, G. F. A. Marquis de l'. Traité Analytique des Sections Coniques et de leur Usage. 4to. Paris. 1776.

——, ——. Method of Fluxions. See Stone, E.

Hospitals. Reasons for the Establishment and Encouragement of St. Luke's Hospital for Lunaticks; with the Rules and Orders. 4to.

——. Memorial concerning the erecting an Orphanotrophy in London. See Bray.

——. Royal Charter establishing a Hospital for Exposed and Deserted Children. 8vo. Lond. 1739.

——. The Same; with an Act of Parliament for confirming and enlarging its Powers. 12mo. Lond. 1740.

——. Considerations on the Necessity and Usefulness of the Royal Charter establishing an Hospital for Exposed and Deserted Young Children. 4to. Lond. 1740.

——. Sketch of the General Plan for executing the Purposes of the Foundling Hospital. 12mo. Lond. 1740.

——. Regulations for Managing the Hospital for Exposed and Deserted Young Children. 8vo. Lond. 1757.

——. Account of the British Lying-in Hospital for Married Women. 8vo. Lond. 1758.

——. Plan of the Magdalen House. 4to. Lond. 1758.

——. Historia Hospitalis S. Elizabethæ extra Muros Monasterii S. Maximini Ordinis S. Benedicti prope Treviros. 8vo. Lond. 1786.

——. Brief Account of the Hospital of St. Elizabeth, in the Electorate of Treves, from the Latin, with Notes, &c. 8vo. Lond. 1786.

——. Account of the New-York Hospital. 8vo. N. York. 1811.

——. Present State of the Asylum for the Relief of Persons deprived of their Reason. 12mo. Phil. 1816.

—— See Charitable Institutions,—Edinburgh,—Massachusetts,—New-York, &c.

Host. Discourse concerning its Adoration. See Church.

Host, Geo. Efterretninger om Oen Sanet Thomas. 8vo. Kiobenhavn. 1791.
Hotchkis, Tho. Discourse on the Imputation of Christ's Righteousness. 8vo. Lond. 1675.
Hotomanus, Ant. De Veteri Ritu Nuptiarum. (Grævius, vol. 8.)
Hotomanus, Fr. Francogallia. 8vo. 1573.
———, —. ———. 8vo. Francof. 1586.
———, —. Franco-Gallia; or an Account of the Ancient Free State of France, &c. tr. from the Latin by Lord Molesworth. 2d ed. 8vo. Lond. 1721.
———, —. De Magistratibus Romanorum.—De Senatu et Senatusconsultis.—De Formulis Antiquis. (Grævius, vol. 2.)
———, —. De Sponsalibus, de Ritu Nuptiarum et Jure Matrimoniorum; item de Spuriis et Legitimatione. (Id. 8.)
Hottinger, J. C. De Decimis Hebræorum. (Ugol. vol. 20.)
Hottinger, Joh. Henr. Promptuarium; sive Bibliotheca Orientalis. 4to. Heidelb. 1658.
———, ———. Etymologicum Orientale. 4to. Francof. 1661.
———, ———. Smegma Orientale. 4to. Heidelb. 1658.
———, ———. Jus Hebræorum. (Ugol. vol. 3.)
———, ———. De Geographia Terræ Chanaan. (Id. 6.)
———, ———. De Variis Orientalium Inscriptionibus.—De Nummis Orientalium. (Id. 28.)
———, ———. Cippi Hebraici. (Id. 33.)
Houbigant, Ch. Fr. Racines Hebraïques, sans Pointes-Voyelles. 8vo. Paris. 1732.
———, ———. Prolegomena in Scripturam Sacram. 2 vol. 4to. Paris. 1753.
———, ———. Biblia Hebraica, cum Notis, et Versione Latina. Accedunt Libri Græci, qui Deutero-Canonici vocantur. 4 vol. fol. Lut. Par. 1753.
———, ———. Notæ Criticæ in Vet. Testamentum. 2 vol. 4to. Francof. ad Mœn. 1777.
Houghton, John. Husbandry and Trade Improved, revised, &c. by R. Bradley. vol. 1. 8vo. Lond. 1727.
Houghton, John. English Grammar. 12mo. Salop. 1766.
Houry, Laurent d'. Almanach Royal, année commune 1789, présenté à sa Majesté, pour la premiere fois en 1699, par Laurent d'Houry, editeur. 8vo.
Household Government, Godlie Forme of. 8vo.
Houser, Henry. Sermon before the Governour, Council, and Assembly, in Jamaica. 4to. Lond. 1673.
Housonus, Jo. Uxore dimissa propter Fornicationem, aliam non licet superinducere. 16mo. Oxon. 1602.
Houstoun, Gul. Reliquiæ Houstounianæ. 4to. Lond. 1781.
Houstoun, James. Works, containing Memoirs of his Life and Travels in Asia, America, &c. 8vo. Lond. 1753.
Houtteville, C. F. La Religion Chrétienne prouvée par les Faits. 4to. Paris. 1722.
———, ———. Method of the Principal Authors for and

against Christianity, from the French; with a Dissertation on the Life of Apollonius Tyanæus. 8vo. Lond. 1739.
Howard, Charles. Thoughts, Essays, and Maxims, chiefly Religious and Political. 12mo. Lond. 1768.
Howard, Edward. On a New Fulminating Mercury. 4to. Lond. 1800.
Howard, John. Trinity Asserted, a Sermon. 4to. Lond. 1700.
———, ——. Sermon in Defence of the Trinity. 4to. Lond. 1701.
Howard, John. On the Medical Properties of Mercury. 8vo. Lond. 1782.
Howard, John. State of Prisons in England and Wales, &c. 3d ed. 4to. Warrington. 1784.
———, ——. The Same. 4th ed. 4to. Lond. 1792.
———, ——, Account of the Principal Lazarettos in Europe, &c. 4to. Lond. 1789.
———, ——. The Same. 2d ed. 4to. Lond. 1791.
Howard, J. C. Discourse before the Humane Society of Massachusetts. 8vo. Bost. 1804.
Howard, Sir Robert. History of Religion. 12mo. Lond. 1694.
———, —————. Doctrines which make for Tyranny displayed. 12mo. Lond. 1697.
Howard, Simeon. Election Sermon. 8vo. Bost. 1780.
———, ————. Sermon at the Ordination of the Rev. Thomas Adams. 8vo. Bost. 1791.
———, ————. Artillery Election Sermon. 8vo. Bost. 1773.
Howe, John. Works; with his Life. 2 vols. fol. Lond. 1724.
——, ——. Sermon on Union among Protestants. 8vo. Lond. 1703.
——, ——. Thanksgiving Sermon. 4to. Lond. 1698.
——, ——. Sermon on Reformation of Manners. 12mo. Lond. 1698.
——, ——. View of Antiquity; being an Account of Some of the Fathers of the Three First Centuries. 8vo. Lond. 1677.
Howe, Nathaniel. Century Sermon at Hopkinton. 8vo. Andover. 1817.
Howe, Richard, Earl, Narrative of the Transactions of the Fleet under the Command of. 8vo. Lond. 1779.
——, ————————, Letter to, on his Naval Conduct in the American War. 8vo. Lond. 1779.
Howe, Thomas. Episcopacy; a Letter to the Rev. Mr. Forster. 8vo. Lond. 1765.
——, ————. See Forster, Tho.
Howe, Sir Wm. (Lt. Gen.) Narrative as to his Command in North America. 2d ed. 4to. Lond. 1780.
——, ————, Two Letters from Agricola to, with Political Observations. 8vo. Lond. 1779.
——, ————. Letter from Cicero to Lord Viscount H——e. 8vo. Lond. 1781.
——, ————. See Galloway, J.

Howel, Laurence. Compleat History of the Bible. 5th ed. 3 vols. 8vo. Lond. 1729.

Howel, Wm. History of the World. 2d ed. fol. Lond. 1680.

Howell, James. French and English Dictionary. fol. Lond. 1673.

———, ———. Inspections into the Character and Consults of the late Long Parliament. 12mo. 1649.

Howell, Wm. Doctrine of the Trinity proved from Scripture, a Sermon. 8vo. Oxford. 1711.

———, ——. Layman's Vindication of the Church of England, against Mr. Howell and Dr. Bennett. See Church.

Howship, John. Observations in Surgery and Morbid Anatomy. 8vo. Lond. 1816.

———, ——. On the Diseases of the Urinary Organs. 8vo. Lond. 1816.

Hubbard, Eben. Sermon on the Death of the Hon. Azor Orne. 8vo. Salem. 1796.

Hubbard, Wm. Narrative of the Indian Wars in New-England. 12mo. Bost. 1775.

———, ——. The Same. 12mo. Brattleborough. 1814.

———, ——. Election Sermon. 4to. Bost. 1676.

———, ——, Memoirs of. (Mass. Hist. Coll. vol. 10.)

———, ——. History of New-England. (Id. 2d Series, vols. 5 and 6.)

Huber, M., et C. C. H. Rost. Manuel des Curieux et des Amateurs de l'Art. 8 vol. 12mo. Zurich. 1797—1804.

Huddesford, Geo. Reply to a Pamphlet, entitled, "A Defence of the Rector and Fellows of Exeter College," &c. 4to. Oxford. 1755.

Huddesford, Wm. Lives of John Leland, Thomas Hearne, and Anthony à Wood. 2 vols. 8vo. Oxford. 1772.

Huddy, Matthew. Sermon at Exon at a Meeting of the Ministers of Devon and Cornwall. 8vo. Lond. 1718.

Hudleston, Richard. Short and Plain Way to the Faith and Church. To which is annexed Charles II. his Papers found after his Decease; as also an account of what occurred on his Death-Bed in regard to Religion. 4to. Lond. 1688.

Hudson, Henry. Divers Voyages and Northerne Discoveries, &c. (Purchas, vol. 3, and N. York Hist. Coll. vol. 1.)

———, ———. Descriptio ac Delineatio Geographica Detectionis Freti, etc. 4to. Amst. 1613.

Hudson's Streights. See North-West Passage.

Hue d'Escures, Ludovicus. Theses Theologicæ de Veritate Bonorum Operum quæ per Christi Gratiam fiunt a Regenitis. 4to. Sedani. 1664.

Huerta, J. L. de la. Exâmen de la Posibilidad de fixar la Significacion de los Sinónimos de la Lengua Castellana. 2 vol. 12mo. Valencia. 1807.

Huerta, Vicent Garcia, de la. Obras Poeticas. 2 vol. 8vo. Madrid. 1786.

———. La Escena Española Defendida. 12mo. Madrid. 1786.

———. Theatro Hespañol. 8 vol. 12mo. Madrid. 1785.

Hues, Rob. Tractatus de Globis. Accedit Breviarium totius Orbis Terrarum P. Bertii. 16mo. Oxon. 1651.
Huetius, P. D. Demonstratio Evangelica. 3tia ed. fol. Paris. 1690.
———, ——. History of Romances, made English by S. Lewis. 12mo. Lond. 1715.
———, ——. Carmina. Vide Poetæ Recentiores, Lat. et Gr.
———, ——. Censura Philosophiæ Cartesianæ. 12mo. Lut. Par. 1689.
———, ——. De Navigationibus Salomonis.—De Situ Paradisi Terrestris. (Ugol. vol. 7.)
Hug, J. Leonhard. Die Erfindung der Buchstabenschrift. 4to. Ulm. 1801.
——, ———. Das Hohe Lied in einer noch unversuchten Deutung. 4to. Freyburg und Constanz. 1813.
Hugenius, Christianus. Opera Varia. 4 tomi in 2 vol. 4to. Lug. Bat. 1724—8.
Hughes, Griffith. Natural History of Barbados. fol. Lond. 1750.
Hughes, Jabez. Lives of the Twelve Cæsars, translated from the Latin of Suetonius. 2 vols. 12mo. Lond. 1717.
Hughes, John. Letters. See Duncombe, J.
———, ——. Poems. See Chalmers, A.
Hughes, John. Complicated Guilt of the late Rebellion. 8vo. Lond. 1745.
Hughes, Obadiah. Sermon on the Death of the Rev. Joshua Oldfield. 8vo. Lond. 1730.
———, ———. Speech at the Interment of the Rev. Wm. Harris. 8vo. Lond. 1740.
———, ———. Sermon on the Death of Mrs. D. Iremonger. 8vo. Lond. 1745.
———, ———. Sermon on the Death of the Rev. S. Wright. 8vo. Lond. 1746.
———, ———. Sermon on the Death of A. Walburge, Esq. 4to. Lond. 1749.
———, ———. Sermon at the Ordination of the Rev. J. Jollie and M. Jackson. 8vo. Lond. 1746.
———, ———. Vide Causa Dei contra Novatores.
———, ———. Sermon on the Plague in France. 8vo. Lond. 1722.
———, ———. Sermon against Popery. 8vo. Lond. 1735.
———, ———. Fast Sermon. 8vo. Lond. 1742.
———, ———. Sermon on a Day of Public Prayer. 8vo. Lond. 1745.
———, ———. Sermon on Reformation of Manners. 8vo. Lond. 1728.
———, ———. Two Sermons on the Nativity of Christ. 4to. Lond. 1749.
———, ———. Peace Sermon. 4to. Lond. 1749.
———, ———. Sermon on Nov. 5th. 8vo. Lond. 1739.
———, ———. Coronation Sermon. 8vo. Lond. 1725.
Hughes, William. Parsons Law. 8vo. Lond. 1673.

Hughes, William. On Original Writs. 4to. Lond. 1655.
Hughes, William. American Physitian. 12mo. Lond. 1672.
Hull, Wm. (Gen.), Trial of. 8vo. Bost. 1814.
——, ————. Report of his Trial, by Lieut. Col. Forbes. 8vo. N. York. 1814.
——, ————. Defence of himself, with an Address to the Citizens of the United States. 12mo. Bost. 1814.
——, ————. Memoirs of the Campaign of the North Western Army of the United States in 1812; with a Sketch of his Revolutionary Services. 8vo. Bost. 1824.
Hulsius, Ant. Nomenclator Biblicus Hebræo-Latinus. 12mo. Bredæ. 1650.
———, ——. De Linguæ Hebrææ Origine, Conservatione, Propagatione, ac Utilitate Oratio. 12mo. Bredæ. 1649.
Hulsius, Henr. De Jehova Deo Rege, etc.—De Schechinah. (Ugol. vol. 24.)
———, ———. De Corpore, Velo, et Sepulcro Moysis. (Id. 33.)
Humane Life, Discourse concerning the Period of. 12mo. Lond. 1677.
Humane Society. Reports for 1783—4. 8vo. Lond.
——— ———. ———— 1785—6. 8vo. Lond.
——— ———, Brief Account of the, for the Year 1788. 8vo.
——— ———. See Massachusetts.
Humbert de Superville, D. P. G. Jésus, Fragment. 8vo. Leide. 1812.
Humboldt, Alex. de. Voyage aux Régions Equinoxiales du Nouveau Continent, fait en 1799—1804, par Alex. de Humboldt et A. Bonpland; redigé par Al. de Humboldt; avec Deux Atlas. Première Partie. Relation Historique. 2 vol. 4to. Paris. 1814—19. Quatrième Partie. Astronomie. 2 vol. 4to. Paris. 1810.
———, ————. Political Essay on the Kingdom of New Spain, tr. from the French by J. Black. 3d ed. 4 vols. 8vo. Lond. 1822.
———, ————. Researches concerning the Institutions and Monuments of the Ancient Inhabitants of America, &c. tr. from the French by H. M. Williams. 2 vols. 8vo. Lond. 1814.
———, ————. Personal Narrative; or Travels in South America, tr. from the French by H. M. Williams. 8vo. Phil. 1815.
———, ————. Versuch über den Politischen Zustand des Königreichs Neu-Spanien. 5 Bände. 8vo. Tübingen. 1809—14.
———, ————. Reise in die Æquinoctial-Gegenden des Neuen Continents. Theil 1. 8vo. Stuttg. und Tübin. 1815.
———, ————. Geographical Distribution of Ferns. (Brande, Journal of Science, vol. 4.)
———, ————. On the Natural Family of the Grasses. (Id. 5.)
———, ————. Philosophical Papers in Nicholson's Journal.
Humboldt, Wilhelm von. Æschylos Agamemnon Metrisch übersetzt. 4to. Leipz. 1816.

Humboldt, Wilhelm von. Lettre à M. Abel-Rémusat, sur la Nature des Formes Grammaticales en général, et sur le Génie de la Langue Chinoise en particulier. 8vo. Paris. 1827.
Hume, David. History of England. 6 vols. 4to. Lond. 1762—44.
——, ——. The Same. 8 vols. 8vo. Lond. 1767.
——, ——. ——; with his Life written by himself. 8 vols. 4to. Lond. 1770.
——, ——. The Same. 8 vols. 8vo. Dublin. 1775.
——, ——. ——. 8 vols. 8vo. Lond. 1786.
——, ——. ——. 6 vols. 8vo. Phil. 1796.
——, ——. ——. 7 vols. 8vo. Phil., &c. 1810.
——, ——. Treatise of Human Nature. 3 vols. 8vo. Lond. 1739—40.
——, ——. Essays and Treatises on Several Subjects. 4to. Lond. 1758.
——, ——. The Same. 2 vols. 4to. Lond. 1768.
——, ——. ——. 4 vols. 8vo. Basil. 1793.
——, ——. His Life, written by himself. 16mo. Lond. 1777.
——, ——. Memoirs of Russia. See Manstein.
Humphrey, Heman. Sermon at the Ordination of the Rev. H. Bingham and A. Thurston, as Missionaries. 8vo. Bost. 1819.
——, ——. Inaugural Address at Amherst College. 8vo. Bost. 1823.
Humphreys, David. Historical Account of the Incorporated Society for the Propagation of the Gospel in Foreign Parts. 8vo. Lond. 1730.
Humphreys, David, (Col.) Miscellaneous Works. 8vo. N. York. 1790.
——, ——. The Same. 8vo. N. York. 1804.
——, ——. Life of Major General Israel Putnam. 12mo. Hartford. 1788.
——, ——. The Same. 12mo. Middletown. 1794.
——, ——. Poem on Industry. 8vo. Phil. 1794.
——, ——. Poem on the Happiness of America. 4to.
——, ——. Discours en Vers, adressé aux Officiers et aux Soldats des différentes Armées Américaines, trad. de l'Anglois par le Marquis de Chastellux. 8vo. Paris. 1786.
——, ——. Valedictory Discourse before the Cincinnati of Connecticut. 8vo. Bost. 1804.
Hünefeld, C. L. De Terra Gosen. 4to. Francof. ad Viad. 1735.
Hungary, Account of the Ancient Kingdom of. 12mo. Lond. 1717.
Hunn, Nathanael. Connecticut Election Sermon. 16mo. N. Lond. 1747.
Hunt, C. A. The Chief Events of Universal History, in Three Tables, on the Plan of the late Professor Bredow. 2d ed.
Hunt, Jeremiah. Essay for Explaining the Scripture-Revelations. 8vo. Lond. 1734.
——, ——. Accession Sermon. 8vo. Lond. 1725.
——, ——. Sermon on Reformation of Manners. 8vo. Lond. 1716.

Hunt, Jeremiah. Sermon on the Death of Mr. Thomas Hollis. 8vo. Lond. 1718.

——, ———. Sermon against Popery. 8vo. Lond. 1735.

——, ———. Sermon on the Death of the Rev. J. Maisters. 2d ed. 8vo. Lond. 1717.

——, ———. Sermons and Tracts. 4 vols. 8vo. Lond. 1748—9.

——, ———. Sermon on the Death of Grey Neville, Esq. 8vo. Lond. 1723.

——, ———. Sermon on the Death of Mr. Samuel Hollis. 8vo. Lond. 1724.

——, ———. Sermon on the Death of Mrs. Hannah Hollis. 8vo. Lond. 1725.

——, ———. Sermon on the Death of the Rev. J. Kinch. 8vo. Lond. 1731.

——, ———. Sermon on the Death of John Hollis, Esq. 8vo. Lond. 1736.

——, ———. Discourse on 1 John iii, 2. 8vo. Lond. 1728.

Hunt, John. Sermon at his Ordination, and at the Instalment of the Rev. John Bacon. 8vo. Bost. 1772.

Hunt, John. Historical Surgery. 4to. Loughborough. 1801.

Hunt, Tho. Dissertation on Proverbs vii, 22, 23. 4to. Oxford. 1743.

——, ——. De Antiquitate, Elegantia, Utilitate Linguæ Arabicæ. 4to. Oxon. 1739.

——, ——. De Usu Dialectorum Orientalium. 4to. Oxon. 1748.

Hunt, Wm. G. Oration in Honor of General Lafayette. 8vo. Nashville. 1825.

——, ———. Character &c. of De Witt Clinton. 8vo. Nashville. 1828.

Hunter, A. Georgical Essays. 8vo. York. 1777.

Hunter, David. Observations on the History of Jesus Christ. 2 vols. 12mo. Edin. 1770.

Hunter, John. Natural History of the Human Teeth. 4to. Lond. 1771.

———, ——. The Same. 2d ed. 4to. Lond. 1778.

———, ——. On the Diseases of the Teeth. 4to. Lond. 1778.

———, ——. On the Venereal Disease. 2d ed. 4to. Lond. 1788.

———, ——. Observations on certain Parts of the Animal Œconomy. 2d ed. 4to. Lond. 1792.

———, ——. On the Blood, Inflamation, and Gun-Shot Wounds; with his Life by E. Home. 4to. Lond. 1794.

———, ——. On the Diseases of the Army in Jamaica, &c. 2d ed. 8vo. Lond. 1796.

Hunter, Wm. Medical Commentaries. 4to. Lond. 1762.

———, ——. Two Introductory Lectures to his Last Course of Anatomical Lectures, &c. 4to. Lond. 1784.

———, ——. Anatomy of the Human Gravid Uterus, English and Latin. fol. Birmingham. 1774.

Hunter, Wm. Description of the Gravid Uterus. 4to. Lond. 1794.
——, ——. Some Account of the Astronomical Labours of Jayasinha. (Asiatic Researches, vol. 5.)
——, ——. Narrative of a Journey from Agra to Oujein. (Id. 6.)
——, ——. On the Pepper of Prince of Wales's Island. (Id. 9.)
Huntingford, Geo. J. Introduction to the Writing of Greek. 8vo. Oxford. 1800.
——, ——. Discourses. 2 vols. 8vo. Lond. 1795—7.
Huntington, Joseph. Thoughts on the Atonement, &c. 8vo. Newburyport. 1791.
——, ——. Calvinism Improved. 8vo. N. Lond. 1796.
Huntingtonus, Robertus. Epistolæ. Vide Smith, T.
Hurault, Phil. Vide Cheverny.
Hurd, Isaac. Discourse before the Humane Society of Massachusetts. 8vo. Bost. 1799.
Hurd, Richard, (Bp.) Twelve Sermons introductory to the Study of the Prophecies. 2d ed. 8vo. Lond. 1772.
——, ——. The Same. 5th ed. 2 vols. 8vo. Lond. 1787.
——, ——. Sermons at Lincoln's Inn. 3d ed. 3 vols. 8vo. Lond. 1785.
——, ——. Moral and Political Dialogues. 8vo. Lond. 1759.
——, ——. The Same. 2d ed. 8vo. Lond. 1760.
——, ——. The Same, with Letters on Chivalry and Romance. 3d ed. 3 vols. 12mo. Lond. 1765.
——, ——. Letters on Chivalry and Romance. 2d ed. 8vo. Lond. 1762.
——, ——. Remarks on his Visitation Charge. 8vo. Lond. 1777.
——, ——. Letter to the Rev. Thomas Leland, in which his late Dissertation on the Principles of Human Eloquence is criticized, &c. 8vo. Lond. 1764.
——, ——. On the Delicacy of Friendship. (Tracts by Warburton and a Warburtonian. See Warburton.)
Hurrion, John. Sermons on the Knowledge of Christ. 8vo. Lond. 1727.
Hurtado de Mendoza. Vide Mendoza.
Husband, Edward. Collection of Remarkable Passages between the King and Parliament, in 1641—3. 4to. Lond. 1643.
——, ——. Collection of Orders, Ordinances, and Declarations of both Houses of Parliament, from March 9, 1642, until December, 1646, &c. fol. Lond. 1646.
Husbandry, Tracts on. 4to. Lond. 1578—86.
Huschke, Immanuel, G. Analecta Critica in Anthologiam Græcam, etc. 8vo. Jenæ et Lips. 1800.
——, ——. Commentatio de Orphei Argonauticis. 4to. Rostochii. 1806.

Hussey, Samuel F. Examination of Asa Rand's Book, called a "Word in Season;" with a Refutation of some of his Charges against the Quakers. 12mo. Salem. 1821.
Hutcheson, Fr. Inquiry into the Original of our Ideas of Beauty and Virtue. 8vo. Lond. 1726.
———, —. The Same. 3d ed. 8vo. Lond. 1729.
———, —. ———. 4th ed. 8vo. Lond. 1738.
———, —. On the Nature and Conduct of the Passions and Affections; with Illustrations of the Moral Sense. 8vo. Lond. 1727.
———, —. The Same. 12mo. Lond. 1728.
———, —. Philosophiæ Moralis Institutio. 12mo. Glasguæ. 1742.
———, —. Short Introduction to Moral Philosophy, tr. from the Latin. 2d ed. 12mo. Glasgow. 1753.
———, —. The Same. 3d ed. 2 vols. 12mo. Glasgow. 1764.
———, —. System of Moral Philosophy. 2 vols. 4to. Lond. 1755.
———, —. Reflections upon Laughter, and Remarks upon the Fable of the Bees. 12mo. Glasgow. 1750.
———, —. De Naturali Hominum Socialitate Oratio. 4to. Glasguæ. 1730.
Hutcheson, Geo. Exposition of the Book of Job. fol. Lond. 1669.
———, —. Exposition of the Small Prophets.—Exposition of St. John's Gospel. 2d ed. fol. Edin. 1657.
———, —. Exposition on John. 4to. Lond. 1657.
Hutchins, Tho. Topographical Description of Virginia, Pennsylvania, Maryland, and North Carolina. 8vo. Lond. 1778.
———, —. Description Topographique de la Virginie, de la Pensylvanie, du Maryland, et de la Caroline Septentrionale, etc., trad. de l'Anglois. 8vo. Paris. 1781.
———, —. Description of Louisiana and West Florida. 8vo. Phil. 1784.
Hutchinson, (Mrs.) Antinomians and Formalists condemned by the Synod of Elders in New-England, &c. 4to. Lond. 1644.
Hutchinson, (Esq.) Of the Authority of Councils; and the Rule of Faith, by William Claggett. 4to. Lond. 1687.
Hutchinson, Aaron. Valour for the Truth, a Sermon. 8vo. Bost. 1767.
———, —. Reply to the Rev. J. Tucker's Remarks on the above. 8vo. Bost. 1768.
Hutchinson, Fr. Historical Essay concerning Witchcraft; with Two Sermons, in Proof of the Christian Religion, and concerning Angels. 8vo. Lond. 1718.
———, —. The Same. 2d ed. 8vo. Lond. 1720.
Hutchinson, John. Abstract from his Works, being a Summary of his Discoveries in Philosophy and Divinity. 2d ed. 12mo. Lond. 1755.
Hutchinson, Lucy. Memoirs of the Life of Colonel Hutchinson (her husband), with her Life prefixed. 4th ed. 2 vols. 8vo. Lond. 1822.

Hutchinson, Mich. Sermon, Jan. 30th. 8vo. Nottingham. 1716.
Hutchinson, Tho. (Gov.) History of Massachusetts. 2d ed. 2 vols. 8vo. Lond. 1765.
———, ———. The Same. 3d ed. 2 vols. 8vo. Salem. 1795.
———, ———. Collection of Original Papers relative to the History of the Colony of Massachusetts-Bay. 8vo. Bost. 1769.
———, ———. Speeches to the General Assembly of Massachusetts, with the Answers of the Council, &c. 12mo. Bost. 1773.
———, ———. See Gold Coins.
———, ———, and A. Oliver, (Lt. Gov.) Copy of Letters sent to Great Britain by them, and other Persons. 12mo. Bost. 1773.
———, ———, ———. Letters, and Remarks thereon; with the Assembly's Address, and the Proceedings of the Lords Committee of Council, &c. 2d ed. 8vo. Lond. 1774.
Hutchinsonians. A Word to them. 8vo. Lond. 1756.
Huth, J. D. De Conversione Hominis Continuata. 4to. Argent. 1697.
Hutter, Elias. Dictionarium Harmonicum Biblicum. 4to. Noribergæ. 1598.
———, ———. Lectiones Evangeliorum et Epistolarum Anniversariæ. 4to. Noribergæ. 1601.
———, ———. Vide Testamentum Novum.
Hutton, Charles. Mathematical and Philosophical Dictionary. 2 vols. 4to. Lond. 1795.
———, ———. Course of Mathematics, revised by R. Adrain. 2 vols. 8vo. N. York. 1812.
———, ———. Papers in the Philosophical Transactions.
Hutton, James. Dissertations on Different Subjects in Natural Philosophy. 4to. Edin. 1792.
———, ———. On the Philosophy of Light, Heat, and Fire. 8vo. Edin. 1794.
———, ———. Theory of the Earth. 2 vols. 8vo. Edin. 1795.
Hutton, Matthew, (Abp.) Sermon before the Society for promoting English Protestant Schools in Ireland. 4to. Lond. 1745.
———, ———. Sermon before the Governors of the London Infirmary. 8vo. Lond. 1746.
Hutton, Sir Richard. Reports in the time of James I, and Charles I. fol. Lond. 1656.
Huxham, John. On the Air and Epidemic Diseases, &c., from the Latin. 2 vols. 8vo. Lond. 1759—67.
———, ———. On Fevers; and on the Malignant Ulcerous Sore-Throat. 8vo. Lond. 1750.
———, ———. The Same. 5th ed. 8vo. Lond. 1767.
———, ———. ———. 8vo. Lond. 1782.
———, ———. Observations upon Antimony. 2d ed. 8vo. Lond. 1767.
———, ———. Papers in the Philosophical Transactions.

Huygens. See Hugenius.
Hyde, Edward. See Clarendon, Earl of.
Hyde, Tho. Syntagma Dissertationum, a G. Sharpe. 2 vol. 4to. Oxon. 1767.
——, ——. De Ludis Orientalibus. 2 vol. 12mo. Oxon. 1694.
——, ——. Veterum Persarum et Parthenorum et Medorum Religio. 4to. Oxon. 1700.
——, ——. Idem. ed. 2da. 4to. Oxon. 1760.
——, ——. Catalogus Impressorum Librorum Bibliothecæ Bodleianæ. fol. Oxon. 1674.
Hyginus Gromaticus, et Polybius Megalopolitanus. De Castris Romanis, cum Notis R. H. Schelii. (Grævius, vol. 10.)
Hyginus, Julius. De Castrametatione. Vide Scriptores de Re Militari.
——, ——. Fabulæ.—Poeticon Astronomicon. Vide Mythographi Latini.
Hymn to the Creator of the World. To which is added, in Prose, an Idea of the Creator from his Works. 8vo. Lond. 1750.
Hyndman, John. Sermon before the Society in Scotland for propagating Christian Knowledge. 8vo. Edin. 1761.
Hyperius, Andreas. De Formandis Concionibus Sacris. 8vo. Halæ. 1781.

I

Ibañez de Echavarri, Bernardo. Reyno Jesuitico. (Documentos de la Compañia en el Paraguay, vol. 4.)

Ibañez de Segovia, Gaspar. Memorias Historicas del Rei D. Alonso el Sabio. fol. Madrid. 1777.

Ibbetson, James. Charge to the Clergy of St. Albans. 4to. Lond. 1766.

———, ———. Plea for Subscription to the Thirty Nine Articles. 3d ed. 8vo. Lond. 1768.

———, ———. Letter to him, occasioned by the above "Plea," &c. 8vo. Lond. 1771.

Ibbot, Benjamin. Sermons at Boyle's Lecture in 1713—14. 8vo. Lond. 1727.

——, ———. The Same. See Boyle's Lecture Sermons.

——, ———. Sermon on the Nature and Extent of the Office of the Civil Magistrate. 8vo. Lond. 1720.

——, ———. Answer to the above. 4to. Lond. 1721.

——, ———. Parable of the Unjust Steward explained, a Sermon. 8vo. Lond. 1719.

Ibenthal, M. Henricus. De Differentiis Vocum Hebraicarum. 4to. Vitembergæ. 1718.

Ichnographiæ Urbium utriusque Belgii. fol.

Ides, E. Ysbrant. Travels from Muscovy to China. (Harris, Coll. vol. 2.)

Ignatius, Sanctus. Epistolæ; item S. Barnabæ Epistolæ; Gr. et Lat.; cum Notis I. Vossii. ed. 2da. 4to. Lond. 1680.

———, ———. Vide Polycarpus,—Cotelerius,—Leslie, C.

Ihre, Joh. Glossarium Suiogothicum. 2 vol. fol. Upsaliæ. 1769.

——, ——. Fragmenta Versionis Ulphilanæ, etc. 4to. Upsal. 1763.

——, ——. Analecta Ulphilana. 4to. Upsalæ. 1769.

Ikenius, Conradus. De Funere, Sepultura, et Luctu. (Ugol. vol. 33.)

Ilg, J. G. De Natis ex Deo non peccantibus, nec peccare valentibus. 4to. Tubingæ. 1748.

Ilgen, Car. Dav. Jobi, Antiquissimi Carminis Hebraici, Natura atque Virtutes. 8vo. Lips. 1789.

——, ————. Opuscula Varia Philologica. 8vo. Erfordiæ. 1797.

——, ————. Scolia, hoc est, Carmina Convivialia Græcorum, etc. 12mo. Jenæ. 1798.

Illgen, Chr. Fr. Vita Lælii Socini Specimen Historico-Ecclesiasticum. 8vo. Lips. 1814.
Illinois. See Lands.
Illuminati, View of the New-England. 8vo. Phil. 1799.
Illyricus. Vide Flacius Illyricus.
Images. Letter shewing what Worship is due to them, according to the Second Council of Nice, &c. 4to. Lond. 1680.
———. Discourse of the Use of them, in relation to the Church of England and the Church of Rome. 4to. Lond. 1687.
Imbonatus, C. J. Bibliotheca Latino-Hebraica. fol. Romæ. 1694.
Imison, John. Elements of Science and Art; a new edition, by T. Webster. 2 vols. 8vo. Lond. 1808.
Imlay, Geo. Topographical Description of the Western Territory of North America. 8vo. Lond. 1792.
——, ——. The Same. 2d ed. 8vo. Lond. 1793.
——, ——. The Same; with a Supplement by J. Filson. 2 vols. 12mo. N. York. 1793.
Impey, Sir Elijah. Original Minutes of the Governor General and Council of Fort William in Bengal, on the Appointment, carried by Mr. Hastings, of Sir E. Impey, to be Judge, &c. 8vo. Lond. 1781.
Impressments. Copies and Extracts of Documents on the Subject of British Impressments of American Seamen. 8vo. Lond. 1812.
——————. See Massachusetts.
Inchiquin's Letters, Reply to the Criticism on, in the Quarterly Review. 8vo. N. York. 1815.
—————— ————. See Dwight, T.
Inchofer, Melchior. La Monarchie des Solipses; trad. du Latin, avec des Remarques, etc. 12mo. Amst. 1722.
Independence. See American Independence.
Index Expurgatorius Hispanus. Vide Sarmiento.
——— Librorum Prohibitorum uque ad Annum 1752. 8vo. Romæ.
India. England and East-India Inconsistent in their Manufactures. 12mo. Lond. 1697.
——. Answer to an Essay on the East-India Trade. 12mo. Lond. 1697.
——. Necessity and Advantage of preserving our own Manufacturies; being an Answer to a Pamphlet, intituled, The Honour and Advantage of the East-India Trade, &c. 12mo. Lond. 1697.
——. Profit and Loss of the East-India Trade stated, &c. 12mo. Lond. 1700.
——. Agreement of the Customs of the East-Indians, with those of the Jews and other Ancient People. 8vo. Lond. 1705.
——. See East-India,—West-India, &c.
Indiana. Memorial to Congress of Sundry Inhabitants of the Counties of Randolph and St. Clair in the Indiana Territory. 8vo. Washington. 1806.
———. See Ohio.
Indians. Conference between Sir William Pepperell and other Commissioners, and the Indians of the Penobscot Tribe. 8vo. Bost. 1753.

Indians. Enquiry into the Causes of the Alienation of the Delaware and Shawanese Indians from the British Interest, &c. 8vo. Lond. 1759.
———. Account of some late Attempts to Christianize the North American Indians. 8vo. Edin. 1763.
———. Farther Appeal in their behalf, &c. 8vo. Lond. 1766.
———. Sitten and Meinungen der Wilden in America. 4 Theile. 12mo. Frankf. am Mayn. 1777—81.
———. Report of the Select Committee of the Society for propagating the Gospel among the Indians and Others in North America. 8vo. 1816.
———. Sketches of the History, Manners, and Customs of the North American Indians, with a Plan for their Melioration, by James Buchanan. 2 vols. 12mo. N. York. 1824.
———. See Conversations,—Researches,—Treaties.
Indies. Beschryvinge van eenige voorname Kusten in Oost- en West-Indien. 4to. Leeuwarden. 1716.
——. See India,—East-India,—West-India.
Indulgence to Tender Consciences most Reasonable and Christian. 4to. Lond. 1687.
Inès de la Cruz, Juana. Poemas. 3 vol. 4to. Madrid. 1725.
Inett, John. Origines Anglicanæ, or a History of the English Church. 2 vols. fol. Lond. 1704—10.
Infant-Baptism, Plain Reasons for. 8vo. Lond. 1750.
Infidelity. Address to the Inhabitants of London and Westminster, in relation to the Bishop of London's Pastoral Letter concerning Infidelity. 8vo. Lond. 1729.
————. Second Address, occasioned by a Second Pastoral Letter. 8vo. Lond. 1730.
————. Question by the Author of the "Address," Whether God is an Arbitrary Being, &c. 8vo. Lond. 1730.
————. See Gibson, E.—See Scepticism.
Ingenhouz, John. Experiments upon Vegetables, discovering their great Power of Purifying the Air in Sun-Shine and Injuring it in the Shade and at Night. 8vo. Lond. 1779.
————, ——. Expériences sur les Végétaux, trad. de l'Anglois. 2 vol. 8vo. Paris. 1787—9.
Ingersoll, Jonathan. Connecticut Election Sermon. 16mo. New-Lond. 1761.
Ingram, Robert. Accounts of the Ten Tribes of Israel being in America. 8vo. Colchester. 1792.
Inheritance, Law of. 2d ed. 8vo. Lond.
Innes, John. Description of the Human Muscles. 12mo. Lond. 1791.
——, ——. The Same. 12mo. Lond. 1804.
Innocentius III, (Papa.) Opera. fol. Coloniæ. 1552.
Inquirer, Impartial, (by J. Lowell.) 8vo. Bost. 1811.
Inquiry, Heads of, relative to the Present State and Condition of his Majesty's Colony of Connecticut, with the Answers thereto. fol. New-London. 1775.

Inquisition, Authentic Memoirs concerning the Portuguese, &c. 8vo. Lond. 1761 and 1769.
Insolvent Debtors, and their Creditors, Act for the Benefit of, passed 3d of April, 1811. 8vo. N. York. 1811.
Institut National des Sciences et Arts, Mémoires de. Sciences Mathématiques et Physiques. (tom. 1—6,) 6 tomes. 4to. Paris. 1798—1806.
——— ——————————. Littérature et Beaux-Arts. (tom. 1—5,) 5 tomes. 4to. Paris. 1798—1804.
——— ——————————. Sciences Morales et Politiques. (tom. 1—5,) 5 tomes. 4to. Paris. 1798—1804.
——— ——————————. Mémoires présentés à l'Institut, par divers Savans. Sciences Mathématiques et Physiques. tome 1. 4to. Paris. 1806.
——— ——————————. Base du Système Métrique Décimal, ou Mesure de l'Arc du Méridien compris entre les Parallèles de Dunkerque et Barcelone, exécutée en 1792 et années suivantes, par MM. Méchain et Delambre. Suite des Mémoires de l'Institut. tome 1. 4to. Paris. 1806.
——— ——————————. Vide Académie.
Institution, Royal. See Great Britain.
Instructor Clericalis, by R. G. 6 vols, 8vo. Lond. 1713—17.
——— ——————. 7th ed. 7 vols. 8vo. Lond. 1727.
Intelligencer in 19 Numbers. 8vo. Lond. 1729.
————, National; 1802—8, and 1818—19. fol. Washington.
————. See Hindoostanee Intelligencer.
Intemperance, Constitution of the Massachusetts Society for the Suppression of. 8vo. Bost. 1818.
————, Report of the Board of Counsel to the Massachusetts Society for the Suppression of. 8vo. Bost. 1820.
Interests of the Empress Queen, the Kings of France and Spain, and their principal Allies, betrayed in the Preliminary Articles, signed at Aix-la-Chapelle, the 30th of April, 1748; from the French. 8vo. 1748.
Interiano, Paolo. Ristretto delle Historie Genovesi. 4to. Lucca. 1551.
Invasions. History of French Invasions from the Revolution. 8vo. Lond. 1744.
———. Account of the Intended Invasion by the Chevalier's Son. 8vo. Lond. 1744.
Inveges, Augustinus. Carthago Sicula. (Græv. Thes. Sicil.)
———, ————. Panormus Antiqua. (Id.)
Inverkeithing, Answer to the Reasons of Dissent from the Sentence of the Rev. Commission of the General Assembly, March 1752, relating to the Parish of. 8vo. Edin. 1752.
Ipswich, Letter from the Second Church in, to their Chebacco Brethren. 8vo. Bost. 1747.
———. Reply to the Above. 8vo. Bost.
———, Declaration of Delegates at, July 21, 1812.
Ireland, Articles of Religion agreed upon by the Clergie of, in 1615. 4to. Lond. 1629.

Ireland. Treatise of Taxes and Contributions, with some Application to Ireland. 4to. Lond. 1662.

———. List of such of the Names of the Nobility, Gentry, and Commonalty of England and Ireland as were attainted of High Treason in Ireland in 1689. 4to. Lond. 1690.

———. Proceedings of the House of Commons in Ireland, in Rejecting the Money-Bill, Vindicated. 8vo. Lond. 1753.

———. List of the Members who voted on the above Question. fol. Lond. 1753.

———. Case fairly stated, &c. 8vo. Lond. 1754.

———. Letter on the Present Crisis of Affairs in that Kingdom. 8vo. Lond.

———. Thoughts on the Affairs of Ireland. 8vo. Lond. 1754.

———. Letter occasioned by the above "Thoughts," &c., by M. B. Drapier. 8vo. Lond. 1754.

———. Pr——te Vindicated, and the Affairs of I——d set in a True Light. 8vo. Lond. 1754.

———. Account of the Revenue and National Debt. 8vo. Lond. 1754.

——— in Tears. 2d ed. 8vo. Lond. 1755.

———. Review of the Rise and Progress of the Incorporated Society in Dublin for promoting English Protestant Schools in Ireland from 1733 to 1755. 4to.

———. Letter to the D——e of B——d. 8vo. Lond. 1757.

———, Debates relative to the Affairs of, in 1763 and 1764, &c. 2 vols. 8vo. Lond. 1766.

———. Sketches of Irish Political Characters of the Present Day. 8vo. Lond. 1799.

———. Letter to the Belfast First Company of Volunteers in the Province of Ulster. 8vo. Belfast. 1782.

———. Transactions of the Association of Physicians in Ireland. 2 vols. 8vo. Dublin. 1817—18.

———. See Britain,—Catholics,—Christianity,—Dublin.

Ireland, John. Paganism and Christianity Compared. 8vo. Lond. 1809.

Ireland, W. M. Remarks on the Medical Properties of the Stramonium. 8vo. N. York. 1817.

Irenæus, Sanctus. Adversus Hæreses, Lat. a D. Erasmo. 4to. Basil. 1534.

———, ———. ———————. Gr. et Lat., cum Notis Variorum, a J. E. Grabe. fol. Oxon. 1702.

———, ———. Idem, a R. Massuet. fol. Paris. 1710.

———, ———. Fragmenta Anecdota, Gr. et Lat., cum Notis et Dissertationibus; item Liturgia Græca J. E. Grabii, etc., a C. M. Pfaffio. 8vo. Hagæ Com. 1715.

———, ———. Dissertationes in Irenæum. Vide Dodwell, H.

Irving, David. Memoirs of George Buchanan. 8vo. Edinburgh. 1807.

———, ———. Memorial of Anne Margaret Anderson, his Wife. 8vo. Edin. 1813.

Irving, Washington. History of New-York, by Diedrick Knickerbocker. 3d ed. 2 vols. 12mo. Phil. 1819.
——, ————. Sketch Book. 2 vols. 8vo. N. York. 1820.
——, ————. Bracebridge Hall. 2 vols. 8vo. and 12mo. N. York. 1822.
——, ————. Tales of a Traveller. Part 1. 8vo. Phil. 1824.
Isæus. Reliquiæ. Vide Oratores Græci, a Reiskio.
Isaiah. See Dodson,—Doederlein,—Lowth,—Stock.
Iscanus, Josephus. De Bello Trojano. Vide Dictys et Dares.
Isernia, Andreas de. In Usus Feudorum Commentaria. fol. Francof. 1598.
Isert, P. E. Reise nach Guinea. 8vo. Kopenhagen. 1788.
Isidorus Hispalensis. Opera Omnia, per J. du Breul. fol. Col. Agrip. 1617.
Isidorus Pelusiotes. De Interpretatione Divinæ Scripturæ Epistolarum Libri IV, Gr. et Lat., a C. Rittershusio. fol. Lug. Bat. 1606.
Isla, J. F. Historia del famoso Predicador Fray Gerundio de Campazas. 4 vol. 8vo. Madrid. 1813.
—, ——. History of Friar Gerund; from the Spanish. 2 vols. 8vo. Lond. 1772.
—, ——. La Juventud Triunfante. 4to. Salamanca. 1727.
Isocrates. Scripta Omnia, Gr. et Lat., ab H. Wolfio. 8vo. Basil. 1571.
————. Opera Omnia, Gr. et Lat., cum Notis, ab A. Augero. 3 vol. 8vo. Paris. 1782.
————. Opera Omnia, cum Animadversionibus Criticis, a W. Lange. 8vo. Halæ Sax. 1803.
————. Orationes et Epistolæ. (Bibliotheca Gr. a Coray.)
————. Orationes. Vide Oratores Græci, a Reiskio.
————. Panegyricus, cum Animadversionibus, a F. A. G. Spohn. 8vo. Lips. 1817.
————. Orations in English. See Gillies, J.
————. H. Stephani Diatribe in Isocratem. Vide Harpocration.
Israeli, J. d'. Romances. 12mo. Phil. 1803.
——, ——. Quarrels of Authors. 2 vols. 12mo. N. York. 1814.
——, ——. Calamities of Authors. 2 vols. 12mo. N. York. 1812.
——, ——. Literary Character illustrated by the History of Men of Genius. 12mo. N. York. 1818.
Italy, State of, in 1687, with respect to the Quietists, Inquisition, &c., being a Supplement to Burnet. 12mo. 1688.
——. Short Account of a late Journey to Tuscany, Rome, and other Parts of Italy. 12mo. Lond. 1741.
——. De l'Italie dans son Etat Actuel et Politique. 8vo. Paris. 1797.
——. Rambles in Italy, in the Years 1816—17, by an American. 8vo. Baltimore. 1818.

Italy, Letters from the North of, addressed to Henry Hallam, Esq. 2 vols. 8vo. Lond. 1819.

Ivernois, Sir Francis d'. Account of the late Revolution in Geneva; from the French. 8vo. Lond. 1795.

Ives, Edward. Voyages from England to India in 1754; and an Historical Narrative of the War in India in 1755—7; also, a Journey from Persia to England. 4to. Lond. 1773.

Izard, (Maj. Gen.) Official Correspondence. See United States.

J

Jablonski, D. E. Thorn Affligée, trad. de l'Allemand par C. L. de Beausobre. 12mo. Amst. 1726.

Jablonski, P. E. Dissertationes Academicæ viii de Terra Gosen, eo Præside, Eruditorum Disquisitioni submissæ. 4to. Francof. ad Viad. 1736.

———, ——. Remphan Ægyptiorum Deus. (Ugol. vol. 23.)

———, ——. Pantheon Ægyptiorum. 8vo. Francof. ad Viad. 1750.

Jablonsky, C. G. Insecten. 6 vol. 8vo. Berlin. 1783—90.

Jacchæus, Gilb. Institutiones Metaphysicæ. 12mo. Lug. Bat. 1628.

———, ——. —————————. 12mo. Cant. 1649.

———, ——. Institutiones Logicæ. 12mo. Oxon. 1675.

Jachiades, Josephus. Paraphrasis in Danielem, Hebr. et Lat. 4to. Amst. 1634.

Jack, Richard. Mathematical Principles of Theology. 8vo. Lond. 1747.

Jackman, Charles. See Pet, A.

Jackson, Arthur. Help for the Understanding of the Holy Scripture, with Annotations on the Historical Parts of the Old Testament. 2 vols. 4to. Camb. 1643—6.

———, ———. Annotations on the Old Testament. 3 vols. 4to. Lond. 1643—58.

Jackson, Charles, of Wexford in Ireland. Narrative of his Sufferings and Escape; with an Account of Atrocities by Irish Rebels. 8th ed. 8vo. Dublin. 1799.

Jackson, Charles. Treatise on the Pleadings and Practice in Real Actions; with Precedents of Pleadings. 8vo. Bost. 1828.

Jackson, James. Eulogy on Dr. John Warren. 8vo. Bost. 1815.

———, ———. Syllabus of the Lectures delivered to the Senior Sophisters in Harvard University. 12mo. Bost. 1816.

———, ———. Text Book of a Course of Lectures on the Theory and Practice of Physic. Parts 1 and 2. 8vo. Bost. 1825—7.

Jackson, John. Remarks on "Christianity as Old as Creation." 8vo. Lond. 1731.

———, ——. Address to Deists. 8vo. Lond. 1744.

———, ——. The Same. 2d ed. 8vo. Lond. 1762.

———, ——. Chronological Antiquities. 3 vols. 4to. Lond. 1752.

———, ——. Memoirs of his Life and Writings, with an Addition to his Chronology, &c. 8vo. Lond. 1764.

Jackson, John. Remarks on Dr. Middleton's Free Enquiry. 8vo. Lond. 1749.

———, ——. Letter to him, occasioned by the Remarks on Middleton. 8vo. Lond. 1749.

———, ——. Defence of Human Liberty, in Answer to Cato's Letters. 8vo. Lond. 1725.

———, ——. Vindication of Human Liberty, in Answer to Collins. 8vo. Lond. 1730.

———, ——. Existence and Unity of God proved from his Nature and Attributes; being a Vindication of Dr. Clarke's Demonstration, &c. 8vo. Lond. 1734.

———, ——. Collection of Queries, in Defence of Dr. Clarke's Scripture-Doctrine of the Trinity, &c. 8vo. Lond. 1716.

———, ——. Dissertation on Matter and Spirit. 8vo. Lond. 1735.

———, ——. Grounds of Civil and Ecclesiastical Government considered; with a Defence of the Bishop of Bangor against Mr. Law. 8vo. Lond. 1718.

———, ——. Modest Plea, &c. continued; or an Answer to Waterland's Queries relating to the Trinity. 8vo. Lond. 1720.

———, ——. Reply to Dr. Waterland's Defence of his Queries. 8vo. Lond. 1722.

———, ——. Observations on Dr. Waterland's Second Defence. 8vo. Lond. 1724.

———, ——. Answer to Bishop Brown's Analogy. 8vo. Lond. 1733.

———, ——. Christian Liberty asserted and the Scripture-Doctrine of the Trinity vindicated against Dr. Waterland. 8vo. Lond. 1734.

———, ——. Animadversions on the Above. 8vo. Lond. 1735.

———, ——. Narrative of the Case of the Rev. Mr. Jackson being refused the Sacrament of the Lord's Supper by Dr. Coney. 8vo. Lond. 1736.

Jackson, John. Reflections on the Commerce of the Mediterranean. 12mo. N. York. 1806.

———, ——. Journey from India towards England. 8vo. Lond. 1799.

Jackson, J. B. Enquiry into the Origin of Printing in Europe. 4to. Lond. 1752.

———, ——. Essay on the Invention of Engraving and Printing in Chiaro Oscuro. 4to. Lond. 1754.

Jackson, J. M. View of the Political Situation of Upper Canada. 8vo. Lond. 1809.

Jackson, Richard. Literatura Græca. 12mo. Lond. 1769.

Jackson, Robert. Remarks on the Medical Department of the British Army. 8vo. Lond. 1803.

———, ———. System of Arrangement and Discipline for the Medical Department of Armies. 8vo. Lond. 1805.

Jackson, S. H. Cautions to Women respecting the State of Pregnancy, &c. 2d ed. 12mo. Lond. 1801.

Jackson, Tho. Works, with his Life. 3 vols. fol. Lond. 1673.

Jackson, William. Visitation Sermon. 4to. Camb. 1675.
Jackson, Wm. (Major). Eulogium on Washington. 8vo. Phil. 1800.
Jacob, Giles. Laws of Liberty and Property. 2d ed. 12mo. Lond. 1736.
——, ——. New Law-Dictionary. 8th ed. fol. Lond. 1762.
Jacob, Wm. Travels in the South of Spain. 4to. Lond. 1811.
Jacobites. See Whigs.
Jacobs. Flora Favershamensis. 8vo. Lond. 1777.
Jacobs, Freidrich. Hülfsbuch zum Griechischen Elementarbuche. Theile i und iv. 12mo. Leipz. 1807—11.
——, ——. Elementarbuch der Griechischen Sprache. 4te Ausg. 4 Theile. 12mo. Jena. 1813—19.
——, ——. Specimen Emendationum in Auctores Veteres. 12mo. Gothæ. 1786.
——, ——. Observationes in Æliani Historiam Animalium et Philostrati Vitam Apollonii. 12mo. Jenæ. 1804.
——, ——. Animadversiones in Euripidis Tragœdias; et in Stobæum. 8vo. Gothæ. 1790.
——, ——. Curæ Secundæ in Euripidis Tragœdias. 8vo. Lips. 1796.
——, ——. Lectiones in Themistii Orationibus. Vide Dionysius Halicarnassensis.
——, ——. Ueber Gelebrte Gesellschaften, ihren Geist und Zweck. 4to. München. 1807.
——, ——. Ueber einen Vorzug der Griechischen Sprache in dem Gebrauche ihrer Mundarten. 4to. München. 1808.
——, ——. Additamenta Animadversionum in Athenæi Deipnosophistas. 8vo. Jenæ. 1809.
Jacobus, J. D. De Foro in Portis. (Ugol. vol. 25.)
——, ——. Acta Barnabæ et Pauli Lycaonica. 4to. Lips. 1714.
Jacomb, Geo. Account of the Proceedings of the Assembly at Exon. 8vo. Lond. 1719.
Jacomb, Tho. Sermon at the Funeral of the Rev. Richard Vines. 2d ed. 4to. Lond. 1656.
——, ——. Treatise of Holy Dedication. 8vo. Lond. 1668.
——, ——. Sermons on the Eighth Chapter of Romans. 4to. Lond. 1672.
Jacotius, Desiderius. De Philosophorum Doctrina. (Gronovius, vol. 10.)
Jacques, John. Ordination by meer Presbyters proved null and void. 8vo. Lond. 1707.
Jacquin, N. J. Selectarum Stirpium Americanarum Historia. fol. Vindobonæ. 1763.
——, ——. Idem. 8vo. Manhemii. 1788.
——, ——. Enumeratio Systematica Plantarum. 8vo. Lug. Bat. 1760.
——, ——. Observationes Botanicæ. fol. Vindobonæ. 1764.
Jadelot. Cours Complet d' Anatomie, peint et gravé en Couleurs Naturelles par M. A. E. Gautier d'Agoty, second fils; et expliqué par M. Jadelot. Partie 1. fol. Nancy. 1773.

ago, Richard. Poems. See Chalmers, A.
Jahn, F. L. Treatise on Gymnasticks, taken chiefly from the German of F. L. Jahn, by Charles Beck. 8vo. Northampton, Mass. 1828.
Jahn, Johann. Einleitung in die Göttlichen Bücher des Alten Bundes. 2 Theile. 8vo. Wien. 1802—3.
——, ———. Introductio ad Libros Sacros Veteris Fœderis in Epitomen redacta. ed. 2da. 8vo. Viennæ. 1814.
——, ———. Archæologia Biblica in Epitomen redacta. ed. 2da. 8vo. Viennæ. 1814.
——, ———. Enchiridion Hermeneuticæ Generalis Tabularum Veteris et Novi Fœderis. 8vo. Viennæ. 1812.
Jahnius, Gottlieb. De Retinendæ Confessionis Privatæ Necessitate. 4to. Vitemb. 1736.
Jahr, Fr. W. De Precibus Gentilium Expiatoriis. (Ugol. vol. 21.)
Jamaica, View of the Proceedings of the Assemblies of, for some Years past. 8vo. Lond. 1716.
———, Representation and Memorial of the Council of, to the Lords Commissioners of Trade and Plantations; with a Preface by Mr. Wood. 8vo. Lond. 1716.
———. Its Importance to Great Britain considered. 8vo.
———, State of, in relation to its Commerce, &c. 8vo. Lond. 1726.
———. See Assiento Trade.
———. Inquiry concerning the Trade, Commerce, and Policy of Jamaica. 4to. Lond. 1759.
———. Proceedings of the Governor and Assembly, in regard to the Maroon Negroes. 8vo. Lond. 1796.
———. Neu-Jahrs-Geschenk aus Jamaika. 12mo. Gottingen. 1780.
———, Privileges of the Island of, vindicated; with an Appendix, containing an Historical Account of the Establishment of the Colony. 8vo. Lond. 1766.
———. Acts of Assembly, from 1681, to 1737, inclusive. fol. Lond. 1738.
———. Acts of Assembly from 1681, to 1754, inclusive. fol. Lond. 1756.
———. Act for raising a Tax by the Poll. 4to. St. Jago de la Vega. 1792.
———. Act to oblige the several Inhabitants of this Island to provide themselves with a sufficient Number of White Men, &c. 4to. St. Jago de la Vega. 1792.
———, History of. See Long, E.,—Sloane, Sir H.
———. See Earthquakes.
Jamblichus. De Mysteriis; necnon Epistola Porphyrii ad Anebonem Ægyptium, Gr. et Lat.; cum Notis, a T. Gale. fol. Oxon. 1678.
————. De Vita Pythagorica; nec non Porphyrius de Vita Pythagoræ; item Anonymus de Vita Pythagoræ apud Photium; Gr. et Lat., cum Notis. 4to. Amst. 1707.
James I. Workes. fol. Lond. 1616.

James I. Truth brought to light by Time; or a Narrative of the First XIV Years of King James Reigne. 4to. Lond. 1651.

——–. Rex Platonicus. Vide Wake, I.

——–. Memorials and Letters relating to the History of Britain in his Reign. Vide Dalrymple, Sir David.

——–. His Majesties Speach in the Starre-Chamber. 4to. Lond. 1616.

——–. Conference with the Bishops. See Barlow, W.

——–, and Charles I, Annals of, from 1612 to 1642. fol. Lond. 1681.

James II. Reflections on his Majesty's Proclamation for a Toleration in Scotland; with the said Proclamation. 4to. 1687.

——–. Reflections on his Majesties Declaration for Liberty of Conscience. 4to. 1687.

——–. Layman's Opinion on the King's Declaration. 4to. Lond. 1687.

——–. Layman's Answer to the Layman's Opinion. 4to. Lond. 1687.

——–. Reasons why the Church of England, as well as Dissenters, should thank his Majesty, for his late Declaration. 4to. Lond. 1687.

——–. Answer to a Petition of the Archbishop of Canterbury and Six other Bishops to his Majesty, touching their not distributing the late Declaration. 4to. Lond. 1688.

——–. Address to the Archbishop of Canterbury and the Bishops upon account of their late Petition, by a Member of the Church of England. 4to. Lond. 1688.

——–. Answer to the late King James' Declaration. 4to. Lond. 1689.

——–. Relation of the Rejoicings in Rome for the Birth of the Prince of Wales. 4to. Lond. 1689.

——–. List of the Names of the Nobility and others attainted of Treason by an Act of the late King James's Pretended Parliament assembled in Dublin. 4to. Lond. 1690.

——–. Death and Dying-Words. (Somers, Tr. vol. 4.)

James, Edwin. Account of Major S. H. Long's Expedition to the Rocky Mountains in 1819—20. 2 vols. 8vo; with an Atlas, 4to. Phil. 1823.

James, E. P. Catalogue of Plants collected during a Journey to and from the Rocky Mountains, in 1820. (Amer. Phil. Tr. N. S. vol. 2.)

James, Robert. Treatise on Canine Madness. 8vo. Lond. 1760.

——, ——. Medicinal Dictionary. 3 vols. fol. Lond. 1743—5.

——, ——. Pharmacopœia Universalis. 3d ed. 8vo. Lond. 1764.

James, Thomas. Strange and Dangerous Voyage to discover a Northwest Passage into the South Sea. 4to. Lond. 1633.

James, Thomas. Bellum Papale, sive Concordia Discors, Sixti Quinti et Clementis Octavi, circa Hieronymianam Editionem. 12mo. Lond. 1678.

James, Thomas. History of the Herculean Straits. 2 vols. 4to. Lond. 1771.
James, Wm. Inquiry into the Merits of the Principal Naval Actions between Great Britain and the United States. 8vo. Halifax, N. S. 1816.
Jameson, Robert. System of Mineralogy. 2 vols. 8vo. Edin. 1804—5.
———, ———. The Same. 3 vols. 8vo. Edin. 1804—8.
———, ———. See Brewster, D.
Jameson, Wm. Fundamentals of the Hierarchy examined and disproved. 4to. Glasgow. 1697.
———, ——. Confutation of Sage's Principles of the Cyprianic Age. 4to. Edin. 1706.
Jamieson, John. Vindication of the Doctrine of Scripture concerning the Deity of Christ, in reply to Priestley. 2 vols. 8vo. Edin. 1794.
———, ——. Use of Sacred History; with Two Dissertations on Moses and the Pentateuch. 2 vols. 8vo. Edin. 1802.
———, ——. Etymological Dictionary of the Scottish Language, Abridged. 8vo. Edin. 1818.
Jane, Joseph. The Vulgar Notion of Imputed Righteousness shewn to be Groundless. 8vo. Bristol. 1766.
Jannotius, Donatus. Dialogus de Republica Venetorum, cum Notis N. Crassi. (Græv. Thes. Ital.)
Janson, Charles Wm. Stranger in America. 4to. Lond. 1807.
Janssonius ab Almeloveen, Theod. Dissertatio de Vitis Stephanorum. 12mo. Amst. 1683.
January Thirtieth, Discourse on Government and Religion, calculated for the Meridian of, by an Independent. 12mo. Lond.
——— ———, Reasons for Abrogating the Observation of. 12mo. Lond. 1715.
——— ———, Week's Preparation for Solemnizing. 12mo. Lond. 1718.
———, ———, Letter to a Clergyman relating to his Sermon on. 12mo. Lond. 1746.
Janus, Dan. Fr. De Vite Aurea Templi Hierosolymitani. (Ugol. vol. 11.)
Janus Etruscus. Elegiæ. Vide Poemata Italorum.
Janeway, James. Address to the Citizens of London after the Dreadful Fire of 1666; with a Relation of the Great Fire of Boston, N. E. in 1760. 12mo. Bost.
Jaquelein, the Marchioness de Laroche. Memoirs; from the French. 8vo. Phil. 1816.
Jarchi, Solomon Ben Isaac. Liber de Lege, seu Commentarius in Pentateuchum. fol. Erfordiæ.
Jardine, Alexander, (Major.) Letters from Barbary, France, Spain, Portugal, &c. 2 vols. 8vo. Lond. 1788.
Jardine, L. J. Letter respecting America. 8vo. Bath. 1795.
Jarrigius, Peter. The Jesuits upon the Scaffold.—The Calumnies of James Beaufes refuted. (Jesuits, Further Discovery of the Mystery of Jesuitisme.)

Jarvis, Samuel F. Discourse on the Religion of the Indians of North America. (New-York Hist. Coll. vol. 3.)

——, ———. Convention Sermon, on Regeneration. 8vo. Bost. 1822.

Jaubert, P. A. Elémens de la Grammaire Turke. 4to. Paris. 1823.

Jaume St.-Hilaire. Exposition des Familles Naturelles et de la Germination des Plantes. tome 1, partie 1; et tome 2. 8vo. Paris. 1805.

Jaupitre, Petrus. De Relatione Bonorum Operum ad Vitam Æternam. 4to. Sedani. 1664.

Jauregui, Juan de. Rimas. 4to. Sevilla. 1618.

———, ———. ———. 8vo. Madrid. 1786.

———, ———. Orfeo. 4to. Madrid. 1624.

———, ———. Farsalia. 2 vol. 8vo. Madrid. 1789.

Java, Alien Law of. 12mo. 1818.

Jay, G. M. le. Biblia Sacra Polyglotta. Vide Biblia Polyglotta.

Jay, James. Letter to the Governors of the College of New-York. 8vo. Lond. 1771.

Jay, John, (Gov.) See Federalist,—Harper,—Remembrancer,—Treaties.

Jean le Maingre, dit Boucicaut, Maréchal de France. Mémoires. (Mém. de France, vol. 6.)

Jean de Troye. Mémoires; autretment dits *La Chronique Scandaleuse.* (Mém. de France, vol. 13.)

Jebb, John. Thoughts on the Construction and Policy of Prisons, with Hints for their Improvement. 8vo. Bury St. Edmunds. 1785.

——, ——. Works, with his Life by J. Disney. 3 vols. 8vo. Lond. 1787.

——, ——. Account of Theological Lectures, now reading at Cambridge, &c. 2d ed. 4to. Camb. 1772.

Jefferson, Tho. (Pres.) Summary View of the Rights of British America. 2d ed. 8vo. Lond. 1774.

———, ———. Notes on Virginia. 8vo. 1782.

———, ———. The Same. 8vo. Lond. 1788.

———, ———. ———. 8vo. Phil. 1794.

———, ———. ———. 9th American edition. 12mo. Bost. 1802.

———, ———. Observations sur la Virginie, trad. de l'Anglois. 8vo. Paris. 1786.

———, ———. On the Discovery of certain Bones of a Quadruped of the Clawed Kind in Virginia. (Amer. Phil. Tr. vol. 4.)

———, ———. Description of a Mould-Board, &c. (Id. 4.)

———, ———. Reports and Messages to Congress. (U. States.)

———, ———. Life of Capt. M. Lewis. See Lewis, M.

———, ———, and A. Burr. Reflections on the Consequences which may ensue, should they have Equal Votes both from the Electors and States. 12mo. N. York. 1802.

Jeffery, John. Sermons and Tracts. 2 vols. 8vo. Lond. 1753.
Jeffery, Tho. True Grounds and Reasons of the Christian Religion. 8vo. Lond. 1725.
——, ——. Review of the Controversy between the Author of a Discourse on the Grounds and Reasons of the Christian Religion, and his Adversaries. 8vo. Lond. 1726.
——, ——. Sermon on the Divinity of Christ. 8vo. Lond. 1726.
Jefferys, Tho. History of the French Dominions in America. fol. Lond. 1760.
——, ——. Description of the Spanish Settlements on the Coast of the West Indies. 4to. Lond. 1762.
——, ——. The Same. 2d ed. 4to. Lond. 1774.
——, ——. Great Probability of a North West Passage. 4to. Lond. 1768.
——, ——. Voyages from Asia to America, &c. 2d ed. 4to. Lond. 1764.
——, ——. West Indian Atlas. fol. Lond. 1775.
——, ——. American Atlas. fol. Lond. 1776.
Jeffrey, Fr. Speech before the Fox Club. 8vo. Lond. 1824.
Jeffrey of Monmouth. British History, translated from the Latin by A. Thompson. 8vo. Lond. 1718.
—— ——. Historia Regum Britanniæ. Vide Rerum Britannicarum Scriptores.
Jeffries, John. Narrative of his Two Aerial Voyages. 4to. Lond. 1786.
Jehringius, J. C. De Regione Tarschisch. (Ugol. vol. 7.)
Jehudah, R. L. Liber Cosri continens Colloquium seu Disputationem de Religione, Hebr. et Lat., cum Notis et Dissertationibus, a J. Buxtorfio. 4to. Basil. 1660.
Jenichen, G. F. Historia et Examen Bullæ Anti-Quesnellianæ. 4to. Lips. 1714.
Jenkin, Robert. Reasonableness and Certainty of the Christian Religion. 2 vols. 8vo. Lond. 1698—1700.
——, ——. Historical Examination of the Authority of General Councils. 4to. Lond. 1688.
Jenkins, John. Art of Writing on a New Plan. 8vo. Andover. 1813.
Jenkinson, Anthony. Voyages into Russia, &c. (Hakluyt, vol. 1, and Eden and Willes.)
Jenks, B. Discourse upon Rom. x, 3. 4th ed. 12mo. Lond. 1755.
Jenks, Francis. Selection from the English Prose Works of John Milton; with a Preface. 2 vols. 12mo. Bost. 1826.
Jenks, Wm. Eulogy on the late Hon. James Bowdoin. 4to. Bost. 1812.
——, ——. Address to the American Antiquarian Society. 8vo. Bost. 1813.
Jennet, Jo. De Justitia per Christi Gratiam Fidelibus inhærente. 4to. Sedani. 1661.
Jennings, David. Sermon on Reformation of Manners. 8vo. Lond. 1737.

Jennings, David. Sermon at the Ordination of the Rev. John Jennings, with a Charge by P. Doddridge. 8vo. Lond. 1742.
———, ———. Jewish Antiquities, with a Dissertation on the Hebrew Language. 2 vols. 8vo. Lond. 1766.
———, ———. The Same. 2 vols. 8vo. Lond. 1823.
———, ———. Scripture Testimony Examined, in Two Discourses. 12mo. Lond. 1755.
———, ———. Sermons to Young People on New-Year's Days. 4th ed. 12mo. Lond. 1752.
———, ———. Abridgement of Samuel Mather's Life of Cotton Mather. 12mo. Lond. 1744.
———, ———, Introduction to the Knowledge of Medals. 8vo. Lond. 1764.
———, ———. On the Use of the Globes and the Orrery. 8vo. Lond. 1752.
Jennings, John. Two Discourses, on Preaching Christ and on Particular and Experimental Preaching. 8vo. Lond. 1723.
———, ———. The Same; with a Translation of Dr. A. H. Franck's Letter on Preaching. 3d ed. 12mo. Lond. 1736.
———, ———. The Same. 4th ed. 12mo. Bost. 1740.
Jenty, C. N. Course of Anatomico-Physiological Lectures. 3 vols. 8vo. Lond. 1757.
Jenyns, Soame. Works, with his Life by C. N. Cole, 4 vols. 12mo. Lond. 1790.
———, ———. Free Inquiry into the Nature and Origin of Evil. 4th ed. 12mo. Lond. 1761.
———, ———. View of the Internal Evidence of the Christian Religion. 12mo. Bost. 1793.
———, ———. The Same. See Christianity.
———, ———. Poems. See Chalmers, A.
Jeremiah. See Blayney,—Pareau,—Rossi.
Jeremias Philadelphus. De Valle Josaphati. (Ugol. vol. 7.)
Jérémie, M. Relation de la Baie de Hudson. Vide Recueil d'Arrests.
Jermin, Mich. Commentary on Ecclesiastes. fol. Lond. 1639.
Jerningham, Edw. Fall of Mexico. 4to. Lond. 1776.
Jerome, St. Vide Hieronymus, Sanctus.
Jerusalem, J. F. W. Betrachtungen über die vornehmsten Wahrheiten der Religion. 2 Theile. 8vo. Braunschweig. 1776—91.
Jervis, Sir John J. White. Refutation of M. M. de Montgaillard's Calumnies against British Policy, &c. 8vo. Lond. 1812.
Jervis, Thomas. Sermons. 8vo. Lond. 1811.
———, ———. Fast Sermon. 8vo. Lond. 1803.
———, ———. Fast Sermon. 8vo. Lond. 1810.
———, ———. Thanksgiving Sermon. 8vo. Lond. 1816.
———, ———. Sermon on the Death of the Rev. John Disney. 8vo. Lond. 1817.
———, ———. Sermon on the Death of the Princess Charlotte Augusta. 8vo. Lond. 1817.
———, ———. Speech intended to have been spoken at Leeds. 8vo. Leeds.

Jessop, Constant. The Angel of the Church of Ephesus no Bishop of Ephesus, &c. 4to. Lond. 1644.

Jesuits. Mysteria Patrum Jesuitarum. 18mo. Lamproli. 1633.

———. Further Discovery of the Mystery of Jesuitisme. 12mo. Lond. 1658.

———. La Morale des Jesuites. Vide Perrault, N.

———. The Moral Practice of the Jesuites, by the Doctors of the Sorbonne, rendered into English. 12mo. Lond. 1670.

———. La Morale Practique des Jesuites. 12mo. Cologne. 1669.

———. Lettre Annuelle du Japon de l'An 1603, escrite par Gabriel de Matos, transl. de l'Italien. 12mo. Douay. 1606.

———. Lettres, Annales des Royaumes du Japon, et de la Chine, escrites par Jean Rodriguez et Matthieu Ricci, trad. de l'Italien. 12mo. Paris. 1611.

———. Relation de ce qui s'est passé en la Nouvelle France en l'année 1637. 8vo. Rouen. 1638.

———. Relation de ce qui s'est passé de plus remarquable ès Missions des Peres de la Compagnie de Jesus en la Nouvelle France, ès années 1645 et 1646. 12mo. Paris. 1647.

———. Le Cabinet Jésuistique. 12mo. Cologne. 1682.

———. Imago Primi Sæculi Societatis Jesu, a Tollenario, Henschenio, et Bollando, etc. fol. Antv. 1640.

———. Account of the Behaviour of the Jesuites for the first Twenty-five Years of Queen Elizabeth's Reign. 4to. Lond. 1689.

———. Nouveaux Mémoires des Missions de la Compagnie de Jesus dans le Levant. 9 vol. 12mo. Paris. 1717—55.

———. Packet from Rome, respecting the Jesuits. 8vo. Lond. 1745.

———. Relaçaõ da Republica, que os Religiosos Jesuitas das Provincias de Portugal, e Hespanha, estabeleceraõ nos Dominios Ultramarinos das duas Monarchias. fol.

———. Erros Impios, e Sediciosos, que os Religiosos da Companhia de Jesus ensinaraõ aos Reos, etc. fol.

———. Sammlung der Neuesten Schrifften, welche die Jesuiten in Portugal betreffen. 4 Bände. 4to. Frankf. und Leipz. 1760—2.

———. Geschichte des Jesuiter Ordens. 2 Bände. 8vo. Berlin und Halle. 1769—70.

———. Delle Cose del Portogallo Rapporto a' PP. Gesuiti. 11 raccolte. 12mo. Lugano. 1760.

———. Raccolta d' Apologie della Dottrina, e Condotta de' PP. Gesuiti in risposta agli Opuscoli che escono contra la Compagnia di Gesù. 9 tom. Fossombrone. 1760.

———. Riflessioni di un Portoghese sopra il Memoriale presentato da' PP. Gesuiti alla Santità di PP. Clemente XIII. 12mo. Lugano. 1759.

———. Critica di un Romano alle Riflessioni del Portoghese, etc. 12mo. Lugano. 1759.

Jesuits. Appendice alle Riflessioni del Portoghese, etc. parte 2da. 12mo. Lugano. 1760.
——. Neue Nachrichten von den Missionen der Jesuiten in Paraguay, etc.; aus dem Spanischen. 12mo. Hamburg. 1768.
——. Auszug aus dem Criminal-Process wider die Jesuiten in Spanien. 12mo.
——. Analisi su i Contratti e la Capacità de Gesuiti. MS. 4to.
——. See Catalogue,—Documentos,—Fleming, C.,—Gazaignes,—Lettres Edifiantes,—Lignac,—Linguet,—Lockman,—Paraguay,—Ripert, &c.
Jesus. See Christ,—Messiah.
Jesu-Worship Confuted. 4to. Lond. 1660.
Jewell, John, (Bp.) Workes. fol. Lond. 1611.
——, ——. Apologia Ecclesiæ Anglicanæ. 16mo. Lond. 1606.
Jewett, Jed. Sermon at the Ordination of the Rev. D. Toppan. 8vo. Newburyport. 1774.
Jewett, J. R. Journal at Nootka Sound. 12mo. Bost. 1807.
Jews. Answer to "Considerations on the Bill for Naturalizing the Jews." 8vo. Lond. 1753.
——. Ninth Report of the Committee of the London Society for promoting Christianity among the Jews, &c.; with a Sermon by Lewis Way. 8vo. Lond. 1817.
——. Eleventh Report of the Same; with a Sermon by Edward Cooper. 8vo. Lond. 1819.
——. Mémoires sur l'Etat des Israélites. Vide Way, L.
——. See India.
Joannes Episcopus Chiemensis. Onus Ecclesiæ. fol. 1531.
Joannes Gerundensis Episcopus. Vide Margaritus.
Joannes. Vide Johannes.
Job. Liber Jobi, Hebr. et Lat., cum Commentario, ab A. Schultens. 2 vol. 4to. Lug. Bat. 1737.
——. Liber Jobi in Vers. Metr. divisus, Hebr. et Lat., cum Notis et Commentario, a R. Grey. 8vo. Lond. 1742.
——. Observationes Miscellaneæ in Librum Jobi, etc. 8vo. Amst. 1758.
——, Book of, in English Verse, with Remarks, by Thomas Scott. 2d ed. 8vo. Lond. 1773.
——, Essay towards a New Version of the Book of, &c. by T. Heath. 4to. Lond. 1756.
——. Hiob, aus dem Hebr. von M. H. Stuhlmann. 12mo. Hamb. 1804.
——. ——, übers. von J. C. W. Augusti und W. M. L. de Wette. 8vo. Heidelberg. 1809.
——. Il Libro di Giobbe, trad. da G. B. de Rossi. 12mo. Parma. 1812.
——, Book of, tr., with Notes, by Bishop Stock. 4to. Bath. 1805.
——, Amended Version of the Book of, with Notes, &c., by G. R. Noyes. 8vo. Camb. 1827.
——, Review of the History of. 8vo. Lond. 1771.
——. Vide Ilgen, C. D. Vide Meintel, J. G.

Jobert, L. La Science des Médailles Antiques et Modernes. 2 vol. 12mo. Paris. 1715.
——, —. Notitia Rei Nummariæ. 12mo. Lips. 1695.
——, —. Knowledge of Medals; from the French. 8vo. Lond. 1697.
Joblot, L. Sur les Microscopes. 4to. Paris. 1718.
Joel, Fr. Methodus Medendi. (Cordus, Dispensatorium.)
Johannes Abbas Burgi S. Petri. Chronicon Angliæ. (Sparke, Hist. Angl. Scriptores.)
Johannes de Fordun. Scotichronicon. Vide Hearne, T.
Johannes Glastoniensis. Chronica. Vide Hearne, T.
Johannes Prior Hagustaldensis. Simeonis Dunelmensis Historia continuata. (Twysden, Scriptores x.)
Johannes. Vide Joannes.
John, (Dr.) Account of Avyar, a Tamul Female Philosopher. (Asiatic Researches, vol. 7.)
John, Saint. Il Vangelo di nostro Signore Gesù Cristo, secondo San Giovanni; trad. in Lingua Italiana e Maltese, secondo la Volgata. 8vo. Londra. 1822.
——, ——, Gospel according to, in the Mohawk and English Languages. 16mo. Lond. See also Brant, J.
——, ——. See Revelation.
Johnson, Charles. History of the Pirates. 2d ed. 8vo. Lond. 1724.
———, ———. Histoire des Pirates Anglois. Vide Oexmelin, A. O.
Johnson, Edward. History of New-England, from the English Planting in the Yeere 1628, untill the Yeere 1652; or Wonder-working Providence of Sions Saviour. 4to. Lond. 1654.
———, ———. The Same. (Mass. Hist. Coll. vols. 2, 3, 4, 7, and 8. New Series.)
Johnson, George. British Penman. Lond.
Johnson, James. Influence of Tropical Climates on European Constitutions. 2d ed. 8vo. Lond. 1818.
———, ———. Influence of Civil Life, Sedentary Habits, and Intellectual Refinement on Human Health and Human Happiness. 8vo. Lond. 1818.
———, ———. On Derangements of the Liver, Digestive Organs, and Nervous System, &c. 2d ed. 8vo. Lond. 1818.
———, ———. On Gout. 8vo. Lond. 1819.
Johnson, John. Ecclesiastical Laws, Canons, &c. of the Church of England until the Reformation. 2 vols. 8vo. Lond. 1720.
———, ——. Clergyman's Vade-Mecum. 6th and 4th ed. 2 vols. 12mo. Lond. 1731.
Johnson, John B. Eulogy on Washington, a Sermon before the Legislature of New-York. 4to. Albany. 1800.
Johnson, (Mrs.) Narrative of her Captivity and Sufferings among the Indians. 12mo. Walpole, N. H. 1796.
Johnson, Richard. Grammatical Commentaries. 8vo. Lond. 1706.
Johnson, Samuel. Remarks on his Scripture-Doctrine of Christ's Divinity, with his Answers, &c. 8vo. Exon. 1729.
———, ———. Works. 2d ed. fol. Lond. 1713.

Johnson, Samuel. Reflections on the History of Passive Obedience. 4to. Lond. 1691.

———, ———. Julian the Apostate. 12mo. Lond. 1682.

———, ———. Constantius the Apostate, being an Answer to Julian the Apostate. 8vo. Lond. 1685.

———, ———. Purgatory proved by Miracles collected out of Roman Catholick Authors. 4to. Lond. 1688.

———, ———. Impossibility of Transubstantiation demonstrated. 2d ed. 4to. Lond. 1688.

Johnson, Samuel, (Pres.) English and Hebrew Grammar, &c. 8vo. Lond. 1767.

———, ——————. Noetica, or the First Principles of Metaphysics and Logic, &c. 8vo. Phil. 1752.

———, ——— ———. Ethica, or the First Principles of Moral Philosophy. 2d ed. 8vo. Lond. 1752.

———, ——————. Sermon on the Beauty of Holiness. 8vo. New-York. 1761.

Johnson, Samuel. Works; with his Life, &c. by Sir J. Hawkins. 14 vols. 8vo. Lond. 1787—8.

———, ———. Works; with an Essay on his Life and Genius, by A. Murphy. 12 vols. 8vo. Lond. 1801.

———, ———. The Same. 12 vols. 12mo. Lond. 1806.

———, ———, Letters to and from, &c., by Mrs. Piozzi. 2 vols. 8vo. Lond. 1778.

———, ———. Plan of a Dictionary of the English Language. 4to. Lond. 1747.

———, ———. Dictionary of the English Language. 2 vols. fol. Lond. 1755—6.

———, ———. The Same. 3d ed. 2 vols. fol. Lond. 1765.

———, ———. ————. 4th ed. 2 vols. fol. Lond. 1773.

———, ———. ————. 2 vols. 4to. Lond. 1786.

———, ———. ————. See Todd. See Worcester.

———, ———. Lives of the English Poets. 4 vols. 8vo. Lond. 1783.

———, ———. The Same. 2 vols. 8vo. Charlestown. 1810.

———, ———. Rambler. 4 vols. 12mo. Edin. 1798.

———, ———. Idler. 2 vols. 12mo. Lond. 1761.

———, ———. Lives of Savage, Drake, and Blake. 3d ed. 12mo. Lond. 1767.

———, ———. Life of the Earl of Rochester. 12mo. Lond. 1782.

———, ———. Remarks on his Life of Milton, &c. 12mo. Lond. 1780.

———, ———. His Life to his Eleventh Year, by himself, with Letters from Miss H. Boothby. 12mo. Lond. 1805.

———, ———. Sermon for the Funeral of his Wife. 8vo. Lond. 1788.

———, ———. Prayers and Meditations. 4th ed. 8vo. Lond. 1807.

———, ———. Poems. See Chalmers, A.

———, ———. False Alarm. 8vo. Lond. 1770.

Johnson, Samuel. Constitution defended, and Pensioner exposed, in Remarks on the False Alarm. 8vo. Lond. 1770.
———, ———. Letter to him on the False Alarm. 8vo. Lond. 1770.
———, ———. Thoughts on the late Transactions respecting Falkland's Islands. 2d ed. 8vo. Lond. 1771.
———, ———. Patriot to the Electors of Great Britain. 8vo. Lond. 1774.
———, ———. Taxation no Tyranny. 4th ed. 8vo. Lond. 1775.
———. ———. "Taxation no Tyranny" candidly considered. 8vo. Lond. See also Congress, Continental.
———, ———. Letter to him, occasioned by his late Political Publications, &c. 8vo. Lond. 1775.
———, ———, Life of. See Boswell,—Hawkins,—Murphy.
Johnson, Wm. Reports of Cases in the Supreme Court of New-York from 1799 to 1803. 3 vols. 8vo. N. York. 1808—12.
———, ——. Reports of Cases in the Supreme Court of New-York. 20 vols. 8vo. N. York and Albany. 1811—23.
Johnson, Wm. Sketches of the Life and Correspondence of Major General Greene. 2 vols. 4to. Charleston. 1822.
———, ——. Nugæ Georgicæ. 4to. Charleston. 1815.
———, ——. Eulogy on Thomas Jefferson. 8vo. Charleston. 1826.
Johnson. See Jonson.
Johnston, (Gov.) Speech on American Affairs. 12mo. Edin. 1776.
Johnston, George. Christianity Older than the Creation. 8vo. Lond. 1733.
Johnston, Robert. Travels through Part of the Russian Empire and the Country of Poland. 4to. Lond. 1815.
Johnston, Wm. Discourse on the Abolition of Death by Christ. 12mo. Lond. 1764.
Johnstone, Abraham, (a Black Man, hanged in New-Jersey.) Address to the People of Colour, &c. 8vo. Phil. 1797.
Johnstonus, Arturus. Psalmi Davidici, Latine, cum Notis. 4to. Lond. 1741.
Joinville. On the Religion and Manners of the People of Ceylon. (Asiatic Researches, vol. 7.)
Joinville, J. Mémoires; avec Observations sur les Mémoires, par Du Cange. (Mém. de France, vol. 1 et 2.)
Jolis, Giuseppe. Saggio sulla Storia Naturale del Chaco. 8vo. Faenza. 1789.
Joly, (M. de.) Pensées de l'Empereur Marc-Aurèle-Antonin, trad. du Grec. 24to. Paris. 1803.
Jonas, Arngrim. Historie of Island. (Purchas, vol. 3.)
Jonas, Runolphus. Grammaticæ Islandicæ Rudimenta. (Antiquæ Literaturæ Septentrionalis, etc. vol. 2.)
Joncourt. Entretiens sur les Differentes Méthodes d'expliquer l'Ecriture et de prêcher, de ceux qu'on appelle Cocceiens et Voetiens dans les Provinces Unies.—Justification de feu Mr. Cocceius contre les "Entretiens," &c. par son Fils. 12mo. Amst. 1707.

Jones, Daniel. Account of West-River Mountain, and the Appearance of there having been a Volcano in it. (Mem. A. A. S. vol. 1.)
Jones, David. Sermon on 1 Tim. vi, 17. 4to. Lond. 1690.
Jones, Hugh. Present State of Virginia. 8vo. Lond. 1724.
Jones, Jeremiah. Method of settling the Canonical Authority of the New Testament. 2 vols. 8vo. Lond. 1726—7.
——, ————. Vindication of the Former Part of St. Matthew's Gospel from Mr. Whiston's Charge of Dislocations. 8vo. Salop. 1721.
Jones, John. Illustrations of the Four Gospels. 8vo. Lond. 1808.
——, ——. Ecclesiastical Researches. 8vo. Lond. 1812.
——, ——. Sequel to Ecclesiastical Researches. 8vo. Lond. 1813.
——, ——. Grammar of the Greek Tongue. 2d ed. 12mo. Lond. 1808.
——, ——. The Same. 3d ed. 12mo. Lond. 1815.
Jones, John Paul. Mémoires, trad. de l'Anglois par André. 12mo. Paris. 1798.
——, ————. Paul-Jones, ou Prophéties sur l'Amérique, l'Angleterre, la France, l'Espagne, la Hollande, etc. par Paul-Jones, Corsaire, Prophète et Sorcier comme il n' en fût jamais. Y joint le Rêve d'un Suisse sur la Révolution de l'Amérique. 8vo. 1780.
——, ————, Life of. See Sherburne, J. H.
Jones, Jonathan. Defence of Religious Liberty. 8vo. Lond. 1729.
——, ————. Answer to the Above. See Smalbroke.
Jones, Rowland. Postcript to the Origin of Language and Nations. 8vo. Lond. 1767.
Jones, Samuel. Communications respecting De Witt Clinton's Discourse before the Historical Society, Spafford's Gazetter of New-York, Smith's History of New-York, &c. (New-York Hist. Coll. vol. 3.)
Jones, Stephen. History of Poland. 8vo. Lond. 1795.
Jones, Thomas. Fourth English Voyage to the East-Indies. (Purchas, vol. 1.)
Jones, Thomas. Sermon at the Opening of the Church of St. Botolph, Bishopsgate, 4to. Lond. 1755.
Jones, Wm. Catholic Doctrine of a Trinity proved. 3d ed. 8vo. and 12mo. Lond. 1767.
——, ——. Letter to a Young Gentleman intended for Holy Orders. 8vo. Lond. 1769.
——, ——. Full Answer to an Essay on Spirit. 8vo. Lond. 1753.
——, ——. The Same. 2d ed. 8vo. Lond. 1770.
——, ——. Remarks on the Confessional. 8vo. Lond. 1770.
——, ——. Three Dissertations on Life and Death. 8vo. Lond. 1771.
——, ——. Essay on the First Principles of Natural Philosophy. 4to. Oxford. 1762.
——, ——. Life of Bishop Horne. 8vo. Lond. 1795.

Jones, Wm. Method of Finding a true Meridian Line. 8vo. Lond. 1795.
——, ——. Catalogue of Instruments. 8vo.
Jones, Wm. On Leaden Cartridges. (Am. Phil. Tr. N. S. vol. 1.)
Jones, Sir Wm. Persian Grammar; with a Catalogue of the most valuable Books in the Persian Language. 5th ed. 4to. Lond. 1801.
——, ————. Poeseos Asiaticæ Commentarii. 8vo. Lond. 1774.
——, ————. Poems. See Chalmers, A.
——, ————. Works, with his Life by Lord Teignmouth. 13 vols. 8vo. Lond. 1807.
——, ————. On Bailments, by J. Balmanno. 8vo. Lond. 1798.
——, ————. Dissertation sur la Litérature Orientale. 8vo. Lond. 1771.
——, ————. Papers in the Asiatick Researches.
——, ————. Inquiry into the Legal Mode of Suppressing Riots. 8vo. Lond. 1780.
Jonnés, Moreau de. Précis Historique sur l'Irruption de la Fièvre Jaune à la Martinique, en 1802. 8vo.
Jonsius, Jo. De Scriptoribus Historiæ Philosophicæ. 4to. Jenæ. 1716.
Jonson, Ben. Works, with Notes by P. Whalley. 7 vols. 8vo. Lond. 1756.
——, ——. Poems. See Chalmers, A.
Jonstonus, Joh. De Festis Græcorum. (Gronovius, vol. 7.)
Jonstonus, Joh. Historia Naturalis. 4 vol. fol. Francof. ad Mœn. 1650—3.
——, ——. Histoire Naturelle, trad. du Latin. fol. Paris. 1773.
Joosten, J. De kleyne wonderlijcke Werelt. 4to. Amst. 1670.
Jordan, Edward. Trial of him and his Wife for Piracy and Murder. 12mo. Bost. 1809.
Jordanes seu Jornandes. Vide Jornandes.
Jorio, Andrea de. Scheletri Cumani Dilucidati. 8vo. Napoli. 1810.
——, ————. Sul Metodo degli Antichi nel dipingere i Vasi, etc. 8vo. Napoli. 1813.
Jornandes. De Regnorum Successione. Vide Rom. Hist. Script.
————. De Getarum, sive Gothorum Origine et Rebus Gestis. 8vo. Lug. Bat. 1697.
Jortin, John. Remarks on Ecclesiastical History. 5 vols. 8vo. Lond. 1751—73.
——, ——. Discourses concerning the Truth of the Christian Religion. 2d ed. 8vo. Lond. 1747.
——, ——. The Same. 3d ed. 8vo. Lond. 1752.
——, ——. Sermons. 7 vols. 8vo. Lond. 1771—2.
——, ——. ————. 3d ed. 7 vols. 8vo. Lond. 1787.
——, ——. Life of Erasmus. 2 vols. 4to. Lond. 1758.
——, ——. Six Dissertations upon Different Subjects. 2 vols. 8vo. Lond. 1755.

Jortin, John. Tracts Philological, Critical, and Miscellaneous. 2 vols. 8vo. Lond. 1790.
——, ——. Miscellaneous Observations upon Authors. 2 vols. 8vo. Lond. 1731—2.
Josef. Vie du Veritable Pere Josef, Capucin nommé au Cardinalat, contenant l'Histoire Anecdote du Cardinal de Richelieu. 12mo. La Haye. 1705.
Josephus Ben Gorion. Historia Judaica, Hebr. et Lat. 4to. Basil. 1541.
Josephus, Flavius. Opera. Princeps Editio. fol. Basil. 1544.
——, ——. ——. Gr. et Lat. fol. Aureliæ Allob. 1611.
——, ——. ——. Gr. et Lat., cum Notis, a J. Hudsono. 2 vol. fol. Oxon. 1720.
——, ——. ——. Gr. et Lat. 2 vol. fol. Amst., etc. 1726.
——, ——. Dell' Antichità de' Giudei, trad. per Fr. Baldelli. 4to. Vinegia. 1583.
——, ——. Works, translated from the Latin and French, by T. Lodge. fol. Lond. 1609.
——, ——. Works, translated from the Greek, with Dissertations, by William Whiston. 2 vols. fol. Lond. 1737.
——, ——. The Same. 6 vols. 12mo. Worcester. 1794.
——, ——. ————. 7 vols. 12mo. N. York. 1815.
——, ——. Works, translated by J. Court; with C. Noldius's History of Herod the Great, &c. fol. Lond. 1755.
——, ——. De Vita sua Liber, Gr., cum Notis H. P. C. Henke. 12mo. Brunovici. 1786.
——, ——. See Forster, N.
Josephus, (Vet. Christ. Scriptor.) Hypomnesticon, Gr. et Lat., cum Notis, a J. A. Fabricio. 12mo. Hamb. 1733.
Josse, A. L. Grammar of the Spanish Language. 2d American edition, by F. Sales. 12mo. Bost. 1825.
——, ——. The Same. 3d Amer. ed. 12mo. Bost. 1827.
Josselyn, John. New-Englands Rarities Discovered. 12mo. Lond. 1672.
——, ——. Account of Two Voyages to New-England.—Chronological Observations of America. 2d ed. 12mo. Lond. 1674—7.
Joubertus, Laurentius. De Gymnasiïs, etc. apud Antiquos.—De Balneis Antiquorum. (Sallengre, vol. 1.)
Jourdan, Adr. Descriptio Africæ et Americæ. MSS. 4to.
Journal of the Academy of Natural Sciences of Philadelphia. See Academy.
——, American, of Science and Arts. See Silliman, B.
——, Boston, of Philosophy and the Arts, by J. W. Webster, J. Ware, and D. Treadwell. 3 vols. 8vo. Bost. 1824—6.
——, Classical. 37 vols. 8vo. Lond. 1810—28.
—— de Commerce. 13 nos. 12mo. Bruxelles. 1760—2.
—— Encyclopédique. 48 vol. 1775—80, et 3 vol. 1781. 12mo. Bouillon.

Journal Général de la Littérature de France. (vol. 21 et 22.) 2 vol. 8vo. Paris. 1818—19.

——— ——————— Etrangère. (vol. 18 et 19.) 2 vol. 8vo. Paris. 1818—19.

———, London Medical and Physical. See London.

——— of Natural Philosophy, Chemistry, and the Arts. See Nicholson, W.

———, New-England, of Medicine and Surgery, &c. (vols. 1—7.) 7 vols. 8vo. Bost. 1812—18.

——— des Mines, publié par l'Agence des Mines de la République. Nos. 1—6. 8vo. Paris. 1795.

——— de Physique, de Chimie, et d'Histoire Naturelle. Vide Delamétherie, J. C.

——— Polytechnique. (tom. 1—3.) 4 vol. 4to. Paris. 1795—1800.

——— des Sçavans, par le Sieur de Hédouville (Sallo), Gallois, de la Roque, etc. depuis 1665 jusqu' à 1728. 89 vol., et 1733, 3 vol. 18mo. Amst. 1685—1733.

———, Quarterly, of Science, Literature, and the Arts, edited at the Royal Institution of Great Britain. (vols. 1—22.) 22 vols. 8vo. N. York and Lond. 1817—27.

———. The Same. New Series. (1—3.) 3 vols. 8vo. Lond. 1827—8.

———. See Academy,—Zeitschrift,—Zoological Journal,—Bulletin,—Review, &c.

——— d'un Voyage sur les Côtes d'Afrique et aux Indes d'Espagne, en 1702—6. 12mo. Paris. 1737.

——— d'un Voyage à la Louisiane, fait en 1720. 12mo. La Haye. 1768.

——— of the Expedition to La Guira and Porto Cavallos in the West Indies, under the Command of Commodore Knolles. 8vo. Lond. 1744.

———, Historical, of the American War. 8vo. Bost. 1793. See also Massachusetts Hist. Coll. vol. 2.

——— of a Young Man of Massachusetts in Dartmoor Prison, &c. containing an Account of the Massacre there. 12mo. Bost. 1816.

———, Maryland; 1783—93. fol. Baltimore.

———, Pennsylvania, and Weekly Advertiser; 1761—3, and 1765—9. fol. Phil.

——— of the Committee of the States from June 4, to August 13, 1784. 8vo.

———. See Colonial Journal,—Congress,—Diurnall,—Gazette,—Massachusetts,—Tagebuch,—United States, &c.

Journey, Short, in the West Indies. 2 vols. 12mo. Lond. 1790.

Joutel. Journal Historique du Dernier Voyage que feu M. de la Sale fit dans le Golfe de Mexique, etc. 12mo. Paris. 1713.

———. Journal of M. de la Sale's Last Voyage to the Gulf of Mexico, &c.; from the French. 8vo. Lond. 1714.

Jouy. Paris Spectator, translated from the French by W. Jerdan. 3 vols. 18mo. Phil. 1816.

Jovellanos, G. M. de. Informe de la Sociedad Económica. 4to. Madrid. 1795.

Jovius, Benedictus. Historiæ Patriæ, sive Novocomensis, Libri Duo. (Græv. Thes. Ital.)
Jovius, Paulus. Vitæ Duodecim Vicecomitum, Mediolani Principum. (Græv. Thes. Ital.)
——, ——. Larii Lacus Descriptio. (Id.)
——, ——. De Romanis Piscibus. (Sallengre, vol. 1.)
——, ——. Historiæ sui Temporis. 2 vol. fol. Florentiæ. 1550—2.
——, ——. Illustrium Virorum Elogia. fol. Florentiæ. 1551.
——, ——. Le Vite di Dicenove Huomini Illustri. 4to. Venetia. 1561.
——, ——. Le Iscrittioni poste sotto le vere Imagini de gli Huomini Famosi, trad. di Latino da H. Orio. 4to. Fiorenza. 1552.
Jowett, Wm. Christian Researches in Syria and the Holy Land, in 1823—4. 12mo. Bost. 1826.
Joyce, John, alias Davis, executed for Murder, Confession of. 8vo. Phil. 1808.
Juan, Don, I. Cronica. Vide Ayala.
Juan, Don, II. Cronica. fol. Logroño. 1517.
Juan de la Cruz. Obras Espirituales. fol. Sevilla. 1703.
Juan, Jorge, y Antonio de Ulloa. Relacion de Viage à la America Meridional. 4to. Madrid. 1748.
Judas. Epistola, Gr. Commentario Crit. et Annotatione Perpet. illustrata, a H. C. A. Haenlein. 8vo. Erlangæ. 1804.
Judiciary, Debates in the Senate of the United States on the. 8vo. Phil. 1802.
Juenin, Gaspar. Institutiones Theologicæ. 2 vol. fol. Lugduni. 1736.
Jugler, Jo. Henr. Elogium Jo. Friderici Jugler. 8vo. Helmst. 1792.
Julian, Antonio. La Perla de la America, Provincia de Santa Marta, etc. 4to. Madrid. 1788.
Julianus Imperator. Opera Omnia, Gr. et Lat., a P. Martinio, etc. 8vo. Paris. 1583.
—— ——. In Constantii Laudem Oratio, Gr. et Lat., cum Animadversionibus et Epistola Critica Wyttenbachii, etc., a G. H. Schæfero.
—— ——. Les Césars, trad. du Grec par Spanheim, avec des Remarques, etc. 4to. Paris. 1683.
—— ——. Idem. 4to. Amst. 1728.
—— ——. Account of his Life. See Johnson, S.
Julius, F. A. Beschreibung einiger Nordamericanischen Holz- und Buscharten. 12mo. Göttingen. 1781.
Juncker, G. J. Conspectus Pathologiæ. 4to. Halæ Magd. 1736.
——, ——. Conspectus Chirurgiæ. 4to. Halæ. 1731.
——, ——. Conspectus Therapiæ. 4to. Halæ Magd. 1725.
——, ——. Conspectus Chemiæ. 2 vol. 4to. Halæ Magd. 1730—8.
——, ——. Conspectus Medicinæ. 4to. Halæ. 1734.
——, ——. Conspectus Physiologiæ. 4to. Halæ Magd. 1735.

Jung, J. P. De Obligatione Evangelicorum Ministrorum Prædicandi Evangelium per Terras Infidelium. 4to. Argent. 1699.
Jüngken, Joh. H. Grund-Reguln der Medicin. 2 Bände. 12mo. Franck. und Leipz. 1701—3.
Junius, Letters of. 2 vols. 12mo. Lond. 1772.
——, ———. 2 vols. 8vo. Lond. 1797.
——, ———, with a Preliminary Essay, &c. by George Woodfall. 2 vols. 8vo. Phil. 1813.
Junius Americanus, Letters of, displaying the Treachery and Tyranny of Administration. 8vo. Lond. 1770.
Junius, Hadrianus. De Annis et Mensibus.—Fastorum Liber. (Græviua, vol. 8.)
——, ———. Lexicon Græco-Latinum. fol. Basil. 1557.
Junius, Franciscus. Opera Theologica. 2 vol. fol. Genevæ. 1613.
——, ———. Grammatica Hebrææ Linguæ. ed. 3tia. 8vo. Genevæ. 1696.
Junius, Franciscus, (F. F.) Glossarium Gothicum. Vide Evangelia.
——, ———. Etymologicon Anglicanum, ab E. Lye; cum Vita Auctoris, et Gram. Anglo-Sax. fol. Oxon. 1743.
——, ———. De Pictura Veterum. fol. Roterodami. 1694.
——, ———. Catalogus Architectorum, Mechanicorum, sed præcipue Pictorum, Statuariorum, etc. fol. Roterodami. 1694.
Jurieu, P. La Politique du Clergé de France, avec les Derniers Efforts de l'Innocence Affligée. 18mo. Amst. 1682.
Jurin, James. Comparison between the Mortality of the Natural Small Pox and that by Inoculation. 8vo. Lond. 1723.
——, ———. Account of the Success of Inoculating the Small Pox in Great Britain. 8vo. Lond. 1724.
——, ———. Account of the Success of Inoculating the Small Pox in Great Britain, for the year 1724. 8vo. Lond. 1725.
Jurine, L. Nouvelle Méthode de classer les Hyménoptères et les Diptères. 4to. Genève. 1807.
——, —. Mémoires dans les Annales du Muséum d'Histoire Naturelle.
Jurisprudence, American, being a few Reflections suggested by "Wheaton on Captures." 8vo. Washington.
Jussieu, Ant. de. Genera Plantarum. 8vo. Paris. 1789.
——, ———. Mémoires dans les Annales du Muséum d'Histoire Naturelle.
Justamond, J. O. Private Life of Louis XV, translated from the French by J. O. Justamond. 4 vols. 8vo. Lond. 1781.
Justice. Treatise on Distributive Justice, chiefly confined to the Consideration of Will Making. 8vo. Lond. 1751.
———. Observations on a late Publication, intituled, "Thoughts on Executive Justice," &c. 12mo. Lond. 1786.
Justice of the Peace. New Survey of the Justice of Peace his Office, by W. S. 12mo. Lond. 1659.

Justice, Alexander. General Treatise of Monies and Exchanges. 4to. Lond. 1707.

Justinianus, Bern. De Venetiis; item de Marci Evangelistæ Vita, ejus Translatione, et Sepulturæ Loco. (Græv. Thes. Ital.)

Justinianus Imperator. Institutionum Libri iv, a F. A. Biener. 8vo. Berol. 1812.

———, ———. The Four Books of Justinian's Institutions, English and Latin, with Notes, by George Harris. 2d ed. 4to. Lond. 1761.

———, ———. Vide Corpus Juris Civilis.

Justinus. De Historiis Philippicis, et Totius Mundi Originibus, cum Notis, etc. in usum Delphini. 4to. Paris. 1677.

———. Historia, cum Notis Minellianis. 12mo. Lips. 1732.

———. Historiæ Philippicæ, cum Versione Anglica, a J. Clarke. ed. 5ta. 8vo. Lond. 1759.

———. Historiæ. Vide Rom. Hist. Scriptores.

Justinus Martyr. Opera;—necnon Tatiani adversus Græcos Oratio; Athenagoræ Legatio pro Christianis; S. Theophili Tres ad Autolychum Libri; Hermiæ Irrisio Philosophorum, etc.; Gr. et Lat., cum Notis; opera Unius ex Monachis S. Mauri. fol. Paris. 1742.

——— ———. Apologiæ Duæ, et Dialogus cum Tryphone Judæo, cum Notis S. Thirlbii. fol. Lond. 1722.

——— ———. Apologies. See Reeves, W.

Justus, Theocrytus. In Apocalypsin Prolegomena. 4to. 1627:

Juvenalis, D. Junius. Satyræ, cum Scholiis Vet., et Commentariis Variorum, ab H. C. Henninio. 4to. Ultrajecti. 1685.

———, ———. Satiræ xvi, cum Commentario, a G. A. Ruperti. 2 vol. 8vo. Lips. 1801.

———, ———. Satires, translated into English Verse, with Notes, by Wm. Gifford. 4to. Lond. 1802.

———, ———. Satire Scelte ridotte in Versi Italiani ed illustrate da M. Cesarotti. 12mo. Parigi. 1805.

———, ———, et A. Persius Flaccus. Satyræ, cum Commentario E. Lubini. 8vo. Hanov. 1619.

———, ———————. Satyræ, cum Notis, etc., a L. Prateo, in usum Delphini. 4to. Paris. 1684.

———, ———————. Idem. 8vo. Lond. 1810.

———, ———————. ———. 8vo. Phil. 1814.

———, ———————. Satyræ, cum Vet. Scholiastæ et Variorum Commentariis. 8vo. Amst. 1684.

———, ———————. Satyræ, cum Scholiis Vet. et Commentariis Variorum, cura M. Casauboni. 4to. Lug. Bat. 1695.

———, ———————. Satyræ Expurgatæ. Accedunt Notæ Anglicæ, in usum Scholæ Bostoniensis, cura F. P. Leverett. 12mo. Bost. 1828.

———, ———————. Vide Collectio Pisaurensis,—Corpus Poetarum Latinorum,—Horatius.

Juvenalis, D. Junius, et A. Persius Flaccus. New and Literal Translation of Juvenal and Persius, with Notes, and the Latin Text, by M. Madan. 2 vols. 8vo. Lond. 1789.
Juvenis, Joannes. De Antiquitate et Varia Tarentinorum Fortuna. fol. Neapoli. 1589.
———, —. Idem. (Græv. Thes. Ital.)
Juventud Triunfante. Vide Isla.

K

Kæmpfer, Engelb. Amœnitates Exoticæ. 4to. Lemgoviæ. 1712.
———, ———. History of Japan, &c. translated from the High Dutch by J. G. Scheuchzer. 2 vols. fol. Lond. 1727—8.
———, ———. Histoire du Japon, trad. en François sur la Version Angloise de Scheuchzer. 3 vol. 12mo. Amst. 1732.
———, ———. Icones Selectæ Plantarum Japonicarum. fol. Lond. 1791.
Kahl, alias Calvinus, Johannes. Magnum Lexicon Juridicum. 2 vol. Coloniæ Allob. 1734.
Kahnert, Andreas. De Resurrectione Impiorum. 4to. Regiomonti. 1704.
Kaimes. See Kames.
Kaiser, G. P. C. Biblische Theologie. 8vo. Erlangen. 1813.
Kalendar. Longworth's Pocket Almanack, and New-York and United States Kalendar. 18mo. N. York. 1816.
———. Historisch-genealogischer Calender, 1784. 18mo. Leipz.
———. Almanac Américain pour l'Année 1802. 12mo. Phil.
———. Calendrier de la Cour, 1812. 24to. Paris.
———. Calendario para las Islas Baleares, 1817, 1821. 12mo. Palma.
———. See Almanac,—Pocket Almanack,—Register, &c.
Kalendarium Vetus Romanum, e Marmore descriptum in Ædibus Maffæorum ad Agrippinam, in Tabula Marmorea, superne fracta. —Kalendarii Fragmentum, quod visitur in Ædibus Capranicorum.—Aliud Vetus Kalendarium, quod in Libris Antiquis præfigitur Fastis Ovidii.—Kalendarium Romanum sub Imp. Constantio, circa Annum Christi CCCLIV compositum, etc. (Græv. vol. 8.)
Kalm, Peter. Beschreibung der Reise nach dem Nördlichen Amerika. 3 Theile. 8vo. Göttingen. 1754.
———, ———. Travels in North America, translated by J. R. Foster. 3 vols. 8vo. Warrington. 1770.
———, ———. The Same. 2d ed. 2 vols. 8vo. Lond. 1772.
———, ———. Account of the Cataracts at Niagara. 8vo. Lond. 1751.
Kals, J. G. Grammatica Hebræo-Harmonica, cum Arabica et Aramæa, etc. 8vo. Amst. 1758.
Kames, Henry Home, Lord. Elements of Criticism. 2d ed. 3 vols. 8vo. Edin. 1763.

Kames, Henry Home, Lord. The Same. 3d ed. 2 vols. 8vo. Edin. 1765.
——, ————. ————. 6th ed. 2 vols. 8vo. Edin. 1785.
——, ————. ————. 2 vols. 8vo. Bost. 1796.
——, ————. Introduction to the Art of Thinking. 2d ed. 12mo. Edin. 1764.
——, ————. Sketches of the History of Man. 4 vols. 8vo. Edin. 1778.
——, ————. Essays on the Principles of Morality and Natural Religion. 8vo. Edin. 1751.
——, ————. Principles of Equity. fol. Edin. 1760.
——, ————. Historical Law Tracts. 2d ed. 8vo. Edin. 1761.
——, ————. The Same. 8vo. Edin. 1769.
——, ————. Loose Hints upon Education. 8vo. Edin. 1781.
Kampen, N. G. van. Medea, naar het Grieksch van Euripides. 8vo. Haarlem. 1811.
Kant, Immanuel. Critik der reinen Vernunst. 3te Aufl. 8vo. Riga. 1790.
——, ————. Critik der practischen Vernunst. 2te Aufl. 8vo. Riga. 1792.
——, ————. Critik der Urtheilskraft. 2te Aufl. 8vo. Berlin. 1793.
——, ————. Grundelung zur Metaphysik der Sitten. 3te Aufl. 8vo. Riga. 1792.
——, ————. Anthropologie in pragmatischer Hinsicht. 8vo. Königs. 1798.
——, ————. Elements of the Critical Philosophy; with Three Philological Essays of J. C. Adelung; translated from the German by A. F. M. Willich. 8vo. Lond. 1798.
——, ————. Die Religion innerhalb der Grenzen der blossen Vernunst. 2te Aufl. 8vo. Königs. 1794.
——, ————. Annotationes quædam Theologicæ ad philosophicam Kantii de Religione Doctrinam. 4to. Tubingæ. 1793.
——, ————. Vide Schmidt-Phiseldek.
Kapff, J. M. De Terrenis Christo Posthabendis. 4to. Tubingæ. 1718.
Karæorum Institutio. (Ugol. vol. 22.)
Karæus, Aaron. Excerpta in Librum Josuæ. (Ugol. vol. 22.)
Karjavine, Phéodore. Remarques sur la Langue Russienne. 8vo. St. Petersbourg. 1791.
Karo, Rabbi Joseph. Annuncians Recta; Interpretationes in Sacrum Codicem. 4to. Amst. 1708.
Karsten, D. J. G. Museum Leskianum. 8vo. Dublin. 1798.
Kastner, C. W. G. Einleitung in die Neuere Chemie. 8vo. Halle und Berlin. 1814.
Kater, Henry. Description of a very sensible Hygrometer. (Asiatic Researches, vol. 9.)

Kavina, P. M. Descriptio Faventiæ. (Græv. Thes. Ital.)
Keach, Benjamin. Glorious Lover, a Divine Poem on Man's Redemption. 3d ed. 12mo. Lond. 1764.
Kearsley, George. Peerage of England, Scotland, and Ireland. 16mo. 1799.
Keate, George. Account of the Republic of Genova. 8vo. Lond. 1761.
Keating, Theodore. Review of a "Review of Dr. Freeman's Sermons," &c. 8vo. Camb. 1821.
Keating, W. H. Considerations on the Art of Mining. 8vo. Phil. 1821.
Keble, Joseph. Statutes at Large. fol. Lond. 1684.
Keckermannus, Bart. Systema Logicæ Minus. 8vo. Hanov. 1606.
——————, ——. Systema Systematum, exhibens Omnia ejus Scripta Philosophica. 4to. Hanov. 1613.
——————, ——. Systema Physicum. 8vo. Hanov. 1623.
Keeling, Bartholomew. Three Discourses on Rom. ix, 3. 8vo. Oxford. 1766.
Keeling, William. Third Voyage of the English to the East-Indies. (Purchas, vol. 1.)
Keene, Edmund, (Bp.) Sermon before the Society for promoting Protestant Working Schools in Ireland. 4to. Lond. 1755.
Keep, John. Sermon before the Domestic Missionary Society. 8vo. Northampton. 1818.
Keill, Jacobus. Tentamina Medico-Physica de Œconomia Animali;—item Medicina Statica Britannica. 8vo. Lond. 1718.
——, ———. Vide Sanctorius.
——, ———. Anatomy of the Human Body Abridged. 9th ed. 12mo. Lond. 1734.
——, ———. The Same. 13th ed. 12mo. Edin. 1760.
——, ———. ———. 15th ed. 12mo. Lond. 1771.
Keill, Jo. Introductio ad Veram Physicam. ed. 4ta. 8vo. Lond. 1719.
——, —. Introduction to Natural Philosophy; from the Latin. 4th ed. 8vo. Lond. 1745.
——, —. The Same. 5th ed. 8vo. Lond. 1758.
——, —. Examination of Burnet's Theory of the Earth, &c. 2d ed; with a Dissertation on the Different Figures of the Celestial Bodies, &c. by M. de Maupertuis. 8vo. Lond. 1734.
——, —. Introduction to the True Astronomy. 6th ed. 8vo. Lond. 1778.
——, —. De Logarithmis. Vide Horsley.
——, —. On the Nature of Logarithms, &c. See Cunn, S.
Keith, George. Immediate Revelation Not Ceased. 2d ed. 8vo. 1676.
——, ———. Protestant Religion maintained, &c. against the Calumnies of one George Keith, a Quaker; by the Ministers of the Gospel in Boston. 16mo. Bost. 1690.
——, ———. See Willard, S.
——, ———, Vindication of the Apostolick and Primitive Manner of Baptizing by Immersion, in a Letter to. 4to. Lond. 1700.

Keith, George. Journal of Travels from New-Hampshire to Caratuck in North America. 4to. Lond. 1706.
Keith, Isaac S. Sermon on the Death of Washington. 8vo. Charleston. 1800.
Keith, James. Evidences of the Divinity of Jesus Christ briefly stated, in Three Sermons. 12mo. Calcutta. 1822.
Keith, Tho. Practical Arithmetician. 2d ed. 12mo. Lond. 1798.
Keith, Sir Wm. History of the British Plantations in America. Part 1. Virginia. 4to. Lond. 1738.
——, ———. Collection of Papers and Tracts. 2d ed. 12mo. Lond. 1749.
——, ———, and Others. Two Papers on the Subject of Taxing the British Colonies in America. 8vo. Lond. 1767.
Kelham, Robert. Dictionary of the Norman, or Old French, Language, &c. 8vo. Lond. 1779.
Kellogg, Elijah. Oration at the Interment of the Rev. Thomas Smith. 8vo. Portland. 1795.
Kelly, Christopher. History of the French Revolution and of the subsequent Wars. 2 vols. 4to. Lond. 1818.
Kelsey, Joseph. Christ Crucified, a Sermon. 4to. Lond. 1691.
Kelyng, Sir John. Reports in Pleas of the Crown. fol. Lond. 1708.
Kemeys, J. G. Reflections occasioned by the late additional Duties on Sugars and on Rum. 8vo. Lond. 1783.
Kemp, Didericus van der. Disputatio Hist. Crit. pro Cornelio Centurione et Sergio Paullo Proconsule in Julianum Imperatorem ad illustr. Act x, 1, et xiii, 7. (Oelrichs, Coll. Opusc.)
Kemp, Fr. Adr. van der. Oration on the Emancipation of the Dutch from the French Tyranny. 8vo. Utica. 1814.
——, ————————. Wreath for the Rev. Daniel Dow. 8vo. Utica. 1806.
——, ————————. Historical Sketches on Calvin and Servetus. MS. 4to.
Kemp, John. Sermon before the Society in Scotland for propagating Christian Knowledge. 8vo. Edin. 1788.
——, ——. Sermon before the Same. 8vo. Edin. 1802.
Kempis, Thomas à. De Imitatione Christi, ex recensione J. M. Horstii. 12mo. Coloniæ. 1675.
Kempius, Johannes. Vide Ainsworth, R.
Kendall, E. A. Travels through the Northern Parts of the United States in 1807—8. 3 vols. 8vo. N. York. 1809.
Kendall, James. Artillery Election Sermon. 8vo. Bost. 1806.
———, ——. Sermon on the Death of Dr. Tappan. 8vo. Bost. 1803.
Kendal, Samuel. Sermon at the Ordination of the Rev. T. M. Harris. 8vo. Bost. 1794.
———, ———. Election Sermon. 8vo. Bost. 1804.
———, ———. Century Sermon at Weston. 8vo. Camb. 1813.
Kennedy, John. New Method of Stating and Explaining the Scripture Chronology. 8vo. Lond. 1751.

Kennett, Basil. Antiquities of Rome. 6th ed. 8vo. Lond. 1717.
———, ———. The Same. 11th ed. 8vo. Lond. 1746.
———, ———. ———. 13th ed. 8vo. Lond. 1763.
———, ———. ———. 14th ed. 8vo. Lond. 1769.
———, ———. Sermons to a Society of British Merchants. 8vo. Lond. 1715.
———, ———. Brief Exposition of the Apostles Creed, according to Bishop Pearson. 8vo. Lond. 1705.
———, ———. Lives and Characters of the Ancient Grecian Poets. 8vo. Lond. 1697.
———, ———. The Same. 2d ed. 8vo. Lond. 1735.
Kennet, White, (Bp.) History of England to the Death of King William III. 3 vols. fol. Lond. 1706.
———, ———. The Same. 2d ed. 3 vols. fol. Lond. 1719.
———, ———. Historical Register of English Affairs before and after the Restoration of Charles II. fol. Lond. 1744.
———, ———. Bibliothecæ Americanæ Primordia. 4to. Lond. 1713.
———, ———. Letter concerning Bishop Merks. 4th ed. 8vo. Lond. 1717.
———, ———. Second Letter concerning Bishop Merks. 2d ed. 8vo. Lond. 1716.
———, ———. Third Letter concerning Bishop Merks. 8vo. Lond. 1717.
———, ———. Character of King James II. 4to. Lond. 1706.
———, ———, Life of. 8vo. Lond. 1730.
———, ———. Address of Thanks to a Good Prince, presented in the Panegyrick of Pliny upon Trajan. 8vo. Lond. 1686.
———, ———. Sermon recommending Charity Schools. 4to. Lond. 1706.
———, ———. Spittal Sermon. 8vo. Lond. 1714.
———, ———. Spital Sermon. 8vo. Lond. 1719.
———, ———. Witchcraft of the Present Rebellion, a Sermon. 8vo. Lond. 1715.
———, ———. Thanksgiving Sermon for the Suppression of the Rebellion. 8vo. Lond. 1716.
———, ———. Advices to the Clergy of the Diocese of Peterborough. 4to. Lond. 1720.
———, ———. Thanksgiving Sermon for a Victory. 8vo. Lond. 1709.
———, ———. Sermon at the Funeral of William, Duke of Devonshire. 12mo. Lond. 1707.
———, ———. Sermon, Nov. 5th. 2d ed. 4to. Lond. 1715.
———, ———. Sermon, Nov. 5th. 4to. Lond. 1729.
———, ———. Sermon, January 31. 2d ed. 4to. Lond. 1704.
———, ———. Answers to the above Sermon, Jan. 31; and Defences of it. 4to. Lond. 1704.

Kennett, White, (Bp.) Sermon, January 30th. 8vo, and 4to. Lond. 1706.
———, —————. Sermon, January 30th. 8vo. Lond. 1708.
———, —————. Sermon, January 30th. 8vo. Lond. 1720.
Kennicott, Benjamin. State of the Printed Hebrew Text of the Old Testament considered. 2 vols. 8vo. Oxford. 1753—9.
————, ————. State of the Collation of the Hebrew Manuscripts of the Old Testament at the End of the Year 1761. 8vo. Oxford.
————, ————. The Same at the End of the Fourth Year, 1763. 8vo. Oxford.
————, ————. Ten Annual Accounts of the Collation of Hebrew MSS. of the Old Testament, begun in 1760, and compleated in 1769. 8vo. Oxford. 1770.
————, ————, Letters to, respecting his Collation of Hebrew MSS; from the French. 12mo. Paris. 1772.
————, ————. Answer to a Letter from the Rev. T. Rutherforth. 8vo. Lond. 1762.
————, ————. Dissertatio Generalis in Vet. Testamentum Hebraicum, cum Notis, a P. J. Bruns. 8vo. Brunovici. 1783.
————, ————. Remarks on Select Passages in the Old Testament; to which are added Eight Sermons. 8vo. Oxford. 1787.
————, ————. Christian Fortitude, a Sermon before the University of Oxford. 8vo. Lond. 1757.
————, ————. Vide Biblia Hebraica.
Kenniston, Levi and Laban, Trial of. See Goodridge, E. P.
Kenrick, John. Horrors of Slavery. 12mo. Camb. 1817.
Kenrick, Timothy. Exposition of the Historical Writings of the New Testament, &c. 3 vols. 8vo. Lond. 1807.
Kenrick, William. Dictionary of the English Language. 4to. Lond. 1773.
———, ————. Grand Question Debated; or an Essay to prove that the Soul of Man is not, neither can be Immortal. 8vo. Dublin. 1751.
———, ————. Reply to the Grand Question Debated. 8vo. Lond. 1751.
Kent, James. Dissertations; being the Preliminary Part of a Course of Law Lectures. 8vo. N. York. 1795.
Kent, William. On Stoves for Hot-Houses. (Horticultural Trans. vol. 2.)
——, ————. Management of Aquatic Plants. (Id. 3.)
Kentish, Edward. Cases of Cancer. 8vo. Newcastle upon Tyne. 1802.
———, ————. On Burns. 8vo. Newcastle upon Tyne. 1800.
Kentucky, Constitution for the State of. 8vo.
————, Description of. 8vo. 1792.
Kepler, Jo. Dioptrice. Vide Gassendus, P.
Ker, Jo. De Lingua Latina Observationes. 8vo. Lond. 1709.

Kerguelen, (M. de.) Relation d'un Voyage dans la Mer du Nord. 4to. Paris. 1771.
Kern, P. E. De Blasphemia in Spiritum Sanctum Gravissima. 4to. Helmst. 1738.
Kerner, Ambrosius, et J. N. Gabriel. Dubia Theologico-Moralia. 4to. Augustæ Vind. 1741.
Kerr, George. Medical Sketches. 8vo. Lond. 1818.
Kerroux, L. G. F. Abrégé de l'Histoire de la Hollande et des Provinces-Unies. 4 vol. 8vo. Leide. 1778.
Kessler, J. C. De Dimidio Siclo, etc. (Ugol. vol. 28.)
Kestner, C. A. Commentatio de Eusebii Auctoritate et Fide Diplomatica. 4to. Gottingæ. 1816.
Keteltas, Abr. Reflections on Extortion, in a Sermon. 8vo. Newburyport. 1778.
Kett, Henry. Bampton Lecture Sermons. 2d ed. 8vo. Lond. 1792.
——, ———. History the Interpreter of Prophecy. 4th ed. 2 vols. 8vo. Lond. 1801.
——, ———. Elements of General Knowledge. 2 vols. 12mo. Phil. 1805.
Kettell, Samuel. See Columbus.
Kettlewell, John. Measures of Christian Obedience. 4th ed. 8vo. Lond. 1700.
Keye, Ottho. Onderscheyt tusschen Koude en Warme Landen. 4to. 'sGraven-Haghe. 1659.
——, ———. Kurtzer Entwurff von Neu-Niederland und Guajana; aus dem Holländischen. 4to. Leipz. 1672.
Keysler, J. G. Travels through Germany, Bohemia, Hungary, Switzerland, Italy, and Lorrain; from the German. 2d ed. 4 vols. 4to. Lond. 1756—7.
———, ——. Antiquitates Septentrionales et Celticæ. 8vo. Hannoveræ. 1720.
Khevenhüller, F. A. Comes de. Regum Veterum Numismata illustrata. 4to. Viennæ.
Kiddell, John. Dignity of the Ministerial Character, &c., a Sermon. 8vo. Lond. 1747.
Kidder, Richard, (Bp.) Judgment of Private Discretion in Matters of Religion defended in a Sermon. 4to. Lond. 1687.
———, —————. Demonstration of the Messias. 3 vols. 8vo. Lond. 1684—1700.
———, —————. The Same. 2d ed. fol. Lond. 1726.
———, —————. ————. See Boyle's Lecture Sermons.
———, —————. Reflections on a French Testament printed at Bordeaux. 4to. Lond. 1690.
———, —————. Commentary on the Five Books of Moses, &c. 2 vols. 8vo. Lond. 1694.
———, —————. Second Dialogue concerning Transubstantiation and the Trinity. 4to. Lond. 1687.
Kiesslingius, J. R. De Pulchris Priscorum Hebræorum Fœminis. 4to. Wittenbergæ. 1729.
Kilborn, Robert. Consecration Sermon. 8vo. Lond. 1728.

Killingworth, Grantham. Observations on "Christianity not founded in Argument." 8vo. Lond. 1765.
————, ————. Supplement to Sermons lately preached at Salters-Hall against Popery. 8vo. Lond. 1736.
————, ————. Essay on the Divine Prescience and Man's Free-Agency, &c. 2d ed. 8vo. Lond. 1766.
Kimball, Daniel. Sermon before the Hingham Peace Society. 8vo. Bost. 1819.
Kimball, Jacob. Essex Harmony. Exeter. 1800.
Kimpton, Edward. History of the Bible. 4 vols. 8vo. Trenton. 1813.
Kimyser, Arnold. Ontdekking van America, etc. 8vo. Dordrecht. 1782.
Kinch, John. Sermon on the Death of the Rev. Dr. John Gale. 8vo. Lond. 1722.
Kinderley, Nathaniel. On the Navigation of Lyn, Wisbeach, Spalding, and Boston, &c. 2d ed. 8vo. Lond. 1751.
Kine Pock. Report from the Committee on Dr. Jenner's Petition respecting his Discovery of Vaccine Inoculation. fol. 1802.
—— ——. See Milton.
King, Arnold. Sermon at the Election of a Lord Mayor. 4to. Lond. 1749.
——, ——. Sermon before the Sons of the Clergy. 4to. Lond. 1751.
King, Daniel. Postscript to my Book, intitled, A Way to Sion, &c. 4to. Edin. 1656.
King, Edward. Essay on the English Constitution. 12mo. Lond. 1767.
——, ——. Morsels of Criticism to illustrate the Scriptures. 3 vols. 8vo. Lond. 1800.
——, ——. Various Antiquarian Papers in the Archæologia.
King, James. Sermon from Luke x, 37. 12mo. Lond. 1708.
King, James. Voyage of Captain Cook. See Cook, J.
King, John. Analysis of the Subject of Extra-Uterine Fœtation, and of the Retroversion of the Gravid Uterus. 8vo. Norwich. 1818.
King, John Glen. Rites and Ceremonies of the Greek Church in Russia. 4to. Lond. 1772.
King, Josiah. Mr. Blount's Oracles of Reason Examined. 12mo. Exeter. 1698.
King, Sir Peter, (Lord Chanc.) Enquiry into the Constitution, &c. of the Primitive Church. 8vo. Lond. 1719.
——, ————. See Slater.
——, ————. History of the Apostles Creed. 8vo. Lond. 1702.
——, ————. The Same. 3d ed. 8vo. Lond. 1711.
——, ————. De Legione Fulminatrice. Vide Mosheim, J. L.
King, Richard. Sermon before the Anti-Gallicans. 4to. Lond. 1751.
King, Rufus. Speech on the American Navigation Act. 8vo. N. York. 1818.

King, William. Poems. See Chalmers, A.
King, William. Essay on the Origin of Evil; from the Latin, with Additions; to which is added a Sermon on the Fall of Man. 4to. Lond. 1731.
——, ————. The Same. 5th ed. 8vo. Lond. 1781.
King, William. Apology, or Vindication of himself. 2d ed. 4to. Oxford. 1755.
——, ————, Letter to, occasioned by the Apology. 8vo. Lond. 1755.
——. ————. Oratio in Theatro Sheldoniano Die Dedicationis Bibliothecæ Radclivianæ. 4to. Lond. et Oxon. 1749.
——, ————. Anecdotes of his own Times. 12mo. Bost. 1819.
King's Evil. Occasional Thoughts on the Power of Curing it, ascribed to the King of England. 8vo. Lond. 1748.
Kingsbury, Benjamin. Theory of Fevers. MS. 4to. 1775.
————, ————. Theory of Generation. MS. 4to. 1785.
Kingsley, James L. Eulogy on A. M. Fisher, Professor in Yale College, who perished in the Wreck of the Albion, April 22, 1822. 8vo. New-Haven. 1822.
———— ,————. See Silliman, B.
Kingston, John. American Hymn Book. 16mo. Balt. 1811.
————, ——. Biographical Dictionary. 2d ed. 16mo. Balt. 1811.
Kinloch. Letters from Geneva and France. 2 vols. 8vo. Bost. 1819.
Kinloch, Robert. Sermon before the Society in Scotland for propagating Christian Knowledge. 8vo. Edin. 1731.
Kipling, Thomas. Codex T. Bezæ Cantabrigiensis, Evangelia et Apostolorum Acta complectens, Quadratis Literis, Gr. et Lat. 2 vol. fol. Cant. 1793.
Kippis, Andrew. Sermon on occasion of a New Academical Institution among Protestant Dissenters, for the Education of their Ministers and Youth. 8vo. Lond. 1786.
——, ————. Century Sermon at the Old Jewry. 8vo. Lond. 1788.
——, ————. Sermons on Practical Subjects. 8vo. Lond. 1791.
——, ————. Vindication of the Protestant Dissenting Ministers with regard to their Application to Parliament. 2d ed. 8vo. Lond. 1773.
——, ————. Life of Captain James Cook. 2 vols. 8vo. Basil. 1788.
——, ————. Life of Dr. Lardner. See Lardner, N.
——, ————. Life of Dr. Doddridge. See Doddridge, P., Family Expositor.
Kirby, Ephraim. Reports of Cases in the Superior Court of Connecticut from 1785 to May 1788, &c. 8vo. Litchfield. 1789.
Kirby, Joshua. Dr. Brook Taylor's Method of Perspective made Easy. See Taylor, B.
Kircher, Athanasius. Prodromus Coptus. 4to. Romæ. 1636.
————, ————. De Musica, etc.—De Musurgia Antiquo-Moderna, etc. (Ugol. vol. 32.)

Kircher, Conradus. Concordantiæ Vet. Testamenti Græcæ, Ebræis Vocibus respondentes. 2 vol. 4to. Francof. 1607.
Kirchmajerus, G. C. Exercitatio ad Taciti Histor. Lib. v. Capita aliquot Priora, de Rebus Moribusque Judæorum. (Ugol. vol. 2.)
Kirchmannus, Joh. De Annulis. Accedunt G. Longi, A. Gorlæi, et H. Kornmanni de iisdem Tractatus. 16mo. Lug. Bat. 1672.
Kirchnerus, C. H. De Deo Ebræorum Montano. 4to. Jenæ. 1746.
Kirkland, James. Appendix to T. Kirkland's Medical Surgery. 8vo. Lond. 1813.
Kirkland, John T. (Pres.) Artillery Election Sermon. 8vo. Bost. 1795.
———, ————. Election Sermon. 8vo. Bost. 1816.
———, ————. Sermon before the Massachusetts Society for the Suppression of Intemperance. 8vo. Bost. 1814.
———, ————. Sermon at the Interment of the Rev. J. Belknap. 8vo. Bost. 1798.
———, ————. Discourse on the Death of Washington. 8vo. Bost. 1800.
———, ————. Fast Sermon. 8vo. Bost. 1798.
———, ————. Sermon at the Ordination of the Rev. J. Pipon. 8vo. Camb. 1800.
———, ————. Dudleian Lecture. MS. 1813.
———, ————. Oration before the Phi Beta Kappa Society. 8vo. Bost. 1798.
———, ————. Address to the Massachusetts Charitable Fire Society. 8vo. Bost. 1801.
———, ————. Answer to Queries respecting the Indians. (Mass. Hist. Coll. vol. 4.)
———, ————. Remarks on Mr. Bailey's Letter respecting the Antiquities of America. (Id.)
———, ————. Life of Fisher Ames. See Ames, F.
———, ————. Life of Gen. Benjamin Lincoln. (Mass. Hist. Coll. vol. 3. 2d Series.)
———, ————. Life of Commodore Preble. 8vo.
Kirkland, Thomas. Inquiry into the Present State of Medical Surgery. 2 vols. 8vo. Lond. 1783—6.
Kirkpatrick, James. Historical Essay upon the Loyalty of Presbyterians in Great Britain and Ireland, from the Reformation. 4to. 1713.
Kirkton, James. History of the Church of Scotland, from the Restoration to the Year 1678; with an Account of the Murder of Abp. Sharp, by J. Russell; edited from the MSS. by C. K. Sharpe. 4to. Edin. 1817.
Kirstenius, Petrus. Grammatica Arabica. fol. Breslæ. 1608.
———, ———. Liber II Canonis Avicennæ. Vide Avicenna.
———, ———. Tria Specimina Characterum Arabicorum. fol. Breslæ.
———, ———. Epistola S. Judæ, Arabice et Latine. fol. Breslæ. 1611.
———, ———. Notæ in Evangelium S. Matthæi. fol. Breslæ. 1611.

Kirwan, Richard. Elements of Mineralogy. 8vo. Lond. 1784.
———, ———. Geological Essays. 8vo. Lond. 1799.
———, ———. Logic. 2 vols. 8vo. Lond. 1807.
———, ———. Estimate of the Temperature of Different Latitudes. 8vo. Lond. 1787.
Kiss of Charity. Inquiry whether the Scriptures enjoin it, &c. 8vo. Bost. 1768.
Kit-Cat Club. See Faber, J.
Kite, B. and T. Philadelphia Directory for 1815. 12mo.
Klein, F. A. De Loquendi Formula in 1 Ep. ad Corinthios, et in Actis Apostol. 8vo. Jenæ. 1816.
Klein, J. T. Ordre Naturel des Oursins de Mer et Fossiles, etc. Lat. et Fr. 8vo. Paris. 1754.
Klenk, Koenraad van. Reisbeschrijving van d'Ambassade van de Heer van Klenk naar Moskovien. 4to. Amst. 1677.
Klenker, J. F. Untersuchung der Gründe für die Aechtheit und Glaubwürdigkeit der Schriftlichen Urkunden des Christenthums. 4 Bände. 12mo. Leipz. 1793—9.
———, ——. Ueber die Apokryphen des Neuen Testaments. 12mo. Hamb. 1798.
Klippel, Gottf. De Zacharia Barachiæ Filio. 4to. Lips. 1720.
Klopstock, F. T. Werke. 10 Bände. 8vo. Leipzig. 1798—1806.
———, ——. Vide Benkowitz, C. F.
Klotzius, C. A. Epistolæ Homericæ. 12mo. Altenb. 1764.
Knaggs, Tho. Sermon on the Death of the Princess Sophia. 8vo. Lond. 1714.
———, ——. Victory Sermon. 8vo. Lond. 1708.
———, ——. Sermon, November 5th. 8vo. Lond. 1716.
———, ——. God with us, a Sermon. 8vo. Lond. 1706.
Knapp, Geo. C. Prolusio de Christo ad Dextram Dei sedente. (Muntinghe, Syl. Opusculorum.)
———, ———. Scripta Varii Argumenti. 2 vol. 8vo. Halæ. 1805.
———, ———. Idem. 2 vol. 8vo. Halæ. 1823.
———, ———. Vide Testamentum Novum.
Knatchbull, Sir Norton. Annotations upon some Difficult Texts in all the Books of the New Testament. 8vo. Camb. 1693.
Knauthius, Christianus. Dissertatio Philologica de Vera Vocis יובל Etymologia et Significatione. 4to. Lips. 1731.
Kneeland, Abner. Lectures on the Doctrine of Universal Benevolence. 12mo. Phil. 1818.
Kneller, Sir Godfrey. See Faber, J.
Knight, Francis. Relation of Seven Years Slavery in Algier. Churchill,) Coll. vol. 8.)
Knight, Gowin. Attempt to explain all the Phænomena in Nature by Attraction and Repulsion. 4to. Lond. 1754.
Knight, Henry. Being and Attributes of God demonstrated in a New Method. 8vo. Lond. 1747.
———, ———. Fast Sermon. 8vo. Lond. 1742.
Knight, H. C. Letters from the South and West, by Arthur Singleton, Esq. 8vo. Bost. 1824.

Knight, J. Extracts from Letters written by Englishmen in the United States to their Friends in England. 8vo. Manchester. 1818.

Knight, James. Visitation Sermon. 8vo. Lond. 1719.

———, ———. Eight Sermons at Lady Moyer's Lecture. 8vo. Lond. 1721.

Knight, Rich. P. Prolegomena ad Homerum. 8vo. Lips. 1816.

———, ———. Analytical Inquiry into the Principles of Taste. 2d ed. 8vo. Lond. 1806.

———, ———. Inquiry into the Symbolical Language of Ancient Art and Mythology. (Classical Journal, vol. 23.)

———, ———. Notice of his Carmina Homerica. (Id. 23 and 24.)

Knight, Samuel. Life of Dr. John Colet. 8vo. Lond. 1724.

Knight, Tho. A. Papers on Horticulture, Physiology, and Botany, in Nicholson's Journal, and in the Philosophical and Horticultural Transactions.

Knighton, Henricus. Chronica. (Twysden. vol. 2.)

Knivet, Anthony. Admirable Adventures and Strange Fortunes. (Purchas, vol. 4.)

Knolles, Richard. Turkish History. Vide Ricaut.

Knollius, Joh. Vocabularium Biblicum Nov. Test. ed. 10ma. 8vo. Lips. 1739.

———, ——. Idem. ed. nova. 8vo. Lips. 1777.

Knorr, Geo. W. Les Délices des Yeux et de l'Esprit, ou Collection Générale de Coquillages. 3 vol. 4to. Nuremberg. 1764—71.

Knowledge, Philosophical Dissertation upon the Inlets to Human. 8vo. Lond. 1739.

Knowler, Wm. The Earl of Strafforde's Letters and Dispatches; with an Essay towards his Life, by Sir George Radcliffe. 2 vols. fol. Lond. 1739.

Knowles, (Commodore.) See Journal.

Knowles, Thomas. Answer to an Essay on Spirit. 8vo. Lond. 1753.

Knox, Henry, (Gen.) Plan for the General Arrangement of the Militia of the United States. fol. N. York. 1790.

Knox, John. Historie of the Reformatioun of Religioun in Scotland. fol. Edin. 1644.

——, ——. The Same; with his Life, &c. fol. Edin. 1732.

——, ——. Sermon, in the publique audience of the Church of Edenbrough, Aug. 19, 1565. 18mo. 1566.

Knox, John. Historical Journal of the Campaigns in North America in 1757—60. 2 vols. 4to. Lond. 1769.

Knox, Robert. Historical Relation of Ceylon. fol. Lond. 1681.

Knox, Vicesimus. Elegant Extracts in Verse. 2 vols. 8vo. Lond. 1800.

——, ————. Elegant Extracts in Prose. 2 vols. 8vo. Lond. 1808.

——, ————. Epistles, Elegant, Familiar, and Instructive, selected from the best Writers. 8vo. Lond. 1791.

Knox, William. Considerations on the Universality and Uniformity of the Theocracy. 8vo. Lond. 1796.

——, ———. The Revealed Will of God, the Sufficient Rule of Men; being a Sequel to the above. 2 vols. 8vo. Lond. 1801.

——, ———. Extra Official State Papers. 8vo. Lond. 1789.

Kobierzykius, Stanislaus. De Luxu Romanorum. (Grævius, vol. 8.)

Koch, C. D. De Nummorum Hebraicorum Inscriptionibus Samaritanis. (Ugol. vol. 28.)

Koch, Chr. Abrégé de l'Histoire des Traités de Paix entre les Puissances de l'Europe depuis la Paix de Westphalie. 4 vol. 8vo. Basle. 1796—7.

——, ——. Table des Traités entre la France et les Puissances Etrangères, depuis la Paix de Westphalie; suivie d'un Recueil de Traités et Actes Diplomatiques qui n'ont pas encore vu le jour. 2 vol. 8vo. Basle. 1802.

——, ——. Observations sur l'Origine de la Maladie Vénérienne, etc. (Institut, Sciences Mor. et Pol. vol. 4.)

Koch, J. G. F. Versuch eines Kriegs-Rechts der Negern in Afrika und Indianer in Amerika. 12mo. Tübingen. 1781.

Koecherus, Jo. Chr. Analecta Philologica et Exegetica in Quatuor SS. Evangelia. 2 tomi in 1 vol. 4to. Altenburgi. 1766.

————, ———. Observationes Selectæ Controversias inter Pontificios et Protestantes illustrantes. 12mo. Jenæ. 1767—70.

————, ———. Vide Grotius.

Koeppelius, J. M. Σφόδρα Χριστιανίζοντες haud raro Ὑπερβολικοί. 4to. Vitembergæ. 1740.

Koës, G. H. C. Probe eines Griechisch-Deutschen Wörterbuchs über den Homer und die Homeriden. 12mo. Copenhagen. 1806.

——, ———. Commentatio de Discrepantiis quibusdam in Odyssea occurrentibus. 12mo. Hafniæ. 1806.

Köhler, J. T. Sammlung neuer Reisebeschreibungen; aus dem fremden Sprachen. Band 1. 12mo. Göttin. und Gotha. 1767.

Kohlius, F. T. Commentationes Criticæ. 12mo. Hamburgi et Kiloni. 1727.

Kolb, Gregorius. Compendium Totius Orbis. 4to. Rottwilæ. 1726.

Kolb, J. C. Erzählungen von den Sitten und Schiksalen der Negersklaven. 12mo. Bern. 1789.

Kolben, Peter. Present State of the Cape of Good Hope, done into English from the German by Mr. Medley. 2d ed. 8vo. Lond. 1738.

Koloff, Henricus. Ludovici de Dieu Aphorismi Theologici Falsi et Erronei Refutati. 4to. Vitembergæ. 1738.

König, J. C. Vide Testamentum Vet. et Nov.

König, J. F. De Vet. Testamenti Natura. 4to. Suobaci. 1692.

Konow, J. P. De Justitia Inhærente, contra Pontificios. 4to. Wittemb. 1687.

Koppe, J B. Vide Testamentum Novum.

Köppen, J. H. J. Anmerkungen zum Homer. 12mo. Hannover. 1787—8.

———, ———. Anmerkungen zu den Oden und Liedern vom Horaz, etc. (Encyclopädie der Lat. Class.)

L

LABAT, J. B. Nouveau Voyage aux Isles de l'Amérique. 6 vol. 12mo. Paris. 1722.
———, ———. Idem. 8 vol. 12mo. Paris. 1742.
———, ———. Voyages du Chevalier des Marchais en Guinée, Isles Voisines, et à Cayenne. 4 vol. 12mo. Amst. 1731.
Labaume, Eugene. Narrative of the Campaign in Russia; from the French. 2d ed. 8vo. Lond. 1815.
Labbæus, Car. Glossaria Latino-Græca et Græco-Latina. fol. Lut. Par. 1679.
———, ———. Idem. 5 Partes. fol. Lond. 1817—26.
Labbe, Philippus. Regulæ Accentuum et Spirituum Græcorum. 16mo. Paris. 1725.
———, ———. Eruditæ Pronuntiationis Catholici Indices, ab E. Leedes. 12mo. Lond. 1751.
———, ———. Fasti Idatiani. (Grævius, vol. 11.)
———, ———. Eclogæ Historicorum de Rebus Byzantinis, etc. (Script. Byz.)
———, ———. Bibliotheca Bibliothecarum; accedit Bibliotheca Nummaria. 12mo. Rothomagi. 1678.
Labillardière, J. J. Mémoires dans les Annales du Muséum d'Histoire Naturelle.
Laborde. Vide Borde.
La Brosse, P. J. (Angelus à S. Joseph.) Vide Angelus.
Lacépède, (Comte de.) Mémoires dans les Annales du Muséum d'Histoire Naturelle.
———, ———. Vide Cépède.
Lachmann, Karl. Ueber die Ursprüngliche Gestalt des Gedichts von der Nibelungen Noth. 8vo. Berlin. 1816.
Lackington, Allen & Co. Sale Catalogue of Books for 1806—8. 8vo. Lond.
———, Hughes and Others. Sale Catalogue of Books for 1819. 8vo. Lond.
Lackner, Christophorus. Galea Martis. 12mo. Tubingæ. 1625.
Laco, Writings of, from the Massachusetts Centinel. 12mo. Bost. 1789.
Lacock, Abner. Strictures on his Report, in the Senate of the United States, on the Seminole War. 12mo. 1819.
Lacombe, J. Dictionnaire du Vieux Langage François. 8vo. Paris. 1766.
Lacretelle. Panorama. Mai, 1820. 8vo. Paris.

Lacretelle. Considérations Politiques et Morales. Mai, 1820. 8vo. Paris.
————. Portefeuille Politique. Mai, 1820. 8vo. Paris.
Lacroix, S. F. Traité du Calcul Différentiel et du Calcul Intégral, avec Suite. 3 vol. 4to. Paris. 1797—1800.
———, ——. Elementary Treatise of the Differential and Integral Calculus, translated from the French; with Notes, &c. 8vo. Camb., (Engl.) 1816.
———, ——. Elémens d'Algèbre. 6me ed. 8vo. Paris. 1807.
———, ——. Complément des Elémens d'Algèbre. 3me ed. 8vo. Paris. 1804.
———, ——. See Farrar, J.
Lactantius, L. C. F. Opera, cum Notis Variorum, studio S. Gallæi. 8vo. Lug. Bat. 1660.
————, ————. Opera, cum Notis Variorum, a J. L. Bünemann. 2 vol. 8vo. Lips. 1739.
————, ————. Opera, cum Notis, a J. B. Le Brun et N. L. Dufresnoy. 2 vol. 4to. Lut. Par. 1748.
————, ————. Divinarum Institutionum Libri vii, etc. 12mo. Lugd. 1556.
————, ————. De Mortibus Persecutorum, cum Notis Variorum, a P. Bauldro. 8vo. Traj. ad Rhen. 1693.
————, ————. Relation of the Death of the Primitive Persecutors, Englished by G. Burnet. 12mo. Amst. 1687.
Lacuna, Andr. à. De Origine Turcarum. (Clauser, de Reb. Turc.)
Lade, Robert. Voyage de l'Afrique, de l'Asie, et de l'Amérique. 2 vol. 12mo. Paris. 1744.
——, ——. Voyages en Différentes Parties de l'Asie, de l'Afrique, et de l'Amérique, trad. de l'Anglois par l'Abbé Prévost. 8vo. Paris. 1810.
Ladies Calling. See Fell, J. See Whole Duty of Man.
Laet, J. de. Histoire du Nouveau Monde. fol. Leyde. 1611.
——, ——. Novus Orbis. fol. Lug. Bat. 1633.
——, ——. Jaerlijcks Verhael van de Verrichtinghen der West-Indische Compagnie. fol. Leyden. 1644.
——, ——. Notæ ad Dissertationem H. Grotii de Origine Gentium Americanarum. 12mo. Amst. 1643.
——, ——. Responsio ad Dissertationem Secundam H. Grotii de Origine Gentium Americanarum. 12mo. Amst. 1644.
Lætus, Geo. Pauli Apostoli Peregrinatio Cæsareâ Romam. 24to. Lug. Bat. 1639.
Lafargue. Œuvres Mêlées. 2 vol. 12mo. Paris. 1765.
Lafitau, J. F. Mœurs des Sauvages Amériquains, comparées aux Mœurs des Premiers Temps. 2 vol. 4to. Paris. 1724.
———, ——. Idem. 4 vol. 12mo. Paris. 1724.
———, ——. Histoire des Découvertes et Conquêtes des Portugais dans le Nouveau Monde. 4 vol. 12mo. Paris. 1734.
Lafontaine. Vide Fontaine, J. de la.
Lafosse, J. F. Avis aux Habitans des Colonies, sur les Principales Causes des Maladies qu'on y éprouve, etc. 8vo. Paris. 1787.

Lagrange, J. L. Théorie des Fonctions Analytiques. 4to. Paris. 1797.

————, ——. De la Résolution des Equations Numériques. 4to. Paris. 1798.

————, ——· Méchanique Analitique. 4to. Paris. 1788.

Laharpe. Vide Harpe, J. F. la.

Lahontan. Vide Hontan, le Baron de la.

Laing, Malcolm. History of Scotland, from the Accession of James VI. to the Throne of England, to the Union in the Reign of Queen Anne. 2 vols. 8vo. Lond. 1800.

——, ————. The Same. 2d ed; with a Preliminary Dissertation on the Participation of Mary, Queen of Scots, in the Murder of Darnley. 4 vols. 8vo. Lond. 1804.

Laire, Fr. Xav. Index Librorum ab Inventa Typographia ad Annum 1500. 2 vol. 8vo. Senonis. 1791.

Lakemacher, J. G. Elementa Linguæ Arabicæ. 4to. Helmst. 1718.

——————, ——. De Gad et Meni. (Ugol. vol. 23.)

Lalamantius, Jo. De Anno Romano. (Grævius, vol. 8.)

——————, —. De Tempore et ejus Partibus.—De Anno Macedonum, seu Græcorum.—De Anno Attico. (Gronovius, vol. 9.)

La Lande. Vide Lande.

Lamarck, J. B. Mémoires dans les Annales du Muséum d'Histoire Naturelle.

————, —— et J. L. M. Poiret. Encyclopédie Méthodique, Botanique. (tom. 1—7,) 7 tomes; et Planches, 9 tomes. 4to. Paris. 1783—1806.

————, ——. Vide Bonnaterre,—Bruguières,—Mauduyt,—Tessier.

Lamb, Catharine. Full Discovery of the False Evidence produced by the Papists against Dr. T. Tenison. 4to. Lond. 1688.

Lambard, Wm. Perambulation of Kent. 4to. Lond. 1596.

————, ——. Eirenarcha. 12mo. Lond. 1592.

Lambe, John. Liberty of Human Nature discussed &c., in a Sermon. 4to. Lond. 1684.

——, ——. Sermon before the King and Queen. 4to. Lond. 1690.

—— ——. Sermon before the Queen. 4to. Lond. 1691.

—— ——. Sermon before the King. 4to. Lond. 1695.

——; ——. Sermon before the King. 4to. Lond. 1696.

——, ——. Sermon before the Lord Mayor. 4to. Lond. 1701.

Lambe, Wm. On Constitutional Diseases. 8vo. Lond. 1805.

——, ——. On the Properties of Spring Water. 8vo. Lond. 1803.

Lambecius, Petrus. Notæ in Kalendarium Vetus. (Grævius, vol. 8.)

————, ———. Commentariorum de Bibliotheca Cæsarea Liber ix, quo continetur Catalogus MSS. Codicum Græcorum Profanorum, etc. (Schelhorn, vol. 5.)

Lambert, (l'Abbé.) Histoire Générale, Civile, Naturelle, Politique, et Religieuse de tous les Peuples du Monde. 14 vol. 12mo. Paris. 1750.

Lambert, A. B. On the Native Country of the Potato, &c. (Quarterly Journal of Science, &c. vol. 10.)
Lambert, A. T. Marchioness de. Mother's Advice to her Son. 16mo. Haverhill, Mass. 1814.
———, ————————. Letter to her Son. See Phillips, J. T.
Lambert, Cæsar. Voyage d'Ægypte. Vide Egypt.
Lambert, John. Travels through Lower Canada and the United States, in 1806—8. 3 vols. 8vo. Lond. 1810.
Lambert, Ralph. Sermon to the Irish Protestants in London. 8vo. Lond. 1708.
Lambert, Wm. Calculations for ascertaining the Latitude and Longitude of the Capitol at Washington. 4to. Washington. 1805.
———, ——. Abstracts of Calculations, to ascertain the Longitude of the Capitol, in the City of Washington, from Greenwich Observatory in England. 4to. Washington. 1817.
Lamberti, Luigi. Vide Odi.
Lambertinus, Prosper, (Pope Benedict XIV.) Casus Conscientiæ. 4 vol. 12mo. Aug. Vind. 1772—5.
Lambertus. Vide Hortensius.
Lambton, Wm. Account of Trigonometrical Operations in India. (Asiatic Researches, vol. 10.)
————, ——. Account of the Measurement of an Arc on the Meridian. (Id. 12.)
Lamétherie, J. C. Vide Delamétherie.
Lamius, B. Vide Lamy.
Lamius, Jo. De Eruditione Apostolorum. 8vo. Florentiæ. 1738.
Lamothe, C. G. Inspiration of the New Testament explained. 8vo. Lond. 1694.
Lampadius, Joh. Mellificium Historicum Integrum, a C. Pezelio propositum, et a Lampadio perfectum. 4to. Marpurgi. 1617.
————, ——. Idem. 2 vol. 4to. Francof. 1628.
Lampe, Frid. A. De Cymbalis Veterum. 12mo. Traj. ad Rhen. 1703.
———, ————. Idem. (Ugolinus, vol. 32.)
———, ————. Exercitationes Sacræ. 4to. Bremæ. 1715.
———, ————. Dissertationum Philolog. Theol. Syntagma. 2 vol. 4to. Amst. 1737.
Lampillas, Xavier. Ensayo Historico-Apologetico de la Literatura Española, trad. del Italiano. 7 vol. 8vo. Madrid. 1789.
Lampridius, Ælius. Commodus Antoninus. Vide Rom. Hist. Script.
Lampridius, Benedictus. Carmen. Vide Sannazarius.
Lamy, Bernard. Apparatus Biblicus; or an Introduction to the Holy Scriptures; from the French, with Notes. 4to. Lond. 1723.
——, ————. The Same. 2d ed. 2 vols. 8vo Lond. 1728.
——, ————. De Tabernaculo Fœderis, de Sancta Civitate Jerusalem, et de Templo ejus. fol. Paris. 1720.
——, ————. De Levitis Cantoribus. (Ugol. vol. 32.)
Lancaster, James. Voyages to the East Indies. (Purchas, vol. 1.)

Lancaster, Peter. Remarks on Bishop Lloyd's Hypothesis of Daniel's Prophecy of the Seventy Weeks. 4to. Lond. 1726.
Lancaster, Wm. Sermon, January 30th. 4to. Lond. 1697.
Lancaster and York. See Union.
Lancelot, Claude. Jardin des Racines Grecques, par J. B. Gail. 5me. ed. 12mo. Paris. 1813.
Lancisius, Jo. Maria. Opera Omnia. 2 vol. 4to. Genevæ. 1718.
Lanckisch, Fr. Concordantiæ Bibliorum Hebraico et Græco-Germanicæ. 4to. Lips. et Francof. 1680.
Lancy, Benjamin, (Bp.) Sermon before his Majesty. 4to. Lond. 1665.
Land-Bank. Settlement of the Land-Bank, established in 1695. fol.
Lande, J. J. F. de la. Astronomie. 2 vol. 4to. Paris. 1764.
——, ————. ————. 3me ed. 3 vol. 4to. Paris. 1792.
——, ————. Voyage en Italie, fait dans les Années 1765—6. 8 vol. 12mo; et Planches, 4to. Venise. 1769.
——, ————. Vide Ephémérides,—Halley,—Montucla.
Landed Property, Certain Ancient Tracts concerning the Management of, reprinted. 8vo. Lond. 1767.
Landen, John. Animadversions on Dr. Stewart's Computation of the Sun's Distance from the Earth. 4to. Lond. 1771.
Landlord and Tenant, Law of. See Woodfall, W.
Landonnière, Réné. Voyage unto Florida. (Hakluyt, vol. 3.)
Landriot, Pierre. Vide Paris, P. L.
Lands, Plan of a Society for the Sale of, in America. 4to. Lond. 1794.
———. Plan de Vente de Trois Cent Mille Acres de Terres situées dans les Comtés de Northumberland et de Huntingdon, dans l'Etat de Pensylvanie. 8vo. Phil. 1794.
———. Verkauf von Ländeyren in Amerika. 8vo. Hamburg. 1793.
———. Plan of Association of the North American Land Company, established February, 1795. 8vo. Phil. 1795.
———. Observations on the North-American Land-Company, lately instituted in Philadelphia. 8vo. Lond. 1796.
———. Memorial of the Ilinois and Ouabache Land Companies to Congress. 8vo. 1802.
———. Account of the Proceedings of the Ilinois and Ouabache Land Companies. 8vo. Phil. 1802.
———. See Georgia,—Non-Resident's Lands,—United States, &c.
Landsdowne, Geo. Granville, Lord. Poems. See Chalmers, A.
Lane, Richard. Reports in the Court of Exchequer from 3 to 9 James I. fol. Lond. 1657.
Lanfrancus, (Cant. Archiep.) Opera, cum Notis, et Vita ejus, a L. Dacherio. fol. Lut. Par. 1648.
Langausen, Christophorus. De Mense Veterum Hebræorum Lunari. (Ugol. vol. 17.)
Langdon, Samuel, (Pres.) Examination of Mr. Robert Sandeman's Letters on Theron and Aspasio. 8vo. Bost. 1769.

Langdon, Samuel, (Pres.) Summary of Christian Faith and Practice. 8vo. Bost. 1768.

———, ————. Dudleian Lecture. 8vo. Bost. 1776.

———, ————. Election Sermon. 8vo. Watertown. 1775.

———, ————. Sermon on the Death of Professor J. Winthrop. 8vo. Bost. 1779.

Lange, N. B. Dänische Sprachlehre. 2 Bände. 12mo. Kiel und Kopenhagen. 1787.

Langeac, M. le Chevalier de. Colomb dans les Fers. 8vo. Lond. 1782.

Langford, William. Charity Sermon. 8vo. Lond. 1748.

Langham, William. Garden of Health. 4to. Lond. 1633.

Langhenez, Bernardt. Four Hollanders Ships Voyage; from the Dutch. (Churchill, Coll. vol. 8.)

Langhorne, John. Poems. See Chalmers, A.

————, ——, and Wm. Plutarch's Lives, translated from the Greek, with Notes. 6 vols. 8vo. Lond. 1770.

————, ——, ———. The Same. 6 vols. 12mo. Phil. 1803.

Langhornius, Dan. Antiquitates Albionenses. 8vo. Lond. 1675.

Langius, C. H. De Crucis Supplicio. 4to. Lubecæ. 1729.

Langius, D. C. De Visionibus Hildegardis. 4to. Vittemb. 1716.

Langius, Joach. Medicina Mentis. ed. 3tia. 8vo. Lond. 1715.

Langius, Josephus. Novissima Polyanthea. fol. Francof. 1617.

Langius, Wilhelmus. De Vetere Anno Romanorum. (Grævius, vol. 8.)

Langlès, L. Sur les Papiers-Monnoies des Orientaux. (Instit. Lit. vol. 4.)

———, —. Les Voyages de Sind-bâd le Marin, et la Ruse des Femmes, Contes Arabes; Traduction Littérale, accompagnée du Texte et de Notes. 12mo. Paris. 1814.

Langres, L'Evêque de. Explication des Evangiles des Dimanches, et de quelques-unes des principales Fêtes de l'Année. 5 vol. 8vo. Breslau. 1800.

Langrish, Browne. Modern Theory and Practice of Physic. 2d ed. 8vo. Lond. 1738.

Langstedt, F. L. Reisen nach Südamerika, Asien, und Afrika. 12mo. Hildesheim. 1789.

Langtoft, Peter. Chronicle. Vide Hearne, T.

Langton, John. New Copy Book. 2 arts. Lond. 1727.

Language. Essay tending to improve intelligible Signals, and to discover an Universal Language. (Amer. Phil. Tr. vol. 4.)

————. Remarks on a Letter to Dr. Waterland, in relation to the Natural Account of Languages. 8vo. Camb. 1731.

Languet, Hubert. Vindiciæ contra Tyrannos; Stephano Junio Bruto Celta, Auctore. 12mo. 1580.

Langwith, Benjamin. Observations on Dr. Arbuthnot's Dissertations on Coins, Weights, and Measures. 2d ed. 4to. Lond. 1754.

Lansius, Thomas. Consultatio de Principatu inter Provincias Europæ. ed. 4ta. 8vo. Tubingæ. 1635.
Lanzi, Luigi. Storia Pittorica della Italia. ed. terza. 6 vol. 4to. Bassano. 1809.
Lanzonius, Petrus. De Coronis et Unguentis in Antiquorum Conviviis. (Sallengre, vol. 3.)
———, ———. De Luctu Mortuali Veterum Adversaria. (Id.)
Lapide, Cornelius à. Commentaria in Omnes Pauli Epistolas. fol. Paris. 1631.
Laplace, P. S. Exposition du Système du Monde. 2de ed. 4to. Paris. 1799.
———, ———. Traité de Mécanique Céleste. (vol. 1—4,) 4 vol. 4to. Paris. 1799—1805.
La Plata. Vide Plata.
Lara, Benjamin. Dictionary of Surgery. 12mo. Lond.
Larcher, P. H. Histoire d' Hérodote, trad. du Grec, avec des Remarques, etc. 7 vol. 8vo. Paris. 1786.
Lardner, Nathaniel. Credibility of the Gospel History. 2d and 3d ed. 17 vols. 8vo. Lond. 1741—62.
———, ———. Collection of Jewish and Heathen Testimonies to the Truth of the Christian Religion. 4 vols. 4to. Lond. 1764—7.
———, ———. Works; with his Life, by Dr. Kippis. 11 vols. 8vo. Lond. 1788.
———, ———. The Same. 5 vols. 4to. Lond. 1815.
———, ———. Vindication of Three of our Saviour's Miracles. 8vo. Lond. 1729.
———, ———. The Same. 2d ed. 8vo. Lond. 1731.
———, ———. Circumstances of the Jewish People an Argument for the Truth of the Christian Religion. 8vo. Lond. 1752.
———, ———. Case of the Demoniacs mentioned in the New Testament. 8vo. Lond. 1758.
———, ———. Dissertation on the Two Epistles ascribed to Clement of Rome. 8vo. Lond. 1753.
———, ———. History of the Heretics. 4to. Lond. 1780.
———, ———. Discourse to Young People. 8vo. Lond. 1735.
———, ———. The Same. 2d ed. 8vo. Lond. 1743.
———, ———. Caution against Conformity to the World; Two Discourses. 8vo. Lond. 1739.
———, ———. Sermons on Various Subjects. 2 vols. 8vo. Lond. 1751—60.
———, ———. Memoirs of his Life and Writings; with Eight Sermons. 8vo. Lond. 1769.
———, ———. Sermon on the Death of the Rev. William Harris. 8vo. Lond. 1740.
———, ———. Remarks upon Dr. Ward's Dissertations on the Scriptures. 8vo. Lond. 1762.
———, ———. Letter on the Logos, with Two Postscripts. 8vo. Lond. 1788.

Lardner, Nathaniel. The Same. (Unitarian Tracts, vol. 7.)
———, ———. Two Schemes of a Trinity considered, and the Divine Unity asserted; Four Discourses on Philip ii, 5—11. (Id.)
Laren, Daniel à. Prolegomena in Apocalypsin. 4to. 1627.
Larochejaquelein. Vide Jaquelein.
Laromiguière. Sur la Détermination de ces Mots, *Analyse des Sensations*.—Sur la Détermination du Mot, *Idée*. (Institut, Sciences Mor. et Pol. vol. 1.)
Larrey, (M. de.) Histoire de France sous le Regne de Louis XIV. (2—6,) 5 vol. 12mo. Nancy. 1719—22.
Las-Casas. Vide Casas, B. de las.
Las Cases, (Count de.) Journal of the Private Life and Conversations of the Emperor Napoleon at St. Helena. 3 vols. 8vo. Bost. 1823.
Lastri, P. M. L'Elogio di Amerigo Vespucci. 4to. Firenze. 1787.
Lasena, Pietro. Dell' Antico Ginnasio Napoletano. 4to.
Lassels, Richard. The Voyage of Italy. 12mo. Paris. 1670.
Latassa, Felix. Bibliotheca Antigua de Aragon. 2 vol. 8vo. Zaragoza. 1796.
———, ———. Biblioteca Nueva de Aragon. 5 vol. 8vo. Pamplona. 1798—1801.
Latch, Jean. Plusieurs tres-bons Cases en la Court de Bank le Roy. fol. Lond. 1661.
Latham, E. Thanksgiving Sermon. 8vo. Derby. 1746.
———, —. Sermon at the Ordination of John Gregory and William Dodge. 8vo. Lond. 1722.
Latham, Henry. Oxford Prize Poem; Coloni ab Anglia ad Americæ Oram missi. (Classical Journal, vol. 6.)
Latham, John. General Synopsis of Birds. 6 vols. 4to. Lond. 1781—5.
———, ———. Supplements. 2 vols. 4to. Lond. 1787—1801.
———, ———. Index Ornithologicus. 2 vol. 4to. Lond. 1790.
Lathrop, John. Sermon at the Dedication of the New South Meeting-House in Dorchester. 8vo. Bost. 1813.
———, ———. Thanksgiving Discourse. 8vo. Bost. 1774.
———, ———. Thanksgiving Sermon. 8vo. Bost. 1808.
———, ———. Sermon on the Death of the Rev. John Eliot. 8vo. Bost. 1813.
———, ———. Sermon on the Sabbath after the Massacre of March 5th, 1770. 8vo. Bost. 1771.
———, ———. Artillery Election Sermon. 8vo. Bost. 1774.
———, ———. Discourse on the Death of his Consort. 8vo. Bost. 1779.
———, ———. Discourse before the Humane Society. 8vo. Bost. 1787.
———, ———. Discourse before the Society for propagating the Gospel among the Indians and Others. 8vo. Bost. 1804.
———, ———. Sermon at the Ordination of the Rev. William Bentley. 8vo. Salem. 1783.
———, ———. Discourse at the Public Lecture. 8vo. Bost. 1797.

Lathrop, John. Dudleian Lecture. 8vo. Bost. 1793.
———, ——. Fast Sermon. 8vo. Bost. 1799.
———, ——. Fast Sermon. 8vo. Bost. 1812.
———, ——. Biographical Memoir of the Rev. John Lothropp. (Mass. Hist. Coll. vol. 1. 2d Series.)
Lathrop, John. Oration, July 4th. 8vo. Bost. 1796.
———, ——. Speech of Caunonicus; a Poem. 4to. Calcutta. 1802.
———, ——. The Same. 8vo. Bost. 1803.
———, ——. Gentleman's Pocket Register, and Free-Mason's Annual Anthology, for 1813. 18mo. Bost.
Lathrop, Joseph. Sermon on American Independence. 8vo. Springfield. 1794.
———, ———. Sprinkling, a Scriptural Mode of Baptism. 8vo. Bost. 1773.
———, ———. Sermons. 2 vols. 8vo. Worcester. 1796.
———, ———. ———. 2d ed. 5 vols. 8vo. Worcester, &c. 1807—9.
———, ———. Sermons on Christian Baptism. 3d ed. 12mo. Northampton. 1803.
———, ———. The Same. 5th ed. 12mo. Bost. 1811.
———, ———. Sermons on the Christian Sabbath. 8vo. Northampton. 1803.
———, ———. Sermon at the Ordination of the Rev. S. Bemis. 8vo. Harvard. 1801.
———, ———. Discourses on Paul's Epistle to the Ephesians. 8vo. Worcester. 1801.
———, ———. Christ's Warning to the Churches to beware of False Prophets, in Two Discourses. 11th ed. 12mo. Bost. 1811.
Latimer, Hugh, (Bp.) Fruitfull Sermons. 4to. Lond. 1604.
———, ————. The Same. 4to. Lond. 1635.
Latin Grammar. Short Introduction of Grammar. 8vo. Lond. 1662.
—— ————, Short Introduction to, for the Use of the University and Academy of Pennsylvania. 6th ed. 12mo. Exeter. 1794.
——, ————. Nouveaux Rudimens de la Langue Latine. 12mo.
—— Language, Pronunciation of the. 2d ed. 8vo. Camb. 1823.
—— Syntax and Prosody, Rudiments of. 8vo. Salem. 1783.
Latour, A. L. Historical Memoir of the War in West-Florida and Louisiana, in 1814—15. 8vo. Phil. 1816.
Latreille, P. A. Genera Crustaceorum et Insectorum. 3 vol. 8vo. Paris. 1806—7.
———, ——. Mémoires dans les Annales du Muséum d'Histoire Naturelle.
Latrobe, B. Henry. Memoir on the Sand Hills in Virginia; with a Supplement by William Tatham. (Amer. Phil. Tr. vol. 4.)
———, ————. Drawing and Description of the Clupea Tyrannus and Omniscius Prægustator. (Id. 5.)

Latrobe, B. Henry. On Two Species of Sphex in Virginia, &c. (Id. 6.)
———, ———. Anniversary Oration before the Society of Artists of the United States. 8vo. 1811.
Latta, James. Practical System of Surgery. 3 vols. 8vo. Edin. 1795.
Lattre, P. A. de. Campagnes des François à Saint-Domingue. 8vo. Paris. 1805.
Laubegeois, Ant. Græcæ Linguæ Breviarium. 12mo. Duaci. 1626.
Laud, Wm. (Abp.) History of his Troubles and Trial. fol. Lond. 1695.
———, ———, Relation of the Conference between him and Mr. Fisher the Jesuit, &c. 4th ed. fol. Lond. 1686.
———, ———, Speech on Tower Hill. (Harl. Miscel. vol. 8.)
———, ———, Life of. (Id. 4.)
———, ———. Vide Baylie, R.
Lauder, Wm. Letter to the Rev. Mr. Douglas, occasioned by his Vindication of Milton, &c. 4to. Lond. 1751.
———, ———. Delectus Auctorum Sacrorum Miltono Facem prælucentium. 2 vol. 8vo. Lond. 1752.
———, ———, Pandæmonium, inscribed to, by Philalethes. 4to. Lond. 1750.
———, ———. Progress of Envy, a Poem, occasioned by Lauder's Attack upon Milton. 4to. Lond. 1751.
Laughton, Richard. Sermon before the King. 2d ed. 8vo. Camb. 1717.
Laugier, (l'Abbé.) Histoire de la République de Venise. 7 vol. 12mo. Paris. 1759—65.
Laugier. Mémoires dans les Annales du Muséum d'Histoire Naturelle.
Laune, Thomas de. See Delaune.
Laureau. l'Amérique Découverte. 12mo. Autun. 1782.
Laurenbergius, Jo. Enarratio Græciæ Antiquæ. (Gronov. vol. 4.)
Laurence. Vide Laurentius. Vide Lawrence.
Laurence, John. Assize Sermon. 8vo. Lond. 1717.
Laurence, Richard. Remarks upon the Systematic Classification of Manuscripts, adopted by Griesbach in his Edition of the Greek Testament. 8vo. Oxford. 1814.
———, ———. Eight Sermons at the Bampton Lecture. 8vo. Oxford. 1805.
Laurent, (l'Abbé du.) Le Compère Matthieu, ou les Bigarrues de l'Esprit Humain. 3 vol. 8vo. Paris. 1796.
Laurentius, Andreas. Historia Anatomica Humani Corporis. fol. Francof. 1599.
Laurentius, Jacobus. Catechesis Heidelbergensis Orthodoxa. 8vo. Amst. 1625.
Laurentius, Josephus. De Rebuspublicis, Suffragiis, ac Conciliis. (Gronovius, vol. 6.)
———, ———. Varia Sacra Gentilium. (Id. 7.)

Laurentius, Josephus. De Sponsalibus et Nuptiis Antiquorum.—De Adulteris, ac Meretricibus.—De Natalitiis, Conviviisque, quæ in iisdem agitabantur.—De Præconibus, Citharœdis, etc.—De Agyrtis, Histrionibus, Acclamationibus, et Osculis. (Id. 8.)
————, ————. De Conviviis, Hospitalitate, Tesseris, et Strenis.—De Prandio et Cœna Veterum, etc. (Id. 9.)
————, ————. De Re Vestiaria. (Id.)
————, ————. De Annis. Mensibus, Diebus, Horis, etc. (Id.)
————, ————. De Professoribus, Oratoribus, Nomenclatoribus, et Litteris. (Id.)
————, ————. De Varietate Navium. (Id. 11.)
————, ————. De Funeribus Antiquorum. (Id.)
————, ————. De Desponsatione Maris Adriatici. (Græv. Thes. Ital.)
————, ————. De Citharœdis, Fistulis, et Tintinnabulis. (Ugol. vol. 32.)
Lauro, Pietro. Arriano di Nicomedia dei Fatti del Magno Alessandro di Greco trad. in Italiano. 4to. Verona. 1730.
Lauts, U. H. Pindars Sentenzen. 12mo. Leipz. 1797.
Lauze de Peren, P. J. Eclaircissemens Historiques en Réponse aux Calomnies dont les Protestans du Gard sont l'Objet, etc. 2 vol. 8vo. Paris. 1818—19.
Laval, (le P.) Voyage de la Louisiane, fait par Ordre du Roy en l'Année 1720, etc. 4to. Paris. 1728.
Laval, Stephen Abel. History of the Reformation in France. 2 vols. 8vo. Lond. 1737—8.
Lavaysse, J. J. D. Voyage aux Iles de Trinidad, de Tobago, de la Marguerite, et de Vénézuéla. 2 vol. 8vo. Paris. 1813.
Lavenden, Theophilus. Travels of Four Englishmen, and a Preacher, into Africa and Asia, in 1600—11. (Churchill, Coll. vol. 7.)
Lavington, Geo. (Bp.) Enthusiasm of Methodists and Papists compared. 8vo. Lond. 1749.
————, ————. The Same. 3d ed. 2 vols. 8vo. Lond. 1752.
————, ————. ————. 2 vols. 12mo. Lond. 1754.
Lavoisier, A. L. Traité Elémentaire de Chimie. 2 vol. 8vo. Paris. 1793.
————, ————. Elements of Chemistry, tr. from the French, by R. Kerr. 5th ed. 2 vols. 8vo. Edin. 1802.
————, ————. Méthode de Nomenclature Chimique, proposée par MM. de Morveau, Lavoisier, Bertholet, et de Fourcroy. On y a joint un Nouveau Système de Charactères Chimiques par MM. Hassenfratz et Adet. 8vo. Paris. 1787.
————, ————. Essays Physical and Chemical, tr. from the French, with Notes, by T. Henry. 8vo. Lond. 1776.
————, ————. Essays on Atmospheric Air, tr, from the French, by T. Henry. 8vo. Warrington. 1783.
Lavoisne, C. V. Complete Genealogical, Historical, Chronological, and Geographical Atlas. fol. Phil. 1820.

Law. Body of the Common Law of England, &c. by E. W. 16mo. Lond. 1655.

——. Les Termes de la Ley; or Terms of the Law expounded. 8vo. Lond. 1671.

——. Grounds and Rudiments of Law and Equity. fol. Lond. 1751.

——. Advice on the Study of the Law. 12mo. Baltimore. 1811.

——. Enquiry into the Law of Nature and Revelation, &c. 8vo. Lond. 1737.

——. Considerations on Criminal Law. 8vo. Lond. 1772.

——. Lex Mercatoria. Vide Malynes.

——. Abridgement of the Laws in Force and Use in Her Majesty's Plantations. 8vo. Lond. 1704.

——. See Government,—United States,—Connecticut,—Massachusetts,—Pennsylvania, &c.

Law, Andrew. Rudiments of Music. 1783.

——, ——. Collection of Hymn Tunes, from the most modern and approved Authors. 8vo.

Law, Edmund, (Bp.) Considerations on the Theory of Religion, &c. 5th ed. 8vo. Camb. 1765.

——, ——. Enquiry into the Ideas of Space, Time, Immensity, and Eternity, &c. To which is added a Dissertation upon the Argument a Priori for proving the Existence of a First Cause, by a Learned Hand. 8vo. Camb. 1734.

——, ——. Considerations on the Propriety of requiring a Subscription to Articles of Faith. 2d ed. 8vo. Lond. 1774.

——, ——. Answer to the Above. 8vo. Oxford. 1774.

——, ——. Observations concerning Literary Property. 8vo. 1769.

Law, John. Money and Trade considered. 16mo. Glasgow. 1750.

——, ——. The Same. (Somers, Tracts, vol. 16.)

——, ——. Proposals and Reasons for constituting a Council of Trade in Scotland. 16mo. Glasgow. 1751.

Law, John. Oration. See Washington City.

Law, Robert. Memorialls; or Memorable Things in Brittain, from 1638 to 1684, edited by C. K. Sharpe. 4to. Edin. 1818.

Law, William. Case of Reason or Natural Religion stated. 8vo. Lond. 1731.

——, ——. Serious Call to a Devout and Holy Life. 6th ed. 8vo. Lond. 1753.

——, ——. The Same. 14th ed. 8vo. Lond. 1802.

——, ——. Letter to the Bishop of Bangor, on his Sermon. 3d and 4th ed. 8vo. Lond. 1717.

——, ——. Second Letter to the Same. 8vo. Lond. 1717.

——, ——. False Notion of a Christian Priesthood confuted; being an Answer to the Above. 1st and 2d ed. 8vo. Lond. 1718.

——, ——. Practical Treatise upon Christian Perfection. 8vo. Lond. 1726.

——, ——. Demonstration of the Errors of a Book called "A Plain Account of the Nature and End of the Sacrament of the Lord's Supper," &c. 8vo. Lond. 1737.

Lawes, Edward. On Pleading. 8vo. Portsmouth, N. H. 1808.
———, ———. On Pleading in Assumpsit, by J. Story. 8vo. Bost. 1811.
Lawrence, Henry. Militia Spiritualis; or a Treatise of Angels. 4to. Lond. 1652.
Lawrence, Nathaniel. Sketch of Tyngsborough, Massachusetts. (Mass. Hist. Coll. N. S. vol. 4.)
Lawrence, Tho. Mercurius Centralis; or a Discourse of Subterranean Shells. 12mo. Lond. 1664.
Lawrence, Tho. Oratio Harveiana. 4to. Lond. 1748.
———, ———. Prælectiones Medicæ. 8vo. Lond. 1757.
———, ———. Fr. Nichollsii Vita. 4to. Lond. 1780.
Lawrence, Wm. Sermon at the Ordination of S. Farrar. 8vo. Bost. 1761.
Lawrence, Wm. On Hernia. 8vo. Lond. 1807.
———, ———. Lectures on Physiology, Zoology, and the Natural History of Man. 8vo. Salem. 1828.
Lawrence. See Laurence.
Lawson, George. Exposition of the Epistle to the Hebrewes. fol. Lond. 1662.
———, ———. Theo-politica. 2d ed. 8vo. Lond. 1705.
Lawson, John. Description of North Carolina. 4to. Lond. 1711.
———, ———. History of Carolina, &c. 4to. Lond. 1718.
———, ———. Beschreibung der Provinz Carolina; aus dem Engl. 8vo. Hamburg. 1712.
Lawson, John. Lectures concerning Oratory. 8vo. Lond. 1759.
Lawton, Charlwood. Jacobite Principles vindicated. (Somers, Tr. vol. 3.)
Lawyer Out-law'd, and the Biter Bit. 8vo. Lond. 1734.
Lawyer's and Magistrate's Magazine. 3 vols. 8vo. 1792—4.
Laxmann, Erich. Sibirische Briefe. 12mo. Göttingen und Gotha. 1769.
Layard, Daniel Peter. Essay on the Bite of a Mad Dog. 2d ed. 8vo. Lond. 1763.
Layer, Christopher, Whole Proceedings upon the Tryal and Attainder of, for High Treason. fol. Lond. 1723.
Laymen. See Church See Whitefield, G.
Layton. See Leighton, A.
Lazare, (le Sieur de S.) Histoires Tragiques de nostre Temps. 8vo. Paris. 1635.
Lazeri, Pietro. Della Consecrazione del Panteon fatta da Bonifazio IV. 4to. Roma. 1749.
Lazius, Wolfgangus. Græciæ Antiquæ variis Numismatibus illustratæ Libri ii. (Gronov. vol. 6.)
Lea, Isaac. Description of Six New Species of the Genus Unio. (Amer. Phil. Tr. vol. 3, New Series.)
Leadbeater, Mary. Cottage Dialogues. 12mo. Phil. 1811.
Leadbetter, Charles. Astronomy. 4to. Lond. 1727.
———, ———. Compleat System of Astronomy. 2 vols. 8vo. Lond. 1728.

Leadbetter, Charles. Astronomy of the Satellites of the Earth, Jupiter, and Saturn. 8vo. Lond. 1729.

———, ———. Uranoscopia; or Contemplation of the Heavens. 8vo. Lond. 1735.

———, ———. Young Mathematician's Companion. 12mo. Lond. 1739.

———, ———. Mechanick Dialling. 8vo. Lond. 1773.

Leake, S. M. Historical Account of English Money. 2d ed. 8vo. Lond. 1745.

Leake, Wm. M. Researches in Greece. 4to. Lond. 1814.

———, ———. Answer to Observations on the Above in the Quarterly Review. (Classical Journal, vol. 10.)

Leaming, Jeremiah. Defence of the Episcopal Government of the Church. 8vo. N. York. 1766.

———, ———. Second Defence. 8vo. N. York. 1770.

———, ———. Convention Sermon. See Seabury, S.

Learning, Essay concerning Critical and Curious; in which are contained Reflections on the Controversie betwixt Sir William Temple and Mr. Wotton, and that betwixt Dr. Bentley and Mr. Boyle, by T. R. 12mo. Lond. 1698.

———. See Literature.

Leases of Cathedral-Churches and Colleges. Tables for Renewing and Purchasing them. 3d ed. 8vo. Lond. 1729.

———, Value of Church and College. 3d ed. 8vo. Lond. 1729.

Leavenworth, Mark. Sermon on the Death of Daniel Southmayd, Esq. 8vo. Bost. 1754.

Leavesly, Tho. Charity Sermon. 8vo. Lond. 1727.

———, ———. Reasons and Necessity of the Reformation, a Sermon at Salters-Hall. 8vo. Lond. 1735.

———, ———. Sermon on Reformation of Manners. 12mo. Lond. 1730.

Le Beau. Vide Beau, C. le.

Leber, Ferd. Prælectiones Anatomicæ, curante J. Wilson. 8vo. Edinburgh. 1790.

———, ———. See Vaughan, W.

Lebeuf, (l'Abbé.) Sur l'Isle d'Oscelle.—Sur l'Usage d'écrire sur des Tablettes de Cire.—Sur Deux Volumes de Poësies Françoises et Latines. (Acad. des Inscrip. vol. 20.)

Leblond, J. B. Description Abrégée de la Guyane Française. 8vo. Paris. 1814.

———, ———. Reise nach den Antillen und nach Südamerika, aus dem Franz. Theil 1. 12mo. Hamb. 1815.

Lebreton, F. Manuel de Botanique. 8vo. Paris. 1798.

Lebrun. Vide Chas, J.

Le Brun, Denis. Traité de la Communauté entre Mari et Femme, etc. fol. Paris. 1754.

Le Cat. Vide Cat, C. N. le.

Le Cène. Vide Cène, C. le.

Lechevalier. Vide Chevalier, J. B. le.

Lechford, Thomas. Plain Dealing; or Newes from New-England. 4to. Lond. 1642.

Le Clerc, J. Sentimens de quelques Théologiens de Hollande sur l'Histoire Critique du Vieux Testament, composée par le P. Richard Simon. 12mo. Amst. 1685. Vide Simon, R.

———, –. Vide Clerc, J. le.

Lécluse, Fl. Manuel de la Langue Grecque. 8vo. Paris. 1802.

Lectures, Abstract of a Course of, on Anatomy and Physiology, as delivered by a Professor of Anatomy, in London. 8vo. Lond. 1784.

Lectureships, Letter to a Bishop concerning, by F. T. 8vo. Lond. 1768.

Lediard, Thomas. Life of John, Duke of Marlborough. 2d ed. 2 vols. 8vo. Lond. 1743.

———, ———. Naval History of England. 2 vols. fol. Lond. 1735.

Ledyard, John, Life of. See Sparks, J.

Lee. Les Etats-Unis et l'Angleterre, trad. sur le MS. de l'Auteur. 8vo. Bordeaux. 1814.

Lee, Andrew. Sermons. 8vo. Worcester. 1803.

—, ———. Comments on Romans ix, in Two Discourses. 8vo. Norwich. 1811.

Lee, Arthur. Observations on certain Commercial Transactions in France. 8vo. Phil. 1780.

—, ———. Extracts from a Letter to the President of Congress, in Answer to a Libel by Silas Deane. 8vo. Phil. 1780.

Lee, Charles, (Gen.) Memoirs, Essays and Letters. 12mo. New York. 1792.

—, ————————. The Same. 8vo. Lond. 1792.

—, ————————, Proceedings of a General Court Martial for the Trial of, July 4th, 1778. fol. Phil. 1778.

Lee, Henry. Free Enquiry into the Meaning of the most excellent Name Jesus. 12mo. Lond.

—, ———. Sophron, or Natures Characteristics of the Truth. 2d ed. 3 vols. 8vo. Lond. 1760.

Lee, Henry, (Gen.) Memoirs of the War in the Southern Department of the United States. 2 vols. 8vo. Phil. 1812.

—, ————————. Oration on the Death of Washington. 8vo. Bost. 1800.

Lee, H. Campaign of 1781 in the Carolinas; with Remarks on Johnson's Life of Greene. 8vo. Phil. 1824.

Lee, James. Introduction to Botany. 3d ed. 8vo. Lond. 1776.

Lee, Rachel, F. A. Essay on Government. 8vo. Lond. 1809.

Lee, Richard H. Life and Correspondence of Richard Henry Lee. 2 vols. 8vo. Phil. 1825.

Leechman, Wm. Temper, Character, and Duty of a Minister of the Gospel; a Sermon. 4th ed. 12mo. Glasgow. 1744.

————, ——. The Same. 6th ed. 12mo. Glasgow. 1755.

————, ——. Sermon on Prayer. 5th ed. 12mo. Glasgow. 1755.

————, ——. Sermon at the Opening of the General Assembly of the Church of Scotland. 8vo. Edinburgh. 1758.

————, ——. Sermons. 2 vols. 8vo. Lond. 1789.

Leechman, Wm. Sermon before the Society in Scotland for Propagating Christian Knowledge. 8vo. Edin. 1768.
Leems, Knud. Account of Danish Lapland. (Pinkerton, vol. 1.)
Leers, J. D. Flora Herbornensis. 8vo. Berolini. 1789.
Leeuw, Isaacus de. De Conceptu Cœlorum apud Sacros Scriptores. 4to. Traj. ad Rhen. 1765.
Leeuwenhoek, Ant. van. Select Works, tr. from the Dutch and Latin by S. Hoole. 4to. Lond. 1798.
Lefroy, T. Reports. See Schoales, J.
Legacy. See Dying Legacy.
Le Gallois. Vide Gallois, M. le.
Legatio Magni Indorum Imperatoris Presbyteri Joannis ad Emanuelem Lusitaniæ Regem ; cum Carminibus C. Graphei ad Damianum de Goes. 12mo. 1532.
Legendre, A. M. Exercises de Calcul Intégral. 3 vol. 4to. Paris. 1816—17.
———, ———. Elements of Geometry ; from the French. 8vo. Camb. 1819.
———, ———. The Same. 2d ed. 8vo. Camb. 1825.
———, ———. See Farrar, J. See Gendre, A. M. le.
Legh, Gerard. Accedens of Armory. 4to. Lond. 1576.
Legrand-d'Aussy. Sur l'Etat de la Marine en France au Commencement du 14me Siècle. (Inst., Sciences, Mor. et Pol. vol. 2.)
—————. Sur les Anciennes Sépultures Nationales. (Id.)
—————. Sur l'Ancienne Législation de la France, comprenant la Loi Salique, etc. (Id. 3.)
—————. Voyage de Jérusalem en 1432—3, par Bertrandon de la Brocquière. (Id. 5.)
Lehmann, J. G. Traités de Physique, d'Histoire Naturelle, de Minéralogie et de Métallurgie, trad. de l'Allemand. 3 vol. 12mo. Paris. 1759.
Leibnitz, Goth. Gul. Essais de Theodicée sur la Bonté de Dieu, la Liberté de l'Homme et l'Origine du Mal.—Réflexions sur l'Ouvrage de M. Hobbes, de la Liberté, de la Nécessité et du Hazard.—Causa Dei asserta per Justitiam ejus, cum Cæteris ejus Perfectionibus, Cunctisque Actionibus conciliatam. 8vo. Amst. 1710.
———, ———, Opera Omnia, cum Vita ejus a J. Bruckero, studio L. Dutens. 6 vol. 4to. Genevæ. 1768.
———, ———. Letter to the Author of the Reflections upon the Origin of Mahometanism. 8vo. Lond. 1712.
———, ———. Letter to Mr. Burnet. See Sharpe, G.
Leichius, J. H. Diatribe in Photii Bibliothecam. 4to. Lips. 1748.
Leigh, Edward. Treatise of Religion and Learning, and of Religious and Learned Men. fol. Lond. 1656.
——, ———. Critica Sacra. 3d ed. fol. Lond. 1650.
——, ———. Antichristi Excidium. 8vo. Lond. 1664.
——, ———. Systeme or Body of Divinity. fol. Lond. 1662.
Leigh, Richard. Where to find a Friend ; a Comedy. 2d ed. 8vo. Lond. 1816.

Leighton, Alexander. Sions Plea against the Prelacy. 4to.
———, ————. The Same. 2d ed. 4to.
Leighton, Robert, (Abp.) Expository Works, and other Remains, revised by P. Doddridge. 2 vols. 8vo. Edin. 1748.
———, ————. Select Works. 8vo. Lond. 1758.
———, ————. Sermons. 8vo. Lond. 1692.
———, ————. Prælectiones Theologicæ, etc. 4to. Lond. 1693.
Leipsick. Vide Commentarii.
Leiste, Christian. Beschreibung des Brittischen Amerika. 8vo. 1778.
Leland, John. Itinerary. See Hearne, Tho.
———, ——. De Scriptoribus Britannicis. 8vo. Oxon. 1709.
———, ——. Cygnea Cantio. 12mo. Lond.
———, ——. Life of. See Huddesford, Wm.
Leland, John. Answer to "Christianity as old as the Creation." 2 vols. 8vo. Dublin. 1733.
———, ——. The Same. 2d ed. 2 vols. 8vo. Lond. 1740.
———, ——. Divine Authority of the Old and New Testament asserted. 2 vols. 8vo. Lond. 1739—40.
———, ——. View of the Principal Deistical Writers in England. 8vo. Lond. 1754.
———, ——. The Same. 3d ed. 2 vols. 8vo. Lond. 1757.
———, ——. The Same; with a View of the Present Times, in regard to Religion and Morals, &c. by W. L. Brown. 5th ed. 2 vols. 8vo. Lond. 1798.
———, ——. Advantage and Necessity of the Christian Revelation. 2 vols. 4to. Lond. 1764.
———, ——. The Same. 2 vols. 8vo. Lond. 1768.
———, ——. Discourses. 4 vols. 8vo. Lond. 1799.
Leland, Thomas. Orations of Demosthenes, &c., translated into English, with Notes. 3 vols. 8vo. Lond. 1763—70.
———, ———. The Same. 3d ed. 3 vols. 8vo. Lond. 1777.
———, ———. Life and Reign of Philip, King of Macedon. 2 vols. 4to. Lond. 1758.
———, ———. The Same. 2d ed. 2 vols. 4to. Lond. 1761.
———, ———. History of Ireland, from the Invasion of Henry II. 3 vols. 4to. Lond. 1773.
———, ———. Dissertation on Eloquence. 4to. Lond. 1764.
———, ———. Letter to him on the Above. See Hurd, R.
———, ———. Answer to the above Letter. 4to. Lond. 1765.
Le Maire. Vide Maire, J. le.
Lémery, Nicolas. Pharmacopée Universelle. 5me éd. 2 vol. 4to. Paris. 1763—4.
———, ——. Course of Chymistry; from the French. 4th ed. 8vo. Lond. 1720.
Le Mesurier. See Mesurier.
Lemnius, Levinus. De Complexionibus. 16mo. Francof. 1619.
———, ———. Herb. Bibl. Explicatio. 16mo. Francof. 1626.
———, ———. De Astrologia.—De Occultis Naturæ Miraculis.—Parænesis. 16mo. Francof. 1626—8.

Lemoine, Abraham. Treatise on Miracles. 8vo. Lond. 1747.
L'Empereur. Vide Empereur, C. l'.
Lempriere, J. Classical Dictionary. 4th ed. 8vo. Lond. 1801.
———, –. The Same. 6th ed. 8vo. Lond. 1806.
———, –. Universal Biography. 2 vols. 8vo. N. York. 1810.
———, –. The Same, by Lord. 2 vols. 8vo. N. York. 1825.
Lendrum, John. History of the American Revolution. 2 vols. 12mo. Bost. 1795.
Lenfant, Jaques. Histoire du Concile de Constance. 2 vol. 4to. Amst. 1714.
———, ———. History of the Council of Constance, translated from the French, by S. Whatley. 2 vols. 4to. Lond. 1730.
———, ———. Histoire du Concile de Pise. 2 vol. 4to. Amst. 1724.
———, ———. See Beausobre, I. de.
Leng, John, (Bp.) Sermon at the Consecration of St. Katherine's Hall in the University of Cambridge. 4to. Camb. 1704.
——, ————. Sixteen Sermons at Boyle's Lecture. 8vo. Lond. 1719.
——, ————. The Same. See Boyle's Lecture Sermons.
Lennep, J. D. à. In Analogiam Linguæ Græcæ; cui præmissa Oratio de Linguarum Analogia. 16mo. Ultraj. ad Rhen. 1779.
———, ———. Vide Valckenærius.
———, ———. Etymologicum Linguæ Græcæ, cum Animadversionibus Variorum, ab E. Scheidio. 2 vol. 8vo. Trajecti ad Rhen. 1790.
Lenoir, Alex. Description Hist. et Chronol. des Monumens de Sculpture réunis au Musée des Monumens Français. 8me éd. 8vo. Paris. 1806.
Lenz, Car. Gott. De Fragmentis Orphicis ad Astronomiam et Agrorum Culturam spectantibus. 8vo. Goettingæ. 1789.
——, ————. Anmerkungen zu Ovids Metamorphosen, etc. (Encyclopädie der Lat. Class.)
Leo, Ambrosius. Antiquitatum necnon Historiarum Urbis ac Agri Nolæ, ut et de Montibus Vesuvio et Abella Descriptio. (Græv. Thes. Ital.)
Leo Grammaticus. Vitæ Recent. Impp. Vide Theophanes.
Leo, John. Observations of Africa. (Purchas, vol. 2.)
Leon, Ant. de. Tratado et Confirmaciones Reales. 4to. Madrid. 1630.
Leon, Luis de. Poesias. 12mo. Madrid. 1790.
——, ———. Obras. 6 vol. 8vo. Madrid. 1804—16.
Leon, Pedro de Cieça de. Vide Cieça.
Leon Pinelo, Antonio de. Epitome de la Bibliotheca Oriental, y Occidental, Nautica, y Geografica. 3 vol. fol. Madrid. 1737—8.
Leonard, Abiel. Sermon at the Ordination of the Rev. George Wheaton. 8vo. Portsmouth. 1772.
Leonardus Chiensis. De Capta Constantinopoli. (Clauser, de Rebus Turcicis.)
Leonhardi, J. Brevis Descriptio Democratici Rhætiæ Reipublicæ Regiminis. 8vo. Lond. 1704.

Leonhardi, J. Account of the Grisons. 8vo. Lond. 1711.

Leoniceno, N. Delle Guerre de Romani. Vide Dion, Cassius.

Leopoldine Academy. Vide Miscellanea Curiosa. Vide Nova Acta.

Lepelletier. Mémoires dans les Annales du Muséum d'Histoire Naturelle.

Le Pluche, (Abbé.) Vide Pluche.

Lerius, Jo. Historia Navigationis in Brasiliam, Gallice scripta, nunc vero primum Latinitate donata. 8vo. 1686.

———, —. Extracts out of his Historie of Brasill. (Purchas, vol. 4.)

Leroux, P. J. Dictionnaire Comique, Satyrique, Critique, Burlesque, Libre et Proverbial. 2 vol. 8vo. Pampelune. 1786.

Le Roy. Vide Roy.

Lery, J. Vide Lerius, J.

Lesbonax. Orationes. Vide Oratores Græci, a Reiskio.

Lescarbot, Marc. Relation Dernière de ce qui s'est passé au Voyage de Poutrincourt en la Nouvelle France. 12mo. Paris. 1612.

————, ——. Histoire de la Nouvelle-France. 2de éd. 2 vol. 12mo. Paris. 1612.

————, ——. Nova Francia. (Churchill, Coll. vol. 8.)

Leslie, Charles. Short and Easy Method with the Deists. 6th ed. 8vo. Lond. 1726.

——, ———. The Same; with a Discourse concerning Episcopacy and the Epistle of St. Ignatius to the Trallians, by J. Checkley. 8vo. Lond. 1723.

——, ———. See Checkley, J.

——, ———. Theological Works. 2 vols. fol. Lond. 1721.

Leslie, John. Experimental Inquiry into the Nature and Propagation of Heat. 8vo. Lond. 1804.

——, ——. Tracts respecting the Election of Mr. Leslie to the Professorship of Mathematics in the University of Edinburgh. 2 vols. 8vo. Edinburgh. 1805—6.

——, ——. Geometrical Analysis, and Geometry of Curve Lines. 8vo. Edinburgh. 1821.

Less, Godfrey. Authenticity, Preservation, and Credibility of the New Testament, translated from the German, by R. Kingdon. 8vo. Lond. 1804.

Lesser, F. C. Théologie des Insectes, trad. de l'Allemand. 2 vol. 8vo. La Haye. 1742.

Lessing, G. E. Fragmente und Antifragmente. 2 Theile. 12mo. Nürnberg. 1788.

———, ——, und J. J. Eschenburg. Zur Geschichte und Litteratur. 3 Bände. 8vo. Berlin und Braunschweig. 1781—93.

Lessius, Leon. De Justitia et Jure, etc. fol. Antv. 1626.

Lessons to a Young Prince, by an Old Statesman, on the present Disposition in Europe to a General Revolution. 6th ed. 8vo. N. York. 1791.

Le Sueur. Vide Sueur.

Leti, Greg. Il Nipotismo di Roma. 16mo. 1667.

Letter from Amsterdam to a Friend in England. 4to. Lond. 1678.

Letter. Answer to the Letter from Amsterdam. 4to. Lond. 1678.

———, Another, from One in the Country to his Friend in Boston, on the Governor's Salary. 8vo. Bost.

——— to a Member of Parliament, concerning the Present State of Affairs at Home and Abroad. 8vo. Lond. 1740.

——— to the late Recorder of N——. 8vo. Lond.

——— from a Member of Parliament, upon the Prince of Wales's Salary. 8vo. Lond.

——— from a Travelling Tutor to a Noble Young Lord, containing good Advice to the Independent Electors of Great Britain. 8vo. Lond. 1747.

———, Second and Third, to the Whigs, by the Author of the First. 8vo. Lond. 1748.

——— from a Russian Sea-Officer, containing Remarks on Mr. de l'Isle's Chart of the New Discoveries; with Observations by A. Dobbs. Also Mr. de l'Isle's Memoir on his Chart; from the French. 8vo. Lond. 1754.

———, Second, to a Friend, giving a more particular Narrative of the Defeat of the French Army at Lake-George. 4to. Bost. 1755.

——— to an honourable Brigadier General, Commander in Chief of his Majesty's Forces in Canada. 8vo. Lond. 1760.

——— from a West-India Merchant, concerning that Part of the French Proposals, which relates to North-America, and particularly Newfoundland. 4to.

——— from a Right Honorable Person (Mr. Pitt); and the Answer to it; translated into Verse, with Notes. 4to. Lond. 1761.

——— from a Merchant in London to his Nephew in North America, relative to the Present Posture of Affairs in the Colonies. 8vo. Lond. 1766. See British Colonies,—Colonies, &c.

——— concerning Libels, Warrants, the Seizure of Papers, &c. 6th ed. 8vo. Lond. 1766.

——— from Farmer Trusty to his Landlord Sir William Worthy, &c. 8vo. Lond. 1769.

——— to the Bishop of Landaff, from a Petitioner. 8vo. Marlborough. 1774.

——— from a Virginian to the Members of the Congress. 8vo. 1774.

——— from an American, now resident in London, to a Member of Parliament, on the Subject of the Restraining Proclamation. 8vo. Lond. 1784.

———, Circular, addressed to the State Societies of the Cincinnati, by a General Meeting at Philadelphia, May 3, 1784. 8vo. Phil. 1784.

———, Circular, from the General Republican Committee, of the City and County of New York, in Vindication of the Measures of the General Government. 8vo. N. York. 1809.

——— to the Hon. Mr. Calhoun, Chairman of the Committee on a National Currency. 12mo. Phil. 1816.

——— from a Congregationalist to a Friend, on the Subject of joining the New Episcopal Church. 8vo. Bost. 1820.

Lettera al Reverendissimo Padre D. Gian Francesco Baldini. 4to. Napoli. 1751.

Lettere Familiari d'Alcuni Bolognesi del nostro Secolo. 2 vol. 8vo. Venez. 1745.

———. Alcune Lettere Piacevoli, Una dell' Arsiccio Intronato, L'altre di M. Alessandro Marzi, etc. 4to. Siena. 1618.

Letters, Four, to a Friend;—concerning Assent to a Revealed Proposition; concerning the Scripture Sense of Heresy; containing Remarks upon Mr. Clubb's Supplement; Remarks upon his Account of the Christian Justification. 8vo. Lond. 1725.

——— of Religion, between Theophilus and Eugenio. Part 1, 2d ed. 4to. Lond. Part 2, 2d ed. 4to. Lond. 1729. Part 3, 3d ed. 4to. Lond. 1735.

———, Three Private, from Persons of Distinction in the Army at Hanau, to their Friends in London. fol. Lond. 1743. See Hanau.

——— to the Earl of Hillsborough, the Marquis of Rockingham, and the Archbishops and Bishops, respecting Grenada, by Pliny junior. 8vo. Lond. 1770. See Grenada.

——— inscribed to the very Loyal and truly Pious Doctor Samuel Cooper. 8vo. Bost. 1775.

———, Thirty, on various Subjects. 2 vols. 12mo. Lond. 1783.

——— to the Yeomanry of the United States, on Funding and Bank Systems, by an American Farmer. 8vo. Phil. 1793. See United States.

——— to the People, by a Farmer, (L. Lincoln.) 8vo. Salem. 1802.

——— from Virginia, translated from the French. 16mo. Baltimore. 1816.

——— to Richard Heber, Esq. on the Waverley Novels. 12mo. Bost. 1822.

Lettre d'un Anglois, contenant une Relation authentique de ce qui s'est passé entre les Cours de Londres et de Versailles, au Commencement des Troubles presents. 8vo. La Haye. 1756.

———. Copie d'une Lettre envoyée d'Angleterre à Dom Bernardin de Mendoze, Ambassadeur en France pour le Roy d'Espaigne. 8vo. 1588.

Lettres Edifiantes et Curieuses, écrites des Missions Etrangères, par quelques Missionnaires de la Compagnie de Jésus. (vol. 1—28, et 31, 23.) 30 vol. 12mo. Paris. 1717—74.

——— d'un François à un Hollandois, au sujet des Différends survenus entre la France et la Grande-Bretagne, touchant leurs Possessions respectives dans l'Amérique Septentrionale. 4to. Paris. 1755.

———, contenantes la Description d'un Voyage, fait de Minorque à Rome, en l'an 1777. 12mo. Francf. et Leips. 1779.

——— d'un Membre du Congrès Amériquain à divers Membres du Parlement d'Angleterre. 8vo. Phil. 1781.

——— Normandes, ou Correspondance Politique et Littéraire. (tom. 5—10,) 6 tomes, et (livraisons 91—7,) 7 livraisons, faisant partie du tome 11me. 8vo. Paris. 1819—20.

Lettres. Vide Recueil.

Lettsom, John C. Memoirs of Dr. John Fothergill. 4th ed. Also Memoirs of Drs. William Cuming, George Cleghorn, A. Russell, and Mr. P. Collinson. 8vo. Lond. 1786.

———, ———. Hints respecting Human' Dissections. 8vo. Lond. 1795.

———, ———. Natural History of the Tea-Tree, &c. 4to. Lond. 1772.

———, ———. Hints designed to promote Beneficence, Temperance, and Medical Science. 3 vols. 8vo. Lond. 1801.

———, ——— und J. Ellis. Geschichte des Thees und Koffees, aus dem Engl. 12mo. Leipz. 1776.

Leun, J. G. F. Vide Paulus, Sanctus.

Leuschnerus, J. C. Commentatio ad Joh. v, 26. 4to. Hirschbergæ. 1753.

Leusden, Joh. Schola Syriaca, una cum Synopsi Chaldaica. ed. 2da. 12mo. Ultrajecti. 1672.

———, ——. Compendium Biblicum, Hebr. et Lat. 12mo. Ultrajecti. 1680.

———, ——. Compendium Græcum Novi Testamenti, cum Versione Latina. ed. 2da. 12mo. Ultrajecti. 1677.

———, ——. Idem. 12mo. Lug. Bat. 1688.

———, ——. ——. ed. 5ta. 12mo. Halæ Sax. 1704.

———, ——. ——. 12mo. Rostochi. 1747.

———, ——. ——. 12mo. Rostochi. 1762.

———, ——. Onomasticon Sacrum. 12mo. Ultraj. 1665.

———, ——. Clavis Hebraica Vet. Test. 4to. Ultraj. 1683.

———, ——. Clavis Græca Novi Test. 12mo. Utraj. 1672.

———, ——. Philologus Hebræus. 4to. Ultraj. 1657.

———, ——. Philologus Hebræo-Mixtus. 4to. Ultraj. 1663.

———, ——. Idem. 4to. Ultraj. 1665.

———, ——. De Dialectis Novi Testamenti, singulatim de ejus Hebraismis. Accessit J. Vorstii Commentariolus de Adagiis N. T. Hebraicis. 8vo. Lips. 1792.

———, ——. Vide Biblia. Vide Testamentum Novum.

Leveillé, A. J. B. F. Vide Scarpa, A.

Lever, Thomas. Sermon at Pauls Crosse. 16mo. Lond.

Lévesque de Pouilly, L. J. Théorie des Sentimens Agréables. 12mo. Paris. 1748.

Lévesque, C. P. Sur l'Homme dans la Vie Sauvage, Pastorale, et Policée. (Instit., Sciences Mor. et Pol. vol. 1.)

———, ——. Sur la Philosophie Ancienne. (Id.)

———, ——. Sur Hésiode.—Sur Homère.—Sur les Mœurs et les Usages des Grecs du temps d'Homère. (Id. 2.)

———, ——. Sur les Anciennes Relations de la France avec la Russie. (Id.)

———, ——. Sur la Constitution de Sparte. (Id. 3.)

———, ——. Sur la Constitution d'Athènes. (Id. 4.)

———, ——. Sur le Retour des Argonautes par le Nord. (Id.)

———, ——. Sur le Government de la France sous les deux premières Dynasties. (Id. 5.)

Léveque, C. P. De la Formation du Langage, considérée dans les plus simples Elémens de la Langue Grocque. (Id.)

———, ——. Sur les trois Poètes Tragiques de la Grèce.—Sur Aristophane.—Sur les Progrès de la Peinture chez les Grecs. (Id., Lit. 1.)

Levi, David. Letters to Dr. Priestley. 8vo. Lond. 1789—93.

Levinz, Sir Creswell. Entries. fol. Lond. 1702.

———, ————. Reports. parts 1 and 2. fol. Lond. 1702.

Lévizac, (l'Abbé de.) Grammaire de la Langue Françoise. 3me éd. 2 vol. 8vo. Paris. 1801.

Lewin, William. Birds of Great Britain. 7 vols. fol. Lond. 1789—94.

Lewis XIV. Vide Médailles.

Lewis XV, Private Life of. See Justamond, J. O.

——— ——. Sacre de Louis XV. Vide Danchet.

Lewis XVI, Correspondence of, with Observations, by H. M. Williams. 3 vols. 8vo. N. York. 1803.

Lewis, Daniel. Election Sermon. 8vo. Bost. 1748.

———, ———. Sins of Youth, a Sermon. 12mo. Bost. 1725.

Lewis, E. African Observer. vol. 1. 8vo. Phil. 1827—8.

Lewis, Edward. Patriot King displayed, in the Life and Reign of Henry VIII, after his Quarrel with the Pope. 12mo. Lond. 1769.

Lewis, Henry R. Code of Laws as established by the Pangerans' Court at Fort Marlborough. 4to. Lond. 1821.

Lewis, John. History of the English Translations of the Bible. 2d ed. 8vo. Lond. 1739.

———, ——. Sermon, January 30th. 8vo. Lond. 1718.

———, ——. The New Testament, translated out of the Latin Vulgat by John Wiclif; to which is prefixt a History of the several Translations of the Bible &c. into English. fol. Lond. 1731.

Lewis, Meriwether, and Wm. Clarke. History of the Expedition under their Command to the Sources of the Missouri, and thence to the Pacific Ocean, in 1804—6, prepared for the Press by Paul Allen; with the Life of Captain Lewis, by Thomas Jefferson. 2 vols. 8vo. Phil. 1814.

———, ————————————. See Gass, P.

Lewis, Thomas. Antiquities of the Hebrew Republic. 4 vols. 8vo. Lond. 1724.

Lewis, William. Experimental History of the Materia Medica. 4to. Lond. 1761.

———, ———. Materia Medica. 4th ed; by J. Aikin. 2 vols. 8vo. Lond. 1791.

Lewis, William. Philosophical Commerce of Arts. 2 vols. 4to. Lond. 1763.

———, ———. Experiments and Observations on American Potashes. 8vo. Lond. 1767.

Lewis, Wm. L. Thebaid of Statius; from the Latin. See Chalmers, A.

Lex Mercatoria Rediviva, by Wyndham Beawes. 4th ed., by Thomas Mortimer. fol. Lond. 1783.
—— ————. See Malynes, G.
Lexicon Talmudicum. 4to. Venet.
Lexicon Trilingue, ex Thesauro R. Stephani, et Dictionario J. Frisii, cum Præfatione J. Sturmii. fol. Argent. 1587.
Leyba Ramirez de Arellano, Fr. de. La Infeliz Aurora; La Mayor Constancia de Muzio Scebola; El Honor es lo Primero; Comedias. 4to.
Leybourn, William. Compleat Surveyor. 2d ed. fol. Lond. 1657.
Leycester, John. Commonwealth. 4to. Lond. 1641.
———, ——. Ghost, a Poem. 4to. 1641.
Leyden, J. On the Language and Literature of the Indo-Chinese Nations. (Asiatic Researches, vol. 10.)
———, –. On the Rosheniah Sect and its Founder. (Id. 11.)
Leyserus, Polycarpus. De Noviter Adornanda Novi Testamenti Græci Editione. 4to. Helmst. 1723.
———, ————. De frustra quæsita Poesi in Codice Sacro Hebræo. (Ugol. vol. 31.)
Leysser, Fr. Wil. a. Flora Halensis. 8vo. Halæ Sal. 1783.
Lezay-Marnezia, Cl. Fr. Ad. de. Lettres écrites des Rives de l'Ohio. 8vo. Paris. 1801.
Lhuyd, Edward. Archæologia Britannica. fol. Oxford. 1707.
Liancourt. Vide Rochefoucauld-Liancourt.
Libanius Sophista. Epistolæ, cum Versione et Notis J. C. Wolfii. 8vo. Lips. 1711.
——— ———. ———. Vide Anecdota Gr. a Wolfio.
——— ———. Orationes et Declamationes, cum Notis J. J. Reiske. 3 vol. 8vo. Altenburgi. 1791—5.
Libellus de Fabularum, Ludorum, Theatrorum, Scenarum, ac Scenicorum Antiqua Consuetudine. (Gronov. vol. 8.)
Liber. See Rabbinical Books.
Liberties, the Peoples Ancient and Just, asserted in the Tryal of William Penn, and William Mead. 4to. 1670.
———, ——————————, in the Proceedings against, and Tryals of Thomas Rudyard, and Others. 2d part. 4to. 1670.
———. See British Liberties.
Liberty of Conscience, the Principles of, stated and defended. 12mo. Edin. 1739.
——— of the Press. Essay on it, chiefly as it respects Personal Slander. 8vo. Lond.
——— ————. Essay on it. 8vo. Phil. 1799.
——— and Free Enquiry, the Cause of, asserted. 8vo. Lond. 1750.
———, Present State of, in Great Britain and her Colonies. 8vo. Lond. 1769.
——— and Independency, Essay on. 8vo. Lond. 1747.
——— and Right. See Great-Britain.
Licetus, Fortunius. De Lucernis Antiquorum Reconditis. fol. Utini. 1653.

Licetus, Fortunius. Pro Urbis Cæsenæ Antiquitate Apologia. (Græv. Thes. Ital.)
Lichfield Cathedral, Some Account of, more particularly of the Painted Glass with which its Windows are adorned. 12mo. Lichfield. 1811.
Liddelius, Duncanus. Ars Medica. 12mo. Hamb. 1617.
Liebentantius, Mich. De Terra Morijah, et Monte Visionis Dei. (Ugol. vol. 7.)
Lieberkühn, Jo. N. Dissertationes Quatuor Medicæ, cura Joannis Sheldon. 4to. Lond. 1782.
Liernur, C. A. Brevis Inquisitio in Resuscitatos Hodiernorum Irenicorum Conatus. 4to. Argent. 1704.
Lieutaud, Josephus. Historia Anatomico-Medica. 2 vol. 4to. Paris. 1767.
———, ———. Synopsis Universæ Praxeos-Medicæ. 4to. Amst. 1765.
Life Boat, a Poem, by a Member of the Humane Society. See Harris, T. M.
Lightfoot, John. Works, with his Life. 2 vols. fol. Lond. 1684.
———, ——. Whole Works, by J. R. Pitman. 13 vols. 8vo. Lond. 1825.
———, ——. Genuine Remains. 8vo. Lond. 1700.
———, ——. Centuria Chorographica in S. Matthæum.—Decas Chorographica in S. Marcum.—Chorographica Pauca in S. Lucam.—Disquisitio Chorographica in S. Johannem. (Ugol. vol. 5.)
———, ——. Descriptio Templi Hierosolymitani.—Ministerium Templi. (Id. 9.).
———, ——. Description of the Temple Service, as it stood in the Days of our Saviour. 4to. Lond. 1650.
———, ——. Horæ Hebr. et Talmud., etc. Vide Episcopius.
———, ——. Harmony of the Old Testament, and Second Part of the Harmony of the Evangelists. 4to. Lond. 1647.
———, ——. Harmony of the Four Evangelists among themselves, and with the Old Testament. parts 1 and 3. 4to. Lond. 1644—50.
Lignac, (l'Abbé de.) Avis Paternels d'un Militaire à son Fils, Jésuite. 12mo. 1760.
Ligon, Richard. History of Barbados. fol. Lond. 1657.
Ligorius, Pyrrhus. Descriptio Villæ Tiburtinæ Hadrianeæ. (Græv. Thes. Ital.)
Lilawati; or a Treatise on Arithmetic and Geometry, by Bhascara Acharya, translated from the Sanscrit by J. Taylor. 4to. Bombay. 1816.
Liljeblad, Samuel. Flora. 12mo. Upsala. 1798.
Lillo, George. Sylvia, an Opera. 8vo. Lond. 1731.
——, ———. Christian Hero, a Tragedy. 2d ed. 8vo. Lond. 1735.
——, ———. Marina, a Play. 8vo. Lond. 1738.
——, ———. Britannia and Batavia, a Masque. 8vo. Lond. 1740.

Lillo, George. Elmerick, a Tragedy. 8vo. Lond. 1740.
——, ——. London Merchant, or the History of George Barnwell. 7th ed. 8vo. Lond. 1740.
——, ——. Account of Scanderbeg. 8vo. Lond. 1735.
Lilly, John. General Abridgment of the Law. 2 vols. fol. Lond. 1719.
——, ——. Modern Entries. 3d ed. fol. Lond. 1758.
Lily, William. English Grammar, or Plain Exposition of Lilie's Grammar in English, by R. R. 12mo. Lond. 1641.
Lima. See Earthquake.
Limborch, Philippus à. Historia Inquisitionis. fol. Amst. 1692.
——, ——. History of the Inquisition, translated by S. Chandler. 2 vols. 4to. Lond. 1731.
——, ——. Theologia Christiana, ed. 4ta.; cum Tractatu de Prædestinatione. fol. Amst. 1715.
——, ——. De Veritate Religionis Christianæ, 4to. Goudæ. 1687.
——, ——. Commentarius in Acta Apostolorum et in Epistolas ad Romanos et Hebræos. 4to. Roterodami. 1711.
——, ——. Historia Vitæ Simonis Episcopii. 8vo. Amst. 1701.
——, ——. Epistolæ Eruditorum Virorum Ecclesiasticæ et Theologicæ. fol. Amst. 1704.
Limner, Karl. Meine Verfolgung in Russland. 8vo. Leipz. 1823.
Limonade, (Comte de.) Le Machiavélisme du Cabinet Français. 4to. Cap-Henry. 1814.
Linage, J. de Veitia. Norte de la Contratacion de las Indias Occidentales. fol. Sevilla. 1672.
Lincoln, Levi. Letters to the People, by a Farmer. 12mo. Salem. 1802.
Lincoln, Levi, (Gov.) Speeches and Messages to the Legislature. 8vo. Bost. 1827—9.
Lind, James. Essay on Diseases incidental to Europeans in Hot Climates. 3d ed. 8vo. Lond. 1777.
——, ——. Versuch über die Krankheiten denen Europäer in heissen Climaten unterworfen sind; aus dem Engl. 12mo. Riga und Leipz. 1773.
Lind, John. Remarks on the Acts of Parliament relating to the Colonies; with a Plan of Reconciliation. vol. 1. 8vo. Lond. 1775.
——, ——. Rights of Great Britain asserted. 8vo. Lond. 1776.
——, ——. Réponse à la Déclaration du Congrès Américain, trad. de l'Anglois par M. Freville. 8vo. La Haye. 1777.
Linda, Lucas de. Descriptio Orbis et Omnium ejus Rerumpublicarum. 8vo. Amst. 1665.
Lindau, Aug. Ferd. Novum in Platonis Timæum et Critiam Conjecturarum atque Emendationum Specimen. 12mo. Vratislaviæ ad Viad. 1815.
——, ——. De Usu et Præstantia Artium et Literarum Græcorum. 12mo. Vratislaviæ. 1815.

Lindenau, B. von, und J. G. F. Bohnenberger. Zeitschrift für Astronomie und verwandte Wissenschaften. Januar—August, 1817, und Mai—August, 1818. 8vo. Stuttgart und Tübingen.

Lindenbrogius, Frid. Codex Legum Antiquarum. fol. Francof. 1613.

Lindsay, H. Essay on 1 Cor. i, 21, against the Infidelity of the Age. 8vo. Edin. 1736.

Lindsay, James. Sermons. 8vo. Lond. 1818.

Lindsay, John. Short History of the Regal Succession, and the Rights of the several Kings recorded in the Holy Scriptures; with Remarks on Mr. Whiston's Scripture Politics, &c. 8vo. Lond. 1720.

Lindsay, John. Voyage to the Coast of Africa. 8vo. Lond. 1759.

Lindsey, Theophilus. Historical View of the State of the Unitarian Doctrine and Worship. 8vo. Lond. 1783.

———, ———. Apology on Resigning the Vicarage of Catterick. 4th ed. 8vo. Lond. 1782.

———, ———. Sequel to the Apology. 8vo. Lond. 1776.

———, ———. Catechist. 12mo. Lond. 1781.

———, ———. The Same. 12mo. Lond. 1792.

———, ———. Vindiciæ Priestleianæ. 8vo. Lond. 1788.

———, ———. Examination of Mr. Robinson's Plea for the Divinity of Christ. 8vo. Lond. 1789.

———, ———. Letter to a Layman concerning the Rev. Mr. Lindsey's Proposal for a Reformed English Church. 8vo. Lond. 1774.

———, ———. Sermon at the Opening of the Chapel in Essex-Street, April 17, 1774. 3d ed. 8vo. Lond.

———, ———. Sermon at the Opening of the New Chapel in Essex-Street, March 29, 1778. 8vo. Lond.

———, ———. Two Dissertations. I. On the Preface to St. John's Gospel. II. On Praying to Jesus Christ. 8vo. Lond. 1779.

Lindsly, Philip. Plea for the Theological Seminary at Princeton, N. J. 8vo. Trenton. 1821.

———, ———. Discourses on the Improvement of Time. 8vo. Trenton. 1823.

Linen Bill. Facts and Observations relative to the Fate of it. 8vo. Dublin. 1753.

Lingard, John. History of England, (to the End of the Reign of Charles I.) 3d ed. 10 vols. 8vo. Lond. 1825.

Linguet, S. N. H. Histoire Impartiale des Jésuites. 2 vol. 12mo. 1768.

Linn, William. Fast Sermon. 8vo. New York. 1798.

Linnæan Society of New-England. Report of a Committee relative to a large Marine Animal supposed to be a Serpent. 8vo. Bost. 1817.

Linnæus, Carolus. Classes Plantarum. 8vo. Lug. Bat. 1738.

———, ———. Genera Plantarum. ed. 6ta. 8vo. Holmiæ. 1764.

Linnæus, Carolus. Species Plantarum. ed. 3tia. 2 vol. 8vo. Vindobonæ. 1764.

———, ———. Supplementum Plantarum. 8vo. Brunsvigæ. 1781.

———, ———. Systema Vegetabilium, a C. H. Persoon. ed. 15ta. 8vo. Gottingæ. 1797.

———, ———. Amœnitates Academicæ. 6 vol. 8vo. Lug. Bat. et Holmiæ. 1749—63.

———, ———. Systema Naturæ.—Fundamenta Botanica. ed. 2da, 8vo. Stockholmiæ. 1740.

———, ———. Systema Naturæ. ed. 12ma. 2 tomi in 3 vol. 8vo. Holmiæ. 1766—7.

———, ———. Flora Suecica. ed. 2da. 8vo. Stockholmiæ. 1755.

———, ———. Fauna Suecica. 8vo. Stockholmiæ. 1761.

———, ———. Philosophia Botanica. 8vo. Vien. Aust. 1763.

———, ———. Museum Reginæ Suecorum, etc. 8vo. Holmiæ. 1764.

———, ———. Clavis Medicinæ. 8vo. Holmiæ. 1766.

———, ———. Instructio Peregrinatoris. 8vo. Lug. Bat. 1762.

———, ———. Materia Medica, curante J. C. D. Schrebero. ed. 5ta. 8vo. Lips. et Erlangæ. 1787.

———, ———. Entomologia, Faunæ Suecicæ Descriptionibus aucta. 4 vol. 8vo. Lugduni. 1789.

———, ———. Bibliotheca Botanica. 8vo. Halæ Salicæ. 1747.

———, ———. Institutes of Botany. See Milne, C.

———, ———. Tour in Lapland. See Smith, Sir James, E.

———, ———. General System of Nature, with his Life, by William Turton. 7 vols. 8vo. Lond. 1802—6.

———, ———. Vide Floræ Lusitanicæ,—Mouton-Fontenille, —Thornton, R. J.

Linnæus, Carolus, (fil.) Decas Prima Plantarum Rariorum Horti Upsaliensis. fol. Stockholmiæ. 1762.

———, ———. Plantarum Rariorum Horti Upsaliensis Fasciculus Primus. fol. Lips. 1767.

Linschoten, J. H. van. Description of the Açores. (Purchas, vol. 4.)

———, ———. Of Goa. (Id. Pilgrimage.)

Lipenius, Martinus. Strenarum Historia. (Grævius, vol. 12.)

———, ———. De Navigio Salomonis.—De Ophir. (Ugol. vol. 7.)

Lipmannus, (Rabbi.) Liber Nizachon, oppositus Christianis, Sadducæis atque Aliis, curante T. Hackspan. Accessit Tractatus, adversus Lipmannum Triumphantem. 4to. Noribergæ. 1644.

Lippi, Lorenzo. Malmantile Racquistato. 8vo. Milano. 1807.

Lipsius, Justus. De Machinis, Tormentis, Telis. 4to. Antv. 1596.

———, ———. Opera Omnia, cum Vita ejus. 4 vol. 8vo. Vesaliæ. 1675.

———, ———. Manuductio ad Stoicam Philosophiam.—Physiologia Stoicorum. 8vo. Paris. 1604.

Lipsius, Justus. Idem. 16mo. Lug. Bat. 1644.
———, ———. De Cruce Libri Tres, cum Notis. 8vo. Lut. Par. 1598.
———, ———. De Vesta et Vestalibus Syntagma. (Græv. vol. 5.)
———, ———. Saturnalium Sermonum Libri Duo, qui de Gladiatoribus. (Id. 9.)
———, ———. De Amphitheatro Liber. (Id.)
———, ———. Miracles of the B. Virgin. 4to. Lond. 1688.
———. ———. Justi Lipsii Sapientiæ et Litterarum Antistitis Fama Posthuma. 4to. Antv. 1607.
Liset, Abraham. Accomptants Closet. Lond. 1660.
L'Isle, (M. de.) Erklärung der Charte von den Neuen Entdeckungen, etc., aus dem Franz. 12mo. Berlin. 1753.
——, ————. Schreiben über die Charte. 12mo. Berlin.
——, ————. Explanation of the Map of the New Discoveries Northward of the South-Sea. See Letter from a Russian Sea-Officer.
Lisle, Henry M. Oration on the Death of Washington. 8vo. Bost. 1800.
Lister, Martinus. Historia Conchyliorum. fol. Lond. 1685.
——, ————. De Araneis et Cochleis. 4to. Lond. 1678.
——, ————. De Conchyliis Bivalvibus Exercitatio Anatomica. 4to. Lond. 1696.
——, ————. De quibusdam Morbis Chronicis. 8vo. Lond. 1694.
——, ————. Dissertatio Medicinalis de Calculo Humano. 4to. Lond. 1696.
——, ————. Journey to Paris in 1698. (Pinkerton, vol. 4.)
Literary Fund Society. See Charitable Institutions.
Literary Gazette, United States. 4 vols. 4to. and 8vo. Bost. 1825.
——— ————, ——————. See Review.
——— Miscellany. 2 vols. 8vo. Camb. 1806.
Literary Property, Enquiry into the Nature and Origin of. 8vo. Lond. 1762.
——— ————, Thoughts on the State of. 8vo. Lond. 1764.
——— ————, Letter concerning. 8vo. 1769.
——— ————, Observations occasioned by the Contest about. 8vo. Camb. 1770.
——— ————. See Warburton. See Maclaurin.
Literatur-Zeitung, Allgemeine. 71 Bände. 4to. Halle, etc. 1804—24.
Literature, Essay upon; or an Enquiry into the Antiquity and Original of Letters. 8vo. Lond. 1726.
————. See Learning.
Lithgow, William. Travels in Candia, Greece, &c. (Purchas, vol. 2.)
Littara, Vincentius. De Rebus Netinis. (Græv. Thes. Ital.)
Littleton, Adam. Dictionary, English and Latin. 4th ed. 4to. Lond. 1703.
Littleton, Thomas. Tenures, in English. 12mo. Lond. 1612.

Liturgia; seu Liber Precum Communium, etc., in Ecclesia Anglicana receptus. ed. 3tia. 12mo. Lond. 1720.
Liturgy. View of the New Directory and Vindication of the Ancient Liturgy of the Church of England. 3d ed. 4to. Oxford. 1646.
——. Account of the Proceedings of the Commissioners, appointed by his Majesty, for the Review of the Book of Common-Prayer. 4to. Lond. 1661.
——. Petition for Peace; with the Reformation of the Liturgy. 4to. Lond. 1661.
——. Two Papers of Proposals concerning the Discipline and Ceremonies of the Church of England. 4to. Lond. 1661.
——. Petition to the King by the Ministers appointed to alter the Liturgy. 4to. Lond. 1661.
——. Copy of the whole Disputation at the Savoy, respecting the Liturgy. 4to. 1661.
——. Brief View of Dr. Gauden's Considerations touching the Liturgy of the Church of England. 2d ed. 4to. Lond. 1661.
——. Primitive Rule of Reformation, according to the First Liturgy of Edward VI, &c. 4to. Lond. 1688.
——. No sufficient Reason for restoring Edward Sixth's First Liturgy. 8vo. Lond. 1718.
——. Objection drawn from the Act of Union against a Review of it. 8vo. Lond. 1740.
——, Christian; or a Devout and Rational Form of Worship. 4to. Lond. 1741.
——. Observations upon it. To which is added, the Journals of the American Convention appointed to frame an Ecclesiastical Constitution for the Episcopal Churches in the United States. 8vo. Lond. 1789.
——. See Clodius, J. C.,—Common-Prayer-Book,—Freeman, J.,—Grabius,—Liturgia,—Mass, &c.
Livermore, Edward St. Loe. Oration, July 17, 1799. 8vo. Portsmouth, N. H. 1799.
Livermore, Samuel. On the Law of Principal and Agent. 2 vols. 8vo. Baltimore. 1818.
Livingston, Edward. Speech on the Third Reading of the Alien Bill. 8vo. Phil.
Livingston, John H. Sermon before the New-York Missionary Society. 8vo. N. York. 1799.
Livingston, William. Funeral Elogium on the Rev. A. Burr, late President of the College in New-Jersey. 4to. Bost. 1758.
——, ——. Letter to the Bishop of Landaff. 8vo. Lond. 1768.
Livius, Titus. Historiæ, cum L. Flori Epitome, etc. fol. Paris. 1510.
——, ——. —— Duobus Libris auctæ, cum L. Flori Epitome, a W. Augusto et N. Carbachio. fol. Moguntiæ. 1518.
——, ——. ——, cum Doctissimorum Virorum Lucubrationibus, Artificiosis Picturis, etc. fol. Francof. ad Mœn. 1578.
——, ——. ——, cum Interpretatione et Notis, etc. in usum Delphini. 6 vol. 4to. Venet. 1714—15.

Livius, Titus. Historiæ, a M. Maittaire. 6 vol. 12mo. Lond. 1722.
——, ——, ————————. 7 vol. 12mo. Lond. 1749.
——, ——. ————, cum Notis Variorum, curante A. Drakenborch. 7 vol. 4to. Amst. et Lug. Bat. 1738—46.
——, ——, ————, ex Recensione A. Drakenborchii, curante A. G. Ernesti. 5 vol. 8vo. Lips. 1785.
——, ——. ————. 13 vol. 8vo. Biponti. 1784—6.
——, ——. ————. Vide Romanæ Historiæ Scriptores.
——, ——. Historiarum Libri Quinque Priores. 12mo. Cant. 1810.
——, ——. Historiarum Liber Primus et Selecta Quædam Capita, a C. Folsom. 12mo. Cantabrigiæ Nov. Angl. 1829.
——, ——. Historiarum Libri xci. Fragmentum 'Ανέκδοτον, a V. M. Giovenazzio et P. J. Bruns. 12mo. Bassani. 1791.
——, ——. History of Rome, from the Latin, with Notis, &c., by George Baker. 6 vols. 8vo. Lond. 1797.
——, ——. Römischer Geschicht Beschreibung T. Livii; und L. Flori Innhalt der verlornen Bücher T. Livii; aus dem Lat. fol. Strassburg. 1581.
Llorente, Jean-Antoine. Histoire Critique de l'Inquisition d'Espagne, trad. du l'Espagnol, sur le Manuscrit et sous les Yeux de l'Auteur, par A. Pellier. 2de éd. 4 vol. 8vo. Paris. 1818.
Lloyd, James. Speech in the Senate of the United States, on the Bill, "Concerning the Naval Establishment," Febuary 28, 1812. 8vo.
Lloyd, P. New Style the True Style, a Sermon. 8vo. Lond. 1753.
Lloyd, Richard. Christian Theology. 8vo. Lond. 1804.
Lloyd, Robert. Poems. See Chalmers, A.
Lloyd, Robert L. Sermon, January 30th. 8vo. Lond. 1710.
Lloyd, Thomas. Debates of the Convention of Pennsylvania on the Constitution proposed for the United States. vol. 1. 8vo. Phil. 1788.
——, ——. Congressional Register. 3 vols. 8vo. N. York. 1789—90.
Lloyd, Wm. (Bp.) Sermon at the Funeral of Bishop Wilkins. 8vo. Lond. 1698.
Lobb, Samuel. Assize Sermon. 8vo. Lond. 1746.
Lobb, Theophilus. Defence of the Christian Religion. 8vo. Lond. 1726.
Lobelius, M. de. Stirpium Historia. fol. Antverpiæ. 1576.
Löber, E C. Nachrichten von Carolina und Georgia, etc. 12mo. Jena.
Lobo, Gerardo. Obras Poeticas Lyricas. 4to. Madrid. 1738.
Lobo, Jerome. Voyage to Abyssinia; from the French, (by S. Johnson.) 8vo. Lond. 1735.
Locatus, Ubertus. De Placentinæ Urbis Origine, Successu, et Laudibus. (Græv. Thes. Ital.)
Locke, John. Two Treatises on Government. 8vo. Lond. 1698.
——, ——. The Same. 6th ed. 8vo. Lond. 1764.
——, ——. Two Letters on Toleration; with Archdeacon Proast's Answers. 4to. Lond. 1689—91.
——, ——. Three Letters on Toleration. 4to. Lond. 1790.

Locke, John. Third Letter for Toleration to the Author of the Third Letter concerning Toleration. 4to. Lond. 1692.
———, ——. Four Letters on Toleration. 4to. Lond. 1765.
———, ——. Abstract of his Essay on Human Understanding. See Gilbert, Sir J.
———, ——. Works. 2d ed. 3 vols. fol. Lond. 1722.
———, ——. ———. 11th ed. 10 vols. 8vo. Lond. 1812.
———, ——. Familiar Letters between him and his Friends. 4th ed. 8vo. Lond. 1742.
———, ——. Judgment on Latin Exercises. See Phillips, J. T.
———, ——. Essay for the Understanding of St. Paul's Epistles; and Le Clerc on Inspiration. 18mo. Bost. 1820.
———, ——. Essay for the Understanding of St. Paul's Epistles; —On Enthusiasm;—Advantages of the Appearance of our Saviour among Men. (Sparks, Collection of Essays, &c.)
———, ——. Paraphrase and Notes on the Epistles of St. Paul. 8vo. Lond. 1823.
Locke, John. Outlines of Botany. 12mo. Bost. 1819.
Locke, Samuel, (Pres.) Convention Sermon. 8vo. Bost. 1772.
Lockman, John. Travels of the Jesuits, translated from the Lettres Edifiantes, etc. 2d ed. 2 vols. 8vo. Lond. 1762.
————, ——. Entertaining Instructer, in French and English. 12mo. Lond. 1765.
Lockwood, James. Connecticut Election Sermon. 16mo. New Lond. 1754.
————, ——. Another. 16mo. N. Lond. 1759.
Locmanus. Fabulæ, Arab. et Lat. Vide Erpenius.
Loder, J. C. Fabulæ Anatomicæ. 2 vol. fol. Vimariæ. 1803.
Lodge, Thomas. Works of Josephus, translated into English. fol. Lond.
Loesner, C. F. Observationes ad Novum Testamentum, e Philône Alexandrino. 8vo. Lips. 1777.
Löffler, J. F. C. Versuch über den Platonismus der Kirchenväter, (aus dem Franz. von Souverain.) 8vo. 1782.
Löfflern, F. S. Jubel-Jahr. 12mo. Leipz. 1725.
Loffredus, Ferrantes. Antiquitates Puteolanæ. (ræv. Thes. Ital.)
Lofft, Capel. Thoughts on the Construction and Polity of Prisons, with Hints for their Improvement. 8vo. Bury St. Edmund. 1785.
Löfling, Peter. Reisebeschreibung nach den Spanischen Ländern in Europa und America in den Jahren 1751 bis 1756, etc., aus dem Schwedischen. 12te Auflage. 8vo. Berlin. 1776.
———, ——. Plantæ Hispanicæ et Americanæ. 8vo. Berlin. 1776.
———, ——. Abstract of the most useful and necessary Articles mentioned in his Travels through Spain and South America; with his Life. 8vo. Lond. 1771.
Logan, John. Sermons. 8vo. Bost. 1804.
———, ——. Poems. See Chalmers, A.
Logicæ Compendium, secundum Principia R. Cartesii. 12mo. Bost. 1758.
——— —————, MS. 4to. (written at Lima.)

Lohrmannus, Gabr. Dissertatio qua demonstratur commentitium ac fictum Electionis Æternæ Absolutum Decretum ex ipsorum Reformatorum Sententia ac Doctrinis omnino consequi. 4to. Jenæ. 1682.
Lojardière. Reise-Beschreibung nach Africa; aus dem Franz. 12mo. Franck. an der Oder. 1748.
Lok, John. Voyage to Guinea. (Hakluyt, vol. 2.)
——, ——. Voyage to Jerusalem. (Id.)
Lolme, J. L. de. Constitution of England. 4th ed. 8vo. Lond. 1784.
——, ——. The Same. 8vo. Dublin. 1793.
——, ——. ——. 8vo. Lond. 1800.
——, ——. History of the Flagellants. 2d ed. 8vo. Lond. 1783.
Lombard, Daniel. Succinct History of Persecutions. 8vo. Lond. 1747.
Lombardus, J. F. Eorum, quæ de Balneis, aliisque Miraculis Puteolanis scripta sunt, Synopsis. (Græv. Thes. Ital.)
Lomejerus, Joh. De Osculis. (Ugol. vol. 30.)
Lommius, Jodocus. Observationes Medicinales. 12mo. Francof. 1643.
——, ——. Idem. ed. 4ta. 12mo. Amst. 1738.
——, ——. ——. 12mo. Edin. 1752.
——, ——. De Curandis Febribus Continuis. 12mo. Lond. 1718.
——, ——. Idem. 12mo. Rotterodami. 1733.
——, ——. On Continual Fevers, translated from the Latin, by T. Dale. 8vo. Lond. 1732.
London, Address to the People of, on the Proclamation for a Fast. 8vo. Lond. 1756.
—— and its Environs Described. 6 vols. 8vo. Lond. 1761.
——. Letter to the Lord Mayor, on his Nomination of Persons for the Office of Sheriffs. 8vo. Lond. 1738.
——, Enquiry into the Legal Constitution of the College of Physicians in. 8vo. Lond. 1753.
——, Medical Observations and Inquiries, by a Society of Physicians in. 3 vols. 8vo. Lond. 1758—67.
——, Medical Transactions, published by the College of Physicians in. 2 vols. 8vo. Lond. 1772.
——, Memoirs of the Medical Society of, instituted in 1773. 4 vols. 8vo. Lond. 1787—95.
—— Practice of Physic. 3d ed. 12mo. Lond. 1778.
——. Transactions of the Society for the Improvement of Medical and Chirurgical Knowledge. 2 vols. 8vo. Lond. 1793—1800.
—— Medical Dictionary. See Parr, B.
—— Medical and Physical Journal, by T. Bradley and Others. 49 vols. 8vo. Lond. 1799—1823.
——, Medico-Chirurgical Transactions; by the Medical and Chirurgical Society. 9 vols. 8vo. Lond. 1815—18.
——. See Arts and Sciences,—Horticultural Society,—Magazines,—Revolution Society,—Royal Society, &c.

Long, Edward. History of Jamaica. 3 vols. 4to. Lond. 1774.
Long, J. Voyages and Travels of an Indian Interpreter and Trader. 4to. Lond. 1791.
——, –. Voyages chez Différentes Nations Sauvages de l'Amérique Septentrionale, trad. de l'Anglois par Billecocq. 8vo. Paris. 1794.
Long, Jacobus le. Bibliotheca Sacra. 2 vol. fol. Paris. 1723.
Long, S. H. (Major.) Expedition to the Rocky Mountains. See James, E.
Long, Roger. Astronomy. 2 vols. 4to. Camb. 1742—64.
Longinus, Dionysius. De Sublimitate, Gr. et Lat., cum Notis Variorum, cura J. Tollii. Accedit Versio Gallica Boilavii. 4to. Traj. ad Rhen. 1694.
————, ——. De Sublimitate, Gr. et Lat., cum Notis, a Z. Pearce. 8vo. Lond. 1762.
————, ——. De Sublimitate, Gr. et Lat., cum Animadversionibus Variorum, a B. Weiske. 8vo. Lips. 1809.
————, ——. On the Sublime. See Smith. W.
Longman & Co. Sale Catalogues of Books for 1814, 1816, and 1822. 3 vols. 8vo. Lond.
Longomontanus, C. S. Astronomica Danica. fol. Amst. 1640.
Longus. Pastoralium de Daphnide et Chloe Libri iv, Gr. et Lat. Accedunt Xenophontis Ephesiacorum de Amoribus Anthiæ et Abrocomæ Libri v, a C. G. Mitscherlich. 8vo. Biponti. 1794.
———. Pastoralia, Gr. et Lat., cum Proloquio P. M. Placiaudii de Libris Eroticis Antiquorum, et Notis G. H. Schäferi. 16mo. Lips. 1803.
———. Les Amours de Daphnis et Chloé, trad. par J. Amyot. 16mo. Lond. 1780.
Longus, Geo. De Anulis. Vide Kirchmannus, J.
Longus, Velius. De Orthographia. Vide Grammatici Vet. Lat.
Longworth, D. American Almanac, New-York Register and City Directory, for the Years 1797, 1810, 1814, 1815, 1816, and 1817. 12mo.
Looker-on. See Roberts, W.
Loon, Gerard van. Histoire Métallique des XVII Provinces des Pays-Bas, depuis l'Abdication de Charles-Quint jusqu'à 1716, trad. du Hollandois. 5 vol. fol. La Haye. 1732—7.
Lope de Vega. Coleccion de las Obras Sueltas. 21 vol. 4to. Madrid. 1776—9.
Lopez, Edvart. Beschrijvinge van 'tKoningrijcke Congo, etc. 4to. Amst. 1658.
Lopez de Zarate, Fr. Obras Varias. 4to. Alcala. 1651.
——————, —. Poema Heroico de la Invencion de la Cruz. 4to. Madrid. 1648.
Lord, Benjamin. Discourse from John i, 12, 13. 8vo. Bost. 1742.
——, ————. Connecticut Election Sermon. 16mo. N. Lond. 1752.
——, ————. Half-Century Discourse. 16mo. N. Lond. 1768.
——, ————. Sermon on the Death of the Rev. Henry Willes. 16mo. N. Lond. 1759.

Lord, Benjamin. Sermon at the Funeral of the Rev. Hezekiah Lord. 8vo. Providence. 1763.
——, ————. Sermon at the Instalment of the Rev. Nathaniel Whitaker. 16mo. N. Lond. 1761.
——, ————. Sermon at the Ordination of the Rev. Levi Hart. 8vo. Providence. 1763.
——, ————. Account of Mrs. Mercy Wheeler's various and singular Deliverances. 3d ed. 12mo. Bost. 1744.
——, ————. Sermon at the Interment of the Hon. Hezekiah Huntington. 12mo. Norwich. 1773.
Lords, History and Proceedings of the House of, from the Restoration in 1660 to 1742. 8 vols. 8vo. Lond. 1742—3.
———. Complete Collection of the Lords' Protests, from the First upon Record, in the Reign of Henry III, to the present Time, &c. 2 vols. 8vo. Lond. 1767.
———. Protest on a Motion to address his Majesty for keeping our Forces at Home, &c. 8vo. Lond. 1746.
———. See Parliament.
Lord's Day, Religious Observance of the. 24to. Lond. 1724.
———. Remarks on its Observation, as a Moral, a Positive, and a Civil Duty, by a Tythingman. 8vo. Camb. 1816.
Lord's Supper. Plain Account of the Nature and End of the Sacrament of the Lord's Supper, not drawn from or founded on Scripture. 8vo. Lond. 1737.
——— ———. Defence of the Plain Account, &c. See Hoadly, B.
——— ———. Letters to the Right Reverend Author of "A Plain Account of the Nature and End of the Sacrament of the Lord's Supper." 8vo. Lond. 1756.
——— ———. See Eucharist. See Sermons.
Lorimer, William. Discourse on the Death and Resurrection of Christ. 8vo. Lond. 1718.
———, ————. Explication of the First Eighteen Verses of the First Chapter of John. 8vo. Lond. 1713.
Loring, Charles G. Oration, July 4th. 8vo. Bost. 1821.
Loring, Israel. Sermon on the Miseries of Hell. 16mo. Bost 1732.
———, ———. Election Sermon. 8vo. Bost. 1737.
Loring, Joseph. Exhibition of Facts, for the Information of the Militia Officers of Massachusetts. 8vo. Bost. 1806.
Lorrain, Paul. Sermon against Popery. 8vo. Lond. 1712.
Lorry, A. C. Tractatus de Morbis Cutaneis. 4to. Paris. 1777.
Loselius, Joh. De Podagra. Accessit Hieronymi Cardani Podagræ Encomium. 12mo. Lug. Bat. 1639.
Loskiel, G. H. Geschichte der Mission der Evangelischen Brüder unter den Indianern in Nordamerika. 8vo. Barby. 1789.
———, ———. History of the Mission of the United Brethren among the Indians in North America, translated from the German by C. I. La Trobe. 8vo. Lond. 1794.
Lossius, Jeremias. De Epispasmo Judaico. (Ugol. vol. 22.)
Louis II, Seigneur de la Trémoille. Mémoires. (Mém. de France, vol. 14.)

Louis XV, Panégyrique de. 12mo. 1748.
Louis le Grand, Médailles sur le Regne de. fol. Baden. 1705.
Louisbourg, Conquest of; a Poem. 4to.
Louise de Savoye, Mère de François I. Mémoires. (Mém. de France, vol. 16.)
Louisiana, Present State of. 8vo. Lond. 1744.
———. Relations de la Louisiane et du Fleuve Mississipi. 12mo. Amst. 1720.
———. Mémoire des Habitans et Négocians de la Louysiane, sur l'Evénement du 29 Octobre, 1768. 8vo.
———, Documents relating to. 8vo.
———. Address to the Government of the United States, on the Cession of Louisiana to the French, &c. 8vo. Phil. 1802.
———, Account of, being an Abstract of Documents, in the Offices of the Departments of State and of the Treasury. 8vo.
———. Representation and Petition of the Representatives elected by the Freemen of the Territory of. 8vo. Washington. 1805.
———. Digest of Martin's Reports of the Decisions of the Supreme Court of the State, from its Establishment in 1813 to August, 1826, by William Christy. 8vo. N. Orleans. 1826.
———. See Journal,—Ohio,—United States.
Love, Discourse on the Duty of. 8vo. Lond. 1742.
Love, John. Vindication of Mr. George Buchanan. 8vo. Edin. 1749.
Love, John. Art of Surveying. 7th ed. 8vo. Lond. 1760.
Loveday, Samuel. Personal Reprobation Reprobated. 8vo. Lond. 1676.
Lovell. A Papist Mis-represented and Represented. 4to. Lond. 1685.
Lovell, Jacobus. Oratio in Funere Henrici Flyntii, Arm. 8vo. Bost. 1760.
Lovell, James. Sketches of Man, "as he is," connected with past and present Modes of Education. 8vo. Bost. 1808.
Lovell, John. Funeral Oration on Peter Faneuil, Esq. 4to. Bost. 1743.
Lovell, Joseph. Meteorological Register for 1822—5. 4to. Washington, 1826.
Lovibond, Edward. Poems. See Chalmers, A.
Lowell, Charles. Sermon at the State Prison. 8vo. Bost. 1812.
———, ———. Sermon on the Execution of H. P. S. Davis for Murder. 2d ed. 8vo. Bost. 1817.
———, ———. Discourse before the Society for promoting Christian Knowledge, Piety, and Charity. 12mo. Bost. 1816.
———, ———. Artillery Election Sermon. 8vo. Bost. 1810.
———, ———. Sermon at the Ordination of the Rev. R. M. Hodges. 8vo. Bost. 1821.
———, ———. Sermon at the Ordination of Mr. Samuel Barrett. 8vo. Bost. 1825.
———, ———. Sermon at the Ordination of Mr. George W. Wells. 8vo. Camb. 1827.

Lowell, Charles. Discourse at the Ordination of Mr. Daniel M. Stearns. 8vo. Bost. 1828.
———, ———. Century Discourse. 8vo. Bost. 1821.
———, ———. Discourse before the Society for propagating the Gospel. 8vo. Bost. 1820.
———, ———. Sermon at the Dedication of the Third Congregational Church in Cambridge. 8vo. Camb. 1828.
Lowell, John. Sermon at Newbury before Col. Titcomb, when going against the French. 8vo. Bost. 1755.
———, ———. Sermon on the Death of Col. Moses Titcomb, who fell in Battle near Lake-George. 8vo. Bost. 1760.
Lowell, John. Oration, July 4. 8vo. Bost. 1799.
———, ———. See Analysis,—Church,—Dexter, S.,—Harvard University,—Inquirer,—Madison, J.,—Morse, J.,—Political Tracts,—Religious Freedom.
Lower, Richardus. De Corde, de Sanguine, et de Catarrhis. ed. 4ta. 12mo. Lond. 1680.
Lowman, Moses. The Argument *a Priori* concerning the Existence and Perfections of God, &c., stated and considered. 8vo. Lond. 1737.
———, ———. Charity Sermon. 8vo. Lond. 1718.
———, ———. Remarks on Dr. Sherlock's Answer to the Bishop of Bangor. 8vo. Lond. 1719.
———, ———. Rational of the Ritual of the Hebrew Worship. 8vo. Lond. 1748.
———, ———. On the Civil Government of the Hebrews. 2d ed. 8vo. Lond. 1745.
———, ———. Paraphrase and Notes on the Revelation of St. John. 4to. Lond. 1737.
———, ———. The Same. 2d ed. 4to. Lond. 1745.
———, ———. ———. 4to. Lond. 1809.
———, ———. Sermon on Reformation of Manners. 8vo. Lond. 1720.
———, ———. Sermon against Popery. 8vo. Lond. 1735.
Lownes, Caleb. Account of the Alteration and Present State of the Penal Laws of Pennsylvania, &c. 8vo. Phil. 1793.
Lowry, Delvalle. Conversations on Mineralogy. 2 vols. 12mo. Lond. 1822.
———, ———. The Same. 12mo. Phil. 1822.
Lowth, Robert, (Bp.) Introduction to English Grammar. 8vo. Lond. 1762.
———, ———. The Same. 2d ed. 12mo. Lond. 1763.
———, ———. ———. 12mo. Lond. 1764.
———, ———. ———. 12mo. Lond. 1783.
———, ———. De Sacra Poesi Hebræorum. 8vo. Oxon. 1763.
———, ———. Idem. ed. 3tia. 8vo. Oxon. 1775.
———, ———. ——. (Ugol. vol. 31.)
———, ———. Vide Michaelis, J. D.
———, ———. Lectures on the Sacred Poetry of the Hebrews, from the Latin, with Notes, by G. Gregory. 8vo. Bost. 1815.

Lowth, Robert, (Bp.) Letter to the Author of "the Divine Legation of Moses Demonstrated." 2d ed. 8vo. Lond. 1766.

———, ————. Letter to him, on the Character of Dr. Bentley given in the Above. 8vo. Lond. 1767.

———, ————. Isaiah, a New Translation, with a Dissertation and Notes. 2d ed. 4to. Lond. 1769.

———, ————. The Same. 3d ed. 2 vols. 8vo. Lond. 1795.

———, ————. Visitation Sermon. 4to. Lond. 1758.

———, ————. Answer to an Anonymous Letter concerning the Election of a Warden in Winchester College. 8vo. Lond. 1759.

———, ————. The Protestant, or the Doctrine of Universal Liberty asserted, in Opposition to Dr. Lowth's Representation of it. 8vo. Lond.

Lowth, Simon. On Church Power. 8vo. Lond. 1685.

Lowth, William. Commentary on the Prophets, in Continuation of Bishop Patrick. fol. Lond. 1727.

———, ———. The Same. 4th ed. fol. Lond. 1739.

———, ———. Vindication of the Old and New Testament. 12mo. Lond. 1692.

———, ———. The Same. 2d ed. 12mo. Lond. 1699.

———, ———. Characters of an Apostolical Church fulfilled in the Church of England, a Sermon on Acts ii, 42. 8vo. Lond. 1722.

———, ———. See Norman, J.

Loyalists. Laws of New-York in force against them, &c. 8vo. Lond. 1786.

————. Laws of Massachusetts relative to them. 8vo. Lond. 1785.

————, Case and Claim of the American, considered. 8vo. Lond. 1783.

————, Particular Case of the Georgia. 8vo. Lond. 1783.

Loysius, G. Pervigilium Mercurii. Vide Hegenitius, G.

Lozano, Christoval. Soledades de la Vida, y Desengaños de el Mundo. 4to. Barcelona. 1722.

Lozano, Pedro. Historia de la Compañia de Jesus en la Provincia del Paraguay. 2 vol. fol. Madrid. 1754—5.

———, ———. Descripcion del Gran Chaco, Gualamba. 4to. Cordoba. 1733.

Lozières, Baudry des. Voyage à la Louisiane, etc. en 1794—8. 8vo. Paris. 1802.

———, ————. Second Voyage à la Louisiane. 2 vol. 8vo. Paris. 1803.

Lubbertus, Sibrandus. De Jesu Christo Servatore, contra F. Socinum. 4to. Leovardiæ. 1617.

Lubecus, Christophorus. De Decisionibus Peniculamenti Hebræorum. (Ugol. vol. 21.)

Lubienietzki, Stanislaus. Historia Cometarum. fol. Amst. 1666.

————, ————. Historia Reformationis Polonicæ. 12mo. Freistadii. 1685.

Lucianus. Works; from the Greek, by T. Francklin. 4 vols. 8vo. Lond. 1781.

———. Dialogues; from the Greek, by J. Carr. 2d ed. 5 vols. 8vo. Lond. 1774—98.

———. Œuvres de Lucien, Traduction Nouvelle, par Massieu. 6 vol. 12mo. Paris. 1781—7.

Lucius, Joannes. De Regno Illyrici.—Inscriptiones Dalmaticæ. (Græv. Thes. Ital.)

Lucilla and Elizabeth, or Donatist and Protestant Schism Paralleled. 4to. Lond. 1686.

Lücke, Friedrich. Grundriss der neutestamentlichen Hermeneutik und ihrer Geschichte. 8vo. Göttingen. 1817.

———, ———. Commentar über die Schriften des Evangelisten Johannes. 8vo. Bonn. 1820.

Lucretius, T. Carus. De Rerum Natura, cum Notis, ad usum Delphini. 4to. Paris. 1680.

——— ———. ———. 4to. Lond. 1712.

——— ———. ———, cum Notis T. Creech. 8vo. Lond. 1717.

——— ———. ———, cum Notis Variorum, curante S. Havercampo. 2 vol. 4to. Lug. Bat. 1725.

——— ———. ———, cum Animadversionibus R. Bentleii et Aliorum, a G. Wakefield. 3 vol. 4to. Lond. 1796—7.

——— ———. Vide Corpus Poet. Lat., et Collectio Pisaur.

——— ———. First Book of the Nature of Things, translated into English Verse, by W. H. Drummond. 12mo. Edin. 1808.

——— ———. Della Natura delle Cose Libri Sei, trad. da A. Marchetti. 8vo. Milano. 1813.

Lüdeke, C. W. Expositio Brevis Locorum Scr. S. ad Orientem sese referentium. 12mo. Halæ Sax. 1777.

Lüdemann, J. H. De Sepulchro Christi ex Petra exciso. 4to. Sedini. 1730.

Ludlam, Wm. Mathematical Essays. 2d ed. 8vo. Camb. 1787.

———, ———. Astronomical Observations, &c. 4to. Camb. 1769.

Ludlow, Edmund. Memoirs. fol. Lond. 1751.

Ludolfus, Jobus. Lexicon Æthiopico-Latinum, cum Grammatica Æthiopica, etc., cura J. M. Wanslebii. 4to. Lond. 1661.

———, ———. Historia Æthiopica. fol. Franc. ad Mœn. 1681.

Ludolph. Panegyrick on George I. 4to.

Ludovicus, Laurentius. Analysis Trium Dialogorum Theodoreti Episcopi Cyri. 12mo. Neustadii. 1604.

Ludwig, Christian. Teutschenglisches Lexicon. 4te Aufl. 4to. Leipz.

———, ———. Dictionary, English, German, and French, revised by J. B. Rogler. 4th ed. 4to. Leipz. 1791.

Ludwig, C. G. Institutiones Historico-Physicæ Regni Vegetabilis. 8vo. Lips. 1742.

———, ———. Adversaria Medico-Practica. 2 vol. 8vo. Lips. 1769—71.

Luther, Martin. Primus Tomus Enarrationum in Epistolas et Evangelia. 12mo. Argent. 1525.
———, ———. Catechesis Græcolatina. 8vo. Basil. 1564.
———, ———. De Kleyne Catechismus; midtsgaders het Kleyne Corpus Doctrinæ, etc. 12mo. Amst. 1641.
———, ———. Collectio Nova Epistolarum, etc., a J. F. Buddeo. 4to. Halæ Magd. 1717.
———, ———. Supplementum Epistolarum, etc., a J. F. Buddeo. 4to. Halæ. 1703.
———, ———. Register aller Schrifften, etc. Vide Schwob.
———, ———. Considerations concerning the Spirit of M. Luther, and the Original of the Reformation. 4to. Oxford. 1687.
———, ———. Answer to "Considerations," &c. See Atterbury.
———, ———. Vide Bibel.
Lutheran Ministerium. See Ministerium.
Luttrell. Account, drawn up 100 years ago, of several Pears then cultivated at Little Chelsea. (Horticult. Tr., vol. 2.)
Lutwyche, Sir Edward. Reports and Entries, by W. Nelson. fol. Lond. 1718.
Lutyens, G. N. Etwas über den gegenwärtigen Zustand der Auswanderungen und Ansiedlungen im Staate von Pennsylvanien in Nord-Amerika. 8vo. Hamburg. 1796.
Luzancy, H. de. Treatise of the Sacraments. 8vo. Lond. 1701.
Lycophron. Alexandra [sive Cassandra], Gr. et Lat., cum Græco Tzetzæ Commentario, et Annotationibus J. Potteri. ed. 2da. fol. Oxon. 1702.
Lycosthenes, Conradus. Apophthegmata, ex Gr. et Lat. Scriptoribus. 8vo. Genevæ. 1633.
———, ———. Idem. 8vo. Lond. 1635.
Lycurgus. Orationes. Vide Oratores Græci, a Reiskio.
Lydius, Jacobus. De Juramento. (Ugol. vol. 26.)
———, ———. De Re Militari, cum Notis Salomonis Van Til. (Id. 27.)
Lydyat, Thomas. Epistola Astronomica de Anni Solaris Mensura. 12mo. Lond. 1621.
Lye, Edwardus. Evangelia Gothica. Vide Evangelia.
———, ———. Grammatica Gothica. Vide Evangelia. Vide Junius, F., (F. F.)
Lye, Thomas. Explanation of the Shorter Catechism. 12mo. Lond. 1702.
Lyman, Joseph. Election Sermon. 8vo. Bost. 1787.
———, ———. Convention Sermon. 8vo. Bost. 1806.
Lyman, Theodore. A Few Weeks in Paris. 12mo. Bost. 1814.
———, ———. Political State of Italy. 8vo. Bost. 1820.
———, ———. Oration, July 4th. 8vo. Bost. 1820.
Lynde, Sir Humfrey. Via Tuta; the Safe Way. 4th ed. 12mo. Lond. 1630.
———, ———. Via Devia; the By-Way. 2d ed. 12mo. Lond. 1632.
Lyne, Richard. Latin Primer. 6th ed. 12mo. Lond. 1817.

Lynford, Thomas. Spittle Sermon. 4to. Lond. 1698.
———, ———. Primitive Christianity Revived, a Sermon. 8vo. Lond. 1709.
Lyon, John. Remarks on the Leading Proofs offered in favour of the Franklinian System of Electricity, &c. 8vo. Lond. 1791.
Lyons, (Mr.) Infallibility of Human Judgment, its Dignity and Excellency. 4th ed. 12mo. Lond. 1724.
Lyserus. Vide Leyserus.
Lyserus, M. Art of Dissecting the Human Body, translated from the Latin, by G. Thomson. 8vo. Lond. 1740.
Lyserus, Polycarpus. Libri Tres Harmoniæ Evangelicæ conscripti a M. Chemnitio, editi opera et studio P. Lyseri. 4to. Francof. ad Mœn. 1608.
———, ———. Dissertatio Philologica ad Esaiæ Cap. iii, 16, 18, illustrandum. (Ugol. vol. 29.)
Lysias. Orationes et Fragmenta, Gr. et Lat., cum Notis, a J. Taylor. 4to. Lond. 1739.
———. Vide Oratores Gr. a Reiskio.
———. Orations of Lysias and Isocrates, translated from the Greek, by J. Gillies. 4to. Lond. 1778.
Lyttelton, Geo., Lord. Observations on the Life of Cicero. 8vo. Lond. 1733.
———, ———. Observations on the Conversion and Apostleship of St. Paul. 8vo. Lond. 1747.
———, ———. The Same. 8vo. Lond. 1767.
——— ———. ———. 8vo. Lond. 1777.
——— ———. ———. See Christianity, Evidences of.
———; ———. History of England, in Letters from a Nobleman to his Son. 2 vols. 12mo. Lond. 1803.
———, ———. Life of Henry II. 2d ed. 4 vols. 4to. Lond. 1767.
———, ———. Letters from a Persian in England to his Friend in Ispahan. 4th ed. 12mo. Lond. 1735.
———, ———. Dialogues of the Dead. 4th ed. 8vo. Lond. 1765.
———, ———. Poems. See Chalmers, A.
Lyttelton, Thomas, Lord. Letter to William Pitt, Earl of Chatham, on the Quebec Bill. 8vo. N. York. 1774.
———, ———. See Littleton.

END OF VOLUME FIRST.

Lightning Source UK Ltd.
Milton Keynes UK
UKHW021618090119
335047UK00005B/459/P

9 780428 680992